FR- 43432

The Price of Emancipation

When colonial slavery was abolished in 1833, the British government paid £20 million to slave-owners as compensation: the enslaved received nothing. Drawing on the records of the Commissioners of Slave Compensation, which represent a complete census of slave-ownership, this book provides for the first time a comprehensive analysis of the extent and importance of absentee slave-ownership and its impact on British society. Moving away from the historiographical tradition of isolated case studies, it reveals the extent of slave-ownership amongst metropolitan elites, and identifies concentrations of both rentier and mercantile slave-holders, tracing their influence in local and national politics, in business, and in institutions such as the church. In analysing this permeation of British society by slave-owners, and their success in securing compensation from the state, the book challenges conventional narratives of abolitionist Britain and provides a fresh perspective of British society and politics on the eve of the Victorian era.

NICHOLAS DRAPER is Teaching Fellow and Research Associate at the Department of History, University College London.

Cambridge Studies in Economic History

Editorial Board

Cambridge Studies in Economic History comprises stimulating and accessible economic history which actively builds bridges to other disciplines. Books in the series will illuminate why the issues they address are important and interesting, place their findings in a comparative context, and relate their research to wider debates and controversies. The series will combine innovative and exciting new research by younger researchers with new approaches to major issues by senior scholars. It will publish distinguished work regardless of chronological period or geographical location.

Titles in the series include:

The Price of Emancipation

Slave-Ownership, Compensation and British Society at the End of Slavery

Nicholas Draper

CAMBRIDGE
UNIVERSITY PRESS

CAMBRIDGE UNIVERSITY PRESS
Cambridge, New York, Melbourne, Madrid, Cape Town, Singapore,
São Paulo, Delhi, Dubai, Tokyo

Cambridge University Press
The Edinburgh Building, Cambridge CB2 8RU, UK

Published in the United States of America by Cambridge University Press, New York

www.cambridge.org
Information on this title: www.cambridge.org/9780521115254

First published 2010

Printed in the United Kingdom at the University Press, Cambridge

A catalogue record for this publication is available from the British Library

Library of Congress Cataloguing in Publication Data
Draper, Nicholas, 1958–
    The price of emancipation : slave-ownership, compensation and British society at the
    end of slavery / Nicholas Draper.
       p.   cm. – (Cambridge studies in economic history – second series)
    ISBN 978-0-521-11525-4
    1. Slaves–Emancipation–West Indies, British–History.   2. Slaveholders–West Indies,
    British–History.   3. Slavery–West Indies, British–History.   4. Slaves–Emancipation–
    Great Britain–History.   5. Slaveholders–Great Britain–History.   6. Slavery–Great
    Britain–History.   I. Title.
    HT1073.D73 2009
    306.3′620941–dc22   2009036858

ISBN 978-0-521-11525-4 Hardback

Contents

Plates

Figures

Tables

Acknowledgements

This book began life as a doctoral dissertation under the supervision of Catherine Hall and Julian Hoppit at University College London, and I owe them both a significant debt of gratitude for their guidance and advice. In Catherine Hall's case, I am particularly grateful for her generous sponsorship of my work within her rather extraordinary network of academic and public historians.

Arriving late to academic history, I have been struck by the kindness of scholars across the world in freely sharing their unpublished material in response to my questions. Specific debts of this kind are acknowledged throughout the text, but I wanted to single out Richard Lobdell of the University of Manitoba for his willingness to turn over the fruits of months of research to me. After the book had gone to press, Bill Rubinstein of the Aberystwyth University very generously agreed to share his extensive accumulated data on the nineteenth-century rich in Britain with the *Legacies of British Slave-ownership* project at University College London. I have also benefited from the close scrutiny and continuing interest of my examiners, Arthur Burns of King's College London and Simon Smith of the University of Hull.

Sections of the book in earlier versions were presented at the *Reconfiguring the British* and *British History in the Long Eighteenth Century* seminars at the Institute of Historical Research in London, and I am grateful both to the organisers for the opportunity to deliver papers and to the participants for the engaged and substantive comments they provided in response. A preliminary version of the findings of the work underpinning this book was published as '"Possessing slaves": ownership, compensation and metropolitan society in Britain at the time of Emancipation 1834–40' in *History Workshop Journal* 64 (Autumn 2007), 74–102, and I am grateful to the editors and staff for its inclusion there.

I was privileged to be able to take up historical research while still employed in the City, and I want to thank my former colleagues, and above all Klaus Diederichs, for their commitment and flexibility in making a dual path possible for several years. Two of those years were spent at Birkbeck, to which I owe a great deal, and where I had in particular the support and encouragement of David Feldman, Frank Trentmann and Michael Berlin.

Finally, I owe a debt beyond words to my family: this book is dedicated to Lalli, Emma, Lucy and Anna.

A note on language

Slave-owners in Britain in the early nineteenth century invested energy in elaborating different categories for themselves, including 'proprietor' and 'planter', and spoke of being 'possessed of slaves', in one of the numerous linguistic and representational strategies adopted to blur the reality of their position. At the same time, the process whereby the British state sanctioned, amassed, evaluated and paid out on claims for compensation from slave-owners in exchange for the freedom (initially partial) of enslaved men and women did not operate, at the metropolitan centre, on the basis of identification of, nor differentiation between, individual enslaved men and women. Instead, it worked in terms of the numbers and categories of 'slaves' treated as abstract commodities. Accordingly, this study reinstates the language of 'slave-owner' to describe those whose asserted title to treat human beings as property was recognised by the state, and uses the term 'slaves' in extracting, analysing and compiling data from the records of the state bodies charged with compensation payments to slave-owners. It uses 'enslaved' in all other contexts.

Abbreviations

ASR	*Anti-slavery Monthly Reporter*
CCED	Clergy of the Church of England Database
DNB	*Dictionary of National Biography*
PP	Parliamentary papers
Thorne	R. G. Thorne, *The House of Commons 1790–1820*, 5 vols. (London: Secker and Warburg for the History of Parliament Trust, 1986)

Introduction

In his autobiography, H. M. Hyndman, the founder of the Social Democratic Federation, Britain's first Marxist party, wrote that his father, John Beckles Hyndman

was an Eton and Trinity Cambridge man, at which college, being then possessed of a very large income, he was a Fellow-commoner ... After taking his degree and having eaten his dinners at the Inner Temple, he was duly qualified to exercise the legal profession, and was called to the Bar. So far as I know, he never had or tried to obtain a brief, but none the less he was entitled to call himself Barrister-at-law, and remained a member of that highly respectable and rigid Trade Union until the day of his death.[1]

One generation back from this caricature of a particular type of English gentleman, however, the lineage changed. H. M. Hyndman came, he said, 'like most well-to-do people of the upper middle class in this island, from decent piratical stock'. His grandfather, who at one period had been 'compelled to play the violin in public houses', became a planter and slave-owner in Demerara (part of what became British Guiana), and had prospered both from extraordinary profits in speculative purchases of estates from alarmed Dutch resident planters at the time of cession of Demerara to Britain, and from 'the ordinary profits of his plantations being steadily forthcoming on a large scale from the beneficial toil of his well-nourished negroes'. 'And here I may add', Hyndman continued,

that, bad as chattel slavery is from every point of view, the big plantations were not by any means bad places for the Negroes in the time of my grand-father. They enjoyed a good standard of life, they were fairly educated, and they were not allowed by law to work more than 45 hours a week. If I had my choice of being a negro slave on a well-kept estate in the West Indies, or a sweated free white wage-earner in one of our great cities for the whole of my life, I know very well which I should prefer.[2]

---

[1] H. M. Hyndman, *The record of an adventurous life* (London: Macmillan, 1911), p. 1.
[2] *Ibid.*, pp. 2–6.

1

Hyndman himself, born in 1842 after Emancipation, sold off the last of his family's plantations as his father's administrator. His family story of the expropriation, transformation and consumption of wealth derived from the enslaved; his rhetorical distancing devices; his ignorance of the nature of plantation slavery; and his contention that colonial enslavement was preferable to wage-labour in Britain; all indeed appear to condense the experience of a broader swathe of British 'well-to-do people of the upper middle class' at the time of Emancipation, more fully than perhaps he intended. His one material omission is the fact that his father John Beckles Hyndman received over £40,000 as compensation for the loss of his 'property' in the 791 enslaved people on his two plantations, out of the total of £20 million compensation that the British government granted to the owners of the enslaved upon Emancipation.[3]

But how truly representative were the Hyndmans, or indeed any of the more famous individual British slave-owners of the 1820s and 1830s, such as John Gladstone – William's father – whom Eric Williams used as such a powerful symbol in *Capitalism and slavery*?[4] Against the background of an historiography generally characterised only by anecdotal examples of British slave-owning, this study aims, in drawing on the records of the Slave Compensation Commission, which between 1834 and 1845 administered the distribution of the compensation paid to British colonial slave-owners, to map more systematically the recipients of this compensation money in metropolitan Britain by geography, class and gender, and to explore their identities and places in British society. In particular, it seeks to answer five questions: how widespread was slave-owning in metropolitan Britain at the end of British colonial slavery; who were these slave-owners and how did they come to own slaves; how did they represent themselves and how were they represented in a society increasingly hostile to slavery; how did these slave-owners secure compensation from the British state in the form and amount they did; and how does the existence of this body of slave-owners fit with established narratives of the end of British colonial slavery?

It has previously been largely assumed that slave-ownership was a marginal activity in Britain by the 1830s; that there was a well-developed

---

[3] National Archives, Kew: HM Treasury papers, Office of Registry of Colonial Slaves and Slave Compensation Commission Records, T71/885, British Guiana Nos. 626 and 627 for 464 slaves on Houstoun plantation (for which John Beckles Hyndman was awarded £24,157 6s 1d) and 327 slaves on Rome plantation (£17,386 9s 10d). All payments in this study are shown before interest, which accrued from 1 August 1834 on all awards.

[4] E. E. Williams, *Capitalism and slavery* (London: Andre Deutsch, 1964), pp. 89–90.

mercantile system of consignment and credit that bled off the remaining profits of a fragile plantation economy for the benefit of a handful of metropolitan merchants concentrated in London, Liverpool and Bristol; and that the conflict over slavery in Britain was played out between the abolitionists, backed by extraordinary public support, and a small number of spokesmen for the West India Committee, a narrow sectional interest fighting in a lost cause.[5] This study argues instead that, in addition to the mercantile interest, large-scale slave-ownership or financial exposure to slavery permeated sections of the Anglican rural gentry class, while small-scale slave-holding was common in a number of urban centres of polite society.

Slavery was not physically present in Britain as it was in the southern USA, Cuba or Brazil, and of course the *distance* from the reality of the experience of oppression played a central part in the representation and self-representation of slave-owners in Britain, by their opponents and themselves. But the abolition of the slave-trade in 1807 did not end Britain's intimate relationship with slavery. Slave-ownership had been converted into financial property and conveyed between generations and sexes by the full range of available techniques of management and control governing other types of property. '[T]he grand object of every West India planter', wrote the London merchant and slave-owner John Robley in 1808, was ultimately to 'place the income derived from property in the West Indies, upon a permanent security at all resembling a revenue derived from a landed estate in Europe'.[6] Slave-ownership within Britain was passed directly by inheritance and by marriage settlement, and indirectly by annuities and legacies, underlining the way in which 'slave-property' had been subsumed into the wider world of landed property norms. Nor was this process of transmission confined to the enslaved attached to large colonial estates: smaller groups of

---

[5] For an early and influential statement of this position, see L. Ragatz, 'Absentee landlordism in the British Caribbean 1750–1833', *Agricultural History*, 5 (1931), 7–24 (p. 12): 'the overwhelming majority [of absentee owners], knowing nothing of plantation-economy and finding themselves hopelessly involved, transferred their hypothecated properties to their creditors, and cut loose entirely from the colonies' after the Napoleonic Wars.

[6] J. Robley, *A permanent and effectual remedy suggested to the evils under which the British West Indies now labour, in a letter from a West India merchant to a West India planter* (London, 1808), p. 4. Robley subsequently moved to Tobago, where he had several children with a 'free mulatto', Eliza M'Kenzie, leaving his wife and children in England (*The Times*, 11 July 1839, p. 7). See also S. D. Smith, *Slavery, family, and gentry capitalism in the British Atlantic: the world of the Lascelles, 1648–1834* (Cambridge: Cambridge University Press, 2006), pp. 342–4. Robley's family in Britain, and the family of his former London partner Charles Brooke, were awarded almost £11,500 for 580 enslaved in Tobago: T71/891, Tobago Nos. 3, 51, 52, 64.

enslaved in the British Caribbean, usually rented out for service work in colonial towns, were routinely bequeathed across generations of absentee owners in Britain.[7]

As a result, after 1807 slavery appears increasingly to have pervaded particular strata and localities of Britain by virtue of direct slave-ownership or indirect financial dependence on the slave-economy.[8] As slave-owning became more widespread, it became 'thinner' and less constitutive of a single identity. It also lost some of its taint as it was transformed into financial assets, into annuities, marriage settlements and legacies. The payment of compensation was central to the final dismantling of the slave system, and when that compensation was offered to slave-owners in the 1830s there was, in effect, a feeding frenzy amongst sections of the British elites over the compensation money, a frenzy that drew thousands of Britons into asserting their ownership of the enslaved once the state attached specific and immediate monetary value to the claims of ownership.

The archive of the Slave Compensation Commission ('the Commission') in which this frenzy can be traced represents an extraordinary resource that has barely been touched by historians. In 1838 the Commission published a Parliamentary Return at the request of Daniel O'Connell listing all the awards made to slave-owners by that date, by which time some 93 per cent of the compensation had been settled.[9] Organised by the colony (and within Jamaica by the parish) in which the enslaved had been registered in the most recent triennial slave-registration, the Return lists over 40,000 awards detailing the unique claim number, the name (although not the address) of the awardee, the number of slaves owned and the amount of compensation awarded.

The Parliamentary Return has been mined selectively by historians for anecdotal material but, as has often been recognised, the summary

---

[7] See Chapter 6, below.

[8] There is no earlier 'census' of British colonial slave-ownership equivalent to the Slave Compensation Commission records, and therefore no systematic proof of the wider dispersion of financial exposure to slave-ownership is available. However, intrinsic to the 'modified primogeniture' that largely governed the transmission of slave-ownership – in which financial claims in the forms of legacies and mortgages (although not by definition annuities for a single life) by dependents other than the primary heir (or heiress) accreted over generations – was an increasing cascade of individuals involved with slavery. The theoretical case is supported by the anecdotal evidence of the Commission records, in which many claims on estates were shared by multiple individuals in Britain. See Chapter 5, below.

[9] *Slavery Abolition Act: an account of all sums of money awarded by the Commissioners of Slavery Compensation*, PP 1837–8, Vol. 48 (215), referred to hereafter as the 'Parliamentary Return' or the 'Return', which lists awards totalling £18,669,401 10s 7d (p. 334).

lists of names in the Return are an inadequate basis for determining the true beneficiaries of slave-compensation. Reliance on the Return, for example, has actively misled the Synod of the Church of England, which was told in February 2006 that Henry Phillpotts, the Bishop of Exeter, had been a slave-owner along with his 'business associates'.[10] In fact, as the underlying records of the Commission clearly show, Phillpotts and his fellow-claimants were trustees and executors under the will of the Earl of Dudley, and while such a role could give very substantial control over and access to funds held under trust, the bald identification of Phillpotts as slave-owner and beneficiary of compensation is not tenable. Again, Richard Sheridan was puzzled to find no sign of the heir of Sir William Young, the Governor of Tobago and owner of five estates in the West Indies, in the Parliamentary Return: the underlying records show the unsuccessful pursuit of compensation by Sir William Young's grandson, who lost it to mortgagees and others with prior claims on the Young estates.[11] The records as a whole thus provide significantly more detail and depth for many of the claims, allowing a more reliable analysis of the identity of the slave-owners, and the construction of a prosopography of the major recipients of compensation.[12]

Emancipation and compensation extended not only to the Caribbean but also to the Cape of Good Hope and Mauritius. Together, these

---

[10] Rev. Simon Bessant to General Synod of the Church of England; see 'Church apologises for slave trade', http://news.bbc.co.uk/1/hi/uk/4694896.stm, 8 February 2006. The same claim was repeated in the House of Commons by Chris Bryant, MP for Rhondda: 'The Bishop of Exeter kept 655 slaves until the time of Abolition of Slavery Act 1833 and he received £12,700 in compensation', Hansard, 6 March 2006, Col. 600:21. See T71/915, p. 58; T71/859, Clarendon Nos. 284 and 320; and T71/858, Vere No. 70 for the erroneous filing of the claims for 'the heirs of the Earl of Dudley'. See T71/962 for a letter of 14 September 1835 to the Commission from the London solicitors Alban and Benbow that points out the error, asks for the compensation to be awarded instead in the names of Phillpotts et al. as trustees and executors, and includes a summary of part of the Earl of Dudley's will; PROB 11/121 for the Earl of Dudley's will itself, proved London 17 September 1833; and The Times, 11 March 1845, p. 6 for the closing of accounts by the trustees and the entry of the late Earl's heir, Lord Ward, into his inheritance.

[11] R. B. Sheridan, 'Sir William Young (1749–1815): planter and politician, with special reference to slavery in the British West Indies', Journal of Caribbean History, 33.1 2 (1999), 1 26; Sheridan was aware of a claim from Young's family that was disputed after the publication of the Return, p. 21. For the correspondence of Sir William Laurence Young of North Dean, High Wycombe with the Commission, see T71/1592, pp. 263–4 (Commission to Sir William Laurence Young MP); T71/1592, pp. 272–3 (Commission to John Ramsey (Young's agent)); T71/1602, 2 October 1835 and T71/1610, 28 September 1835 (Young to the Commission). The claims he pursued included T71/877, Antigua No. 282; T71/891; Tobago No. 64; T71/880; Grenada No. 691; and T71/892, St Vincent Nos. 559, 577.

[12] For a more detailed discussion of some of the limitations and issues of the underlying records as a source, see Chapter 4, below.

two colonies received £3.35 million of the total compensation of £20 million.[13] However, the demographics of the slave-owners of these two important arenas both differed from the predominantly anglophone and anglo-centric owners of the Caribbean. The Cape of Good Hope was characterised by many small slave-owners, generally of Dutch-Boer extraction; Mauritius remained a francophone plantocracy. This is not to say that there were no linkages between these slave economies and metropolitan Britain: it was axiomatic at the time of Emancipation, and remains so in much of the subsequent literature, that Mauritius in particular had rapidly become dependent on British mercantile credit.[14] Nevertheless, because of the different cultural and national backgrounds of the slave-owners, this study, focused as it is on the British metropolitan slave-owners, does not seek to analyse these two non-Caribbean colonies.[15]

Much of the energy and most of the excitement of the recent literature of late colonial slavery has been devoted – appropriately – towards retrieving, documenting and seeking to understand the experience of the *enslaved*. In focusing instead on the metropolitan slave-owners, this study aims to bring into view the identities, actions, rhetoric and behaviours that slavery as an economic system entailed for elite groups of overwhelmingly (but not exclusively) white men and women in Britain, without implying in any way a privileging of these histories over those of the men and women impacted so directly, brutally and continuously

[13] National Debt Office: Abolition of Slavery Act 1833, Registers of compensation paid to slave owners, NDO4/26 Awards actually paid. The Cape received £1,241,355 16s 9d, and Mauritius £2,110,950 0s 4d.

[14] See for example A. J. Barker, *Slavery and antislavery in Mauritius 1810–1833: the conflict between economic expansion and humanitarian reform under British rule* (London: Macmillan, 1996), p. 5: 'With most Mauritius estates mortgaged to British creditors and with nearly all sugar exports from the island, largely as a consequence of loan conditions, flowing into the London market, the colony's economic dependence on Britain [by 1833] was almost complete'; and P. Burroughs, 'The Mauritian Rebellion of 1832 and the abolition of British colonial slavery', *Journal of Imperial and Commonwealth History*, 4.3 (May 1976), 244–65 (pp. 245–6): 'British merchants and creditors ... by 1832 apparently held mortgages on all but one of the island's sugar plantations.'

[15] In addition, Bermuda and the Bahamas, accounting for £178,000 in compensation, have been omitted from the quantitative analysis: neither had significant concentrations of slave-ownership or material levels of absentee ownership: National Debt Office: Abolition of Slavery Act 1833, registers of compensation paid to slave-owners, NDO4/26 Awards actually paid. The Bahamas received £128,294 10s 7d, and Bermuda £50,397 11s 7d. The Bahamas had 39 claims over £500, amongst which Lord Rolle, who received compensation of £4,333 6s 9d for 337 slaves, was easily the largest claimant and the only slave-owner readily identifiable as an absentee in this period (Return, p. 149; Bahamas No. 960).

by enslavement over many centuries, and whose exploitation was undertaken in large measure on behalf of British slave-owners. Such an investigation of the British slave-owners, whose presence and nature as historic actors this study seeks to (re-)establish is essential both to exploring how Emancipation happened as and when it did, and – it is argued – to beginning to understand how the extent and limits of Britain's complicity in slavery can be conceptualised. If Colley and others are correct in asserting that anti-slavery became a key ingredient in the making of British identity in the late eighteenth and early nineteenth centuries, what did this imply for slave-owners who lived in Britain and stood so directly in opposition to the prevailing social and ethical currents, and how were they reconciled to the nation?[16] The absentee slave-owner, as an essentially liminal figure, should therefore be an ideal field of enquiry in the 'new imperial history'. In fact, with the notable exception of an unpublished dissertation by Alexandra Franklin, very little work has been done that brings modern historiographical concerns to bear on British slave-owners.[17]

Much of the literature that touches on the absentee slave-owners continues to treat absenteeism, in Eric Williams' phrase, as 'the curse of the Caribbean', foregrounding the consequences for the *colonial* societies of absenteeism and treating those consequences as entirely negative. Lowell Ragatz set out the basis for this conventional approach. He traced three phases in the creation of the absentee slave-owner (or 'landlord', as Ragatz significantly labelled such slave-owners): the prosperity

[16] L. Colley, *Britons: forging the Nation 1707–1837* (New Haven: Yale University Press, 1992), pp. 370–81. According to James Walvin, by the beginning of the nineteenth century, anti-slavery had become 'a defining quality of being British; a proof of the distinctive and divinely-inspired qualities of the British people'. Quoted in A. Lester, *Imperial networks: creating identities in nineteenth-century South Africa and Britain* (London and New York: Routledge, 2001), p. 25.

[17] A. Franklin, 'Enterprise and advantage: the West India interest in Britain 1774–1840', Ph.D. thesis, University of Pennsylvania, 1992. Franklin examined the records of the West India Committee, as the organised expression of the West India interest in Britain, with a 'new imperial' sensibility, to pose questions of identity and representation beyond the conventional analysis of the Committee as a sectional pressure-group. For more traditional accounts of the 'West India' lobby in Britain, see L. M. Penson, *The colonial agents of the British West Indies* (London, 1924; reprinted London: Frank Cass & Co., 1971); 'The London West India interest in the eighteenth century', *English Historical Review*, 36.143 (1921), 373–92; 'The origin of the Crown Agency Office', *English Historical Review*, 40.158 (1925), 196–206; A. E. Furness, 'George Hibbert and the defence of slavery in the West Indies', *Jamaican Historical Review*, 5.1 (1965), 56–70; D. Hall, *A brief history of the West India Committee* (St Lawrence, Barbados: Caribbean University Press, 1971); and, more recently, A. J. O'Shaughnessy, 'The formation of a commercial lobby: the West Indies, British colonial policy and the American Revolution', *Historical Journal*, 40 (1997), 71–95.

of the sugar-economy in the mid eighteenth century, which allowed the owners both to educate their children in England (*sic*) and to retire there themselves; the period from 1775 to 1815, when large numbers of estates passed into the possession of inhabitants of England (*sic*) by inheritance; and the period from 1815 to 1834, when 'the greater part of them fell into the hands of creditors, chiefly West Indian traders in London and the outports, through foreclosing of mortgages'.[18] But his focus was on the destructive impact of absenteeism in the colonies, its social results seen as increasing the disproportion between blacks and whites, the debasement of colonial society (by the removal of the 'natural' governing elite of principal land-owners to Britain), and the passing of local pride and feeling in the colonies.[19] Douglas Hall's challenge to this traditional model of absenteeism, in which he called for more focus on the specifics of time and place rather than reliance on generic models of absenteeism, enriched the discussion by emphasising the diversity of experience underlying the category of 'absentee'.[20] More recently, Trevor Burnard returned to the question of absenteeism in eighteenth-century Jamaica, in order to test its true extent, to deepen Hall's suggestive work about the diversity of 'absentee' experiences and to qualify, if not overturn, the notion of absenteeism as an unmitigated disaster for the colonies.[21]

The *resident* slave-owners have received attention within the context of the 'new imperial history', concerned to integrate metropole and colony and to bring to bear perspectives of race and gender on the local slave-owning communities. Christer Petley has examined the slave-owning society of St James's parish in Jamaica and looked at the collision between colonial and metropolitan values.[22] Barry Higman has recently provided texture to the lives and work of the attorneys, the necessary corollary of absentee ownership.[23] David Lambert's recent work exemplifies the 'new imperial history', meticulously applying a by-now familiar theoretical framework to Barbadian society at the time

---

[18] Ragatz, 'Absentee landlordism', p. 7.

[19] *Ibid.*, p. 18.

[20] D. Hall, 'Absentee proprietorship in the British West Indies, to about 1850', *Journal of Caribbean History*, 35.1 (2001), 97–121 (originally published in *Jamaican Historical Review*, 4 (1964), 15–35).

[21] T. Burnard, 'Passengers only: the extent and significance of absenteeism in eighteenth-century Jamaica', *Atlantic Studies*, 1.2 (2004), 178–195.

[22] C. Petley, 'Boundaries of rule, ties of dependency: Jamaican planters, local society and the metropole 1800–1834', Ph.D. thesis, University of Warwick, 2003. See also J. P. Greene, 'Liberty, slavery and the transformation of British identity in the eighteenth-century West Indies', *Slavery & Abolition*, 21.1 (April 2000) 1–31.

[23] B. W. Higman, *Plantation Jamaica 1750–1850: capital and control in a colonial economy* (Mona, Jamaica: University of the West Indies Press, 2005).

of abolition.[24] In focusing on Jamaica and Barbados, such recent works have tended to reinforce the bias of historiography to the old colonies, those in most perceptible decline towards the end of British colonial slavery.

Little work has been done directly on the social dimensions *in Britain* of absentee metropolitan slave-owning in the nineteenth century, to trace how the stock eighteenth-century character of the 'West Indian' was modified and normalised in the early decades of the nineteenth century.[25] These metropolitan slave-owners are largely invisible in the historiography of abolition. Seymour, Daniels and Watkis concluded that 'there is little evidence to suggest that colonial land-ownership [i.e. slave-ownership] was a sufficient distinction to exclude such people from British elite society, although in certain situations such connections could cause fractures', and argued, based on the case of their subject Sir George Cornewall, that ownership of colonial property was not an anomaly, but an addition to a varied portfolio of interests.[26] But sensible though their first conclusion seems, there is no empirical material adduced in support of it; and the second conclusion, on the 'portfolio' model of slave-owning, is not supported by the analysis later in this study for British rentier-owners, although it has more validity for a group of mercantile investors.

Histories of specific slave-owning families in Britain both raise the question as to how representative such families were, and confirm the value of the Slave Compensation Commission records. Pares on the Pinney family, Checkland on the Gladstones and most recently Smith on the Lascelles (subsequently the Earls of Harewood) have all delineated the processes of wealth-creation from slavery.[27] None was particularly interested in the identity and social tensions of a slave-owning

[24] D. Lambert, *White creole culture, politics and identity in the age of Abolition* (Cambridge: Cambridge University Press, 2005).

[25] F. W. Pitman, 'The West Indian absentee planter as a British colonial type', *Proceedings of the Pacific Coast Branch of the American Historical Association* (1927), 113–27, is suggestive, but addresses mainly the origins of absenteeism rather than the identity of the absentee in Britain.

[26] S. Seymour, S. Daniels and C. Watkis, 'Estate and Empire: Sir George Cornewall's management of Moccas, Herefordshire and La Taste Grenada 1771–1819', *Journal of Historical Geography*, 24.3 (1998), 313–51.

[27] R. Pares, *A West India fortune*, (London: Longman, 1950); S. G. Checkland, *The Gladstones: a family biography 1764–1851* (Cambridge: Cambridge University Press, 1971); Smith, *Slavery, family, and gentry capitalism.* There are also smaller-scale studies of individual absentee slave-owners, including: C. Taylor, 'The journal of an absentee proprietor, Nathaniel Phillips of Slebech', *Journal of Caribbean History* 18.1 (1984), 67–82; and V. E. Chancellor, 'Slave-owner and anti-slaver: Henry Richard Vassall Fox, 3rd Lord Holland 1800–40', *Slavery & Abolition*, 1.3 (December 1980), 263–75.

family in private and public life, although there is abundant evidence in each of their efforts to 'normalise' their slave-derived wealth through redeployment into other forms of property, especially landed property, in Britain. All three also allow a testing of the methodology of this study by providing details from family papers of the results of the compensation process, which in each case corroborate the conclusions drawn from an examination of the Commission records.

This book, in seeking to redress the past neglect of the British slave-owners, is not a history of Emancipation, but an analysis of British slave-owning at the time of Emancipation through the prism of 'slave compensation'. The compensation paid to slave-owners has itself attracted little attention from historians. The only general history of the compensation process is an unpublished thesis written over seventy-five years ago, a traditional but exhaustive administrative history that focuses on the organisation of the Commission before ending with an analysis of the relationship between Emancipation and the Great Trek.[28] Eric Williams drew on the Parliamentary Return of compensation payments to highlight individual slave-owners, and the examples he selected have tended to recur in the historiography.[29] More recently, Kathleen Mary Butler broke new ground in her examination of the impact of slave-compensation on Jamaica and Barbados.[30] Butler's method of combining research in the colonial mortgage registers with the metropolitan records of compensation yielded valuable detailed examples of the interaction of mercantile creditors and slave-owners, and she highlighted the role of women as slave-owners and private creditors in the colonies. Ultimately, her focus of interest was the *local* impact of compensation in the two colonies, rather than its dimensions in metropolitan Britain, with which this study is concerned: she was uninterested in British slave-owners as such, and her conclusions tended to reinforce the traditional 'mercantile'

---

[28] R. E. P. Wastell, 'The history of slave compensation 1833 to 1845', M.A. thesis, University of London, 1933. The Parliamentary Return itself has been analysed by Richard Lobdell, who drew from it statistics on the apparent structure of slave-ownership in each colony by number of owners, size of holding and sex. Professor Lobdell kindly made available to me his unpublished findings: R. A. Lobdell, 'The price of freedom, financial aspects of British slave Emancipation 1833–38. Notes on research in progress', unpublished paper delivered at the Annual Meeting of the Social Sciences History Association, Pittsburgh (October 2000).

[29] Williams, *Capitalism and slavery* highlights compensation payments to the Bishop of Exeter, p. 43; Earl St Vincent, p. 44; the Baillie family, p. 62; the Miles family, pp. 74–5; William Beckford and the Hibberts, p. 88; John Gladstone, p. 90; Henry Goulburn and the Earl of Balcarres, p. 94; and Joseph Marryat, p. 105.

[30] K. M. Butler, *The economics of Emancipation: Jamaica and Barbados, 1823–1843* (Chapel Hill: University of North Carolina Press, 1995).

interpretation of compensation flowing very largely to metropolitan creditors.

Examination of the slave-compensation process from the perspective of domestic British slave-owners also provides a new route into the questions raised by Eric Williams, both as to the relationship between abolition of the slave-trade and the economics of British colonial slavery and as to the relationship between slavery and Britain's industrial and commercial transformation.[31] Of Williams's four key theses (that racism was a result, not a cause, of slavery; that Britain's Industrial Revolution was heavily dependent on the slave-economy; that the slave-economy suffered a decline after the American Revolution; and that abolition of the slave-trade and of slavery itself was motivated not by disinterested humanitarianism but by rational economic calculation), the material and arguments presented here on British slave-ownership at the end of colonial slavery are directly relevant to all but the first.[32] It is important to emphasise at the outset that it is fully recognised that the data and analysis in this study do indeed concern British colonial slavery at the *end* of its existence, whereas Williams's primary focus was on wealth-creation in the eighteenth century. It will become clear, however, that Commission records not only represent a comprehensive census of slave-ownership as of a single date (1 August 1834) but also express processes of transmission, inheritance and financial structuring dating back to the eighteenth century, and therefore capture some of the period of Williams's key concerns, by which the analysis is in turn illuminated.

In the light of Williams's work, therefore, this study seeks in part to explore the extent to which the co-existence of the continued private

---

[31] Williams, *Capitalism and slavery*. For a summary of the voluminous literature stimulated by Williams, see for example C. L. Brown, *Moral capital: foundations of British abolitionism* (Chapel Hill: University of North Carolina Press, 2006), pp. 15–17.

[32] B. L. Solow and S. L. Engerman (eds.), *British capitalism and Caribbean slavery: the legacy of Eric Williams* (Cambridge: Cambridge University Press, 1987), p. 1. For all the ebbs and flows of historiography of the past sixty years, there is now widespread if not universal acceptance of the 'weak' form of Williams's argument, that industrialisation and commercial transformation were partly shaped by the slave-economy. J. E. Inikori, *Africans and the Industrial Revolution in England: a study in international trade and economic development* (Cambridge: Cambridge University Press, 2002) sought to re-ignite the 'strong' version of the Williams thesis – that the Industrial Revolution depended on the slave-economy and could not have occurred without it – in his wide-ranging re-appraisal of the Industrial Revolution and the Atlantic world. The reception of Inikori's book tended to confirm the consensus around the 'weak' form of linkage: see J. E. Inikori, S. D. Behrendt, M. Berg *et al.*, 'Roundtable: reviews of Joseph Inikori's *Africans and the Industrial Revolution: a study in international trade and economic development* with a response by Joseph Inikori', *International Journal of Maritime History*, 15.2 (December 2003), 279–361.

profitability of slavery with its declining importance at the national level gave rise to tensions that were ultimately mediated by the payment of compensation. But the study also allows us to re-examine the refutation of Williams implicitly constructed by Rubinstein in his extensive work on the prosopographies of the nineteenth-century rich.[33]

Rubinstein's studies of the wealthy in Britain potentially provide a basis for confronting the 'systemic' contentions of Williams and Inikori with the empirical evidence showing how diverse were the sources of wealth in nineteenth-century Britain. However, there are significant problems with Rubinstein's material as evidence for the linkage or lack of it between Britain's economic development and slavery. First, there is an unacknowledged limitation: by focusing on deaths only from the early nineteenth century onwards, Rubinstein by definition misses the mass of eighteenth-century wealth derived from slavery (a limitation that this study in part shares). Second, Rubinstein does not identify (as Inikori did) trades that had broader economic links to slavery. Thus Rubinstein can write of Bristol that 'there were virtually no fortunes here whose origins lay in the slaving and mercantile past of that town' immediately after specifying 'nearly all of its wealth-holders belonged to two families, the tobacco-manufacturing Willses and the Frys, the Quaker sweets manufacturers': there is no acknowledgement of the central role of slavery in the supply of tobacco, chocolate or sugar to these industries.[34] Ultimately, Rubinstein brushes away the linkages between Britain and slavery: 'Very few wealth-holders earned their fortunes in 'immoral' trades such as slave-trading or plantation-owning based on slavery. Most of these were at the lesser wealthy level ... No English millionaire ever made his money from the slave trade or the employment of slaves.'[35]

This study aims in part to examine that judgement in the light of the evidence from the slave-compensation process. In so doing, it inevitably bears on the international discussions of restitution or reparations for slavery that have their origins in the USA, have found traction in the Caribbean and in Africa, and that were greatly stimulated in Britain by the commemoration in 2007 of the bicentenary of the abolition of the slave-trade.[36]

---

[33] W. D. Rubinstein, *Men of property: the very wealthy in Britain since the Industrial Revolution*, 2nd edn (London: The Social Affairs Unit, 2006).

[34] *Ibid.*, p. 135.   [35] *Ibid.*, p. 141.

[36] See the summary in A. Rupprecht, 'Excessive memories: slavery, insurance and resistance', *History Workshop Journal*, 64 (Autumn 2007), 6–28.

John Torpey coined the term 'entrepreneurs of memory' for the activists, theologians, therapists, attorneys, historians, educators and the 'activist injured' engaged in (re-)establishing the relationship between past injury and present disadvantage as a precursor to seeking restitution, reparations or compensation for the injured.[37] But what else is the historian's function, if not to re-establish the relationship between past and present and in doing so to constrain memory within the disciplines of history? The reparations paid by Germany to Holocaust survivors in the aftermath of the Second World War, by Japan to Korean 'comfort women' and by the USA to internees of Japanese descent, as well as the restitution by Swiss banks returning deposits to Holocaust survivors, have all involved historians accessing and evaluating records, often on a privileged basis.[38] The debates about restitution or reparations for slavery in the USA have created a new specialisation for historians in researching the involvement of financial institutions in antebellum slavery: such research is as a cost of doing business for suppliers to the city of Chicago, for example, and for insurance companies in California. Specific firms and institutions are responding to the findings of historical research by seeking in effect a settlement with their pasts, a settlement that has predictably been hard to reach.[39]

But this is also charged territory for historians. As Rupprecht has observed, the act of disclosure by a financial institution of its prior linkages to slavery has itself become the event and the act of atonement: the content of the disclosure appears to matter less.[40] And such 'directed' histories are rarely complete, rarely capture all the elements of

---

[37] J. Torpey, *Making whole what has been smashed: on reparation politics* (Cambridge, MA: Harvard University Press, 2006), pp. 19–20.

[38] For one perspective on the comparison of the campaign for reparations for slavery with recent precedents, see R. E. Howard-Hassmann and A. P. Lombardo, 'Framing reparations claims: differences between the African and Jewish social movements for reparations', *African Studies Review*, 50.1 (April 2007), 27–48, and R. E. Howard-Hassmann, *Reparations for Africa* (Philadelphia: University of Pennsylvania Press, 2008).

[39] See, for example, the work for Bank One and JPMorgan Chase described in the press release from History Associates Incorporated dated 20 January 2005, www.historyassociates.com; ABN AMRO Bank NV, *Predecessors of ABN AMRO Bank NV and their connection to African slavery in the United States and the Americas* (April 2006), www.abnamro.com/com/about/history/pdf/hai_report.pdf; Brown University, *Slavery and justice, report of the Brown University Steering Committee on Slavery and Justice*, www.brown.edu/slaveryandjustice; and P. Flaherty and J. Carlisle, *The case against reparations*, National Legal and Policy Center, www.nlpc.org.

[40] 'This has enabled the process to be transformed rapidly from evidence of corporate complicity into evidence of corporate responsibility': Rupprecht, 'Excessive memories', p. 11.

inter-linkage between a financial institution and the slave-economy.[41] Yet despite their disclaimers, such histories are effectively positioned as representing the last word, based as they are on privileged access to archives and to resources.

A common assumption, little examined, governing the debate about reparations, on the part of both advocates of reparations and their opponents, is the *systemic* collective responsibility of white Britain (or America) for slavery.[42] Randall Robinson's manifesto in *The debt: what America owes to Blacks* is explicit that collectively the American state and the white American people should bear the cost of reparations.[43] David Horowitz, in his refutation, sought to undermine the notion of collective responsibility, and then treated the refutation of collective responsibility as the refutation of the concept of reparations altogether.[44] But part of the impetus behind this study has been a concern to locate the accountability for slavery more precisely. As Rhoda Howard-Hassmann argued, 'it is possible to sort out different levels of responsibility on the part of different actors'.[45] Who benefited from slavery? Most immediately, it was the slave-owners and those who supplied them with slaves, credit and goods. Since Adam Smith, there has been a continued and, in the end, inconclusive debate as to the impact of the West Indian colonial economies on national wealth.[46] But British colonial slavery was without a doubt *privately* profitable, at some periods and in some colonies spectacularly so. Those profits were extracted in the first instance from the appropriation of the labour of the enslaved. But the profits

---

[41] See Chapter 7, below, pp. 245–246 for comments on the incomplete scope and misleading conclusions of the original Citizens Financial Group, Inc. and Royal Bank of Scotland Group, *Historical research report: predecessor institutions research regarding slavery and the slave trade, May 25 2006, undertaken for Citizens Financial Group, Inc. and the Royal Bank of Scotland Group*, www.citizensbank.com/pdf/historical_research.com.

[42] An exception is the class-based analysis by B. Dalbey, 'Slavery and the question of reparations', *International Socialist Review*, 26 (November–December 2002), 74–80.

[43] R. Robinson, *The debt: what America owes to Blacks* (New York: Plume, 2001).

[44] D. Horowitz, 'Ten reasons why reparations is a bad idea for blacks – and racist too' (1 March 2001), www.frontpagemag.com/Articles/Printable.aspx?GUID={23D875BO-65A3–44; and D. Horowitz, *Uncivil wars: the controversy over reparations for slavery* (San Francisco: Encounter Books, 2002).

[45] R. E. Howard-Hassmann, 'Moral integrity and reparations for Africa', in J. Torpey (ed.), *Politics and the past: on repairing historical injustices* (Lanham, MD: Rowman and Littlefield 2003), pp. 193–215 (p. 206).

[46] See R. B. Sheridan, 'The wealth of Jamaica in the eighteenth century', *Economic History Review*, NS 18.2 (1965), 292–311; 'The wealth of Jamaica in the eighteenth century: a rejoinder', *Economic History Review*, NS 21.1 (1968), 46–61; R. P. Thomas, 'The sugar colonies of the Old Empire: profit or loss for Great Britain', *Economic History Review*, NS 21.1 (April 1968), 30–45; Smith, *Slavery, family, and gentry capitalism*, pp. 139–73.

for owners of the enslaved in British colonies were also sustained by a system of protective tariffs under which higher duties were paid by the British people on foreign-grown tropical produce, especially sugar. These duties as a whole in turn helped fund the expansion of the British state while shielding the wealthier sections of the population from more progressive taxation regimes. A section of the British elite thus utilised its political influence for more than two centuries to defend its interest at the expense of the enslaved and at the expense of the mass of the British people. When that system was brought down, by the combined effect of resistance by the enslaved and popular political activity by abolitionists, the slave-owners received one final transfer payment in the form of slave-compensation. The process of paying that compensation allows clear identification of who in Britain at that time owned slaves and who benefited from the compensation. A real enquiry into Britain's 'debt to slavery' does not end with the slave-owners and their creditors at the time the system came to an end, but it can start there, and this study is a contribution to that enquiry.

The study is organised to provide context both for absentee slave-ownership and for the decision to compensate the slave-owners on Emancipation, and then to present detailed analysis of the British slave-owners who received compensation in the 1830s. Accordingly, Chapter 1 explores the ways in which British slave-owners represented themselves and were represented in the period of contestation over Emancipation between the revival of the abolitionist campaign in 1823 and the end of Apprenticeship in 1838. It draws particularly on the attacks on British slave-owners by abolitionists in the *Anti-slavery Monthly Reporter* (*ASR*) to show the form and nature of pressure exerted on these slave-owners, and on the evidence of a number of Select Committees in the 1830s to analyse how such slave-owners positioned themselves in response to such pressure in a new public sphere. The specific debates within the Emancipation controversy over the award of compensation to the slave-owners are examined separately in Chapter 2, tracing both the intellectual bases of advocacy of, and antagonism to, the principle of compensation, and the evolution of the practical scheme of payments ultimately adopted. Compensation was an integral part of the wider discourses of slavery and anti-slavery for both planters and abolitionists throughout the period between 1823 and the Emancipation Act 1833, and although the controversies over slavery and compensation are presented below in distinct chapters for ease and clarity of narrative, the two belong together. Rather than recapitulate some of the work on the parliamentary and extra-parliamentary history of the 'West India interest' in its organised manifestation as the West India Committee, these two chapters focus on analysing the discourse and representational strategies, and illustrating the social and political experience, of a broader swathe of slave-owners confronted by a society increasingly hostile to slavery.[47]

Chapter 3 looks at the mechanisms by which compensation was distributed and Chapter 4 presents the overall results of the analysis of the structure of British colonial slave-ownership as captured in the records of the compensation process. Chapters 5, 6 and 7 then analyse in more detail the composition of, respectively, large-scale rentier, 'widow and orphan' and merchant slave-owners and beneficiaries of compensation, and trace typical paths to ownership for these three broad categories of slave-owners. Chapters 5 and 6 also examine the language and terms in which respectively the large- and small-scale rentier slave-owners presented themselves in their dealings with the Slave Compensation Commission, while Chapter 7 seeks to highlight, in the case of the commercial interests engaged in slave-owning, first some 'uses of proceeds' in terms of reinvestment of the compensation money in other enterprises and, second, some continuities between recipients and beneficiaries of slave compensation and firms and institutions active today. Chapter 8 presents conclusions as to the structure and significance of British slave-ownership in the Age of Reform.

---

[47] This study does not attempt to address the interesting question of how the *enslaved* saw, and negotiated with, the metropolitan slave-owners.

1 The absentee slave-owner: representations and identities

The British absentee slave-owner's world spanned metropole and colony: whether or not the absentee physically moved between the two, his or her income in the metropolis depended on the outcome of forced labour processes thousands of miles away, and the experience of the enslaved and their immediate oppressors in the colonies was in turn shaped by the absence of the legal owner and ostensible locus of authority. The presence of slave-owners in Britain severely complicated the binary divisions of metropolitan virtue/colonial vice in the discourse of liberty, Britishness and abolition. Absentee slave-owners experienced a position of ambiguity: tied to the colonies but not of them, in British society but seen (certainly until the early nineteenth century) as 'West Indian', insulated from the accusation of personal cruelty but nevertheless living from the fruits of slavery, often making claims to gentility but at times the object of an overwhelming national movement of profound hostility towards the 'sin' of slavery.

These British slave-owners participated both as subjects and objects in the 'war of representation' over slavery between the revival of abolitionism in Britain in the early 1820s and the end of Apprenticeship in 1838.[1] A conflict ostensibly about a colonial system thousands of miles away proved to be deeply embedded in metropolitan society, not only as the site of imperial power but as the home of many slave-owners, large- and small-scale, influential and obscure. While it may be true (at least of the first half of the nineteenth century), as Cooper and Stoler suggest, that 'it is not clear that the idea of ruling an Empire captivated European publics for more than brief periods or that a coherent set of agendas and strategies for rule was convincing to a broad metropolitan population', it is categorically the case that access to metropolitan government and influence over it through shaping elite (and occasionally even popular) metropolitan opinion were

---

[1] C. Hall, *Civilising subjects: metropole and colony in the English imagination 1830–1867* (Cambridge: Polity Press, 2002), p. 107.

integral to both local and metropolitan discourses of colonialism.[2] Examples abound throughout the literature of struggles in the metropole over the appropriation of the production of colonial knowledge, from Thomas Clarkson's account of the abolitionists' efforts to establish the true mortality of British sailors in the slave-trade to Lester's account of William Gladstone and Sir Rufane Donkin attempting to exclude witnesses from Buxton's Select Committee on Aborigines (British Settlements) in 1835–6.[3]

In the extended contestation in Britain over slavery, new techniques and new institutional contexts allowed individual slave-owners to speak on their own behalves, but also exposed them to greatly increased scrutiny by their opponents. In particular, as this chapter explores below, the set-piece parliamentary battles of the Select Committees on slavery in 1832 and on Apprenticeship in 1836 provided forums in which individual slave-owners were confronted with the contradictions of their position in extended Committee sessions, the evidence from which was then subject to extraordinary public scrutiny. The 'war of representation' was not a confrontation between two monolithic camps. There were tensions and contradictions within each side. Nor did the struggle over slavery *dominate* British politics and public life. There were limits to the contestation. Slavery was only one of a number of highly divisive issues in British public life at the time, issues with which it was sometimes intertwined: religious freedom, parliamentary reform, reactions to factory industrialisation, control of the indigenous British poor.[4] It is perfectly possible to find private diaries of the time that make no, or only passing, mention of the abolition of slavery.[5] In political diaries, the abolition of slavery can attract less space than minor ministerial appointments.[6] The conflict over slavery was sometimes confined to private pressure within the bounds of friendship or association. The Rev. William Frend, for

[2] F. Cooper and L. A. Stoler (eds.), *Tensions of Empire: colonial cultures in a bourgeois world* (Berkeley: University of California Press, 1997), p. 6.

[3] T. Clarkson, *The history of the rise, progress and accomplishment of the abolition of the African slave trade by the British Parliament*, 2 vols. (London: 1808, reprinted Bibliobazaar, 2008), Vol. I, pp. 127, 177, 197–8, 235, 267; Vol. II, pp. 11, 16, 35–6, 121–3; A. Lester, *Imperial networks: creating identities in nineteenth-century South Africa and Britain* (London and New York: Routledge, 2001), pp. 109–10.

[4] See A. Burns and J. Innes (eds.), *Rethinking the Age of Reform* (Cambridge: Cambridge University Press, 2003) for the sheer range of institutions and practices subject to contested reform projects.

[5] E.g. Rev. F. E. Witts, *The diary of a Cotswold parson 1783–1854*, ed. David Verey (Stroud: Sutton Publishing, 1978; 2nd edn 2003).

[6] E.g. C. F. Greville, *A Journal of the reigns of King George IV and King William IV*, 2nd edn, ed. Henry Reeves, 3 vols. (London: Longman, 1874).

example, repeatedly pressed Robert Hibbert of East Hyde (cousin of the London merchant and pro-slavery advocate George Hibbert, and founder of the Unitarian Hibbert Trust) over Hibbert's slave-owning in Jamaica, but remained friendly with him.[7] Elsewhere, slave-owning was elided. When Sydney Smith's daughter Emily became engaged to George Hibbert's son Nathaniel in 1827, Smith wrote to Lady Grey to tell her of the engagement, but characterised George Hibbert as 'the Indian', rather than *West* Indian, merchant: Nathaniel he described as 'Mr Hibbert of the North Circuit ... a sensible high-minded young man who will eventually be well off'.[8]

Attacking an opponent for his slave-owning does not appear to have been a reflexive response for those engaged in other forms of social conflict with slave-owners. It is possible to find trenchant criticism of slave-owners couched in terms of *arrivisme* but not explicitly invoking slave-owning. Thus, when the slave-owner Charles Rose Ellis was made Lord Seaford in 1826, Greville reported the strictures: '[E]verybody cries out against Charles Ellis' peerage; he has no property, and is of no family, and his son is already a peer ... it is thought very ridiculous, and that he would have done much better to have declined it.'[9]

Again, in a Sheriff's Court case in Launceston in 1823 – in which Sir Rose Price, the owner of Worthy Park estate in Jamaica, brought a prosecution under an old statute whereby if 'any of the inferior class of tradesmen, or other idle and dissolute persons, should presume to shoot on any park, manor &c. they should be deemed and taken as wilful tres- passers, even if no previous notice should have been given to them not to trespass' – counsel for the defendant (an apothecary) said:

[I]n the present case, here was Sir Rose Price, whose family sprang up as but yesterday, and who was himself what he was from trade, presuming, under this statute, to stigmatize an honest and industrious tradesman as one of 'the inferior class', an 'idle and dissolute person'. Would the jury sanction such arrogance in the application of such as statute?[10]

Finally, Peel dismissed George Watson Taylor, the MP for Devizes, who squandered the fortune of his wife – the niece of the major Jamaican slave-owner Simon Taylor – in terms of his cultural pretensions, not

---

[7] J. Murch, 'Memoir of Robert Hibbert' (1874), in *The book of the Hibbert Trust* (printed by direction of the trustees for private circulation, 1933).

[8] S. Smith, *Selected letters of Sydney Smith*, ed. N. C. Smith (Oxford: Oxford University Press, 1956; 2nd edn, 1981), p. 119: Smith to Lady Grey, 13 September 1827.

[9] Greville, *Journal*, Vol. I, p. 85, quoted in B. W. Higman, *Montpelier, Jamaica: a plan- tation community in slavery and freedom 1739–1912* (Mona, Jamaica: University of the West Indies Press, 1998), p. 31.

[10] *The Times*, 7 April 1823, p. 3.

his slave-owning: 'No man ever bought ridicule at so high a price', Peel said, when Watson Taylor's *objets de vertu* were sold off in 1832.[11]

Yet there clearly was social and political conflict over slavery and abolition. The rhythm of the 'war of representation' was uneven between 1823 and 1838, with peaks of parliamentary and extra-parliamentary activity between 1823 and 1826, 1831 and 1833, and again between 1836 and 1838.[12] Canning's Resolutions in 1823 had provided a basis for a consensus around the official government policy of amelioration, and had been supported by 'West Indian' MPs, including Charles Ellis, Joseph Marryat, George Watson Taylor and Thomas Wilson.[13] Each side subsequently invoked the Resolutions: the abolitionists in seeking to make real the commitment to amelioration, and the anti-abolitionists in underscoring the implied commitment to compensation. As the Tory minister Robert Wilmot Horton said, 'it was doubtless very easy to compose those resolutions, but the terms involve a tremendous and responsible difficulty'.[14]

---

[11] R. G. Thorne, *The House of Commons 1790–1820*, 5 vols. (London: Secker & Warburg for the History of Parliament Trust, 1986), Vol. v, p. 498.

[12] These peaks, of course, correlate not only with domestic British political rhythms but also with key moments at which resistance by the enslaved broke out into open armed conflict or its imminent threat.

[13] On 15 May 1823, Thomas Fowell Buxton's resolution,

> which first raised the question of ultimate emancipation ... was withdrawn after much debate, being superseded by the following resolutions of Mr Canning; they were adopted without a division: – 'That it is expedient to adopt effectual and decisive measures for meliorating the condition of the slave population in his Majesty's colonies; That through a determined and persevering, but at the same time judicious and temperate enforcement of such measures, this House looks forward to a progressive improvement in the character of the slave population, such as may prepare them for a participation in the civil rights and privileges which are enjoyed by other classes of his Majesty's subjects; That this House is anxious for the accomplishment of this purpose at the earliest period that shall be compatible with the well-being of the slaves themselves, with the safety of the colonies, and with a fair and equitable consideration of the interest of private property' ... [W]ithin a fortnight instructions were sent to the governors of every slave colony to introduce the following reforms: – religious instruction was to be provided; Sunday markets were to be abolished; slave evidence was to be admissible; slave marriage was to be legalised; slave property was to be protected; manumission was to be facilitated; families were not to be separated by sale; arbitrary punishment, and the corporal punishment of females were to be abolished; the driving-whip was to be abandoned; and savings banks were to be established. (George Stephen, *Antislavery recollections in a series of letters addressed to Mrs Beecher Stowe* (London: Thomas Hatchard, 1854), pp. 61, 90–1)

[14] Rt Hon. R. Wilmot Horton, *Speech of the Rt Hon. R. Wilmot Horton in the House of Commons on the 6th of March 1828 on 'Moving for the production of the evidence taken before the Privy Council, upon an Appeal against the compulsory manumission of slaves in Demerara and Berbice'* (London: John Murray, 1828), p. 32.

The controversy over compulsory manumission in Demerara and Berbice in 1826–7 should have been an inflection point in the gradual realisation that the consensus around amelioration was not a stable one: instead, the specific Demerara issue was effectively parked, as the wider debate about slavery lost salience and political energies were focused on Catholic Emancipation and the prospect of parliamentary reform. Brougham's renewed motion on abolition in 1830 raised the temperature over slavery again in parliamentary and electoral politics between 1830 and 1833. Edward Protheroe Jr, for example, the scion of a slave-owning Bristol family, supported Brougham's motion, 'although in so doing he should displease many of his friends and raise serious obstacles to his return to Parliament' as MP for Bristol, as indeed he did.[15]

Nor did the passage of the Abolition Act in 1833 end the conflict. Contestation over the early end of the period of Apprenticeship intensified from 1836 to 1838, and the fault lines in British society over slavery are visible in the debates over Free Trade in the 1840s, and in the Governor Eyre controversy as late as 1867.

Against this background, this chapter examines, first, some of the new forums and mechanisms in which such contestation between British slave-owners and their opponents occurred and by which it was controlled, and second, the rhetorical themes and devices of the discourses that governed that struggle.

The public sphere

Slavery had obviously been the object of significant public debate and contestation in the early 1790s, and again at the time of the abolition of the slave-trade in 1807. By the 1820s, the mechanisms of Parliamentary Returns, the reporting of parliamentary debates and the appointment of Select Committees had become increasingly established, augmenting the flow of information as to what was being said in Parliament and providing new powers to individual MPs to command information from an increasingly orderly state apparatus.[16] The number of

---

[15] *ASR*, 64 (August 1830), Vol. III, p. 333. The slave-owner James Evan Baillie stepped forward as a rival Whig candidate against Protheroe in the 1830 election; in the following year, the two united on a Reform ticket against the Tory West Indian Richard Hart Davis; Peter Marshall, *Bristol and the abolition of slavery: the politics of emancipation* (Bristol: Bristol Branch of the Historical Association, 1975).

[16] P. Jupp, *British politics on the eve of reform: the Duke of Wellington's administration 1828–30* (London: Macmillan, 1998), pp. 195–227.

returns requested tripled from the 1780s to the 1820s, and the number of copies printed of key returns rose from a thousand to two-and-a-half thousand.[17] In the struggle over amelioration and emancipation in the 1820s and 1830s, there was more intense usage of these forums and parliamentary tools by both sides. What were new in the 1820s and 1830s were those tools that gave the potential to foreground the individual British slave-owner. Key amongst these were the triennial slave-registers, established originally as the brainchild of Zachary Macaulay and James Stephen, two abolitionists with direct personal experience of the slave-system, who understood the uses to which such periodic censuses of the enslaved could be put.

This constitution of an enhanced public space in which not only the nature of slavery but also the position of the identified individual slave-owner could be debated and discussed was not itself uncontested. The slave-owning London banker William Alers Hankey protested bitterly (but vainly) in his public *Letter to Thomas Wilson* of the violation of his privacy by the abolitionists: 'I require them to show what right the constitution of their own, or of any public institution, gave them to intrude into my private affairs, and found charges against me of having violated my own principles in the management of my property.'[18] Sturge and Harvey, in response, disclaimed any such intention to intrude, but denied that 'the interests of the slave population of our colonies, are the private concerns of any individual *proprietor*'.[19] What they did not do was to point to Hankey's own decision to enter the public sphere as a witness to the House of Commons Select Committee on the Extinction of Slavery in 1832, which placed Hankey at the centre of the 'war of representation'.[20]

The slave-registers

Within the expanded public sphere, the slave-registers in particular provided a key resource to the anti-slavery campaigners for identifying the owners of slaves and tracking the mortality of the enslaved. Established initially for Trinidad and St Lucia by Orders in Council in 1812 and 1814, slave-registers were instituted in all major colonies between 1816 and 1817, while the central Slave Registry Office in London was founded in 1819. The registers obliged a triennial return of slaves in the colonies,

---

[17] *Ibid.*, p. 196.
[18] W. A. Hankey, *Letter to Thomas Wilson Esq.* (London, 1833), quoted in J. Sturge and T. Harvey, *The West Indies in 1837* (London: Hamilton Adams & Co., 1838) p. lxxii.
[19] *Ibid.*   [20] See below, pp. 54–58, 62–63, 68–69.

generally organised by estate.[21] Howick drew on these in the House of Lords in 1833 to highlight mortality on the British Guiana estates of John Gladstone and others. The *ASR* used the registers relatively sparingly, generally only 'naming names' when the slave-owner had brought himself forward into the discussion of slavery, or when it was highlighting specific abuse in the colonies. However, it was capable of selectively publishing mortality tables, as it did in November 1829, when it published a comparison of the number of enslaved owned in 1824 and 1826 by eleven absentee 'proprietors', including the MPs John Foster Barham and Joseph Marryat, showing in every case a decline in the absolute number of enslaved: 'the Names [of British slave-owners] we have selected will be allowed to be of the first respectability and on the Estates of all of them the number of women is equal to, or more than, the number of men'.[22]

John Henry Deffell, the London merchant, intervened publicly in 1832 when the *ASR* misread the background of slaves on Deffell's Salt Spring plantation in Jamaica. He wrote twice to *The Times* to correct the *ASR*'s facts about the movement of slaves on and off the estate (which had distorted the analysis of mortality), the second time enclosing copies of his private correspondence with Thomas Pringle, the secretary of the Anti-slavery Society. However, Deffell was careful to confine himself to the recitation of facts, to present himself as defending his attorney W. S. Grignon rather than himself, and to avoid addressing the wider issues Pringle invited him to debate: 'It is neither my intention, nor my wish, to enter into a controversy with Mr Pringle on the question of Negro slavery.'[23]

Parliamentary Select Committees

In the year immediately preceding the Emancipation Act of 1833, two Commons' Select Committees, scrutinising the West Indies from

---

[21] B. W. Higman, *Slave populations of the British Caribbean 1807–1834* (Baltimore: Johns Hopkins University Press, 1984), p. 80. See *ibid.*, pp. 7–37 for discussion of the registers as historical sources.

[22] *ASR* No. 54 (November 1829), Vol. III, p. 146. The *ASR* meant that sexual imbalances could not explain the declines in the enslaved populations.

[23] *The Times*, 27 March 1832, p. 3; 3 April 1832, p. 1. The *ASR* had focused on mortality on the estate under Grignon's management in discussing the causes of the Jamaica slave rebellion, *ASR* No. 94 (10 March 1832), Vol. V, p. 111. A footnote on Grignon as the attorney of Salt Spring said: 'it belongs to Mr Deffell of London, and had upon it in 1826 177 slaves, being a decrease of 56 from 1821, when there were upon it 233. This is a decrease of 5 per cent per annum.' Deffell pointed out in the *Times* correspondence that he had only acquired the estate in June 1825, when it had had 126 slaves: Deffell had added 51 slaves, and there remained 177 slaves on the estate in 1831; Grignon had had no role prior to 1825.

different perspectives, and a Committee of the House of Lords (dupli-
cating to an extent the work of one of the Commons' Committees),
had provided public forums for a number of slave-owners in Britain to
define themselves in relation to their ownership of slaves.[24] A fourth
Select Committee, on Apprenticeship, sat in 1836.[25] The transcripts
of the interviews of witnesses before these Committees can be read as
revealing the construction of rival identities by and for a group of men
(and all the witnesses, of course, were men) who both owned slaves and
occupied positions of status or authority in a Britain that was generally
hostile to slavery. The tensions inherent in this ambiguous position of
the British slave-owner gave rise to contradictions in evidence to the
Select Committees that illuminate the moral, social, political and intellectual situation of absentee slave-owners on the eve of Emancipation.[26]
These tensions were in turn exploited by the abolitionists, who provided detailed commentary on the evidence and involvement in the
slave-economy of the slave-owners.[27]

The Commercial Committee completed its work and produced
a final report; the Extinction of Slavery Committee, however, was

[24] These were: the House of Commons' Select Committee on the State of the West
India colonies (1832: the 'Commercial Committee'); the House of Commons' Select
Committee on the Extinction of Slavery throughout the British Dominions (1832: the
'Extinction of Slavery Committee'); and the House of Lords' Committee on the
Condition and Treatment of the Colonial Slaves (1832: the 'Lords' Committee').

[25] The House of Commons' Select Committee appointed to inquire into the working of
the Apprenticeship system in the colonies, conduct of the Apprentices laws, regulations etc. (1836: the 'Apprenticeship Committee').

[26] Work has previously been done that draws on these transcripts, but none so far
has explored the self-representation of the slave-owner. See in particular D. Paton,
'Decency, dependency and the lash: gender and the British debate over slave
Emancipation 1830–1834', Slavery & Abolition, 17.3 (December 1996), 163–84; and
O. M. Blouet, 'Earning and learning in the British West Indies: an image of freedom
in the pre-Emancipation decade 1823–1833', Historical Journal, 34.2 (June 1991),
391–409. Both draw on the records of the Extinction of Slavery Committee. Paton's
close reading of the evidence taken by the Extinction of Slavery Committee revealed
the terrain of shared assumptions common to abolitionists and slave owners as to
the position of women, including belief in marriage rather than consent as the key to
morality in sexual relations, and categorisation of sexual violence as a sub-category
of the larger problem of 'fornication', rather than as a problem in itself. Paton also
revealed the 'invisibility' to the Committee of the enslaved woman as worker: whereas
at least 50 per cent of field labour was female, the Committee's vision of a post-
Emancipation society explicitly placed the woman in the home, maintained by her
husband, consistent with the 'separation of spheres' underway in domestic British
households and, indeed, the withdrawal of women from field labour after the end
of Apprenticeship in 1838. For this withdrawal, see for example Thomas C. Holt,
The problem of freedom: race, labour and politics in Jamaica and Britain, 1832–1938
(Baltimore: Johns Hopkins University Press, 1992), pp. 152–3.

[27] See for example anon., A letter from Legion to His Grace the Duke of Richmond the
Chairman of the Slavery Committee of the House of Lords containing an exposure of the

overtaken by the end of the parliamentary session, publishing its evidence with only a brief introduction, and no conclusion other than that the evidence 'discloses a State of Affairs demanding the earliest and most serious attention of the Legislature'.[28] Their purposes were clearly different. The first Committee engaged with the West India trade and the economics of sugar production under slavery since the abolition of the slave-trade, while the second Committee looked ahead to a post-Emancipation world and focused on two main points to be investigated: 'That the slaves, if emancipated, would maintain themselves, would be industrious and disposed to acquire property by labour … [and second] that the dangers of convulsion are greater from Freedom withheld than from Freedom granted to the Slaves'.[29] The Extinction of Slavery Committee therefore dealt more directly with issues affecting the moral standing of slave-owners, but the Commercial Committee nevertheless provided opportunity and stimulus to its witnesses to situate themselves in relation to their ownership of slaves and all its implications. None of the Committees dealt directly with the question of compensation to the slave-owners for emancipation. The Commercial Committee addressed whether any previous government act or policy (including abolition of the slave-trade) had contributed to the present distress of the West India trade, and if so whether and in what form compensation *for the past* was necessary. The Extinction of Slavery Committee explicitly treated as beyond its remit 'the important question of what is due "to the fair and equitable consideration of the Interests of Private Property", as connected with Emancipation'.[30] Nevertheless, an important subtext throughout the three reports is the positioning of slave-owners and their opponents on the question of compensation to slave-owners for emancipation.[31]

The composition of the Committees reflected their different concerns. The witnesses for the Commercial Committee, reflecting its focus, were drawn (although not equally) from all branches of the West India trade (slave-owners, West India merchants, a sugar-refiner, ship-owners, ship-brokers) together with a handful having experience of other sugar/slave regimes to provide comparisons. Two witnesses to

---

character and evidence of the colonial side produced before the Committee (London, [1832]); *Analysis of the Report of a Committee of the House of Commons on the extinction of slavery, with notes by the editor, printed for the Society for the Abolition of Slavery throughout the British dominions* (London, 1833); and *Abstract of the Report of the Lords Committee on the condition and treatment of colonial slaves* (London, 1833).

[28] *Report from the Select Committee on the extinction of slavery throughout the British dominions*, PP 1831–2, Vol. 20 (721), p. 4.

[29] *Ibid.*, p. 3.   [30] *Ibid.*, p. 4.

[31] See Chapter 3, below, pp. 88–90.

the Commercial Committee (William Burge, who as MP and agent for Jamaica was a member of the Committee as well as witness, and Joseph Marryat) sat subsequently as members on the Extinction of Slavery Committee. The Commercial Committee's was a 'technocratic' slate of witnesses, almost all of whom had vested interests in the West India trade: it did not include prominent advocates of 'free sugar', for example. It drew on a number of colonies for witnesses.

By contrast, the Extinction of Slavery Committee and the Lords' Committee were major parliamentary set-piece battles in the 'war of representation' between the abolitionists and their opponents. Most of the key Commons' representatives of the two sides sat on the twenty-five-strong Extinction of Slavery Committee when it was established on 24 and 30 May 1832, including Dr Lushington, Thomas Fowell Buxton, Lord Howick and Sir James Graham on the abolitionist side, and Viscount Sandon, William Burge (the agent for Jamaica) and Joseph Marryat on behalf of the slave-owners. The Lords' Committee was dominated, the *ASR* complained, by slave-owning peers. The heavily overlapping slates of witnesses for the Extinction of Slavery and Lords' Committees were compiled on an overtly partisan basis.

The Extinction of Slavery Committee first called and listened to witnesses in support of its two (pro-emancipation) hypotheses, and then subsequently called those perceived to be critical of the hypotheses. What becomes clear from the transcripts is that this was not a debate susceptible to such complete polarisation. Witnesses on both sides fell into contradiction or produced statements that must have surprised and dismayed their own supporters. The initial pro-emancipation witnesses were very largely missionaries, both Anglican and dissenting, but included a couple of 'prizes' (notably William Taylor) in the form of those with experience as planters, whose credibility became a central issue for the Committee. The bulk of the evidence, which the Committee acknowledged as a weakness, dealt only with Jamaica, at the expense of other colonies.

Of the twenty-seven witnesses to the Commercial Committee, fifteen later received compensation as slave-owners or mortgagees. Of the thirty-three witnesses to the Extinction of Slavery Committee, nine subsequently received compensation (as did the family of one abolitionist witness). Only one of these recipients of slave-compensation (Peter Rose) defined himself as resident in the Caribbean and only temporarily in Britain.[32] The self-biographies of the remaining twenty-three

---

[32] Rose had returned to England from British Guiana to represent the 'grievances which [the planters of that colony were] suffering under from the dissolution of the Courts

slave-owners highlight the diversity of the category of 'absentee'. Some had never been to the West Indies at all, a few had visited their estates for a period of one or two years, several had lived for an extended period in the West Indies before returning to Britain. Some depended for their livelihood on their slave-ownership; for others, it was a small part of much wider wealth. These different experiences, different adjacencies to slavery and different degrees of financial reliance shaped different claims on authority to speak, and different strategies of representation, on the part of the slave-owners. At the same time, there were common themes, especially around compensation, that united the disparate group of slave-owners.

The question-and-answer Committee format itself, of course, constrained and shaped the discourse of the witnesses (and of the Committee members), limiting and sometimes undermining their self-representation. The Committee members also operated within their own frameworks of thought and representation. They were on occasion startlingly well-informed about the detail of the topography of estates or, more unsettlingly, about personal circumstances of the witnesses. The abolitionists prepared meticulously for these set-pieces: George Stephen recalled how he had assisted Lord Suffield in the Lords' Committee:

As all the antecedents of every witness called by the West Indian peers were well known to me, as the solicitor of the Anti-slavery Society, I prepared over-night a short statement of them, and a list of questions to be put to the witness, the questions branching out into others, according as the answer might be expected: this sufficed for the first day's cross-examination of each witness: while the examination in chief was going on, Lord Suffield made copious notes of it, and those notes enabled me to prepare the cross-examination for the following day.[33]

Naming names

The abolitionists appear to have focused public attacks only on slave-owners in Britain who themselves emerged publicly as opposed to abolition. Occasionally, such attacks extended to slave-owners whose estates

---

of Justice and all the other institutions of the colony which took place 21st of July last' (*Report on the extinction of slavery*, Q. 1445–7, p. 182. Rose had spent half the previous twenty years in Britain serving as a Justice of the Peace in Aberdeen, when he was in Britain between 1820 and 1825, and again in 1833: C. McAlmont, 'Peter Rose: the years before 1835', *History Gazette*, 19 (April 1990), 2–9.

[33] Stephen, *Antislavery recollections*, p. 61. The transcripts themselves are limited by the lack of identification of the questioner: questions are simply numbered consecutively.

were the sites of particularly vivid examples of oppression, or at least of examples that ran concordantly with specific abolitionist concerns. Thus, in late 1830, the *ASR* highlighted the persecution of George Amah, an enslaved man and Baptist preacher on the Bogue estate in Vere owned by John Morant of Brockenhurst Park near Lymington, and reproduced from the Jamaican anti-slavery paper *The Watchman* the editorial on the case: 'Mr Morant, no doubt, supposes that his Negroes are happy and contented, and living in the enjoyment of liberty of conscience. The foregoing, however, but clearly proves he is mistaken.'[34]

George Stephen highlighted some of the limitations on the abolitionist 'naming of names'. If the abolitionists did not cite specific estates and owners in alleging incidents of cruelty, he said, they were charged with falsehood; if they did name specifics, their witnesses were subject to persecution and retaliation. As a result, there was reliance on official records such as the returns of the Fiscal for Berbice to document 'cases sufficiently numerous to prove such guilt to be systematic and not individual'. Stephen used the case of 'Mr [Nathaniel] Wells of Piercefield, Monmouthshire', the son of a white planter and an enslaved black woman, who served as deputy-lieutenant and who, Stephen told his audience, could be named 'because he was not less ignorant than yourselves of the circumstances I am about to state': after Wells had left his estate in St Kitts to settle in England, the number of enslaved had fallen from 140 in 1812 to 86 in 1819.[35]

Leadership or advocacy of the 'West India body', of course, entailed public identification as a slave-owner and drew abolitionist assaults. In 1826, the *ASR* focused on the Secretary of State Viscount Dudley and Ward after he had signed a pamphlet from 'the great colonial mart in Albemarle Street [i.e. the West India Committee]'.

This Nobleman has of late taken so conspicuous a part as an advocate of colonial interests, and has laboured with so much zeal to discredit the efforts of the Anti-slavery Society, that it becomes a matter of some moment to ascertain the degree in which he has acquired a title to guide the public opinion on this point.

The *ASR* went on to examine Dudley's support in 1807 for the abolition of the slave-trade, given explicitly because 'it would tend to the emancipation of the Negroes', to highlight the decline of the enslaved population on his estates at a time when American slave-populations

---

[34] *ASR* No. 71 (November 1830), Vol. III, p. 491.
[35] *Ibid.* No.74 (January 1831), Vol. IV, pp. 62–3, reporting a speech by Stephen in Oakham, 26 October 1830.

were known to be growing, and to confront Dudley with the contradictions between his position in 1807 and his actions and experience in the 1820s.[36]

When the lawyer and slave-owner Fortunatus Dwarris produced an anti-abolitionist pamphlet in 1828, the *ASR* referred back to Dwarris's role in the 1822–6 Commission of Legal Inquiry in the West Indies: 'we shall have little more to do, in the fulfilment of a great part of our task, than to try Mr Dwarris the pamphleteer, by the evidence of Mr Dwarris the Commissioner'.[37] The *ASR* went on to contrapose Dwarris's anti-abolitionist arguments with the criticisms he had made of the colonial legislatures earlier in the decade.

The *ASR* in mid 1831 focused on the signatories of the West India body's address, enclosing an abstract of the West India colonial laws, 'extensively circulated ... by hundreds of thousands'.

We have inserted the forty-one names subscribed to this paper by way of securing a lasting record of them. They are names which ought not to be forgotten ... they themselves, if they opened their eyes, could not but know, at the very time they affixed their signatures to this paper, that it was destitute of even the shadow of the truth.[38]

Did not the Jamaica laws, and their own attempted vindication of them, 'wear an air which in the case of less honourable men would be deemed somewhat akin to imposture?', asked the A*SR*.[39] On the retention of the cart whip, it said:

And not only are those, it would seem, ready to fight for it, who actually wield it, who exult in its explosions, and whose lust for power is gratified by directing and witnessing its application; but by forty-one chosen advocates of the West India body, residing among ourselves, mixing in our assemblies, joining our convivial parties, occupying seats in the imperial senate, and claiming the name and character of English gentlemen ... forty-one eminent planters who vauntingly tell us that, by the humane law of that island [Barbados] women when flogged, are to be flogged *decently*, and *with the military cat*, and that 'pregnant women' are no longer to be flogged but merely confined.[40]

Involvement in organised ameliorationist efforts, especially religious instruction, tended to create public profile, complexity and vulnerability for absentee slave-owners. Two Scottish slave-owners, William Stothert and Archibald Stirling, were respectively a director and the

---

[36] *Ibid.* No. 10 (March 1826), Vol. I, p. 174.
[37] *Ibid.* No. 37 (June 1828), Vol. II, p. 237.
[38] *Ibid.* No. 82 (June 1831), Vol. IV, pp. 290–2.
[39] *Ibid.*   [40] *Ibid.*, pp. 301–2.

brother of a second director (William Stirling, himself a slave-owner) of the Scottish Missionary Society, an Edinburgh-based organisation of the United Secession Church. Stothert and Archibald Stirling invited the Rev. George W. Blyth to go out to proselytise on their Jamaican plantations; Stirling subsequently invited a second missionary, the Rev. John Chamberlain. On Blyth's return on leave in 1831, he was reported to have commented favourably on slavery, and a letter of the same year by him to the *Edinburgh Christian Instructor* was seen as insufficiently critical of what he had witnessed. The *Scottish Missionary and Philanthropic Register* in 1833 published 'An apology for the Scottish missionaries in Jamaica', drafted by the secretary of the Scottish Missionary Society, which sought to address 'the conclusion that they have been unfaithful, because they have not been persecuted'.[41]

Stirling was singled out subsequently by the Anti-slavery Society in an aside to its analysis of the evidence of the Lords' Committee. The Society invoked the case of eight enslaved men executed on the Duke of Manchester's authorisation for rebellion and conspiracy in St Mary's parish in Jamaica between 1823 and 1824: indemnities had been paid by the colonial government for the executed men.

All these poor creatures, except the first, belonged to an estate called Frontier, the property of Archibald Stirling Esq., a Scotch gentleman, who stands high in reputation in Scotland as a religious character, but who seems to have pocketed £605 as the price of the blood of these seven innocent and murdered men.[42]

In the metropole, slave-ownership itself was thus not a sufficient ground for public attacks: public espousal of anti-abolitionist causes, however, was. As a result, some of the anti-abolitionists took refuge in anonymity or attempted anonymity. George Hibbert began an assault on the Rev. Thomas Cooper, who had spent three years on the estates of Hibbert's cousin Robert Hibbert, through a letter in *The Times* under the name of 'An Enquirer'.[43] Cooper quickly obliged Hibbert to disclose his authorship. Again, the brewer and slave-owner Benjamin Greene in Bury St Edmunds published a pamphlet attacking the abolitionists the

---

[41] J. H. Proctor, 'Scottish missionaries and Jamaican slaveholders', *Slavery & Abolition*, 25.1 (April 2004), 51–70.

[42] Anon., *Abstract of the report of the Lords' Committee on the condition and treatment of colonial slaves* (London, 1833), pp. 8–9.

[43] Thomas Cooper, *Correspondence between George Hibbert, Esq. and the Rev. T. Cooper relative to the condition of the Negro slaves in Jamaica extracted from the Morning Chronicle, also a Libel on the character of Mr & Mrs Cooper published in 1823 in several of the Jamaica journals, with notes and remarks* (London, 1824).

Rev. J. Orton, a Wesleyan minister, and Joseph Phillips of Antigua: initially anonymously, but the pamphlet was 'understood (and has been since avowed) to be the production of Benjamin Greene, the well-known pro-slavery champion in that place'.[44] Greene eventually left Bury St Edmunds, where he had published an anti-abolitionist newspaper, to resettle in London, apparently as a result of a related libel trial.[45] When John Gladstone launched his assault on James Cropper in response to Cropper's 'The impolicy of slavery' in the *Liverpool Mercury* of 31 October 1823, Gladstone's initial response was over the name of 'Mercator' in the *Liverpool Courier*, and Gladstone wrote an anonymous letter to William Cobbett attacking Cropper.[46]

But in Britain, despite the pressures exerted on individual slave-owners, there was no *systematic* effort to identify and assail absentee slave-owners, whereas there was indeed pressure exerted to force disclosure by public servants in the colonies. This disparity of treatment between metropole and colony tends to underline the importance of the artificial but pervasive fiction that slavery was a colonial rather than a domestic matter. The power of official scrutiny as applied to slave-owners in the colonies is vividly illustrated by some of the tortured and defensive responses published in the 1827 Parliamentary Return of those 'Public Functionaries' in all the slave-colonies who were engaged in the slave-economy.[47] In order to obtain this collation, the metropolitan state had intervened through its mechanisms of colonial government. Earl Bathurst's dispatch covering the request had included an instruction that Governors and Lieutenant-Governors in colonies in which 'Property in Slaves' existed would be prohibited from holding 'that species of property'. In some colonies, the Governors simply tabulated the factual replies from officials and clergymen affected by the compulsory disclosures, but in Jamaica the verbatim replies of the officials were included. William Burge, the Attorney-General who was

---

[44] *ASR* No. 74 (January 1831), Vol. IV, p. 69.
[45] Richard G. Wilson, *Greene King, a business and family history* (London: Bodley Head & Jonathan Cape, 1983), pp. 39–43.
[46] S. G. Checkland, *The Gladstones: a family biography 1764–1851* (Cambridge: Cambridge University Press, 1971), pp. 190, 192. Although these examples appear clear-cut, anonymity might be explained in other ways, notably the desire to highlight the argument rather than the arguer. Abolitionists also corresponded in the press under noms de plume, and *ASR* articles were unsigned.
[47] *Slaves in the Colonies: return to an address of the Honourable the House of Commons dated 8th March 1826 for A Return of all the Public Functionaries ... in all the Slave Colonies belonging to His Majesty, who are Proprietors of Slaves, or of Plantations worked by Slaves; or who are in occupancy or concerned in the management of slaves, either as Attorney, Manager, Trustee, Mortgagee, Executor or otherwise*, PP 1826–7, Vol. 22.1 (111), (146).

in Britain in the 1830s as agent for Jamaica, disclosed five domestic slaves and continued:

My wife is entitled, for her life, with a power of appointment amongst her children, to a coffee plantation called Warwick, in the parish of Manchester, and of [sic] certain slaves thereon. Plantation and 50 slaves in strict settlement for her benefit ... This settlement was made long before her marriage with me ... I always had a great objection to possess landed property or slaves.[48]

Lewis Bowerbank, of St Catherine's Rectory, acknowledged nine slaves of his own: 'I have also in right of my wife a claim to the fifth of a sugar estate called Dumbarton situated in the parish of St Anne. Upon this property there are, I believe, from 190 to 200 slaves; it is however under the sole direction and management of an attorney, appointed jointly by the parties, and it is not at all subject in these respects to my interference or control.'[49] The Rev. S. H. Cooke of St David said he had no slaves other than domestics.

The plantation called Mt Gotham, in the parish of St Catherine, together with the slaves thereon, although given in by Mrs Brooks, in my name, are not in fact mine; never having held the said plantation and slaves, by any other title than the will and pleasure of Mrs Brooks, whose property they are, for her natural life; and that I have not been in the occupancy, or concerned in any way with the management of the said plantations and slaves, since 1821.[50]

All three of these uncomfortable Jamaicans, it should be noted, sought and were awarded slave-compensation in the 1830s, despite their protestations a decade earlier.[51] But the power of official enquiry to discountenance them is clear. Neither the disclosure obligation nor the state's discouragement of slave-ownership on the part of senior officials, however, was ever extended to the absentee slave-owners of metropolitan Britain.

---

[48] *Ibid.*, p. 22.   [49] *Ibid.*, p. 24.   [50] *Ibid.*, p. 26.

[51] Burge was then in Britain as an MP and agent for Jamaica; he claimed unsuccessfully on behalf of his wife for the compensation on Warwick but lost to the London merchants W. R. & S. Mitchell (T71/860, Manchester No. 452). He did receive £97 7s 11d compensation, however, in December 1835 as 'owner and in right of wife' for 4 slaves (T71/852, St Catherine No. 309). Bowerbank did not gain compensation for Dumbarton (T71/857, St Ann No. 565) but in November 1835 he was awarded £207 9s 10d for 13 slaves (T71/852, St Catherine No. 216). Most strikingly, Stephen Hope Cooke and his wife claimed the reversionary interest in 55 of 61 slaves on Mount Gotham, and in February 1836 were awarded £1,178 8s 11d with Frances Virgo Brooks, the tenant-for-life (T71/852, St Catherine No. 349).

Supporters of the slave-owners

Slave-owners in Britain, abetted by slave-owners in the colonies, built both their own organisational bodies and a wider coalition amongst non-slave-owning supporters. Anti-abolitionism was expressed in an organised form by the various West India Committees, especially the London Committee, and by the island 'agents': paid representatives of the colonies in London.[52] In part, this coalition was sustained through financial power. The levy raised by the West India Committee on imports of West India produce to fund its anti-abolitionist activity was described by the *ASR* as 'secret-service money'.[53] Spokesmen for the West India interest were subsidised in a variety of ways. Peter Borthwick, subsequently MP for Evesham, and editor and owner of the *Morning Post*, was hired by the West India interest to make a series of speeches in defence of slavery, and engaged in a programme of set-piece debates with the abolitionist George Thompson in 1832 and the early months of 1833. Of James MacQueen, the anti-abolitionist editor of the *Glasgow Courier*, Henry Nelson Coleridge, generally a temperate and sympathetic observer of the West Indians (although opposed to slavery), warned the resident slave-owners of the West Indies that in the war of representation 'they should know that the excesses of MacQueen are as justly reprobated as those of Stephen'.[54] MacQueen acknowledged that he himself 'became possessed of slaves' in the late 1820s, and later jointly received compensation with his partner Alexander MacDonnell, but in the mid 1820s he was widely regarded as simply a paid agent of the slave-colonies.[55] MacQueen was central to the libel cases around Mary Prince, which pitched pro-slavery advocates and their publishers against the editor and publishers of the *History of Mary Prince*, the famous autobiographical narrative of an enslaved woman striving for freedom in London: Thomas Cadell,

---

[52] See L. M. Penson, *The colonial agents of the British West Indies* (London, 1924; reprinted London: Frank Cass and Co., 1971). Agents amongst the recipients of compensation included George Hibbert, William Burge, Anthony Browne and John Pollard Mayers; for the West India Committee, see D. Hall, *A brief history of the West India Committee* (St Lawrence, Barbados: Caribbean University Press, 1971).

[53] *ASR* No. 6 (November 1825), Vol. I, pp. 52–3.

[54] [H. N. Coleridge], *Six months in the West Indies in 1825* (London: John Murray, 1826), pp. 309–10. For MacQueen, see D. Lambert, 'The "Glasgow king of Billingsgate": James MacQueen and an Atlantic proslavery network', *Slavery & Abolition* 29.3 (June 2008), 389–413. I am grateful to David Lambert for kindly making a draft of this paper available to me.

[55] See for example *ASR* No. 13 (June 1826), which reports that MacQueen was voted £3,000 by the Jamaican Assembly.

the London publisher of Blackwood's magazine, was sued by Thomas Pringle over an article by MacQueen published in November 1831, because MacQueen in Glasgow was outside the jurisdiction of the court of Common Pleas.[56] MacQueen met Cadell's costs, and paid £150 to Foss, his barrister, and £185 to Blackwood's, which appears to have been off-set by 'a present from the people of Mauritius'; he received a further contribution of £68 from Trinidad. However, his expectations of additional support from the West Indies appear to have been disappointed.[57]

But it is not enough to characterise the anti-abolitionist allies of the slave-owners simply as venal. The British slave-owners and West India merchants drew wider support from a number of prominent individuals who did not themselves own slaves, but who were willing at particular junctures to align themselves publicly with the slave-owners. At a great City meeting of the West India interest and its supporters in April 1832, where allegedly over 6,000 were present, a dozen of the 32 MPs who attended were included neither in Judd and Higman's 'West India' interest, nor in the wider circle of MPs tied to the slave-economy.[58] Such 'disinterested' men had obvious value to the slave-owners, and were actively solicited to appear in anti-abolition public forums. Very often, these were military and especially naval men with service in the West Indies, with a value-system in which violence was not necessarily a source of unease, and probably with social circles that were robustly anchored in the armed services. Admiral Sir Byam Martin, for example, seconded the first resolution at a public meeting in the City of the West India planters and merchants of 27 May 1833:

The gallant officer said it might be right that he should state that he was not a West India proprietor. He had not a farthing of property in the colonies, and was entirely unconnected with any person trading there, but he had accepted the invitation to second the resolution proposed by the noble Lord [Combermere], under the feeling that it was the bounden duty of every man to come forward and lend a helping hand to the cause of the colonists at a time when he saw them in a most perilous situation.[59]

---

[56] S. Thomas, 'Pringle v. Cadell and Wood v. Pringle: the libel cases over "The history of Mary Prince"', *Journal of Commonwealth Literature*, 40.1 (2005), 113–35.

[57] Lambert, 'The "Glasgow king"', p. 401.

[58] For a list of these MPs, see Appendix 4. G. P. Judd IV, *Members of Parliament 1734–1832* (New Haven: Yale University Press, 1955), pp. 93–4 lists 'West India merchants' and 'Members in the West India interest'. B. W. Higman, 'The West India interest in Parliament 1807–33', *Historical Studies*, 13.49 (October 1967), 1–19 (p. 3, Table I) uses Judd's data with the addition of six MPs.

[59] *The Times*, 28 May 1833, p. 5.

At the same meeting, two other Admirals, the ninth Lord Colville and Sir Robert Stopford, proposed and seconded motions, and Admiral Douglas was amongst those in attendance. Lord Colville said he 'had no personal interest in the West India colonies, yet he was neither uninterested in, nor ignorant of their state and condition'.[60]

In other cases, the non-slave-owning supporters of anti-abolitionism were representatives of constituencies closely linked to the slave-economy. Sir Michael Shaw Stewart, for example, explained at the same May 1833 meeting that 'as representative for the county of Renfrew, in which was situate the two important ports of Greenock and Port Glasgow, he could not but feel deeply interested in the question of the West India colonies, without which those ports would never have arisen from insignificance to their present important height'.[61]

George Frederick Young, MP for Tynemouth, similarly established his own credentials at the 1833 meeting 'as representative of an important seaport, and as chairman of one of the largest associations of ship-owners in the kingdom'.[62]

The Times's leader challenged the legitimacy of the intervention of Young and of John Horsley Palmer, the former Governor of the Bank of England, as 'volunteer orators' at the May 1833 meeting: 'What right, for instance, had such *disinterested* gentlemen as Mr [George Frederick] Young or Mr Horsley Palmer ... to figure at a meeting where the West Indians could so abundantly speak for themselves[?]'[63] But Horsley Palmer was an example of an important segment of the financial and political elite that espoused concern for the credit structure of the City in the wake of the 1825–6 bank crisis and, above all, united with the slave-owners over the central principle of 'property'.[64]

Finally, amongst the 'disinterested' anti-abolitionists were those who *presented* themselves as independent of the slave-economy, and appear to have been accepted as such. Thus Jeremiah Harman,[65] the Russia merchant and former governor of the Bank of England, proposed one of the resolutions at the 6 April 1832 West India meeting in London. 'In doing so he stated that he stood there as an individual wholly unconnected and uninterested, but he was bold to assert that there was not a man in the kingdom who was more sensible than himself of the alarming state in which the colonies were placed ...'[66]

---

[60] *Ibid.*   [61] *Ibid.*   [62] *Ibid.*
[63] *Ibid.*, 29 May 1833, p. 2.
[64] See Chapter 3, below, pp.82–83.
[65] See Chapter 7, p. 247 fn, 45 below for the possibility that Jeremiah Harman was not entirely disinterested, although whether he had any beneficial interest in the claim detailed there is unclear.
[66] *The Times*, 6 April 1832, p. 1.

Key rhetorical themes and devices

Both sides in the war of representation were conscious that they were constructing competing discourses in which the analysis of the other side's representational strategies was a key to the struggle. This analysis was conducted on occasion in strikingly modern terms: '[t]he truth is, there has never been, and never will be, in the grammar of slave-holders, any present tense for the oppressions of slavery', said the *ASR* in critiquing the trope deployed by slave-owners over a half-century or more, which held that while the enslaved may have suffered in an always-distant past, their current state was invariably much improved.[67]

A number of consistent themes recur, for all the tensions and counter-currents those competing discourses over slavery contain. These key themes include: (1) the desirability of ultimate emancipation; (2) the nature of responsibility and agency under an absentee system; (3) the importance of distance – spatial, political, economic and social – from slavery, distance that defended the British slave-owner but also undermined his authority to speak of slavery; (4) the compromised nature of the 'Englishness' of the slave-owner; (5) the contradictions of the ameliorationist or even abolitionist slave-owner; (6) the importance of *inheriting* as opposed to purchasing estates in reconciling a British or English identity with slave-ownership; (7) the differences between the 'gentle' absentee and the deracinated returned 'planter' for whom slavery had provided social mobility and wealth; (8) the pervasiveness of slave-owning within British society, syndicating the guilt of slavery and implicating the abolitionists themselves; (9) the condition of the poor in metropolitan Britain compared with the enslaved in the colonies; and finally, (10) the central issue of compensation to the slave-owners on emancipation (discussion of slave-owning and debates over compensation were increasingly intertwined in the 1820s, largely because the slave-owners consistently and determinedly linked the two). The following sections of this chapter deal with each of these themes in turn, with the exception of compensation, which is dealt with in Chapter 2, below.

The desirability of ultimate emancipation

The degree to which defence of slavery as a positive good had disappeared from the discourse around abolition in the 1820s is striking. Very few anti-abolitionists provided overt defences of slavery as such. The

---

[67] *ASR* No. 40 (September 1828), Vol. II, p. 294.

common sense in Britain had moved sufficiently that the stock rhetoric, and in many cases presumably the conviction, of the anti-abolitionists became not the desirability of slavery but the need for improvement over a potentially long period prior to emancipation.

There were exceptions, especially, perhaps, outside official documents. Thus, in late 1830, a Captain Browne, a Jamaican planter, delivered at a Reading anti-slavery meeting 'as audacious a defence, or rather eulogy, of West India slavery as we have recently met with ... too preposterously mendacious to be seriously replied to ... he had been in the colonies – he had witnessed the happiness of the slaves, and the humanity of the planters'.[68] In the 1826 Surrey election, Charles Nicholas Pallmer was reported to have defended his slave-owning on the grounds that 'he had been the instrument of introducing within the pale of the Christian Church a thousand slaves, not nominally but really'. 'The statement, coming from that gentleman', said the *ASR*, 'surprised us not a little because we can have no doubt whatsoever that it is altogether untrue; and that he has suffered himself to be deceived by his informant'.[69]

To a Briton – to any man who has been bred up in the enjoyment of rational freedom – the exchange for a state of Slavery would prove the greatest of calamities: but not so the wretched sons of Africa – to them the change has been the very opposite ... The Negro has been rescued from barbarism and the darkness of Paganism in his native Africa to participate in the pure light and the inseparable blessings of Christianity ...

wrote George Saintsbury in 1829.[70] But with the exception of a few outbursts from unreconstructed slave-owners, often but not always returned planters who had made their fortune from humble beginnings through direct participation in slavery, overt pro-slavery discourse was suppressed. Anti-abolitionists generally incorporated positive endorsements of slavery only by reference or allusion. For example, John Rock Grosett, MP for Chippenham, slave-owner, tenant of Lacock Abbey and later Assemblyman in Jamaica in the late 1830s, quoted the late Bishop Watson of Llandaff: 'Slavery in the mysterious dispensation of Providence is a lot authorized by the supreme law-giver, the great Architect of the Universe.'[71]

---

[68] *Ibid*. No. 74 (January 1831), Vol. IV, p. 49.
[69] *Ibid*. No. 13 (June 1826) Vol. I, p. 196.
[70] G. Saintsbury, *East India Slavery*, 2nd edn (London 1829; reprinted Shannon: Irish University Press, 1972), pp. 32–3.
[71] J. R. Grosett, MP, *Remarks on West India Affairs*, 2nd edn (London, 1825), p. 55.

The prevailing rhetoric of the slave-owners was thus ameliorationist from the early 1820s onwards.

There is no class of your Majesty's subjects more desirous than your petitioners to enable the slaves to acquire their freedom on terms compatible with the well-being of the slaves themselves, the safety of the colonies, and a fair and equitable consideration of the interests of private property ... They are bold to assert, before your Majesty that slavery is as repugnant to their feelings as to those of any other class of your Majesty's subjects ...

declared the sixty-five 'London Proprietors and Mortgagees' who petitioned against compulsory manumission in Demerara and Berbice in an appeal to the Privy Council in 1826.[72] Yet despite their rhetorical stance, these petitioners were very publicly and formally (and successfully) contesting a cornerstone of the ameliorationist policy.

Distance, power and responsibility in absentee ownership

In the early nineteenth century, land-owners commonly lived away from their estates in England and Scotland without triggering a problematisation of 'absenteeism', while the system of curacy was originally a recognition, if not a remedy, for the gaps left by church pluralists. The language and stigmatisation of 'absenteeism' as a social problem in British discourse were therefore constructed for particular types of non-residence. Absenteeism as a category in fact had its origins in Ireland prior to its routine application to the West Indies. Johnson's *Dictionary* defined absentee as 'a word commonly used with regard to Irishmen living outside their country'. Absenteeism in Ireland was routinely condemned, its complexity overlooked and its extent conventionally exaggerated.[73]

Widespread absentee ownership of British colonial slaves had become established in the eighteenth century, and fundamentally reflected the earning power of the slave-economy under conditions of protection of the domestic sugar market. Owners lived in Britain and incurred the agency costs of attorneys and consignees not only because they preferred to do so, but because they could afford to do so. Fear was one factor that encouraged absenteeism. By removing the slave-owner from personal contact with the enslaved, absenteeism lifted the slave-

---

[72] In the Privy Council: Demerara & Berbice, Petition and Memorial of the London proprietors and mortgagees to His Majesty in Council against compulsory manumission in those colonies, TS11/978.

[73] A. P. W. Malcomson, 'Absenteeism in eighteenth-century Ireland', *Irish Economic & Social History*, 1 (1974), 15–35; N. D. Palmer, 'Irish absenteeism in the eighteen-seventies', *Journal of Modern History*, 12.3 (September 1940), 357–66.

owner out of the 'philosophy of fear' that informed the world-view of the resident white owner, attorney or overseer.[74] The West Indies occupied a position as threat and as promise to Britons, offering risk and opportunity, and was often represented as a charnel-house for whites. '[In 1798] I had an offer to go to the West Indies to follow my business. But fortunately I was advised to ask higher terms than was given and another young man was satisfied with less terms than I required. Thus I was fortunately prevented going to that grave of our countrymen, the West Indies', wrote Sir Peter Laurie, Lord Mayor of London, in 1832.[75]

It became an established trope that British absenteeism was unique. Henry Nelson Coleridge in the mid 1820s provided the classic expression:

The French colonists, whether Creole or Europeans, consider the West Indies their country; they cast no wistful look towards France; they have not even a pacquet [metropolitan-colonial mail-service] of their own; they marry, educate and build in and for the West Indies and the West Indies alone. In our colonies it is quite different; except for a few regular Creoles, to whom gratis rum and gratis coloured mothers for their children have become quite indispensable, every one regards the colony as a temporary lodging place, where they must sojourn in sugar and molasses till their mortgages will let them live elsewhere ... The French colonist deliberately expatriates himself; the Englishman never.[76]

But of course, absenteeism in fact was far more nuanced and complex. It was uneven between colonies: Barbados (as Coleridge acknowledged) had established an indigenous planter society, but maintained also many Anglo-Barbadian families. And Britons arrived at owning slaves as absentees by many different paths, not simply by returning to Britain as a slave-owner after living and working in the slave-colonies.[77]

The inherently damaging effect of absenteeism was contested. Its benefit in financing domestic British consumption was an axiom of the slave-owners and their supporters. The Duke of Wellington, in presenting a petition from the 'bankers, merchants and people of Belfast' in favour of abolition but with compensation, emphasised 'it is a fact,

---

[74] M. J. Steel, 'A philosophy of fear: the world view of the Jamaica plantocracy in a comparative perspective', *Journal of Caribbean History*, 27.1 (1993), 1–20.

[75] P. Laurie, *The Journal of Sir Peter Laurie*, ed. Elizabeth Shepherd (London: The Saddlers Company, 1985), p. 21.

[76] Coleridge, *Six months*, pp. 143–4.

[77] See the analysis of rates of absenteeism in Chapter 4, below (p. 152), and Chapters 5 (pp. 186–201) and 6 (pp. 211–224) for 'paths to ownership' by absentees.

which must never be overlooked, that the fortunes of the West India proprietors are expended in this country'.[78] British slave-owners came forward voluntarily into the public domain as individuals in defence of absenteeism. H. P. Simmons of Liverpool published his letters to Earl Grey between 1832 and 1834.[79] They displayed the common trope of the special relationship between the enslaved and their absentee master, a bond expressed on the master's occasional visits to his estates, but disrupted by the activities of the abolitionists:

I have now been the possessor of property for thirty years in Barbadoes, and during the whole of that period I can look back with the greatest pride and satisfaction, and declare that I have on no one occasion so acted towards my slaves as to feel regret ... Until this my last visit, I have invariably found them impressed with a just sense of my kindness, and rendering me an adequate return by their assiduity and devotion to my interest ... We have to contend against a junta of hypocritical fanatics, hireling calumniators, unjust judges and renegade statesmen.[80]

This 'special relationship' formed an important part of the identity of the absentee. It is very visible in 'Monk' Lewis's journal of his visits to his estates in Jamaica between 1816 and 1818.[81] Bonds of obligation were imagined by the slave-owners. 'I think it very ungrateful in them towards me to act thus', wrote Joseph Foster Barham when the enslaved on the Springfield estate, which he had bought in 1819, refused to transfer en masse to Barham's Mesopotamia estate, some twelve miles distant by foot.[82] The relationship with the absentee owner also formed part of the discourse of the enslaved with certain white audiences. Sturge and Harvey heard commentary illuminating this relationship in a number of cases from apprenticed black labourers on their visit between 1836 and 1837.[83]

---

[78] *The Debates in Parliament – Session 1833 – on the Resolution and Bill for the Abolition of Slavery in British colonies, with a copy of the Act of Parliament* (London, 1834), pp. 32–3.

[79] Simmons was a Creole, resident in Britain, the owner of Vaucluse estate in Barbados: T71/897, Barbados No. 2041. See also Lambert, *White creole culture*, p. 174.

[80] H. P. Simmons, *A letter to the Rt Hon. Earl Grey on the West India question by H. P. Simmons Esq.* (Liverpool, 1833), pp. 1, 28.

[81] M. G. Lewis, *Journal of a Residence among the Negroes in the West Indies* (originally, *Journal of a West India Proprietor, kept during a residence in the island of Jamaica*) (first published posthumously, London: John Murray, 1834; reprinted Stroud: Nonsuch Publishing, 2005).

[82] R. Dunn, '"Dreadful Idlers" in the cane fields: the slave labour pattern on a Jamaica sugar estate 1762–1831', *Journal of Interdisciplinary History*, 17.4: *Caribbean slavery and British capitalism*, (Spring 1987), 795–822 (p. 820).

[83] Sturge and Harvey, *The West Indies*, Appendix, pp. xlviii (Edward Barrett), lvi (Richard Quarrell), lix (Lady Holland).

Distance protected the absentee slave-owners, but it also compromised their authority. Increasingly, they were held responsible for what happened on their estates, and their inability or unwillingness to effect amelioration became a weapon in the hands of their opponents. The slave-owner sought authority without responsibility; the abolitionist tended to conceive the absentee as responsible without authority. Yet the responses drawn forth by absenteeism were complex. There were different strands discernible in the abolitionist position on absentees: one was that the humane owners in Britain were regrettably let down by their colonial agents (but remained responsible for them); the second was that the character of absentee owners differed, that they could even be virtuous and instruments for good as well as for evil; the third was that whatever the behaviour of the slave-owners, the system's own logic produced cruelty and oppression; and the fourth and most fundamental was that there were inevitable and irreducible contradictions between slave-owning and Christianity. These strands were neither consistent nor consistently employed, and the second two became more prominent as the fragile ameliorationist consensus of the mid 1820s failed.

As an illustration of the first strand, Lord Combermere, the former Governor of Barbados, was subject to assault over the oversight of his Nevis estate. At the General Meeting of the Anti-slavery Society in Exeter Hall on 23 April 1831, Sir James Mackintosh emphasised that having selected attorneys and overseers, Combermere thought he might 'with perfect satisfaction to his feelings and conscience' return from the West Indies, leaving his slaves as an example of what could be accomplished by a beneficent master. Unfortunately, 44 of 240 slaves had since died: 'here we had the whole system of the West Indies concentrated within the narrow limits of a private estate'.[84] Two months later, the *ASR* returned to the same case, to report on the Board of Magistrates that had been convened in Nevis to investigate the conduct of Combermere's manager, prompted by the unusual mortality. 'The whole of these proceedings were communicated by the Secretary of State to Lord Combermere. His Lordship has professed to feel deep horror at the inhuman and abominable conduct of his manager, Mr Walley. He has not, however, explained to Lord Goderich how he came to place, in that man's hands, the uncontrolled power over his slaves with which he appears to have been invested.' Walley had been indicted in 1827 for murder of a slave, and Combermere, said the *ASR*,

[84] *ASR* No. 76 (February 1831), Vol. IV, p. 260.

had friends in Nevis, whom he could and should have consulted as to Walley's character.[85]

In an example of the 'virtuous' proprietor, the *ASR* singled out one slave-owner, James Beckford Wildman, for exemption from the strictures laid on others. Wildman had spent three years on his Jamaican estates, and appeared to carry through on his commitments to religious instruction. His evidence to the Select Committees was praised and his collaboration with the Church Missionary Society (CMS) applauded.[86] The *ASR* in November 1831 carried tributes to the work of the CMS, 'aided by the laudable efforts of Mr Wildman, the proprietor of Papine Estate'; two pages on there is a further allusion to his 'laudable zeal' and several pages later another reference to Wildman 'whom we have already more than once had occasion to eulogise'.[87]

Wilberforce superficially appeared to continue to articulate the old notions of virtuous proprietors and vicious agents in one of his last speeches, at a meeting at Bath on 22 October 1830, but he did so within an analytical framework that underscored the irreducible systemic exploitation inherent in colonial slavery, and left no room for positive intervention by absentee proprietors: their character was irrelevant.

The greater part of the West India proprietors are resident in this country. However humane they may be, the slaves are far more affected by the disposition and temper of the individuals immediately over them – their book-keepers and more especially their drivers and other servants on the estate ... The attorneys or managers naturally wish to render the receipts as great, and the outgoings as small as can be effected ... there is always a necessary tendency to render the expenses of the estate, by far the greater part of which consists in the maintenance of the slaves, as little, and their produce, in other words their labour, as great as possible.[88]

But Brougham in 1825 had pointed to the more fundamental conflict between absentee slave-owning and Christianity:

I know indeed many West India proprietors who I am persuaded do all that those can do, by directions of lenity, and charity and humanity, who are absent owners who are living nearly 4,000 miles from the unhappy objects of their compassion and who, for necessity, leave over them delegates, invested with a power so absolute, that it might almost be called an impiety to God, to grant it over any of our fellow-creatures.[89]

---

[85] *Ibid.* No. 83 (July 1831), Vol. IV, pp. 320–3.
[86] '[I]n much of what he says we entirely acquiesce': *Ibid.* No. 104 (December 1832), Vol. V, p. 441.
[87] *Ibid.* No. 90 (November 1831), Vol. V, pp. 470–7.
[88] *Ibid.* No. 74 (January 1831), Vol. IV, p. 52.
[89] *Ibid.* No. 1 (June 1825), Vol. I, p. 5.

In other words, the very appointment of an attorney, regardless of his character and behaviour, was construed as sinful.

Distance undercut the beneficial intentions of the absentees. The *ASR* reported from *The Watchman* criticism by the Committee of the Jamaican Auxiliary Church Missionary Society of the oppression of attempted religious observance by the enslaved on the Coley estate in St Thomas-in-the-East, belonging to Sir G. H. Rose and others:

How does [Alexander Barclay, the pro-slavery advocate] account for it, that with all the laudable zeal manifested by Sir George Rose for the religious instruction of his slaves, he should have been unable to effect his purpose, or even to screen the Christian part of them from persecution on account of their religion at the hands of the very managers of his property?[90]

'His slaves, we do not hesitate to say, owe Lord Seaford nothing', said the *ASR* in its review of the evidence to the Lords' Committee.

Even the kindness he may have meant them, if not intercepted in its distant progress, has reached them only through hearts and hands known to them, not by any interchange of affection, but by the stern exaction of their unintermitted toil. While they have been surrounding him with every enjoyment which wealth can purchase, they have been wearing out their lives, by night as well as by day, in bitter bondage, under the frown or lash of unfeeling task-masters.[91]

Sturge and Harvey cited the *Christian Record*'s strictures on a proprietor who 'concluded that giving instructions by letter in Scotland, and carrying them into full effect in Jamaica, meant the same thing', and continued 'This is a misconception, to which the West India proprietors, resident in Great Britain, are notwithstanding so prone, that we know not how to avoid considering it a *determined self-deception*.'[92]

The absence of slave-owners from their estates was conceded to be a problem even by some of the absentees themselves. 'Monk' Lewis, dying of yellow fever on his second return journey from Jamaica to England in early 1818, left his Jamaican estates to trustees, to be divided between his sisters, Lady Fanny Lushington and Mrs Sheddon, on condition that the persons who should become entitled to the estates should reside upon them for three months every third year. This condition was struck down by the courts.[93]

---

[90] *Ibid.* No. 65 (August 1830), Vol. III, p. 384.
[91] *Ibid.* No. 105 (February 1833), Vol. V, pp. 493–4.
[92] Sturge and Harvey, *The West Indies*, p. lxxiii.
[93] *The Times*, 30 January 1830, p. 5: Court of Chancery, *Lushington* v. *Sewell*.

Absenteeism and the authority of knowledge

Distance played an ambivalent role in the representation and self-representation of the British slave-owners. Not only did it raise the issues of responsibility and authority for what happened on the estates, as discussed in the previous section: it also compromised the authority of the absentee slave-owners to *represent* what happened, or what they believed happened, there. Distance was a defence, insulation against direct implication in the physical realities of slavery. Yet lack of first-hand experience of slavery compromised the epistemological authority of the absentees, not solely from ignorance but also from a more deliberately constructed counter-reality, as the *ASR* suggested of Lord Seaford:

Now it is perfectly natural that Lord Seaford should be anxious to persuade himself and others that there is nothing, in this dependence of his on the slavery of his fellow-creatures, which should wound his self-esteem, or ablate the confidence of the public in his statements respecting the condition of society, and that he should endeavour, nay that he should even succeed in the endeavour, to hide from his own view the deformity of the system with which he is so very closely and profitably connected.[94]

'We believed many very well-meaning proprietors of West India property, who resided away from their estates, were the unconscious instruments of disseminating false intelligence as to the real state of things upon their plantations', said Lord Milton in 1825.[95] The authority of absentee slave-owners to represent slavery was further eroded by the consistent playing of the 'ruination' card by the West India interest. 'It cannot be unreasonable to question the real superiority of that knowledge which, in defiance of this practical refutation [i.e. the survival by the slave-economy of the Amelioration Orders of 1824 and 1830], is still claimed by the gentlemen connected with the colonies', observed Lord Goderich in late 1831.[96] Finally, the West India interest on occasion gave their opponents easy openings to challenge their authority of knowledge. George Hibbert (who never visited the West Indies) was significantly embarrassed when on behalf of the Jamaican Assembly he forwarded to Sir Robert Peel at the Home Office documents purporting to be the Proclamation of Boyer the President of Haiti, and extracts from the *Code rural*, which showed imposition of military discipline

[94] *ASR* No. 40 (September 1828), Vol. II, p. 294.
[95] *Ibid.* No. 1 (June 1825), Vol. I, p. 3.
[96] *Ibid.* No. 92 (January 1832), Vol. V, p. 38: Goderich's 5 November 1831 address to Governors of Crown Colonies.

on the free black fieldworkers.[97] The latter was quickly shown to be inauthentic. Hibbert blamed misunderstanding with the Jamaican Assembly, but the accusation of forgery lingered.

The Select Committees were forums in which these contests of authority were played out. Andrew Colvile, who introduced himself as 'a West India merchant ... and also connected with the Colonies as a proprietor and planter', and who was instrumental in the development of the Hudson Bay Company, was asked in the Commercial Committee whether he had had the opportunity of familiarising himself with the West Indies, and replied, 'I have had those means of making myself acquainted with the interests and affairs of the West India colonies as far as any person can do who is resident in this country, and has never been to the colonies.'[98]

Colvile's detailed knowledge was drawn largely from the accounts of his estates, an abstract and dematerialised expression of the underlying reality.[99] Pressed for the authority on which he claimed that the slaves worked with less alacrity than in the past, he conceded: 'I am speaking merely from information and conversation.'[100] Considerable gaps were revealed in his detailed understanding of conditions on his estates and of the broader political economy of slavery. When asked whether he could speak of the quality of soil in Demerara (where he also was a large-scale slave-owner) versus that of other West Indies islands, he replied: 'Not accurately. I would suggest that that question would be better answered by a planter who has been resident in those countries.'[101]

Parliamentary set-pieces involved the staged collision of different authorities and different knowledge. There was significant debate, for example, within the Extinction of Slavery Committee over the reliability and authority of William Taylor's evidence. Taylor had been appointed the attorney of James Beckford Wildman's estates in Jamaica in February 1829, when Wildman returned home to Britain after himself living on the island between 1826 and 1829. Taylor evolved a scheme to move to a free labour system, and had later offered to buy out Wildman to put it into practice. Taylor submitted to the Committee a financial analysis that showed the potential profitability of a free labour system at the level of the plantation. This became a key and contested text for the Extinction of Slavery Committee, with rival estimates re-casting Taylor's work being submitted by three witnesses with

---

[97] HO 44/17 7a, b: 'Geo. Hibbert sends to Mr Peel documents under instructions from Assembly of Jamaica, 12th July 1827'.
[98] Evidence of Andrew Colville [*sic*], *Report on the extinction of slavery*, Q. 252–3, p. 43.
[99] *Ibid.*, Q. 254, p. 43.   [100] *Ibid.*, Q. 395, p. 56.   [101] *Ibid.*, Q. 442, p. 59.

planting experience, all of whom calculated a loss between £800 and £1,100 per annum against Taylor's calculation of an annual profit of £800 under what the anti-abolitionist witness Robert Scott called his 'chimerical' schemes.[102]

Absentees and Englishness

As noted earlier, the presence of slave-owners in Britain disrupted the easy antagonisms of metropole–colony, of virtue–vice, of liberty–oppression. When Ralph Cleghorn, a free coloured man who later became President of Nevis, wrote in 1833 to Zachary Macaulay seeking preferment to the sinecure of Patentee of the Provost Marshals' Office, with an income of £1,400 currency per annum, Cleghorn captured the particular meanings of 'Englishness' that governed the abolitionist discourse. He explained that he had been in England from the age of 5 until 1823, in St Kitts from 1823 to 1824, in London from 1824 to 1825, in St Kitts as a merchant between 1826 and 1829 and in London as representative of the free coloureds between 1829 and 1830:

[s]o that you perceive my whole residence in the West Indies has never exceeded at any one time 3 years. And I can most conscientiously declare, that I never (and I trust I never shall) imbibed any other feelings upon the subject of West Indian manners and policy than that of disquiet and opposition, which is only strengthened and increased as I know more of them. My education was liberal and although perhaps ill dev[el]op[e]d has at least been English – English are my ideas and my feelings are English – Thank God for it. I have had not a single relation in the West Indies but my wife[,] and her only sister is the only inmate of my house. Though Creole women they are blessed with English notions, having breathed the air of liberty in England.[103]

But a letter from 'M. H.' to the *ASR* in 1828 on compensation included the indignant aside that '[P]ersons, calling themselves Englishmen, contend, with pertinacity and even rage, for the uninterrupted exercise of a tyranny which has been proved, by woful [*sic*] experience, to have produced the most deplorable effects, and which operates as a bar to all improvement both of master and slave'.[104]

The abolitionists also sought initially to divide absentee owners from the local colonists. In 1824, the *Edinburgh Review* had reflected on the

---

[102] William Shand recalculated a loss of £884 in his evidence (*Report on the extinction of slavery*, pp. 542–4), Robert Scott a loss of £889 (p. 345) and James Simpson a loss of £1,082 (p. 383).

[103] Ralph B. Cleghorn to Zachary Macaulay, 29 June 1833, reproduced in V. L. Oliver, *Caribbeana*, 6 vols. (London: Mitchell, Hughes and Clarke, 1909), Vol. VI, pp. 141–3.

[104] *ASR* No. 42 (November 1828), Vol. II, p. 331.

reaction in the colonies to ameliorationist promptings from Britain: 'To the most gentle and moderate advice, to the suggestions of the most respectable of the West India proprietors resident in England, they [the resident colonists] reply only in ravings of absurd slander, or impotent defiance.' The *Edinburgh Review* went on to say that it could almost have forgiven those with a real stake – 'the Chandoses, the Ellises, the Hibberts, the Mannings, the Pallmers etc.' – for displaying violence of language against abolition. But these absentees had not shown such violence. And why not? 'They live in England and understand and participate in English feelings. The colonists, on the other hand, are degraded by familiarity with oppression.'[105] But later in the 1820s, as a part of the abolitionist movement lost faith in amelioration, the focus on the position and responsibility of the absentee slave-owners increased. When Alexander Macdonnell, a Demerara planter and later secretary of the West India Committee, published a pamphlet on the West India question, the *ASR* responded: 'Mr Macdonnell further labours to prove that the feelings of proprietors resident in England and of the colonists are identical. So much the worse for the proprietors resident in England! We have always suspected it, notwithstanding their repeated disclaimers of any such identity.'[106]

As assaults on the absentees became more absolute, the contradiction between the claims to status in the metropole and slave-ownership in the colony became irremediable. James Evan Baillie, as candidate for Bristol, was described by the *ASR* as 'a great West India proprietor and merchant, who, though *spoken of* as a highly respectable gentleman, has nevertheless a deep stake in the perpetuation of that system of cruelty and crime, Negro slavery'. The *ASR* went on to quote a letter from 'Libertas' in the *Bristol Mirror* of 1 July 1830 on Baillie's public entrance into the Bristol hustings: 'I stood in silence, contemplating the procession, and whilst viewing it as it passed, I thought how many human backs had been lacerated – sighs heaved – groans uttered – and sales of human beings effected to have produced the ostentatious display. I turned away, Sir, from the guilty pageantry!'[107]

Gentility versus deracination

It has been argued that the rentier male absentee risked falling between the 'aristocratic' manliness of the planter – whose masculinity was based on physical activity, personal dominance and sexual

[105] *Edinburgh Review*, October 1824, cited in *ASR* No. 53 (October 1829), Vol. III, p. 115.
[106] *ASR* No. 56 (January 1830), Vol. III, p. 173.
[107] *Ibid.* No. 65 (August 1830), Vol. III, p. 361.

prowess – and the newer, middle-class virtues of hard work, probity and sexual continence.[108] Whereas members of the Extinction of Slavery Committee attacked the flogging of slave women as 'unmanly', the pro-slavery discourse characterised abolitionism as a feminised 'delusion'. In connection with the West Indies, much of the abolitionist discourse around the slave-owners as a result was couched in terms of anti-aristo-cratic stereotypes: the alleged immorality and personal violence of the slave-economy were seen as archetypally aristocratic over and against the emerging norms of bourgeois self-discipline and systematic, imper-sonal justice and punishment. The literature suggests that at different times and impacted by different local conditions there was, throughout the Empire, an effort to govern the use of violence. Justice and punish-ment were to be removed from the personal sphere and institutional-ised. 'Arbitrary, personalised and often brutal aristocratic authority was being replaced by a ... more modern and systematic, philanthropic state of discipline.'[109] Anti-slavery, of course, was seen as the quintessential British bourgeois project, extending to the enslaved abroad the notions of self-governing rational individualism that characterised approaches to managing the poor at home.

The absentee slave-owner, however, could lay claim to neither the 'aristocratic' manliness of the planter-settler nor (unless he were a mer-chant rather than a rentier) the new middle-class virtues of work and renunciation of violence outside their appropriate institutional context. The absentee slave-owner therefore can be read as further complicating the re-definition of manhood within Britain and within the Empire. The rentier male was complicit in, for example, the flogging of women. But the returning planter who had made his fortune in the West Indies, though rarer than in the eighteenth century, still carried the taint of immediate and personal contact with, and complicity in violence and sexual exploitation of, the enslaved.

Such a returning slave-owner was deracinated and seen as incapa-ble of aligning his values with those of a newly hegemonic respectabil-ity in the metropolis. The returnee slave-owner James Simpson had expressed alarm to the Extinction of Slavery Committee in 1832 at

---

[108] Paton, 'Decency', pp. 172–7. Paton points out in addition, however, that the newly forged manliness of the middle class was not self-evident in light of earlier stand-ards of masculinity and was striving to establish itself. This follows Davidoff and Hall's contention that '[e]arly nineteenth century [middle class] masculine identity was fragile, still in the process of being forged and always measured against the background of condescension from the gentry as well as the long tradition of artisan pride'; L. Davidoff and C. Hall, *Family fortunes: men and women of the English middle class 1780–1850* (London: Hutchinson, 1987), p. 229.

[109] Lester, *Imperial Networks*, p. 129.

a scheme by the ameliorationist William Taylor to segregate slaves by gender, and thus to interdict book-keepers from converting each estate into a brothel:

It was a great mistake in Mr Simpson to expect that his sneer against such a project would be received in the Committee of the British House of Commons with the derision with which it would have been listened to in a company of attorneys and overseers meeting at his dinner table in Kingston. It furnishes a melancholy exemplification of the state of morals and manners in Jamaica.[110]

The retired planter Robert Scott's testimony to the same Committee is direct and plainly, even brutally, phrased: he does not rely on the conventional formulae and the representational strategies that characterise other witnesses. 'I am a proprietor', he opened. He had lived in Jamaica between 1802 and 1826, and again for a few months from 1828 to 1829. 'I have certainly seen punishments inflicted which I have disapproved of, but not very frequently.' When asked whether he felt that after the withdrawal of the power of flogging females, it would still be possible to make them work at field labour, he said: 'I think it is likely that they would become excessively troublesome; they are, generally speaking, the much worse to manage than men.' He was closer than many other witnesses to an apparent defence of slavery: 'I think the general state of slaves in Jamaica is much better than what the people of this country have any idea of: I do think they are not so ill off in any respect as people here imagine.' Yet when pressed on the stock comparison of the enslaved with the English peasantry, he responded: 'I do not mean to say that a slave and a free man are to be brought into comparison at all, because the very idea of being under compulsion must be very bad.'[111]

The exchanges between Scott and Committee members on poor relief are also illuminating:

Q: Do the poor laws of England prevail there?
SCOTT: I do not know what the poor laws of England are; but I know that in Trelawny they have from £1,500 to £2,000 a year raised for paupers.

Scott had denied that there was any preference given to poor whites over blacks in the distribution of poor relief in Trelawny, of which he believed himself directly knowledgeable. His questioner produced accounts that showed white recipients receiving two-thirds of the £1,508 spent in 1821. Later, Scott was asked whether he had any knowledge of poor relief in Jamaica as a whole. Ruefully, he said: 'Not

---

[110] *Report on the extinction of slavery*, p. 147.
[111] Evidence of Robert Scott, *ibid.*, Q. 4934–5, p. 330; Q. 5047, p. 336; Q. 5067, p. 337; Q. 5116, p. 340.

except as to the parish in which I live [*sic*]; and I found that I was not very correct in stating my opinion of that from recollection.'[112] So Scott appears as a displaced figure: he knows little about the England where he is resident, yet his knowledge of Jamaica is flawed and inferior to that of his opponents.

William Taylor shares, from a different point of view, this ambiguous position between metropole and colony. He had been in Jamaica at separate times in 1816–23, 1824–5, 1826, 1827 and 1829–31, originally as a partner in Simpsons & Co. of Kingston, and then, as noted above, as attorney for James Beckford Wildman. He was excoriated by the anti-abolitionist witnesses, including his ex-partner James Simpson, as incompetent as a merchant and as a planter. Yet he remained deeply identified in his social being in England with the 'Jamaican' community:

Q: Are not most of your relatives and connexions West Indians?
TAYLOR: They are West Indians all of them I think.
Q: Have you been upon terms of intimacy with many persons whose great interest is in the West Indian islands?
TAYLOR: All my friends and intimate associates are West Indians, Jamaica people.[113]

Contradictions of the ameliorationist British slave-owner

The energies of abolitionists were increasingly devoted to tearing away the veil of amelioration. One of the key devices was to revive memories of opposition to the abolition of the slave-trade amongst slave-owners. At the General Meeting of the Anti-slavery Society in the spring of 1832, Buxton attacked Lord Seaford: as Charles Ellis, Seaford had opposed the end of the slave-trade in 1807, on the grounds that the trade was a mechanism for converting Negroes to Christianity; however, in defending amelioration Seaford subsequently maintained that prior to 1823 no slaves were Christians, but that by 1832 they all were.[114] The Rev. Thomas Cooper wrote of George Hibbert in 1824 that 'as he regarded the abolition of the slave-trade as an impolitic and unnecessary measure, he cannot be expected to view an attack on slavery itself with a friendly eye'.[115]

Elsewhere, abolitionists sought to confront slave-owners with the asserted realities of amelioration, and to exploit the tensions and

---

[112] *Ibid.*, Q. 5057–60, p. 336; Q. 5135–7, p. 340; Q. 5327, p. 354.
[113] Evidence of William Taylor, *ibid.*, Q. 640–1, p. 55.
[114] *ASR* No. 96 (May 1832), Vol. v, p. 147.
[115] Cooper, *Correspondence*, Preface, p. iii.

contradictions of the ameliorationist absentee. Again, the abolitionist position itself was not entirely consistent. The singling out of James Beckford Wildman as a virtuous proprietor has been noted above, but abolitionist discourse was increasingly expressing the fundamental contradiction between slave-owning, however conducted, and Christianity. The interplay between Taylor's and Wildman's evidence to the Extinction of Slavery Committee reveals the limits and contradictions inherent in the position of the 'improving' absentee slave-owner. Wildman had emerged publicly in Britain as a reforming slave-owner in 1830, when he had sought the support of the Colonial Office to pursue the neighbouring white planter who had savagely assaulted an enslaved woman, Eleanor James, owned by Wildman and living and working on one of his estates. There had been no redress available through the Jamaican courts and the case was taken up by abolitionists in Britain after Wildman had made it public.

Wildman lived at Chilham Castle in Kent and served as MP for Colchester between 1820 and 1826. Jane Austen had urged her niece Fanny Knight against marrying Wildman, not out of any concern for his character or status as a slave-owner (on which she was silent), but because, she said, she was reluctant for Knight to marry at all.[116] Wildman had three Jamaican estates, Papine in St Andrew, Salt Savannah in Vere and Low Ground in Clarendon. Inspired in part by Joshua Steele's experiments in Barbados a generation earlier, Wildman had determined 'to govern [his slaves] by mild and equitable laws, and to let them feel all the benefits of freedom without the name'.[117] When he first arrived in Jamaica in 1826, he testified he had found his slaves 'perfectly destitute of all religious instruction'. He told the Committee that:

the great object I had when I became acquainted with the mode of management of estates, was, to do away with the system of punishment, driving as it is called, and to endeavour to get them to work, using the whip when it was necessary, merely as a punishment for crime, but never as a stimulus to labour; and I have found the effect of that most valuable.[118]

[116] J. Austen, *Jane Austen's Letters*, ed. D. Le Faye (Oxford: Oxford University Press, 1995), pp. 328–31: Letter from Jane Austen to Fanny Knight 20 February 1817: 'Mr JW frightens me – He will have you – I see you at the Altar ... Do not imagine I have any real objection, I have rather taken a fancy to him than not, and I like Chilham Castle for you; – only I do not like you sh[oul]d marry anybody.'
[117] Evidence of James Beckford Wildman, *Report on the extinction of slavery*, Q. 7920, p. 519.
[118] *Ibid.*, Q. 7782, p. 511.

Wildman volunteered an anecdote about his punishment early on of a slave for 'very great impertinence' in defying Wildman and desiring that Wildman part with him. 'I did punish him and gave him 16 or 17 stripes, and then he begged very hard, and promised he would not do the like again, and he returned to his work.' So fear of the whip, a Committee member asked, had never been removed? 'No certainly not, when they committed crime; the way in which I used the whip in the few instances, and I am thankful they were but few, were those in which I should have sent a man to gaol had complaint been made before me as a magistrate in this country.'[119] It emerged later in Wildman's testimony that in fact the whip was still carried by the driver under Wildman's reformed regime:

> a very old Negro, who had been the head man a great number of years, begged I would not take [the whip] away from the driver, because it kept up his authority; and he undertook that it should not be used at all if I would let it be carried into the field, and I agreed to it.[120]

Wildman nevertheless had drawn odium amongst his fellow planters for his efforts at amelioration. When he began to introduce schools on his estates for the enslaved, he said, 'I was set forth in the papers as an enemy to the Colony: I was told, if I meant to burn down my own estate, I had no right to burn down those of others.'[121]

Wildman, in response to questioning, was highly critical of William Taylor's management of the estates after Wildman's return to England. 'I lost £1,400 last year, and should have lost everything if his management had continued', was his first response to questions about Taylor's stewardship of his estates.

> He [Taylor] seemed to throw up the thing altogether; he got it into his head that the duration of slavery in any shape was iniquitous, and he seemed to abandon the whole thing ... He seemed to abandon the idea of produce altogether: his letters turned exclusively upon the question of the right or wrong of slavery, and I could get very little else out of him.[122]

Taylor had, amongst other things, discontinued the whip being taken into the fields.

Taylor's testimony, which preceded that of Wildman, was consistent with Wildman's yet reached a different conclusion. 'Was it understood', Taylor was asked, 'that in case the interest of the proprietor and the prosperity of the slaves should come into collision, that the interest of

---

[119] *Ibid.*, Q. 7855–6, pp. 515–16.
[120] *Ibid.*, Q. 8060, p. 529.   [121] *Ibid.*, Q. 8046–8, p. 528.
[122] *Ibid.*, Q. 7847; Q. 7850, p. 515; Q. 7875, p. 517.

the proprietor was to be made secondary to the interest of the slave?'. 'That was the principle I went upon, and I never receded from it; that his pecuniary interest was to be decidedly secondary to the better interests and well-being of the slave', but after two years 'I felt it was impossible to work the system upon that principle.' Taylor said he had discovered that it would not work upon the principle of humanity: that it required a harsh and coercive principle. 'My neighbours advanced before me, simply because they could and did make use of a power which I would not make use of.'[123]

Taylor had communicated this to Wildman, and Taylor was requested to read out a letter that he had sent to Wildman in October 1830.

I must now advert to the subject on which you have remarked in your last letter, namely, the civil condition of your Negroes ... I cannot refrain from being explicit on the subject ... I do not think then that your estates can possibly be made to yield under the combined system of religion, humanity and slavery. There is in the latter, as it exists in Jamaica, a repugnance to unite with the two former. By our system, we take away the motive that leads to labour in the neighbouring estate, the dread of the lash; we cannot substitute that which makes the English labourer industrious, namely the fear of want, for the law of Jamaica compels the slave proprietor to feed his slave, to clothe him and to house him.

The only solution, Taylor concluded, was Emancipation. 'In the middle state we are perplexed and retarded in our operation, simply because there is not sufficient stimulus.'[124] Taylor was kicking away one of the key supports of the absentee planter, the possibility of the amelioration of slavery. For Taylor, the threat of violence was intrinsic to slavery: to reject violence was necessarily to reject slavery. In making public the letter to Wildman conveying this conclusion, Taylor was seeking to deprive Wildman not only of an illusion, but of the protection of ignorance that it was an illusion.

The Rev. Thomas Cooper went a step further in seeking to strip the ameliorationist defence from Robert Hibbert. Cooper, in discussing the impact of education on the enslaved ('slavery supposes their degradation, considers them as animals, goods and chattels; instruction considers them men'), reported:

I told Mr Hibbert that I considered that if the slaves were taught to read, they will certainly cease to be slaves; that in proportion as they are enlightened, they will be dissatisfied; when they clearly see what their real condition is, they will

---

[123] Evidence of William Taylor, *ibid.*, Q. 189–91, p. 23.   [124] *Ibid.*, Q. 192, p. 23.

themselves alter it; and on my admitting that, he begged me to discontinue teaching reading.[125]

William Alers Hankey's evidence shows the interplay of innocence/ ignorance and the difficulty in which an ostensibly 'abolitionist' slave-owner could find himself. Hankey was senior partner in Hankey & Co., a private bank established in the City in 1685 that was one of the antecedents of the National Westminster Bank (now owned by the Royal Bank of Scotland). Hankey was constrained in his initial self-identification by the leading tack taken by his questioner(s):

Q: You are a West Indian proprietor?
HANKEY: I am.
Q: Possessing slaves?
HANKEY: Possessing slaves.
Q: Have you never visited the property yourself?
HANKEY: I have not.[126]

But Hankey had a number of aspects of his identity and public personality that he wanted to convey to the Committee. First was his distance from the detailed commercial and physical dimensions of slave-owning. He answered questions on the number of slaves, and the number of hogsheads of sugar produced by his estate, but was then asked a supplementary question about the definition of hogshead: 'Our hogsheads are usually called heavy hogsheads, I suppose from 14 to 16 hundred [weight]: but my recollection may not be perfectly accurate upon that point: I am much more of a banker than a West India merchant.'[127] He came back to this when asked a little later about the returns on capital available to slave-owners at the then-current price of sugar:

I am not sufficiently a West India merchant to have very extensive and accurate views: it is but a secondary object of attention to myself and it is in the management of Messrs Thomson, Hankey Plummer & Co. so that I really do not profess to be personally and intimately acquainted with all those considerations that necessarily enter into the character of a merchant.[128]

Distance protected Hankey from the questioning endured by more active planters about the physical violence of slavery; it also reduced his responsibility for the pace of amelioration of his own slaves. He was asked what measures he had taken to prepare his own slaves for

---

[125] Evidence of Rev. Thomas Cooper, *ibid.*, Q. 1704, p. 139; Q. 1706, p. 140.
[126] Evidence of William Alers Hankey, *ibid.*, Q. 4555–6; Q. 4563, p. 307.
[127] *Ibid.*, Q. 4561, p. 307.
[128] *Ibid.*, Q. 4585, p. 309.

freedom. 'They are very slight and incipient, but they are these: I have given instructions to the attorney, at his discretion, to stop some of the supplies that are ordinarily granted to the negroes', and pay cash instead, 'to teach them the application of money'. The experiment was too recent to have yielded results: the instruction 'was given to the attorney when he was in England last; he sailed only in January [1832]'. A Committee member sought to confirm that Hankey had given a certain sum of money in lieu of stores.

HANKEY: I have given permission for the attorney to do that, but as to the precise nature or extent of that commutation, if I may so call it, I did not conceive myself to be a sufficient judge, and left it to his discretion. I have the highest confidence in his judgment to do that.

Q: You would not trust yourself, not having local experience, to regulate even that matter?

HANKEY: Certainly not: he knows my determination and my wish to act as far as I can consistently in furtherance of the object, and I have in him that kind of confidence that he will not counteract or thwart unnecessarily my wishes. I have committed the management of that detail to his hands.[129]

Hankey was thus willing, indeed eager, to give up the authority of expertise in commercial and plantation matters: but the second point that he sought to convey to the Committee was his claim to a different form of authority, the moral authority of the active reformer. 'I am now talking not merely from personal experience as it regards my own property, but from some considerable opportunities of knowing the subject, from the situation in which I have, for several years, stood as treasurer to the Missionary Society', he said, in answer to a question about the impact of instruction of the enslaved. This prompted further questioning to clarify that Hankey had been for sixteen years treasurer to the non-denominational London Missionary Society.[130]

Finally, Hankey sought to convey his commitment to 'amelioration' and his embrace of the consequences of amelioration for slavery. As a West India proprietor, he was 'most decidedly' in favour of religious instruction for the enslaved.

Q: Has the result of your experience, as treasurer to this [Missionary] Society, led you to the conclusion, from the progress of civilisation among the slaves, that when instructed they have become more obedient and tranquil?

HANKEY: Quite so. I believe their value, even in the market, has risen in proportion as they have been so instructed: we have had instances of that; a

---

[129] *Ibid.*, Q. 4624–5, pp. 311–12; Q. 4634–5, p. 312.
[130] *Ibid.*, Q. 4567–72, pp. 307–8.

slave has been regarded as more valuable in consequence of his having been instructed by the missionaries of our own and other societies.

Q: ... [I]s it your opinion that slavery can long continue, the slaves possessing this knowledge [of the debates underway in Britain about abolition] and being so stimulated?

HANKEY: I think not.[131]

However, once Hankey had set out these markers of identity, the contradictions within his position came savagely home. He was asked what, from his wary response, he recognised as a leading question:

Q: Have you, as relates to your own property, been prepared to anticipate the period when emancipation may be forced upon you?

HANKEY: I have not anticipated it, as far as I am aware: may I beg to know to what the question refers?[132]

Hankey was then confronted with the fact that the Rev. William Knibb had told the Committee that 'a gentleman' had agreed to the emancipation of his slaves on condition that Knibb took on the instruction of those slaves. The Committee had asked for the name of the gentleman concerned, and Knibb had returned 'and discovered yours'. 'With my permission', Hankey acknowledged, but then denied that he had an agreement with Knibb. 'Mr Knibb must have in some degree misunderstood me on that point; I am not prepared to anticipate the general measure at this moment. I am rather prepared to wait for those measures which I trust the government of this country will see its duty to adopt in reference to the general question.'[133] Not surprisingly, one or more Committee members pressed Hankey repeatedly on the nature and causes of the misunderstanding with Knibb. Had Hankey told Knibb that he would emancipate his slaves? 'I never understood Mr Knibb to put that question to me in that form.' Would Hankey state the nature of his communication with Knibb?

I had a long conversation with Mr Knibb of several hours. I invited him to my house to spend the afternoon and evening, that we might have a full opportunity of discussing the whole question, and consequently the conversation as it were dilated over too wide a surface for me to be able to say precisely what the tenor was on any particular point. Besides one cannot be supposed, on impressions arising from such temporary communications, to have made up one's mind on so important a point *instanter*, so as to lay down any thing as a precise statement on which one was inclined to act. I certainly should not send out Mr Knibb or any other man at this moment to my estate with a letter of manumission or any such document ... I am not prepared to do that.[134]

---

[131] *Ibid.*, Q. 4565, p. 307; Q. 4572, p. 308; Q. 4579, p. 308.
[132] *Ibid.*, Q. 4580, p. 309.   [133] *Ibid.*, Q. 4581–2, p. 309.
[134] *Ibid.*, Q. 4592–3, p. 310.

Hankey was asked whether he had expressed in any terms his abhor-rence of the existing state of slavery, and replied: 'I am not aware: I am ready to express it in very strong terms.'[135] Asked whether he expressed his desire to co-operate in any system of emancipation, he framed his reply carefully: 'I dare say I did, because I am at all times ready to co-operate in any proper system to effect emancipation. I must of course hold myself a judge of the tenor of any system I should co-operate in, except that it was adopted by authority.'[136]

Committee members returned again to this discrepancy later in the testimony. Was it a desultory conversation between Hankey and Knibb? 'It was a very diffuse conversation.' Was there anything that was likely to give rise to misunderstanding? 'Mr Knibb is a man of ardent feelings, and the construction he might put, under the influence of those feel-ings, put upon the terms he might use, I cannot answer for: I have had conversations with the Secretary of the Baptist Society, upon the same topics, over and over again.'[137]

The Committee apparently (and understandably) concluded that Knibb had had an adequate basis for his account to the Committee of Hankey's posture, because, when Knibb was later recalled to the Committee, there was no further questioning of him about the meeting with Hankey in the light of Hankey's own testimony.

Two other areas of Hankey's positioning and his social identity were disclosed by his testimony. The first was his claim to move easily in abo-litionist circles. He spoke of his 'kind and friendly and somewhat offi-cial association' with the managers of the Baptist Missionary Society (to which Knibb belonged), 'most of whom I know, and in whom I place the greatest confidence'. He expressed that he was a friend to the object of the Anti-slavery Society, 'but not to the means by which it carries on its object', which drew clarificatory questioning:

Q: You originally belonged to the Africa Society, the object of which was to watch the execution of the laws for the abolition of the Slave Trade, but when it assumed its new character and new functions of interfering with the state of slavery, you withdrew from it?

HANKEY: No, I am a member to this day of the African Society.

Q: Did not the Anti-Slavery Society emanate from the African Society?

HANKEY: It might arise out of it, but they are distinct. I never became a mem-ber of the Anti-Slavery Society for that reason; had their measures been more in accordance with my own opinions, I would have supported the one as well as the other; I may be in ignorance.[138]

---

[135] *Ibid.*, Q. 4596, p. 310.   [136] *Ibid.*, Q. 4597, p. 310.   [137] *Ibid.*, Q. 4614–16, p. 311.
[138] *Ibid.*, Q. 4637–9, p. 313.

The corollary of this was that he explicitly avoided contact with the West India lobby. Had Hankey held no communication with 'the West India body'? 'Never'. He had in fact attended one meeting of the West India lobby, concerning the Demerara uprising of 1823, but for the purpose of standing ready to defend missionary exertions in the West Indies from any unfounded charges that might be made against missionaries.[139] But anxiety about his social standing is betrayed in his answer to the questions as to whether slavery would fall by insurrection:

> It must fall for the general effect produced by it on the one hand upon the Negro, whatever that may be; and it must fall from the social consequences affecting the proprietors themselves. A period, I am persuaded, will come beyond which the proprietor cannot hold that unjust possession which he now has of his fellow man as a slave.[140]

The second area of Hankey's positioning was the religious context. He characterised the London Missionary Society as strictly non-denominational: 'all are employed', save that the Baptists and Methodists had their own Missionary Societies. Were they all Christians? 'Yes, provided their principles are what we ourselves deem to be orthodox, generally speaking in harmony with the Church of England; we disagree entirely with the Unitarians, we have no association with them in the least; we would not employ a Unitarian missionary.' Against this background, it is a little surprising to find towards the end of Hankey's testimony his answer to the question, seemingly isolated from the immediate context, as to whether he was himself a member of the established church. 'I am not; I am a dissenter.'[141]

Paths to slave-ownership

In defining and representing themselves, and in being defined and represented, British slave-owners displayed awareness that their 'path to ownership' was potentially a source of protection or of vulnerability. Inheritance rather than the purchase of an estate appears to have constituted a partial extenuation.

W. R. K. Douglas, the MP, younger brother of the Marquess of Queensberry and Tobago slave-owner who had chaired the Acting Committee of the West India body, defined his connection with the West Indies to the Commercial Committee in a form that foregrounded inheritance, distance and authority:

---

[139] *Ibid.*, Q. 4640–2, p. 313.   [140] *Ibid.*, Q. 4660, p. 315.
[141] *Ibid.*, Q. 4569–70, p. 308; Q. 4676, p. 316.

I succeeded to an extensive property in the West Indies about 10 years ago, and by the will under which I succeeded, I was especially directed to correspond myself with the managers of the different estates in the management of them, so that I might make myself as much master of the subject as a person never having been in the West Indies, could.[142]

Even forty years later, this defence of inheritance appears to have retained resonance. Jerom Murch, the biographer of Robert Hibbert in 1874, said of Hibbert's purchase of the Georgia estate in Hanover:

For a long time I was under the impression that this estate, like his other interests in the West Indies, came to him by inheritance. I now find that it was not so, and it is right to state that, though he was always an eminently kind master, he had no repugnance to this kind of property on moral grounds.[143]

Abolitionists did not invariably accept the defence of inheritance. The *ASR* referred sarcastically to the Tory minister Mr Goulburn 'having had the misfortune to succeed to a property in the colonies'.[144]

Paths to ownership were carefully navigated in the set-piece Parliamentary Committees.[145] Because of the concentration of witnesses with Jamaican property, and the absence of witnesses from newer and recently expanded slave economies such as Demerara, there were few witnesses who had in fact purchased their estates. William Shand positioned himself and was positioned by the Committee as an attorney and a planting expert with between 18,000 and 20,000 slaves on the estates he managed in his period in Jamaica from 1791 to 1823 (he also returned there briefly from January 1825 to May 1826). Only later in his evidence did it emerge that he was himself a substantial slave-owner as a result of purchase, with 1,200 slaves.[146] Even James MacQueen, the anti-abolitionist polemicist, used the odd circumlocution 'I became possessed of West India property' in his self-description in front of the Commercial Committee.[147]

---

[142] Evidence of W. R. K. Douglas, *Report from the Select Committee on the commercial state of the West India colonies*, PP 1831–2, Vol 20 (381), Q. 620, p. 78 (hereafter *Report from the Commercial Committee*).
[143] Murch, 'Robert Hibbert', pp. 22–3.
[144] *ASR* No. 10 (March 1826), Vol. I, p. 122.
[145] However, Robert Scott's path of inheritance, typically of him, did not emerge except through questioning; *Report on the extinction of slavery*, Q. 5301, p. 353: 'Did you buy your property? No, I succeeded to it.'
[146] Evidence of William Shand, *Report on the extinction of slavery*, Q. 6459, p. 434 (which contains an allusion to his two estates in Clarendon); Q. 7020–1, p. 466, in which Shand is asked when he had become a 'proprietor of slaves': 'I think about 1801.'
[147] Evidence of James M'Queen [sic], *Report from the Commercial Committee*, p. 104.

Members of the Extinction of Slavery Committee were knowledge-able about the personal circumstances of witnesses and their links to slave-ownership. The Rev. Wiltshire Stanton Austin, an Anglican cler-gyman – a native of Barbados who had been in England since being obliged to leave Demerara in 1824 in the wake of his support for John Smith over the Demerara rising – appeared as a pro-abolition witness to the Committee. After he explained his role in seeking to manage the reception amongst the enslaved in Demerara of news of the 1823 Parliamentary Resolutions, he hit this exchange:

Q: Is not your father a proprietor?
AUSTIN: My father is a West India proprietor in the colony of Surinam.
Q: Is he a slave proprietor?
AUSTIN: He is.
Q: Have you resided with him?
AUSTIN: I have: I managed his property for about 18 months, when I was about 18 years of age.[148]

Austin went on to explain that he would return to the West Indies only after Emancipation, but drew further questioning:

Q: Are you heir to your father's estate in Surinam?
AUSTIN: I am joint heir; but I have other not inconsiderable property in other reversionary interests in the West Indies.
Q: With reference to these reversionary prospects, taking the mere question of monetary interest, are you of opinion that it would be for your interest, as well as consistent with your feeling, that emancipation should be granted?
AUSTIN: My reversionary interest[s] must suffer, I admit, by emancipation, because they consist chiefly, if not entirely, of securities on slave property, and if the slaves were emancipated of course I might lose. I have no rever-sionary interest in land, or at least to a very trifling amount.[149]

Austin, therefore, was apparently tenant in tail to mortgages over slaves, divorced from the land and thereby also divorced from the 'protection' offered to slave-owners by ownership of the land related to the slaves. Finally, Austin was asked whether he was acquainted with either La Belle Alliance or the Land of Plenty estates in Demerara. He acknowl-edged that these estates belonged to his uncles.[150]

---

[148] Evidence of Rev. Wiltshire Stanton Austin, *Report on the extinction of slavery*, Q. 2229–31, p. 179.
[149] *Ibid.*, Q. 2279–80, p. 183.
[150] The Austin family collected compensation on these two estates in 1836: £19,514 0s 5d for 369 slaves on Land of Plenty to John and Mehatebel Austin as executors of William Austin, and £20,511 19s 7d for 415 slaves on La Belle Alliance to John Austin as sequestrator of the estate of Edward Austin (T71/887, B[ritish] G[uiana] Nos. 2258 and 2265 respectively).

As Austin's example suggests, the network of slave-property was extensive, and few witnesses who had been connected with the West Indies escaped involvement in it. The evidence of Vice-Admiral Sir Charles Rowley, the former Commander-in-Chief who 'would not have' slaves on his tour of duty (although he hired 'regular servants'), for example, includes the following:

Q: Have you any connection with the West Indies?
ROWLEY: None.
Q: No property?
ROWLEY: Not the least.
Q: Have your relatives any property there?
ROWLEY: No, a gentleman who married a daughter of mine has, in Antigua.[151]

While the Extinction of Slavery Committee, combining abolitionist and anti-abolitionist members and witnesses, was usually well-informed enough to clarify ownership and connections, there were examples of distancing that appear simply disingenuous. Samuel Baker, who was of particular interest to the Committee because he had been in Jamaica at the time of the 1831 uprising of the enslaved, presented himself as follows on 6 August 1832:

Q: In what line of life are you?
BAKER: A merchant in London.
Q: Are you interested at all in West India property?
BAKER: In receiving consignments from the island I am interested.
Q: Have you not large concerns in the island of Jamaica?
BAKER: As a merchant; we are not considered extensive merchants; I speak comparatively. Our interest is large in the island certainly.
Q: Have you mortgages upon any of the estates?
BAKER: Not now; jointly I believe my partner may have mortgages, but I am not clear about that.[152]

Baker's account was incomplete. His partner was Thomas Phillpotts, who had been a witness to the Commercial Committee.[153] Their firm of Samuel Baker, Phillpotts & Co. of 144 Leadenhall Street was

---

[151] Evidence of Vice-Admiral Sir Charles Rowley, *Report on the extinction of slavery*, Q. 7672–4, p. 504. Rowley's daughter, Elizabeth Sophia, had married Peter Langford Brooke of Mere Hall in Cheshire, who received £8,098 15s 2d for 629 slaves on Langford, The Wood and Jonas estates (T71/877, Antigua Nos. 28, 105, 308); *A genalogical and heraldic history of the commoners of Great Britain and Ireland enjoying territorial possessions or high official rank but uninvested with heritable honours, by John Burke*, 5 vols. (Liverpool, 1828, 1841), Vol. III, p. 627.
[152] Evidence of Samuel Baker, *Report on the extinction of slavery*, Q. 7428–32, p. 490.
[153] Evidence of Thomas Phil[l]potts, *Report from the Commercial Committee*, pp. 61–8.

a significant recipient of slave-compensation in its own name: and Phillpotts was awarded more individually.[154]

It emerged only towards the end of William Alers Hankey's testimony that his ties were more extensive than the ownership of the single estate he presented at the outset, because he was a significant mortgagee as well. He was asked whether he was mortgagee of an estate called Arcadia, which he acknowledged – 'upwards of 40 years ago' – but went on to say: 'I have through life been a good deal connected with the West Indies; I was mortgagee in possession for several years as executor of two other considerable estates in the West Indies.'

Q: That is the only estate now remaining?
HANKEY: Yes, except that I am yet mortgagee of New Hope and Albany Estate.[155]

When Hankey then talked of 'the assignment which made me a proprietor ... and which made me reluctantly what I am now', he drew two separate lines of questioning, one predicated on the sanctity of property and one representing a qualified challenge, rare in the Committee, to the property argument.

Q: Your ancestor from whom you derived that mortgage, as well as every other person purchasing property in the West Indies, purchased it knowing it was a property saleable under the laws of the land?
HANKEY: It was not purchased, it was taken on advances.
Q: Purchasers in the West Indies and mortgagees in the West Indies are, in your opinion, under the same solemn sanction of law as other property?
HANKEY: I think so.
Q: Do not you think that at the time the purchase was made, the ancestor of the present proprietor was aware that it was an unjust act to make that purchase?
HANKEY: I really do not think he had any such feeling: it is to be recollected it is a feeling which has risen up very much in modern times; the moral turpitude of it has been ever the same, but the public feeling upon it has become different.[156]

The pervasiveness of slave-ownership

In counter-attacking their opponents, the anti-abolitionists did invert the charge of slave-ownership against the abolitionists at times. Thomas

[154] Samuel Baker and Thomas Phillpotts were awarded £3,708 4s 4d for 170 slaves on the Bogue estate after counter-claiming as judgement creditors (T71/873, St James No. 50) and £4,282 15s 2d for 240 slaves on the Twickenham Park estate as judgement creditors and mortgagees (T71/852, St Catherine No. 473). Phillpotts had further claims in St Ann (T71/857, St Ann Nos. 65, 86, 357).
[155] Evidence of William Alers Hankey, *Report on the extinction of slavery*, Q. 4620–1, p. 311.
[156] *Ibid.*, Q. 4684–6, p. 317.

Fowell Buxton himself was drawn into a public correspondence with Christopher Bethell Codrington in 1832, in which Codrington skilfully deployed information he had about Buxton's slave-owning antecedents piece-by-piece to tempt Buxton into an indiscreet denial. Buxton avoided disaster, but was driven in the end to acknowledge the truth of his slave-owning antecedents. The correspondence began conventionally enough. Codrington, whose family had held Barbuda under a lease from the Crown for a century-and-a-half, and owned several estates on Antigua, published an *Address to the Electors of Gloucestershire* in April 1832, which set out the established defence of slavery but accepted the principle of Emancipation:

I have lived among my Negroes, and seen their comforts, and I will assert (defying all contradiction), that a more happy and contented class of beings never existed, until cursed with the blessings of the Antislavery Society ... Still, gentlemen, I will say that no man can be more desirous of their emancipation than myself, because no man would benefit more by it, if it answered its desired object ... I have bought my Negroes, and cultivated my land, on the pledged faith of England. Secure me from loss, or give me compensation, and you may offer manumission to the above Negroes tomorrow.[157]

Buxton, provoked by references to himself in Codrington's *Address*, replied on 28 April 1832, to ask how there could be a dispute between Codrington and himself: 'I had never, in private or in public, mentioned your name, or commented on your conduct. I ought perhaps to take shame for my ignorance – but the fact is, I was not conscious that there lived such a person as Sir Christopher Bethell Codrington.' Given that Codrington had sat in the House of Commons for a West Country constituency only a few years before Buxton was elected for Weymouth, this was a provocative position to take. Buxton challenged Codrington to refute any statement on slavery that Buxton had made, and asked, if slavery was so good, why Codrington would free his slaves; and, if benefits result from freeing them, why compensation would be necessary.[158]

Codrington returned in the autumn of 1832, with a public letter to Buxton. The Anti-slavery Society had 'destroyed the property of the planter, taken away the means of subsistence from the widows and fatherless ... changed the character of the Negro from a happy and contented being ... to that of a rebel and a murderer'.

---

[157] 'Correspondence between Sir C. B. Codrington and T. F. Buxton on the subject of slavery', reprinted in *ASR* No. 103 (November 1832), Vol. VI, p. 301.
[158] *Ibid.*, p. 302.

Let me not be told, *by you*, that man cannot *be the property of man*. I have heard (perhaps I have heard in error) that you have yourself received the benefit of this species of property ... Were those slaves, from whose sale (the last instalment of which was made just eleven years ago) you profited, sold again, into slavery, to swell that decrease [in slave numbers] you now so pathetically describe?[159]

'You taunt me with the sale of my slaves, and with the profit which I derived from them', Buxton replied, and said that the charges against him alluded to by Codrington dated back to 1824. He provided a summary of the charges: that in 1771 Buxton had prevailed on a Mrs Barnard to place £20,000 in a West India house, that in 1783 he had sent a Mr Crosby to the West Indies to sell Negroes, that Buxton had inherited £170,000 from Mrs Barnard in 1792 as husband of her niece and as executor, and that he had again sent out a gentleman to sell Negroes. However, said Buxton, he had not been born until 1786.

I never had a Negro to sell ... I repeat I never was the master of a slave – I never bought one, or sold one, or hired one. I never owned a hogshead of sugar or an acre of land in the West Indies ... There was a Mrs Barnard. She was my grandfather's sister. She embarked a sum of money in a West India house, the greatest part of which she lost. The remnant descended to some of my near relations. So far is true. But it is also true that in that property I have never happened to be a partaker. I am not, and, to the best of my knowledge, NEVER HAVE BEEN, THE OWNER OF A SHILLING DERIVED FROM SLAVES.[160]

'You have honoured me with an introduction to your grandfather's sister', sneered Codrington,

but you have omitted to introduce me to your grandfather himself ... there are obstinate people who still assert that your grandfather had considerable property and slaves in the island of Barbadoes: that some 35–36 years ago he sent out the late Mr Holden to dispose of that property ... it was disposed of for a large sum of money, a proportion of which was invested in property in Weymouth, which gave right of voting, and in virtue of which property you possess your present influence in that borough.[161]

In response, Buxton denied any influence in Weymouth, about which Codrington was 'grossly deceived', but was obliged to qualify his position:

I have already told you that some of my near relatives inherited the remnants of property derived from the West Indies: but that to the best of my knowledge and belief (and in the difficulty of ascertaining exactly the source from

[159] *Ibid.*, pp. 303–4.   [160] *Ibid.*, p. 306.   [161] *Ibid.*, p. 308.

which property is derived, it is impossible to say more) no part of that property descended to me.

He was driven to conclude by asking: 'Should I owe less obligation to the Negro, if I had even remotely participated in the fruits of his oppression?'[162] In fact, Buxton had further connections with slave-owning. His wife was the niece of Mary Woodley, who was awarded £2,925 4s 2d for 172 slaves on St Kitts settled on her by her father William Woodley: one of the trustees of Mary Woodley's marriage settlement was the Rev. Gerard Noel, a prominent abolitionist who spoke at the third annual meeting of the Anti-slavery Society in 1828.[163]

The anti-abolitionist cleric Nathaniel Sotham, who had been a minister for the Society for the Propagation of the Gospel in the West Indies, threatened Zachary Macaulay in a pamphlet published in Cheltenham in 1825:

There are several who were well acquainted with facts which occurred, while Mr Macaulay acted as overseer upon a respectable property in that island [of Jamaica]; and who were well informed of the circumstances which led to his quitting that employment. He may recollect the names of Mr M'Lewd and Mr Cuthbert, and those names may bring to his mind circumstances which he perchance may have forgotten. This recollection, too, may induce him to hesitate before he again accuses a West Indian planter of maltreating his Negroes.[164]

Again, in the 1830 Bristol election, placards in support of the slave-owner James Evan Baillie attacked his Whig abolitionist opponent Edward Protheroe Jr, himself the scion of a slave-owning family:

Should he [Protheroe] appear on the hustings, tell him that it is from the West Indies, and the West Indies ALONE, that he owes his every shilling!! His father and grandfather amassed ALL their wealth as West India merchants, and consequently his money is the produce of Slave labour. Tell him, then, if he wishes to act at accordance with his *avowed* principles, he should *first* resign the wealth derived from such a source.[165]

'The English working man'

A second strand in the counter-attack by slave-owners on the abolitionists was the comparison between the allegedly privileged condition of

[162] *Ibid.*, p. 310.
[163] T71/879, St Kitts No. 705; *ASR* No. 36 (May 1828), Vol. II, p. 33.
[164] N. Sotham, *Plain facts on the question of West India slavery seriously examined by the test of truth and real observation* (Cheltenham, 1825), p. 22.
[165] Marshall, *Bristol and the abolition*, p. 9.

the enslaved and the hardships endured by the English working man. This was an established general trope, common to radicals such as Cobbett, who was equally hostile to compensation for the planters and abolitionist solicitude for the enslaved, as well as to the slave-owners and their supporters, over many years.[166] Benjamin Greene, the Suffolk slave-owner, wrote a public letter to Buxton in the spring of 1832, to ask how Buxton could reconcile his treatment of his own brewery workers, and especially their employment on Sundays, with his 'repeated exclamations against the sale (limited as it is) of some articles of their own produce by the slaves on a Sunday morning, and against permitting their masters to claim on other days more than ten hours of their time as the limit of daily labour'. Greene, himself a brewer, said that maltsters had to be employed every Sunday from October to April, and that he had every reason to believe Buxton kept his draymen and brewers to their labour '14, 15, 16 and 17 hours a day'. Greene went on to suggest that Buxton had either forgotten his Spitalfields brewery 'or, peradventure, you are deeply skilled in that species of sophistry, that mental and moral charlatanerie, which spreads a healing balm over one's own errors ... but does not diminish, nay rather increases, our abhorrence of the same misdeeds on the part of our neighbours'. He challenged Buxton to 'the most minute inspection, the most scrupulous comparison between your servants and my slaves, in their individual, moral and social state'.[167]

The potential moral *superiority* of the relationship between owner and enslaved over that between employer and workman was also asserted. *The Times*, although increasingly hostile to the planters in the years immediately prior to the Abolition Act, reported approvingly in 1829 that the Anglo-Jamaican John Blagrove,

who died in April 1824, and the owner of 1,500 slaves in Jamaica, by the following clause in his will, marks at once his feelings for his slaves, which few men would bestow upon the free labourers of England. We suspect however that Mr John Blagrove has not nor will have many imitators in the colonies;

'And lastly to my loving people, denominated and recognized by the law as, and being in fact my slaves, in Jamaica, but more estimated and considered by me and my family as tenants for life, attached to the soil, I bequeath a dollar for every man, woman and child as a small token of my regard for their faithful and affectionate service and labours to myself and my family, being reciprocally

---

[166] See for example P. Hollis, 'Anti-slavery and British working-class radicalism in the years of reform', in C. Bolt and S. Drescher (eds.), *Anti-slavery, religion and reform: essays in memory of Roger Anstey* (Folkestone: W. Dawson, 1980), pp. 294–315; and, for a revisionist view, S. Drescher, 'Cart whip and Billy Roller: antislavery and reform symbolism in industrialising Britain', *Journal of Social History*, 15 (1981–2), 3–24.

[167] Letter, March 27 [1832] from Benjamin Greene, Bury St Edmunds, to Fowell Buxton, MP, *The Times*, March 31, 1832, p. 7

bound in one general tie of master and servant in the prosperity of the land, from which we draw our mutual comforts and subsistence in our several relations (a tie and interest not practiced on by the hired labourer of the day in the United Kingdom), the contrary of which doctrine is held only by the visionists of the puritanical orders against the common feeling of mankind.'[168]

'Look at the examination before the House of Commons upon the Factory Bill', said the hired anti-abolitionist speaker Peter Borthwick in his Edinburgh lecture in March 1833:

Who were they that turned the promoters of that bill out of the House of Commons? Who opposed the amelioration of Home Slavery? Who opposed Mr Sadler when he stood for the representation of Leeds, knowing that, upon his return, depended the carrying of a bill for the amelioration of this condition of our own poor? Why, the Macauleys [sic] and other liberators of the Slaves in our own colonies![169]

And indeed historians have come to see more clearly the linkages within abolitionist thought between ideologies of 'free labour' in the colonies and the development of a factory proletariat in metropolitan Britain.[170]

Representations and identities in the Apprenticeship period and beyond

Contention and conflict did not end with the passage of the Abolition Act. The period of Apprenticeship saw continued campaigning by abolitionists to bring it to an immediate end. A Select Committee of the House of Commons sat in 1836, and reprised the set-piece confrontation between the owners of Apprentice labour and abolitionists.[171] Sturge and Harvey, and the US abolitionists Thome and Kemball, both made tours of the islands between 1836 and 1837 to report on the progress of Emancipation. In their account, Sturge and Harvey appeared to have no systematic approach to 'naming and shaming', sometimes citing owners of estates of which they were critical, sometimes passing over ownership

---

[168] *Ibid.*, 5 June 1829, p. 3. *Ibid.*, 13 April 1824, p. 4 had reported the death of John Blagrove 'of Jamaica and Ankerwyke House Bucks. aged 70'.

[169] P. Borthwick, *Report of a lecture on colonial slavery and gradual emancipation, delivered at the Assembly Rooms on Friday March 1 1833* (Edinburgh, 1833), p. 5.

[170] See for example Holt, *The problem of freedom*; D. B. Davies, *The problem of slavery in the age of Revolution, 1770–1823* (Ithaca, NY: Cornell University Press, 1975); H. Temperley, 'Capitalism, slavery and ideology', *Past and Present*, 75 (May 1977), 94–118; S. Drescher, *The mighty experiment: free labour versus slavery in British Emancipation* (Oxford: Oxford University Press, 2002).

[171] *Report from the Select Committee appointed to inquire into the working of the Apprenticeship system in the colonies, conduct of Apprentices, laws, regulations etc.*, PP 1836, Vol. 15 (560) (hereafter *Report from the Apprenticeship Committee*).

in silence. They identified Robert Wallace, the MP for Greenock, by name as the owner of the Glasgow estate in Westmoreland:

We are quite willing to believe that the proprietor of this estate has been kept in ignorance of the treatment of his negroes; and it is not without regret that we bring these facts under his notice and that of the public in the present manner; but we are strongly impressed by the conviction, that there are no estates more oppressively and even cruelly managed than those of many liberal humane and even religious proprietors in England.[172]

They did also re-engage with William Alers Hankey, identifying him (though not interestingly by name) and devoting part of an Appendix to him. The 'proprietor of Arcadia', they wrote, had published a pamphlet in January 1833[173] vindicating himself as a Christian slave-owner:

When we contrast his sentiments with the past history and present state of Arcadia, we cannot but regard his experience as one of the most unhappy examples, of the consequences resulting from the dereliction of the plain principles of Christian duty, for a course of expedience and compromise … Of all the partners in colonial iniquity, none are more guilty than the professedly liberal and especially the Christian proprietors, resident in England; and it is in discharge of a most painful duty, that we presume to place them, in the person of an eminent individual of their number, at the bar of public opinion.[174]

Sturge and Harvey went on to a point-by-point refutation of Hankey's defence, attacking in turn each of the conventional positions of the absentee: the principled opposition to slavery subject to due regard for the interests of the owners and the fitness of the slaves to be freed, the defence of distance, the inability to impose the owner's will upon the attorney. They concluded:

The proprietor of Arcadia pleads ignorance, inexperience and want of confidence in his own judgement … In matters of such importance, none of these pleas has the smallest weight … He might have ascertained, without leaving his counting-house, that the number of slaves on Arcadia was decreasing, though there was no disproportion of the sexes, and that this was owing in great part to the night labour during crop … [A] Christian slave owner can only exercise a conscience void of offence towards God and towards man, by emancipating his slaves … The attempt to discover and pursue a middle course demands, not only a sacrifice of principle but, if they are non-residents, involves them in the participation of evil, which it is fearful to contemplate.[175]

---

172 Sturge and Harvey, *The West Indies*, p. 252.
173 Hankey, *Letter to Thomas Wilson*.
174 Sturge and Harvey, *The West Indies*, Appendix, Section 6, p. lxxi.
175 *Ibid.*, pp. lxxiv–lxxv.

Nor did bitterness and contention over slavery end with Emancipation in 1838. On the one hand, some arenas of conflict dropped away. Abolitionists and some former slave-owners found common cause in the Society for the Extinction of the Slave Trade and the Civilization of Africa. Amongst the eighty-seven members of the Provisional Committee in February 1840 were a handful of former slave-owners, including Lord Seaford, the MPs Henry Goulburn and John Irving and, most strikingly, James MacQueen, who had previously particularly offended the abolitionists.[176] It is easy to see how the interests of the British owners of colonial estates worked by free labour after Emancipation were consistent with the effective suppression of the international slave-trade, but it is noteworthy how quickly the previous antagonisms were subsumed in new institutions.

Elsewhere, however, bitterness survived. There was very significant friction over the importation of 'hill coolies' into the colonies of Trinidad and British Guiana: efforts led by a group of British metropolitan slave-owners and merchants, and bitterly opposed by anti-slavery campaigners.[177] Domestic British politics continued to show at the local level signs of division. At the Cambridge election in May 1840, the successful candidate was assailed in the *Cambridge Independent Free Press*:

Sir Alexander Cray Grant, slave-owner, slave-driver, and slave-trader, was a most respectable representative of the Tories, lay and clerical, gown and town, voters and non-voters, bullies, burgees and bigots, of the borough of Cambridge; but ... it was too bad to force upon a Christian constituency a man to represent them who was also the representative of the cat and the cart-whip, and amongst the banners of whose triumph should be placed high up in front a black's head and cross-bones ... the Tories of the University wanted a whole hog man to carry out their desperate principles at that critical moment, and ... they would have had him, although he had in his day cut the flesh from the backs of half the black women of the West Indies.[178]

During the campaign in the following year, in June 1841, a flag depicting Grant witnessing the flogging of a black woman was exhibited in the town and at the hustings. Grant was again elected, and in his victory address indicated that he had information as to the character of John Shechan, the editor of the *Cambridge Independent Free Press* and

---

[176] Society for the Extinction of the Slave trade and the Civilization of Africa, *Prospectus of the Society for the extinction of the slave trade and the civilization of Africa, instituted June 1839* (London, 14 February 1840). See Lambert, 'The "Glasgow king"', pp. 19–23.

[177] [J. Scoble], *Hill Coolies: a brief exposure of the deplorable condition of the Hill Coolies in British Guiana and Mauritius, and of the nefarious means by which they were induced to resort to these colonies* (London: Harvey & Darton, 1840).

[178] Quoted in *The Times*, 25 November 1841, p. 6.

author of the article attacking Grant the previous year. Sheehan wrote to Grant to say that he had only done what he considered his public duty to his party in attacking Grant on public grounds, and had never made the most distant allusion to Grant's personal honour or private character, but now sought from Grant an apology or, implicitly, a duel. In the elaborate series of interventions by third parties that followed, it appears that the norms governing the conduct of this kind of 'affair of honour' had become contested and uncertain, and Grant ultimately went to court to avoid fighting a duel with Sheehan or potentially with Sheehan's bellicose second, Sir John Doyle, who was contemptuous of Grant's use of the courts to protect himself.[179] The court upheld the 'rule', effectively an injunction, against Doyle, but discharged without costs the rule against Sheehan: the court held that Sheehan's conduct was unjustifiable in calling Grant a slave-trader (although not apparently a slave-owner and slave-driver), that it was 'impossible that such observations would not have deeply wounded the feelings of the person to whom they were applied', and that he could be held 'morally responsible' for the 'obnoxious flag' of 1841; nevertheless, Grant's insinuations were unwarrantable.[180]

Fault-lines around slavery within British society continued to be evident in the debates around Free Trade in the 1840s and into the Eyre controversy a generation later. Of 146 'merchants, bankers and traders of the city of London' petitioning against the repeal of the Corn Laws in June 1846, 18 had been recipients of slave-compensation.[181] Following the ending of favourable duties for West India sugar in late 1846, of forty signatories of a petition to the Commons to allow free use of sugar and molasses in breweries, half had been recipients of slave-compensation.[182] As Disraeli wrote of the complexity of the sugar issue, 'It is that all considerations mingle in it; not only commercial but imperial, philanthropic, religious, confounding and crossing each other, and confusing legislature and nation lost in a maze of conflicting interests and contending emotions.'[183]

In 1854, the London merchants Thos Daniel & Co. addressed a public letter to the Duke of Newcastle protesting against the 'misrepresentations'

---

[179] *Ibid.*   [180] *Ibid.*, 29 November 1841, p. 6.

[181] *Ibid.*, 17 June 1846, p. 6 for signatories of the petition.

[182] *Ibid.*, 21 January 1847, p. 7.

[183] B. Disraeli, *Lord George Bentinck: a political biography*, p. 530, cited in W. E. Carroll, 'The end of slavery: imperial policy and colonial reaction in British Guiana', Ph.D. thesis, University of Michigan, Ann Arbor, 1970, p. 243.

of the Anti-slavery Society in representing the West Indian planters as wasteful and inefficient.[184]

Governor Eyre's behaviour after the Morant Bay rebellion in Jamaica in 1865 polarised English society along fissures represented as aristocratic versus bourgeois values: '[J. S.] Mill and [Peter] Taylor, in whose names the prosecution [of Eyre] is carried on, are the objects of the fiercest odium on the part of the whole upper-class mob ... Plutocracy, styling itself aristocracy, has displayed its character in this affair with a distinctiveness which is really fearful', wrote Goldwin Smith, Regius Professor of History at Oxford, who undertook a lecture tour to raise funds for the anti-Eyre Jamaica Committee.[185] Thirty years after Emancipation, of the sixty-six members of the Eyre defence committee in 1867, ten are identifiable as recipients of slave-compensation or direct descendants of such recipients.[186]

Conclusion

How effective were the abolitionist assaults in the 'war of representation'? The abolitionists had certainly, and at a relatively early date, succeeded in changing the field of discourse around slavery: it had become unacceptable to be a proponent of slavery as a positive good. The *ASR* reported Lord Dudley and Ward (later the Earl of Dudley) saying, in a parliamentary speech in 1826, 'Not only without but within the walls of Parliament there existed, he might say, but one opinion ... he heartily wished that the West India system had never existed at all. It was morally wrong, and if it was morally wrong, it could not be politically right.'[187] William Gladstone was perceptibly uncomfortable when confronted in the Select Committee on Apprenticeship in 1836 with the idea of the existence of a 'pro-slavery' party before Emancipation.[188]

The abolitionists sought to undermine the rhetorical distancing devices of slave-owners: an anti-abolitionist must, by definition, be a defender of slavery. Just as the slave-owners designated their opponents as 'anti-colonialists', so the abolitionists strove to break through the screen of 'the West India system', or 'the colonial system'. Lord Suffield, for example, sought to re-denominate Lord Dudley in 1826 as

---

[184] T. Daniel & Co., *A letter to His Grace the Duke of Newcastle on West India affairs called forth by the misrepresentations of the Anti-slavery Society* (London, 1854).

[185] Bernard Semmel, *The Governor Eyre controversy* (London: MacGibbon & Kee, 1962), pp. 166–7.

[186] Appendix 13.

[187] *ASR* No. 10 (March 1826), Vol. I, pp. 111–12.

[188] *Report from the Apprenticeship Committee*, pp. 181–2.

'the Noble Lord who was the most able and ready advocate of slavery, or rather the most ready and able apologist for the West India system'.[189] The effectiveness of re-inscribing 'slavery' on the slave-owners of course depended on the success of the cultural work of the abolitionists over the previous half-century in making 'slavery' a signifier of profound sin and depravity, not only in its practical impact on the enslaved but in its effects on the enslavers.

The impact *in the colonies* of metropolitan campaigns of the abolitionists was emphasised by resident and absentee slave-owners in order to explain resistance and rebellion amongst the enslaved. Yet it was also perhaps more sincerely acknowledged to be corrosive of the self-esteem of colonial slave-owners. 'They are Englishmen', said Richard Barrett, 'their literature is English; every ship takes them the lamentations and curses of the real and mock friends of the slave. Every newspaper, every magazine and review paints, in the darkest colours, the wretchedness of the crime of slavery.'[190]

If it is true that the assault on slavery had a demoralising effect in the colonies, the impact must have been greater in Britain itself, where the culture of anti-slavery was deeply established. Lord Holland was anxious about the effect of the Lords' Committee for which the West India interest pressed, in his view ill-advisedly, in 1832:

And tho' some exaggeration of the evils of slavery and the cruelty of the masters and drivers have no doubt been industriously circulated, I am far from believing that the truth of the case will so entirely refute these allegations as many West Indians imagine. Sure I am that a few insulated instances of barbarous severity and injustice (of which there must needs be many) will be quite sufficient to stamp on the whole system the character of cruelty, in a public predisposed to receive such impressions, at this moment.[191]

The *ASR* was clearly concerned to promote its own impact, but carried a suggestive piece in late 1829 on its success in establishing its discourse in Britain. It reproduced in August of that year from the *Jamaica Royal Gazette* an 'Extract of a letter from a respectable West India proprietor (in London) dated 2nd April 1829', which included the admission 'Our line is the defensive: we cannot advance without almost the certainty of defeat and ruin', and urged the Jamaica Assembly to read the *ASR* in order to understand better the prevailing mood in the metropolis. The

[189] *ASR* No. 12 (May 1826), Vol. I, pp. 174ff.
[190] R. Barrett, 'The speeches of Mr Barrett and Mr Burge', 1833, quoted in C. Petley, 'Boundaries of rule, ties of dependency: Jamaica planters, local society and the metropole 1800–1834', Ph.D. thesis, University of Warwick, 2003, p. 252.
[191] Lord Holland *et al.*, *The Holland House Diaries 1831–40*, ed. A. D. Kriegel (London: Routledge, 1977), 29 February 1832, p. 142.

speeches of Lord Seaford, reported the London absentee, had 'brought down on his Lordship the accumulated wrath of the Saints.'[192] Serjeant Spankia, the chosen counsel for Cadell, Wood and MacQueen in the Mary Prince libel trials, withdrew in what his replacement called 'a political funk'.[193]

The Antiguan resident planter Armstrong, whom Thome and Kimball met during Apprenticeship, invoked the pressures on the metropolitan slave-owners:

In the year 1833, when the abolition excitement was at its height in England, and the people were thundering on the doors of Parliament for emancipation, Mr Armstrong visited that country for his health. To use his own expressive words, he 'got a terrible scraping wherever he went'. He said he could not travel in a stage-coach, or go into a party, or attend a religious meeting, without being attacked. No one the most remotely connected with the system could have peace there. He said it was astonishing to see what a feeling was abroad, how mightily the mind of the whole country, peer and priest and peasant, was wrought up. The national heart seemed on fire.[194]

But there is less evidence that slave-owners were *systematically* subject to social sanction. Elizabeth Heyrick in 1824 had called for differentiation: 'the whole nation must now divide itself into the active supporters, and the active opposers of slavery'.[195] Yet this division never fully materialised. In many social and cultural institutions, there was clearly co-habitation between abolitionists and slave-owners, and even those who publicly quarrelled over slavery found common ground in other causes to rebuild collaboration. Thus John Gladstone and James Cropper, after a bitter exchange over slavery in 1823–4, when Gladstone accused Cropper of being motivated in his hostility to slavery by his interests in East India sugar, nevertheless found common cause in jointly campaigning in the late 1820s against the East India Company's remaining monopoly.[196] Tensions occurred within families such as the

---

[192] *ASR* No. 51 (August 1829), Vol. III, pp. 34–5.

[193] Thomas, 'Pringle v. Cadell', p. 125.

[194] J. A. Thome and J. H. Kimball, *Emancipation in the West Indies* (New York, 1838), p. 125.

[195] E. Heyrick, *Immediate not gradual emancipation*, quoted in C. Midgley, 'Slave sugar boycotts, female activism and the domestic base of British anti-slavery culture', *Slavery & Abolition*, 17.3 (December 1996), 137–62 (p. 153).

[196] See *The Times*, 26 February 1829, p. 4 for details of a public meeting of merchants in Liverpool 'for the purpose of taking into consideration the best means of removing the restrictions imposed upon commerce by the present Charter of the East India Company ...', at which John Gladstone and James Cropper both spoke, and together moved and seconded the final resolution, to raise a subscription for the Committee on which they both sat.

Gladstones but such tensions appear to have had limited impact on Gladstone's public positioning on slavery. Ultimately, slave-owning did not constitute an *exclusive* identity for the absentee slave-owner: he or she had, and took, opportunities to assume alternative identities: local, regional, religious, philanthropic.

Wilberforce addressed Lord Holland carefully in 1830 'in your other character of a West India proprietor': although critical of Holland, Wilberforce did not make slave-owning the essence of Holland's identity but allowed him it as an additional identity, separate from his political and social position in the metropolis.[197]

The argument (made both by slave-owners and by some abolitionists) that slavery was a *national* sin appears to have eased the divisions in society, real though they were, over the implications. The counsel for the Demerara and Berbice planters at the Privy Council appeal over compulsory manumission in 1827 quoted George Canning's speech of 19 May 1826:

I do maintain that we, having all concurred in the guilt of rearing and fostering this evil, are not to turn upon the planters and say 'you alone shall suffer all the penalty: we determine to get rid of this moral pestilence which infects our character as much as yours, which we have as much contributed to propagate as you, but you, as spotted lepers, shall be banished from our society, and cast to utter ruin to expiate our common crime'.[198]

But if national atonement for the 'national sin' served to re-integrate slave-owners, such re-integration was not unqualified. As the Rev. Thomas Cooper remarked, the crime of slavery might in a great degree be a national crime, but 'the Planters seem determined, by a strange and desperate line of conduct, to plunge themselves more deeply than any other class of the community, into this abyss of sin and suffering'.[199]

---

[197] V. E. Chancellor, 'Slave-owner and anti-slaver: Henry Richard Vassall Fox, 3rd Lord Holland 1800–40', *Slavery & Abolition*, 1.3 (December 1980), 263–75 (p. 267).
[198] Quoted in Carroll, 'The end of slavery', p. 85.
[199] Cooper, *Correspondence*, p. iv.

2 The debate over compensation

The debate over compensation was central to the conflict over slavery itself in the 1820s and 1830s, informing the rhetorical structures of both sides. In the aftermath of Canning's Resolutions in 1823, their importance in embedding the principle of compensation was recognised. Slave-owners were uneasy that the principle was not as explicit as desired. 'The principle of indemnity and compensation ought not only to be fully and unequivocally admitted, but a guarantee to that effect should be given to the colonies, on the general property of the country. The equity of the right to indemnity cannot be denied; the justice of the country cannot refuse it', wrote the MP John Rock Grosett in 1824.[1] The slave-owners fought to maintain compensation as an integral part of the discourse on Emancipation, while a number, but not all, of the abolitionists sought to disentangle the two: 'the emancipation of the Negroes, and the remuneration of their masters, are two essentially distinct things, and ought always to be kept separate', maintained Charles Stuart.[2]

The previous chapter has argued that the discourse of amelioration was established as hegemonic in the 1820s. This chapter explores how the debate over compensation in the context of Emancipation was conceived and structured by both sides, and how slave-owners were ultimately successful in establishing the principle of unconditional compensation and in reaching a financial settlement with the state. It examines first the conceptualisation and contestation of the enslaved as property, at a time when other forms of property established or sanctified in the eighteenth century were under scrutiny, then looks at the main precedents for compensation that shaped how the *principle* of compensation was thought about and spoken of in the context of

---

[1] J. R. Grosett, MP, *Remarks on West India affairs*, 2nd edn (London, 1825), p. 102.
[2] C. Stuart, *The West India question: an outline for immediate emancipation and remarks on compensation*, reprinted from *English Quarterly Magazine & Review*, April 1832 (New Haven, 1833), p. 19.

Emancipation: a series of discourses that are examined in the third section. The chapter then looks at how both the form and amount of compensation were conceived and ultimately negotiated, before concluding with an analysis of the financial implications of compensation for the slave-owners and the British state.

'Property in men'

The legal background and context

Although the debate about 'property in men' was a moral rather than legal debate, it took the form it did partly because the legal framework governing slave-ownership was so underdeveloped. English law had neither positive statute nor prohibition. The weakness of the positive endorsement of slavery under English statute law was inadvertently highlighted by Lord St Vincent in Parliament in 1833, when he recited what was presumably intended to be a compelling history of legislative recognition of slavery: he drew sequentially upon an act of William III that exempted the importation of Negroes from duty; two acts under George III that dealt with mortgage law; and the Act establishing slave-registers, in which 'the right of property in slaves was expressly acknowledged'.[3] For its recent endorsement under English common law, the slave-owners in the early 1830s invoked Lord Stowell's 1827 judgement in the case of *The Slave, Grace*, which the slave-owners construed as declaring the slaves in the colonies to be the inalienable property of their masters. Yet the abolitionists had little alternative framework: the decisions of the Somerset case were famously ambiguous. Only with the passage of the Abolition Act itself did the British Parliament directly address the legality of colonial slavery, sanctioning 'property in men' through the provision of compensation at the same time as it was striking down such ownership.

The legal position of ownership of slaves under *colonial* law was relatively diverse and relatively complex.[4] The Caribbean colonies did not have a single, uniform legal system: for example, there was a prolonged

---

[3] *The Debates in Parliament – Session 1833 – on the Resolution and Bill for the Abolition of Slavery in British colonies, with a copy of the Act of Parliament* (London, 1834), 3rd series, Vol. 18, pp. 360–1: 3 June 1833.

[4] See M. Craton, 'Property and propriety: land tenure and slave property in the creation of a British West Indian plantocracy, 1612–1740', in J. Brewer and S. Staves (eds.), *Early modern conceptions of property* (London and New York: Routledge, 1995), pp. 497–529 for the piecemeal development of colonial law.

struggle in Trinidad over the replacement of Spanish law by English law. Mortgage debt over slaves was not recognised in St Lucia until late in the life of slavery, and elsewhere the operation of mortgage lending was complicated by the extension into many of the colonies as part of the English common law heritage of the 'equity of redemption', one of the devices by which land was increasingly privileged over other forms of property.[5] The ownership of slaves was not codified locally until the eighteenth century, and ambiguity remained as to whether they constituted real property or personalty.[6] In addition to the estate as the unit of land and slaves, the enslaved were owned in groups or 'gangs' of slaves unattached to land but hired out to land-owners, as well as domestic servants and urban artisans, typically held in smaller numbers, all of whom represented property to be transmitted.

Despite the ambiguities, slave-owners remained entitled to buy and sell slaves after the abolition of the slave-trade in 1807, although the sale of slaves between colonies was increasingly constrained.[7] Initially, a licence was required from the exporting colony, and in the case of the new colonies an import licence was also necessary, limited to a 3 per cent increase in the existing population of the enslaved. In 1818, the movement of slaves between the Bahamas and Dominica to Demerara-Essequibo was explicitly permitted, although in 1819 a more general prohibition on the movement of unregistered slaves was put in place. Between 1825 and 1828, only the British Privy Council could grant licences to move slaves, and then only where it was essential to the welfare of the enslaved. After 31 July 1828 all movement between colonies was prohibited, except for fishermen and domestics.[8] Within colonies, the sale of estates and the attached slaves was still entirely possible, although there were increasing restrictions on the sale of enslaved away from estates if it meant the break-up of families.

[5] D. Sugarman and R. Warrington, 'Land law, citizenship, and the invention of "Englishness": the strange world of the equity of redemption', in Brewer and Staves (eds.), *Conceptions of property*, pp. 111–43. See also S. D. Smith, *Slavery, family, and gentry capitalism in the British Atlantic: the world of the Lascelles, 1648–1834* (Cambridge: Cambridge University Press, 2006), p. 69 for the impact of the 1732 Colonial Debts Act.

[6] See for example the assertion by the London and Bristol merchants Daniels that 'negroes in Montserrat are by Law chattel property and consequently not dowerable'. Thos Daniel & Sons to Commission, T71/1610, 8 March 1836. See also Craton, 'Property and propriety', pp. 515–17.

[7] D. Eltis, 'The traffic in slaves between the British West Indian colonies 1807–1833', *Economic History Review*, NS 25.1 (1972), 55–64.

[8] B. W. Higman, *Slave populations in the British Caribbean 1807–34* (Baltimore: Johns Hopkins University Press, 1984), p. 80.

Contested forms of property

Against the background of legal ambiguity or silence under English law, contention over 'property in men' was one of a wider series of parallel discussions over what could and could not be owned in the Age of Reform.[9] Property in office was the subject of sustained erosion in the attack on 'Old Corruption'.[10] In 1835, the Whigs established an inquiry into colonial sinecures. Charles Greville was contorted with embarrassment over his West Indian sinecure as Secretary of Jamaica, although he fought successfully to keep it: 'I feel unutterable disgust, and something akin to shame ... A placeman is in these days an odious animal ... The funds from which I draw my means do not somehow seem a pure source; formerly those things were tolerated, now they are not ...'[11]

More robustly, Thomas Grenville, his family under pressure to cede the income from their sinecures, notably the Tellership, complained: 'The spirit of the times is making war upon many other properties equally protected and recognised by law; tithes for lay and Church properties are equally menaced, but nobody will expect a gratuitous surrender of them.'[12] Earl Grey apologised for the attack by the Whig MP Thomas Creevey on the Buckingham-Grenvilles' Tellership, which was 'vested property, with which you cannot interfere without shaking the security on which all property stands'. Reflecting Grey's attitude, losses of offices were often compensated through commutation into pensions. There was a forlorn radical critique of such compensation by Wade and others: 'the sinecures were abuses, and they ought to have been swept away without equivalent'. 'If other classes are injured by reform and improvement, what compensation do they receive for their loss? The workman suffers by the substitution of machinery ... and the farmer by alterations of the currency; but ... no fund is provided to make up the loss of their capital and industry.'[13]

The loss of patronage of rotten boroughs, by contrast, was uncompensated, although claims were made that the Reform Act was

---

[9] Brewer and Staves, 'Introduction', in *Conceptions of property*, pp. 1–18; P. J. Marshall, 'Parliament and property rights in the late eighteenth-century British Empire', in Brewer and Staves, *Conceptions of property*, pp. 530–44.

[10] P. Harling, *The waning of 'Old Corruption': the politics of economical reform in Britain 1779–1846* (Oxford: Clarendon Press, 1996); W. D. Rubinstein, 'The end of "Old Corruption" in Britain 1780–1860', *Past and Present*, 101 (November 1983), 55–86; E. J. Evans, *The contentious tithe: the tithe problem and English agriculture, 1750–1850* (London: Routledge & Kegan Paul, 1976).

[11] C. C. F. Greville, *A Journal of the reigns of King George IV and King William IV*, 2nd edn, ed. H. Reeves, 3 vols. (London: Longman, 1874), Vol. III, pp. 275–6.

[12] Harling, *The waning of "Old Corruption"*, p. 212.

[13] *Ibid.*, pp. 145–6.

expropriation. Above all, debates over the commutation of tithes followed closely the patterns of the discussions of compensation for slave Emancipation.[14]

Slave-owners and 'property in men'

Against this background, the start-point of the slave-owners was the sanctity of property. The theme runs repeatedly and repetitively through slave-owner discourse in the 1820s and 1830s. 'Your memorialists will not waste a moment in advancing arguments to establish their right of property in their slaves. To suppose it could be doubted, would be to bring into question the title to all property whatever', wrote the London Berbice and Demerara slave-owners and mortgagees in their 1826 petition to the Privy Council.[15] Henry Simmons recognised the importance of establishing the slaves as property and of deflecting the argument that the owners would retain their estates post-Emancipation:

I maintain, my Lord [Earl Grey], that possessing this property under the sanction of British law, it is plunder to deprive me of it without full compensation … [A]lthough Mr Stanley most artfully and insidiously attempts to blink the question [of compensation] by talking of the land being our property, I would beg to remind this proud and flippant young man that the English government paid America one million for those Negroes who were received by the English admiral at Halifax, in 1815, so that the Negroes as well as the land were justly considered property.[16]

Denominating slaves as a conventional class of property was key to the anti-abolitionist arguments on compensation. Robert Wilmot Horton, the former Secretary of State and MP, was one of the most sophisticated and concrete advocates of this normalisation of slave-property.

Let me suppose the case of a Yorkshire proprietor, who dies possessed of a Plantation and slaves in the West Indies. His eldest son succeeds to his Estate in Yorkshire. To one half of his younger children, he leaves his West Indian plantation and to the other his property in the funds. At the time of his death, what reason had he to suppose that the integrity of one class of property was

---

[14] Evans, *The contentious tithe*, esp. pp.118–19 on Thomas Greene's abortive proposals of 1828.

[15] London Proprietors and Mortgagees, *Demerara & Berbice: Petition and Memorial of the London proprietors and mortgagees against compulsory manumission in those colonies* (November 1826), p. 4.

[16] H. P. Simmons, *A letter to the Rt Hon. Earl Grey on the West India question by H. P. Simmons Esq.* (Liverpool, 1833), pp. 18–19, 34. He was alluding to the provisions of the Treaty of Ghent for payment by the British for the enslaved removed to Nova Scotia at the end of the American Revolution; see S. Schama, *Rough crossings: Britain, the slaves and the American Revolution* (New York: HarperCollins, 2006), pp. 134–5.

not to be preserved, equally with that of the others? If he had any such reason, it would have been an unwarrantable partiality, to have devoted one part of his family to beggary and pauperism, by giving them, as their portion, a property upon the continuance of which they could not depend.[17]

Wilmot Horton went on to express, moreover, the way in which the fruits of slave-property could and did permeate metropolitan society:

The possible justice of such case might be placed in a stronger point-of-view. Five years before his death, this Yorkshire proprietor might have been exclusively an owner of West Indian property; but he might have sold three-fourths of it, vesting two of these fourths in land, and the other in the funds. If confiscation is to be the result of guilty wealth, why is not the property in England to be confiscated, as well as that of the West Indies?[18]

It was an important part of the representational strategy of the slave-owners to constitute themselves as 'proprietors', as owners of *land* rather than as owners of slaves. Land was both politically and legally privileged as a form of property.[19] The comparison with absentee gentleman farmers in Britain was used to illuminate the owner–agent relationship, a Committee member in 1832 asking William Shand to compare the absentee attorney nexus with that of 'a gentleman in London with a large farm in Scotland'.[20] Key to the re-framing of slave-owners as land-owners is the opening of the *Report from the Commercial Committee*:

[T]he case ... is one of severe distress affecting the Proprietors of the Soil, in countries which, acquired in various modes, and at several periods, have become integrated parts of the British Empire: and if it be true that it is necessarily through commercial transactions that the means of maintaining themselves and their dependants are obtained by these Proprietors, it is not less true, that it is rather as Landowners than as Merchants, that they appear before the House. They are thus entitled to the benefit of any distinction which may be made in favour of those interests which are fixed and permanent, as compared with the fleeting and occasional objects of commercial enterprise.[21]

[17] Rt Hon. R. Wilmot Horton, *1st and 2nd letters to the Freeholders of the County of York, on Negro slavery, being an enquiry into the claims of the West Indians for an Equitable Compensation by the Rt Hon. R. Wilmot Horton* (London: Edmund Lloyd, Harley Street, 1830), pp. 42–3.

[18] *Ibid.*

[19] Land was, for example, outside the ambit of the bankruptcy laws (J. Hoppit, 'Risk and failure in English industry *c.* 1700–1800', Ph.D. thesis, University of Cambridge, 1984, p. 37); as noted above, the mortgagor-land-owner was advantaged relative to the mortgagee by the legal entitlement to the 'equity of redemption': Sugarman and Warrington, 'The strange world of the equity of redemption'.

[20] *Report on the extinction of slavery*: evidence of William Shand, Q. 7003, p. 465.

[21] *Report from the Commercial Committee*, p. 3. This of course highlighted the potential tensions between owners and those with mercantile claims on 'slave-property'.

West India property was acknowledged to be a different form of property, not because it entailed slave-ownership, but because of the 'peculiar disability' of the West India planter to relieve himself by any transfer or altered direction: the argument was that West India property was uniquely illiquid as a result not only of the depressed economic circumstances but also of the abolitionist campaign. 'I think that it is quite impossible to sell a West India estate at the moment', asserted Alexander Macdonnell, the Secretary to the Committee of West India merchants, to the Commercial Committee in January 1832.[22] The Commercial Committee concluded that '[t]he agitation of the slave question in Great Britain has tended to diminish the feeling of confidence of the West India proprietor in the security of his property, to check the investment of capital, and to increase the difficulty of effecting sales and mortgages'.[23]

However, Augustus Hardin Beaumont, a newspaper-owner and editor in Jamaica, identified a contradiction amongst the absentee owners in Britain, a contradiction reflecting the success of the abolitionists in shifting the discourse over slavery.[24] Beaumont spoke of:

the delusion kept up by the slave owners resident in Britain: their timidity prevents their stating the nature of their property. What is their property? Is it the satisfaction of civilizing their slaves, and rendering them fit for Emancipation? No, the property in slaves which the British Parliament sold them, is in the rights, the natural – the *born* rights of the Negro – a right to his labour – to all he can acquire, to the possession of him as a mere chattel – destitute of will – subject to absolute power. Cruel as this may be, it is the contract between Parliament and the Slave Owners.[25]

A petition in 1824 from 'the planters and merchants of the British West India colonies' sought to defuse the argument that the immorality of slavery compromised the sanctity of property rights, but in so doing introduced potentially a radical critique of property rights per se: 'We might ask, how much of the property of your Majesty's

---

[22] *Ibid.*, Q. 69, p. 28. [23] *Ibid.*, p. 21.

[24] Beaumont, born in America, was forced out of Jamaica in the early 1830s for his embrace of compulsory manumission and his opposition to the flogging of women, and ultimately became the editor of the Chartist newspaper *The Northern Liberator*. For Beaumont's extraordinarily picaresque life, see W. H. Maehl, Jr., 'Augustus Hardin Beaumont: Anglo-American radical (1798–1838)', *International Review of Social History*, 14 (1969), 237–50.

[25] A. H. Beaumont, *Compensation to Slave Owners fairly considered in an appeal to the common sense of the people of England*, 4th edn (London, 1826), p. 8.

subjects – property held the most sacred – could shew a title in its origin free from injustice or violence.'[26]

Such calls to the defence of 'property' appear to have mobilised a section of the British elite with no direct stake in slave-ownership in support of the slave-owners in the later stages of the battle over compensation. The MP Robert Dundas moved one of the resolutions at the London meeting of the West India interest in April 1832:

He came there totally unconnected with any West India interest. He derived no portion of his income from any connexion with that country, but ... asked for those injured and depressed colonies only, what every individual in this country would expect if his property was to be taken from him, – namely strict justice. No person was more anxious than he was to ameliorate the condition of the slaves in the West Indies, but he should consider it unworthy of any Englishman, or any person who held a title to property in this country, – he should consider it derogatory if they accepted relief only on the condition that they complied with the orders in council.[27]

'Mr Fitzgerald, M.P.' extrapolated a wider threat to property in the same meeting.[28] 'He ... called upon the fundholder to make common cause with the West India proprietor against the innovation upon property. The fundholder knew not how soon his own turn might come. [Hear.]'[29] John Horsley Palmer, former Governor of the Bank of England, also spoke of the security of the financial system:

He concurred in all that had been said upon the propriety of emancipation with due regard to the rights of property ... the reckless spoliation of the Ministerial plan ... would endanger the whole frame of society. The property of the planter had been secured by a hundred acts of Parliament, and no minister had a right to tamper with that property. (Hear, hear.) It tended to shake the credit and confidence of the country. The events of 1825 proved what was the effect of confidence and credit shaken; but he feared those events would be but as nothing in comparison with the results to be anticipated from the passing of the proposed measures, for he would maintain that in such event there would be no security to the funded property in this country. (Cheers.) The funded property was but secured by one act of Parliament, while the property of colonists now assailed had the protection of one hundred statutes, which seemed to avail but little against the first proposition of gross violent spoliation.[30]

[26] 'Petition of the planters, merchants and others interested in the British West India colonies,' March 1824, quoted in Grosett, *Remarks on West India Affairs*, p. 113.
[27] *The Times*, 6 April 1832, p. 1.
[28] Probably Thomas Fitzgerald of Fane Valley, elected for the Irish constituency of Louth in 1833.
[29] *The Times*, 28 May 1833, p. 5.
[30] *Ibid.*

Although this intervention was greeted with scorn by *The Times* (and indeed in the intensity of its reaction may be read concern as to the power of Horsley Palmer's scaremongering), it is not unreasonable to infer that genuine concern existed in City circles over the impact on the credit system of a catastrophic collapse of the slave-economy through expropriation, especially against the background of the 1825–6 financial crisis.[31] Compensation which allowed an orderly reduction of debt appealed not only to the direct recipients but to those exposed indirectly or even systemically to West India credit.

The critique of 'property in men'

The fundamental principle of defining the enslaved as 'property' was contested by a section of the abolitionists. Brougham expressed the most absolute form of such contestation:

Let us hear no more of this being a question of property – of man being the property of man. As long as men loathe rapine, despise fraud or abhor blood, so long will men, true to that principle, and true to the feelings of their common nature, reject with abhorrence, and put from them with indignation, the vain and guilty phantasy, that man can be the property of his fellow creatures.[32]

A meeting of the Surrey Anti-slavery Society at Epsom in 1827 passed a resolution in the light of the appeal to the Privy Council against compulsory manumission in Demerara:

That the right of property asserted by the planters in Demerara in kidnapped aliens, and in their own countrymen, is a fearful specimen of the pervading principle of all the colonial legislatures – a principle which, if it should ever be tolerated by any ministers or any legislative authorities in England, would

---

[31] 'Leader', *The Times*, 29 May 1833, p. 2:

The allusion made by the ex-Governor to the panic of 1825, and his comparison of the security of funded property to that of property in our fellow man, would excite our horror, if it did not provoke our ridicule ... Because a planter can no longer authorize his driver to apply the cartwhip to the back of his fellows, and treat a gang of slaves like a team of horses, – therefore he may tremble for his dividend at the Bank; and because freedom is henceforward to be the birthright of black as well as white children, – therefore the English landed proprietor may be stripped of the inheritance of his family, or deprived of the titles to his estate!! It is in such perversions of fact and reasoning, or in such stupid exaggerations as these, which heat the minds or increase the obstinacy of the interested parties at home, – which indisposes both them and their agents in the colonies to listen to terms, or which prevent them from co-operating cordially with the Government, by representing it as their greatest enemy, – that the chief danger of emancipation lies.

[32] Brougham, speech of 13 July 1830, quoted in Wilmot Horton, *1st and 2nd letters*, p. 49.

shake the British constitution to its foundation, and proclaim to the astonished world that its watchful guardians never sleep except when rich men trampled underfoot the stranger, and him that is ready to perish.[33]

Robert Otway Cave, the MP for Leicester, provided a more carefully delineated denial when he 'maintained that West India proprietors possessed, and could possess, no legal property in persons who were equally British subjects themselves'.[34] Lord Goderich contested the equivalence of colonial slaves and metropolitan real property but saw this as qualifying rather than vitiating the comparison: 'Much is said on the abstract question of the right of the owner to his slaves, which is compared to that which an Englishman possesses in his land.' But, he said, the house and land of an Englishman have no interest in whether they are his property or not: a slave naturally does. 'Property in inanimate matter and in a rational being cannot stand precisely on the same basis', because of the rights of the alleged slave.[35]

Some of those who conceded questions over the legitimacy of 'property in men' could nevertheless concede the principle of compensation. The Bishop of Bath and Wells, addressing an anti-slavery meeting in Bath on 22 October 1830, said that he was not an advocate of instantaneous Emancipation, and went on to say that 'he was also favourable to some form of compensation being made to the slave-owners, however defective in a moral point of view might be their title'.[36]

Lord Suffield in 1826 responded to the call for compensation by saying that it seemed to him to come from the wrong quarter. Britain had spent £150 million and suffered 50,000 dead defending the West Indies, and still incurred a cost of £2 million to £3 million per annum. 'Surely the mother country should be indemnified for this vast exhaustion of blood and treasure?' But, he said, England would rather pay £6 million (i.e. annually) for no slavery than £3 million for it. 'Thus compensation, however unreasonable in principle, would readily be granted.'[37] By 1833, Suffield was arguing that sentiment had turned away from compensation. He said that he had been at an abolitionist meeting in Camberwell two to three years previously where the minority favoured compensation: but 'at a meeting which took place a few days ago ... the idea of compensation was scouted altogether, on the ground that the

---

[33] *ASR* No. 30 (November 1827), Vol. II, Resolution 14.
[34] *Ibid*. No. 64 (August 1830), Vol. III, pp. 339–40.
[35] *Ibid*. No. 92 (January 1832), Vol. V, p. 17.
[36] *Ibid*. No. 74 (January 1831), Vol. IV, p. 57.
[37] *Ibid*. No. 12 (May 1826), Vol. I, reporting Suffield's speech in the House of Lords.

West India proprietors can have no claim to a right of property in the body and soul of any human being whatever'.[38]

Amongst some of the aristocratic Whig abolitionists, however, was an expressed contempt for money in the context of Emancipation, which suggested that the slave-owners simply cared more about compensation than their opponents. Viscount Howick dismissed the issue in a rather grand manner:

However large the claim of the West Indians for compensation may be, I do not hesitate to say that it should not stand in my way for a moment, as weighed against the importance of putting an end to the sufferings of the slaves ... the victims of that guilt must not continue for one hour to suffer, while we are haggling about pounds, shillings and pence.[39]

The precedents for compensation

The arguments of both sides around compensation were shaped and structured by previous experience of government intervention in property rights. Compensation for compulsory purchase of land for 'improvement' projects was an important point of reference, for it crystallised both the contingent rather than absolute nature of property rights and the wider notion of the legitimacy or otherwise of 'property in men'. As an established qualification to the absolute nature of property rights, the abolitionists used compulsory purchase to legitimate legislative intervention in slave-ownership, while the slave-owners used it to justify compensation. Commissioners had been appointed in 1799, for example, to investigate claims for compensation from the West India, London and subsequently East India docks, and a total of £677,382 was awarded.[40] Slave-compensation differed significantly in its modes of organisation and implementation from compulsory purchase, but its principle was the same.

The British state also had a tradition of making emergency loans to slave-owners and merchants, as it had in St Vincent and Grenada in the late 1790s, and in St Vincent again after the volcanic eruption of 1812. The state had granted outright relief in Barbados after the hurricane of 1831. There was thus an established model of financial support to

---

[38] *The Debates in Parliament – Session 1833 – on the Resolution and Bill for the Abolition of Slavery in British colonies, with a copy of the Act of Parliament* (London, 1834), p. 39.
[39] Viscount Howick, speech of 13 April 1831, reported in *ASR* No. 94 (March 1832), Vol. v, pp. 85–6.
[40] *The Times*, 18 October 1828, p. 3.

the slave-colonies. The West Indian interest had an equally long tradition of calls for relief, as their opponents registered. In June 1830, the
ASR carried a supplement on 'the Case of the West Indian planters,
or pauperism on a great scale', in which it sarcastically appraised the
constant appeals of the West Indians, as in 1792 and 1805, and spoke
sorrowfully of the evidence amongst 'the body of not quite 2,000 sugar
planters' of all the evils that attend pauperism: 'a want of exertion and
self-dependence, recklessness of the future, improvidence, waste, prof-
ligacy etc.'.[41] This is a powerful illustration of how the newly hegemonic
values of independence, thrift and self-reliance were harnessed rhetoric-
ally against slave-owners as well as practically against the 'undeserving
poor' in Britain in the Age of Reform.

American Loyalist compensation provided an *administrative* parallel,
but was not apparently invoked in support of the principle of slave-
compensation.[42] Slave-owners such as H. P. Simmons, as noted above,
focused instead on the payment made to America by the British government under the Treaty of Ghent.

There had been efforts amongst the West India interest to mobilise in
pursuit of compensation at the time of the abolition of the slave-trade
in 1807. William Manning had introduced a parliamentary motion for
compensation. But the fragmentation of the West India interest around
the slave-trade undermined any coherent effort. The interests of the
slave-traders were not inherently identical to those of the slave-owners.
The owners of slaves in the established slave-colonies were ambivalent about the continuation of slave shipments to estates in the newer
and expanding sugar-colonies. And both groups were opposed to the
shipment of slaves to non-British colonies. Moreover, property in the
slave-trade was a more difficult concept than property in slaves, even
for those who held it. Nevertheless, some of the rhetoric surrounding
compensation at the time of the abolition of the slave-trade reappeared
in the 1820s and 1830s.

Thomas Clarkson had published three letters in 1807 on compensation in the context of abolition of the slave-trade.[43] The first, from
January 1807, was in response to a petition to the House of Lords
for compensation. He had heard, he said, of thieves being punished
by death; he had heard of thieves and receivers being punished; 'but
I never yet heard, that men in any country had a compensation for

---

[41] Supplement to *ASR* No. 61 (June 1830), Vol. III, p. 275.
[42] See Chapter 3, below, p. 116.
[43] T. Clarkson, *Three letters (one of which has appeared before) to the Planters and Slave-
Merchants principally on the subject of compensation* (London, 1807).

abstaining from inequity, or that they were to be indemnified for losses which might arise out of a violation of all religion, provided they would abandon the crimes which occasioned them'.[44] In his second letter he attacked William Manning, who had tabled the question of compensation in the House of Commons: 'And are you serious in asking for compensation? That compensation is due somewhere there is no doubt. But from whom is it due? It is due from you to Africa! ... In all other countries, except in defenceless Africa, or the Colonies of Nations planted on the discovery of the New World, you would have been condemned to death had you gone there on the same errand.'[45]

The principle of compensated Emancipation

The rhetorical structure of Augustus Hardin Beaumont's pamphlet in 1826 exemplified the main framework to which anti-abolitionists adhered. The frontispiece of Beaumont's pamphlet reproduced two quotations

DUKE OF DEVONSHIRE 'I consider the claims of the West Indian to compensation, if his property were destroyed, as the claim of a Receiver of stolen goods'

VISCOUNT ST VINCENT 'I am descended from one of the Receivers of that period; the noble Duke is descended from one of the thieves. Had I been present at the meeting [at which the Duke spoke], I would have asked the noble Duke who stole those goods, who sold them, who pocketed the money for them? Who, but the people of England?'[46]

The relationship between slave-owner and slave, Beaumont acknowledged, was that between the receiver and the party robbed; but that between the slave-owner and the people of England was that between receiver and thief, because the slave-owners had been compelled to purchase slaves. Beaumont pointed to the intervention of the British Parliament in South Carolina in 1769 and in Jamaica in 1774 to thwart efforts to prohibit slavery or to limit the import of slaves. These were established tropes of the anti-abolitionists. But Beaumont went on to analyse the opposition of different classes to the pledge of compensation, in terms that reflected the perspective of the planter community in the colonies. He saw five classes of opponents to compensated Emancipation in 1826. The first was that of many West India proprietors in Great Britain, who believed Emancipation was remote and dreamt of a return to the old level of profits. The second was that of the merchant gentlemen who

---

[44] *Ibid.*, p. 6.   [45] *Ibid.*, pp. 6, 8.
[46] Beaumont, *Compensation to slave owners fairly considered*, Frontispiece.

received consignments of West India produce, and who wanted only a continuance of their commissions. The third was composed of the many interested in East India sugar, who sought uncompensated abolition. The fourth comprised many liberal and philanthropic men who would contemplate compensation only when injury was sustained. And the final category was that of 'talking philanthropists', abolitionists committed to opposing absolutely the principle of compensation to slave-owners.[47]

If Beaumont was right that in the mid 1820s some absentees would not engage on compensation because they would not yet engage on Emancipation, it remains true that those who *did* engage with Emancipation were consistently mindful of the issues of property rights and compensation. By the 1830s, when Emancipation was less remote, compensation was even more salient for the slave-owners. Disparate though the slave-owners were in background and representation in the Extinction of Slavery Committee, the issue of compensation is assidu-ously threaded through individual testimonies. The single polemical point Robert Scott endeavoured to convey to the Committee is on compensation. When asked whether he had contemplated a free labour regime in Jamaica, Scott answered:

No, I have never contemplated anything of the sort, because I cannot conceive the thing possible; but, if this country is tired of this odious system, there is one plain way of doing the thing: and if the people of this country are satisfied that it ought to be done, why do they not adopt it, that is, to compensate the pre-sent proprietors, and then make the experiment in any way they think proper. If it answers, the country will not lose by it; but at all events, as a proprietor, I would protest against any experiments being so tried with my property ... It is my firm opinion that property would be of no value in the event of emanci-pation; but if I am wrong, why do not the country take the responsibility upon themselves?[48]

Wildman dealt only obliquely with the question, resisting an invita-tion to commit unconditionally to Emancipation:

Q: The Committee are to understand, that when you mentioned you would consent to the emancipation of the Negroes, being themselves prepared, you viewed it as a sacrifice due to humanity, at the direct expense of your own interests?

WILDMAN: When I mentioned that, I was alluding to Steele's plan: if I could have brought that into operation, I should have felt confident I should still have a good return from the estates.[49]

---

[47] *Ibid.*, pp. 16–18.
[48] Evidence of Robert Scott, *Report on the extinction of slavery*, Q. 5182, p. 344; Q. 5365, p. 355.
[49] Evidence of James Beckford Wildman, *ibid.*, Q. 8287, pp. 541–2.

Hankey's early testimony on compensation was allusive rather than direct, when he had said that 'if my own interest as a proprietor were to be entirely [sub]merged, I hope that my views of obligation, moral, religious and social would lead me to say the sacrifice must be made: I hope so'. He was reminded, presumably by an anti-abolitionist member of the Committee, that 'your other means are ample and you are aware how many there are who have no other means whatever'. Hankey continued: 'I am ready, in prosecution of a great principle to make any sacrifice it may involve, hoping at the same time that it would not ultimately be a sacrifice.' Clearly conscious of his lack of clarity, he reverted to the subject as his testimony drew to a close in a revealing addendum:

There is one point on which it suggests itself to my mind, I may have been misunderstood, and that is the subject of compensation; I consider that the subject of compensation to proprietors should be part of the general measure to be adopted by the legislature, certainly not that it should distinctly precede it; but that it should be a part.[50]

He accepted that the enslaved could not owe compensation, 'but the nation does in my opinion; slavery is a national act and it has involved national consequences; it derives resources from it'. He pointed to the fact that 'the Legislature took £800 from me' in stamp duty on the assignment to him of his estate, 'though it did not make me a farthing better [off]'.[51] He had, he said, 'signed many [abolitionist] petitions to the Legislature, but I have ever declined to sign a petition that did not either more or less directly involve the consideration of compensation'.[52]

The existence of a network of vulnerable individuals dependent on the slave-economy became an established trope of the anti-abolitionists. George Saintsbury's defence of the continuation of slavery against the attack of the East India sugar interest made the case that in the event of abolition, the cost of switching from West India sugar to East India sugar would be high, and that the ethical justification for such a switch was questionable given the realities of forced labour in the East Indies. Those costs included explicitly the impact on the absentee rentiers:

So if it be the colonial proprietors, and the Negro labourers, and the unoffending offspring of both, that we seek to get rid of – if it be the thousands of our fellow countrymen and neighbours, hospitable families or dependent widows

---

[50] Evidence of William Alers Hankey, *ibid.*, Q. 4589–90, pp. 309–10; Q. 4680, pp. 316–17.
[51] *Ibid.*, Q. 4682, p. 317.   [52] *Ibid.*, Q. 4644, p. 313.

and orphans, deriving their subsistence from the colonies, but residing in every county and almost every parish throughout England – if it be these that we desire to destroy, doubtless the power is in our hands.[53]

A recurring ritualised element in the Commercial Committee was the request from the Committee for examples of hardship in Britain arising from West India distress. Witness after witness followed the same pattern of bringing the suffering back home:

I certainly know of a case where persons who had an income of between £2,000 and £3,000 per annum from the West Indies, have been obliged to send money out to keep up their properties, and last year I took means to ascertain the truth of a case I had heard of, children in this country, who were bred up in affluent circumstances, being sent to the workhouse, there being no funds to pay for the expenses of their education.[54]

I know a widow lady now resided in England, who has an annuity from a sugar estate in Trelawny, which is under receivership in the Court of Chancery, it is a prior lien upon the estate, but from the present distressed times, the receivers have not money enough to pay her £100 a year after the payment of contingencies and she is literally starving.[55]

What is striking is the extent to which abolitionists acquiesced in the 'widow and orphan' arguments. Even the strongest form of rejection of such arguments was not absolute, but qualified:

But our apologist [for slavery] contends that 'all holders of slave property are not wilfully, consequently, not guiltily such. There are many who have never seen the estates from which they derive their emoluments, or the slaves by whom they are cultivated. There are many widows and orphans who are the unconscious stipend[i]aries of this wicked system, and are entirely dependent on the income they derive from it. Are these to be cast provisionless and pennyless on the wide world?' No, certainly. We demand justice for the slave at the expense of no injustice in any other quarter. Only prove that the parties in question become provisionless and pennyless by slave emancipation, and the public, as well as the Government, will be cheerfully disposed to render them ample compensation.[56]

The 'national crime' argument syndicated the costs of abolition and at the same time allowed the anti-abolitionists also to extend the

[53] G. Saintsbury, *East India slavery*, 2nd edn (London, 1829; reprinted Shannon: Irish University Press, 1972), pp. 4–5.
[54] Evidence of Alexander Macdonnell, *Report from the Commercial Committee*, Q. 68, p. 28.
[55] Evidence of Thomas Phillpotts, *ibid.*, Q. 483, p. 62.
[56] Anon., *Letters on the necessity of a prompt extinction of British colonial slavery chiefly addressed to the more influential classes, to which are added thoughts on compensation* ([London], 1826).

attack on those abolitionists whose ancestors – not always remote – had themselves been slave-owners. R. Alexander had asserted in 1830:

He who owns slaves now is surely not a more responsible party than he who owned them ten or twenty or thirty years ago; who converted them into money, and who now lives in splendour upon the fortune then acquired. If restitution is to be made, it is not the present holders of slaves alone, but former holders, who ought to be compelled to make the sacrifice. The greater part of the fortune of Mr Fowell Buxton was derived from slaves. He is consequently as responsible as Mr Goulburn or any other present proprietor of slaves. Mr Protheroe, of Bristol, is as responsible as Sir Thomas Lethbridge or Lord Seaford. Mr Zachary Macaulay ought to contribute to the compensation fund nearly three times as much as my Lord Chandos; Lord Calthorpe is as responsible as the Marquis of Sligo. In short, there are very few noble or eminent families in this country, who have not at one time or another, possessed or inherited property in slaves. Surely these persons are as much entitled to make restitution and contribute to the sacrifice, as you, the present contemned and slandered Proprietors and Planters of the West Indies.[57]

For abolitionists, too, the stress on the contingent rather than absolute nature of property rights carried implicitly the logic of compensation. The *ASR* in 1830, responding to a pamphlet by Alexander Macdonnell, secretary of the West India Committee, exclaimed: 'As for the "spoliation of the rights of property", [d]oes the case of the West Indies differ from the case of the East Indies, or of the London Bridge?'[58] When William Burge, the agent for Jamaica, insisted in the House of Commons that slaves were a freehold property, and that to compel a man to dispose of his freehold property against his will was unjust, Lord Howick feigned amazement: 'These observations shocked me more than I can describe. Is it not the ordinary practice of the British legislature to compel a man to dispose of his own freehold property when it is for his convenience?' Railroads and turnpikes involved compulsory purchase of property 'neither acquired nor held by guilt, or with the shadow of injustice'.[59]

The ultimate success of the slave-owners and their supporters in defining the terrain of discussion on the principles of property and compensation are illustrated by the prevailing cross-party discourse. At Whitehaven in 1832, the London banker Matthias Attwood vied

---

[57] R. Alexander, *The fate of the colonies, a letter from R. Alexander Esq. to the proprietors and planters of the West Indies resident in the colonies* (London, 1830), cited in Wilmot Horton, *1st and 2nd letters*, pp. 43–4. The evidence offered by the Compensation records for the ubiquity or otherwise of slave-ownership amongst the British political elite is analysed in Chapter 4, below.

[58] *ASR* No. 56 (January 1830), Vol. III, p. 173.

[59] *ASR* No. 82 (June 1831), Vol. IV, p. 305.

with his local rival Isaac Littledale in condemnation of slavery, but did so within the rhetorical framework of Canning's Resolutions, which allowed them both simultaneously to condemn slavery and uphold a commitment to 'property'. Littledale was reported as follows:

> With respect to slavery, he was of opinion that it should be abolished as soon as possible, in a manner which, whilst it relieved the suffering of the Negroes, would not subject the estates of the planters to devastation. It was acknowledged on all hands, that the abolition of slavery was desirable ... He would give his support to any measure which would bring about the abolition of slavery with safety to all parties.

while Attwood's victory address was reported after winning the election:

> What he was about to say would not be for gaining votes, for the contest was over; but he found he could go further in the Emancipation of the Negro than Mr Littledale felt disposed to go ... He [Mr Attwood] would yield to no man in his detestation of slavery as a general principle, and would go to any length to emancipate the Negro, if it could be done without injury to the slave, and with indemnity to the planters. In wiping out the stain of slavery, they must, in justice, contend for the indemnification of the planters, who had acted in conformity with the existing law.[60]

Forms of Emancipation and forms of compensation

Even once the principle of compensation was so firmly embedded in the discursive field around Emancipation that it could not be shifted, the *form* of compensation (and indeed the form of Emancipation) remained open and contested.

Lord Seaford, alert to the precedents from the northern states of the USA, attacked in 1828 a proposal to free children of slaves born after a set date, 'by which act, the property of every owner of a slave would have been at once converted from a property in fee to a life interest'.[61]

A number of the abolitionists who countenanced compensation tended to focus on *demonstrated* loss. An intervention by Rev. Archdeacon Moysey saved the same 1830 Bath meeting at which the Bishop of Bath and Wells had spoken in favour of compensation from breaking up in disagreement, by brokering an 'amicable compromise' drawing on Canning's Resolutions. '[A]s the sense of several of the speakers

---

[60]   *The Poll Book of the election of a representative in Parliament for the borough of Whitehaven* (Whitehaven, 1832), pp. 49, 58–9.

[61]   Speech of Lord Seaford in Parliament, 23 June and 18 July 1828, reported in *ASR* No. 40 (September 1828), Vol. II, p. 300.

was favourable to a remuneration for such losses as could be actually proved to arise from abolition; and as, moreover, the exact nature of that compensation, and the manner in which it could be effected, was not to be decided here, but in Parliament', he proposed the addition of a clause to the abolitionist motions expressing confidence in the justice of Parliament and the wish to protect as far as possible the interests of individuals and property in the colonies. This was acceptable to all sides, including apparently the anti-abolitionist camp.[62] The *ASR* in January 1831 conceded the right of the owners to prefer a claim for compensation, but denied that the award of compensation was automatic: it likened the position of the owners to that of coach-masters, waggoners or bargemen affected by the London and Manchester railway.[63] This was not, of course, a commitment to compensation, certainly not to upfront compensation. Two further such contingent abolitionist commitments to compensation were provided: by the *Anti-slavery Society Report* of April 1823, which had said 'the colonists say that they shall sustain a great actual loss by this proposed change of system. If so, they will of course have an opportunity of preferring and establishing their claim to Indemnity'; and by 'Anglus', an abolitionist writing to *The Times* in 1824: '[T]he crime of creating and upholding the slavery of the West Indies is a national crime, and not the crime of slave-holders alone. For the loss, therefore, which individuals may incur by its abolition, they have a claim upon the public.'[64]

Wilmot Horton identified two classes of abolitionists 'entertaining principles totally different' on compensation. The first group considered slavery a national crime and, if a 'pecuniary mulch' were necessary, believed the cost should be shared; the second group denied the claim of right or equity on the part of the slave proprietors, but considered the question 'one of mere liberality', believing the public with equal justice might or might not grant compensation. But this was a simplistic division. There were also abolitionists who acknowledged the *right* to compensation but only if damage were demonstrated; and there were abolitionists such as Charles Stuart and Elizabeth Heyrick who remained bitterly opposed to compensation at all.

On the side of the slave-owners, too, what compensation meant in practice was also disputed. In the 1830 election campaign in Bristol, Christopher Claxton, the captain of a West Indiaman who co-ordinated anti-abolitionist activity on behalf of 'the Friends of the

---

[62] *Ibid*. No. 74 (January 1831), Vol. IV, p. 57.
[63] *Ibid*., p. 89.
[64] Both cited in Wilmot Horton, *1st and 2nd letters*, pp. 1, 36–7.

Trade of Bristol – of Order – of the Sacred Institutions – of the Laws – of the Church – of the State – and of Practical as well as Theoretical Emancipation', brought forward two motions at a re-convened anti-slavery meeting, the original meeting having broken up in violent disorder. The first motion, which was passed, was for abolition 'with fair and equitable regard to the rights of property involved', i.e. a Canning Resolution; the second, which was thrown out on the grounds that compensation should be determined by Parliament, called for 'compensation for the value of the slave before the agitation of this question reduced the same ... and a security for the land and works, in the event of free labour failing, provided the planter fairly tries the experiment, to be decided by constitutional authorities'.[65]

Part of the process of settling compensation was the establishment of a common sense that it was in concept financially feasible. Early estimates of the capital committed in the West Indies tended to preclude the notion of compensation. George Hibbert had placed a value of £70 million on West Indian capital in the 1790s. The Reverend Bickell in the mid 1820s ruled out any capacity of the British government 'with the immense debt already on their hands and which presses so heavily on all classes of people' to afford the 'one hundred and twenty or thirty millions more' as satisfaction to West India property, 'for that is the value which those moderate gentlemen in the colonies, set on their ill-gotten wealth'.[66] John Rock Grosett in 1825 used as a valuation yardstick the compensation paid by Great Britain to America under the Treaty of Ghent and the convention of St Petersburg, which fixed a value of £266,197 11s for 3,061 loyalist slaves, or £90 sterling each, implying a value of some £70 million for the colonial slaves as a whole. William Burge gave evidence to the House of Lords' Committee on slavery in 1832 that Jamaica was 'worth' £58 million, and the whole of the West Indies £101 million.[67]

Moving away from these high values was a precondition of arriving at a negotiated settlement for compensated Emancipation. Joseph Foster Barham had set out in an 1823 pamphlet an annual income (i.e. owner's profit) of £3 per slave, or £2.4 million per annum for the entire colonial slave-economy of 800,000 slaves. The Anti-slavery Society re-worked these figures in 1825 using £2.1 million per annum as the base, capitalising it at 16 years' purchase (based on 6 per cent colonial interest

[65] *ASR* No. 74 (January 1831), Vol. IV, pp. 58–61.
[66] Rev. R. Bickell, *The West Indies as they are: or a real picture of slavery but more particularly as it exists in the Island of Jamaica* (London: J. Hatchard, 1825), p. 5.
[67] Anon., *Abstract of the report of the Lords' Committee on the condition and treatment of colonial slaves* (London, 1833), p. 82.

rates and characterising it as 'property exposed to much comparative hazard') for a total capital value of £33.6 million.

At 3.5 per cent [the yield on government securities in Britain], this sum would be completely liquidated by a perpetual annuity of £1,176,000, a sum less than what is now made to pay to the West Indies, in consequence of the mode of regulating the drawback on sugar, and exclusive of all other charges, whether civil or military ... What we pay, however, we pay to uphold and aggravate slavery. A less sum, if Mr Barham be right ... would be sufficient to buy out the whole system; and even if that were thought too large a step to take at once, yet by the appropriation of less than a third of what we now pay, we might redeem from their bondage the whole of the female population, and thus extinguish Slavery in a single generation.[68]

The *ASR* marginally modified the figures in 1831, setting £2 10s as the income per slave (because of the decline in the price of colonial produce), a total of £2 million per annum. This stream it valued, given colonial interest rates of 6 per cent, at no more than 15 years' purchase, or £30 million as the capital value of the slave-economy. At 3.5 per cent, £30 million would yield £1.05 million per annum: but only half of this was attributable to the slaves and half to the land and works. This was an important conceptual revision to the analytical approach: it rested on recognition of the premise that underpinned *all* contemporary thinking about Emancipation, i.e. that the slave-owners would retain their estates (and implicitly on the further assumption, which was contested, that free labour would allow profitable exploitation of it). Therefore, it concluded, a payment of £525,000 per annum would fully compensate the planters, and would be affordable. The *ASR* also looked at an alternative calculation, based on a price per slave of £30 sterling, or a total value for all colonial slaves of £24 million, requiring at 3.5 per cent a total annuity of £840,000, which it said was less than two-thirds the cost in bounties and duties to protect 'this criminal and profitless system'.[69] Both approaches to capitalising the value of Barham's overall income figure in the first instance relied on an adjustment of a risky colonial income stream into a risk-free British government return.

Augustus Hardin Beaumont made a similar risk-adjustment in his notional example of a proprietor with a capital of £100,000 and 'a clear revenue of even £10 per cent'. Under compensated Emancipation, Beaumont said, the proprietor's 'loss of actual revenue is balanced by his share of the price of undoing the wrong committed by the whole of

---

[68] 'Antislavery Society Annual Report 1825', quoted in Wilmot Horton, *1st and 2nd letters*, pp. 28–9.
[69] *Ibid.*, pp. 96–7.

Table 2.1 *A. H. Beaumont's 'accounting entries' for compensation to slave-owners.*

Dr. British Nation	A–C with	West India Proprietor *Cr.*	
To annual value of property for which West Indian paid £100,000............	£10,000	By sum secured as compensation affording a revenue of.................	£5,000
		By security, in the event of a Revolution, when otherwise you would get nothing..............	£4,000
		By your proportion of Humanity, Justice, and common Honesty to Blacky.................	£1,000
	£10,000		£10,000

Source: Beaumont, *Compensation for slave owners fairly considered,* p. 8.

his Nation, and by the change of an insecure tenure of property for one of more stability'. Beaumont drew up a ledger, as shown in Table 2.1.

The key point in the reasoning of both Beaumont and the Anti-slavery Society was that the income of the planters would fall moving from a risky investment to a lower-risk re-investment in government securities or in domestic British credit-markets, even if the full market value of the slaves were paid as compensation. In Beaumont's example, to provide even the reduced level of annual income of £5,000 at lower rates of return prevalent in Britain would require a capital sum of the full value of the £100,000 outlay.

Contestation of the future of 'free labour' was central to the debate on compensation. 'If indeed it can be shewn, that Free-Labour would be as profitable to proprietors in the West Indies as Slave Labour, compensation would cease to affect the question of the abolition of slavery', was Wilmot Horton's stark statement. Wilmot Horton put the burden of proof on the abolitionists, and said that he had in 1824 induced the Society of Arts to offer a gold medal or a premium of fifty guineas for a satisfactory account of a method to diminish the [slave-]labour content of sugar, cotton or coffee production by mechanisation or livestock management, 'yet not one Abolitionist has ever come forward, to shew in what manner this desirable change might be accomplished'.[70] Wilmot Horton's logic was not accepted by all slave-owners, for the danger of

[70] Wilmot Horton, *1st and 2nd letters,* pp. 27–8.

his position was evident: it opened the door to retrospective compensation only when damage was demonstrated. Hence the emphasis by slave-owners in the Select Committee on the calculation of free-labour costs, which in their estimates consistently yielded a significant penalty to free labour over slave-labour.

British metropolitan merchants were a focus of particular hostility from abolitionists on the question of compensation, reflecting a continuing distaste for 'trade' and again a privileging of landed property:

> The great and efficient, tho' less obtrusive parties, in the delusions practised and the clamours raised on this subject, are not the planters, but the consignees and mortgagees of their produce – the merchants of London, Liverpool, Bristol and Glasgow ... while they themselves have been aggravating the distress of the planters and thriving on their spoil, have been urging them to raise high the cry of poverty. They have speculated, with a perfect knowledge of all the circumstances of the case, in the colonial trade, and they must be considered as standing on precisely the same footing with speculators in every other branch of commerce, and as bound to abide by the result of their speculations, whatever it may be.[71]

The *ASR* estimated the return of the consignees, 'the ordinary advantages', as between 12 and 20 per cent per annum, including interest, insurance freight and commissions, implying a replacement of capital every 8 to 12 years (the *ASR* must have made allowance for costs of 3.5 to 7.5 per cent to generate this payback period). When W. R. K. Douglas defended the consignee system to the Commercial Committee as compensation for the risks of the trade, the *ASR* asked 'but what, after all, is this but evading the law forbidding usury?'[72]

The negotiation of compensation

Against this background of differing opinion on both sides, the Whig government formally and informally negotiated a package of compensation with representatives of the West India interest.[73] Howick conducted private discussions with John Moss and Patrick Maxwell Stewart in parallel with official negotiations. These representatives of the slave-owners were not the conventional Jamaica consignees who had historically dominated the West India Committee. Moss was a

---

[71] *ASR* No. 75 (February 1831), Vol. IV, 'The Question of Compensation Calmly Considered', p. 102.
[72] *Ibid.* No. 97 (June 1832), Vol. V, p. 198.
[73] For the detailed sequence in Parliament, see I. Gross, 'The abolition of Negro slavery and British parliamentary politics 1832–3', *Historical Journal*, 23.1 (March 1980), 63–85.

Liverpool banker and slave-owner in British Guiana. Maxwell Stewart, who owned slaves in Tobago, was an MP, the son of a baronet whose title dated from 1667 and the brother-in-law of the Duke of Somerset, as well as a London merchant.[74]

The journal of Thomas Raikes, the London rentier son of the merchant of the same name, and related by marriage to Jamaican slave-owners, captures the anxieties and secrecy surrounding these negotiations in the early months of 1833.[75] On 4 February he recorded 'the government has been much alarmed at the effect caused by their rash project of emancipating the slaves in the West India colonies, and have given assurances today to the deputation of proprietors, which have in some degree calmed their fears for the present'.[76] The following day he noted that the king's speech 'omits entirely West India projects'. On 11 February, he reported that the government had stopped the sailing of the Jamaica packet, from fear that the news that 'the question of emancipating the negroes has been again agitated here'[77] would trigger fresh insurrections in Jamaica and Demerara. On 20 February 'the West India proprietors are in great alarm: they hear that the bill for the emancipation of the slaves is drawn up, and all will be made public in the next week. A meeting on this subject is to be held at Apsley house on Tuesday next.'[78] On 26 February, 'the West India delegation went up to the Government by appointment at one o'clock. They returned bound to secrecy as to the nature of the emancipation bill, which will not be divulged for two to three days.' By 8 March, the Emancipation proposals had still not been divulged, and the subject 'engrosses much conversation'.[79]

There seems little doubt that compensation is intended to the proprietors, the funds for which can only be raised by a loan. The Government asserts that the country demands the abolition of slavery. If it can be done at the cost of one unfortunate class, well and good; but I believe the philanthropist has very little inclination to contribute any part thereof out of his own pocket.[80]

On 6 April, Goderich was forced out of the Colonial Office.[81] On 9 April, 'the news from Jamaica is very bad. Lord Mulgrave, the new governor,

---

[74] G. S. R. Kitson Clark, *The making of Victorian England* (London: Methuen, 1965; first published 1962), p. 295.

[75] T. Raikes, *A Portion of the Journal kept by Thomas Raikes Esq. from 1831 to 1847* ([London], 1856).

[76] *Ibid.*, p. 157.   [77] *Ibid.*, p. 159.   [78] *Ibid.*, p. 162.

[79] *Ibid.*, p. 164.   [80] *Ibid.*, p. 167.

[81] For an account of the sacrifice of Goderich in order to create a vacancy as Secretary of State for Stanley, see Greville, *Journal*, Vol. II, pp. 365–6.

has been assaulted in the streets. Everything seemed to announce a serious insurrection in the island.'[82] Finally, when the opening public position of the government was put forward in Stanley's Resolutions of 14 May 1833, Raikes commented: 'it is so complex in its machinery, that none think it practicable: and as it is not sufficiently decisive for the Abolitionists, and much too severe on the West India interest, it gives equal dissatisfaction to both parties'.[83]

Stanley's Resolutions were not internally consistent (and it is hard to avoid the view that they were intended as no more than an opening shot). Stanley, working on a profit of £1.5 million from the West Indies at a 10 times multiple, arrived at a loan of £15 million that he intimated might be converted into a 'gift': 'This sum of £15 million may be considered as the purchase money of one-fourth of the labour of the slave.' It would be accompanied by 12 years' apprenticed labour, for 75 per cent of which time the former slave would work for his master; out of the other quarter of the time, he should save up to redeem himself.[84]

Buxton opposed, not the compensation, but the Apprenticeship: 'the Rt Hon. Gentleman said, that the money was to be paid either by the country or by the Negro ... I will oppose the payment of a single farthing by the Negro.'[85]

The counter-proposal of the West India body was for a grant of £20 million to the slave-owners and a loan for an additional £10 million secured on the properties. Patrick Maxwell Stewart explained in Parliament that since the £20 million would go largely to the repayment of debt, the loan of £10 million was 'indispensably necessary to the success of future cultivation in the colonies'.[86]

On 10 June, Stanley told the House of Commons that the £15 million loan was not enough, but that he had the assurance of the West Indians that a grant of £20 million would command the support of the metropolitan slave-owners and they would use their influence with the colonial legislatures to gain their acquiescence. The motion was carried 286 to 77.[87]

Contestation of the compensation continued after the negotiations of May and June. The abolitionists succeeded in reducing the period of Apprenticeship from twelve years to six. Before the debate

[82] Raikes, *Journal*, pp. 157–76.
[83] *Ibid.*, p. 187.
[84] *The Debates in Parliament 1833*, pp. 77–9.
[85] *Ibid.*, p. 103.
[86] R. B. Sheridan, 'The West India sugar crisis and British slave Emancipation, 1830–1833', *Journal of Economic History*, 21.4 (December 1961), 539–51 (p. 547).
[87] *Ibid.*

on resolving the Abolition of Slavery Bill into committee proceeded on 23 July 1833, petitions were presented by William Ewart from the Association of Merchants of Liverpool trading to the Brazils, 'against the grant of £20 million sterling, as compensation to the West India merchants [sic]', and by John Arthur Roebuck from the inhabitants of Bath,

stating that they viewed with alarm the bill for the emancipation of slavery ... and objecting to a grant of compensation so large as [£]20,000,000; also a petition from Bristol praying that compensation might only be granted to the West India planters in proportion to the actual loss sustained by the emancipation of the Negroes, and that no money might be granted until that emancipation was complete.

'Mr Trelawny' presented a petition from Tavistock (Devon), against the provisions of the West India Bill. At the same time, however, Sir Richard Vyvyan presented a petition from planters, mortgagees and others interested in West India property, against the provisions of the Slavery Abolition Bill, and praying to be heard by counsel against the same.[88]

The process culminated in the Slavery Abolition Act of 28 August 1833 (or, to give its full and revealing title, *An Act for the abolition of slavery throughout the British colonies, for promoting the industry of the manumitted slaves, and for compensating the persons hitherto entitled to the services of such slaves*). The Act provided for the award of £20 million (plus interest from 1 August 1834) to the owners of 'slave-property' in the British colonies other than Ceylon and St Helena, and the imposition of a period of forced labour known as 'Apprenticeship' that bound the enslaved to unpaid labour for a further period after 1 August 1834: four years in the case of those working as domestic servants and six years for those classed as fieldworkers.[89]

Economics of compensation

Although there has been and continues to be controversy over the 'decline thesis' for the slave-economy as an explanation for abolition of the slave-trade in 1807, there has been a reasonable measure of consensus between both the advocates and opponents of 'decline' that by the time of Emancipation in 1834 the slave-economy was indeed fatally

---

[88] *The Times*, 30 July 1833, p. 1.
[89] *An Act for the abolition of slavery throughout the British colonies, for promoting the industry of the manumitted slaves, and for compensating the persons hitherto entitled to the services of such slaves 28 August 1833* (3 and 4 Wm IV cap. 73).

weakened financially, and that the compensation process allowed a liquidation of an effectively bankrupt sector.[90]

However, this conventional reading obscures some important complexities, in particular the variable prosperity across colonies, the question as to who bore the consequences of 'distress' and the evaluation of the financial effects of the compensation on the slave-owners, mortgagees and dependents. Part of the difficulty in reaching a reasoned assessment is the partisan nature of contemporary commentary. Both slave-owners and abolitionists had a vested interest in presenting the West Indies' slave-economy as 'distressed'. The abolitionists were constrained to argue that slave-labour was inherently inefficient; and that any profits accruing to the slave-owners were a function of high sugar-duties protecting the British domestic market. The slave-owners had a more difficult task: they had to maintain at the same time that the West Indies contributed significantly to Britain's national wealth and that the planters individually were in financial distress, in part because of the disruptive effects of the anti-slavery agitation on labour productivity. There was clearly a short-term crisis in the sugar-economy in the early 1830s as an immediate backdrop to Emancipation. But this is not to say that returns were in fact inherently low across the Caribbean for an extended period prior to this. Major fortunes were still being built post-1807 in British Guiana and to a lesser extent in Trinidad. Ward's work on the profitability of individual estates in the older colonies qualifies the picture of a bankrupt plantation sector. The profitability of the estates he examined certainly declined in the 1820s, but it is striking that with one exception none of the estates was loss-making: and his definition of profitability appears to be after all charges of management, i.e. after attorneys' fees and consignees' commissions. In the 'value chain' of the plantation economy, the absentee owner stood behind a number of claims on the earnings of the plantation: that the owners remained net beneficiaries indicates the high underlying profitability of the slave-economy.

Ward found in the 'old colonies' high though variable returns in the last quarter of the eighteenth century and the first quarter of the

---

[90] The historiography of the 'decline thesis' is summarised in C. L. Brown, *Moral Capital: foundations of British abolitionism* (Chapel Hill: University of North Carolina Press, 2006), pp. 15–16. Williams characterised the slave-owners by the 1830s as 'an outworn interest, whose bankruptcy smells to heaven in historical perspective'; E. Williams, *Capitalism and slavery* (London: Andre Deutsch, 1964), p. 211. Drescher argued that decline followed the abolition of the slave-trade in 1807, and that an expanding slave-system had thereby been fatally undermined; S. Drescher, *Econocide: British slavery in the era of Abolition* (Pittsburgh: University of Pittsburgh Press, 1977).

nineteenth century, returns varying between 2 and 3 per cent, and 12 and 14 per cent, per annum.[91] To place these returns in context, British government securities generally yielded 3 or 3.5 per cent, domestic British interest rates were 5 per cent per annum and 'colonial interest' was 6 per cent per annum. It was the risk (including liquidity), not the return, that disqualified West India property from the function fulfilled first by foreign government bonds and then by railway shares. The conventional risk–return preference was typified by the Leeds businessman Joseph Henry Oates, warning his brother Edward Oates against seeking excessive returns in his investments: 'I fear you will look out for something great, some 8 or 10% and lose your principal altogether.'[92]

Examples from Jamaica and from British Guiana point in different directions. Even after the abolition of the slave-trade, the boom in the coffee sector in Jamaica drew in new emigrants from Britain. John Mackeson of the Kent brewing family married in 1805 into a family of Jamaican slave-owners, and Mackeson had debated whether his wife's estates could support his staying in England as a rentier:

This sweet girl's property is infinitely greater than my most sanguine imagination had an idea of. I understand that if her estates are converted into money that it will produce in this country at least £10,000 sterling ... PS. I have just had a long conversation with Mr Wyllys, the brother of Olive, and he has agreeably surprised me with the information that the estates in the West produced from £1,000 to £1,200 yearly. That, added to what I possess, do you think it will be sufficient inducement for me to settle in this country [i.e. England]?[93]

But Mackeson did go to Jamaica in 1807 with his wife and his brother-in-law, who owned the Mount Lebanus sugar estate in St Thomas-in-the-East. In 1812, Mackeson had 98 slaves of his own, 'which I would not take less than £10,000 sterling for'. Although the coffee boom faded, Mackeson was back in England by 1816, living in Bath, and still expected, after paying off £5,000 in debt, to clear £3,000 per annum

---

[91] J. R. Ward, 'The profitability of sugar planting in the British West Indies 1650–1834', *Economic History Review*, NS 31.2 (1978), 197–213. See also R. K. Aufhauser's conceptual rather than empirical 'Profitability of slavery in the British Caribbean', *Journal of Interdisciplinary Study*, 5.1 (Summer 1974), 45–67.

[92] R. J. Morris, *Men, women and property in England 1780–1870: a social and economic history of family strategies amongst the Leeds middle classes* (Cambridge: Cambridge University Press, 2006), p. 14.

[93] A. E. Furness, 'The Jamaican coffee boom and John Mackeson: a Blue Mountain coffee planter 1807–1819', *Jamaican Historical Review*, 3.3 (March 1962), 10–21.

to cover his yearly expenditure of £1,300.[94] Mackeson was awarded £2,446 9s 8d compensation in 1835 for 132 slaves he still owned.[95]

For the Mesopotamia estate in Jamaica, Joseph Foster Barham's consignee Plummer & Co. deposited £47,583 into Barham's bank account over twenty years between 1805 and 1825. Thus post-abolition of the slave-trade, the estate – owned by the Barhams since 1728 – produced on average almost £2,400 per annum of profit to the Barhams, after all the agency costs of attorney and consignee. The years 1821 and 1822 were notably poor ones, however, and Dunn believes it unlikely that the Barhams extracted much further income from Mesopotamia between 1825 and Emancipation.[96]

Checkland's work on the Gladstone family fortune shows the impact of the high returns from the West Indies, but especially from the new territories of British Guiana. John Gladstone's purchase of the Success estate in two tranches between 1812 and 1816 cost £80,000 for an asset yielding him £10,000 per annum.[97] His net worth rose by half, from £333,000 to £502,550 between 1821 and 1828; within this, the capital value of the West India component accounted for the bulk of the increase, rising from £200,000 to £300,000.[98]

It is important to recognise that the indebtedness of the British West Indian estates, which has become an inseparable part of the received picture of late colonial slavery, was not primarily the result of the funding of operating losses. It arose mainly from the extraction of value by the owners, who borrowed against future revenue streams from their slave-worked property in order to fund investment or consumption at home, and to provide for dependants in the form of annuities and legacies secured on the land and slaves of their West India estates.[99]

---

[94] *Ibid.*, p. 19. For the coffee boom, see also S. D. Smith, 'Sugar's poor relation: British coffee-planting in the West Indies 1720–1833', *Slavery & Abolition*, 19 (1998), 68–89, reprinted in G. J. Heuman and J. Walvin (eds.), *The slavery reader* (London and New York: Routledge, 2003).

[95] T71/860, Manchester No. 358. His brother-in-law made a counter-claim as trustee to the marriage settlement of Mackeson and his wife Olive, which appears to have been resolved amicably.

[96] R. Dunn, '"Dreadful idlers" in the cane fields: the slave labour pattern on a Jamaica sugar estate 1862–1831', *Journal of Interdisciplinary History*, 17.4 (Spring 1987), 795–822 (p. 820).

[97] S. G. Checkland, *The Gladstones: a family biography 1764–1851* (Cambridge: Cambridge University Press, 1971), pp. 194–5.

[98] *Ibid.*, p. 179.

[99] David Cannadine makes a similar point that the indebtedness of the British landowners was not per se an index of distress; D. Cannadine, 'Aristocratic indebtedness in the nineteenth century: the case re-opened', *Economic History Review*, NS 3.4 (November 1977), 624–50.

The aggregate slave-economy – although not every estate – was thus indeed leveraged by the time of Emancipation, and as such was highly geared to fluctuations in product prices, since few costs were even semi-variable.[100]

Against this background, what did the structure and level of the compensation payments represent to the slave-owners? Three structural features of the compensation impacted unevenly across the totality of the slave-owners.

The first, and starkest distinction, was that the Abolition Act provided for an *ad valorem* rather than per capita distribution of the compensation: in other words, rather than dividing the total £20 million equally across the number of slaves in all the colonies, it recognised that differences existed economically between the colonies, and that slaves had more value in the new and productive territories of British Guiana and Trinidad than they did in Jamaica or Barbados. This was of course deeply divisive amongst the slave-owners, and was highly contested within the slave-owning body.[101]

The second differentiation was within colonies by class of slave. Through a process termed 'inter-colonial apportionment', each colony was allotted a share of the monetary compensation based on the number of registered slaves and the average price of the enslaved in the period from 1821 to 1828. Then in a subsequent step this fixed amount was allocated within each colony between categories of slaves: although the average sum per slave and the total were fixed for each colony, there was a scale of payment derived for each sub-class of slave. 'Gaming' of the process was possible by slave-owners seeking to establish higher classifications than appropriate for their slaves, but this was a zero-sum game within each colony, and was policed by the local Assistant Commissioners and registry officials.[102]

---

[100] Chancellor, for example, indicates the Vassall estates of Lord Holland requiring a 'subsidy' of £1,200 in 1828. His figures show in fact an operating loss of £220, with the remainder of the shortfall attributable to £700 of annuity payments and the repayment of a mortgage; V. E. Chancellor, 'Slave-owner and anti-slaver: Henry Richard Vassall Fox, 3rd Lord Holland 1800–40', *Slavery & Abolition*, 1.3 (December 1980), 263–75 (p. 266).

[101] See D. Taylor ' "Our man in London": John Pollard Mayers, agent for Barbados, and the British Abolition Act 1832–3', *Caribbean Studies*, 16 (1977), 60–74.

[102] See J. Azeez, 'The compensation controversy', *History Gazette* 12 (September 1989), for an example of the struggle within a colony (British Guiana) over slave classification; and K. M. Butler, *The economics of Emancipation: Jamaica and Barbados, 1823–1843* (Chapel Hill: University of North Carolina Press, 1995), p. 33 for the re-classification by the local Commissioners of 1,166 Barbadian apprentices between June 1837 and June 1838.

The final, and subtler, difference related to the effective privileging of land as a form of property in the design of the compensation. After the period of Apprenticeship, the erstwhile owners of land and slaves would still retain the land and would be able to hire labour for wages. But those owners without land who hired out their slaves, either as agricultural gangs on the estates of other slave-owners or as service-workers in the urban economies of the colonies, would have nothing. The case of Dorothy Little of Bristol, who owned fourteen unattached slaves in St James, provides examples of a number of different facets of the finances of slave-compensation, not least of the alertness of slave-owners to the financial implications of the structure of compensation. She was seventy years old, the widow of the Rev. Simon Little, formerly Rector of Hanover in Jamaica, who died in 1802, since when Mrs Little had been resident in England. She had, she said, 'with the greatest attention read every debate in the House of Commons on the West India question and I have not seen my case mentioned by any one MP'. She received an annuity from the Clergy Fund of Jamaica, 'much reduced in late years and now £32 sterling only per annum' and was increasingly insecure as a result of the threat to the fund from 'anarchy and revolution' in Jamaica, but relied primarily on the income from renting out the enslaved people whom she owned. In May 1834 she asked whether the power of attorney she was sending out to Jamaica

had any influence over the valuation of my Negroes, as I have no relation or friend now in the island who I can flatter myself will feel any great interest in my welfare ... I am anxious to ascertain if there is a prospect of my getting full and fair compensation for my unattached field labourers, they will I fear be put down [i.e. classified] as inferior labourers, for out of the whole number (14) 10 of them are females, but from that very circumstance they have been more valuable to me than if they had been very strong men, for they have more than doubled their original number, and of course doubled my income. I speak strongly on this subject as my existence depends on the rent of these few negroes, and what am I to do when seven-eighths of my income are taken away?

The rental of her slaves had never been less than £80 sterling per annum during the fifteen years previous to 1832, when the valuation was reduced and rental fixed at £80 currency or £57 3s sterling. The compensation at £26 per slave, she calculated, would not exceed £364 sterling, the income on which would be no more than £12 14s 9d (she clearly assumed re-investment of the proceeds in British government securities yielding 3.5 per cent per annum). She was afraid that the owner of the estate in future would refuse to rent any infirm slaves, throwing one aged slave and two children upon her support.

She complained of 'the breach of the immutable principles of Religion and Justice which will be committed in thus depriving an aged widow of her property without any fault alleged on her part'. She highlighted the disparity of treatment between those who were owners of slaves only (as was she) and those with estates: at the end of seven years (i.e. 1840, the intended end of the Apprenticeship period for agricultural labourers) the former would have nothing: it was inequitable. 'She believes there are many in her situation, but that they are principally widows and orphans and she is sorry to perceive that the large Proprietors have not had the generosity to put forward their particular situation.'[103]

It is thus not possible to speak of the slave-owners as a whole in terms of the impact of the compensation package. But, on average, Fogel and Engerman calculated that the package of cash plus interest plus the value of the six-year Apprenticeship totalled 96 per cent of the market value of the enslaved, comprising 49 per cent cash and 47 per cent from the Apprenticeship.[104] Their estimate of the net present value of Apprenticeship appears high as a result of their use of six years for all of the enslaved including domestic servants, and their adoption of a discount rate, drawn from work on Jamaica in the eighteenth century, as high as 11 per cent. John Gladstone himself attached a value to the Apprenticeship period of £5 million sterling.[105] Despite the efforts of Buxton, the enslaved therefore paid between a fifth and one-half of the cost of their freedom.

The value in today's terms of the monetary compensation finally agreed and passed in the Abolition Act can be considered in various ways. Pure consumer price escalation suggests the compensation would be worth perhaps £1.8 billion, and that H. M. Hyndman's father received the equivalent of £3.6 million.[106] However, inflationary adjustments are notoriously difficult: urban property values, for example, would suggest a much higher equivalence today. Setting the compensation in the context of public spending provides a different dimension. The British state of the 1830s was much smaller than it is today, and at 40 per cent of government receipts or expenditure, £20 million was a huge

---

[103] Dorothy Little, cover letter to Lord Stanley enclosing her petition to the House of Lords, T71/1608, 27 September 1833; Little to Commission, T71/1608, 12 May 1834, 5 March 1835 and 31 March 1835.

[104] R. W. Fogel and S. L. Engerman, 'Philanthropy at bargain prices: notes on the economics of gradual emancipation', *Journal of Legal Studies*, 3.2 (June 1974), 377–401.

[105] R. E. P. Wastell, The history of slave compensation 1833 to 1845', M.A. thesis, London University, 1933, p. 233.

[106] J. O'Donoghue and L. Golding, 'Consumer price inflation since 1750', *Economic Trends*, 604 (2004), 38–46.

amount: it would equate to almost £200 billion today.[107] Conversely, the state was also much more indebted in the 1830s in the aftermath of the Napoleonic Wars than it is today, and as a comparable increase in the national debt, the current equivalent of the compensation would be £13 billion.[108] Finally, in relation to the size of the economy, the £20 million compensation would be equivalent to around £76 billion.[109]

The financing of the compensation

Whatever measure of scale is adopted, there is no question that the amount of compensation was highly material to the British state, and its financing represented a significant funding operation for the government and the City.[110] The government's willingness to incur new obligations of such size reflected the general financial confidence prevailing in the mid 1830s. While the financial crisis of 1825–6 was still a recent memory, the immediate economic and monetary background to the commitment to, and funding of, the compensation to slave-owners was favourable, with good harvests, the expansion of joint-stock banking under the 1833 Bank Act and an incipient boom in railway stocks. By the time this period of stability and confidence gave way to a new crisis centred on the Bank of England between 1836 and 1839, the compensation money had been raised.[111]

---

[107] B. R. Mitchell and P. Deane, *Abstract of British historical statistics* (Cambridge: Cambridge University Press, 1962), p. 396 (1834 gross public expenditure £50.2 million); ONS time series date online, www.statistics.gov.uk/StatBase/TSDseries1. asp, Series ANLP (Central government: current expediture) (2006 central government expenditure £480 billion).

[108] Mitchell and Deane, *Statistics*, p. 402 (1834 national debt £781.3 million); ONS time series data, Series RUTN (Public sector finances: net debt £billion) (2007 Q3 national debt £516.9 billion).

[109] Mitchell and Deane, *Statistics*, p. 366 (1831 gross national income £340 million); ONS time series data, Series YBHA (GDP at current market prices, current prices seasonally adjusted) (2006 gross domestic profit £1.3 trillion).

[110] R. J. Barro, 'Government spending, interest rates, prices and budget deficits in the United Kingdom, 1701–1918', *Journal of Monetary Economics*, 20 (1987), 221–47, reprinted in R. J. Barro, *Macroeconomic policy* (Cambridge, MA: Harvard University Press, 1990) pp. 341–72. Barro compared the scale of the transfer payments of compensation to 'a medium-sized war', and characterised the compensation as one of the two episodes he found in 200 years of 'budget deficits run for no reason – that is, deficits that are not endogenous responses to wartime, recession, expected inflation and so on' (the other example was the product of the temporary interruption to tax revenues caused by legislative deadlock in fiscal 1909–10). Barro found no evidence of the compensation funding having a significant impact on long-term interest rates. Short-term rates, however, did rise from a trough in 1833 into the financial crisis of 1836–9; Barro, *Macroeconomic policy*, pp. 367–9.

[111] A. Andreades, *History of the Bank of England 1640 to 1903*, 3rd edn (London: P. S. King, 1935) pp. 256–68.

The idea of funding the compensation through a specific new tax had been canvassed during the parliamentary debates, but the 1833 Abolition Act itself provided for the Treasury to raise a loan through the issue of new government securities to fund the compensation payments, and capped the interest rate on them to a small premium to the market rate on existing government debt.[112] Because of the time necessary to set up and implement the process of distributing the compensation money (see Chapter 4, below), funds were not required until the summer of 1835, after the departure of Peel's administration in April. At that stage, the new Chancellor, Thomas Spring Rice, set out to raise £15 million, on a schedule of instalments designed to match expected compensation payments over the coming months. The remaining £5 million was accounted for by Mauritius and the Cape of Good Hope – which were on a slower timetable in processing claims – and by Barbados, compensation for slave-owners of which had been delayed by the inability of the Barbados assembly to pass acceptable enabling legislation for Emancipation. The owners of enslaved in Barbados would ultimately receive compensation in stock rather than cash.[113]

Through the Bank of England, Spring Rice invited potential bidders for the contract to raise the loan to a meeting to hear an outline of the terms of the tender. At the initial meeting on 29 July 1835, those present included 'Messrs Rothschild, Montefiore, Sir J. R. Reid, Messrs Irving, Baring, Mildmay, J. L. Goldsmid, Ricardo, Robertson, Hobhouse, Ward &c. &c.'.[114] Although the prices of government securities were unsettled in the immediate aftermath of this meeting, the market expected that a number of syndicates would continue to compete in the tender.[115] However, on 30 July, 'a very unexpected incident occurred' when Baring Brothers & Co. and Reid, Irving & Co., 'who

---

[112] Lobdell, 'The price of freedom: financial aspects of British slave Emancipation 1833–38. Notes on research in progress', unpublished paper delivered at the Annual Meeting of the Social Sciences History Association, Pittsburgh (October 2000), p. 7. I am indebted to Professor Lobdell for identifying several of the sources used in this section.

[113] Wastell, 'Slave compensation', pp. 104–5; Butler, *The economics of Emancipation*, pp. 36–7; Lobdell, 'The price of freedom', pp. 7–8.

[114] 'Proceedings at the Preliminary Meeting respecting the Loan of 15,000,000 *l* to be raised, under the authority of the Act 3 & 4 Will. IV c. 73 for the Compensation of Owners of Slaves', PP 1835, Vol 51 (463); reprinted in, for example, 'Slave Compensation Fund, Return relating to the West India Compensation', PP 1836, Vol. 49 (597), pp. 23–4. Five of the named loan contractors – Rothschild, Sir John Rae Reid, John Irving, Baring and Mildmay – themselves claimed compensation as slave-owners or mortgagees over slaves.

[115] 'Business and Finance', *The Times*, July 30 1835, p. 5: 'It is understood, however, that none of the lists originally formed are to be abandoned in consequence of what passed at the Treasury meeting this morning.'

had formed a very powerful list to bid for the contract', announced their withdrawal. *The Times* reported that the withdrawal had been 'very freely commented on by the monied interest in general', especially by those who had joined the Barings syndicate 'who complain loudly of having been sacrificed to some secret coalition or private arrangement with the other competitors for the loan'. *The Times* adopted the more charitable explanation that the size of the loan and the critical turn of events in France (where the king had escaped assassination) had cooled the Barings' commercial appetite, but commented that '[i]t is only unfortunate in this view of the case that their resolution was not taken yesterday, as all these circumstances were known shortly after the meeting with the Treasury broke up'.[116]

On the following day, the syndicate formed by Ricardo, Maubert and Mieville also withdrew, leaving the Rothschild syndicate as the sole bidder. *The Times* reported that rumours of insider-dealing ahead of the announcement of the Ricardo syndicate's withdrawal had been investigated and proved unfounded. The newspaper also returned to the Barings withdrawal, which had attracted remarks

so severe ... by those who are deprived by it of the benefit they expected to reap ... that it were greatly wished that [Barings] had thought it proper, if not to the public, to some of their private friends, to accompany the abandonment of the list with some explanation as to their real motives. Till this is done some unpleasant feeling will remain on the subject.[117]

Hence, on 3 August 1835, only the Rothschild syndicate submitted a bid, and this was in excess of the sealed limit tabled by the Treasury. The Rothschild syndicate after some reflection accepted the limit, and was awarded the contract, signed by Nathan Mayer Rothschild and Moses Montefiore.[118]

The participation by Rothschild and Montefiore has been placed, both at the time and subsequently, in the context of their international philanthropy.[119] John Finlaison, the Actuary of the National Debt

---

[116] 'Money-market and City Intelligence', *ibid.*, 31 July 1835, p. 3.
[117] *Ibid.*, 1 August 1835, p. 6.
[118] *Ibid.*, 4 August 1835, p. 4.
[119] For Montefiore, see for example A. Green, 'Rethinking Sir Moses Montefiore: religion, nationhood and international philanthropy in the nineteenth century', *American Historical Review*, 110.3 (June 2005), 631–58. Green notes that Montefiore's participation came ten years after he had nominally retired from business, and that 'clearly it testified to his personal commitment to the antislavery cause'. The heavily edited diary of Moses Montefiore alludes to the loan, but the bulk of the text comprises a transcription of the 'Money-market and City Intelligence' article from *The Times* of 4 August 1835: M. Montefiore, *Diaries of Sir Moses and Lady Montefiore, comprising their life and work as recorded in their diaries from 1812 to 1883*, ed. Dr L. Loewe

and Government Calculator, closed his official report to the Lords Commissioners of His Majesty's Treasury on the debt issue with a tribute to Rothschild:

Lastly, in concluding this report, I would most humbly crave permission to express admiration of the high-spirited contractor who courageously undertook the Loan, and in a few weeks fulfilled his contract, on terms the very lowest that were consistent with his own safety. Better qualified, perhaps than any living man to appreciate the value of public credit, that eminent position has, on this occasion, given England the full benefit of her inestimable preeminence among nations, in the great attributes of unshaken fidelity in her engagements, of unimpaired, increasing and all but unlimited resources.[120]

However, the very existence of Finlaison's report points to controversy over the terms of the loan. Spring Rice had made a defensive speech on the loan on 3 August, in which he expressed his disappointment about the collapse of the competitive bidding process that he had attempted to put in place, expressed his awareness that the loan was a departure from all previous loan raisings (in that he, as Chancellor of the Exchequer, had – and had used – the delegated power under the Abolition Act to execute a definitive agreement rather than, as had previously been customary, entering into a conditional contract subject to confirmation by Parliament) and concluded 'a more advantageous loan had never been contracted'. The Radical MP and advocate of retrenchment Joseph Hume (himself entangled in slave-ownership through his wife's family) subsequently tabled twelve resolutions on 4 September 1835, which triggered Finlaison's response.[121] The thrust of Hume's resolutions was that the whole design of the funding was flawed, that it would have been more economical to pay all the slave-owners in stock rather than raise a loan, and that in any event the

(London: The Jewish Historical Society, 1983; facsimile of the two-volume 1890 edn), pp. 97–9. The transcription in the edited diary omits the detail that when Rothschild and Montefiore arrived for their ten o'clock appointment to present the only bid for the loan, 'through some misunderstanding they were kept waiting till 20 minutes past 11 before Lord Melbourne and the Chancellor made their appearance'. The Rothschild Archive, in reporting that '[f]rustratingly, scant information can be found in the Archive about the loan of 1835 that hastened the end of the slave trade by compensating the plantation owners', makes no reference to Rothschild's own claim to compensation as mortgagee of slaves; M. Aspey, 'Nathan Rothschild's company: Jews, Quakers and Catholics', *Rothschild Archive: Annual Review*, April 2003–March 2004, pp. 24–9, www.rothschildarchive.org/ib?/doc=/ib/articles/annualreview. See below, p. 000.

[120] J. Finlaison, 'To the Right Honourable The Lords Commissioners of His Majesty's Treasury. The Report of John Finlaison, Actuary of the National Debt, and Government Calculator', 7 March 1836. The report is printed in 'Slave Compensation Fund, Return relating to the West India Compensation', PP 1836, Vol. 49 (597), pp. 3–26.

[121] For Hume's relationship with William Hardin Burnley, see Chapter 4, below, p. 158.

stock issued should have been 3.5 per cent rather than 3 per cent of government stock. Hume concluded that the loan scheme as implemented had cost the country over £1 million more than his alternative. Spring Rice was affronted, characterising this as a resignation matter should Hume's charges be upheld. Spring Rice drew support from two West Indian MPs, both slave-owners: Sir John Rae Reid and Patrick Maxwell Stewart. Nevertheless, it was agreed that Hume's resolutions should be examined by Finlaison. This was an arcane discussion that depended on the assumed price at which the 3.5 per cent stock could have been issued and on the likelihood of falling interest rates in the future (which would disproportionately benefit the issuer of higher-denomination stock): the controversy rumbled on beyond Finlaison's reply to Hume.[122] But it became clear in Finlaison's report that the terms of the Rothschild loan differed from those presented by Spring Rice in Parliament. Hume had assumed, as apparently did others, that the Rothschild syndicate had contracted to provide £15,000,000 net of the 2 per cent discount allowed for paying upfront rather than in instalments over one year; in fact, the contract treated the discount as a deduction from the £15,000,000, so that the government received (and of course only paid interest on) £14,701,875.[123] Spring Rice had made play, both in his speech of 3 August and in his response to Hume on 4 September, of the interest rate of £3 7s 6d to £3 7s 8d, although at the end of the 3 August speech he did qualify this as the interest on the permanent debt. In fact, Finlaison calculated the interest rate to be £3 9s 686/100d, or ten basis points above the level Spring Rice had stated to Parliament. Finlaison dealt with this in his Report by focusing on a demonstration that the true interest rate was within the maximum set in the 1833 Act, rather than defending Spring Rice's account.

There was also controversy over the role of the Bank of England in financing the payment of subscriptions, since it was possible to borrow from the Bank on the security of the stock at a lower rate than the discounted stock yielded, providing a riskless arbitrage profit to the holders of the stock, and markedly increasing both the lending by, and deposits at, the Bank in the autumn of 1835. John Horsley Palmer, an influential director of the Bank who served as Governor between 1830 and 1833, was called on to explain these transactions amongst others

[122] See for example R. Page, *A critical examination of the twelve resolutions of Mr Joseph Hume, respecting the loan of fifteen millions for slave compensation* (London: Pelham Richardson, 1839), which corrected some details of Hume's calculation but upheld his overall argument at Spring Rice's expense.

[123] PP 1836, Vol. 49 (597), p. 3.

when Select Committees of the House of Commons in 1840 and 1841 examined the Bank of England's role and performance in the crises of 1836 and 1839.[124]

Conclusion

The idea of payment of compensation to slave-owners in exchange for the freedom of their slaves had, as argued above, divided the anti-slavery movement in the 1820s and early 1830s. The legitimacy of the notion of 'property in men' had been challenged as a matter of principle, in a period when other forms of property established in the eighteenth century, such as public office or patronage of rotten boroughs, were also increasingly contested. But there was also acquiescence in the practical consequence of Canning's Resolutions of 1823, which had set out the demand for Emancipation 'with a fair and equitable consideration of the interests of private property'. The owners – and many others – took this last phrase to be a commitment to compensation. Substantial disagreement took place within the political nation as to the mode and the amount of compensation, however, and those tensions are visible beneath the fragile consensus between abolitionists and slave-owners around amelioration in the mid 1820s. The emergence of 'immediatism' amongst the abolitionists and the formation of the Whig government in 1830 triggered a more intense though still intermittent and protracted negotiation between the state and the slave-owners over the form of Emancipation and the nature of compensation.[125]

Compensation for 'slave-property' was consistent with the common sense of property rights, as opponents of compensation recognised. 'There is among the higher and middle ranks of society so prevailing a disposition to admit the justice of the claims of the Planters to compensation, in the event of the emancipation of their slaves', complained one pamphleteer as early as 1826, going on sadly to cite the Liverpool abolitionist Adam Hodgson's concession that 'it would be robbery, under the garb of mercy, to compel one class of individuals to atone for the injustice of a nation'.[126] This common sense was contested: it was better, said Charles Stuart, 'that a few criminal individuals should suffer

---

[124] E.V. Morgan, *The theory and practice of central banking 1797–1813* (Cambridge: Cambridge University Press, 1943), p. 105.

[125] J. R. Ward, 'Emancipation and the Planters', *Journal of Caribbean History*, 22.1–2 (1988), 116–37 argued that the reality of compensation, and indeed abolition, was not clear to 'the planters' before the 1830s, but a reading of the West India discourse on both sides places compensation centrally from 1823 onwards.

[126] Anon., *Letters on the necessity of a prompt extinction*, pp. 183–4.

a pecuniary loss, than that hundreds of thousands of innocent people should continue bereaved of all that is most unalienably the real property of man.'[127] But the major political debate came to be about the structure of Emancipation and the *form* of compensation within it, not about the principle.

---

[127] Stuart, *The West India question*, p. 30.

3   The distribution of slave-compensation

The Abolition Act with its provision of compensation to slave-owners triggered what could be characterised as a feeding frenzy in Britain amongst those who owned slaves, those whose families had once owned slaves, and those such as annuitants, mortgagees and legatees who benefited financially in other ways from slavery. Thousands of men and women resident in both Britain and the colonies stepped forward to lay claim to compensation. The process of amassing, evaluating, arbitrating and paying these claims was truly an integrated process between metropole and colony. Claims had to be filed in the colonies themselves, with supporting information drawn from the local registry of slaves; but the regulatory and administrative framework was designed and controlled in Britain, and payment was made at the National Debt Office in London. The records generated in these processes provide a unique 'census' of slave-ownership in the Age of Reform, and also reveal the unprecedented scale and scope of the bureaucratic challenge confronting the British state in establishing mechanisms to manage the distribution of the £20 million compensation.

The Slave Compensation Commission

The Abolition Act established Commissioners of Arbitration ('the Slave Compensation Commission' or 'the Commission') with a professional staff to administer the compensation. The Commission, whose offices were at 25 Great George Street until 1838 and then at 12 Manchester Buildings, was briefly chaired by the lawyer Charles Christopher Pepys (later Lord Chancellor and first Earl of Cottenham) and subsequently by John Bonham Carter, the MP for Portsmouth.[1] It comprised three salaried members, James Lewis (ex-speaker of the Jamaican

---

[1] The rump of the Commission moved again, around 1842, to what is now Gwydyr House in Whitehall, which currently houses the Wales Office. I am grateful to Peter Newbitt of the Wales Office for this information.

Assembly), Hastings Elwin and Henry Frederick Stephenson (both lawyers) and three non-salaried members, John George Shaw-Lefevre (of the Colonial Department and later Vice Chancellor of London University), Thomas Amyot (the Registrar of Slaves) and Samuel Duckworth (a barrister). In January 1835, two further Commissioners were appointed, R.W. Hay and James Stephen, both of the Colonial Department. The Secretary, Henry Hill, had been Secretary to the Commission of Colonial Legal Inquiry for ten years.[2] The Commission also used outside expertise, drawing on new disciplines of statistics and actuarial work. The calculations of average slave prices, for example, were done by Charles M. Willinck, the Secretary of the University Life Assurance Office.[3] In handling over 45,000 individual claims from owners of 800,000 enslaved, the Commission built on the resource provided by the slave-registers, an instrument of governmentality of which, as noted above, abolitionists had made good use in confronting slave-owners with mortality rates for the enslaved on specific estates. Boards of Assistant Commissioners were established in each of the colonies, nominated by the Governors, responsible for the local colonial tasks of reconciling claims to the slave-registers and classifying slaves by category. The Commission published its proposed Rules on 18 April 1834, in accordance with the Abolition Act, subject to a six-month period of appeal. Delays in the colonies and in the approval of the Rules caused the Commission's initial timetable to be revised; but adjudication of uncontested claims, beginning with Jamaica, slipped only by a quarter, from 1 July to 1 September 1835.

In contrast to the American Loyalist compensation or to compulsory purchase for infrastructure improvements, the distribution of slave-compensation was designed as an orderly bureaucratic process with published rules and formal procedures, consistent with other findings on the increasing professionalism of government in the 1830s.[4] Slave-compensation differed from its precedents in establishing a uniform and transparent framework for evaluating claims: the monetary amounts were given, not negotiated, and were set by formula, with differentiation first between colonies and then within colonies amongst classes of slaves, but with the explicit assumption that within categories slaves were homogeneous, interchangeable units of property. Once the

[2] R. E. P. Wastell, 'The history of slave compensation 1833 to 1845', M.A. thesis, London University, pp. 35–8.
[3] *Ibid.*, p. 62.
[4] For the growing professionalism of government in this period, see Z. Laidlaw, *Colonial connections 1815–45: patronage and the information revolution in colonial government* (Manchester: Manchester University Press, 2006).

tariff had been established and the slaves classified for each colony, there was no further room for discussion or negotiation over the level of compensation.

By contrast, earlier compensation claims were effectively bilateral (and often bad-faith) negotiations between individual owners and arbitrators over specific pieces of property acknowledged (unlike the enslaved in the context of compensation) to have unique characteristics. Chapter 2 highlighted the importance of 'improvement' schemes in shaping the *principle* of compensated expropriation: the practice of compulsory purchase provided a more cautionary precedent. The Commissioners for the London docks' compensation schemes, for example, which sat from 1799 to 1824, made 1,376 awards totalling £677,382. But the claims of individual owners amounted to £3,705,419: only three out of the 1,376 awards were made for the full amount originally claimed. When these discrepancies emerged in a summary published by the Lords of the Treasury in 1828, they drew attention to 'the power of the imagination of the mercantile classes'. 'A Correspondent' to *The Times* highlighted some of the most invidious examples of 'the wide misconception which people are apt to make of the value of that which belongs to them'. Amongst the thirty-nine cases singled out in *The Times* were three by individuals who later also claimed slave-compensation, including Sir William Abdy (who claimed £10,000 from the Docks Commissioners and was awarded £2,600) and John Atkins (who claimed £5,125 in one case in which he was awarded £1,000, and who abandoned altogether another claim for £8,000).[5] The Commission of Enquiry into the Losses, Services and Claims of the American Loyalists, which between 1783 and 1790 had received 3,225 claims, did not make public its General Rules and Principles, and appears to have been characterised by apparent favouritism towards larger claimants and by fraudulent efforts on the part of claimants.[6]

However, while there were by contrast many signs of recognisably modern modes of government in the compensation process, the correspondence of slave-owners with the Commission also highlights its novel character in a period of transition in the nature of government. Henry Hill, the secretary, was known to a number of the slave-owners: several letters to the Commission extended personal greetings

[5] 'Compensation claims on the public purse, from a correspondent', *The Times*, 18 October 1828, p. 3.
[6] E. R. Fingerhut, 'Uses and abuses of the American Loyalists' claims: a critique of quantitative analyses', *William and Mary Quarterly*, 3rd series 25.2 (1968), 245–58; W. Brown, *The King's friends: the composition and motives of the American Loyalist claimants* (Providence: Brown University Press, 1965).

to him and his family. A number of correspondents continued to proceed on the traditional basis of more personalised government, petitioning ministers, or petitioning the Commissioners themselves. John Sandbach of Liverpool wrote to Viscount Sandon in 1835, stating that he and his family were legatees under the will of the late owner of Ramble plantation in Manchester, Jamaica, but that he had been unable to obtain any information about the compensation, and was thus appealing to Sandon for help: 'Having been a canvasser for your lordship at the most recent election, and a member of your subcommittee at Edge Hill, will I hope induce your lordship to excuse my being thus troublesome.'[7]

While such networks of patronage were activated, the records carry no indication that decision-making as to awards was thereby influenced, and the Commission (at least until it was overwhelmed with the volume of work in the summer of 1835) appears uniformly responsive to all correspondents, usually replying by the following day to each of the mass of letters it received.[8] Nevertheless, patronage did on occasion secure a fuller response than might otherwise have been obtained. For example, the Hon. James King of Gantry Castle in Tipperary, brother of Lord Kingston and parliamentary candidate for the County of Cork in 1837 and the University of Dublin in 1841, writing via Sir George Grey, intervened on behalf of the 'poor widow and children' of the late Gerald Shaw, who had 'recently called on him': the Commission secretariat gave King in response to his request an estimate of the value of the compensation in St Vincent ('perhaps it may be for £25 to £30 each'), whereas elsewhere it declined to give such estimates.[9]

The very nature of the Commission's work, its bureaucratic procedures with a clear framework of rules and a quasi-legal system of arbitration were alien to many of the claimants who interacted with it, and some claimants offended the Commission's sense of regularity and order. The Rev. Alex Scott of Bath received back through the post 'the enclosed documents, purporting to be Counterclaims in respect of certain slave property in the colonies of Antigua and Tobago . . . not having

---

[7] Letter from John Sandbach to Viscount Sandon, T71/1606, 5 February 1835.
[8] The temperature rose perceptibly as the Commission moved towards arbitration in the summer of 1835. The Commission apologised to James Covernton Jr of Wargrave near Maidenhead for the delay in sending him details of the slave registry, 'which has been owing to the extreme pressure of business in the Office these many days past'. Commission to Covernton, T71/1592, p. 217, 27 August 1835.
[9] T71/1592 pp. 180, 346 (letters from Commission to King); T71/1610 (letter from King to Commission). See *The Times*, 14 August 1837, p. 2; 23 June 1841, p. 5 for King as parliamentary candidate. Lucinda Shaw received £139 6s 3d for six slaves: T71/892, St Vincent No. 51.

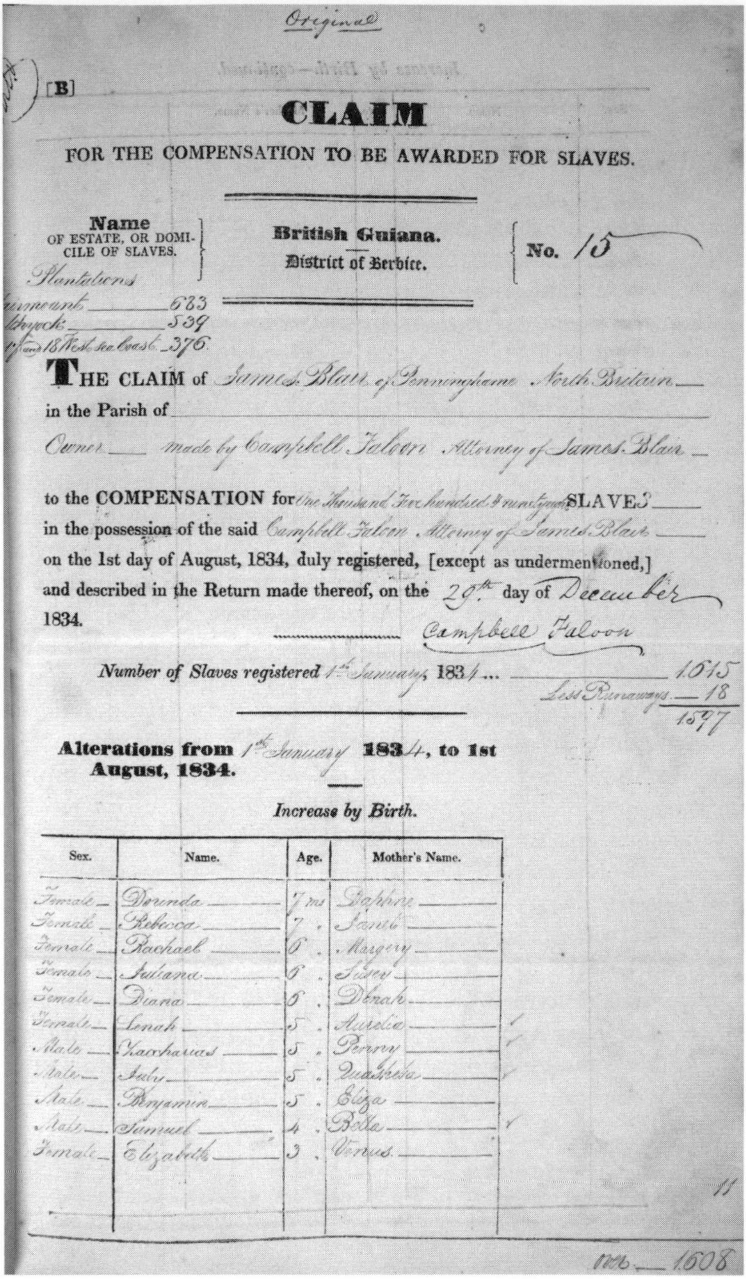

Plate 1 James Blair claim. Individual compensation awards in some colonies, notably British Guiana, could amount to tens of thousands of pounds. This claim by the MP James Blair for the 1,598 enslaved on his Blairmont estate in British Guiana gave rise to the largest single compensation payment, £83,530 8s 11d.

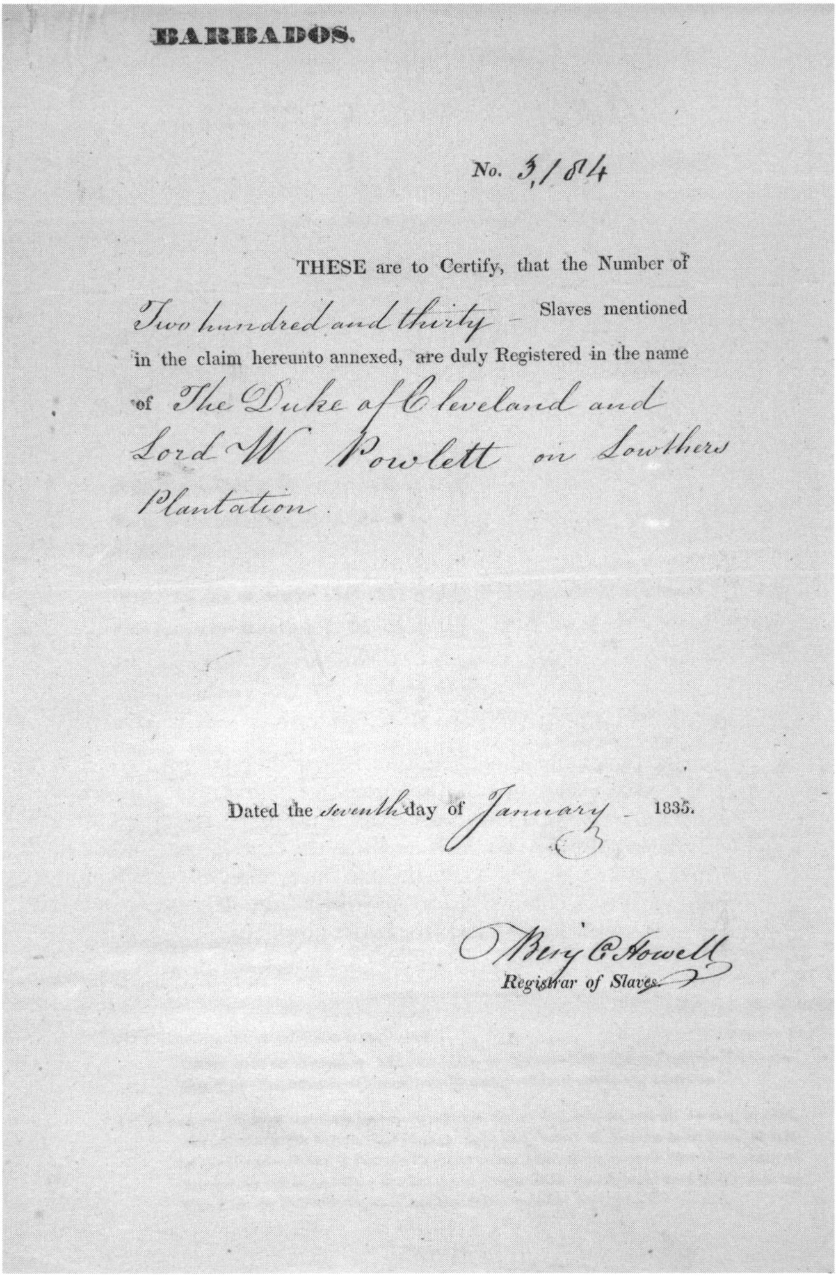

BARBADOS.

No. 3,184

THESE are to Certify, that the Number of

Two hundred and thirty — Slaves mentioned in the claim hereunto annexed, are duly Registered in the name of *The Duke of Cleveland and Lord W. Powlett on Lowthers Plantation.*

Dated the *seventh* day of *January* 1835.

Beny C. Howell
Registrar of Slaves

Plate 2 Duke of Cleveland certificate. Claims had to be accompanied by certificates from the local slave registrar confirming prior registration of the enslaved in the name of the claimant, such as this endorsement of the Duke of Cleveland's claim over 230 enslaved in Barbados.

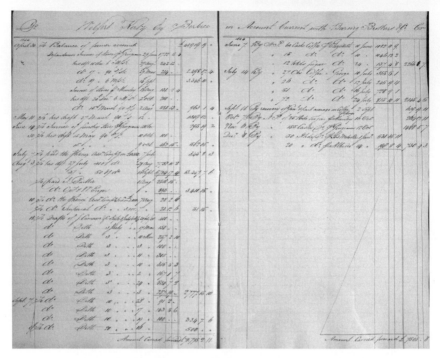

Plate 3   Baring Brothers account. British merchants provided large-scale credit to slave-owners, secured on estates and on the enslaved living and working upon them. Here is the 1824 'Account Current' with Baring Brothers of Wolfert Katz, the largest slave-owner in British Guiana, produced by Barings' as evidence of their counter-claim for Katz's compensation, in which ultimately they reached a settlement with Katz's executors after his death.

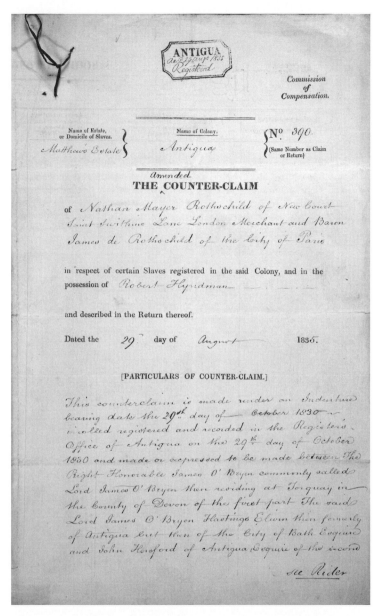

ANTIGUA
Registered

Commission
of
Compensation.

Name of Estate, or Domicile of Slaves.	Name of Colony.	N° 390.
Matthews Estate	*Antigua*	(Same Number as Claim or Return)

Amended
THE COUNTER-CLAIM

of *Nathan Mayer Rothschild of New Court Saint Swithins Lane London Merchant and Baron James de Rothschild of the City of Paris*

in respect of certain Slaves registered in the said Colony, and in the possession of *Robert Hyndman*

and described in the Return thereof.

Dated the *29* day of *August* 1835.

[PARTICULARS OF COUNTER-CLAIM.]

This counterclaim is made under an Indenture bearing date the 29th day of October 1830 inrolled registered and recorded in the Register's Office of Antigua on the 29th day of October 1830 and made or expressed to be made between The Right Honorable James O' Bryen commonly called Lord James O'Bryen then residing at Torquay in the County of Devon of the first part The said Lord James O' Bryen Hastings Elwin then formerly of Antigua but then of the City of Bath Esquire and John Hersford of Antigua Esquire of the second

see Rider

Plate 4   N. M. Rothschild counter-claim. British bankers as creditors pursued slave compensation to recover debts owed by slave-owners. This counter-claim by Nathan Mayer Rothschild, arising from an assignment to Rothschild by Lord James O'Bryen of a debt secured on enslaved men and women in Antigua, was ultimately successful.

St. CHRISTOPHER
Registered

Commission
of
Compensation.

Name of Estate, or Domicile of Slaves.	Name of Colony.	Nº 592
Bell Tete	St Christopher	(Same Number as Claim or Return)

THE COUNTER-CLAIM

of *James William Freshfield. James William Freshfield the Younger & Charles Hoye Freshfield of 5 New Bank Buildings London situated under the firm of Freshfield & Sons*

in respect of certain Slaves registered in the said Colony, and in the possession of *Hugh Pyley Semper*

and described in the Return thereof.

Dated the *31* day of *August* 1835

[PARTICULARS OF COUNTER-CLAIM.]

The counterclaimants claim the compensation money to be awarded in respect of the slaves comprized in the above named claim of Hugh Pyley Semper.

The Bell Tete Estate and Negroes were in and prior to the year 1829 the property of Messrs Mannings & Anderdon. They delivered the Title deeds of the said Bell Tete Estate to the counterclaimants for the purpose of advising them as to their legal rights on the said Estate and the counterclaimants retained them until the firm of Mannings & Anderdon became Bankrupt which happened in the year 1831 and still hold them.

The said Messrs Mannings and Anderdon have contracted for the sale of the said Estate and Negroes to the Claimant but he has not paid for the same and the Title deeds have never been delivered up by the counterclaimants who have a lien thereon for law charges against the said Messrs Mannings and Anderdon amounting to £402.15.4 which has not yet been discharged. They therefore claim that the compensation money in respect of the slaves on the Bell Tete Estate and which are comprized in the above mentioned claim may be applied towards satisfaction of their said debt of £402.15.4 upon payment of which they are ready to deliver up the said Title deeds to the owner of the Estate.

Freshfield & Son

Plate 5   J. W. Freshfield claim. British law firms were highly active in the compensation process as agents of the slave-owners, but this counter-claim for slave-compensation by the partners in the law firm Freshfield & Sons as principals formed part of their pursuit of outstanding legal fees owed to the firm.

LIST to which the foregoing **Certificate** refers.

Jamaica, Clarendon

Number of Claim.		Name.	Designation.	Sum.		
1	1	John Biddulph and Samuel Pepys Cockerell	of Whitehall Place Lincoln's Inn	£ 959	12	5
2	2	John Biddulph and Samuel Pepys Cockerell	of Whitehall Place Lincoln's Inn	3945	11	10
3	3	George Hay Dawkins Pennant	Pennants	4,509	7	3
4	4	George Hay Dawkins Pennant	Kupius	3,065	9	2
5	5	Rowland Mitchell and Samuel Mitchell		2,509	16	~
6	6	Arthur Mackenzie	Clarendon	468	12	5
7	7	John Biddulph and Samuel Pepys Cockerell	of Whitehall Place Lincoln's Inn	2729	5	8
8	11	John Biddulph and Samuel Pepys Cockerell	of Whitehall Place Lincoln's Inn	2429	16	6
9	12	Edward Thompson	Chapelton	29	3	1
10	13	William Beckford		2,570	2	3
11	14	William Rose	Clarendon	817	13	2
12	16	John W. Johnson	Welcome	224	10	9
13	18	Thomas P. Cottrell	Mount Lyall	10	19	9
14	19	Isulilla Catherine Douglas	Welcome	32	2	1
15	21	Margaret Murdock	Clarendon	32	9	9
16	22	Ellen Wilmot	View Plantation	31	5	11
17	23	Alexander McDowell	Content	73	5	3
		Lewis Hastings Edwards		£ 33055	3	3
		Henry Frederick McLeaon				

Plate 6 Clarendon list. The Commissioners of Compensation, having approved an award to a slave-owner, sent details to the Treasury in order to authorise payment. Of the seventeen awards listed in this example for Clarendon in Jamaica, eight were made to British absentee owners.

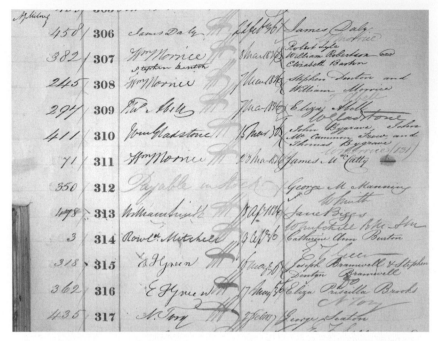

Plate 7   Gladstone signature. Payments were physically made at the National Debt Office of the Bank of England, where the recipient of the payment signed for the payment. Agents often attended on behalf of the awardees themselves. Here William Gladstone appears next to the prints of number 310, signing for the compensation on behalf of a group of slave-owners in Manchester, Jamaica.

Plate 8   Silver-gilt ewer. The West India Committee of absentee
slave-owners and West India merchants presented silver plate to the
full-time Slave Compensation Commissioners in appreciation of their
work. This ewer, made by R. & S. Garrard in 1841, was given to the
Commissioner James Lewis and incorporates his coat-of-arms.

been drawn up in the form prescribed by the Rules'.[10] The Commission returned to the Rev. Robert Allen of Barcombe, Lewes a memorandum left in the letter-box of the Commission that same morning withdrawing his counter-claim: 'it must be obvious to you that a more formal document than that in question will be required'.[11]

What is striking, although unsurprising, is the absence of the enslaved as individuals, indeed as people, from the records of the Commission. There are a handful of cases where the enslaved themselves erupted into the Commission's records as they sought to use the procedures of Emancipation to their benefit, or where individual slaves were named. In St Vincent, for example, two enslaved mariners, Joe aged 48 and Sam aged 28, 'claimed and obtained their freedom under the 3rd section of the Abolition Act. They have been in England.'[12] Again in St Vincent, two enslaved women, Abba and Kitty Brown, formerly belonging to James Wilson, MP for York, filed proceedings in the colonial court against Wilson's executors to obtain their freedom.[13] George Westby petitioned the Commission from 38 Dorset Square in London on behalf of Mrs Mary Tate of Honduras (and on his own behalf, it emerged). Mary Tate had bought an enslaved woman called Integrity for £320 currency with a loan from Westby: the father of Integrity was to pay off the loan in instalments and so free his daughter. But upon the Emancipation Act, the mother of Integrity claimed her own freedom for being in England thirty or forty years before, and freedom for Integrity herself 'on being born at sea'.[14] In a savage irony, four enslaved women in Honduras 'named and described in the foregoing registry viz. Maria, Mary Ann, Harriet and Mary, were accidentally drowned up the River Sibun when on their passage to Belize for the purpose of being valued, as officially notified to me [the Registrar] by Alexander France', who was nevertheless compensated for the dead enslaved.[15] But with these

---

[10] Commission to Rev. Alex Scott, T71/1592, p. 135, 12 May 1835.

[11] Commission to Rev. Robert Allen, T71/1592, p. 212, 22 August 1835. Correspondence continued with Allen until 1837, well after the adjudication of the claim in Barbados he pursued, despite an exasperated Commission telling him in November 1836, 'it is neither necessary nor regular that any further correspondence should take place on this subject'. See Commission to Rev. Robert Allen, T71/1593, 12 December 1835, 28 March 1836, 29 June 1836, 12 October 1836, 17 November 1836, 22 November 1836 (advising him that he was entitled to appeal to the Privy Council), 21 January 1837 (directing him to the Accountant-General's office for details of payment). Allen was unhappy with his share in the award of £1,259 6s 11d on Mapps Estate, contested within the Allen family, T71/897, Barbados No. 2954B.

[12] T71/500, St Vincent No. 426, p. 278.

[13] T71/892, St Vincent No. 568. Similar examples can be found at T71/894, Trinidad No. 1301; and T71/900, Barbados No. 5141.

[14] Westby to Commission, T71/1609, 14 May 1835.

[15] Note from James MacDonald, Registrar, T71/251, Honduras No. 212, p. 233.

few exceptions, the compensation process was structured by different categories of information than the identity of the enslaved: 'The names of individual slaves afford no clue in this Office to the Claims for compensation which may have been filed for them, the Valuation Returns merely specifying the numbers and classes of the slaves claimed and not their names', the Commission advised Margaret McGie of Edinburgh, who was seeking to establish a counter-claim for several slaves in St Elizabeth, Jamaica.[16]

Disseminating information on compensation in Britain

Knowledge of the Abolition Act and its consequences was dispersed unevenly amongst British slave-owners and other beneficiaries of slavery, and gave rise to anxiety and dislocation amongst claimants. Initially, of course, the Act provided only a framework for the distribution of compensation. The Compensation Commission itself was charged with determining the inter-colonial apportionment and the elaboration of the rules by which to govern the distribution of the compensation. Accordingly, for the first year of its operation it had little specific guidance to offer potential claimants, at a time when it was bombarded by general enquiries as to process. When Mary Sutherland wrote from Melina Place, Westminster Road, London in March 1834 that

I am an annuitant to the extent of £200 a year on certain estates in St Vincent belonging to a deceased Brother, and my children are legatees on the same estates to the amount of £5,000, the sum now due me amounts to £600 ... I very respectfully beg to ascertain from you, whether before the said fund shall pass from the control of the government, any portion of it is intended to be appropriated for annuitants and Legatees ... The question is of the utmost importance to me and my family, as the annuity is *all* I have to look forward to in life; failing it, I have no other prospect than *positive starvation*! As this is a National Measure, it would appear but equitable that all parties concerned shall bear their due proportion of the loss arising from it,

the Commission could only respond with a holding message, although annuitants and legatees whose incomes were secured on the enslaved were indeed eligible to claim compensation.[17]

---

[16] Commission to Margaret McGie, Shakespeare Square, Edinburgh, T71/1593, pp. 185–6, 28 April 1836.

[17] Letter to Rt Hon. Lord Stanley from Mary M., T71/1610, St Vincent bundle, 10 April 1834. 'The cases of the annuitants and legatees who will be affected by the recent Act of Parliament will be provided for in the Rules which the Commissioners are now engaged in framing': Commission to Sutherland, T71/1592, p. 18.

Even once the Commission had established the framework for its operation and published its rules, potential claimants had uneven access to sources of information. Many slave-owners belonged to networks of West Indians close enough to the metropolitan centres to be fully informed. But not everyone was so connected, and those who were not were aware of their disadvantage. Sir William L[aurence] Young of North Dean, High Wycombe, the grandson of Sir William Young, the 2nd baronet, sought to file a late counter-claim: 'my only excuse that I can give is that not being connected at present with the West India interest, I imagined that claims of the different parties would not be gone into till after the loan had been contracted by the Government'.[18]

Others, often the most substantial owners, relied on agents in London, generally either their merchant-consignees or solicitors. But the use of intermediaries did not signal indifference to the process, the timing or the outcome. John Pusey Wint of Boulogne, for example, used the merchant Edmund Francis Green, who pressed the Commission for the date of the hearing for Wint's claim on the Ryde estate in Manchester, Jamaica after Green had applied at the Compensation Office on 25 September and 19 October 1835 and been told to apply again on 26 October, 'Mr Wint being naturally extremely anxious to hear from me on this subject'.[19] G. Jago of Trelleck Terrace, Pimlico acted for the Duke of Buckingham and Chandos for his claims in St Andrew, £6,630 5s 6d of which was paid to the Marquis of Breadalbane and the Hon. G. Neville as trustees of a marriage settlement of 11 May 1819 for £20,000. Jago wrote to the Commission early in the compensation process 'directed by his Grace the Duke … to ascertain what sum will be awarded and at what period the same will be payable'.[20] A handful of aristocrats in uncontested cases dealt directly with the collection of their awards. The Rt Hon. Charles, Earl of Romney wrote to discover the day on which he could receive the certificate for his award of £4,324 18s 11d for 258 slaves on his eponymous estate in St Kitts, adding in a rather magnificent *de haut en bas* line: 'I should also be obliged to you if you would inform me, where your office is.' He did, however, manage to find the National Debt Office to receive payment on submission of his certificate.[21]

[18] Young to Commission, T71/1602, Bundle 2 (miscellaneous official correspondence, January to December 1835), 2 October 1835.
[19] T71/860, Manchester No. 94; E. F. Green to Commission, T71/1606, 19 October 1835.
[20] T71/865, St Andrew Nos. 114, 150; Jago to Commission, T71/1607.
[21] T71/879, St Kitts No. 636; Romney to Commission, T71/1609, 12 December 1835. Romney's signature for the payment itself appears in NDO4/11, where his identity was vouched for by John Martin.

The main official communication mechanism, however, was the press. Initially, the Commission confined publication of its announcements to the *London Gazette*. The agent in the Gazette Office in Edinburgh wrote to the Commission in 1834 on publication of the Commission's Rules to point out that he had been subject to repeated applications for information concerning compensation, 'and as that is to be found in the *London Gazette* alone, one copy of which is filed at this office and not more than five in Scotland besides', he had on his own initiative 'in order to the better dissemination of a matter so important to the community of Scotland' printed it in the *Edinburgh Gazette*. He was writing to request payment of the same allowance as to the *London Gazette* ('our charges being similar').[22] The Commission declined to pay, but subsequently selected one West India merchant firm in each of what it deemed the relevant major provincial urban centres to republish its notices in the local newspapers.[23]

Rentier claimants remained puzzled, despite the efforts of the Commission. Frank Howard wrote from Eastbourne in late 1835: 'I observed an advertisement in the papers that the Commission would proceed to compensation to the claimants in various parishes in Jamaica and other colonies, up to No. 100 of the uncontested claims, but I did not see the name of St Vincent: was it intentionally, or by negligence of the printers, omitted?'[24] In fact, the uncontested St Vincent claims were adjudicated and awarded at weekly sessions of the Commission in January and February 1836.

Outside London and the main urban centres, the problem of communication was exacerbated. There was confusion on quite basic issues, notably on the difference between the value of the slaves and the compensation to be paid, and on the relationship between the loan raised to fund the compensation and the awards themselves.[25] In a number of

---

[22] Gazette Office, Edinburgh to Commission, T71/1602, Bundle 2, 25 April 1834.

[23] For the refusal, see Commission to Gazette Office, T71/1592, p. 30, 2 May 1834. The firms were: Charles Payne (Bristol), C. & W. Shand (Liverpool), A. Milne (Glasgow), Thos Wilson (Dublin): Circular request, T71/1592, 8 September 1835.

[24] Letter from Frank Howard, 20 Sea House, Eastbourne, T71/1610, St Vincent bundle, 1 October 1835. Howard was the husband of Charlotte Bolton, mortgagee.

[25] See for example the Commission writing to Joseph Padmore of Cheltenham as late as 1836 to explain why he received £135 18s 4d and £1,790 9s 3d for slaves valued at £350 and £4,610 respectively, T71/1593, p. 137, 11 March 1836; and the letter to the Commission from H. G. Burke of Killimor Castle, Loughrea, Ireland, T71/1602, Bundle 1, 4 December 1836: 'About this time twelve months I received my proportion of the fifteen millions then ordered to be apportioned among the several slave owners. I am informed that the remaining 5 millions are shortly to be decided. Please inform me if so, and to say, whether it is to the Gazette I am to look for further information thereof.'

cases, claimants were simply too late to register their claims or counter-claims as a result of the difficulty of information flows.

The obligation to file claims in the colonies obviously placed burdens on slave-owners in Britain, just as the obligation to receive payment in London created difficulty for colonial (and indeed many provincial British) slave-owners. There was distress where claims had not been filed. Allan Laing of Inner Temple, whose claim was noted above, complained in seeking consent to file a late counter-claim in Dominica: 'I had fully relied upon my Agent Mr Laidlaw, who is one of the Assistant Commissioners in the Island ... the sum due is a large one.'[26]

Mundane challenges arose from distance and from the need for documentation. Cordelia Duncombe wrote from Clifton in 1836 requesting consent to file a late claim in Antigua: she used her social connection with Henry Hill to frame her approach ('I trust your good wife and sister are as well as when I last had the pleasure of seeing them'), setting out that her late father had inherited forty slaves from her grandfather, and had had no debts other than family ones, including a bond in favour of her aunt. The bond had been thought lost, but had recently been discovered amongst old papers in Antigua: its value was £1,000 sterling. Catherine Warner wrote from Paris in 1837 asking for a further delay in the adjudication of Colonel Warner's estate in Dominica: 'By letters I have just received from Trinidad in reply to my application for a copy of my marriage settlement, and to produce which you kindly granted me a delay in your decisions, I am promised that the deed shall be sent for to Dominica and forwarded to London without loss of time.'[27]

The mechanics and cost of payment were also a source of concern. In principle, payment should have been simple for absentee owners in Britain, certainly simpler than for residents in the colonies. But costs and difficulties arose. Richard Atkinson of Kirkby Lonsdale, a mortgagee with '(to me) considerable claims on an estate in British Guiana', wrote to Stanley early in 1834 of:

one circumstance connected with my claim (and no doubt with that of many other persons)[:] it is payable in England and if I have to send out to make the claim in the West Indies in addition to what I should probably loos [sic] in the amount of the claim[,] I shall probably have to pay 10 p[er]cent on the amount I may actually receive, a cruel hardship of which those only can judge whose means are like mine limited.[28]

---

[26] A. S. Laing, Inner Temple to Commissioners, T71/1609, Dominica No. 288, 8 December 1835.

[27] Catherine Warner to Commission, T71/1609, Dominica bundle, 22 September 1837.

[28] Richard Atkinson to Stanley, T71/1610, Guiana bundle, 3 February 1834.

The Commission told Thomas Hopkinson of 3 Cockspur Street in 1836 that it could only have regard to the rights of the respective parties: 'they cannot enter into the question raised by you as to an anticipated charge of 10 per cent commission on monies so received'.[29]

The system of the Commission issuing certificates for payment by the National Debt Office also gave rise to practical problems and presented opportunities for manipulation. The Commission had defended the system ('not more than two instances have occurred in which these certificates have passed into the wrong hands'), but Henry Hill the secretary was compelled to write to J. C. Clarke of 4 Water Lane in 1836: 'I am directed by the Commissioners of Compensation to point out to you the propriety of delivering the Certificate to Mr Sanguinetti who appears to be the proper party to present the same for payment at the National Debt Office', since he held a power of attorney from W. & E. Law, the owners of the slaves.[30] Again, in July 1836 the Commission wrote to Robert Morrison of 53 St Paul's Churchyard to say the Commission understood 'you decline to give up the Certificate of Award which you obtained at this Office in January last, altho' you hold no authority whatever for keeping possession of the same', but did not doubt that Morrison would see the necessity of returning it. The Commission's sanction was no more than to issue a new certificate and cancel the old one, as they warned Morrison, if he did not show his authority.[31]

Contested claims

The Commission was charged with unpicking the various types of claims of ownership or entitlement amongst different colonial and metropolitan parties that had accreted over specific slaves or groups of slaves.[32] The Commission's obligation was to (re-)impose a binary relationship

---

[29] Commission to Hopkinson, T71/1593, p. 68, 19 January 1836.
[30] Commission to Colvile & Co., T71/1593, pp. 39–40, 16 January 1836; Commission to J. C. Clarke, T71/1593, p. 136, 11 March 1836.
[31] Commission to Morrison, T71/1593, p. 240, 21 July 1836, 30 July 1836.
[32] The Commission could only consider financial claims that were deemed by colonial law to represent a lien on the enslaved or the estate. It turned away as outside its remit claims by general unsecured creditors of slave-owners. There are about a dozen cases in the records of British tradesmen trying to recover debts from defaulting customers: for example J. H. Froelich and the executors of Geo. Draeger, tailors of 37 Suffolk Street, claiming against nine residents of Barbados, Antigua and St Vincent for sums ranging from £12 to £214, T71/1602, Memorial, 9 January 1836. There are at least four British schoolteacher creditors attempting to recover unpaid bills for board and education, including Thomas Hunt of Hammersmith, owed £154 by Edward de Poullain of Grenada, T71/1609, petition from Thomas Hunt, schoolmaster, 24 November 1835.

on owner and slave as a matter of legal and economic reality, to define simply the owner and the owned. In fact, the complexity of the owner-ship relationship was enormous, and was highly contested amongst rival claimants. As a result of the cumulative accretion of different claims – whether of ownership or of financial obligation – 'slave-property' was fought over within families, between families, between mortgagor and mortgagee, between owner and consignee, between trustees and benefi-ciaries, and between executors and legatees. Some 3,500 awards were formally 'contested' or 'litigated', i.e. subject to counter-claims filed by rival claimants: the bulk of these were for large-scale awards, although there were disputes over the compensation for single slaves. In addi-tion, the Commission paid compensation in 156 cases into the Court of Chancery in England and in 199 cases into colonial courts, to await court judgements in pre-existing suits as to the appropriate party to receive compensation.[33] Beyond such formally contested claims, more were subject to rival claims but evidence in the Commission records suggests negotiated settlements were reached between competing claim-ants in order to avoid the delay imposed on formally contested awards. For every successful claimant in a contested case, there was a corre-sponding disappointed party, and the records contain a litany of rancour and bitterness over failure in the compensation process.

Such contested claims were predictably the focus of significant anxiety as conflicts were worked out between creditors and owners, amongst different classes of creditors, between trustees and executors on the one hand and beneficiaries on the other, amongst different fami-lies and within a single family. J. Brocklebank from Liverpool wrote in 1836 asking the Commission to stay the award of compensation to the mercantile Dennistoun family of Glasgow for the Milton estate in Trinidad. His cousin, William Bosworth, he said, had purchased the estate for £6,000, subsequently dying intestate. The Dennistouns had claimed the compensation 'on the pretence that the said Wm Bosworth was merely the agent':

If this statement is a fact, why did the aforesaid Robert Dennistoun & Co. go to the expense and trouble of searching into the aforesaid William Bosworth's relations and next of kin? Why did they employ a Mr Crums, an att[orne]y in Liverpool, to tamper with us by offering at one time £50, at another £100, if

---

[33] These Chancery and Colonial Court (or 'List E') claims, accounting for some £1 million in compensation, are not recorded in any detail in the Commission records beyond payment of the compensation into the respective courts, except for a handful of cases determined by the courts during the life of the Commission. In most cases, only the identity of the competing litigants, not the outcome, can be determined from the Commission records. See Chapter 4, below, pp. 150–151 for further analysis.

we, whose names are annexed to the enclosed document, would sign an acquittance to all claims upon the estate called 'Milton'?[34]

Some potentially contested cases were settled between the rival claimants rather than arbitrated by the Commission. The Commission had no power to force claimants and counter-claimants to settle, but clearly facilitated agreement where it could. Its sanction was the declaration of an award as 'contested' or 'litigated' and the payment of the compensation money to the Accountant-General to be invested in government stock for the benefit of the ultimate awardee. Awards so designated went to the bottom of the pile, since the Commission was committed to resolving all uncontested claims before it turned to the contested ones. With no direct experience even by the Commission of the mass management of claims, and the precedent of lengthy delays in Chancery, claimants could not predict how long – how many years – they might wait for contested claims to be resolved. It is clear that some claimants expended much effort in avoiding claims falling into the 'contested' category, and that the threat of the delay was a point of negotiating leverage. For example, R. M. Reece wrote on behalf of Alexander Mackenzie concerning the Waterloo and Orange Hill estates in St Vincent to highlight to the Commission 'a probability that in a certain event my client may be induced to withdraw the counterclaim lodged by him in time to prevent the money to be appropriated to those estates to be paid to the Accountant-General'.[35] Charles Paul of 'Whittington Rectory nr Radstock Bath' claimed for 126 slaves on the Kingstown Park estate in St Vincent, and acknowledged to the Commission his awareness of the existence of counter-claims. Given, he said, that 'all parties are anxious to avoid any delay in the payment of the compensation, and fearing lest the existence of a counter-claim should cause the case of Kingstown Park to be classed under the "disputed claims"... I write to know by what means such inconvenience can be avoided'.[36]

Consequently, there are numerous references to negotiation towards sharing of awards, in some of which the outcome is explicit. Thus in the case of the Bon Air estate in Grenada, Louisa Maltby of Charlotte Street, Portland Place – widow, executrix and devisee of Rowland Maltby, the mortgagee of the estate – 'claims £2,691 but hereby consents to receive one half of the compensation money', i.e. £1,686 11s 4d (the other half

[34] J. Brocklebank, 28 Scotland Terrace, Liverpool, T71/1611, Trinidad bundle, 9 February 1836.
[35] T71/892, St Vincent Nos. 449, 450; Reece to Commission, T71/1610, 13 January 1836. Mackenzie was ultimately awarded over £1,000 from the Waterloo estate.
[36] T71/892, St Vincent No. 552; Charles Paul to Commission, T71/1610, 14 November 1835.

was shared between the owners Edward and Peter Gibbs and the tenants in common, the de Bellot family).[37] In a complex case over the Boarded Hall estate in Barbados, owned originally by the merchant Sir George Harnage but mortgaged to the late Sir Edward Nagle, claimants and counter-claimants included the trustees of a settlement first created in 1791 of an annuity of £150 per annum on Lady Harnage, in case she survived her husband Sir George ('£3,000 to be raised after both were dead for their children'), and Dame Mary Nagle of Hampton Court, annuitant £700 per annum for life and £3,750 due in arrears. With the consent of all parties, the money was paid jointly to Nagle's executors and the trustees of the Harnage settlement.[38]

There was recourse from the Commission's decisions in cases of continued disagreement amongst claimants. There was an appeal mechanism to the Privy Council, but it was invoked in only a handful of cases, and the Commission's verdict overturned in even fewer.[39]

Some potential claimants simply applied too late to the Commission. Ellen Blades of Kirkby Lonsdale approached the Commission in late 1839 identifying herself as one of the daughters of John Renny, who had died around nineteen years previously leaving two estates, Swamp Head and Norris Head, in Jamaica. She was well-informed, specifying the number of slaves (198 and 210 respectively) and referring to provisions of the will that prevented the property from being sold or mortgaged. She wanted to know what had happened to the compensation: 'I am the wife of an outpensioner of Chelsea Hospital – we have been buffeted about in the world – suffered many privations – which has hitherto been the means of preventing us from establishing our claim on the above property.' But the award had been paid out three years previously.[40] Harriott Strachan, with two other executors and trustees, had claimed £4,641 3s 3d for 231 slaves on Norris estate and £3,326 14s 7d for 170 on Swamps as the widow of Thomas Renny Strachan of Tarrie near Arbroath, who had died in 1823. Harriott Strachan herself

---

[37] T71/880, Grenada No. 565, and T71/1229, counter-claims. Mrs Maltby appears to have reached the same agreement on the Duquesne estate, Grenada No. 684, where she was again awarded half the total compensation, i.e. £1,666 15s 9d.

[38] T71/898, Barbados No. 3653.

[39] According to Wastell, there were seven appeals, only one of which was successful. The underlying records show Notices of Appeal in at least fourteen, in two of which (St Vincent No. 689 and British Guiana No. 269) the Privy Council ordered a minor re-allocation of the compensation amongst contending groups of claimants, and in another (Trinidad No. 1599) it overturned the judgement of the Commission and awarded the compensation to Henry Davidson as mortgagee.

[40] Letter from Ellen Blades, T71/866, St David Nos. 104, 122; T71/1607, 31 October 1839.

died about thirty years after her husband, and the estates of which she had been 'life-renter' passed by her husband's wishes to the son of Sir David Carnegie of Kinnaird.

In a small handful of cases, even after an award was made the Commission attempted to retrieve the compensation in the light of new evidence. In general, it simply told applicants that they were too late, that jurisdiction had passed out of their hands, but some cases appear to have been so invidious that it sought to retrieve the compensation. So, for example, it wrote to the Rev. Stephen Isaacson in Dorking, who had collected compensation for a slave in British Guiana, enclosing an affidavit from a Mr Reid and asking for repayment of the compensation; and to William Carter in Worthing, asking for compensation he had received in error to be paid to Mr Harker, the agent of Miss Catherine Carter of Jamaica.[41]

The Commission formally closed its business in 1840, although claims were still handled into the mid 1840s, with James Lewis remaining to oversee the tail of claims, including dealing with families who continued to pursue compensation already awarded. Robert Dall, for example, had been awarded £1,809 5s for 107 slaves on the Cedar Valley estate in St George, Jamaica in 1835. In 1842, James S. Mitchell of Edinburgh, wrote that Dall's wife (who had a life interest) had died, and that her relatives wanted to know how the claim was awarded, when and for how much. The relatives knew, said Mitchell, that Dall had been in London in 1835 'for the purpose of arranging the settlement of his business'.[42] Again, even after compensation was paid, trade creditors in Britain nevertheless continued to pursue the recipients, although the Commission by that stage was only a potential source of information rather than a possible point of leverage for the creditors. The Edinburgh wine merchants Adams, for example, wrote to the Compensation Commission as late as 1843 to inquire whether any claim had ever been made by C. J. Warner and, if so, how much had been paid. [43]

Conclusion

The Commission early in its proceedings had been subject to criticism of its pace of work. *The Times* in December 1835 alluded to discontent

[41] Commission to Rev. Stephen Isaacson, T71/1593, pp. 115, 381, 20 February 1836, 28 January 1837; Commission to William Carter, T71/1593, pp. 215–16, 17 June 1836. Isaacson also collected £60 4s for three slaves in Barbados in right of wife Anna Maria Miller Killikelly, T71/897, Barbados No. 2432.

[42] T71/869, St George No. 206. Mitchell to Commission, T71/1607, 18 June 1842.

[43] Adams to Commission, T71/1610, St Vincent bundle, 22 May 1843.

with 'their dilatory mode of doing business', highlighting the 'mere routine' nature of the uncontested claims, and quoting approvingly the letter of protest to the Commission of an unnamed 'most respectable merchant', who had said: 'As to the plan of doling out these [uncontested] adjudications by 100 or 200 in weekly apportionments, it does not meet the views or reasonable expectations of any one above the intellect of a child.'[44]

There was, however, belated recognition of the achievement of the Commission in arbitrating and settling such a volume of claims in a short period, certainly relative to the pace of suits in Chancery at the time. Documents were occasionally lost and mistakes in payment were made. There were the standard frustrations of dealing with a bureaucracy that at times was over-stretched. James Beckford Wildman wrote testily to the Commission in late 1835: 'Having had two useless journeys to London for the purpose of receiving the compensation due to me for an estate in Clarendon No. 109 and St Andrew No. 149 I take the Liberty of requesting you to inform me when I may apply at the Office with the certainty of not being again disappointed.'[45]

Disappointment was also experienced with the level of compensation. Eliza Lawrence Hay, originally of Guernsey but subsequently of Hotwells, Bristol, was awarded compensation for 50 slaves on Pitfour in St James. 'In the return ... the amount of their value was £2,155 – for which I have only received £833 16s 4d. Since my return to England from Guernsey I have enquired of many of my friends and find their compensation has been far higher in proportion than mine. On it depends the chief part of my support.'[46] Her expression of concern indicates her participation in a social network of slave-owners in Britain, but also its limitations: her compensation as a proportion of the slave values could not have been materially lower than that of her friends.

Nevertheless, the system, while creaking on occasion, very largely worked. E. Witter Bucknor, a spinster of Hatfield who had arrived from Jamaica in 1824, grew concerned 'in a matter (to me) of such great importance' that W. S. Grignon of Montego Bay, to whom she had left a power of attorney, had not registered her slaves, and that a search by

[44] *The Times*, 25 December 1835, p. 2.
[45] Wildman to Commission, T71/1608, Various parishes bundle, 27 October 1835. The Commission was nettled ('I have to acquaint you that the Commissioners of Compensation have endeavoured to give every facility in their power to the parties interested in the compensation Fund to make themselves acquainted with the course of proceedings in this Office', for example, through newspaper advertisements), Commission to Wildman, T71/1592, p. 312, 28 October 1835.
[46] T71/873, St James No. 158; Elizabeth Lawrence Hay to the Commission, T71/1608, 17 June 1836.

Pitcairn & Amos, West India broker, on her behalf at the Compensation Commission Office 'revealed nothing': in fact, the Commission's own search discovered that Grignon had after all registered the claim as Miss Bucknor's attorney, and she was paid £391 13s 11d for the eighteen enslaved she had owned hired to the Hopewell estate in Hanover.[47]

Towards the end of the main Commission's work, the West India Committee formally thanked the Commissioners, who, the Committee said,

have displayed the greatest ability in the management of a commission so entirely novel in its nature and its duties, and in the arrangement of a system by which upwards of 50,000 [*sic*] claims have been considered and determined with an accuracy and despatch perfectly unprecedented ... the justice and impartiality with which the Commissioners have adjudicated on the important interests submitted to their decision will be best exemplified by stating that notwithstanding the above number of cases and the legal intricacy of many of the counter-claims and conflicting securities, there have been scarcely any appeals to the superior tribunal provided by the Act [i.e. the Privy Council].[48]

The West India Committee moved to what had been its standard practice for servants of the colonial interest, and launched a subscription for plate to be presented to James Lewis, Hastings Elwin and Henry Frederick Stephenson.[49] This implies a degree of 'regulatory capture' of the Commission by the West India Committee that is not borne out by the records, but it does tend to suggest more profoundly and fairly that the official London 'West India interest' was well-satisfied, not only with the implementation of payments but also with the whole compensation scheme.

---

[47] T71/915, Hanover No. 94; Bucknor to Commission, T71/1608, 28 August 1835; a handwritten note on the letter confirms the existence of the claim.

[48] *The Times*, 4 May 1839, p. 1.

[49] *Ibid*. The silver-gilt ewer presented to James Lewis was sold at auction by Sotheby's in London on 18 December 2007; Sotheby's, *Important silver, gold boxes and* objets de vertu (London: Sotheby's, 2007), p. 116.

4   The structure of slave-ownership

The Commission published a Parliamentary Return in March 1838 of awards made up to that date, which gives by colony the names of awardees, the number of slaves and the monetary value of each award.[1] As noted in the Introduction, the Return does not give the location of the claimant, the estates for which claims were made, the capacity in which the claimant made the claim (whether as owner, tenant-for-life, trustee, executor, mortgagee, annuitant) or the 'path to owner-ship'. Much of this additional information, however, has been pieced together from the underlying records of the Commission and other sources, and this and the following two chapters draw on those records to provide as complete a picture as possible of the ownership of the enslaved in the colonies of the West Indies and the Caribbean, which accounted for just under 83 per cent of the total compensation of £20 million.[2] The overall universe of awards analysed in the remainder of this study is shown in Table 4.1, which highlights the weight of Jamaica and British Guiana in the overall totals for monetary compensation, followed by Barbados and Trinidad. Barbados had almost as many enslaved as British Guiana, but owners of the enslaved in Barbados received less than half as much monetary compensation because the unit price of the enslaved, and hence the compensation, was so much lower in Barbados.[3]

---

[1] *Slavery Abolition Act: an account of all sums of money awarded by the Commissioners of Slavery Compensation*, PP 1837–8, Vol. 48 (215) (hereafter 'the Parliamentary Return' or 'the Return').

[2] Mauritius, the Cape of Good Hope, Bermuda and the Bahamas account for the remainder.

[3] This table is built up claim-by-claim from the Parliamentary Return and the under-lying records of the Commission. The National Debt Office's own calculations show minor discrepancies, but total to £16,449,500, within 1 per cent of the above figures; NDO4/26 'Awards actually paid'. It should be noted that there were multiple awards to many individuals. Lobdell calculates for these colonies that the 'net' number of individuals, after eliminating multiple awards, was 82 per cent of the 'gross' num-ber of claims; R. A. Lobdell, 'The price of freedom: financial aspects of British slave Emancipation 1833–38. Notes on research in progress', unpublished paper delivered

Table 4.1   *Overall distribution of compensation.*

Colony	Awards	No. of slaves	Compensation		
			£	s	d
Anguilla	213	2,260	35,669	2	0
Antigua	1,027	29,003	424,391	2	4
Barbados	5,344	83,225	1,714,561	1	7
British Guiana	2,674	84,075	4,281,032	11	0
Dominica	871	14,266	277,737	8	8
Grenada	993	23,729	615,671	16	8
Honduras	290	1,896	100,691	5	4
Jamaica	13,240	311,455	6,121,446	10	0
Montserrat	229	6,392	103,556	1	10
Nevis	304	8,792	149,611	13	5
St Kitts	767	17,514	293,331	17	8
St Lucia	861	13,232	331,805	5	4
St Vincent	757	22,786	579,300	7	10
Tobago	338	11,592	233,367	14	1
Trinidad	2,052	20,428	1,021,858	11	5
Virgin Islands	267	5,135	72,635	13	11
Total	**30,227**	**655,780**	**16,356,668**	**3**	**1**

Categorisation of slave-owners

There was undoubtedly significant mobility between the metropole and colonies for slave-owners in the 1820s and 1830s, as there had been in earlier periods, and in seeking to develop an approach and structure for analysing the extent and nature of metropolitan slave-ownership, it is important not to reduce the complexity and diversity of the lived experience of movement. Families and individuals displayed elaborate patterns of journeying backwards and forwards across the Atlantic for social, educational, medical and commercial reasons. Absentees such as Matthew 'Monk' Lewis famously visited their estates and recorded their travels; others, such as Benjamin Buck Greene, lived and worked in the West Indies for a number of years supervising the estates of immediate family and of wider networks of kin and associates. Colonists who played important roles in local politics nevertheless spent considerable periods of time in Britain: Peter Rose of British Guiana, as already seen, served as a Justice of the Peace in Scotland for several years in the 1820s. The compensation process itself, by virtue of centralising payment in London, appears to have accelerated these patterns of

at the Annual Meeting of the Social Sciences History Association, Pittsburgh (October 2000)', p. 9.

movement, with slave-owners ordinarily resident in the colonies coming to London to collect their own compensation. Temporary residence in England at the time of the compensation process was accordingly by no means uncommon. Forster Clarke, for example, registered his own slaves in Barbados in 1834, but personally collected his own compensation money in London in 1836: when Thome and Kimball visited Clarke's Horton plantation in 1837 they described it as 'an estate owned by Forster Clarke, Esq., an attorney for 22 estates, who is now temporarily living in England'.[4] Elizabeth Samuells, 'of Trelawny (but now of Holloway and about to sail for Jamaica)', assigned her compensation for five enslaved to the London merchant Petty Vaughan before she left Britain.[5]

Such movement, in both directions, was of course part of the process by which slavery 'came home' to Britain and by which the colonies were bound into Britain by ties of kinship, information and commerce. Nevertheless, without neglecting the importance of these exchanges, it is possible to move beyond a sense of slave-owners as undifferentiated members of 'the Atlantic community' and to establish some structure in the analysis of the patterns of metropolitan slave-owning. Four categories of differentiation have been deployed in analysing the slave-owners that require discussion: 'absentee' versus 'resident', 'rentier' versus 'merchant', large-scale versus small-scale rentier, and classification by geography within Britain.

The first division is between 'absentee' and 'resident'. In the use of this distinction it is not intended to minimise the mobility between colony and metropole, nor is it intended in deploying the category of 'absentee' to blur the diverse experiences of those within it, who comprised radically different individuals: metropolitan inheritors of estates who may never have visited their property, returnee slave-owners who had built up their own estates before retiring to Britain, mortgagees who had foreclosed, owners of two or three slaves who had inherited them or acquired them while on a tour of duty in the West Indies, or annuitants and legatees financially dependent on the slave-economy but remote from it not only physically but also socially and culturally. The category of 'resident' is probably still more precarious, because

---

[4] J. A. Thome and J. H. Kimball, *Emancipation in the West Indies* (New York, 1838), Barbadoes, Chapter 1. T71/556, p. 48 for Clarke's registration. Clarke was awarded £4,837 7s 8d for 205 enslaved on Horton. He was also attorney for the Society for Propagation of the Gospel's Codrington estate and the Earl of Harewood's Belle, Thicket and Mount St George estates, amongst others.

[5] Vaughan to Commission, 7 April 1835, T71/1608, Trelawney No. 207.

of the continuing tradition of seeking to earn a fortune in the colonies
and then to return to Britain. A common form of mobility was thus
that of retirement from the colonies to the metropole, as was the case
with William Miller, 'the Attorney-General'. When Miller testified to
the Select Committee on Apprenticeship, set up in 1836 to examine
the working of the system of forced labour under the Abolition Act, he
portrayed himself as definitively back from Jamaica, and as the owner
of very few enslaved.[6] A 'resident' can thus be seen in many cases as
simply a potential absentee intercepted by premature death.

Nevertheless, as short-hand, 'absentee' and 'resident' have been
retained as categories because they allow quantification of the extent
to which slave-ownership had become truly a metropolitan as well
as a colonial phenomenon. The 'absentee' category includes all those
who at the time of the payment of the compensation were domiciled
in Britain and Ireland and not clearly simply visiting the metropole.
Thus it excludes, for example, Forster Clarke, as noted above known to
be only a temporary visitor to the Britain. The study also picks up and
identifies separately: 'foreign' absentees (mainly Dutch but also French
and a handful of Spaniards and Italians) living in continental Europe
and owning slaves or holding mortgages over slaves in colonies that had
come into Britain's possession in the decades preceding Emancipation,
'West Indian' absentees living elsewhere in the Caribbean (or in the
remaining British colonies in North America) and owning slaves in
another colony, and absentees living in the United States. It does not
seek to address the 'internal' absentees, those who lived for example in
Kingston while owning estates in the parishes of Cornwall in the west
of Jamaica.

'Resident' describes those domiciled in the West Indies at the time of
Emancipation but not known to be visiting: an unknown, but it would
appear not insignificant, proportion of these later returned or, if Creole
(i.e. born in the West Indies), emigrated to Britain after the period of
Emancipation. 'Resident' identification is held to a lower standard than
'absentee' in attributing claims in the analysis which follows: registration by the individual of ownership of slaves in the most recent triennial registration, or signing of the claim form for compensation (both
by definition activities that could only take place in the colonies) have
each been taken as sufficient proof of 'resident' status in the absence of

---

[6] Evidence of William Miller, *Report from the Select Committee appointed to inquire into the
working of the Apprenticeship system in the colonies, conduct of Apprentices, laws, regulations
etc.*, PP 1836, Vol. 15 (560), pp. 189–90.

any other off-setting information. In order to classify a slave-owner as 'absentee', it is not enough that his or her compensation claim or slave registration was undertaken by an attorney: an additional piece of evidence, such as an attribution within the records as an absentee, or an address in Britain or identification from other primary or secondary material, has been required.

There are, nevertheless, slave-owners who truly defy categorisation, living between the colonies and the metropole and taking on hybrid identities. An example of such hybridity is shown by the death-notice 'at Park-place, Highgate, deeply lamented, Lucy, widow of the late James Sadler Esq. of Wey-hill and Port Morison plantations, in the Island of Jamaica, and of Highgate, England aged 59'.[7] Again, Andrew Gregory Johnston, who claimed for 147 enslaved in Portland and who died in Jamaica, was described as 'of Fritton-Hall Suffolk and Anchovy-Valley'.[8] John Adams Wood, the Antiguan slave-owner who brought Mary Prince to Britain, spent most of the last years of his life in London, where he was very active in the compensation process until his death there in 1836.[9] Such slave-owners have been categorised as 'Transatlantic' in the analysis that follows. As shown below, such examples, while interesting, appear in fact rare relative to those capable of starker classification.

The second category is of 'mercantile' versus 'rentier' owners. There were significant commonalities between the two: both absentee merchants and absentee rentiers relied, by definition, on the management of the enslaved by intermediaries, and were thus distanced both geographically and personally from the realities of enforcing the slave system. As Morgan demonstrated for eighteenth-century Bristol merchants, the distinction was not simply between rentier-*owners* and mercantile *creditors*: many metropolitan merchants owned estates and slaves in the colonies alongside absentee aristocratic and gentry

[7] *The Times*, 9 October 1850, p. 7. James Sadler had claimed for compensation for 114 enslaved on his Weyhill estate in St Mary, only for John Sheppard of Swindon, Wiltshire, the trustee of Sadler's marriage settlement, to counter-claim. Lucy Sadler, as James's agent, admitted the counter-claim, and £1,949 7s 0d was awarded to Sheppard and his co-trustee Edmund Kibblewhite on 5 November 1838; T71/856, St Mary No. 94.

[8] T71/868, Portland No. 33. Johnston lost his claim for compensation to Pitcairn & Amos, the London merchants who were his mortgagees. *The Times*, 27 April 1850, p. 9 and 16 June 1864 carry death-notices for Johnston and his daughter respectively. Johnston was a signatory of calls to arms by the West India interest in London in the early 1830s, but also held office in Jamaica in the late 1830s.

[9] John Adams Wood was awarded compensation on more than two dozen claims in Antigua, many of them small claims where he appears to have purchased the right to compensation by assignment from the original slave-owner.

rentier-owners.[10] In other respects, too, the distinction was not always clear-cut. For example, the journal of Samuel Boddington, senior partner in a leading London West India merchant firm, is an account of a rentier lifestyle, an agreeable leisured life rooted in the circle of Lord and Lady Holland and membership of the King of Clubs, in which slavery and compensation receive not one line. Yet Boddington continued as an active merchant throughout this period and received very substantial compensation from the Commission (and does record in his journal the deaths of his mercantile partners).[11] More problematically, the mercantile/rentier categories are not stable over time: merchants aspired to and (if successful enough financially) achieved rentier status later in life for themselves (or secured it for their heirs). John Bellingham Inglis, for example, a partner in the London merchant firm of Inglis Ellice at the time of Emancipation and recipient as mortgagee of compensation for 165 slaves in St Lucia, died in London in 1870 aged ninety-one, and was described then as 'a person of sedentary and literary pursuits', the owner of bonds, especially of Turkish bonds, which were the subject of a suit over Inglis's will between his executors and his maidservant.[12] Even such a relentlessly mercantile figure as George Hibbert came to rentier status towards the end of his life: his succession to an estate of 'an uncle by his wife', Rogers Parker of Munden, Hertfordshire, made him finally 'independent of the hazards and anxieties of commerce'.[13]

Again, however, there is a meaningful distinction to hold in place at least in the period of the compensation process, between active capitalists engaged in enterprise directly related to the slave-economy – even if that was not their exclusive focus – and passive capital for whom 'slave-property' represented a source of income without any form of active involvement in the supply of goods or financial services to the colonies. S. D. Smith has recently advanced the notion of 'gentry capitalism' to capture the involvement of local networks of commercially active landed families such as the Harewoods in the eighteenth century in international (especially colonial) trade and enterprise.[14] But the Harewoods as slave-owners passed from active enterprise to rentier status over generations: while it is perhaps difficult to specify the tipping

---

[10] K. Morgan, 'Bristol West India merchants in the eighteenth century', *Transactions of the Royal Historical Society*, 6th series 3 (1993), 185–208.

[11] S. Boddington, Journal 1815–43, Guildhall Library MS 10823/5.

[12] T71/884, St Lucia Nos. 763, 859 (the latter shared with two rival creditors). See *The Times*, 22 January 1873, p. 11 for the lawsuit.

[13] [J. H. Markland], *A sketch of the life and character of George Hibbert Esq., FRS, SA & LS* (printed for private distribution, 1837).

[14] S. D. Smith, *Slavery, family, and gentry capitalism in the British Atlantic: the world of the Lascelles, 1648–1834* (Cambridge: Cambridge University Press, 2006), pp. 1–9.

point, the family was recognisably rentier by the 1830s. 'Passive capital' does not necessarily imply lack of interest: as Smith demonstrates, Edward Lascelles launched a major audit into the unsatisfactory returns of his estates in 1799.[15] The bulk of annuitants and financial dependents other than owners, however, were truly remote from the management of the underlying estates.

This study has also segregated within 'passive capital' on the one hand the larger rentier-owners, who typically owned the estates to which the enslaved were attached as well as the enslaved themselves, and on the other the smaller-scale rentier-owners, who typically owned between one and ten enslaved people but held no land in the colonies. The study has used a division of the claims between those above £500 and those below £500 to differentiate between large-scale and small-scale, but the distinction is not clear-cut: some 'small-scale' dependents in Britain with claims below £500 held legacies or annuities secured on underlying estates in the colonies, or owned coffee or pimento estates with smaller workforces than characterised sugar-plantations.[16]

The final differentiation is within Britain by geography. Slave-owners, whether merchants or large or small-scale rentiers, have been characterised in the analysis below by geography, attributed for example as belonging to 'London' or 'Bristol'. This is probably the least rigorous category of analysis. Ambiguities inevitably arise: a few in the case of merchants with ties and presences in two or more financial communities, but more with large-scale rentiers, many of whom had both London and country addresses. Compounding these methodological difficulties in determining regional locations of individual slave-owners is the presence in many claims of agents or intermediaries acting on behalf of the beneficial owners. Very little detail may be disclosed for these beneficial owners beyond their names and sufficient indication of metropolitan British status to enable their classification as absentees, and secondary sources do not always provide reliable evidence of the owners' addresses within Britain, especially in the case of women beneficiaries. While the conclusions presented below for the geography of mercantile claimants are robust, the mapping *within* Britain of the rentier claimants at this stage should thus be regarded as indicative.

There has long been recognition that, as a result of the presence of intermediary agents, the Parliamentary Return detailing payments

---

[15] *Ibid.*, pp. 229–30. See also the discussion of absentee owners as progressive if distant managers, in W. A. Green, 'The planter class and British West Indian sugar production, before and after Emancipation', *Economic History Review*, NS 26.3 (1973), 448–63.

[16] See below, pp. 147–148 for further discussion of the £500 cut-off.

by the Commission does not tell the whole story of the compensation because the recipient of the compensation cannot be assumed to
have been the beneficiary.[17] Separation of beneficiary from recipient
could arise in one of two ways. The first was if the recipient named
in the Return were acting not on his or her own account, but as trustee or executor for unrelated beneficiaries. Certainly, as noted in the
Introduction, the Parliamentary Return lists have recently misled the
Synod of the Church of England about Henry Phillpotts, the Bishop
of Exeter.[18] However, as this example indicates, the records of the
Commission underlying the highly summary Return data do frequently
clarify the nature of the recipients' roles. In principle, the claim forms
issued and recorded by the Commission required claimants to state the
capacity in which they acted, and in the bulk of cases they did, together
with some indication of the beneficiary (as in the example of the Bishop
of Exeter). In general, the more contested a claim, the more information as to the claimants, the beneficiaries and their background is present in the Commission archives.

The second and potentially more material reservation has been over
'mercantile interception', the suspicion that metropolitan merchants
had, as creditors, appropriated compensation that nominally had
been awarded to a proprietor. Pares expressed the concern in analysing the Parliamentary Return that 'the compensation ... paid directly
to the factors [i.e. metropolitan merchants] was only the visible part of
the iceberg; beneath the surface the factors obtained, in payment of
their due, the compensation money of many planters who ostensibly
received it themselves'.[19] But the underlying records of the Commission,
including the ledgers of the National Debt Office (NDO) recording
the signatures of those who actually *collected* the compensation money,
suggest that such interception – which undoubtedly occurred – generally left traces. In almost all instances where the secondary literature identifies 'mercantile interception' based on family and business

---

[17] Unfortunately, the mode of payment does not allow dogmatical assertions reinforced
by statistical proof [as to who benefited from compensation] ... Only a wearisome
inspection of each claim could prove whether the payment passed to the colonies or
remained in England; and the regulation which permitted the transfer of the money
to an agent armed with a Power of Attorney, and insisted that all payments should
be made in England, would render even that unprofitable. (R. E. P. Wastell, 'The
history of slave compensation 1833 to 1845', M.A. thesis, London University, 1933,
pp. 145–6.

[18] For Phillpotts and church reform, see A. Burns, *The diocesan revival in the Church of
England c. 1800–1870* (Oxford: Clarendon Press, 1999), pp. 168–73, 180–4.

[19] R. Pares, 'Merchants and planters', *Economic History Review*, Supplement 4 (Cambridge:
Cambridge University Press, 1960), p. 49.

papers or official colonial mortgage records, there are indications in the Slave Compensation records. For example, Pares identified that Peter Huggins, 'who received his own compensation', discharged his debts to the Pinneys after receiving £10,000 in compensation.[20] While the Parliamentary Return does indeed show Huggins as the recipient for four awards on Nevis, the underlying records show first that Charles Pinney counter-claimed as mortgagee, second that he withdrew the counter-claim and third that he collected the payments at the NDO.[21] Again, Butler, using colonial mortgage records, highlighted the award of compensation for the Clermont estate in Barbados (despite a counter-claim by the Liverpool mortgagees Barton, Irlam & Higginson) to Charles Bradford [sic] Lane, 'who almost immediately transferred his compensation to the merchants in partial repayment of his debt'.[22] The Commission records show the counter-claim by the mortgagees, the award to Lane, and a note that Lane was willing to admit the counter-claim.[23] Based on the consistency of such evidence, in awards under which a merchant had filed a counter-claim against a proprietor and then dropped that counter-claim, but had nevertheless physically collected the compensation or recorded an agreement with the slave-owner, there are such strong grounds for suspecting mercantile interception that such cases have been categorised in the analysis below as 'mercantile'.

What the analysis of the records cannot capture are cases where merchant and proprietor simply settled privately: but the whole structure of the compensation process, in which owners might simply fail to meet their obligations to creditors or unexpected counter-claims could come from any direction to challenge an owner's or creditor's right to compensation, suggests that few merchant-creditors with material financial exposure to an owner would refrain from filing a counter-claim as a matter of course. Only one clear case of such a 'gentleman's agreement', leaving no traces in the Commission records, has been found in the secondary literature: that of John Gale Vidal, indebted to the London merchant firm of W., R. & S. Mitchell for the compensation on Shenton in St Thomas-in-the-Vale. Vidal, however, had a close relationship with the Mitchells as their local attorney.[24]

[20] *Ibid.*, p. 317.
[21] See T71/882, Nevis claims Nos. 133–6 for Huggins's awards on the Clarke's, Mountravers, Scarbrough's and Parris estates for a total of £8,541 5s 3d for 474 slaves; NDO4/9 for Chas Pinney of Pinney & Chase's signature for these awards.
[22] K. M. Butler, *The economics of Emancipation: Jamaica and Barbados, 1823–1843* (Chapel Hill: University of North Carolina Press, 1995), p. 61.
[23] T71/895, Barbados No. 488. Letter from John Hopton Forbes to Commission, T71/1280, 18 May 1836.
[24] Butler, *The economics of Emancipation*, pp. 59–60.

Altogether, sixty-three cases of mercantile interception have been identified, amounting to a total of £272,823 in compensation. This is without doubt an under-accounting, but the foregoing suggests that the margin of error is unlikely to be so material as to distort the conclusions presented below.[25]

Composition of slave-owners

The start-point for this study has been a database constructed initially by computerising the Parliamentary Return data for just over 30,000 awards for the West Indies and Caribbean, excluding Bermuda and the Bahamas. The database has then been significantly expanded by a series of further steps. First, the awards made after 1838 (and therefore excluded from the Return) have been identified from the various Registers of Claims and incorporated. Second, the Registers of Claims have also been used to identify the names of the estates involved in the major claims and, critically, the *capacity* in which the awardees acted (whether as owners, mortgagees, trustees, executors or administrators). Third, the records of the NDO have been used to identify who physically visited it to sign for and collect the compensation.

For the purposes of further analysis, the 30,000 awards to owners of the enslaved in the colonies analysed in this study have then been divided into two size categories: awards of £500 and above, and those below £500. Because of variable values for the enslaved between different colonies, an award for £500 covers different numbers of enslaved, from eight or nine in British Guiana to twenty to twenty-five in Jamaica and thirty-five in Antigua. A single monetary cut-off has nevertheless been used because the focus of the work is on the flow of monetary compensation to (metropolitan) owners: care should be taken in reaching conclusions about the comparative structure of the slave-economy *in the colonies* from differences in monetary awards. The £500 threshold was selected as a level that on the one hand captured over 80 per cent of the total compensation and on the other produced a manageable population of awards for comprehensive claim-by-claim research. In aggregate, as is widely recognised, the majority of *slave-owners* owned only a handful of slaves: 18,000 of the awards went to owners of fewer

---

[25] Of the dozen or so cases described by Butler of compensation being applied to reduce mortgage debts (*ibid.*, pp. 44–73), all but the Vidal case are either precisely portrayed, or are identifiable as mercantile interception, in the Commission records. Analysis of the top twenty-five merchant recipients of compensation (Appendix 15) shows nine cases of suspected mercantile interception in addition to thirty-four confirmed cases, suggesting the under-counting may be by 20 per cent.

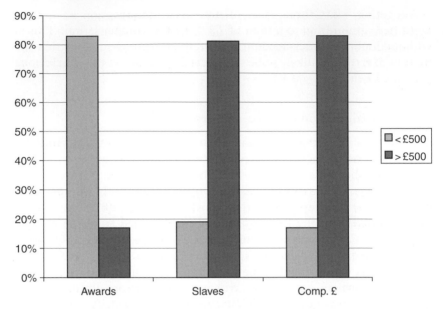

Figure 4.1   Composition of awards by size (above or below £500 per award).

than five enslaved, and therefore fall into the second category, of awards below £500. The overwhelming majority of these small-scale owners of enslaved were resident in the colonies, largely urban owners of enslaved men and women engaged as domestic servants or in other areas of the service economy. Conversely, the majority of the *enslaved* were held on sizeable production units of fifty or more enslaved people, and fall into the first category of award. Hence, the 5,044 awards above £500 accounted for only one-sixth of the total number of awards but five-sixths of the total number of enslaved and of the compensation money awarded (Figure 4.1). The conclusions of this study would not be materially impacted had *all* the awards been systematically analysed, because the smaller awards were overwhelmingly resident. A higher cut-off set by a common number of slaves (for example, twenty-five or fifty) or by a higher common monetary amount would have increased the perceived ratio of absentees in the whole, because it would have excluded the 'tail' of resident slave-owners now captured by the £500 cut-off.

For the 5,044 major claims above £500, a comprehensive attempt has been made to identify the awardee and (where different) the benefici-ary, and to classify them by sex, status (resident or absentee, merchant or rentier) and geography.[26] This identification and classification has again drawn on the Register of Claims (which somewhat inconsistently provides addresses and descriptions of the awardees), and on other parts of the Slave Compensation Records, notably the original claims and counter-claims and the letter-books of the Commission, but also on a wide range of other primary and secondary sources. For awards below £500, no such systematic effort has been made to identify the slave-owners behind the 25,000 such awards. Instead data have been recorded where the Commission records allow ready identification of absentees, or where the research on claims above £500 has identified individuals who were also involved in claims below £500.[27]

Of 4,730 contested and uncontested awards over £500 (not including the Chancery and List E cases), the recipients in 4,543 (96 per cent), accounting for 98 per cent of the monetary compensation paid on such awards over £500 (and 80 per cent of the overall monetary compensation), have been positively identified from the Commission records, from other primary sources or from secondary sources, so that the individuals named as recipients are known to be resident or absentee, and their function (whether owner, mortgagee, trustee, executor) is known (Table 4.2).[28] In the vast majority of cases in which claimants were acting as trustees or executors, the underlying beneficiaries have also been identified.

The unidentified claimants are not concentrated disproportionately in any one colony, but are most numerous in Jamaica, British Guiana and Trinidad. In the latter two, the unidentified are generally holders of a relatively small number of slaves (ten to twenty) and/or appear to be slave-owners of Dutch, French or Spanish origin, whose economic and social position, whether resident or absentee, falls outside the main thrust of this analysis. In the case of Jamaica, the unidentified are disproportionately women – for whom naming practices, limited active involvement in economic enterprise and lack of access to public office make identification more difficult. There is also likely to be a disproportionate number of 'free coloureds' living in the colonies amongst

---

[26] In 314 of the 5,044 awards above £500, the compensation was paid into suits in Chancery in England or in colonial courts (so-called 'List E' awards), so that only the parties to the suits, not the eventual recipients of the compensation, are captured in the Commission records. These Chancery and List E claims are dealt with separately in the analysis and discussed on pp. 150–151 below.

[27] Recipients have been identified in 2,638 awards below £500.

[28] The data in this study supersede the preliminary figures published in N. Draper, ' "Possessing slaves": ownership, compensation and metropolitan society in Britain at the time of Emancipation 1834–40', History Workshop Journal, 64 (Autumn 2007), 74–102. The revisions are not material to the conclusions presented in that article.

Table 4.2 *Awards over £500 and identification rates.*

	Awards > £500, A	Of which: Chancery, B	List E, C	Contested and un-contested awards > £500, D = A – (B + C)	Iden-tified contested and un-contested awards > £500	% identi-fied con-tested and uncontest-ed awards > £500 by value
Anguilla	16	0	0	16	13	81
Antigua	161	5	5	151	149	99
Barbados	578	1	8	569	563	99
British Guiana	646	2	15	629	605	96
Dominica	143	1	0	142	136	96
Grenada	170	8	1	161	146	91
Honduras	43	0	0	43	36	84
Jamaica	2,267	99	111	2,057	1,978	96
Montserrat	45	3	0	42	39	93
Nevis	65	1	8	56	53	95
St Kitts	114	11	2	101	98	97
St Lucia	131	0	5	126	126	100
St Vincent	147	4	8	135	129	96
Tobago	84	7	0	77	73	95
Trinidad	406	0	2	404	378	94
Virgin Islands	28	2	5	21	21	100
Total	**5,044**	**144**	**170**	**4,730**	**4,543**	**96**

this group of unidentified holders, again because their limited access to public office precludes their ready identification. Of all these omissions, it is likely to be that of women that leads to modest systematic under-counting of the proportion of 'British' slave-owners.

The parties to the litigation have been identified in 90 per cent of the 144 awards over £500 made into Chancery suits in Britain. These suits in many cases continued into the 1850s or beyond, and the ultim-ate beneficiaries of the compensation cannot be determined without a systematic examination of the Chancery records case-by-case. It is possible to conclude, however, that these Chancery cases, predictably, were largely contested amongst absentee slave-owners and creditors. No Chancery suits have been found that involved only colonial resi-dents on both sides, while approximately 10 per cent appear to have been between absentees and residents. Similarly, the parties to litiga-tion in the colonial courts have been identified in 86 per cent of the

170 List E awards above £500. Fourteen of these cases appear to have involved only absentees and thirty-three only residents; the bulk pitted residents against absentees. Again, without scrutiny of the colonial court records it is not possible to identify the ultimately successful party in these cases.[29]

Absentee slave-owners

Of the 4,730 awards over £500 (excluding the Chancery and List E cases), 2,086 have been positively identified as absentees. Because absentees predictably held a disproportionate share of larger production units – i.e. the estates – these absentee awards represent almost two-thirds of the compensation paid on claims above £500. Again, there is significant variation by colony (Table 4.3).

The grouping of colonies in Table 4.3 by chronology of settlement (which follows Higman's classification) tends to suggest a correlation between the passage of time and the level of absenteeism.[30] But there are exceptions. As has been recognised, Barbados was an atypical colonial slave society, with a majority of resident slave-owners. Very high levels of absenteeism are shown for the other original sugar-colonies, and for those seized in 1763 with the exception of Dominica. By contrast, the newer territories of St Lucia and Trinidad, where British rule was overlaid on pre-existing francophone or Hispanic planter communities, which typically were more inclined to residency than British slave-owners, have lower rates of absenteeism. Of St Lucia in the mid 1820s, Henry Nelson Coleridge said 'at present, it is a British colony in little more than name. The religion is Romish, and the spirit of its ministers bigoted and intractable. The people are French in language, manners and feelings.'[31]

British Guiana has a relatively low 'simple' rate of absenteeism, but the absentees owned very large-scale production units, so based on the proportion of the enslaved and the value of compensation attributable

---

[29] It is probably reasonable to estimate that between 80 and 100 per cent of the compensation in Chancery awards, and between 40 and 60 per cent in List E colonial court awards, ultimately passed directly to absentees.

[30] Higman, *Slave populations in the British Caribbean 1807–34* (Baltimore: Johns Hopkins University Press, 1984), pp. 50–71. The '1st phase' colonies are those settled by Britain in the seventeenth century (other than non-sugar marginal economies), '2nd phase' are former French possessions seized in 1763 and '3rd phase' are colonies finally seized by Britain during or after the Napoleonic Wars.

[31] [H. N. Coleridge], *Six months in the West Indies in 1825* (London: John Murray, 1825), p. 130.

Table 4.3 *Absentee claims over £500.*

	Contested and uncontested awards > £500	Absentee awards > £500	% absentee rate by number ('simple' absentee rate)	% absentee rate by value ('economic' absentee rate)
1st-phase sugar-colonies				
Antigua	151	120	79	85
Barbados	569	134	24	38
Montserrat	42	31	74	85
Nevis	56	39	70	77
St Kitts	101	84	83	89
Virgin Islands	21	11	53	73
Jamaica	2,057	956	46	66
2nd-phase sugar-colonies				
Dominica	142	40	28	38
Grenada	161	101	63	81
St Vincent	135	82	61	80
Tobago	77	71	92	98
3rd-phase sugar-colonies				
British Guiana	629	264	42	70
St Lucia	126	19	15	22
Trinidad	404	134	33	44
1st-phase marginal colonies				
Anguilla	16	0	0	0
Honduras	43	0	0	0
Overall	**4,730**	**2,086**	**44**	**65**

to British slave-owners, it was economically an absentee society. The 'simple' rate of absenteeism below 50 per cent and the economic rate of 66 per cent for larger claims for Jamaica appear low relative to estimates as high as 85 per cent that have gained currency; but the £500 cut-off (equivalent in Jamaica, as noted, to between 20 and 25 slaves) is lower than thresholds generally applied by other historians who, in seeking to isolate the 'plantation economy', look at larger units. Of the 939 awards for more than 100 slaves found in the Commission records for Jamaica (equivalent to compensation of around £2,000), 615 went to absentees (and one to a US absentee and one to a 'Transatlantic' owner), while a further 83 went into Chancery suits in Britain, implying overall absenteeism for these large estates of at least 75 per cent, consistent with other analyses of nineteenth-century Jamaican absenteeism.[32]

---

[32] B. W. Higman, *Plantation Jamaica 1750–1850: capital and control in a colonial economy* (Mona, Jamaica: University of the West Indies Press, 2005), p. 18: 'In 1832 ... 54 per

For the smaller and far more numerous claims below £500, systematic work has not been undertaken claim-by-claim, but the records of the Commission, especially the letter-books, have been used to identify absentee British slave-owners amongst the claimants, while claims for less than £500 have also been traced for those identified as absentees and residents by the work on claims above £500. Just over 1000 awards amongst the claims below £500 have been identified as going to absentees. Many of these smaller awards bring rich anecdotal material with them, but the aggregate quantitative impact is small: the compensation to identified absentees in awards below £500 in aggregate amounts to around £150,000, or around 1 per cent of the total compensation paid for the Caribbean colonies (see Figure 4.2).

As noted above, not all the absentees were British or lived in Britain. The British government paid over £400,000 to 'foreign' absentees, overwhelmingly Dutch with continuing interest in the slaves of British Guiana (see Table 4.4). It is striking how few owners of the enslaved in British Caribbean colonies lived elsewhere in the Caribbean. The notion of 'networks of Empire' has limited relevance to the structure of slave-ownership. There was some movement of slave-owners and slaves between the colonies, notably from Barbados to Trinidad, but in general the 'hub and spoke' model, with Britain at its centre, is the more convincing account of the relationships between metropole and colony. Many of those with interests in the West Indies were also involved in colonisation projects in Australasia or Canada: but almost invariably their connections were mediated through London, not made directly between colonies. Power – political power, economic power, information – was concentrated in the metropolis in the slave-compensation process, even though that process itself undoubtedly embraced metropole and colony in the same frame.

It is also worth noting that as far as the immediate impact *on Britain* was concerned, the flows of compensation to absentees from slaves in British Guiana approached those from Jamaica (over £2.5 million versus £4 million), each of which exceeded the combined flow from all the other colonies together. The compensation from Trinidad was not that far short of Barbados (£450,000 versus £600,000). Assessments of the end of slavery that depend on the traditional historiography of Jamaica and Barbados risk missing almost half the picture.

cent of the enslaved lived on properties owned by absentees, almost all of them outside Jamaica. Of the dominant sugar estates, 81 per cent belonged to non-resident proprietors.' Absenteeism in the 1830s varied substantially within Jamaica by parish, ranging from 41 per cent of claims over £500 in St Andrew to 87 per cent in Trelawny.

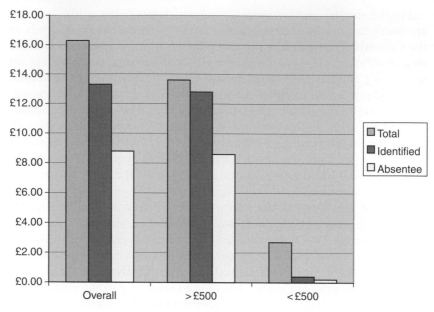

Figure 4.2   Overall distribution of awards (£ millions).

Table 4.4   *Absentee awards by area of residence.*

	Number of claims				
	> £500	< £500	Total	Slaves	Compensation (£)
Britain and Ireland	1,986	911	2,897	314,058	7,741,824
'Foreign'	57	18	75	8,182	402,728
USA	7	15	22	866	18,216
'West Indian'	5	35	40	482	14,654
Transatlantic	31	53	84	3,770	115,309
Total	**2,086**	**1,032**	**3,118**	**327,358**	**8,292,731**

Slave-owning was overwhelmingly a commercial or an individual undertaking: the recipients of compensations were partners in mercantile enterprises and banks, or were private individuals. There are very few institutions or public organisations evident as slave-owners in the Compensation records. One famous exception, of course, was the Society for the Propagation of the Gospel in Foreign Parts: its Treasurer, John Heywood Markland (who also served as Secretary of the West India Committee in 1832), was awarded £8,558 2s 2d for the

410 enslaved on the Society's Codrington estate in Barbados.[33] Local colonial charities and institutions such as workhouses were awarded compensation money in a small number of claims.[34] In Trinidad, the Crown itself pursued slave-compensation for the arrears of taxes of slave-owners.[35] The British state does not otherwise appear as an owner in the Compensation records: the enslaved it used as 'Pioneers' in military support roles appear in general to have been hired rather than owned.[36] In Britain, a handful of other institutions appear in the compensation process. The Minister and Elders of Kilmarnock lodged a counter-claim for the compensation for fifty-two slaves on the Down Castle estate in Trelawny, as legatees for £332 under the will of the former owner Thomas Paterson.[37] The Commissioners of Greenwich Hospital were involved in a number of claims that went to Chancery in the suit of *Pratt* v. *Willis*, and the Hospital had owned the Golden Vale estate in Jamaica between 1793 and 1811.[38] But in general, the linkage between slave-ownership and British public institutions was indirect: slave-owners subscribed funding to institutions, rather than the institutions owning slaves directly.[39]

The importance of the metropolitan merchants in the compensation process has long been recognised. The data suggest, however, that their relative importance has also been overstated. A claim-by-claim analysis, including cases of suspected 'mercantile interception', shows that just under £4 million of the compensation from the West India colonies flowed to merchants in the metropolis, representing one-quarter of the total compensation and just under one-third of the identified compensation (see Table 4.5). Absentee rentiers – those without mercantile involvement who nevertheless drew on the slave-economy for the profits of direct ownership or for legacies, annuities and mortgages – account for the same proportion of the compensation as the merchants. This suggests a different pattern than that previously accepted for metropolitan ownership of the enslaved, and raises questions as to how such ownership fitted with British society in its abolitionist moment.

---

[33] T71/899, Barbados No. 4215.

[34] See for example the award of some £5,500 for 283 slaves on the Knockpatrick Estate to six residents identified as the Commissioners of Munro and Dickenson's Charity; T71/860, Manchester No. 95.

[35] See for example T71/894, Trinidad No. 1426, which records a counter-claim from 'HM the King as judgement creditor' and for which George Baillie was awarded £88 11s 6d for 'the use of Her Majesty'.

[36] See below, pp. 175–176 for the example of enslaved 'Pioneers' in Jamaica.

[37] T71/874, Trelawny No. 395.

[38] For the Commissioners of Greenwich Hospital, see for example T71/853, St Dorothy No. 123.

[39] See the further discussion below, Chapters 5 and 6.

Table 4.5   *British rentier versus British merchant absentees.*

	Claims > £500		Claims < £500		Total	
	Number	Value	Number	Value	Number	Value
Rentiers	1,043	£3,852,474	491	£75,755	1,534	£3,928,229
Merchants	916	£3,700,645	313	£56,279	1,229	£3,756,924
Total	**1,959**	**£7,553,119**	**804**	**£132,034**	**2,897**	**£7,685,153**
(Unassigned)	(27)	–	(107)	–	(134)	(£56,671)

Excludes Chancery and List E awards and 'Transatlantic' owners; includes identified 'mercantile interception'.

Political dimensions of British slave-ownership

The 3,000 or so British absentee awards (of which around one-third were contested) involved perhaps some 10,000 claimants in metropolitan society in different capacities (assuming an average of 2.5 claimants for each successful uncontested award, and 5 individuals each on average as successful and unsuccessful claimants in the generally more complex contested awards).[40] The absolute number of absentees thus remains small: the population of Great Britain and Ireland after all was 26.6 million in 1841. But the absentees were concentrated socially and geographically, and, it is argued, had significance beyond their numbers.

For example, over 100 MPs who sat in Parliament between 1820 and 1835 have been identified in the records of the Compensation Commission, of whom over three-quarters were owners and the remainder trustees or executors.[41] Higman placed the 'West India interest' in the unreformed Parliament of 1831 as thirty-one MPs, falling to nineteen in the Commons of 1833.[42] The analysis of the compensation data, however, suggests that fifty MPs in 1831 and forty-two in 1833 had a sufficient direct interest in slavery to be personally part of the compensation process. This analysis takes no account of spokesmen in the House of Commons for the West India interest who had no

---

[40] The proportion of absentee awards that were contested ranged from below one-fifth in St James or Hanover, to one-quarter in Barbados and British Guiana, to over half in St Kitts and Antigua. The average number of individuals per award is based on a random sample of thirty-two uncontested claims and twenty-seven contested claims from three colonies (Antigua, Tobago and Trinidad) and two parishes within Jamaica (Vere and Trelawny). No account is taken of Lobdell's 'net versus gross' calculation.

[41] See Appendix 1.

[42] Higman identified a total of ninety-one 'West India' MPs over the whole period from 1807 to 1833; Higman, 'The West India interest', pp. 3–4.

direct stake in slavery by 1833, such as Sir Richard Vyvyan or Richard Hart Davis. Nor does it take account of family relationships, such as Christopher Bethell Codrington's son, who sat for Gloucestershire in 1833 and 1835, or W. S. S. Lascelles and Henry Lascelles, one of whom sat for Northallerton in every Parliament from 1820 to 1835.

Even amongst MPs for the new industrial areas, linkages to the slave-economy occur, although in general in the geography of British slave-owning it is noteworthy how few slave-owners came from the manufacturing areas of Yorkshire, the West Midlands or, apart from Liverpool and its hinterland, from Lancashire. Nevertheless, William Feilden, the MP for Blackburn, filed a counter-claim alongside his wife (the daughter of the slave-owner Catherine Haughton-Jackson) for a moiety of three legacies of £6000 currency each under the 1792 will of Mary James secured on Burnt Ground Pen and its slaves in Hanover.[43]

It should also be noted that there was not invariably a direct 'read across' from slave-owning to anti-abolitionism (or indeed to wider anti-Reform reaction) amongst the MPs benefiting from compensation. In many cases, of course, there was: the bulk of the slave-owning MPs were seen as Tory enemies of Reform. *The Times*, in examining the list of those attending the City meeting of the West India interest of 29 May 1833, came to the conclusion that this was a group characterised by party-political loyalties.

We find the names of very few who either are not generally staunch Tories, or who would not resolutely oppose the existing Administration on any other given question as well as on that of West Indian slavery. We may therefore conclude, that in fact a political as much as a colonial object brought them together, and determined their united movements. In support of this inference, need we mention the political bias of the noble chairman [the Earl of Harewood], who is resolved never to honour the House of Lords with his presence because it submitted to the public dictation in passing the Reform bill? Need we mention the party of Lord Combermere, of Lord Selkirk, of Lord Colville, of Lord Saltoun, of Admiral Sir B. Martin, of Sir J. Reed, of Sir Alexander Grant, of Sir R. Vyvyan, of Mr Irving, or of various other gentlemen whose names are inserted in the different reports of the meeting?[44]

To these could be added slave-owners who served as Tory ministers, such as Henry Goulburn. However, *The Times* did note exceptions to its classification of the attendees, such as Sir Michael Shaw Stewart, MP for Renfrewshire, and said 'these either supported their own colonial

[43] T71/1212, Counter-claim on Hanover No. 19. The award was made in the name of Philip Haughton James, with whom Feilden and his wife had counter-claimed.
[44] Leader, *The Times*, 29 May 1833, p. 2.

interests, or represented constituents so deeply involved in colonial property or prejudice, as to detach them, on this occasion, from their usual liberal principles of action'. While slave-owning was predictably associated by many of its critics with a reactionary Toryism, in fact, slave-owning spanned a political spectrum significantly broader than the Tory party. The Whig organiser and colonial entrepreneur Edward Ellice was awarded slave-compensation in Jamaica. The reformer and radical MP Joseph Hume, married to the sister of the Trinidad slave-owner William Hardin Burnley, drew criticism for his qualified anti-slavery and his espousal of the cause of compensation for slave-owners.[45] 'Not a few of them [the West India proprietors in Parliament]', acknowledged the *ASR* in 1825, 'are the strenuous advocates of popular rights, and the sworn enemies to oppression, at least in Europe'.[46]

In support of this, surprisingly few slave-owning MPs appeared amongst the 'Ultras' in revolt against Wellington's administration. Of seventy-six Ultras in the Commons, only seven appear in the Slave Compensation records, roughly in line with the proportion of slave-related MPs in the House as a whole.[47] A higher proportion of Canningites who joined or supported the government were slave-owners.[48] Of 161 Whig MPs identified by Jupp in the 1828–9 period, 6 were slave-owners and 6 more appear in the Compensation records in capacities other than owner.[49] In 1826, slave-owners appeared in roughly equal numbers on both sides of the vote on Lord John Russell's

[45] See the letter of Joseph Hume in *The Times*, 3 January 1833, p. 3, in which Hume published also correspondence of his opponents 'Candidus' and Sandford Arnot. Arnot had alleged that Hume, through his wife, was heir-at-law to slave-property, and 'Candidus' wrote of 'the pain of seeing the advocate of liberty all over the world the stickler for slavery in one corner of it'.

[46] *ASR* No. 6 (November 1825), Vol. 1, p. 52.

[47] P. Jupp, *British politics on the eve of reform: the Duke of Wellington's administration 1828–30* (London: Macmillan, 1998), Chapter 7, Appendix 4, pp. 314–15. The seven comprise: two of Jupp's twenty-four 'Group 1' Ultras in the Commons (Henry Bright and Charles Nicholas Pallmer); none of the twenty 'Group 2' (violent Ultras or moderate Ultras who voted against the government on three or more occasions); three of the seventeen 'Group 3' moderate Ultras (Neill Malcolm, P. J. Miles and Sir George Rose); and two of Jupp's fifteen 'Group 4', MPs who were at one stage linked with the Ultras but who became friends of the government in the 1830 session (Henry Dawkins and George Watson Taylor).

[48] *Ibid.*, Chapter 7, Appendix 1, pp. 312–13. Of ten Canningite peers, three (De Walden, Dudley and Seaford) were slave-owners; of twenty-three Canningite MPs, four (W. R. K. Douglas, A. F. Ellis, W. Lascelles and Sir James Scarlett) were slave-owners or the heirs of slave-owners.

[49] *Ibid.*, Chapter 7, Appendix 7: the slave-owners were Ralph Bernal, G. Byng, R. Gordon, Lord W. Powlett, E. Protheroe and A.W. Robarts. W. J. Denison, Sir R. Heron and four Barings also appear in the Compensation records as agents, trustee and mortgagees respectively.

resolutions against bribery at the elections.[50] Of the fifty MPs in the 1831–2 Parliament identified in the Slave Compensation records, fewer than half (twenty-two) appear in the minority opposing the second reading of the Reform Bill on 17 December 1831.[51]

So slave-owning, although concentrated in the Tory interest, crossed the spectrum of British politics. Even on the question of Emancipation itself there was not a uniform view amongst the slave-owning MPs. Lord Holland placed a partisan interpretation on the 'party of West Indians, tremendously numerous and attended by respectable classes and individuals, which shewed a very hostile and formidable spirit against our plan [of Emancipation] and our Ministry' in April 1833.[52] The Holland House Whigs included amongst their younger members abolitionists such as Viscount Howick, but they were led, of course, by a slave-owner in Lord Holland himself and included Richard 'Conversation' Sharp, the society wit and for many years the partner of Samuel Boddington in the West India merchants Boddington, Philips & Sharp. Both Boddington and Sharp were members of the King of Clubs, and both served (Boddington very briefly) as MPs. Holland occupied a profoundly ambivalent position as an ameliorationist absentee slave-owner, rupturing with Wilberforce in 1823 over Holland's refusal to commit to the 'gradual extinction of slavery', and assuming membership of the Standing Committee of the West India proprietors in April of the same year.[53]

Edward Protheroe Jr and James Evan Baillie split the Whig vote in Bristol in 1830, Protheroe running on an abolitionist platform and Baillie contesting as the anti-abolitionist candidate of the West India merchants. But in 1831, the two combined forces on a pro-Reform platform to fight the Tory (and anti-abolitionist) Richard Hart Davis. In contesting Liverpool in 1830, William Ewart embraced the need for immediate steps towards abolition; and during the period of Apprenticeship in 1837, in contesting Lyme Regis the supporters of William Pinney (the son of John Frederick Pinney, a major slave-owner

---

[50] 'List of sixty-two', *The Times*, 27 May 1826, p. 3. Of sixty-two voting for, six were slave-owners (R. Bernal, H. Bright, E. Ellice, Hon. W. J. Powlett, A. W. Robarts, J. Scarlett) and of fifty-nine voting against, six (James Blair, W. R. K. Douglas, J. R. Grosett, Sir G. F. Hill, J. Irvine, John Plummer) were slave-owners, as was one of the two Tellers (Goulburn), while Wilbraham Egerton appears in the Compensation records as a trustee.

[51] 'List of the Minority on the second reading of the Reform Bill', *The Times*, 22 December 1831, p. 2.

[52] Lord Holland *et al.*, *The Holland House Diaries 1831–40*, ed. A. D. Kriegel (London: Routledge, 1977), entry for 27 April 1833, p. 212.

[53] V. E. Chancellor, 'Slave-owner and anti-slaver: Henry Richard Vassall Fox, 3rd Lord Holland 1800–40', *Slavery & Abolition*, 1.3 (December 1980), 263–75 (pp. 264–6).

and recipient of compensation) ran a ferocious anti-slavery campaign against Renn Hampden, the Barbadian slave-owner. In most such cases, pro-abolition sentiment by those tied to the slave-economy went hand-in-hand with consistent demands for compensation, but according to Gross, Alexander Baring, the retired senior partner of Baring Brothers, actually voted against compensation in 1833.[54]

Religious dimensions of slave-ownership

Strong evidence of Anglicanism runs through the compensation recipients, both merchants and rentiers. Almost 150 Anglican clergy-men in Britain and Ireland appear in the Compensation Commission records.[55] Many, predictably, were serving as trustees and to a lesser extent as executors, but more were slave-owners or other beneficiaries. In the context of almost 10,000 livings in England, this is not a large number: only 1 per cent of Church of England clergymen were involved directly. Nevertheless, ownership again was concentrated in particular sub-groups, and slave-owners were prominent in institutions representing a newly re-assertive Anglicanism.[56] British slave-owners predictably were the backbone of the Society for the Conversion, Religious Instruction and Education of Negro Slaves, re-animated, as the *ASR* bitterly remarked, only when abolitionist sentiment returned in 1823.[57] But away from direct involvement in the West India slave-economy, the subscription lists for the Anglican King's College London contain multiple slave-owners: 15 of 111 initial donors of £50 to £100 in 1828 later collected slave-compensation.[58]

---

[54] For Protheroe, see P. Marshall, *Bristol and the abolition of slavery: the politics of eman-cipation* (Bristol: Bristol Branch of the Historical Association, 1975); for William Ewart, see *The poll for an election of an MP for the Borough of Liverpool, taken between Wm Ewart and J. E. Denison, to which are added history of the election etc.* (Liverpool: J. Gore, 1830). For the Lyme Regis campaign, see the leaflets from the Pinney Papers exhibited online at PortCities Bristol, www.discoveringbristol.org.uk. For Baring, see I. Gross, 'The abolition of Negro slavery and British parliamentary politics 1832–3', *Historical Journal*, 23.1 (March 1980), 63–85 (p. 79). I am sceptical of Gross's claim, since compensation was not put to a separate vote outside the context of the Abolition Act: it was presumably the Act as a whole against which Baring voted.

[55] Another forty or so colonial clergy appear in the records, most as beneficiaries. See Appendices 5 and 6 for the absentee clergymen.

[56] See Burns, *The diocesan revival*, pp. 1–22 for the argument that the re-assertion of Anglicanism pre-dated the conventionally ascribed timing of the 1840s and 1850s.

[57] Two-thirds of the subscribers to the Society in the subscription lists of 1823–4 are identifiable as recipients of slave-compensation in the 1830s: *The Times*, 29 July 1823, p. 7 and 25 March 1824, p. 2 show the subscription lists.

[58] Appendix 11.

Again, as with the political spectrum, while the majority of slave-owners could be identified with mainstream Anglicanism, there were exceptions. William Alers Hankey, as seen previously, was a dissenter, Robert Hibbert a Unitarian. H. M. Hyndman's father, John Beckles Hyndman, was a 'really decent Christian and Anglican churchman of the straitest sect of the Low Church variety'. Deeply moved by the death of his sister Catherine 'he deemed it right to expend a very large sum, not less certainly than £150,000, upon building and endowing churches for her memory, the incumbents of which were always to be Anglican Low Churchmen as Low as Low could be'.[59] But overall a close identity with established religion runs through the slave-ownership.

Such allegiances and identities continued beyond Emancipation. When in 1843 the National Society for Promoting the Education of the Poor in the Principles of the Established Church throughout England and Wales established a sub-committee to raise funds for schools in manufacturing and mining districts, 10 of the 100 contributors of £100 and 7 out of 104 donors of £50 in the second appeal had received slave-compensation.[60]

Absentee ownership and the complications of race

Slave-ownership in the colonies was by no means the exclusive preserve of whites, as communities of 'free coloureds' had evolved who were active in commercial and capitalist activities, including the ownership of slaves.[61] Slave-ownership in Britain itself was also impacted by the complexities of race, in a number of different ways. It was an established pattern for male slave-owners who spent extended periods of time in the colonies to father children with enslaved females or with free women of colour. In many cases, the children of such relationships were provided for through transfer of property, including slave-property, by the slave-owner in vivo or by will. A white male slave-owner returning or migrating to Britain might therefore have encumbered his slave-property with annuities and legacies in favour of his 'reputed' children by enslaved or free women of colour. In addition, such children if freed were sometimes brought to Britain to be educated and in some cases to reside

---

[59] H. M. Hyndman, *The record of an adventurous life* (London: Macmillan, 1911), p. 7.
[60] See Appendix 12.
[61] Amongst the extensive literature on the social structure of race and sexuality in the slave colonies, see for example G. Heuman, *Between black and white: race, politics and the free coloureds in Jamaica* (Westport, CT: Greenwood Press, 1981); E. L. Cox, 'The free coloureds and slave emancipation in the British West Indies: the case of St Kitts and Grenada', *Journal of Caribbean History*, 22.1–2 (1988), 68–87; C. K. Brathwaite,

there permanently, in order to keep them away from the consequences of 'mixed blood' in the racially stratified societies that characterised the slave colonies. The records of the Slave Compensation Commission do not allow identification of slave-owners or other claimants by race, so it is not possible to provide a systematic account of slave-ownership by people of colour in Britain. The records do however contain details of absentee slave-owners of colour identified from secondary sources.

One or two of these British slave-owners of colour are well-known. For example, Nathaniel Wells of Piercefield in Monmouthshire, born the son of William Wells of St Kitts and an enslaved woman, Juggy, in St Kitts in 1779, was sent to Britain for his education, inherited the bulk of his father's estate in 1794 and married Harriet Este, only daughter of the chaplain to King George II. Shortly after his wedding, Wells bought the Piercefield estate near Chepstow for £90,000 in 1802, serving as Sheriff of Monmouthshire in 1818 and later as deputy lieutenant. Joseph Farington the painter and diarist described him as 'a West Indian of large fortune, a man of very gentlemanly manners, but so much a man of colour as to be little removed from a Negro'. Wells received £1,400 9s 7d in compensation in 1837 for the eighty-six slaves he owned on the Fahies and Astons estates.[62]

At the other end of the spectrum as far as scale of ownership is concerned, free coloured domestic servants or family companions who accompanied their colonial employers to Britain might well possess slaves. Mary Trepsack, Elizabeth Barrett Browning's 'Treppy', had been brought into the Barrett family in Jamaica by Edward Barrett, Elizabeth's grandfather, then came with the family to England and was an important presence in Elizabeth's early life at Hope End and later in London. Trepsack was awarded £226 17s 10d for eleven slaves she owned on the Barrett family's Cinnamon Hill and Cottage estates in St James.[63] A claimant who appears to have been the servant of a Jamaica returnee Hannah Barnes (herself a slave-owner and recipient of slave-compensation), a free coloured woman named Margaret Taylor, was awarded £29 3s 1d for one enslaved woman, Margaret Taylor Bennett, domiciled in Kingston, of whom Margaret Taylor 'became possessed ... by purchase from the savings alone of her own industry'.[64]

'London Bourne of Barbados 1793–1869', *Slavery & Abolition*, 28.1 (April 2007) 23–40.

[62] 'Nathaniel Wells', *Dictionary of national biography*. T71/879, St Kitts No. 685.

[63] T71/873, St James Nos. 258, 656, where she is given respectively as 'Miss Tripsack England owner-in-fee' and 'Miss Tripsack London owner-in-fee'. The *Jamaica Almanac* for 1831 shows her correctly as Mary Trepsack, owning twelve slaves.

[64] T71/863, Kingston No. 2659; petition received 12 November 1835 from Margaret Taylor, 'a person of colour late of Kingston, Jamaica but now residing at Dawlish

In other cases, the impact in the compensation process of sexual relationships between white slave-owners and women of colour spanned generations. For example, Dugald Campbell, the owner of Salt Spring state in Hanover, had provided in his will (made in London in November 1813 and proved there in 1818) annuities of £100 per annum to the three daughters and the son of Susanna Johnson, secured on the Salt Spring estate. Dugald Campbell was almost certainly the father of these children. In Susanna Johnson's own will, also made in 1813, she described herself as a free woman of colour, and detailed the thirty-one slaves conveyed on trust to the four children by an earlier indenture of July 1803. All four of her children at the time of her will were in London, including Ann Pool Johnson, who was the beneficiary of twelve enslaved under the 1803 deed. The Compensation records of the 1830s show multiple echoes of these relationships. First, the compensation for Salt Spring was subject to a suit in the Jamaican Court of Chancery between the annuitants and the Campbell family. Second, George Johnson (Susanna's son, described as a quadroon in the 1823 Hanover census) was awarded £686 9s 8d for thirty-two slaves on the Cave Valley settlement. Third, trustees for Ann Pool Ritherdon were awarded £274 18s 6d for twelve more slaves on the Cave Valley settlement. She was the daughter of Ann Pool Johnson, Susanna Johnson's daughter, who had married an East India Company civil servant in Britain.[65]

The father of Samuel Jackson Prescod, the abolitionist newspaper editor and leader of the free coloureds of Barbados who was a delegate to the General Anti-slavery Convention in London in 1840, was William Hinds Prescod, an absentee slave-owner living at Alstone Lawn in Cheltenham from around 1820. W. H. Prescod was born in Barbados, studied in England and was admitted to the bar at Middle Temple in 1797, and returned to Barbados to work as attorney to his uncle William Prescod. Between 1806 and 1812, he appears to have had four children by Mary Lydia Smith of Barbados. When William Prescod died in Gower Street in London in 1815, W. H. Prescod became the

in the county of Devon' who came to England 1830 as attendant to a Lady 'with whom she has ever since resided', T71/1607. This appears to refer to Hannah Barnes, the widow of Joseph Barnes of Kingston, who was awarded compensation for nine slaves in Kingston and counter-claimed as annuitant on Cumberland Pen. T71/862, Kingston No. 1856; T71/852, St Catherine No. 502; Hannah Barnes, Barton Cottage, Dawlish to Commissioners, T71/1608, 21 November 1835; Commissioners to Barnes, T71/1592, 11 August 1835.

[65] T71/872, Hanover No. 465 for Salt Spring; T71/872, Hanover No. 477 (George Johnson); Hanover No. 478 (Thomas Knocker, North Naylor Savery and Robert Ritherdon as trustees for Ann Pool Ritherdon); Dugald Campbell's will, PROB 11/1600; Susanna Johnson's will, IRO Spanish Town Wills, Vol. 87, p. 95, both transcribed on www.jamaicafamilysearch.com.

life tenant of his uncle's former estates. At the time of compensation, W. H. Prescod settled 25,000 Dutch guilders in 5 per cent bonds in trust for Mary Lydia Smith and her 4 children. All the children other than Samuel Jackman received compensation for one slave each; W. H. Prescod received compensation for the 122 slaves of which he was owner-in-fee on Barry's, and trustees were awarded the money for the estates on which Prescod was tenant-for-life.[66]

Conclusion

Absentee slave-owners and creditors as a whole received the bulk of the compensation paid by the state, accounting for almost two-thirds of the value of the compensation for the larger claims over £500, and between 55 and perhaps as much as 60 per cent of the total slave-compensation paid in the West Indian and Caribbean colonies.[67] Within these overall figures for absentee awards, British metropolitan absentees, mercantile and rentier, accounted for the vast bulk, and received in aggregate over half the total slave-compensation. Rentier-owners in Britain were as important as merchants amongst the recipients and beneficiaries of slave-compensation. Mercantile interception was less ubiquitous than has been assumed.

It is reasonable to ask whether this overall picture of slave-owning in the 1830s presents a distorted view of the structure of slave-ownership as a result of any major changes of ownership prior to, and perhaps triggered by the prospect of, Emancipation. In other words, were there unusual changes in the pattern of slave-ownership in the prelude to Emancipation, from speculative purchasing activity and from panic-driven selling?[68] Ward argues that the shape and form of compensation

[66] G. O. Phillips, 'Barbadian legacy: the unacknowledged earlier life of William Hinds Prescod', *Cheltenham Local History Society Journal*, 16 (2000), 14–17. T71/900, Barbados No. 5306 for Barry's; T71/896, Barbados Nos. 1763 and 1764, and T71/900, Barbados No. 5245 for Prescod's children. T71/898, Barbados Nos. 3223 and 3225, T71/899, Barbados Nos. 4306 and 4307, and T71/900, Barbados No. 5305 for awards to William Hinds and John Gay Goding as trustees for remainder under the will of William Prescod. W. H. Prescod also served as trustee of the absentee Barbadian slave-owner Ward Cadogan of Brinckburn Priory, Northumberland and Northbrook House, Exeter; T71/899, Barbados Nos. 4726, 4763. See Chapter 5 below, pp. 182–183 for Prescod's travails over his compensation.

[67] £8.29 million identified as paid to absentees; plus between £0.4 and £0.5 million paid into Chancery; plus between £0.2 and £0.3 million List E cases, out of a total of £16.36 million analysed; plus small incremental amounts for undiscovered 'mercantile interception' of awards to residents and undiscovered absentee awards below £500.

[68] This question is distinct from the issue of speculative activity in the compensation process itself, for which evidence certainly exists; see Chapter 7, below, pp. 263–264.

was so uncertain as to discourage speculative activity ahead of the Abolition Act. He contests Craton and Walvin's assertion that Rose Price was acquiring slaves on Worthy Park in Jamaica as a speculation on compensation in 1830, arguing that there was no evidence 'that it was the expectation of compensation which sustained the market for slaves during the last period'.[69] Certainly, the overwhelming impressionistic evidence from the database on compensation is that there was broad continuity of slave-ownership, often over many generations. More rigorous analysis using St James's parish in Jamaica as an example suggests that *voluntary* transfers were relatively rare in the 1820s, but that there was steady turnover in ownership of estates because of mortality.

In the slightly longer run, the evidence from the Slave-Compensation process controverts Ragatz's bald assertion that 'by the 1830s, most of the Caribbean estates were in the hands of new owners'.[70] There clearly is evidence for a shift towards mercantile ownership, but by the 1830s, *pace* Ragatz, there had not been a wholesale transfer of estates from absentees to their metropolitan creditors after the Napoleonic Wars.

Slave-owning in Britain was predominantly an Anglican, Tory phenomenon. But while the typical slave-owner fell into this category, slave-owning transcended religious and political divisions: it flowed and mutated across generations and sexes over time. Overall, the level of slave-ownership and other links to the slave-economy amongst MPs revealed by the Compensation records, significantly higher than previously thought, suggests first that the political influence of slave-owners was probably greater in the 1820s than hitherto believed, and may not have collapsed as completely in the Reformed House of Commons as conventionally assumed. Second, slave-ownership was not a bar, although it was an obstacle, to electoral success, even after 1832. Third, slave-owners were not a homogeneous bloc: but on compensation, their interests had come to be almost entirely aligned by 1833.

[69] J. R. Ward, 'Emancipation and the planter', *Journal of Caribbean History*, 22.1–2 (1988), 116–37 (p. 121).
[70] L. Ragatz, 'Absentee landlordism in the British Caribbean 1750–1833', *Agricultural History*, 5 (1931), 7–24 (p. 12).

5   The large-scale rentier-owners

The large-scale non-mercantile claimants of slave-compensation resident in Britain were typically owners or beneficiaries not only of the enslaved but of the colonial estates to which the enslaved were attached. They were thus absentee land-owners as well as slave-owners, and this dual nature of their property defined many facets of their relationships with slavery.

As discussed earlier, the category of 'rentier' is neither homogeneous nor entirely fixed. Nor is the division of 'large-' and 'small-scale' owners complete: a number of small-scale claimants were minor annuitants or legatees of large-scale colonial estates. Nevertheless, there is value in segregating this grouping of large-scale slave-owners and examining it separately both from the mercantile community and from the smaller-scale slave-owners: its motivations, representations and behaviours had some distinctive features. Although social networks overlapped in centres of concentration of 'West Indian' slave-owners where mercantile, large-scale and small-scale rentiers co-habited, generally there were differences of social class between large-scale and small-scale rentiers as well as between rentiers and many merchants. This chapter therefore seeks to quantify the extent of large-scale slave-ownership amongst absentee rentier-owners in Britain, to explore the composition of this rentier grouping, and to illustrate the complexity of ownership of slave-property by tracing some of the paths to ownership within it.

The chapter also uses the records of the Commission to examine aspects of the identities and self-representation of this rentier grouping in its correspondence with the Commission. Of course, this was a particular form of discourse, shaped by perceived norms of inter-action with government bodies, but those norms themselves were in their formative stages, and it is possible to trace other more subjective elements even where the formal constraints were observed. It may also be questioned to what extent the slave-owners who corresponded with the Commission were representative because, while there are hundreds of individuals captured by the letter-books, many significant owners relied on agents to intermediate with the Commission, and so do not appear in the letter-books at all. However, their voices are perhaps muffled rather than lost, since their agents' letters often transmit or purport to transmit anxieties emanating from the slave-owners themselves.

Composition of rentier-ownership

Of the 5,044 awards for compensation over £500, just over 1,000 were made to individuals or groups of individuals resident in Britain who had no direct commercial linkages with the West India trade and who have been classified as 'rentiers' (in addition, almost 500 smaller awards have been identified where absentee rentier-owners in Britain owned only a handful of slaves). Absentee rentier and mercantile awards are thus roughly evenly split. However, given that many rentier awards involved more individuals than equivalent mercantile awards, around 7,500 of the estimated 10,000 or so total British claimants were non-mercantile individuals. To place this in approximate context, Colquhoun estimated (for a generation earlier) that there were 20,000 heads of families and 160,000 family members who could be classified as 'Gentlemen and ladies living on income', and an additional 7,000 heads of families with almost 80,000 members amongst the peerage, baronets, knights and esquires.[1] Again, there were perhaps a quarter of a million fund-holders by the late 1820s of a national debt of some £800 million. Slave-owning, therefore, was not as common in absolute terms as investing in government securities, but was at least as widespread in proportion to the size of the capital involved.[2]

The nobility and peerage

A number of the British slave-owners are the traditionally known and readily identified aristocratic absentee owners of large colonial

[1] P. Colquhoun, *A treatise on indigence* (1806), reproduced in P. Hilton, *A Mad, bad and dangerous people? England 1783–1846* (Oxford: Oxford University Press, 2006), pp. 127–8. If these numbers still obtained in the 1830s, and assuming that the 7,500 rentier individuals estimated to be in the compensation process represented some 2,000 to 3,000 families, then as many as 1 family in 10 of the elite were involved enough in the slave-economy to appear in the Compensation records.

[2] Taking £20 million as an approximation for total British *rentier* capital in slaves and land in the West Indies, £800 million as the national debt, and 7,500 and 250,000 as the respective universes of investors. The £20 million is derived from the £4 million actually received by (1) scaling up to 100 per cent of the value of the slaves from the approximately 40 per cent represented by the cash compensation, and (2) applying the rule of thumb that the land and the slaves each constituted half the value of an estate.

Table 5.1 *British nobility and peers appearing in the Compensation records.*

	Owner	Trustee/ executor	Combined	Total of respective ranks in peerage
Dukes	2	1	3	28
Marquesses	1	0	1	34
Earls	10	6	16	223
Viscounts	0	2	2	74
Barons	12	3	15	257

See Appendix 8. Totals of respective ranks are sourced from *A genealogical and heraldic dictionary of the peerage and baronetage of the British Empire, by John Burke* (London: Henry Colburn, 1828). Hilton, *A mad, bad and dangerous people?*, p. 134 lists only the English aristocracy.

vestates, such as Lord Holland, the Earl of Harewood, and the Duke of Buckingham and Chandos.[3] The issue is to determine how representative such anecdotal examples are. The evidence shows that of 616 members of the English, Scottish and Irish peerages, 37 (6 per cent) were involved in the compensation process, of whom 25 were beneficially interested in the exploitation of the enslaved (see Table 5.1).

In some cases, such as the Harewoods, noble titles (and, indeed, slave-ownership itself) had followed the wealth accrued over decades or centuries of different forms of involvement in the slave-economy. Charles Rose Ellis, raised to the barony as Lord Seaford in 1826, is another example of slave-ownership as the platform for ennoblement.[4] James Scarlett, made Lord Abinger in 1834, owed his elevation to a

[3] V. E. Chancellor, 'Slave-owner and anti-slaver: Henry Richard Vassall Fox, 3rd Lord Holland 1800–40', *Slavery & Abolition*, 1.3 (December 1980), 263–75; S. D. Smith, *Slavery, family, and gentry capitalism in the British Atlantic: the world of the Lascelles, 1648–1834* (Cambridge: Cambridge University Press, 2006), and the related article by J. Walvin, 'The colonial origins of English wealth: the Harewoods of Yorkshire' (kindly provided to me in draft and subsequently published in *Journal of Caribbean History*, 39.1 (2005), 38–53); L. L. Sturtz, 'The "Dimduke" and the Duchess of Chandos: gender and power in Jamaican plantation management – a case study or, a different story of "a man [and his wife] from a place called Hope"', *Revista/Review interamericana*, 29.1–4 (1999). The Duke of Buckingham withdrew one claim in St Dorothy in favour of Ambrose Humphr[e]ys, the mortgagee: 'The cause of the Duke's signature not appearing (the Duchess's being substituted) is a severe attack of Gout in his Grace's right hand' (G. W. S. Jago to Commission, T71/1608, Various parishes bundle).

[4] The title inherited in 1803 by Ellis's young son Charles Augustus, Lord Howard de Walden, was derived independently of the family's involvement in the colonial slave-economy, and the London estate that underpinned the family's modern wealth came only in 1879 as a result of an earlier marriage with the heiress of the Duke of Portland.

legal career that culminated in his appointment as Lord Chief Baron of the Exchequer, but he was a Creole, the scion of a slave-owning family in Jamaica, and was himself a slave-owner, awarded £626 2s 2d for thirty enslaved on Spring Grove in Manchester parish.[5]

More commonly, as in the cases of Lord Holland and the Duke of Buckingham, marriage to commoners had brought ownership of slaves into established aristocratic families. For example, the Duke of Cleveland and his son Lord William Powlett were awarded £4,854 16s 9d for 233 enslaved on the Lowther estate in Barbados, which had come into the family through inter-marriage with the Lowthers: the Duke's mother (Margaret Lowther, who married the second Earl of Darlington) and his wife (his cousin, the daughter of Katherine Lowther and the Duke of Bolton) were both descendants of the Lowther family of Barbados.[6] The Duke of Cleveland, of course, had sources of wealth in Britain that dwarfed in importance his ownership of slaves. In other cases, there was more active female agency in the transmission of slave-property within the aristocracy. Mary Salter Dehany, the heiress of the slave-owner Philip Dehany, was engaged to the eleventh Earl of Caithness. When the Earl died before their marriage, Dehany adopted the Earl's niece Wilhelmina Traill, and bequeathed the estates and enslaved in Barbados and Jamaica to her.[7]

The second path to ownership for aristocratic families, other than inter-marriage with the female offspring of a slave-owning family, was through the acquisition of estates and enslaved while on military or official service in the colonies. Howe Peter Browne, the second Marquis of Sligo, was Governor-General of Jamaica in 1834–5, and was awarded £5,526 9s 1d compensation for the enslaved on two estates in St Dorothy – 119 on Kelly's and 167 on Cocoa Walk – and counter-claimed, apparently unsuccessfully, as a judgement creditor of William Garvey Clarke on the Woodfield estate in St Ann.[8] The Earl of Romney, whose difficulty over the treatment of the enslaved on his estates was noted earlier in Chapter 1, received £4,324 18s 11d for 258 enslaved on Romney's in St Kitts and shared in a further £2,944 4s 6d for 174 enslaved on Lamberts.[9]

---

[5] T71/860, Manchester No. 398. The claim was made by Robert Davies, 'Adm[inistrat] or of Christian Johnston Williams and Attorney of James Scarlett the real owner'.

[6] T71/898, Barbados No. 3184. The Duke of Cleveland and Lord William Powlett are described as 'owners in fee'.

[7] *Ibid.* No. 3612. Traill was awarded £4,361 11s 9d for 205 enslaved on the Salters estate in Barbados. She died at Hayes Place, the house left to her by Mary Salter Dehany, in 1862, aged 77 (*The Times*, 12 August 1862, p. 1).

[8] T71/853, St Dorothy Nos. 6, 100; T71/857, St Ann No. 202.

[9] T71/879, St Kitts Nos. 635, 636.

Prof. Gainsborough R.A.   G. Sanders

Honble Charles Marsham & Sisters.

Proof

London Henry Graves & Comp^y 6 Pall Mall 1878

Plate 9   Hon. Charles Marsham, by George Sanders, after Thomas
Gainsborough, 1878 (1787). A minority of the British nobility and
peerage were slave-owners at the time of Emancipation, including
Charles, second Earl of Romney (shown here as child with his
sisters), whose family had long held property in St Kitts. Romney
pursued his claim for compensation carefully, but spared the
enslaved on his estates the years of Apprenticeship, freeing them
immediately in 1834.

Plate 10   Earl of Dudley, by Frederick Christian Lewis Sr, after
John Slater, 1826 or after. Absentee slave-ownership was transmitted
through marriage and inheritance. John William Ward, Earl
of Dudley, Secretary of State from 1827 to 1828, had inherited
'slave-property' in Jamaica from his maternal grandmother. His
compensation was paid to his executors and trustees, including the
Bishop of Exeter, after Dudley's death in 1833.

Plate 11   James Scarlett, by Henry Cousins, after Sir Martin Archer
Shee, March 1837. Colonial slave-owners moved to Britain and
established themselves in metropolitan society. James Scarlett,
the first Lord Abinger, Attorney-General and Chief Baron of the
Exchequer, came from a Jamaican slave-owning family and himself
received compensation for the enslaved on Spring Grove estate in
Manchester parish.

Plate 12 Sir Edward Hyde East, by G. B. Black, after George Chinnery. Sir Edward Hyde East, MP, distinguished judge and Chief Justice of Calcutta, came from a Jamaican slave-owning family and was a major recipient of slave-compensation.

Plate 13 Adam Sedgwick, by Samuel Cousins, after Thomas
Phillips, 1833. Slave-compensation spread beyond the immediate
slave-owners. Adam Sedgwick, Canon of Norwich, Woolwardian
Professor of Geology at Cambridge and teacher of Darwin, was
awarded compensation for the enslaved on the Providence estate in
Jamaica as trustee under the will of the deceased owner.

The Earls of Balcarres had followed a route to ownership redolent of 'Old Corruption'. The seventh Earl filed counter-claims on eleven different awards in Jamaica for slaves hired out by the Kingston merchants George Atkinson and James Hozier to the colonial government in support functions on military bases, and provided a slightly embarrassed account of the background to his claimed right to compensation:

The counterclaimant in this case labours under some difficulty in asserting his counterclaim in this country, in as much as there do not appear to be on hand the deeds between the parties by which their respective rights were ascertained and fixed: the counterclaimant however states that under an agreement entered into between his late father, the Rt Hon. Alex. Earl of Balcarres formerly governor of this colony [between 1794 and 1801], and the predecessors of the firm of the present claimants Messrs Atkinson and Hozier [,] his said father became entitled to one third of the whole of the slaves then employed by the Government as Pioneers and also to one third of those who might be thereafter purchased and placed in that Establishment.[10]

Title for the slaves was taken by the existing firm, and as any partner retired the interest was transferred to the succeeding firm. Until the death of the sixth Earl in 1825, Atkinson and Hozier rendered accounts to him charging him for purchases of slaves and crediting him for receipts from hire or sale of slaves, and 'by letters and otherwise invariably recognized his Lordships right to a participation in a full third of the rent and profit of all the Pioneer Negroes, and also his claim to a full third of the Negroes themselves'. The seventh Earl had continued to receive accounts current, although title was held by Atkinson and Hozier who, until three or four years previously, acted as the seventh Earl's attorneys on his own Jamaican estates. The seventh Earl, the counter-claim concluded, stood 'ready to maintain and prove' the circumstances of his claim, one-third of the compensation being 'both legally and equitably the property and of right payable and belonging to the counterclaimant'.[11] Balcarres's counter-claim drew a wounded response from Atkinson and Hozier (the latter then in London), who said that they 'have not only never denied his right of participation but have always been ready and willing that he should receive and be paid the same': Balcarres's name, they said, had been omitted from the claim not to cut him out, but because his name was not on the slave-register in 1832, nor indeed had been since registration had begun in 1817. Deliberately or otherwise, this arrangement of the Balcarres family had thus been shielded from scrutiny by abolitionists. Balcarres did have

---

[10] T71/1201, Portland No. 163, Appendix: 'Particulars of counterclaim'.
[11] *Ibid.*

more straightforward ownership of slaves: he was awarded £9,352 14s 10d for 474 slaves held in his own name on Marshall's Pen and Martin Hill in Manchester.[12]

The Earl of Northesk and his brother, John Jervis Carnegie, combined the two routes of service and marriage. The two were sons of Admiral William Carnegie, the seventh Earl of Northesk, and Mary Ricketts, the daughter of the slave-owner William Henry Ricketts and Mary Jervis. They shared the award for 200 enslaved on the Canaan estate in Westmoreland with their uncle, Edward Jervis Ricketts, the second Viscount St Vincent, brother of Mary Ricketts and nephew of the first Viscount St Vincent.[13]

Overall, however, it was clearly a small minority – 6 per cent – of the British aristocracy who owned slaves by the 1830s. Those who did had acquired slaves either during colonial/military/naval service in the Caribbean, or through marriage, and had held on to them in some cases for generations. But in the absence of these two paths, Britain's great land-owning families apparently had limited appetite to make discretionary investments in the slave-economy by the early nineteenth century.

The gentry

Baronets

It is possible to extend the quantitative analysis of slave-ownership from the nobility and peerage into the upper reaches of the gentry, although measuring the extent of slave-ownership becomes more difficult amongst the mass of 'the landed gentry' because the universe becomes harder to define: even if it is possible to count heads of slave-owners by a variety of criteria, it is more difficult to define the category and so evolve measurement of the 'dark figure' of non-slave-ownership.

Baronets, however, can be identified relatively readily. There are seventy-five baronets appearing in the Compensation records, of whom fifty-six were beneficially interested in slavery, as slave-owners or mortgagees.[14] The remainder were trustees or executors, often for close family members. Thus, again, around 6 per cent of all baronets

---

[12] T71/860, Manchester No. 204.

[13] T71/871, Westmoreland Nos. 232A, 232B. Viscount St Vincent is described as 'tenant for life of one moiety and trustee of the other except as to four, of which he is owner in fee'. Half the award went as Westmoreland No. 232A to Northesk and Carnegie; the other half went to St Vincent, Sir William Parker (1st Baron of Shenstone and a cousin of St Vincent's wife), and Francis Love Beckford, another absentee slave-owner, presumably as trustees.

[14] Appendices 9 and 10.

were slave-owners or mortgagees and a further 2 per cent were sufficiently connected to assume roles as executors or trustees to men and
women whose assets included slaves.[15] All but three of these baronets were absentees. The absentee baronets were concentrated in the
'old colonies': Jamaica had the most in absolute terms with seventeen,
but relative to the slave-populations in each colony, St Kitts (with ten),
Antigua (with nine) and Grenada (with eight) were all disproportionately represented. This preponderance of older colonies, together with
the fact that the modal decade in which the baronetcies of slave-owners
in 1834 were first created was the 1810s, suggests that the eighteenth-
century heritage of wealth-creation from slavery and its transmission to
Britain created upward social mobility for slave-owners, but only with
a time-lag of several decades. By contrast, the complexion of capital
deployed in Trinidad and British Guiana was newer and rawer, and
slave-owners in those newer colonies had either not had the time by the
1830s to assume heightened respectability or were confronted by new
standards in which the heightened respectability conferred by title was
more difficult for slave-owners to secure.

Most of the baronets were very substantial slave-owners. The jurist
and East India judge Edward Hyde East (born in Jamaica) owned 1,211
human beings. Sir Henry Willock, ambassador to Persia, contested
claims as heir-at-law of his brother Frank Gore Willock for the compensation over 801 enslaved. But there were minor claims: the Irish baronet
Sir George Frederick Hill was awarded compensation for a single slave
in Trinidad. For many, as with Edward Hyde East and Henry Willock,
the thrust of their energies went into imperial projects elsewhere in the
world, whereas for others, such as Sir George Cornewall, management
of their estates in Britain and (more remotely) the West Indies was their
métier. Few appear to have been primarily 'West Indians' in identity
in the sense that they sought out public controversy over slavery: Sir
Christopher Bethell Codrington and Sir Rose Price were exceptions to
this, although seven of the seventy-three baronets attended the April
1832 City rally of the West India interest and its friends. Ultimately,
the qualification for baronetcy was likely to have been ownership of
land in Britain (including land purchased with the profits of slavery),
and such land took on greater salience in defining the public persona of
a slave-owner than his slaves in the West Indies except at moments of
crisis around abolition.

As another measure of slave-ownership's penetration of the landed
gentry, in each of the triennial rounds of nominations for the post of

---

[15] *The peerage of the British Empire as at present existing, by Edmund Lodge* (London: Saunders
& Otley, 1843) lists 904 active baronetcies for the United Kingdom.

Sheriff from 1819 to 1834 (with the notable exception of 1825), between five and ten of the hundred or so nominees appear as recipients of slave-compensation. The Sheriff nomination was not universally coveted, and there were cases of men clearly seeking to be excused nomination, but the lists of nominees do also show upward mobility by both London and provincial merchants such as Joseph Timperon and Thomas Hartley, alongside more established gentry slave-owners.[16] Consistent with Smith's work on the Harewood family in the eighteenth century, regional networks remain readily identifiable into the nineteenth century, such as that around the brewer and slave-owner Benjamin Greene and his son Benjamin Buck Greene in Suffolk, who managed both their own and other plantations on St Kitts on behalf of local neighbours in Suffolk.[17]

Given the permeation of the landed gentry by slave-owners, individuals engaged in slave-owning inevitably figure in the development of institutions of culture and leisure that were founded or reinforced in the nineteenth century and are still prominent today. Thus John Whyte Melville, one of the major forces behind the Royal and Ancient Golf Club of St Andrews (of which he was elected Captain in 1823 and again in 1883, serving also as Chairman of the merged club in 1877), Grand Master of freemasonry in Scotland 1864–6, deputy-lieutenant of the county, whose wife was a daughter of the Duke of Leeds, was a slave-owner. He received £2,781 14s 10d in 1835 for 131 slaves on Melville Hall in Dominica. In November 2003, a proposal was debated by the local council, apparently in ignorance of his slave-owning, to erect a plaque to him at St Andrews to celebrate the linking of town, gown and golf club.[18] George Alexander Fullerton, a founder member of the Royal Yacht Club (now the Royal Yacht Squadron), had assumed the name of his great uncle and inherited not only Ballintoy Castle in County Antrim and Tockington Manor in Gloucestershire, but also slaves in Jamaica: Fullerton was awarded £9,325 1s 11d for 415 slaves on the Ballintoy, Penny's and Hopewell plantations.[19]

The geography of British rentier slave-ownership

Large-scale rentier-ownership was primarily concentrated in rural areas in the south and south-west of England, and in East Anglia.

[16] Appendix 14.

[17] R. G. Wilson, *Greene King, a business and family history* (London: Bodley Head and Jonathan Cape, 1983), pp. 32–59.

[18] T71/881, Dominica No. 151. For Melville, see www.standrewscc.net/archive/0311 agenda.pdf.

[19] St Ann claims Nos. 60, 497, 573. See J. Barker, *Lady Georgiana Fullerton: a Bourne-mouth benefactor*, at www.rc-churches.net/diocese/history/lgfl.html.

There was comparatively little slave-owning rentier interest in the out-ports, primarily because the rentier interest, which emerged over generations from mercantile roots, tended to migrate to the hinterlands of these port cities, and thus appears in Gloucestershire, Wiltshire and Somerset rather than Bristol, and in Cheshire rather than Liverpool (see Table 5.2). There were for the same reasons also clusters of slave-owners in the north-west around Whitehaven and in the north-east around Newcastle. Something of this effect is again visible for London vis-à-vis the Home Counties. London nevertheless remained an important locus of rentier interest.

There were geographic concentrations of large-scale but especially of smaller-scale slave-ownership in provincial centres of genteel leisure: notably Cheltenham, Bath and Clifton, as well as along the south coast, including Southampton and Brighton. Each of these towns had between twenty and fifty identifiable slave-owners. There were slave-owners amongst the British expatriate communities in continental Europe, notably in Boulogne, 'where so many impoverished English gentry resort to'.[20] Conversely, as noted previously, there were very few rentier-slave-owners in the industrial cities of Lancashire and Yorkshire, or from the West Midlands. Slave-property is conspicuously absent from the milieu of the Leeds middle classes studied by Morris, and the major financial transaction he identified around slavery is the donation of £500 by one woman, Mary Marriott, to the Anti-slavery Society in London; but, as Morris points out, linkages with slavery even within this quintessential domain of urban middle-class anti-slavery were not entirely absent, one branch of the Oates family that he studied being linked to family members in Jamaica.[21]

There is, however, a disproportionate Scottish presence amongst the claimants.[22] Scots make up some 15 per cent of the absentee awards, against 10 per cent of the population of Great Britain and Ireland.[23] Edinburgh had some fifty slave-owners or claimants identifiable in the

[20] Rev. F. E. Witts, *The diary of a Cotswold parson 1783–1784*, ed. David Verey (Stroud: Sutton Publishing, 1978; 2nd edn 2003), p. 64.

[21] R. J. Morris, *Men, women and property in England 1780–1870: a social and economic history of family strategies amongst the Leeds middle classes* (Cambridge: Cambridge University Press, 2005), p. 4.

[22] The prominence of Scots in the slave-economy has long been recognised, although the over-representation has not been systematically quantified. D. Hamilton, *Scotland, the Caribbean and the Atlantic world 1750–1820* (Manchester: Manchester University Press, 2005) shows evidence suggesting Scots accounted (by different measures) for one third of the whites in Jamaica and around half the planters in Tobago, Dominica and St Vincent in the 1760s (pp. 22, 63).

[23] This figure includes only Scots in Scotland, and does not include members of the 'diaspora' such as the Baillie family of Bristol or Neill Malcolm of London, both of

Table 5.2   *Geographic distribution of rentier awards over £500.*

	London	Liverpool	Bristol	Other
Awards by number				
Jamaica	184	5	19	335
Barbados	20	3	11	62
1st phase colonies	44	0	3	102
2nd phase colonies	58	1	1	85
3rd phase colonies	48	4	1	45
Marginal colonies	0	0	0	0
Total	**354**	**13**	**35**	**629**
Awards by value (£)				
Jamaica	588,000	22,000	47,000	1,009,000
Barbados	76,000	13,000	39,000	220,000
1st phase colonies	117,000	0	6,000	257,000
2nd phase colonies	211,000	5,000	2,000	315,000
3rd phase colonies	550,000	18,000	11,000	325,000
Marginal colonies	0	0	0	0
Total	**1,542,000**	**58,000**	**105,000**	**2,126,000**

Values rounded to nearest £1,000. Twelve rentier claims worth £21,000 have not been allocated by geography, generally where the records signal an awardee as absentee or 'Great Britain' but no further information has been found on the individual.

Compensation records, many falling into the 'widows and orphans' category. But even for this centre of slave-ownership, when the Duke of Wellington tabled a petition from Edinburgh citizens for 'a gradual and safe abolition of slavery and compensation to the planter ... signed by 2,468 persons and ... well-entitled to attention, no less on account of the respectability of the petitioners than by reason of the justice of the sentiments contained in the petition', he was upstaged by Lord Suffield, who said he had already presented an abolitionist petition from the same city signed by 21,000 or 22,000 of the male adults.[24]

Within London there was a very marked concentration of slave-owners around Marylebone, with every third or fourth house in streets such as Portland Place, Harley Street/Upper Harley Street and Wimpole Street/Upper Wimpole Street being occupied in the first decades of the nineteenth century by families involved as beneficiaries in the slave-compensation process.[25]

whom were major slave-owners and substantial land-owners in Scotland, Hamilton; *Ibid.*, pp.197–201.

[24] *The Debates in Parliament – Session 1833 – on the Resolution and Bill for the Abolition of Slavery in British colonies, with a copy of the Act of Parliament* (London, 1834), 3rd series, Vol. 17, pp. 837, 839, 2 April 1833–30 May 1833.

[25] See Appendix 17.

The nature of 'West India property' for absentee rentiers

'[T]he grand object of every West India planter', wrote the London merchant John Robley in 1808, was ultimately to 'place the income derived from property in the West Indies, upon a permanent security at all resembling a revenue derived from a landed estate in Europe'.[26] It has been argued that land-owners in England did indeed conceive of West India property in the same frame as their estates in Britain.[27] In many cases this cannot have been meaningful: many absentees (including Sir George Cornewall) never visited their slave estates. Cornewall, after he had taken possession of La Taste in 1798 and installed a manager, sought regular accounts 'to become as much acquainted as, at this distance, I can, with every thing that related to the Estate, the mode of managing it, its produce, its stock etc.'.[28] Nevertheless, transmission of 'slave-property' was managed in the same way as that of landed property in Britain. The characteristic unit of estate and slaves was physically indivisible, but was capable of being encumbered with annuities and legacies, and subjected to strict settlement and to marriage settlements.[29]

Primogeniture (or at least single non-partible inheritance, since a number of examples exist of younger sons receiving West India estates while eldest sons inherited estates in Britain) remained prevalent amongst absentee estate-owners, but it was qualified by the creation of monetary claims secured on the estate, and in a significant minority of cases estates were bequeathed equally. It may be that such equal inheritance was more characteristic of merchants or returning planters than rentier families where the estate had already been owned for one or more absentee generations. In British Guiana, for example, the compensation for the Schepmoed plantation was split and shared in equal thirds between Charles Henry Fraser; George Frederick Rich and his wife Jane Agnes Wilhelmina, née Fraser; and Sir Alex Woodford and

---

[26] J. Robley, *A permanent and effectual remedy suggested to the evils under which the British West Indies now labour, in a letter from a West India merchant to a West India planter* (London, 1808), p. 4.

[27] See for example S. Seymour, S. Daniels and C. Watkis, 'Estate and empire: Sir George Cornewall's management of Moccas, Herefordshire and La Taste Grenada', *Journal of Historical Geography*, 24.3 (1998), 313–51.

[28] *Ibid.*, p. 333.

[29] For English landed property, see J. Habakkuk, *Marriage, debt and the estate system* (Oxford: Clarendon Press, 1994); and S. Staves, 'Resentment or resignation? Dividing the spoils among daughters and younger sons', in J. Brewer and S. Staves (eds.), *Early modern conceptions of property* (London and New York: Routledge, 1995), pp. 194–220. For the antithetical values of 'bourgeois' management of property, see Morris, *Men, women and property*.

his wife Charlotte Mary Ann Fraser. Clearly the three Fraser siblings had equal ownership in the underlying plantation.[30]

Entail, of course, introduced complexity into the ownership of slaves and into the compensation process. Under entail, a tenant-for-life enjoyed the profits or rents of property until death, when the property went to the remainder-man or -men (who could be male or female). This form of ownership potentially imposed on the Commission the need to assign values to the respective interests. John Vernon of Boulogne asked whether, for property in strict entail, the whole of the compensation would be invested by trustees, or whether a proportion of the compensation would be allotted to the tenant-for-life and a proportion to the heir in tail, according to their respective ages. He went on to pose an ostensibly hypothetical question to the Commission: the proportions of compensation to each party 'supposing the age of the tenant for life to be 56 and the age of the heir intail 23 and the compensation money for the Negroes to be 6,000 [pounds sterling]'.[31] However, the Commission wisely formulated a simpler approach for itself: it refused to deal with the sub-allocation and required the tenant-for-life and the remainder-men to agree in writing to payment of all compensation to the tenant-for-life, all to the remainder-men or all to both jointly. Failing such an agreement, the compensation would go to trustees to be invested in 3 per cent consols, the dividends to go to the tenant-for-life and the principal to the remainder-men on death of the tenant-for-life.[32] W. H. Prescod of Cheltenham was, as already noted, the largest single slave-owner in Barbados, having 1,223 slaves valued at £67,045, but with the exception of the Barry estate he held the estates as tenant-for-life under the will of William Prescod. Under what he construed as the guidance of the Commission, Prescod agreed to the awards being paid to the trustees alone, William Hinds and John Gay Goding of Speightstown.[33] He immediately regretted the decision, which was

[30] T71/885, British Guiana No. 426A,B. The claim is missing in the *Slavery Abolition Act: an account of all sums of money awarded by the Commissioners of Slavery Compensation*, PP 1837–8, Vol. 48 (215) ('the Parliamentary Return' or 'the Return'), but appears in the Register of Claims. Again, on the Eden Estate in St James, the owners had respectively died thirty and ten years previously, but their heirs in Britain 'for years have divided the rents and profit of the Estate according to their proportions'; T71/873, St James No. 31A–F; C. E. and W. E. Bernard to Commission, T71/1608, 26 October 1835.

[31] Vernon to Commission, T71/1609, 19 August 1835.

[32] See for example Commission to Conrade Coulthurst, Sandiway nr Northwich Cheshire, T71/1593, pp. 163–4, 14 April 1836, setting out these alternatives. Coulthurst consented for the award to be made to the remainder-men, who appear to have been four Coulthurst sisters; T71/1899, Barbados No. 4950.

[33] T71/898, Barbados Nos. 3223, 3225; T71/899 Nos. 4306, 4307, 5305. For Prescod's own claim on Barry's see T71/899, Barbados No. 5306. K. M. Butler, *The economics*

bascd on the Commission simply outlining the alternatives, and rapidly sought the help of the Commission against the remainder-men of the estates, with whom his relationship had broken down: 'It appears to me, that the next Heirs under the will of my late Uncle will, if they can, invade my just rights ... it is plain they will put their hands into my pocket.'[34] The Commission was, understandably, disinclined to involve itself: 'The board is not authorised', it told Prescod, 'to give any direction where a Trust has already been created and the Trustees are in the exercise of the duty they have undertaken'.[35]

The gendered transmission and control of property are central to understanding how slave-ownership was dispersed and disseminated within British metropolitan society. The distinctive contribution of women to the British abolitionist movement, both of the slave-trade but particularly of slavery itself, has been recognised.[36] However, British women were also inter-connected with the slave-economy as owners, beneficiaries and dependants, and little work has been done on such women as a whole.[37] In contrast to women carving out roles in abolitionist movements, which provided contested entry into a public sphere of meeting and campaigning, women in Britain who owned slaves had little incentive by the 1820s and early 1830s to seek public identities based on slave-ownership. Mrs Carmichael's narrative represents a rare pro-slavery intervention, drawing on a period of residence in St Vincent between 1820 and 1823.[38] But the compensation process provides a window into the generally closed world of slave-ownership, and obliged or gave the opportunity to British women to assert their ownership of the enslaved. Litigation, especially in Chancery, also provided a forum in which women as slave-owners entered a public world. Analysis of the role of women in the slave-compensation process bears out Davidoff and Hall's more general contention that the *forms* in which property in

of Emancipation: Jamaica and Barbados, 1823–1843 (Chapel Hill, University of North Carolina Press, 1995), p. 85 characterises Prescod's compensation as going to his 'attorneys and creditors' but this appears to be a misreading of the entail.

[34] Commission to W. H. Prescod, T71/1593, p. 145, 19 March 1836; Prescod to Commission, T71/1611, Barbados bundle, 8 September 1836.

[35] Commission to Prescod, T71/1593, p. 264, 9 September 1836.

[36] See for example C. Midgley, 'Slave sugar boycotts, female activism and the domestic base of British anti-slavery culture', *Slavery & Abolition*, 17.3 (1996), 137–62.

[37] Beckles has used a narrative by Mrs Carmichael to look at women resident in the colonies as slave-owners; Butler has established the active role played by women in Barbados in the local slave-economy, especially as small-scale providers of capital. H. M. Beckles, *Centering woman: gender discourses in Caribbean slave society* (Kingston, Jamaica: Ian Randle Publishers, 1999) pp. 106–124; Butler, *The economics of Emancipation*, pp. 92–108.

[38] Mrs A. C. Carmichael, *Domestic manners and social condition of the white, coloured and Negro populations in the West Indies* (London: Whittaker & Co., 1833). The Carmichaels

nineteenth-century Britain was transmitted were determined by sex: '[p]atterns of ownership were closely related to patterns of control. It was primarily women who were the beneficiaries of "passive" property yielding income only: trusts, annuities, subscriptions and insurance.'[39] Women in Britain received compensation directly and indirectly: the whole nexus of legacies, annuities and settlements around West India estates reflects the attempts to direct and limit the financial status and flexibility of wives and daughters, while providing for them materially. Transmitting West India property to daughters posed the same challenges as any other form of property given the legal principle that 'the husband and wife are one person in law'. Marriage settlements remained common amongst the estate-owners in an effort to mediate conflict between males (father and husband, husband and future husband), underscoring the 'gentry' nature of ownership.[40]

Nevertheless, despite the adoption of metropolitan norms of managing West India property across generations and sexes, the hope expressed by Robley, that West India property would become the equivalent of metropolitan landed property, was never realised after the abolition of the slave-trade. West India property offered neither the stability nor the social cachet of English land. It lacked the conventional domestic structure of landlord–tenant: there was almost no rental of colonial slave-worked land by tenant-farmers. Instead, the absentee slave-owner remained directly dependent on the level of profits achieved by the agents – attorneys, managers and overseers – he or she had in place, who were generally rewarded on a commission basis linked to revenue rather than profit.

Neither did West India property offer the liquidity and security of government stock. It therefore did not form one of the options for a rentier portfolio for the mass of the urban middle class. In the life-cycle from entrepreneurial to rentier capital, West India property had little part to play. Although there *were* instruments potentially allowing passive investment, no institutional framework developed after the failure of the West India Company scheme of the mid 1820s to get off the ground.[41] Rentier assets in the form of mortgages constructed from West India

subsequently moved to Trinidad before returning to Britain and settling in Jersey. Mrs Carmichael's husband, John Wilson Carmichael, was awarded £981 18s 0d for twenty-two slaves in Trinidad in 1836; T71/894, Trinidad No. 1463.

[39] L. Davidoff and C. Hall, *Family fortunes: men and women of the English middle class 1780–1850* (London: Hutchinson, 1987), p. 277.

[40] *Ibid.*, p. 263.

[41] The West India Company was intended to raise £4 million in capital to receive consignments of West India produce in return for advances made on mortgage and other good security. Prime movers behind it were the London West India merchants who

property retained the risk characteristics of the underlying slave-economy and did not meet the demand of an expanding urban middle class
for diversification and liquidity. That pent-up demand, of course, was
shortly to be met by domestic and international railway securities. The
failure of 'West India property' – i.e. slaves – to represent an investment
alternative appears to have been a problem of practice as much as one of
principle, although other forms of property did become tainted: Morris
argues that slum-property on the Mabgate estate in Leeds, for example, became an unacceptable form of property for 'a family network
with aspirations to join and sustain its place among the liberal elite of
Leeds' public life'.[42] One route for rentier capital to gain exposure to the
slave-economy was in lending to West India houses in London, but this
appears not to have drawn the urban middle-class investor: on Manning
& Anderdon's bankruptcy in 1831, several 'members of the landed gentry' were amongst the creditors who had lent money, in amounts of
between £5,000 and £20,000, at 5 per cent interest.[43]

Because the slave-economy, especially sugar production, was subject to short-term fluctuations in profitability, and because the owners'
profits, annuities and legacies stood in priority behind the commissions
and fees of attorneys and consignees (which were related to revenue
rather than profit), the income from a leveraged estate was disproportionately variable. There is plenty of evidence for disruptions to income
of British absentees – ahead of the 1831–2 crisis in the sugar-economy
of the British Caribbean – in the complaints of mortgagees, legatees
and annuitants in Britain to the Compensation commission. Eleanor
Brumskile of the County of Dublin petitioned Stanley in 1834 as the
eldest daughter and administrator of William Brereton, claiming one-
quarter of the 'remuneration' on the Guiana property of her father and
late brother: 'I am with the rest of my sisters left large legacies on the
Estate, one shilling of which we have not received.'[44] Penelope Ballard

---

appear to have wanted to bring external capital to bear. William Manning's motion
to bring the bill to a second reading was contested not only by abolitionists and Free-
Traders, but by Huskisson on the more general grounds that companies should seek
a royal charter before seeking limited liability in Parliament; 'From a correspondent',
The Times, 23 April 1824, p. 2, and 'Politics and Parliament', 11 May 1824, p. 2.
Ragatz implies the company did operate for a period on a reduced capital; L. Ragatz,
*The fall of the planter class in the British Caribbean, 1763–1833: a study in social and eco-
nomic history* (New York and London: The Century Co., 1928), pp. 381–2. There is
no evidence of the West India Company in the Compensation records.

[42] Morris, *Men, women and property*, p. 294.
[43] R. B. Sheridan, 'The West India sugar crisis and British slave Emancipation, 1830–
1833', *Journal of Economic History*, 21.4 (December 1961), 539–51 (p. 544).
[44] Eleanor Brumskile née Brereton of Bray in County of Dublin, petition to Lord
Stanley, T71/1610, Guiana bundle, 8 May 1834. The compensation for the Peter Hall

and Elizabeth Crabb wrote to the Commission in 1835 concerning an annuity established on the Spring Path estate in Hanover for their deceased great aunt and mother: 'the payments were very irregularly made and in some years altogether withheld, the last payment in part was about the years 1819 or 1820'.[45]

Whatever the structural profitability of the slave-economy ahead of Emancipation, evidence for the impact of the 1831–2 crisis on rentiers dependent on the older colonies appears to be unarguable. The London diarist Thomas Raikes recorded in his journal in June 1832 'the irremediable distress which has this year overtaken all the West Indies proprietors, many of whom, my intimate friends, have laid down some a part, some the whole, of their establishments'.[46]

The compensation process itself tended to disrupt flows, as agents and mortgagors positioned themselves for Emancipation. Richard Atkinson of Kirkby Lonsdale, in writing to Stanley on other issues concerning his claims, commented in passing on his mortgage on an estate in Guiana: 'any payment on acc[oun]t of which is of course stopped from the time your measures were brought before the House of Commons'.[47]

Paths to ownership

There were three main paths by which non-mercantile residents in Britain came to own slaves or be entitled to compensation: as returnees or migrants from the West Indies, having purchased or inherited estates and the enslaved attached to them while in the colonies; by inheritance in Britain, either directly as owners of land and slaves or of unattached slaves, or indirectly as holders of annuities or monetary legacies secured on West India property; and by marriage, either directly or under the control of a marriage settlement (the slave-property thus transmitted was, by the 1820s and 1830s, almost invariably the result itself of earlier inheritance). There is very little evidence of direct purchase by absentee *rentiers* of investments in West India property in the 1820s and 1830s.

---

estate she was referring to was awarded to Baillie, Ames & Baillie of Bristol as mortgagees, but in a unique case the Commission, having misfiled the counter-claim from Thomas Brereton as executor of Wm Brereton, re-opened its adjudication; T71/885, British Guiana No. 629; Commission to Evan Baillie, T71/1593, 18 April 1836.

[45] Penelope Ballard (late Crabb) and Eliz. E. Crabb, 6 Augustin Place, Clapham Road, Surrey to Commission, T71/1608, Cornwall & others, Hanover bundle, 8 June 1835.

[46] T. Raikes, *A Portion of the Journal kept by Thomas Raikes Esq. from 1831 to 1847* ([London], 1856), p. 50, entry for Tuesday 12 June 1832.

[47] Atkinson to Stanley, T71/1610, Guiana bundle, 3 February 1834.

Retirement and returnees

The scale of the decline of the white population in much of the British West Indies, especially Jamaica, in the first decades of the nineteenth century indicates both a reduction in the rate of emigration from Britain and an increase in the flow of returnees.[48] Fewer Britons were finding their way to the Caribbean, especially to the older sugar-colonies, after the abolition of the slave-trade, so that new 'slave-property' was not being established except in the newer territories of British Guiana and Trinidad, and this (at least initially, before it was replaced in a natural life-cycle by rentier property) was very largely mercantile capital. However, amongst those returning as retirees to Britain in the decades immediately before Emancipation were men who had made their fortune, even in the older colonies, in the period after the abolition of the slave-trade. William Miller, 'the Attorney-general', appears exceptional both in the scale of his management activities in Jamaica – he had been attorney for forty-eight properties – and in his apparent lack of ownership of the enslaved. William Burge had urged the Select Committee on Apprenticeship to call Miller as a witness in 1836: 'Mr Miller has quitted Jamaica entirely, has no property in the island, and never, I believe, had any slave property. He is a gentleman of very large fortune, who was a great many years resident in Jamaica, a very extensive attorney; he lives now in Bryanston Square.'[49] Miller was called: he explained that he had been thirty-seven years in Jamaica until June 1835, and had 'no interest whatever' to return to Jamaica.

Q: Were you a proprietor of slaves?
MILLER: No, I had a few domestics.
Q: But were you not a planter?
MILLER: I am a planter by profession. I was agent for a number of
  proprietors.[50]

By contrast, William Shand had been in Jamaica from 1791 to 1823, and again between 1825 and 1826, and acted as an attorney for many

---

[48] B. W. Higman, *Slave populations in the British Caribbean 1807–34* (Baltimore: Johns Hopkins University Press, 1984), p. 77, shows an overall decline of the white population between 1810 and 1830 from 63,995 to 55,694. Within this, British Guiana, Trinidad and St Vincent showed increases; Barbados, St Kitts, Nevis, Antigua, Tobago and Grenada, declines of between 5 per cent and 20 per cent; and Jamaica, a fall of one-third, accounting alone for the whole decline in the region's white population.

[49] Evidence of William Miller, *Report from the Select Committee appointed to inquire into the working of the Apprenticeship system in the colonies, conduct of Apprentices, laws, regulations etc.*, PP 1836, Vol. 15 (560), pp. 189–90.

[50] *Ibid.*, pp. 199–200.

estates, but had returned to England as the owner of 1,200 slaves of his own.[51] Robert Scott had been a resident in Jamaica between 1802 and 1826, and for a few months from 1828 to 1829. He was awarded nearly £5,000 compensation for his 246 slaves on his Kinloss estate in Trelawny.[52] Thomas Rossiter was born in Tiverton, Devon in 1772, and married in Spanish Town in December 1796: he returned to Tiverton around 1808, and retained his ownership of slaves, being awarded £1,064 9s 4d for fifty-five enslaved on the Retreat estate in 1835 and dying in 1839.[53]

Inheritance

It was not, however, the retirement to Britain of 'planters' that created the bulk of slave-owners living in Britain in the 1830s: it was inheritance by heirs in Britain who in many cases had few active connections with the West Indies. Ownership through inheritance, as discussed above, was represented as a mitigant of slave-ownership.[54]

In the newer colonies, wealth-generation was often sufficient for inheritors to achieve rentier status in a single generation, as was the case with H. M. Hyndman's father or with James Blair. Blair was the recipient of the largest single compensation award: £83,530 8s 11d for 1,598 enslaved on the Blairmont plantation in British Guiana. Blair had inherited the estate from his uncle Lambert Blair, who was originally from a mercantile background in Ireland. Both men married into the Stopford family of the Earls of Courtown. In 1818, James Blair was elected as MP for Saltash and subsequently for Wigtown in Scotland, where he owned the Penninghame estate. Blair was, however, active in defence of his slave-property as a prime mover in the organisation of the absentee interest, appearing as the first-named member of the committee appointed by the proprietors and mortgagees of Demerara and Berbice to carry on an appeal to the Privy Council against compulsory manumission in 1826. On his death in 1841 he left his estate to his wife's family.[55]

---

[51] Evidence of William Shand, *Report from the Select Committee on the extinction of slavery throughout the British dominions*, PP 1831–2, Vol. 20 (721), p. 428 (hereafter *Report on the extinction of slavery*). Shand's compensation was tied up in Chancery in *Oswin* v. *Shand* (Clarendon Nos. 128, 143, 415; St John No. 20).

[52] Evidence of Robert Scott, *Report on the extinction of slavery*, p. 330; and T71/847, Trelawny No. 116.

[53] T71/855, St Thomas-in-the-Vale No. 130.

[54] See Chapter 1 above, pp. 59–60.

[55] T71/885, British Guiana No. 15. *The Times*, 17 June 1818; 11 September 1841. R. G. Thorne, *The House of Commons 1790–1820*, 5 vols. (London: Secker and Warburg for the History of Parliament Trust, 1986), Vol. iii, p. 216.

Inheritance of estates in the older established colonies, by contrast, spanned several generations and tended to distance the owner from the owned by the 1830s. British landed dynasties had grown up amongst descendants of early slave-owners, and in many cases estates and the enslaved attached to them passed down absentee families over a period of 100 years or more. Over half of the thirty-three 'Gentry families' identified by Sheridan as in Antigua before 1680 can be found still as absentee slave-owners in the records of the Slave Compensation Commission a century-and-a-half later, including the Tudways of Wells and the Williams family.[56] The Tudways' Parham estate averaged an annual profit of £2,349 between 1820 and 1826, against £5,000 per annum between 1799 and 1819. Robert Charles Tudway, who was nominated as Sheriff of Somerset in 1839 and later served as MP for Wells, was awarded £8,560 9s 2d for 557 slaves in 1835, after the death of his father John Paine Tudway in 1835.[57] R. C. Tudway was a member of the provisional committee of the Antigua Railway Company in 1845, as was Rowland Edward Williams, a descendant of Colonel Rowland Williams, the Lieutenant-Governor of Antigua in 1675.[58] Williams had served with the Tenth Royal Hussars; had married the daughter of the then Governor, Major-General Sir Patrick Ross, in Antigua in 1828, when he was described as of 'Weston-Green Surrey and Antigua'; and was resident at Weston Green at the time of compensation, when he was awarded £3,569 8s 0d for 245 enslaved on his St Clare's and Clarendon estates. In addition, Williams, who was appointed a magistrate for Middlesex in 1843 but was also a member of the Council of Antigua in the 1840s, received compensation as trustee of the marriage settlement of Henry Anthony Hardman of Southampton, who had assigned his mortgage over Monteros estate into trust in 1819.[59]

Amongst the descendants of those identified by Sheridan as eighteenth-century migrants to Antigua was John Tollemache, the son of Vice-Admiral John Richard Delap Tollemache, grandson of John

---

[56] R. B. Sheridan, 'The rise of a colonial gentry: a cast study of Antigua 1730–1775', *Economic History Review*, NS 13.3 (1961), 342–357. Appendix I, p. 355 identifies twenty-nine of the thirty-three gentry families in Antigua before 1680 as 'absentees'; of these, seventeen are identifiable in the Slave Compensation records.

[57] T71/877, Antigua Nos. 327, 328, 330 for the awards on Parham Lodge, Parham Old Works and Parham New Works. In each case the claim was lodged by John Payne [sic] Tudway of Wells as tenant-for-life. J. R. Ward, 'The profitability of sugar planting in the British West Indies 1650–1834', *Economic History Review*, NS 31.2 (1978), 197–231 (pp. 210–11) for Parham's financial performance.

[58] *The Times*, 8 October 1845, p. 15; 15 October 1845, p. 15;

[59] *The Times*, 2 April 1828; 28 August 1843; T71/877, Antigua Nos. 115, 1047; T71/877 No. 11A.

Delap Halliday and Lady Jane Tollemache, and great grandson of John Halliday, the Collector of Customs on Antigua between 1739 and 1777. John Tollemache inherited 6 estates and the 822 enslaved attached to them on his father's death in 1837, for whom he was awarded £12,669 2s 7d in compensation after he reached a settlement with two counter-claimants, executors of Daniel Hill of Antigua, 'for a sum found due by Masters Report in Chancery' of £10,453 15s 9d. Tollemache, whose family seat was at Helmingham in Suffolk, bought 26,000 acres of land in Cheshire in 1840; was elected as MP for Cheshire South in 1841; and built, between 1842 and 1851, the faux-medieval Peckforton Castle.[60]

Property changed in character over time as inheritance distanced it from its mercantile or planter origins: thus the Hon. John Barham of Stockbridge House in Hampshire, MP and owner of the Mesopotamia estate at the time of compensation, was the fourth generation of owners to be absentee and continued the distinct rentier characteristics established by his father and grandfather, both named Joseph Foster Barham.[61]

Annuities by their nature were generally a single-generation device for supporting a dependant. The compensation process allowed many annuitants and legatees in Britain, usually but not exclusively women, to recoup arrears. Hence, for example, Elizabeth Gale Vidal of Ideford in Devon was awarded £1,050 for the three-and-a-half years' arrears on her annuity of £300 secured on the Berkshire Hall estate in St Thomas-in-the-Vale.[62] A male annuitant, James Gray, was an annuitant for £150 per annum during the life of his aunt Sarah Gray, the absentee owner of the Friendship sugar estate in Hanover: Gray had mortgaged his annuity to the Hankey banking firm in London, who counter-claimed against Sarah Gray for the compensation.[63] The typical amounts of the annuity were between £100 and £150, presumably intended to be adequate for a small measure of financial independence to a relative perceived to have no need for major outlays on housing or extensive domestic service. Elizabeth Scott enjoyed an exceptionally high annuity of £800 per annum under the will of John James Scott, her husband, secured on a number of Jamaican estates.[64] Elizabeth Pinnock had £1,200 per

---

[60] T71/877, Antigua Nos. 39, 40, 58, 82, 83, 123; *The Times*, 12 January 1876, p. 10.

[61] T71/871, Westmoreland No. 319. For the Mesopotamia estate, see Richard S. Dunn, 'A tale of two plantations: slave life at Mesopotamia in Jamaica and Mount Airy in Virginia, 1799–1828', *William and Mary Quarterly*, 3rd series 34.1 (January 1977), 32–65.

[62] T71/855, St Thomas-in-the-Vale No. 60. T71/1378 carries details of the award. The Parliamentary Return shows this as awarded to the London merchants Rowland and John Mitchell, and two others, who were in fact respectively trustees for Elizabeth Gale Vidal and a second claimant, William Clark of Hackney.

[63] T71/872, Hanover No. 7.

[64] Including the Retreat estate with 201 slaves; T71/867, St Thomas-in-the-East No. 295.

annum in lieu of dower under the will of James Pinnock, dated 1809, but the level was set unfeasibly high before the decline of sugar prices, and by 1834 the arrears were £17,100.[65]

Not only direct ownership of the enslaved but also loans against slave-property were heritable. Brewer has pointed to a private market in credit in eighteenth-century Britain, and the Slave Compensation records support the argument that a significant credit capacity at one stage existed outside the intermediation of banks and other financial institutions.[66] Richard Pares highlighted that some annuitants on slave estates were not only family members, but also small (private) investors who lent capital sums of money to be repaid for annuities over one, two or three lives.[67] While there is little evidence of large-scale *new* lending by private individuals on West India property in the early nineteenth century, there are certainly traces of such lending in the past. Edward Lambert wrote from Bath in 1834 concerning a mortgage for £7,000 he held in Nevis: 'It has been in the family, whose representative I am on this reason, for nearly a century.'[68] As well as mortgages, other debts secured against the estate, notably court judgements, were heritable. Allan S. Laing of the Inner Temple was awarded two-thirds of the compensation for the Springfield estate in Dominica as the executor of the will of his late father, who was a judgement creditor for £1,875 7s 6d.[69]

Marriage

Marriage disseminated slave-ownership further within Britain, creating new families of slave-owners and new ties to the slave-economy. Jane Kerby, the widow of Thomas Norbury Kerby of Antigua (who was himself a descendant of one of Sheridan's seventeenth-century Antiguan settler families), was at the time of compensation living in a grace-and-favour apartment in Hampton Court. Her claim, with Jane Young of Brocke Street in Bath, as tenants-for-life for compensation for 217 enslaved on Stephen Blizard's estate, was contested by the trustees of the marriage settlement of her daughter the Hon. Anne Byam Stapleton (née Kerby), the widow of the Hon. Miles J. Stapleton,

---

[65] *Ibid.*, No. 265.

[66] J. Brewer, 'Commercialisation and politics', in N. McKendrick, J. Brewer and J. H. Plumb (eds.), *The birth of a consumer society: the commercialisation of eighteenth-century England* (London: Europa Publications, 1982), pp. 197–262.

[67] R. Pares, *A West India fortune* (London: Longman, 1950), pp. 248–9.

[68] Edward Lambert to Commission, T71/1609, Grenada bundle, 25 September 1834, 20 October 1834. Lambert went on to say that the arrears of interest amounted to as much as the principal.

[69] T71/881, Dominica No. 288.

son of Sir Thomas Stapleton the sixteenth Baron le Despencer. Sir Thomas Stapleton himself had married into another Antiguan slave-owning family, his wife Elizabeth being the daughter of Samuel Elliott of Antigua.[70]

Marriage also incorporated new families into the networks of trusts and trusteeships that characterised the way in which slavery penetrated British society. For example, George Henry Dashwood, the MP for Buckinghamshire and High Wycombe, was awarded compensation for the Spring, Ashton Hale and Over Hill estates in Barbados as one of the devisees-in-trust of his brother-in-law Harrison W. Sober, whom Dashwood's sister Elizabeth had married in 1821.[71]

Control over males brought into the family by marriage was a repeated theme for slave-property. Lord Holland had taken his wife's name in order to preserve her inheritance of the estates of her grand-father, Florentius Vassall: she had given them up to her first husband Sir Godfrey Webster on their divorce in 1796, but they reverted to Lady Holland as tenant-for-life after Webster's suicide in 1800.[72] In the compensation process, Webster's son (also Sir Godfrey Webster) was awarded part of the compensation as remainder-man of his mother.

In the absence of specific arrangements of marriage settlements or trusts, 'couverture' applied to slave-property and slave-compensation. William Stirling of Scotland was awarded £122 15s 6d for four slaves on Content in St James, Jamaica, 'in right of wife'.[73] Stirling, of Kenmore County Lanark and Glasgow was a director of the Baptist Missionary Society, and with his brother Charles was awarded directly £6,671 10s 3d for 321 slaves on Content. While his wife owned in her own name a handful of enslaved, probably domestic servants, she had no inde-pendent access to the compensation. But the Commission used £200 as the cut-off for the value of award above which it would, in the case of a husband claiming compensation on behalf of his wife, require the wife to be 'examined separately', i.e. to swear a separate affida-vit.[74] Thus the Hon. George Grantley Berkeley and his kinsman Robert

---

[70] T71/877, Antigua No. 363; CCED No. 543; S. E. Parker, *Grace and favour: a hand-book of who lived where in Hampton Court Palace 1750–1950* (East Molesey: Hampton Court, 2005), p. 41. Anne Byam Stapleton also received compensation in 1837 for twelve slaves owned by her mother Jane after the latter's death; T71/877, Antigua No. 812. Two other claims by Samuel Warner as administrator of Thomas Norbury Kerby – the Commander-in-Chief of Antigua and Montserrat and descendant of an early Antiguan family, who had died in 1819 – went to the Colonial Court; T71/877, Antigua Nos. 339, 349; *The Times*, 27 January 1820, p. 2.

[71] T71/897, Barbados No. 2034; T71/899, Barbados Nos. 4598, 4925.

[72] Chancellor, 'Slave-owner and anti-slaver', pp. 263–4.

[73] T71/873, St James No. 178.

[74] E.g. Commission to Lt Col. Hugh Hay Rose, Edinburgh T71/1593, pp. 18–19, 12 December 1835.

Berkeley shared £14,000 for two estates in Guiana belonging to their respective wives, daughters and co-heiresses of Paul Benfield, the East India nabob and financier, 'the said Henrietta Sophia Berkeley and Caroline Martha Berkeley having under deeds duly executed consented that the award should be made to them and their husbands conjointly'.[75] How much protection this truly offered is unclear, but Ellen Murray, the wife of Lieutenant-General John Murray, the former Governor of Guiana, was awarded the compensation for five slaves in Guiana, despite Murray having made the claim 'nom uxoris': 'she alone having signed the Power'. Certainly, women tried to use the mechanisms of the Commission to secure more autonomy. Sarah and Mary Ann Rogers, of 2 Cadogan Place, awarded £7,036 12s 11d as a share of the compensation on two plantations in Guiana, wrote to the Commission requesting that the compensation be paid directly to them and not to their agents 'in Demerary' who had filed the original claim as representatives, Benjamin Hopkinson and Hugh Rogers: unusually amongst women recipients, the two Rogers women also signed to collect their own compensation at the National Debt Office.[76]

Conflicts of course arose from regulation and control of property within marriages: conflicts that were often heightened in the compensation process, and that are most easily visible where the relationship between husband and wife had broken down. Thus Francis Glasse and his wife Eliza of London contested the compensation for the Java estate in Manchester. Francis counter-claimed as the annuitant of £100 per annum under the will of his brother-in-law the Hon. W. Stimpson of Jamaica. Eliza responded:

Mrs Eliza Glasse begs to inform the Commissioners that she is intitled under her brother's will the Planter Wm Stimpson an annuity of £100 p.a. – he dying some years ago left Java plantation to my son Francis Philip Glasse he unfortunately dying last year left the entail of the Property to me his mother ... but being a divided family I fear it cannot be settled, only by the Chancellor.[77]

[75] T71/885, British Guiana Nos. 217, 493. Grantley Berkeley, an MP and sportsman, may be at least as representative of British slave-owners as, say, John Gladstone. Berkeley kept a pack of staghounds at Cranford: on one occasion the hunt pursued a deer through Regent's Park and cornered it on the steps of a house at No. 1 Montague Street, Bedford Square. When *Fraser's Magazine* published an unfavourable anonymous review of Berkeley's novel *Berkeley Castle*, Berkeley whipped the publisher Fraser, severely injuring him; *Victoria County History, Middlesex*, Vol. 2 (ed. William Page, 1911), pp. 260–2, available at www.british-history.ac.uk/source.aspx?pubid=84; (George Charles) Grantley Fitzhardinge Berkeley, *Dictionary of national biography*.
[76] T71/885, British Guiana No. 576A–D; letter from Sarah Rogers and Mary Ann Rogers to Commission, T71/1610, 30 October 1835.
[77] T71/860, Manchester No. 464; Eliza Glasse, No. 1 Wilton St., Grosvenor Place to Commission, T71/1606, 3 December 1835.

Compensation for slave-property on the Unity Valley Estate in Portland, Jamaica, was bitterly contested between William Pearson and his wife, after Pearson counter-claimed for one moiety by virtue of inter-marriage. James Vanhouse, the couple's trustee, London consignee and manager under the Court of Chancery intervened: 'Mr Pearson has never paid to my knowledge one shilling towards the support of his wife and four children, since the execution of the deed by which I act now, above 12 years, and there is due above £5,500 arrears of annuity.' Mrs Pearson told the Commission that they were losing one-third of the crop on the estate (because of the Apprenticeship system), that the difficulty could only be met by the payment in question (i.e. the compensation), and that her husband's counter-claim was acknowledged to be intended only as an obstruction.

My children have only my energy to look forward to for their advancement in life ... I will only further trouble you with the judgement of Lord Stowel in the Ecclesiastical court, 'that such a series of brutal and unmanly conduct on the part of a husband had scarcely on any occasion been brought before him and that he must be mad'.

She wrote again to tell them that Pearson had offered to withdraw his counter-claim if Vanhouse paid him: 'MR VANHOUSE let him have it depending on his honor! After he obtained it, he renewed his counterclaim.'[78]

Marriage settlements were intended to protect but also to regulate wives' property, restricting access by women as well as men. Jackson Barwise wrote to the Commission in 1835 to say he understood the Commission had an application from Mrs Delauncy for compensation on Pear Tree Grove and Retreat Estate in St Mary, in which she had a part interest. 'Any such payment w[ould] not be valid', trustees – including Barwise – having been appointed under her marriage settlement: 'the money must be at our disposal for the benefit of her children, not hers'.[79] Richard Trench had written from Elms Lodge, Southampton in 1834:

As trustee to the marriage settlement of Anthony Hardman Esq. I am advised to give you notice that his interest in the Montero estate and in the slaves thereon in the Island of Antigua, are subject to the uses thereof the Trust and thus it will be necessary to have the consent of all the Trustees before any compensation money for slaves so included shall be advanced by you.

[78] T71/868, Portland No. 246A,B; Vanhouse to Commission, T71/1607, 20 November 1835; Mrs A. H. B. Pearson to Commission, T71/1607, 2 March 1836.
[79] Barwise, 16 Blackman Street, Borough to Commission, T71/1606, St Mary, 24 August 1835. Peartree Grove estate appears under St Thomas-in-the-Vale No. 132, a List E claim in which the compensation was paid into the colonial courts.

Hardman was the mortgagee of the estate, and wrote in turn to the Commission in 1836, having been served with the counter-claims of Trench and his co-trustee Rowland Williams as assignees of the mortgage: 'I give you hereby notice that you are NOT TO PAY that CLAIM TO THEM without MY JOINT signature being affixed in discharge of the same.' The Commission awarded the compensation to Trench and Williams notwithstanding Hardman's objection.[80]

Property brought by marriage, of course, was almost invariably itself the fruit of earlier inheritance. Thus Peter Langford Brooke of Mere Hall, a member of a long-established gentry family and Sheriff of Cheshire (and, as noted previously, the son-in-law of the Extinction of Slavery Committee witness, Admiral Sir Charles Rowley), collected £8,098 15s 2d for 629 slaves on the Jonas, Langford and The Wood estates in Antigua. These had come into his impeccable 'county' family by the marriage of his grandfather to a daughter of Jonas Langford, an Antigua planter. Brooke also was a counter-claimant for compensation on Laroche's estate in Antigua against his brother (and heir), Thomas Langford Brooke, together with the other trustees of the marriage settlement of Eliza Brooke (Thomas's wife), which provided for '£150 per annum pin money, £8,000 for children, £800 per annum as jointure'.[81] Again, Richard Bridgens, the architect and furniture-designer, moved to Trinidad for several years with his wife Maria after she inherited the St Clair plantation there.[82]

In many cases, the trustees of marriage settlements and annuities that included 'slave-property' point towards the existence of social networks of people tied to the slave-economy. Thus Abel Rous Dottin, MP, was trustee (together with the agent for Barbados, John Pollard Mayers and others) of a deed of 10 April 1819 for securing to Caroline Cumberbatch (née Chaloner) a sum of £356 per annum for life, and securing to Abraham Parry Cumberbatch her husband 'the estate etc. ... for life with remainder to all his children (except his eldest son) by his previous and then intended marriages)'; the claim involved a

---

[80] T71/877, Antigua No. 11A; Trench to Commission, T71/1609, 16 December 1834 (filed erroneously under Antigua No. 161); H. Anthony Hardman Belle, Vue Lodge, Bitterne, Southampton to Commission, T71/1609, 28 September 1836.

[81] T71/877, Antigua Nos. 28, 105, 308; Antigua No. 392. V. L. Oliver, *Caribbeana*, 6 vols. (London: Mitchell, Hughes and Clarke, 1909), Vol. v, p. 88; *A genealogical and heraldic history of the commoners of Great Britain and Ireland enjoying territorial possessions or high official rank but uninvested with heritable honours, by John Burke*, 4 vols. (London: Henry Colburn, 1833), Vol. iii, p. 627.

[82] Bridgens published a volume of drawings based on the sketch-books he kept, *West India Scenes*, in 1836. The Bridgens received only a fraction of the compensation for the thirty-five slaves on St Clair, the bulk going to Eliza Safe, a creditor of the estate,

compromise with Elizabeth Susannah Jones of Manchester Street, Middlesex, widow and counter-claimant for an annuity of £150 per annum.[83] However, Dottin was also a slave-owner in his own right and was awarded £3,885 16s 3d for 189 slaves on the Coverley plantation in Barbados.[84]

There is evidence that such trustee roles involving slave-property were undertaken out of a sense of duty, being potentially onerous and carrying risk. In a polemical letter after Emancipation opposing the naval blockade of Africa and the abolition of preferential duties on colonial sugar as mutually incompatible, an anonymous 'trustee of a West India property' and captain of the Royal Navy claimed that under the trust deed, he was personally liable to the consignees of the estate for its whole debt to them. One of his co-trustees enjoyed 'the privilege of Parliament' and the other had 'broad lands': the Captain had only his half-pay and a life insurance policy.

[T]hough as a private individual, I am not even in my tailor's debt, yet, as a trustee of a West Indian estate, I make a rather bad figure in a balance sheet; and yet, does the fault lie with myself? I accept an unpaid trust for a near relation without the desire of gain, but in the hope of serving another.[85]

William Frater of Jamaica was executor and trustee for the heirs of Turnbull for the Spring Garden estate in Trelawny. He was assailed by legatees and by merchant creditors, but refuted the claims of the legatees by stating that 'as Exor. he is bound to satisfy 2 judg[ement]s ag[ain]st his Testator & remaining unpaid – which have a prior claim to the legacies of the counterclaimants'.[86]

Such trusteeships and executorships, which preceded the slave-compensation process, suggest a commingling of slave-owners and wider British society as slave-property increasingly featured as one part of estates and bequests of wider property. The compensation process itself generated the need for more such roles. The '4th Rule' of the Compensation Commission specified that it should appoint trustees in cases in which any compensation or interest thereon 'belong to or be vested in any married woman, infant, lunatic or person of insane or unsound mind, or person beyond the seas, or labouring under any

---

but the couple were awarded £374 7s 6d under a second claim, which identified Richard Bridgens as of 29 George Street, New Road, London, and Maria Bridgens as 'of Aranca'; T71/894, Trinidad Nos. 1455, 1456A,B.
[83] T71/899, Barbados Nos. 4948, 4612.
[84] T71/898, Barbados No. 3210.
[85] 'Letters to the Editor', *The Times*, 4 December 1847, p. 8.
[86] T71/874, Trelawny No. 697.

other legal or natural disability or incapacity for the protection of whose rights and interests it may be necessary to make provision'.[87]

Such appointment was not automatic, and some claimants preferred to avoid the cost and complexity of trusts. Eliza Metcalfe ('widow, relict, admix and a devisee of Geo. Metcalfe, of Halton, County of York') was tenant-for-life on three estates in Dominica, with no trustees appointed. Her London solicitors, Baxendale, Tatham, acknowledged that under the 4th Rule the Commissioners could appoint trustees, 'but the parties who are intitled in remainder expectant on Mrs Metcalfe's death, have come to an understanding with her, for an immediate division of the fund, which would render it unnecessary to appoint trustees'.[88] By contrast, Ellis Anderson Stephens's claim for Byde Mill estate in Barbados was opposed by the counter-claims of his four daughters and their husbands (all living in England), subject to his life-interest: he admitted their counter-claims and trustees were appointed to invest their compensation money.[89]

Trustees might be professional agents, or family members otherwise unconnected with slave-ownership, or slave-owners themselves. Constrained as they were by the wider legal framework, as well as by the rules of the Commission, some women nevertheless sought to play active roles. 'I presume I can be the trustee to my son, when the money is to be invested', asked Charlotte Pinnock of Wellington Parade, Gloucester in 1835.[90] Jane Elizabeth Nusum of Clifton successfully counter-claimed as executrix of her brother and heiress-at-law of her late father and brother, holding an execution judgement dating back to 1799 for £2,000 currency on William Hall's Grove estate in Barbados.[91]

Lunacy threatened to disrupt the continuity of ownership for 'slave-property' as for other forms of wealth. J. Phipps Hood of St John,

---

[87] Extract from *London Gazette*, 18 April 1834, T71/1622. The original language of the 4th Rule provided for trustees to be nominated on behalf of the parties interested and approved by the Commissioners, but the 1835 final Rules provided for the Commissioners to appoint trustees directly.

[88] T71/881, Dominica Nos. 4, 5, 275. Baxendale, Tatham to Commission, T71/1609, 4 December 1835. A letter from Robarts & Co., Eliza Metcalfe's London bankers, gives her own address as Rigg House nr Hawes, Yorks.; Robarts to Commission, T71/1609, 29 September 1835; T71/1609.

[89] T71/898, Barbados No. 3777.

[90] Charlotte Pinnock to Commission, T71/1608, Various parishes bundle, 27 July 1835. The claim was for compensation of £829 3s 11d for thirty-three slaves at Clifton in St Andrew, awarded in the name of James Townson as trustee to George Pinnock; T71/865, St Andrew No. 496.

[91] T71/899, Barbados No. 4547A; Commission to Nusum, T71/1593, p. 367.

New Brunswick positioned himself as the agent of Elizabeth Phipps of Gloucester for the compensation for eighteen slaves in St Andrew, resisting the claim filed by Joseph Gordon. Hood had left Jamaica in 1825, giving a power of attorney to Gordon, but he had returned in 1831: 'I have further to observe that I am the only person who ever received a power from Miss Phipps, and upon her decease the property becomes mine.' However, the Commission then received a letter from a W. G. Balton stating that Elizabeth Phipps was a lunatic and praying that the compensation money should not be paid to Hood. The Commission finally revoked the original award in 1843 and made a new award in favour of the Rev. Charles Gostling Turner of Ilchester Place, North Brixton, 'the committee of E. Phipps lunatic'.[92]

There were major awards caught up in lunacy proceedings, including in Chancery suits for John Tharp and John Willett Willett. In the case of the Tharp family of Chippenham Park in Cambridgeshire, in 1801 John Tharp of Jamaica had disinherited his children and passed his estates and slaves to his grandson (also John Tharp) when the latter reached the age of 24: until then, the estate was vested in trustees, including Simon Taylor; the absentee slave-owner Sir Simon Haughton Clarke; Sir Gilbert Affleck; and one of Tharp's London consignees, George Hibbert. John Tharp the grandson was declared lunatic after his marriage to Lady Hannah Hay but before his majority, and the family was embroiled in a prolonged suit over the conduct of Hibbert and the MP Philip John Miles as consignees. The suit was still underway at the time of compensation, and the money for 2,277 slaves on 9 estates in Trelawny and 98 slaves on Chippenham Park Pen in St Ann was paid into Chancery in *John Tharp the elder and others* v. *John Tharp the younger and others*.[93]

In the case of John Willett Willett, the Chancery suit was not a forum of contention but a means of managing the estate of the lunatic by the 'committee', his brother Henry Ralph Willett. The two were sons of John Willett Adey, who had changed his name to John Willett Willett after his adoption by his father's cousin, Ralph Willett, and was subsequently elected as MP for New Romney in 1796 and 1802. Ralph Willett in turn had been a slave-owner in St Kitts, bought the Merley estate at Canford in Dorset in 1751, built a house there and become Sheriff of the county in 1760: his estate was worth £10,000 per annum when John Willett Adey inherited it in 1796. The family still held the

[92] Hood to Commission, T71/865, St Andrew No. 359, 5 March 1835.
[93] S. M. S. Pearsall '"The late flagrant instance of depravity in my Family": the story of an Anglo-Jamaican cuckold', *William and Mary Quarterly*, 60.3 (July 2003), 549–82; T71/874, Trelawny Nos. 384, 396–7, 529, 532, 533–7; T71/857, St Ann No. 480.

St Kitts estates of Red Gate and Bevon Island at the time of compensation, and nearly £6,000 was paid into Chancery for the 351 enslaved on them.[94]

The Commission's insistence on the appointment of trustees for infants in awards above the £200 threshold (below this level the guardian could receive the money on behalf of the children), and the definition of 'infant' often as under 25, meant that there were some notably composed 'infants' in the compensation process. Robert James Hale[s] of Brownham Place, Hotwells, Bristol inherited 'a gang of slaves' in St John in Jamaica from his father, which, he wrote to the Commission, were currently in the possession of Martha Rachel Swinhoe: he himself nominated as his trustees Henry A. Hawkins and Elizabeth Hale, widow (presumably his mother). When Swinhoe died shortly afterwards, it was discovered that she was entitled to the rent and profits of the property until Robert Hale was 21 (as opposed to until her death), so the trust had to be re-structured and another trustee added.[95] Thomas Henly of New City Chambers, Mariner, had recently reached his majority: his late guardian and brother-in-law Joseph Reay had died shortly before, 'having destroyed himself'. Henly was now entitled to his share of the compensation for thirty-two slaves on Mango Valley in St Mary, which had been registered to Henly and his sister Catherine Reay jointly, without allocating them between the two. More than twenty were Henly's property, he claimed, 'and they are of a description quite as valuable as his sister's'. He offered 'his perfect conviction that his sister if on the spot would offer no opposition to the prayer of his petition', viz. that he should get half the compensation money now and that half be held over to be shared, as he had had no benefit during his minority from the labour of the Negroes that had been 'appropriated to the entire use and benefit of his said guardian'.[96]

Again, the trustee role in the context of slave-compensation appears to have been taken on out of obligation rather than desire. The London merchant John Bloxam Elin, for example, declined to act as trustee for Ann Byrne, the tenant-in-tail of slave-property in St Elizabeth, who had petitioned for Elin and E. F. Green to act upon the trusts under the will of William Shaw; a substitute was inserted.[97] Conversely, however,

---

[94] Habakkuk, *Marriage, debt and the estates system*, p. 455; T71/879, St Kitts Nos. 747, 748.
[95] T71/854, St John No. 259A,B. Robert James Hale[s] to Commission, T71/1606, 14 November 1836, 15 December 1836; Commission to Henry Hawkins, High St., Bideford, T71/1593, 16 February 1837. Hawkins and Hale were initially awarded £1,299 5s 5d as trustees.
[96] T71/856, St Mary No. 324. Letter and petition from Henly to Commission, T71/1606, 30 November 1835.
[97] T71/870, St Elizabeth No. 696.

the role was a paid one, at least for the commercial men who engaged in it. The London merchant Robert Kite, who was trustee with Michael L'Hoste of Jamaica to Mr and Mrs Daly and the infant children of the late Alexander Campbell, approached the Commission in 1837: 'in preparing the awards ... I request that you will make provision for the payment of my Commission & Charges out of the principal sums to be transferred'. Kite explained that he could not say exactly how much the charges would be, but requested £100 be awarded to him, with a promise that he would invest the balance if his charges were not that high.[98] Where family members, clergymen or MPs were appointed as trustees, by contrast, networks were established around slavery and the slave-economy, further broadening their reach into British metropolitan society.

Finally, the very nature of the structures put in place to manage and control property, including slave-compensation, created tensions and anxieties. John McHugh, the only residuary legatee in London of the late Dr Robert Garraway of Roseau in Dominica, asked whether it was too late to file a late counter-claim to prevent the executors from receiving the compensation: 'I have reason to doubt them.'[99] John Martin of Greenock explained that 'a relative who resided in Kingston Jamaica died last spring and by will (not a trust will) bequeathed my mother, two sisters and myself Land etc. in that island and about 140 negroes'. Martin and an individual in Kingston were appointed executors; it was a condition of the will that, should the property be sold, the proceeds would be placed in British funds and were not liable to be called upon by the legatees for two years. 'I was immediately informed by gentlemen of the highest respectability that the property had fallen into the hands of one who had gone through his own property and was in all probability not the most likely to take proper care of a stranger's.' Martin sent out his brother-in-law, but the full powers he gave him were not recognised in Jamaica, and the other executor refused to give up the property. '[A]ll I wish is to secure to the females any residue of the compensation.' He asked the Commission to control the award until the legatees asked for it. The Commission could not do this: but appears to have made the award to Elizabeth Martin as heiress of John Scott.[100]

[98] Robert Kite to Commission, T71/1608, Various parishes bundle, 30 May 1837. The Commission rejected his request; Commission to Kite, T71/1594, p. 66, 31 May 1837.
[99] McHugh to Commission, T71/1609, 26 October 1835.
[100] T71/852, St Catherine No. 688; Martin to Commission, T71/1606, 31 October 1834, 12 January 1836.

The Court of Chancery remained the primary forum in which trustees and executors were held to account for their stewardship of assets, including of slave-property and of compensation. Edward Finiston of Brecart, County Antrim counter-claimed as executor of John McCorry for the balance of purchase money for the New Antrim estate in Dominica, 'my counterclaim being made on behalf of an orphan child, destitute of the means of education and dependent on precarious Subsistences'. McCorry had died in 1825 in Dominica, bequeathing the estate to his infant daughter, left under Finiston's protection.

[McCorry's] exors in Dominica allege they sold all his slaves and property soon after his death tho they had no power under his will to do so ... I have frequently applied to them to have the proceeds of the sale invested for the child ... It is now obvious that in place of acting as Exors they have made themselves the heirs of their deceased friend.

In fact, the executors, Alexander Robinson and James Matthews, had sold the estate to J. H. Newman (who filed the original claim for compensation) for £11,000 currency, but received only £3,000. After the Commission awarded the compensation (£904 18s) to Robinson and Matthews, Mary Ann McCorry launched a suit in Chancery against Matthews enjoining him from receiving the money.[101]

Conclusion

The passage of legislation providing compensation in exchange for ownership of slave-property legitimated slave-ownership and made the undesirable desirable. No slave-owner has been found who declined compensation, although some may have contributed their compensation to other causes. Lord Rolle, who granted immediate freedom to his slaves and therefore voluntarily gave up the period of Apprenticeship, nevertheless pursued compensation with vigour, claiming for a runaway slave and only dropping that claim on being informed that it would otherwise delay receipt of all his compensation. The language of entitlement permeates the letters of claimants of compensation. Sir William Laurence Young became vehement in contemplating that he might be too late to file a counter-claim:

The munificence of Parliament has placed a large sum of money at the disposal of the Commissioners to reimburse West India proprietors for the interest they possessed in their slaves, but it never was in contemplation of the legislature to

---

[101] T71/881, Dominica No. 285; T71/1609: Finniston to Stanley, 24 January 1834; Memorial, 29 June 1835; Finniston to Commission, 19 September 1836.

confer a boon upon those who by fraud and the most iniquitous proceedings have become possessed of the property of others.[102]

Stephen Briggs wrote from Weir End, Ross in Herefordshire in 1835 to ask about the compensation for the Spring, Friendship and other estates on the Island of Bequia, which had belonged to C. J. Warner, who by his will had left £5,000 to each of his three daughters:

> The eldest daughter married Dr Baillie; the next Thomas Osborn Esq., and the Third was my wife [who died without children]. If Dr Baillie, or Mr Osborn have received anything, I am precisely in the same situation with them as to the right of sharing and should be most obliged for such information as you should be pleased to give me.[103]

Whatever the language of their discourse or the ultimate success or failure of efforts to secure compensation by individual claimants, the compensation process had in many cases restored value to slave-ownership or transformed a hard-to-realise value thousands of miles away into an immediately redeemable claim in Britain. In response, thousands of British men and women claimed and contested for compensation, actively seeking the identity as slave-owners that few had previously embraced.

The compensation process thus lays bare a cadre of genteel rentier-slave-owners in Britain, located within identifiably 'polite' layers of British society. In the years before Emancipation, such ownership became more widespread as transmission across generations (through inheritance) and amongst generations (through marriage) created new exposures to the slave-economy. Slave-ownership became surprisingly widespread within specific traditional tiers: ownership permeated the rural gentry of southern England to a degree not previously understood.

Slave-owning had thus become normalised and, in particular circles, common within networks of people connected with the West Indies by birth or marriage. For some established families, the identity of slave-ownership was diluted as colonial estates and the enslaved attached to them became commingled with other property, especially landed property, in Britain. At the same time, the circle of those dependent on the slave-economy was widened beyond the actual slave-owners by a system of annuities and legacies that drew further value out of the slave-economy and eventually encumbered the estates. Compensation

---

[102] Young to Commission, T71/1602 Bundle 2, 2 October 1835.
[103] Letter from Stephen Briggs, Weir End, Ross, Herefordshire, T71/1610, St Vincent bundle, 31 October 1835. In fact, the award was made to Thomas Osborn; T71/892, St Vincent Nos. 691, 696.

restored liquidity and value to many of these obligations, and was thus fiercely contested amongst thousands of Britons.

It has been argued that British rentier families such as the Harewoods were not rich because they owned sugar-plantations; they 'were planters *because* they were rich'.[104] But specifically, they were planters because they were rich from participating in West Indian trade as merchants and money-lenders. There is little evidence that rentier Britons with no prior connection to the West Indies made discretionary investments in the slave-economy in the 1820s and 1830s: most had inherited their slaves or their financial dependence on slaves, or made loans secured against slaves in the past. In that sense, many slave-owners in Britain were 'reluctant planters'.[105] But no rentier recipients and beneficiaries of slave-compensation have been found who were so reluctant as to free their slaves or pass up the compensation payments from the British state.

[104] Walvin, 'The colonial origins', p. 3.
[105] S. D. Smith's characterisation of the Lascelles, in *Slavery, family, and gentry capitalism*, p. 177.

6 'Widows and orphans': small-scale British slave-owners

The existence in Britain of a community of 'widows and orphans' dependent on the slave-economy was an established trope of the anti-abolition movement in the 1820s and 1830s, but has drawn little attention subsequently.[1] Although in aggregate these small-scale rentier beneficiaries of slavery (defined for the purpose of this study as pursuing claims under £500) accounted for only a small fraction of the overall slave-compensation, they nevertheless represent a strand of the story of how slave-ownership 'came home' to Britain, and numbered (including unsuccessful claimants) several thousand people.[2] The existence and extent of this small-scale slave-ownership in Britain is a minor but novel finding from the investigation of the Slave Compensation records. Most such smaller-scale slave-owners, though not all, were female. The general difficulties for early-nineteenth-century Britain of reliably identifying individuals of modest means and limited social position are compounded in the case of women compensation claimants by naming practices (for example, describing women in street directories simply as 'Mrs Smith') and the lack of opportunity for women to participate in public life (and therefore to appear in official discourse), and hence it has not been possible in every case to trace the paths to ownership and life-stories of women identified as slave-owners or beneficiaries of

[1] See Chapter 2, above, pp. 89–90 for the use by the anti-abolitionists of the rhetoric of 'widows and orphans' in a Britain dependent on slavery.
[2] This study has identified 491 awards under £500 to rentier absentees totalling £75,755 in compensation, and a further 107 awards to absentees who could not be classified reliably as either rentier or merchant. In contrast to the analysis of awards over £500, which is based on a systematic name-by-name search of all such awards and is intended to be comprehensive, the identification of these 598 awards does not result from a name-by-name search for absentee rentiers amongst the 25,000 awards under £500: instead, the absentees have been identified where the Slave Compensation Commission gave British addresses for the claimants, or where the claimant was identified through research of the larger awards (such as the Hon. Anne Byam Stapleton, who had one award above £500 and one below; T71/877, Antigua Nos. 363, 812). As a result, the figures in this study are likely to understate the extent of small-scale slave-ownership in Britain.

204

slavery resident in Britain. Amongst those who can be identified, and for whom their various paths to ownership of single or small groups of enslaved can be traced, ownership fell into three categories.

First, some of the claimants of amounts below £500 were absentee owners of small estates, generally devoted to tropical crops other than sugar such as coffee or pimento, where the labour force comprised perhaps fifteen to twenty enslaved. Second, others were the beneficiaries of relatively modest annuities and legacies secured on larger colonial estates and on the enslaved attached to the estates. The Rev. William Vernon, for example, of Grindleton Parsonage, near Clitheroe, Lancashire in 1834, had an annuity of £11 2s 6d per annum ten years in arrears on his brother's estate in Antigua, but told the Commission that 'in order to enable my brother to effect certain arrangements with his merchants in London, I engaged some months ago not to make any demand for principal money or arrears of interest and annuity until the Estates should have produced enough to enable him to liquidate his Debt with his merchants'. Rev. Vernon had since been informed of a counter-claim on the estate: 'My brother Captain Vernon who is living in Boulogne did not inform me that there was such a thing as a counter-claim – had he done so, my reply would have been that "I should make my claim on the Government".'[3]

Finally, a third class of small-scale absentees owned enslaved men and women outside the context of the plantation. Such enslaved people worked in gangs of agricultural labourers or as artisans and domestic servants in colonial towns and villages, in both cases rented out by their absentee owners. They were categorised as 'unattached' in the records of the Slave Compensation Commission. In contrast to the owners of colonial estates, who had the possibility of continuing to cultivate their land through the waged labour of their former slaves, the owners of the unattached enslaved were left empty-handed after the end of Apprenticeship, as Dorothy Little and others recognised.[4] Robert Dundas Clunie, 'late of the Island of Jamaica now resident in London' protested at the valuation of his artisan slaves, 'sundry valuable coppersmith and plumber negroes' trained, he said, at a cost of more than £200 each, and as head tradesmen subject to only four years' Apprenticeship, after which his stream of rental income would come to an end.[5]

[3] Rev. William Vernon to Commission, T71/1609, Antigua bundle, 27 October 1834.
[4] See Chapter 2, above, pp. 105–106 for Dorothy Little's analysis of her position as an owner of unattached, enslaved people.
[5] R. D. Clunie to Commission, T71/1602, 19 March 1834. Clunie and Henry Lowndes were awarded £678 19s 2d for twenty-three slaves under two separate claims: T71/855, St Thomas-in-the-Vale No. 322, and T71/865, St Andrew No. 480.

In general these small-scale slave-owners came recognisably from a different and more modest social background than the larger-scale owners. But there were exceptions to this. Henrietta Dallas, for example, of 18 Henrietta Street, Cavendish Square, the daughter of Sir George Dallas, Bart, contested successfully as legatee of her nephew Sir Peter Parker, Bart, the claim of her sister Lady Parker to compensation for ten slaves in Antigua. The slaves had been registered in Lady Parker's name in 1821, when her son the baronet was still a minor.[6] The Hon. (later Sir) Thomas Bladen Capel, Admiral of the Blue and fourth son of the Earl of Essex, was awarded £79 16s 8d for three slaves in St Elizabeth, Jamaica. He had married in 1816 Harriet Catherine Smyth, the daughter of a Jamaican slave-owner Francis George Smyth: these were presumably slaves once owned by his wife.[7] When Frances Cockburn Sims, the daughter of Charles James Sims of Jamaica, was awarded compensation for twelve slaves on Farm Pen in St Andrew, her lawyers Freshfield & Sons explained to the Commission that she was 'at present with Admiral Sir George Cockburn in Bermuda'. Cockburn, the 'burner of the White House' in the War of 1812, was Frances Sims' brother-in-law, the husband of her sister Mary. Frances herself went on to marry in 1837 George Arthur Annesely, Viscount Valentia, only son of the Earl of Mountnorris.[8] Sir Tomkyns Hilgrove Turner, the soldier and courtier who brought the Rosetta Stone to Britain and who was Governor of Bermuda immediately prior to Emancipation, was executor of Francis Jennings, a slave-owner active in Jamaica in the late eighteenth century, and in that capacity Hilgrove Turner shared an award for four slaves in Vere.[9] The nexus of slave-ownership, marriage, and naval or military service as engines of social mobility in Britain thus runs through even the cadre of small-scale slave-owners. But in addition, as would be expected, the circumstances of many smaller-scale slave-owners point to less privileged existences in Britain.

[6] T71/877, Antigua No. 728. Statement in support of counter-claim of Miss Henrietta Dallas, T71/1223 [n.d]. If Henrietta Dallas died, the next legatee was her brother Sir Robert Charles Dallas, also of 18 Henrietta Street (who was himself the recipient of compensation for the Mountraven estate in Grenada; T71/880, Grenada No. 692).

[7] T71/870, St Elizabeth No. 820. The slaves had been registered to Capel in 1832; T71/176, p. 177. Francis George Smyth owned Goshill and Longhill Pen in St Elizabeth, and was active in Jamaica in 1780 (National Archives 3012Z/T/6). The *Dictionary of national biography* entry on Bladen is silent on Smyth's background, describing him simply as 'of Upper Brook St.'.

[8] T71/865, St Andrew Nos. 76, 384. Letter from Freshfield & Sons to Commission, T71/1607.

[9] Sir T. Hilgrove Turner, Great Britain and William Davidson, Great Britain, ex[ecut]or and devisee in trust of Francis Jennings, T71/858, Vere No. 163; 'Hilgrove Turner', *Dictionary of national biography*.

The compensation process might be expected to have posed particular challenges for these smaller-scale slave-owners, who generally had fewer monetary resources and less access to the infrastructure of mercantile consignees and agents than the large-scale slave-owners. Conversely, the importance of the compensation money to this group motivated them to become engaged in the compensation process personally rather than through intermediaries, and encouraged resourcefulness and persistence. As a result, the records of the Commission bring to visibility this otherwise hidden cadre of small-scale owners.

Some smaller-scale owners were clustered together in urban centres of gentility where recognisable communities of 'West Indians' remained connected, and the owners thus caught up with the requirements of the compensation process as a result of incidental flows of information within these informal networks in Britain. There was, for example, evidently a circle of Trinidadian absentee slave-owners to which Mary Hunt of Woolwich Common belonged. In an effort to reclaim a debt from the hire of 'her Negroes' to a whale fishery in Trinidad, she explained (in a letter written for her by another owner of slaves in Trinidad) in 1837 that 'it was by the merest chance that a gentleman mentioned it at my house last week, that he was expecting a power of attorney to receive Mr Joell's compensation'.[10] She then entered a counter-claim against the Joell family (which was resident in Trinidad) and shared in the award.

Again, Maria Macandrew of 56 Cumberland Street, Edinburgh was a frequent correspondent with the Commission and government ministers in the summer and autumn of 1835 and the winter of 1835–6. She clearly maintained a network of Tobago contacts, since she told the Commission she held powers of attorney for Mrs E. Clark (who received £37 0s 10d for five slaves) and Mrs A. Steel (who got £31 3s 5d for one slave), both residents of Tobago. Macandrew wrote to the Commission in July 1835 to ask whether her name was on the list of owners, whether it was for two or three slaves and whether the payment was to be made in England or not. She followed up by writing in September and October to Glenelg and to the Commission separately to ask about the timing 'and the sum which will be allowed me for my

---

[10] Letters from Eliza Jesse, T71/1611, Trinidad bundle, 8 December 1837; and Mary Hunt, 11 December 1837. The letters are in the same hand, but the second one, signed by Mary Hunt, says: 'Mrs Jesse was shocked at her want of attention in signing her own name to a letter she was kind enough to write for me.' Mary Hunt was awarded £80 0s 0d under the contested claim, in which Henry Joell was awarded £63 19s 3d, and the sons-in-law of Richard Joell – 'of unsound mind' – a further £405 7s 10d; T71/883, Trinidad No. 922A–C. Eliza Jesse was awarded a total of £1,776 10s 9d for thirty-four slaves; T71/894, Trinidad Nos. 1860, 1902, 2062.

three negroes in that island valued at £155'. In April 1836 she told the Commission, 'I am a poor widow with a large family to provide for and my only dependance is on the payment of the compensation money for some Negroes in the Island of Tobago.' Macandrew received £74 13s 11d for her three slaves in May 1836.[11]

Early in the slave-compensation process, before the Commission had codified and published its rules there was simply a paucity of information for everyone. Maria Isabella Flockton, for example, wrote from Spa Cottage, Bermondsey in mid 1834: 'I own some property in the Island of St Vincent, and although the period is fast approaching for the proposed Emancipation of the Negroes, I am totally ignorant of the means to be used in obtaining the compensation; and also what writings or documents will be found helpful.'[12] Henry Samuel Beer, writing in January 1835 from Clifton Villa in the very heart of the absentee West Indian community centred on Bristol and its suburbs, sought general information about the status of claims, 'having endeavoured in vain to obtain information in this quarter'.[13] However, reflecting the spread of financial ties to slave-ownership throughout Britain, many second- and third-generation descendants of slave-owners and their families appear to have been outside any 'West Indian' networks of association or kinship, and so had no access to information even once the compensation process and procedures were established. Henry French Palmer, a wine merchant in Cambridge, was awarded £466 17s 7d for twenty-three slaves in Clarendon, property that had come through his wife: he was, he said, 'unacquainted with West India affairs'.[14] Family and birth background in the colonies did not necessarily anchor Creoles in networks of absentee 'West Indians'. Capt. John George Cox was the son of Herbert Palmer Cox and Jane Alexander of St Vincent, and grandson of Harry Alexander the first President of St Vincent, but nevertheless

[11] Macandrew to Commission, T71/1610, 18 July 1835; Macandrew to Glenelg, T71/1610, 27 September 1835; Macandrew to Commission, T71/1610, 7 October 1835; Commission to Macandrew, T71/1593, 6 February 1836 and 16 April 1836; Macandrew to Commission, T71/1610, 13 April 1836; T71/891, Tobago Nos. 80, 96, 136. Macandrew's own path to ownership is not clear: she was described as executrix and devisee of Henrietta Gordon.

[12] Letter from Maria Isabella Flockton, T71/1610, St Vincent bundle, 16 June 1834. The award of £442 13s 6d was made on 22 February 1836 to Webster Flockton; T71/492, St Vincent No. 460. The earlier registration of slaves was made by Wm Sayer for Webster Flockton, in right of his wife, the late M. I. Cruikshank; T71/500, p. 12.

[13] Beer to Commission, T71/1607, 30 January 1835. Beer was awarded £73 13s 10d for four slaves in the town of Port Royal; T71/864, Port Royal No. 82.

[14] T71/859, Clarendon No. 359. Henry Palmer to Commission, T71/1606, 10 August 1835 and 5 December 1835.

wrote to the Commission in some puzzlement from Porlock in Somerset in October 1835 ('Having two apprentices in the Island of St Vincent named Louise and John – for whom I claim compensation – may I be permitted to know how and how much?'), and again in February 1836, when he acknowledged 'this is a subject with which I am totally unacquainted'.[15]

Distance from the colonies gave rise to particular difficulty for those with no surviving network in the colonies and for those who never had access to one. As noted earlier, claims on behalf of absentee proprietors had, by the Rules, to be filed by their agents with the Assistant Commissioners in the colonies: the claims were then collated and forwarded to London. The letter-books are therefore filled with inquiries from small-scale British slave-owners seeking to confirm that the registration of their claims had been effected on their behalf. Eliza Thomas of Edinburgh wrote to the Commission in August 1836 that her late brother Mr Sholto Archibald had left two female slaves in Dominica named Denise and Eve with their children in the charge of Mr Thomas Dawbiney [sic]: 'I as the nearest relation of the said Sholto Archibald beg of you to inform me whether the said female Negroes have been given in by Mr Daubney.' She wrote again three weeks later to emphasise that Daubney was not entitled to the slaves.[16] Mary Scarlett and her daughter Louise of South Lambeth had their slaves (numbering thirty-one and five respectively) duly registered by their attorney in St James, William Reynolds, but he died before the slaves were valued.[17] Sarah Anne Rawlins 'late of the Island of St Kitts now Residing at No. 1 Bilby Place Kennington' wrote to the Commission that she had two female slaves but had received no compensation, 'not having any person filing an [Extract] for me'. The slaves, since her husband's death in St Kitts, had been working to maintain themselves 'by my wish, thinking when Emancipation took place I should with other slave owners receive the compensation granted by a Humane and Generous Government ... I

---

[15] T71/892, St Vincent No. 488. J. G. Cox to Commission, T71/1593, 7 October 1835, and Cox to Commission, 18 February 1836; Commission to Capt. J. G. Cox, HP, 40th Regiment, Porlock, T71/1593, 22 February 1836. He was awarded £44 17s 10d for the two enslaved in February 1836.

[16] T71/881, Dominica No. 859: Eliza Theresa Thomas to Commission, 10 August 1836; Eliza T. Thomas, formerly Eliza T. Dowdy, to Commission, 31 August 1836. She was successful in her claim, being awarded (under her maiden name of Eliza Archibald, widow) £52 7s 3d for five slaves on 19 December 1836.

[17] T71/873, St James No. 815A–C. Mary Scarlett and Louise Scarlett to Commission, T71/1608, 20 August 1835. Mary Scarlett received £465 5s 2d for '31 slaves domiciled on Cinnamon Hill', and Louisa Scarlett £46 10s 6d for her share in four further slaves.

have three children entirely dependant [*sic*] upon me. I have no income but my own exertion to support my family.'[18]

Rebecca Mackenzie wrote from 16 St Andrews Square, Edinburgh and Mount Lodge, Portobello near Edinburgh in pursuit of two claims in Antigua that brought her into conflict with other parties.

I regret to find that Mr Gilchrist has returned my six slaves left me by my sister Grace Dow in his name as her Executor ... I have only to pray that you would show this to the Commissioners so that the above claims might remain until they hear from me which shall be as soon as I get an answer from Mr J. Gilchrist of Antigua[,]

she asked on the first claim. On the second, Rebecca Mackenzie told the Commission she had laid a counter-claim against James Gilchrist, which he acknowledged, saying

he would not put any obstacle in the way of receiving my share, say the half of the compensation for the slaves of Mrs Martha Dow deceased. My brother William Dow having put in a claim for one half, Mr Musson lays claim as a creditor of my late brother Charles Dow supposing he had a share of the said slaves, but he could have none, for he disposed of one half of the Negroes left by my late mother ... My brother and I are the only Heirs and persons entitled to receive the compensation money.

James Gilchrist was awarded the compensation in both cases, his status as executor trumping that of Rebecca Mackenzie as legatee or heiress-at-law.[19]

Even once claimants had succeeded in filing a claim in the colonies, anxiety continued. James Walker of the Colonial Office wrote to the Commission about 'a poor lady of the name of Burman, a Widow, whose claim to one slave had been recognised and returned from Barbadoes', saying that she was now 'at a loss as to what course she should adopt to obtain her compensation'. She was awarded £38 16s 9d a month later.[20]

Distance meant also the lapse of time, especially if two points of the Empire were connected through the metropole. Thus Alexander Campbell wrote from Oban in 1837 to ask whether he needed to send out for a new power of attorney from his son who was with the East

---

[18] Sarah Anne Rawlins to Commission, T71/1609, 5 November 1836. She received £22 6s 7d for one slave; T71/879, St Kitts No. 165.

[19] Rebecca Mackenzie to Commission, T71/1609, 29 January 1836; Rebecca Mackenzie to Commission, T71/1609, unnumbered bundle, 26 August 1835. T71/877, Antigua Nos. 820, 831.

[20] T71/897, Barbados No. 2435 identifies Mary Burman as 'in England'. Walker to Commission, T71/1611, 15 March 1836.

India Company in Calcutta, which, as he pointed out, would take at least twelve months and possibly two years if either letter were lost.[21] Campbell described his son's claims as 'a small trifle'. His awards amounted to £196 5s 7d for ten slaves in St Catherine and £19 10s 10d for one slave in Kingston.[22]

Fixed transaction costs such as stamp duty also loomed large on smaller claims. Anna Maria Fraser of Douglas Row, Inverness wrote to Spring Rice, the Colonial Secretary, in mid 1834 to explain that she had, since the death of her father William Fraser of Goldstone Hall in Guiana, been dependent on her friends in Scotland for support, and that prior to arriving in Britain 'the only money I possessed I laid out in the purchase of a negro slave who stands registered in my name in [Berbice]'. Fraser now needed to create a power of attorney in Berbice to allow the slave to be registered for compensation:

This slave is all the property I possess in the world and my means preclude ... being at the expense of this formal conveyance ... Under the circumstances I have been advised to apply to you for the information whether a mandate on unstamped paper will be a sufficiently legal power to vest my attorney with the necessary authority for uplifting the Govt compensation.[23]

Paths to ownership

For small-scale slave-owners and financial dependants on slavery resident in Britain, the paths to ownership conceptually were the same as for the large-scale rentiers: purchase of slaves while in the West Indies, either as Creoles or on crown service prior to return or migration to England; inheritance; and marriage.

Returnees and colonial migrants to Britain

Returnees and Creole migrants (i.e. those born in the colonies but later moving to Britain) were frequently not large-scale owners. Margaret Kennedy, widow, 'formerly of Dominica but now of Bathphiland Ireland' was awarded £26 16s 4d for one slave whom she owned on Dominica.[24] E. Witter Bucknor, the spinster from Hatfield noted earlier,

---

[21] Alex. Campbell to Commission, T71/1608, Various parishes bundle, 8 March 1837; and to James Lewis, 24 July 1837.

[22] T71/852, St Catherine No. 530; T71/863, Kingston No. 2601.

[23] Anna Maria Fraser to Spring Rice, T71/1610, Guiana bundle, 26 June 1834. Fraser was awarded £35 9s 10d for one slave in November 1835; T71/885, British Guiana No. 181.

[24] T71/881, Dominica No. 148.

inherited a certain number of 'Negroes' on her mother's death when both were in Jamaica in 1793: 'from indisposition and other causes I was inclined to leave Jamaica and visit Great Britain' in 1824, where she had stayed since, owning eighteen slaves hired to the Hopewell estate in Hanover.[25]

Even amongst the smaller awards there is evidence that slave-owning families, especially in Jamaica and Barbados, spanned the Atlantic. Elizabeth Wood Senhouse, a Creole born to the slave-owner Samson Wood in Barbados around 1755, married into the Anglo-Barbadian slave-owning and naval Senhouse family, which had branches deeply embedded in British county society, such as the Senhouses of Nether Hall in what is now Cumbria. She was widowed in 1800, subsequently migrated to Britain and was living in Watford when she filed her claim as owner of two slaves. She died in December 1834 before the compensation was awarded, and the money was paid to two of her sons, Sir Humphrey Fleming Senhouse and Samson Senhouse, as executors. A third son, Edward Hooper Senhouse, acted as her attorney in Christ Church, Barbados. Edward Hooper Senhouse himself first married Elizabeth Bishop Spooner, the daughter of the Hon. John Spooner, the acting Governor of Barbados who died in 1819 at 46 Upper Gower Street. John Spooner's son, also John Spooner, was still living in Gower Street at the time of compensation, when he, and, separately, Anna Maria Spooner (again of 46 Upper Gower Street) were awarded a number of small claims. John Spooner as mortgagee also contested his former brother-in-law Edward Hooper Senhouse's compensation for the Lower Gray's estate.[26]

John Strachan wrote from Caithness on his claim to fourteen slaves in St Ann: 'I hope there will be no stop[p]age or delay in paying me, I am truly a native of St Ann Jamaica or say a Creole, the above is my property left me by Father and mother.' He put his birth date as 1764, said he had fought in the Maroon wars ('I am no imposter'), and included repeated references to the £700 value of the slaves.[27] The Rev. Joseph Duncan Ostrehan of Sheepscombe Parsonage, Painswick in Gloucestershire

---

[25] T71/915, Hanover No. 94, p. 10; E. Witter Bucknor to Commission, T71/1608, 28 August 1835.

[26] T71/900, Barbados No. 5287 (the Parliamentary Papers list gives 'Samuel Stenhouse', but this is more likely to be Samson Senhouse); *A genealogical and heraldic dictionary of the landed gentry of Great Britain and Ireland, by John Burke and John Bernard Burke*, 2 vols. and supplement (London: Henry Colburn, 1846, 1849), Vol. i, pp. 217–18; T71/897, Barbados No. 2380; T71/900, Barbados Nos. 5289, 5290 for the Spooners' awards. T71/900, Barbados No. 5286 for the Lower Gray's claim.

[27] T71/857, St Ann, No. 335. Strachan to Commission, T71/1606, 24 October, 18 November, 20 November 1835.

had been born in Barbados, benefited from slave-compensation after inheriting slaves from his sister Lucretia, and later served in India as chaplain of Vizianagaram.[28] The Rev. Renn Dickson Hampden, the subject of the successive 'Hampden controversies' and ultimately Bishop of Hereford, was born in Barbados in 1793 into a slave-owning family, but came to England aged six. Thirty-five years later, Lt-Col. Thomas Moody of Waltham Abbey wrote to the Commission to say he had 'had a request from the Rev. Dr Hampden of St Mary Hall Oxford to enquire after some domestics left to him in Barbadoes': Hampden was awarded £1 18s 10d for one slave in 1836.[29]

Returnees who were small-scale owners had often been in the West Indies on military, naval or imperial service. James and Elizabeth Christian Carr wrote to Palmerston in 1834, 'knowing your Lordship to be a man of feeling', Elizabeth Carr explaining: 'I have two female slaves at Barbadoes … I am a native of Barbadoes, was married in 1828 to James Carr, he was then in his Majesty's service, the day after our marriage the ship that he was master of arms of was order [sic] to England, it was HMS Aurora.' The two slaves, Nell and Aurora, were aged between ten and eleven.[30] The Carrs tracked the progress of their claim assiduously through frequent correspondence with the Commission. James Carr later complained from Guernsey that he had received only '£28 and some shillings … my claim was for two head people at Barbadoes', even though his wife had clearly identified the slaves two years previously as young female domestics. 'I should also wish to dispose of the 7 years [sic] apprenticeship of each slave', he wrote.[31] Susannah Lynch Harper (née Heath) of Lord Russell Place, Edinburgh, who received two awards for three and four slaves in Jamaica, was the widow of Robert Harper, Lieutenant of the 77th Regiment of Foot. They had married in Hanover, Jamaica in 1827, and Mrs Harper's attorney in Jamaica was William Heath, so she appears to

[28] T71/891, Barbados No. 1013. The award was made to Bezsin K. Reece, constituted attorney and also trustee under the marriage settlement of the Rev. Joseph Duncan Ostrehan … heir-at-law to Lucretia Ostrehan; Frederick George Lee, *Dictionary of national biography*.
[29] T71/897, Barbados No. 2521; Moody to Commission, T71/1611 [n.d.]; *The Times*, 20 December 1847, p. 5; Letter from Edward Renn Hampden, *The Times*, 27 April 1868, correcting the death notice for Renn D. Hampden; Renn Dickson Hampden, *Dictionary of national biography*.
[30] Letter to Palmerston, T71/1611, 8 January 1834.
[31] James Carr to Commission, T71/1611, 9 May 1836. See also other letters concerning process between James Carr and the Commission, T71/1592, 20 January 1834 and 21 June 1834; T71/1593, 19 January 1836, 11 May 1836 and 23 January 1837; and T71/1611, 20 November 1835. T71/895, Barbados No. 970.

have been a Creole of Jamaican family who had followed her husband back to Britain.[32]

Margaret Watts, granddaughter of Monica Kirwan of an Antiguan slave-owning family, married Lt-Col. Samuel Watts of the 4th West India Regiment, but the two were living in Llangollen in Wales at the time of compensation. Margaret Watts and her sister Sarah McHugo had inherited thirty-five slaves from their mother Mary Haverkam, Margaret's share of which Samuel Watts claimed in right of his wife; in addition she was awarded £39 0s 7d for three additional slaves. At the time of her death in 1846, Margaret, by then widowed, was living at 6 Rodney Terrace, Cheltenham.[33] Widowhood was not the only reason for the wives of slave-owners to appear as actors in the compensation process. Emily Pakenham Huggins, the daughter of the Yates naval family of Alverstoke, which itself had strong Jamaica connections, intervened successfully to secure compensation after writing to the Commissioners in 1835 about a claim 'due to my husband', Edward Rodon Huggins, who was Purser on the Andromache and 'a small West India proprietor on the East India station' serving with Lord Napier on his expedition to China: 'the task of bringing to a settlement his affairs in Jamaica devolves to me'.[34]

The Anglican church, as well as the armed forces, generated a stream of slave-owners migrating or returning to Britain, often the widows of clergymen. Jane Elizabeth Bunting, the widow of the Rev. Anthony Bunting, chaplain to the Garrison at Port Antonio, was awarded £252 4s 4d for thirteen slaves on her own account and a further £126 7s 8d for six slaves as guardian to Sarah A. Bunting. After Anthony Bunting died around 1831, his widow came to Britain, where she died at Newport Pagnell aged sixty-one in 1857.[35] The medical profession also created patterns of mobility amongst small-scale slave-owners. Mary Harvey (or Harvie) Cobham, widow, of 17 York Place, Edinburgh was awarded

---

[32] T71/872, Hanover No. 375; T71/873 St James's No. 780. Susannah Harper to Commission, T71/1608, 18 September 1835; Commission to Susannah Harper, T71/1592, 23 September 1835.
[33] T71/877, Antigua Nos. 554, 822. Letter from Barron & Co. to Commission, T71/1223, 15 May 1837. *The Times*, 16 March 1846, p. 9.
[34] Letter from Emily Pakenham Huggins, Lipson near Plymouth, T71/1606, 4 September 1835; Letters from Commission to Emily Huggins, T71/1592, pp. 232, 236. Edward Rodon Huggins was awarded £385 0s 2d for twenty-three slaves under two awards; T71/852, St Catherine Nos. 253, 489. Emily Huggins was the daughter of the naval officer Thomas Legall Yates and Mary Beckford of the slave-owning family. Her cousin, also Thomas Legall Yates, was a merchant in Kingston, returning home to Alverstoke shortly before his death in 1835: his executor Barnaby Maddan was a major recipient of slave-compensation on behalf of Yates's estate.
[35] T71/868, Portland Nos. 131, 183. *The Times*, 12 January 1857, p. 1.

£42 14s 5d for two slaves in Barbados: she had written to the Slave Compensation Commission in July 1836 explaining that she was seeking to recover debts from John Alleyne Beckles (a resident Barbados planter) and others as administrator of Francis Cobham. She had married Francis Cobham MD of Barbados in Edinburgh in 1820; by the 1840s, she appears to have migrated to Australia, where at least two of her daughters by her late husband were married.[36]

Creole widows born in the colonies also appear to have gravitated towards Britain after losing their husbands. Wilhelmina Petgrave (née Johnson) of Westmoreland was widowed shortly after her marriage to Ezekiel Charles Petgrave of St James in 1826. She bore a son after her husband's death and was awarded £167 4s 9d for nine slaves on Richmond Hill as executrix of her husband in 1835, by which time she had moved to Britain, where she remained, living in Devon and dying at Bath in 1888.[37]

As well as widows and servicemen, returnees or migrants also included commercial men who retired to Britain. Henry George Windsor, partner in the merchant firm of Windsor & Milne, was married in Barbados in 1821 and was serving as a vestryman on the island in St Michael parish in 1833, but by the time of compensation, when he was the awardee in several small claims, he had retired to Budleigh Salterton in Devon.[38]

The newspaperman Augustus Hardin Beaumont, the early advocate of compensated Emancipation, was one of the few absentees clearly seeking to 'game' the compensation system. In the compensation process, he filed dozens of counter-claims for slaves in Jamaica. His strategy appears to have been to identify incomplete claims and claims where he could secure small judgements in Jamaica, and then hold them up for a settlement.[39] A number of claimants indignantly denied any connection

---

[36] Mary Harvey Cobham to Commission, T71/1611, 29 July 1836; Commission to Mrs F. Cobham, 17 York Place, T71/1593, 2 August 1836. T71/899, Barbados No. 4364. *Edinburgh Monthly Magazine* (later *Blackwood's*), 1820, p. 705). James Graham, *Australian dictionary of national biography.*

[37] T71/873, St James No. 21. V. L. Oliver, *Caribbeana*, 6 vols. (London: Mitchell, Hughes and Clarke, 1909), Vol. iii: *Families: McIntosh and Petgrave of Jamaica.* 1861 Census; 1888 *England and Wales Births Marriages and Deaths*, both available at www.ancestry.co.uk.

[38] T71/895, Barbados Nos. 113, 291; T71/896, Barbados No. 1036; T71/899, Barbados No. 4377; T71/900, Barbados No. 5044; Windsor to Commission from 137 Leadenhall Street, T71/1611 [n.d.].

[39] See for example the letter of J. Mulholland of London concerning the claims on the Harmony Hill and Ann Grove estates in St George, Jamaica:

I take the liberty of calling your attention to [the] nature [of Beaumont's counterclaims]. A very slight examination (I submit) will shew that Mr Beaumont has taken judgement against the two properties ... for the same sums of money and on dates corresponding, thus locking up two large sums, for amounts in themselves trifling,

with or knowledge of Beaumont. The Commission was correct in its dealings with him, but sought to limit his activity within their own regulations.[40] Beaumont himself was aware of the Commission's disapproval, but justified his behaviour by reference to the circumstances of his forced departure from Jamaica.

> I cannot conceal from myself the fact that my being concerned in so many counterclaims places me in rather an invidious situation before the Commissioners but perhaps they will consider that the hardship is rather on me who am kept out of enjoyment of money which is due me by so many persons and the justice of my claim which is established by the court of justice ... I am anxious not to appear litigious nor vexatious to the Commissioners ... I could state to the Commissioners the very extraordinary causes (mostly political) which have made me a plaintiff in so many judgments would it not be irrelevant and however they may be pleased to think, I feel that the enforcement of these small demands is the most painful duty in which I was ever engaged, but I cannot consent to please the planters of Jamaica by yielding to them my rights as an atonement for proposing in the legislative assembly the abolition of flogging for women ... All this statement is beside the consideration of my counterclaims LEGALLY, but I have a right to remove the MORAL obloquy which my proceedings if unexplained might subject me to.[41]

After Beaumont's death in 1838, his solicitor George Burn wrote to consent to give up an appeal on the award of the Commission's costs against Beaumont: 'I beg leave to express to you a hope that the Commission will instruct you to impose on the widow as little (if any) expense as possible – she has given up all her late husband's property to a judgement creditor excepting a Piano Forte, every article of furniture has been converted into cash for him.'[42]

Inheritance

In the context of the larger-scale rentier-slave-owners, this study has emphasised that the management of 'slave-property' adhered largely

and for which I am quite ready to arrange with Mr Beaumont when he returns to this country. (T71/869, St George Nos. 256, 258; Mulholland to Commission, T71/1607)

[40] See for example the letter from the Commission to Beaumont, 15 January 1836, T71/1593, p. 62: 'an application has been made ...to request that you should be called upon to shew by which authority you have filed the counterclaim ... on behalf of Mr Whitelocke'; and the letter to the Commission from Vizard & Leman, the Commission's own solicitors, in May 1837: 'We have obtained from the [Privy] Council Office certificates of the default of Mr Beaumont in giving security under the act for costs on the 2 appeals Nos. 564 and 892 so that he cannot proceed as to these two' (T71/1608, Various parishes bundle, 30 May 1837).

[41] Beaumont to Commission, T71/1606, 10 February 1836.

[42] Burn to Commission, T71/1608, Kingston bundle, 8 November 1838.

Plate 14   J. A. Hankey, by Maull and Polyblank, 1855. Mercantile
involvement in slavery was also often passed from generation to
generation. John Alexander Hankey, Sheriff of Sussex, was the
nephew of the London merchant Thompson Hankey, became
a partner in the family firm of West India merchants and was
a major recipient of slave-compensation in Grenada.

Plate 15   John Bolton, by Thomas Crane, 1835. Slave-ownership continued to create new wealth in Britain even in the period of abolitionist campaigning. John Bolton, the Liverpool magnate and philanthropist, had started life as a store clerk in St Vincent in 1773 and died 'a gentleman in mind and manners' in 1837.

Plate 16   Samuel Boddington, by William Drummond, circa. 1835.
Slave-ownership was not an obstacle to social acceptance. Samuel
Boddington, a London merchant and slave-owner with estates
throughout the British Caribbean, was closely connected with the
Holland House circle and was a member of the elite Whig King
of Clubs.

Philip John Miles Esq.ᵣ M.P.

Plate 17   P. J. Miles, by John Young, 1822. Philip John Miles of Bristol, MP for Westbury and Corfe Castle, was one of the very few British non-landed millionaires in the first half of the nineteenth century: his wealth derived from his business as a West India merchant and large-scale slave-owner in Jamaica.

Plate 18 West Hill, House of D. H. Rucker. Wealth derived from slavery funded the social aspirations of many London West India merchants. This picture by Humphrey Repton shows West Hill, the Wandsworth home of D. H. Rucker, a merchant and mortgagee of 'slave-property', in 1810.

Plate 19 Otterspool House. Mercantile communities in the 'out-ports' equally benefited from slavery. John Moss, the Liverpool banker and slave-owner who negotiated secretly over compensation with Lord Howick and the Whig government on behalf of the slave-owners in the spring of 1833, built this house at Otterspool around 1812.

to the norms for transmission of landed property in Britain. But the owners of 'unattached' enslaved people also transmitted them as property through willing them to their heirs as specific legacies or as part of the residual estate. William Rothwell of Liverpool, for example, traced his children's inheritance: under his father-in-law Henry Hough's will of 1800, three slaves were bequeathed to Mary Ohlson for the term of her natural life, then to Hough and Ohlson's three children, Jane, Olive and Elizabeth, and to their heirs forever. By 1826, the number of slaves had increased to twelve. Elizabeth, William Rothwell's wife, had since died, leaving four children, 'who are now the sole heirs'.[43]

Smaller-scale claimants were also beneficiaries of annuities or legacies secured on larger estates. Eliza Fraser of Edinburgh was a resourceful and persistent correspondent with the Commission in pursuit of a legacy of £100 from her godfather George Huie of Jamaica, but ultimately failed to secure it in the face of opposition by the executors. 'The Board, following the course which they have invariably pursued in all conflicting claims between executors and legatees, adjudged the money to the persons entrusted by the Testator with the administration of his estate, and passed the award accordingly in favour of the Executors, who are of course responsible to the legatees for the due application of the monies received by them thereunder', explained the Commission.[44]

William Maule of Sunnybank, Falkland, Fifeshire wrote to explain that: 'James Moyes late of Cornwall left my mother Janet Moyes or Maule one fifth share of his estate and as I am her only son, whatever slave money may belong to me I want it to remain where it is as the Settlement made by my mother is very doubtful.' But the Commission, consistent with its principle, awarded the fifth share (£311 15s 6d) to Francis Deas, 'trustee of the Band of Provision executed by Janet ... sister of James Moyes and dated 11th March 1820'.[45]

---

[43] Rothwell to Commission, T71/1606, 27 September 1834. The letter is classified under St Mary, but in fact the claim referred to is St George No. 264. T71/869, St George No. 264 shows a claim by Jane Wilson, tenant-for-life, and a counter-claim from a group of infants by Wm Rothwell, their father and guardian, 'entitled as remaindermen in fee in expectancy under the will of Henry Hough deceased dated 1 January 1800'. Rothwell to Commission, T71/1607, 27 June 1835 identifies Mary Ohlson as grandmother of the children; Commission to Rothwell notifying him of a claim by Mrs Mary Ahlson [sic], T71/1592, pp. 165–6. The award of £227 7s 3d was made to Rothwell and Joseph Jeffreys Broster, presumably a trustee, as the Commission insisted on the appointment of trustees where minors were entitled to awards above £200.

[44] Commission to W. Maconochie, Edinburgh, T71/1594, pp. 83–4, 13 June 1837.

[45] T71/870, St Elizabeth No. 175D; Maule to Commission, T71/1608, 28 April 1837.

Marriage

Given the principles governing property between man and wife, marriage most frequently brought small-scale slave-ownership from the wife's family to the husband. The Commission wrote to John Adam in Glasgow in 1835 for example, acknowledging receipt from him of a copy of a counter-claim lodged in St Vincent by John Barbour, 'the attorney of Jane Wilson, now Jane Adam, and which you are desirous should be recognized as the counterclaim of yourself and Mrs Adam'.[46] The money was awarded in both their names.

Francis White, the former Deputy Secretary of Berbice but by 1835 living at Richmond Terrace in Earl's Court, was awarded £68 8s 0d for one enslaved person after he filed a counter-claim as 'owner or proprietor by marriage on the 16th November 1833 with the claimant Anna Wilhelmina Von Ommeron as appears by Certificate', and produced proof of his inter-marriage and his wife's consent.[47] Thomas Osborn of Frenchay (near Bristol) was awarded the compensation for nine slaves in St Vincent after submitting an affidavit from George Worrall, a magistrate in Gloucestershire, that Osborn's wife Deborah Margaret 'had appeared and being examined separate and apart from her said husband did declare that of her own free will she did consent and agree that the compensation money ... should be paid over to her said husband'.[48] In a counter-example, Sarah Clutterbuck, the wife of the Rev. Lewis Clutterbuck of Newark Park near Wotton-under-Edge in Gloucestershire and daughter of William Balfour of Edinburgh and Jamaica, pursued and received her own compensation for twelve slaves in St James without reference to her husband: 'in what way am I to proceed to procure the money as a personal attendance as specified in the letter would be expensive and inconvenient?', she asked the Commission in 1837.[49]

James Rymer, a surgeon in Ramsgate, described the elaborate background to his and his wife's compensation claim in Dominica. In 1816, he had married the natural daughter of the late John Robinson of Dominica, under whose will £500 was due to his daughter on her

[46] Commission to John Adam, 83 Queens Terrace, Glasgow, T71/1592, p. 158, 18 June 1835. John and Jane Adam were awarded £231 17s 2d for eight slaves on 11 November 1839; T71/892, St Vincent No. 526.

[47] T71/885, British Guiana No. 490.

[48] T71/892, St Vincent No. 357. Deborah Margaret Osborn was the daughter and co-heiress of C. J. Warner: for other claims on Warner's estate, see Chapter 5 above, p. 202.

[49] Sarah Clutterbuck to Commission, T71/1608, 17 June 1837. The award had been made earlier, in January 1836: T71/873, St James Nos. 439, 440.

wedding day, provided the executors consented. They did consent but said they had no money to pay. Rymer's mother-in-law had intended to settle £4,000 upon her daughter, but given the impossibility of the executors paying the £500, 'my wife's mother paid me down £500'. Rymer and the executors then made over the £500 to Rymer's wife, giving her interest in her lifetime and the principal to her children after her death; the marriage settlement also specified that until the original legacy of £500 should be paid into the Bank of England ('not one farthing has been paid'), it should attract interest at 5 per cent. The acting trustee to the marriage settlement, Skeffington Robinson (a London merchant), had kept back the £2 10s 0d interest 'under the plea of what he … calls interest on Legacy Duty!'.[50] Rymer was counter-claiming against Skeffington Robinson's claim as residuary legatee. His wife, Elizabeth, had made the first approach to the Commission, seeking information on the last date for filing counter-claims.[51]

William Marcus Coghlan, an Artillery Lieutenant en route to Bombay, wrote a detailed account of the struggle over twenty slaves left to his wife Mary Jane Marshall by her grandmother's husband, Dr Laurence Hunter. The slaves had been claimed by Thomas Legall Yates of Kingston, as holding a mortgage on Dr Hunter's property greater than the value of that which he had already seized, under plea that Captain Coghlan, CB RN, Miss Marshall's stepfather, had made a written engagement to deliver them up ('Capt. Coghlan denies this – and had no right to anyway)'. William Coghlan concluded: 'the right which I have to these negroes is so obvious that I cannot doubt but your Hon. Board will consider me fully warranted in this application'.[52]

The geography of small-scale ownership

As is clear from the individual examples, there was a concentration of small-scale ownership in a handful of towns and cities throughout Britain. As with the larger-scale rentier-owners, there were few owners in the newly industrialising towns of the West Midlands or Lancashire and Yorkshire. One exception was the Adams family of Walsall, who received £74 2s 6d for a single enslaved person in Trinidad, and a second was George Washington Anderson of Yardley Village, Birmingham,

---

[50] Rymer to Commission, T71/1609, Dominica bundle, 11 August 1835.
[51] Elizabeth Rymer to Commission, T71/1599, 16 June 1835.
[52] William Marcus Coghlan, Ryde, Isle of Wight, T71/1606, St Mary, 29 January 1834. He was on-board ship for Bombay, but a 'country wind' had put it back to port. The award was made to Barnaby Maddan as executor of Thomas Legall Yates, who lodged the original claim but died shortly after his return to England; T71/856, St Mary No. 101.

who was awarded £131 8s 1d for two enslaved in British Guiana.[53] There were a handful of individual owners scattered throughout rural Ireland, such as Eliza Elvira Glen of Newtown Limavady (County Derry), who owned a single enslaved person in Trinidad and received £64 0s 1d, but again Scottish absentees are disproportionately represented amongst smaller-scale slave-owners, including those owning small groups of enslaved, such as Angel d'Arcueil Henghan of Guiburn, Annan in Dumfriesshire (who was awarded compensation for four slaves) or those sharing in the ownership of a single enslaved person, such as Agnes and Martha Montgomerie of Perthshire.[54] Individual colonies had their own patterns of metropolitan ownership, and Scottish ownership was still more concentrated in certain colonies. For example, of the eleven awards in Tobago identified to absentee small-scale owners, nine were resident in Scotland. There were small-scale slave-owners amongst the British diaspora in continental Europe, such as Eliza Jane Warner of Tours who owned two slaves in Trinidad, or Mary Grant Gordon of Brussels who owned twenty-four slaves in Antigua.[55] But most were concentrated in London, such as Judith Baillie, who received compensation for six slaves in Trinidad, in the genteel towns of the south and south-west of England, and as noted previously in Edinburgh.[56]

The sense of entitlement

As with the large-scale rentier-slave-owners, the letter-books of the Commission show evidence of the sense of entitlement that the Abolition Act created amongst small-scale owners of the enslaved and the relatives of such owners. At the same time, the discourse between claimants and the Commission was of course also conducted within the framework of prevailing norms of communication. The letter-books suggest in particular differences in representation between men and women, with men tending to talk of their rights, women of their needs and vulnerability.

---

[53] T71/893, Trinidad No. 273 identifies the awardees Charles Adams and Charles Haden Adams as 'Walsall in England'. T71/886, British Guiana No. 1281; T71/887, British Guiana No. 2574; letter to Commissioners from P. M. James, magistrate for Worcestershire, attesting to the identification of G. W. Anderson, T71/1610, 18 January 1836; Commissioners to G. W. Anderson, T71/1593, 20 January 1836.

[54] T71/893, Trinidad No.114, Commissioners to Mrs Eliza Glenn, T71/1593, p. 177; T71/893, Trinidad Nos. 383, 830.

[55] T71/893, Trinidad No. 903; T71/877, Antigua No. 1055. Mary Grant Gordon was the widow of Francis Grant Gordon of England, and had come to own the slaves for whom she received compensation in lieu of an annuity of £200 per annum.

[56] T71/893, Trinidad No. 677.

William N. Furnace wrote to Spring Rice from the Chief Secretary's Office Dublin Castle about three slaves (including Richard, a mason 'capable of earning £30 British p. annum') whom he had owned with his aunt in Antigua since 1825, 'since which time I never received a penny as compensation':

As my inquiries relative to the above slaves and also my demands for money on their account have been met with evasions, [and] I have not, to this day, got one farthing on their account, I feel impelled to request your interference in the matter, at least as far as to enable me to obtain such portion of their ransom [*sic*] as justly belongs to me.[57]

F. A. Loinsworth, the Deputy Inspector General of Army Hospitals in Bombay, wrote from Bath to claim for two domestic servants who were with him in England. The Commission pointed out that 'the Persons who were formerly slaves of Mrs Loinsworth and yourself were on 1st August last, and had indeed been for a considerable time previously, residing in England and consequently free', and that the Act specifically embraced only those in a state of slavery on 1 August 1834.[58] Loinsworth persisted: he acknowledged they were in England on 1 August 1834, 'yet by more than one Decision of the English courts of justice, they would have become, or returned, to a state of slavery had they returned to the West Indies prior to the passing of the abolition Act, and as slaves could have been sold by Mrs Loinsworth and myself'. He therefore reiterated his request for compensation, 'as it could never be contemplated by the framers of the Act, to deprive Individuals of their Property without some compensation in return'.[59] The Commission was unmoved.[60]

In a similar case, Frederick William Martiny, 'an inhabitant of Belize but at present residing at 38 Allsop Terrace New Road', petitioned the Commission about a slave purchased for £300 currency and given as a nurse by Mary Wall of Honduras (Martiny's mother-in-law) to his daughter Emily in 1831. Two years later, Martiny came to England for his health, bringing his daughter and her nurse, 'to whom she had naturally become attached ... not aware that by bringing the said slave to England he should be injuring his Child's property or rights'. The Commission declined to consider the request for compensation, despite Martiny's willingness to take the slave back to Honduras and pay her passage 'which will not be less than twenty guineas'.[61]

---

57 William N. Furnace to Spring Rice, T71/1609, Antigua bundle, 28 July 1834.
58 Commission to Loinsworth, T71/1592, p. 168, 1 July 1835.
59 Loinsworth to Commission, T71/1609, Grenada bundle, 2 July 1835.
60 Commission to Loinsworth, T71/1592, p. 169, 4 July 1835: 'they see no reason to alter their opinion upon this case'.
61 Letter and petition from F. W. Martiny, T71/1609, 14 May 1835. Martiny did collect £96 5s 4d for four slaves; T71/878, Honduras No. 209.

Matthew Adam, the Rector of the Royal Academy in Inverness, kept a tenacious grip on the compensation awarded to him 'being in right of my late wife Ellen Moffat, proprietor of a pimento-plantation named Rural Retreat in St Ann' in October 1836. The Commission had alerted Adam to the existence of a counter-claim by Philip Pinnock, but appears to have proceeded with the award to Adam while the Assistant Commissioners in Jamaica were still deliberating on the counter-claim. In May 1837, the Commission wrote to Adam to 'recommend to you to refund the sum which you have received in this case'. Adam told them he had written to his attorney in Jamaica, Charles Brown, on 31 October 1836 to discover the origins of Pinnock's claim, 'and if satisfied I would not avail myself of the Decision in my favour'. However, in April 1842 Henry Todd of Edinburgh wrote to the Commission to say that he only now had a power of attorney from Pinnock, 'a poor man ... to proceed here with an action here against Adam the claimant who had surreptitiously obtained an award and drawn payment of the compensation, pending a reference made by his Attorney and the counter-claimant to the Assistant Commissioners who preferred Pinnock' (Pinnock was the executor of a judgement creditor of Adam's father-in-law). Adam was unabashed. He asked the Commission whether there had been different sets of Rules produced by the Commission in the mid 1830s (the other side had clearly produced what he thought was a different set), and, he alleged, 'much suspicion of collusion between Brown and Pinnock existed'.[62]

The language of women, by contrast, tended to be more deferential. 'May I also entreat of you from respect to my departed Husband to watch over as far as may be consistent with the propriety of your office, the interests of myself my Daughter and Grandchildren', wrote Hannah Barnes from Barton Cottage, Dawlish in late 1835, identifying herself as the widow of Joseph Barnes of Kingston, Jamaica.[63] Maria Isabella Flockton of Bermondsey closed her letter to the Commission 'with my apologies for the freedom I am using' in approaching them.[64]

---

[62] T71/857, St Ann No. 46. Adam to Commission, T71/1606, 21 August 1835; Commission to Matthew Adam, T71/1593, 3 October 1836; Commission to Adam, T71/1594, 20 May 1837; Henry Todd, 39 York Place, Edinburgh to Commission, T71/1606, 19 September 1842; Adam to Commission, T71/1606, 26 January 1844.

[63] [Mrs] H[annah] Barnes to Commission, T71/1608, Various Parishes bundle, 21 November 1835. She was awarded directly £157 8s 0d for nine slaves; T71/862, Kingston No. 1856. Her husband's executors were awarded £1,253 2s 10d as a share of the compensation for 267 slaves on Cumberland Pen; T71/852, St Catherine No. 502.

[64] Letter from Maria Isabella Flockton, T71/1610, St Vincent bundle, 16 June 1834. See above, p. 208.

The Commission was inclined to suggest women claimants take professional advice or appoint an agent as a matter of course; whereas only in response to visibly hopeless men did they do the same.[65] The Commission would not engage with women seeking its counsel (few men sought advice, although many sought information). Mrs Eliza Cooper van der Horst wrote from Bristol in 1838, sensibly attempting to get a reading from the Commission as to the strength of her case before she incurred the expense of launching a counter-claim in Antigua, but the Commission was unhelpful: she was free to file a counter-claim, it told her, but it was for her consideration whether she needed help and whether the prospect of success warranted the expense: 'the Commissioners are unable to offer an opinion'.[66]

Slave-compensation and rentier absentee finances

For many small-scale slave-owners, the compensation played a significant role in their short-term financing. It is clear from the intensity of scrutiny and the time and attention bestowed on the compensation question by many claimants that the amounts of money involved were material *to them*. Hannah Barnes, for example, wrote of her income from Jamaica: 'myself, my daughter and her children are entirely dependent for support on what we receive from [my late husband's] Estate: that in consequence of the non-receipt of our remittances for many months past, I am much in want of money'.[67]

There is limited evidence of a market in buying and selling awards within Britain. In the colonies, there was a common pattern of sale of claims to intermediaries, but in Britain there are few apparent examples of it. Hester Smith of 26 Brunswick Place, City Road, formerly of Nevis, appears to have acted as a dealer in compensation claims, acting either alone or with Christiana Smith of the same address as assignee on eight small claims from residents in parishes throughout Nevis.[68]

[65] For suggestions to women to seek professional advice or a London agent, see for example Commission to Mrs Penelope Ballard [Clapham, Surrey], T71/1592, p. 149; and Commission to Eliza Fraser, Morningside, Edinburgh, T71/1592, p. 197, 10 August 1835. Eliza Fraser, at least, did not take the advice but continued herself. For an example of the Commission suggesting to a male claimant he seek help from 'some professional Gentleman', see Commission to James Rymer, T71/1592, p. 201, 13 August 1835.

[66] Commission to Mrs Eliza Cooper van der Horst, T71/1594, pp. 169–70, 10 February 1838.

[67] [Mrs] H[annah] Barnes to Commission, T71/1608, Various parishes bundle, 21 November 1835.

[68] T71/882, Nevis Nos. 9, 53, 67, 147, 192, 238, 255, 277, totalling £640 12s 2d. The two women were also awarded £91 14 s 11d for five slaves of their own in Charlestown, T71/882, Nevis No. 202.

One or two claimants mistook the early payment of uncontested claims for a form of discounting by the Commission itself: Hannah Barnes told the Commission that she had heard 'that there is a Person at the Office, who discounts the non-contested claims' under the sanction of the Commissioners, and she sought to do the same if she could do so 'without great loss'.[69]

The compensation allowed the payment of arrears for annuitants and in some cases the restructuring of the finances of estates. Thus George Goodman from Leighton Buzzard wrote to the Commission to say that he had heard that £5,000 had been awarded to trustees under the will of Henry Smithson on the claim for compensation on the New Forest estate in Guiana, and asked when the money would be paid and at what rate of interest: 'a relation of mine who is an annuitant under the will has been written to, to say whether she will take a promissory note for a sum which may be agreed upon (in lieu and in discharge of her annuity) until the compensation money becomes payable, when the money expressed in such a note of hand is to be paid to the Annuitant'.[70]

A few slave-owners over-extended themselves in anticipation of compensation. Thomas Monkhouse of the Isle of Man had an annuity of £150 per annum from the Hampstead property in St Ann, and was awarded £347 6s 10d by the Commission in 1837; however, he received only £200 of this from his agents (Hamilton Brown in Jamaica and MacKarness & Higgin in London): by 1842 Monkhouse was, said George Duck of Castletown, Monkhouse's trustee, 'now in abject poverty and worse than that considerably involved as he contracted some debts under the expectation of regular receipts from Jamaica', but had had nothing for five years. 'Mr Monkhouse's household furniture is now under arrest for his debts and will be sold and he will be himself incarcerated in Gaol unless he can get some relief soon.'[71]

If the slave-owner were already insolvent, then the compensation process recognised the claims of the assignees of the insolvent. For example, Joseph Bolton and Jeremiah Underwood, both butchers, of Pentonville and City Road respectively, were awarded £333 17s 7d (plus interest) as the assignees of the estate and effects of Mary Ann Portless, an insolvent debtor, for nine slaves Portless owned in Demerara.[72]

---

[69] Barnes to Commission, T71/1608, Various parishes bundle, 21 November 1835.
[70] T71/885, British Guiana No. 356. Geo. Goodman to Commission, T71/1610, unnumbered bundle, 10 June 1835.
[71] T71/857, St Ann No. 472.
[72] T71/887, British Guiana No. 2487. See also *The Times*, 2 October 1837, p. 4 for the subsequent insolvency of the solicitor used by Bolton and Underwood.

Conclusion

Small-scale slave-ownership by *identified* absentees in Britain accounts for about 2 per cent of the 25,000 awards under £500. Unknown further numbers of small-scale British absentees have not been identified in the records, but it is quite clear (and has always been understood) that the overwhelming majority of small-scale owners of slaves were resident in the colonies, and that, in contrast to the large-scale claims over £500, the vast majority of the slave-compensation money paid in awards under £500 went to slave-owners outside Britain. Nevertheless, the compensation process lays bare a group of slave-owners distant from the colonies, often pleading poverty, who were financially dependent on the fruits of their ownership of small numbers of enslaved men and women thousand of miles away, and whose existence helped legitimate the political claims for compensation to the slave-owners. At the same time, these owners were a means by which slavery came home to Britain, through the agency of ordinary Britons who had actively or passively embraced slave-ownership as a means of support.

The story of Ann Gibbons of Ardagh near Newport in the county of Mayo brings together many of the themes of entitlement, the agency of women and its limitations, the language of patronage, the conflict between executors and legatees, conflict within families, and the difficulties of distance that characterise this group of British slave-owners. She submitted a Memorial from 5 Richards Buildings, Shoe Lane in 1837:

That your Honourable Board's Mem[orialis]t has travelled with her daughter under an expense the badness of her circumstances can ill afford from the Western provinces of Ireland to lay the claims of her sick husband Peter Gibbons before His Majesty's First Minister Lord Viscount Melbourne who with his usual humanity and justice which has so uniformly marked his administration has directed Mem[orialis]t by letter to lay her case before your Hon. Board.

The uncle of Peter Gibbons, the original proprietor of Rosemount, had died in 1800 leaving £500 ('now thirteen hundred pounds with interest') to his nephew Peter. However, the uncle's widow Rosetta was remarried to William Hughes, whom she made joint executor of the will of her first husband. Hughes did not pay the legacy, despite repeated applications from Gibbons, 'Hughes well knowing that poor Gibbons was not in circumstances to go to law'. Gibbons commenced proceedings but 'for want of pecuniary means' stopped. Hughes and his wife had both now died intestate; shortly after the deaths, a gentleman in Jamaica had sent Gibbons a power of attorney to enable him to take possession of the estate, but Gibbons had refused 'until the claim should be laid before you'.

That so convinced was the Marquis of Sligo of the justice of the Mem[orialis]t's claim that although on the immediate eve of departure from this country when the Mem[orialist] arrived in London and consequently engaged in preparing for a journey he signed the memorial to Lord Melbourne, being himself fully convinced of the truth of her Story and of the injury which had been done to herself and her infirm husband and Large and unprotected female family ... in addition to the extreme ill health of the Mem[orialis]t's Husband through which she a delicate and friendless woman has been obliged to journey to his Metropolis her extreme poverty is such that she is scarcely able to procure the necessarys of life or pay for the obscure lodging at which she is forced to sojourn much less to obtain the aid of legal advice to assist her ... Mem[orialist] flings herself for redress and commiseration on your Honble. Board.

This was followed later in the year by another Memorial, from Francis Walters of Castlebar, County Mayo, who alluded to the presence earlier in London of 'Anne Gibbons' [sic] and her daughter Sabina in pursuit of this claim and recounted the same factual background to the claim by Peter Gibbons, but said that with his subsequent death his children became rightful heirs, and Ann Gibbons could not claim their right,

as if she got it she would soon spend it foolishly as she had already done with £500 that was got from Jamaica and left her children ever since in poverty by means of her extravagance ... as soon as she heard of said Hughes and his Wife being dead she (said Anne Gibbons the most unnatural of women) caused Sabina her daughter and Mem[orialis]t's wife to rob him of a large sum of money and took her off to England leaving two other daughters behind in poverty. Mem[orialist] further states that it was on account of said property that he married the daughter of said Peter Gibbons and hopes your Hon. Board will protect him and give him his portion of said compensation money ... being one-third.

However, as the Commission wrote to Mrs Ann Gibbons originally, it was too late. The Commission had awarded the whole of the £2,372 5s 7d to William Hughes in November 1835, and it was out of their jurisdiction: 'under the circumstances, it is not in the power of the Commission to afford you any relief'.[73]

---

[73] Memorial of Ann Gibbons, T71/1607, 1 June 1837; Commission to Mrs Ann Gibbons, 5 Richards Buildings, Shoe Lane, T71/1594, p. 70, 30 June 1837; Memorial from Francis Walters of Castlebar, County Mayo, T71/1607, 16 October 1837. T71/865, St Andrew No. 254 shows the award was made to William Hughes as owner-in-fee.

7   Merchants, bankers and agents
in the compensation process

Metropolitan merchants have long been seen as dominating the receipt of slave compensation.[1] As the previous two chapters have sought to demonstrate, such emphasis risks obscuring the extent to which British rentier slave-owners were not only recipients but beneficiaries of slave-compensation. Nevertheless, mercantile participation in the whole compensation process, extending from the leading role of British merchants in agitation for *compensated* Emancipation through their intermediation as agents in the distribution of the compensation to their receipt of compensation as principals, remains fundamental to the overall picture of absentee slave-ownership and compensation.

The presence of metropolitan merchants in the compensation process has been seen primarily as a function of their status as creditors of slave-owners, whether absentee or resident, in the absence of indigenous credit institutions and mechanisms in the colonies. In the traditional merchant-creditor model, the consignee role of the metropolitan agent for a colonial estate was potentially so highly profitable for the merchant that in order to obtain or perpetuate the consigneeship, the merchant was willing to extend credit to the slave-owner on account. In order, in turn, to secure such advances, the merchant might take a mortgage over the estate and the enslaved people attached to it. Metropolitan mercantile involvement in slave-ownership has thus been largely portrayed as the reluctant corollary of the consignee system. While confirming the importance of such traditional creditor relationships, however, the Slave Compensation Commission records also highlight the *active* deployment of new capital by metropolitan merchants after the abolition of the slave-trade. This new capital, especially in the new colonies

---

[1] For example R. Pares, 'Merchants and planters', *Economic History Review*, Supplement 4 (Cambridge: Cambridge University Press, 1960), p. 49: 'in the 1830s the West Indies were sold up largely for the benefit of the factors'; K. M. Butler, *The economics of Emancipation: Jamaica and Barbados, 1823–1843* (Chapel Hill: University of North Carolina Press, 1995), p. 140: 'by the mid-1840s, British merchants and financiers controlled the original indemnity'.

232

of Trinidad and British Guiana, was mobilised as mortgage-lending to planters but also as direct investment in slave-owning. Williams used John Gladstone as an exemplary figure in this context, and the analysis underpinned by the Compensation records allows judgements as to how representative John Gladstone was as a modern capitalist, treating slave-ownership as part of a broader portfolio of investments that were periodically rearranged and restructured.[2]

If the importance of the metropolitan merchants to the slave-economy in this period is well-documented, less work has been done on the importance of the slave-economy to the metropolitan merchants.[3] This chapter seeks to put forward some preliminary measures for assessing how important the colonial slave-economy was to commercial communities in Britain by the 1830s, when Britain, and London in particular, was consolidating a position of leadership as the source of new capital for the development of the Americas, and thereby offering massive new opportunities for the providers and agents of capital flows in areas away from the traditional colonial slave-economy.[4] A core of 'West India merchants', whose business was largely or exclusively devoted to the slave-colonies, was supplemented in the slave-compensation process by the participation of scores of bankers and merchants who were mainly dedicated to other trades, some of which were themselves directly slave-related (such as the American cotton trade) while others were more remote from slavery, such as the Russia trade.[5] These merchants and bankers frequently had only one or two claims in the compensation process: it is clear that while the amount of the compensation money was not negligible to them, and they fought very hard to secure it if

---

[2] E. Williams, *Capitalism and slavery* (London: Andre Deutsch, 1964), pp. 89–90; S. G. Checkland, *The Gladstones: a family biography 1764–1851* (Cambridge: Cambridge University Press, 1971), p. 327.

[3] For the central role of the metropole in the finance of the slave-trade and colonial slavery, see for example R. B. Sheridan, 'The commercial and financial organisation of the British slave trade 1750–1807', *Journal of Economic History*, 53.1 (March 1987), 249–63; and S. G. Checkland, 'Finance for the West Indies, 1780–1815', *Economic History Review*, NS 10.3 (1958), 461–9.

[4] R. W. Hidy, 'The organization and functions of Anglo-American merchant bankers, 1815–1860', *The Journal of Economic History*, 1, Supplement: *The tasks of economic history* (December 1941), 53–66.

[5] See, however, J. E. Inikori's argument that almost every branch of overseas trade was 'slave related'; *Africans and the Industrial Revolution in England: a study in international trade and economic development* (Cambridge: Cambridge University Press, 2002); and the critiques in J. E. Inikori, S. D. Behrendt and M. Berg, 'Roundtable: reviews of Joseph Inikori's *Africans and the Industrial Revolution: a study in international trade and economic development* with a response by Joseph Inikori', *International Journal of Maritime History*, 15.2 (December 2003), 279–361, especially that by N. Zahedieh, pp. 325–9.

contested, nevertheless the West Indian slave-economy itself was not central to their economic well-being and viability. Such merchants participated in financing British colonial slave-ownership on an opportunistic rather than dedicated basis. It is at the level of the individual port that the commercial, political and social influence, and position of these slave-owning and slave-related merchants can best be evaluated: as already noted, there had been no equivalent of the East India Company to institutionalise in joint-stock form the West India colonial endeavour. Nevertheless, it is worth noting that these discrete mercantile communities did at times collaborate in the formation and articulation of the 'West India interest' in Britain.

Aggregate mercantile involvement in compensation

Metropolitan merchants as a whole have been identified as beneficiaries in awards amounting to some £3.76 million of compensation. Their relative importance varies across the different colonies. Metropolitan merchants accounted in total for around one-third of Jamaica's compensation, less than one-tenth of Barbados's, but over half the compensation of Trinidad and British Guiana (Table 7.1). With a proportionately lower rate of absenteeism, Barbados does not appear to have given rise to the same elaborate networks of debt-financed legacies and annuities that ultimately hampered other first- and second-phase colonies. Conversely, as a long-settled colony Barbados had not generated recent heavy capital needs, in contrast to the expansive new third-phase slave colonies such as Trinidad and British Guiana.

In aggregate, London merchants outweighed all outports combined for all colonies other than the third phase, having by far the largest number of merchants active in the slave-economy. But the single largest *individual* mercantile recipients of compensation money (the top twenty-five metropolitan merchants received £1.7 million in total) tended not to be the London-based Jamaican consignees who have dominated the historiography, but instead were merchants active in the more capital-intensive new territories and, second, a group of less well-known merchants with activities across a number of colonies, as Table 7.2 highlights.

Paths to ownership

Merchants in the compensation process can be broken down into broadly two groups. The first are the traditional consignees, the London and Bristol merchant firms who had, since the late eighteenth century,

Table 7.1   *Geographic distribution of mercantile awards over £500.*

	London[a]	Liverpool	Bristol	Other
Awards by number				
Jamaica	262	39	34	30
Barbados	16	15	2	0
1st-phase colonies	76	21	21	10
2nd-phase colonies	100	10	11	21
3rd-phase colonies	115	51	12	67
Marginal colonies	0	0	0	0
Total	**571**	**136**	**80**	**128**
Awards by value				
Jamaica	£814,000	£95,000	£92,000	£86,000
Barbados	55,000	40,000	8,000	0
1st-phase colonies	173,000	54,000	44,000	23,000
2nd-phase colonies	369,000	18,000	41,000	77,000
3rd-phase colonies	757,000	506,000	87,000	366,000
Marginal colonies	0	0	0	0
Total	**£2,168,000**	**£713,000**	**£272,000**	**£552,000**

Rounded to the nearest £1,000. One award over £500 is unassigned. The 313
smaller mercantile awards below £500 totalling £56,279 are not reflected in the
table, but show much the same distribution.
[a] Geographic affiliation of these merchants is not without ambiguities. The important
   firm of T. & J. Daniel is categorised as 'London' in this table, but Thomas Daniel
   remained an important figure in Bristol even after his firm had shifted its centre of
   gravity. Sandbach Tinne had its origins in Glasgow, while George Wildes of London
   had an important sister-firm in Liverpool, Wildes Pickersgill.

marketed sugar and other colonial produce from the West Indian
estates; procured and despatched supplies to the estates; and provided
credit to slave-owners, generally secured by mortgage. In some cases,
these merchants had come to own slaves through foreclosure, taking
control of debtors' estates, sometimes many years prior to the compensation process: they (or their heirs) thus appear in the Compensation
records as claimants, sometimes designated as mortgagees-in-possession, but more often simply as owners or with no specific designation
at all. In other cases, and more commonly, such merchants laid claim
to the compensation money as mortgagees, or other secured or judgement creditors, by means of a counter-claim against the slave-owner to
whom they had previously lent money on the estates and the enslaved.
Such differentiation within the compensation process is only one of
time: many consignee-merchants had both types of exposure to the
slave-economy. For example, the London merchants James Trecothick,
John Henry Roper, William Coles and Francis Thwaites were awarded

Table 7.2   *Twenty-five largest mercantile beneficiaries.*

Rank	Firm	City	Main colonies	Compensation
1.	Davidsons, Barkly	London	Various	£164,875
2.	Sandbach Tinne	Liverpool	British Guiana	£150,452
3.	T. Daniel & Co.	London/ Bristol	Barbados, British Guiana	£140,824
4.	Chauncy, Lang	London	Grenada, St Vincent, British Guiana	£121,664
5.	John Gladstone	Liverpool	British Guiana	£109,934
6.	Hall, M'Garel	London	British Guiana	£101,056
7.	H. D. & J. E. Baillie	Bristol	British Guiana	£76,036
8.	J. Campbell Sr	Glasgow	British Guiana	£73,565
9.	W., R. & S. Mitchell	London	Jamaica	£61,289
10.	R. Bogle/Bogle, King.	Glasgow	British Guiana, Trinidad	£59,059
11.	C., W. & F. Shand	Liverpool	British Guiana	£58,584
12.	J., T. & A. Douglas	Glasgow	British Guiana	£57,862
13.	Reid, Irving	London	Virgin Islands, Jamaica, St Kitts	£49,580
14.	Wm Fraser, Alexander	London	Jamaica	£49,405
15.	T. & W. King	London	British Guiana	£47,961
16.	Pinney & Case/J. F. Pinney	Bristol	Nevis	£44,458
17.	Joseph Wilson & Co.	Dublin	Trinidad	£41,444
18.	P. J. Miles	Bristol	Jamaica	£41,019
19.	J. & H. Moss	Liverpool	British Guiana	£40,353
20.	J. Marryat	London	Trinidad	£38,956
21.	G., W. & S. Hibbert	London	Jamaica	£38,603
22.	Barton, Irlam & Higginson	Liverpool	Barbados	£37,465
23.	T. & H. Murray	Liverpool	British Guiana	£36,917
24.	Timperon & Dobinson	London	Jamaica	£36,575
25.	H. & J. Cohen	London	Jamaica	£35,959

Includes mercantile interception; excludes trustee and executor awards. See Appendix 15 for details.

£622 15s 1d as the owners of Herbert's estate in Antigua.[6] But the same group also counter-claimed as mortgagees against Abraham and Langford Redwood, the absentee owners of the Cassada Garden estate in Antigua.[7]

The second, and less numerous, group are those merchants, predominantly from Liverpool and Glasgow, who invested directly in

[6] T71/877, Antigua No. 117.

[7] T71/877, Antigua No. 103. Abraham Redwood (whose father founded the Redwood Library of Rhode Island) admitted the counter-claim for one moiety, and each side was awarded half the compensation, or £1,428 9s 5d. In the 1840s, Roper and Langford Redwood both served as members of the provisional committee of the Antigua Railway Company, *The Times*, 8 October 1845, p. 15.

the expansion of the slave-economy in the new territories of Trinidad and British Guiana – both by lending money and also by purchasing estates – of whom John Gladstone is the best-known example. Such slave-owners invested ingenuity and effort in bringing slaves to these colonies, despite the obstacles progressively erected to the inter-colonial slave-trade after 1807. Investment increasingly took the form of purchasing and consolidating existing estates rather than financing new ones. Consignee relationships were also established for these territories, but generally with newer merchant firms outside the circles of the traditional Jamaican consignees. Hence, for example, Robert Bogle & Co. of Glasgow held a mortgage dated March 1820 over the Golden Fleece estate in British Guiana for '£11,664 12s 6d subject to deduction as to bales of cotton'.[8]

Merchants in both categories, of course, were not in many cases geographically fixed. In order to conduct their business, they needed to have an infrastructure in the colony they served. In mature slave-economies, this function appears to have been fulfilled largely by the attorney system. In many cases, metropolitan merchants of the 1830s connected with the established colonies had never been to the islands in whose trade they carried on business and where in many cases they had become slave-owners. This was notoriously true of George Hibbert, the MP, agent for Jamaica and Chairman of the West India Dock company. But in expansive slave-territories, local representation appears to have been key. Thus for example the major Liverpool firm of Sandbach Tinne had a partner, George Rainy, resident in British Guiana, and the Liverpool partners had themselves been active in British Guiana in the 1790s. Metropolitan merchants include other examples of men who had either returned or (if Creole) moved permanently to Britain and remained active for a period rather than following a route of retirement and rentier participation, such as Archibald Edmonstone, who had been a minor colonial official and proprietor of 100 slaves in Demerara employed in wood-cutting, and had retired to Scotland, dying in 1837 but apparently maintaining his business in British Guiana.[9]

[8] T71/885, B[ritish] G[uiana] No. 198A,B.
[9] Edmonstone appears in the Compensation records under Archibald Lapslie, 'partner representing the firm of Archd Edmonstone & Co. of Parish St Mark': Lapslie was awarded £6,734 5s 7d for 127 slaves at Waratilla Creek, and Edmonstone himself signed at the National Debt Office in London for the compensation money; T71/886, British Guiana No. 1176; MLN Testaments, www.scottap.com/family/Lanark/MLNTestaments/MLNTestaments1E.html (which show Edmonstone, 'formerly in Demerara, now res. Stirling' in 1834 when his 'brother german' Robert died in Edinburgh). NDO4/8 for Edmonstone's signature.

Metropolitan Britain, although overwhelmingly dominant, was not the only centre of credit-provision to the slave colonies. In a number of territories that had come relatively recently under British sway, older networks of financial dependence centred on earlier colonial metropoles are evident. Thus in British Guiana there are a number of very substantial claims by Dutch merchants and mortgagees resident in Holland; in Trinidad there are more limited linkages to French creditors, as well as to Hispanic creditors on the mainland of Latin America; in St Lucia there are still traces of an intra-Caribbean francophone network centred on Martinique.[10]

One noteworthy absence is that of the British insurance companies, whose development in maritime insurance at least had been intimately bound up with the slave-trade. In the mid eighteenth century, London insurance companies were lending short-term to London merchants; by the end of the century, insurance companies had become major mortgagees of British landed estates and remained so at least into the mid nineteenth century.[11] But through neither route – as creditors of distressed West India merchants or mortgage lenders on West India estates and slaves – do insurance companies appear in the Slave Compensation records.

Mercantile interception

Merchants came into conflict in the compensation process, with each other but also in particular with the slave-owners for whom they acted as consignees and lenders. The issue of 'mercantile interception' – awards where metropolitan merchants, as opposed to resident or absentee slave-owners, were in fact beneficiaries although not named as awardees – has been discussed previously, and the argument made that in most cases the underlying records of the Compensation Commission betray evidence of such interception.

It is important to note that in addition to 'mercantile interception' as defined in this study, there were of course many awards in which the

---

[10] In British Guiana, for example, J. J. Bysterus Heemskerk of Amsterdam, a liberal politician and newspaper owner, was awarded over £40,000 as mortgagee on four estates (T71/885, B[ritish] G[uiana] Nos. 637, 662, 696, 713) and a group of Amsterdam merchants led by Jan Frederick Scharff were awarded £12,000 as mortgagees (T71/885, British Guiana Nos. 154, 290, 357). In Trinidad a group of French mortgagees led by Fabien Jacques de Sallier were awarded £2,582 1s 7d (T71/894, Trinidad No. 1606). In St Lucia, the heirs of Louis Joseph Hardy de St Omer of Martinique were awarded £3,621 1s 5d as mortgagees of 142 slaves (T71/884, St Lucia No. 876).

[11] S. D. Smith, *Slavery, family, and gentry capitalism in the British Atlantic: the world of the Lascelles, 1648–1834* (Cambridge: Cambridge University Press, 2006), p. 152;

merchants are directly named as awardees having intervened as cred-itors. In some cases, the whole management of the claim was devolved to the creditor metropolitan merchant by the debtor slave-owner. For example, in Antigua the slave-owner Samuel Warner claimed for 246 slaves on his Belle Vue estate. The Liverpool merchant William Shand counter-claimed as mortgagee, and Samuel Warner signed a letter of attorney to Shand and another 'appointing them as his attorneys to relinquish his claim wholly or in part to the compensation and to admit such counterclaims as shall appear proper': Shand subsequently took £3,674 13s 1d of the compensation and Warner the residue, £337 19s 3d; both are named as awardees in the Parliamentary Return and the underlying records.[12] In more numerous cases, the counter-claim of the mortgagee was admitted by the original slave-owner claimant, and an apparently amicable settlement agreement reached with the com-pensation being awarded to the mortgagee. Thus William Forsyth of Plantation Friends in British Guiana admitted a counter-claim from the London bankers Smith, Payne & Smith as mortgagees, and the whole compensation of £14,689 12s 3d for 272 slaves was awarded in the name of George Robert Smith, one of the bank's partners.[13]

In a minority of cases, contestation amongst slave-owners or rival claimants and mortgagees was mediated by the Commission. Thus the London merchants Hall, M'Garel counter-claimed on the Endragt and Mon Repos plantations in British Guiana against an original claim by William Atwick Hamer as attorney and trustee of the Hamer estate: Hall, M'Garel held a mortgage dating from 1816 for £22,679 0s 3d plus inter-est of £1078 0s 6d. The award was bitterly contested by a second coun-ter-claimant, Lieutenant Michael Hamer, 'alias Michael Greatheed Hamer of 87 Blackman St Borough as youngest legitimate son and as having a life interest'. At the Arbitration Board (the Commission's ses-sion for hearing contested claims), documents were produced in evi-dence that Hamer had signed away his rights (for consideration) in the 1820s. When Hamer continued to complain of the process followed by the Commission in arbitrating the award, and claimed he had been unfairly excluded from the process, the Commission lost patience with him, writing to him that Mr Boys of the solicitors Forbes, Hale & Boys 'proved upon oath that he had duly served you the counterclaim with

---

D. Cannadine, 'Aristocratic indebtedness in the nineteenth century: the case re-opened', *Economic History Review*, NS 30.4 (November 1977), 624–50 (pp, 636–7).
[12] T71/877, Antigua No. 351. The co-attorney appears to have been the London stock-broker Joseph Wartnaby, although the manuscript entry is indistinct.
[13] T71/885, British Guiana No. 167. Smith, Payne & Smith held two mortgages for £8,050 and £14,868 and upwards.

notice that a Replication [i.e. a response] to your counterclaim had been filed in this office – he also put in two letters from you with an admission to that effect'.[14]

Finally, there are examples of true 'mercantile interception' that are not explicit but have left evidence in the underlying records suggesting what had probably really happened to the compensation. Chauncy & Lang, as mortgagees for £9,716 13s 8d, lodged a counter-claim against Capt. George Warren on Taymouth Manor and Farm in British Guiana. The Compensation records carry the note 'Replication of George Warren admitting counterclaim and consenting that compensation be awarded to counterclaimants Chauncy & Lang'. But the counter-claim was then withdrawn, and Warren appears as the recipient of the whole compensation (£18,344 9s 6d): it appears most likely that Chauncy & Lang 'intercepted' a portion of the compensation to cover their mortgage.[15] As noted previously, in all cases where merchants issued counter-claims and withdrew them, but went on to collect the compensation money at the National Debt Office, the awards have been classified as 'mercantile', so strong is the suspicion of mercantile interception.

Women and mercantile compensation

Mercantile involvement in the compensation process at first appears resolutely masculine. There are no examples evident in the Compensation records of women actively involved in merchant firms engaged in the West India trades.[16] Partly, of course, this may reflect naming practices, firms trading exclusively under the names of the male partners whatever the involvement of women. At the turn of the century, a handful of women had invested under their own names in the West India Docks, suggesting active participation in and control over investment decisions by women within the mercantile community, from which the Docks' investors were almost exclusively drawn.[17]

However, closer inspection reveals a more complex pattern of involvement by women in mercantile receipt of compensation. Women were

---

[14] Letters from Commission to Lt Hamer, 10 December 1835, 9 December 1836, T71/885, British Guiana No. 555. T71/1593.

[15] T71/885, British Guiana No. 618.

[16] In the mid century, two women were partners in private banks: The Rt Hon. Sarah Sophia Child, Countess of Jersey, in Child & Co., and Ann Tisdall in Tisdall & Ward; see J. W. Gilbart, 'A ten years retrospect of London banking', *Journal of the Statistical Society of London*, 18.4 (December 1855), 333–44 (p. 340).

[17] N. Draper, 'The City of London and slavery: evidence from the first dock companies', *Economic History Review*, 61.2 (May 2008), 432–66 (p. 437).

certainly beneficiaries of merchant fathers, husbands and brothers converting mercantile capital into rentier capital through marriage settlements, legacies or annuities. Cecilia Douglas of Glasgow, for example, was the sister of three brothers who formed the West India firm of J., T. & A. Douglas: she married Gilbert Douglas, another West India merchant, in 1794, and outlived all her male relatives. She was awarded £3,013 12s 7d for her half-share in the Mount Pleasant estate on St Vincent in 1836.[18] Again, Cecilia Blake had been brought to Dublin by her father's cousin, the Dublin merchant Valentine O'Connor, when her father (and O'Connor's agent) Bryan Blake died in St Vincent in 1801. O'Connor left Cecilia £500 on his death in 1813, but Cecilia's brother Martin successfully contested provisions of the will by which O'Connor specified the sale of his share of the Mount William estate in St Vincent, which he had bought from Bryan Blake before the latter's death. The original purchase was revoked, and Cecilia Blake was awarded £5,052 14s 9d compensation for the 188 slaves on the estate in 1837.[19]

But women, of course, also inherited the mercantile capital in the firms themselves when husbands or fathers died before retirement. Margaret Higgin was one of three executors and trustees of Isaac Higgin, a deceased partner in Higgin & Whitely & Co. of 18 London Street. Together with her co-executors, and trustees John Anderson and Thomas Graham, Margaret Higgin was awarded £11,067 4s 4d for 607 slaves on 5 estates in St Ann.[20] Together with Graham (Anderson was in Jamaica), Margaret Higgin signed for the compensation at the National Debt Office.[21] Mary Higgin, under the will of a second deceased partner, John Higgin, was awarded a further £3,867 11s 10d for 193 slaves on the Great Pond estate, on which John Higgin had been the assignee of a judgement debt dating from 1801.[22] Similarly, Maria Lang was executrix and devisee-in-trust with Charles Porcher Lang under the will of her husband, Robert Lang, a deceased partner in the London merchant firm of Chauncy, Snell & Lang: she shared in awards in Grenada and British Guiana.[23]

---

[18] T71/892, St Vincent No. 490A; J. G. Smith and J. O. Mitchell, *The old country houses of old Glasgow gentry* (Glasgow: James MacLehose & Sons, 1878), LXXIX: Orbiston House.

[19] T71/892, St Vincent No. 470. V. L. Oliver, *Caribbeana*, 6 vols. (London: Mitchell, Hughes and Clarke, 1909), Vol. IV, pp. 252–5.

[20] T71/857, St Ann Nos. 11, 12, 725, 727, 728.

[21] NDO4/3 for Higgin and Graham's signatures.

[22] T71/857, St Ann No. 302.

[23] T71/880, Grenada Nos. 759, 786; T71/887, British Guiana Nos. 2316, 2334, 2340.

London merchants and bankers

Over 150 London merchants have been identified in the compensation process as beneficiaries of compensation; dozens more appear to have acted only as agents. Of these London merchants, about one-half were firms that appear to have had British colonial slavery as their main or exclusive business. Of forty-seven leading London 'West India merchants' who signed a protest to Goderich in April 1832 setting out a minatory critique of the Orders in Council of November 1831 and an explicit claim to compensation, forty-six appear as recipients of slave-compensation later in the 1830s.[24] This core of forty-six merchants together accounted for £1.14 million or just over half the total compensation flowing to all London merchants. In addition to the signatories of the 1832 Protest, a further thirty-two firms have been identfied that feature amongst the London mercantile claimants or recipients of compensation and appear as 'West Indian merchants' in London trade directories of 1832 to 1834.

Outside this core of dedicated West India merchants was a larger circle of merchants who appear to have participated in the slave-economy on an opportunistic basis. Some London merchants engaged in colonial slavery were also actively involved in the affairs of the East India Company as it restructured. Others combined interests in slavery with involvement in new colonisation in Australia or Canada. George Fife Angas, for example, was a Honduras merchant of 2 Jeffries Square, London, who acted as agent in collecting compensation of some £7,000 for resident Honduran owners.[25] He later was the 'leading spirit' in the colonisation of South Australia and established the South Australian Company, the Bank of South Australia and the Union Bank of Australia, serving as London chairman of all three firms until he left England in 1850 to settle in South Australia, where he died in 1879.[26] Andrew Colvile, a prime mover in the 'Hill Coolie' importations into British Guiana after Emancipation, was heavily involved with the Hudson's Bay Company and later became chairman of the Royal Mail Steam Packet Co.[27]

---

[24] 'Copy of a protest transmitted by the West India mercantile body of London to the Right Hon., Lord Viscount Goderich, 9th April 1832', *The Times*, p. 3. The signatories not receiving compensation were Cottam & Morton. The only leading West India firms not appearing as signatories were Ellice; Kinnear (the firm of the Whig Secretary of State Edward Ellice); Reid, Irving & Co.; and Joseph Marryat & Sons, a firm embedded in the colonial politics of Trinidad.

[25] T71/878, Honduras Nos. 51, 199, 231, 244. NDO4/10 shows Angas's signing for the compensation for these awards.

[26] Obituaries, *The Times*, 24 May 1879, p. 9.

[27] E. S. Meany, *Origin of Washington geographic names* (Seattle: University of Washington Press, 1922), p. 54; Sir James William Colvile, *Dictionary of national biography*.

Four of the top ten metropolitan mercantile recipients of compensation were exclusively London-based (the Daniels of Bristol and London were also in the top ten), and only one of these (W., R. & S. Mitchell) was a traditional Jamaica consignee. Nevertheless, London merchants overwhelmingly dominated the Jamaica consignee trade. There was significant continuity over half a century for many of the London firms. A memorial from London merchants of 1846 to the Earl of Clarendon included as signatories the Hibberts, Davidson & Co., Timperon & Dobinson, and J. Marryat, all names recognisable within the West India interest as early as the 1790s.[28]

Despite the visibility of *mercantile* credit, British banks were also engaged in financing the slave-economy by the 1820s and 1830s. Of sixty London banking firms listed in 1835, thirty have been identified in the Slave Compensation records, both as principals and agents.[29] Sixteen of these banks were involved solely as agents in collecting the compensation from the National Debt Office and, presumably, banking it on behalf of the awardee. R. Barclay of Barclay, Bevan & Tritton, for example, collected on behalf of John and Henry Moss of Liverpool the £40,353 18s 3d payment to the Mosses for 805 slaves on Anna Regina in British Guiana, the second largest single compensation award made. Partners in four further firms (Coutts & Co.; Curries & Co.; Smith, Payne & Smith; and Williams Deacon) acted as trustees or executors for slave-owners as well as (in three of the four cases) agents for collecting the compensation. Coutts & Co. was the most actively involved agent amongst the London banking firms, with a notable proportion of Scottish absentees amongst the slave-owners for whom it acted, including the largest single payment: that to the MP James Blair for £83,530 8s 11d for 1,598 slaves on the Blairmont estate, again in British Guiana. In addition, Sir Edmund Antrobus and William Colthurst acted as trustees, together with the solicitor Oliver Farrer, of the marriage settlement of George Watson Taylor, in which capacity they were awarded over £40,000 for a number of estates in Jamaica.

The involvement of London banks on behalf of their slave-owning clients, in what after all were basic processes of collection and deposit of large payments made in London to those clients mostly living elsewhere in Britain, appears unremarkable because, of course, the compensation process transformed ownership of human beings into financial claims and financial assets, abstract, fungible and respectable. Even

---

[28] Included in Thos Daniel & Co., *A letter to His Grace the Duke of Newcastle on West India affairs called forth by the misrepresentation of the Anti-slavery society* (London, 1854), pp. 25–6.

[29] See Appendix 16 for full details.

trusteeships and executorships dealt in assets or records of assets physically distant from the realities of slavery.

Beyond the agency and trusteeship functions, however, ten London banks (and possibly an eleventh) were direct beneficiaries of the slave-compensation process, having lent against the security of slaves. The largest recipient was Smith, Payne & Smith, the unimpeachably Evangelical banking house, which was the leading creditor of the collapsed West India merchant Manning & Anderdon, and which had secured its lending against mortgages on that firm's estates and slaves.[30] Hankey & Co., the banking firm of William Alers Hankey, which he had been careful to distinguish from his family's West India merchant firm in his testimony to the Extinction of Slavery Committee in 1832, was awarded £5,777 8s 0d for slaves on Arcadia in Trelawny, and lodged counter-claims as mortgagee against Sir Edward Hyde East on his estates in St Mary and elsewhere.[31] The firm of Bosanquet Anderdon was awarded £3,953 10s 0d for 243 enslaved on Nevis under two claims as mortgagees and assignees, and a further £2,018 0s 8d with the official assignee George Lackington for 115 enslaved owned by William Maynard on Nevis; in a further claim by William Maynard, 'an amicable arrangement' appears to have taken place between Maynard and his creditors, amongst them Bosanquet and Lackington, over the compensation for 107 enslaved on New River.[32] The partners of the London banking firm of Sir James Esdaile were mortgagees-in-possession of the Hazelymph estate in St James.[33]

Overall, of twenty-one London predecessor banks of today's Royal Bank of Scotland Group active at the time of Emancipation, six (Dorriens, Magens, Mello & Co.; Sir James Esdaile; Robarts Curtis; Smith, Payne & Smith; Vere Sapte; and Hankey & Co.) have been identified as receiving compensation as mortgagees of slave-property; partners in three more (Coutts & Co., Curries & Co. and Williams Deacon Labouchere) acted as trustees or executors of slave-owners, as well as agents in the case of Coutts and Williams Deacon; and six acted solely as banking agents (Barnard Dimsdale; Joseph Denison & Co.; Drummonds; Sir J. W. Lubbock; Prescott Grote; and Glynn Mills).[34] One London predecessor of Lloyds TSB was a beneficiary (Bosanquet

[30] R. B. Sheridan, 'The West India sugar crisis and British slave Emancipation, 1830–1833', *Journal of Economic History*, 21.4 (December 1961), 539–51.
[31] T71/874, Trelawny Nos. 25, 26, 27; St Mary Nos. 11, 14, 15, 153.
[32] T71/882, Nevis Nos. 76, 132.
[33] T71/873, St James No. 5.
[34] See Appendix 16 for references to the sources underpinning the summary in this paragraph.

Anderdon), and four acted as banking agents (Barnetts Hoares, Sir T. H. Farquhar, Praed & Co. and Stevenson Salt).[35] Two London predecessors of Barclays (Barclays, Bevan & Tritton and Goslings) acted as banking agents, while a partner of Cocks, Biddulph was a trustee and possibly mortgagee of James Dawkins's estates in Jamaica.[36]

In 2006, Citizens Financial Group Inc., a US subsidiary of the Royal Bank of Scotland, published an *Historical research report* of an investigation into the surviving records of the predecessor firms of the parent and subsidiary 'to identify any links between these predecessors and the slave trade or slavery which are documented in their records'.[37] The report identified, as the sole case of a predecessor firm owning slaves, an instance arising from a loan secured by mortgage in Grenada in 1766 by Hankey & Co., which was foreclosed in 1767. It also acknowledged that the individual partners of Hankeys 'appear to have been part-owners of the Arcadia estate Jamaica' from the 1790s.[38] It further identified a loan by Prescott, Grote & Prescott on a coffee-plantation in Dominica as the second known case of mortgage-lending secured by slaves.[39] The Report therefore apparently did not discover the lending against the security of slaves by five out of the six predecessor firms identified in the Slave Compensation records, including two firms (Dorriens, Magens, Mello and the large-scale beneficiary Smith, Payne & Smith) whose archive records were expressly researched for the study.[40] Nor did the report

[35] In addition, Simon Halliday, a partner in an earlier embodiment of Sir T. H. Farquhar (Herries Farquhar Halliday Davidson & Co. of St James's Street), was a creditor and kinsman by marriage of Gilbert Mathison: Halliday took possession of the Castle Wemyss estate in 1823 when Mathison was pressured by his Glasgow merchant. See U. Halliday, 'The slave owner as reformer: theory and practice at Castle Wemyss estate, Jamaica 1808–1823', *Journal of Caribbean History*, 30.1–2 (1996), 65–82.

[36] Only London banks have been systematically researched. Provincial predecessor banks also appear in the Compensation records. For example, a predecessor of HBOS, Sir William Forbes of James Hunter & Co. of Edinburgh, was awarded compensation as judgement creditor of Helen Watt, gentlewoman, for slaves in Jamaica; T71/860, Manchester No. 348; T71/1190.

[37] Citizens Financial Group Inc. and Royal Bank of Scotland Group, *Historical research report: predecessor institutions research regarding slavery and the slave-trade*, 25 May 2006, www.citizensbank.com/pdf/historical_research.pdf.

[38] Citizens Financial Group and RBS Group, *Historical research report*, p. 5 & p. 6.

[39] *Ibid.*, p. 6. This mortgage is not apparent in the Compensation records twenty years later.

[40] Smith, Payne & Smith appears twice in the report, once in the context of owning 'American stocks' between 1820 and 1828, and once in acknowledging that two partners of the bank, Edward and Rene Payne, owned a merchant firm 'which is not a RBSG predecessor' and had links to European slave-colonies in the Caribbean during the 1770s; Citizens Financial Group and RBS Group, *Historical research report*, pp. 6–7. The Report also provides a list of fourteen British firms (including Hankey & Co.; Prescott's Bank; Robarts Curtis; and Smith, Payne & Smith) where partners

identify amongst the '[b]usiness ties to individuals or institutions that owned slaves' any of the relationships of predecessor firms with slave-owners, such as Coutts with a dozen recipients of slave-compensation. In May 2009 RBS reportedly revised the original report in response to press attention to the role of Smith, Payne & Smith discussed above.[41]

Boyle's 1835 list of sixty 'London bankers' utilised in the above analysis does not include what became known as the 'merchant banks', such as Baring Brothers or N. M. Rothschild. These merchant banks appear to have had exposure only to one or two slave-owners, but such exposures could be very high. Thus Baring Brothers lodged counter-claims on six estates in British Guiana against Wolfert Katz, the largest slave-owner in the colony, under what seems to have been a single, but very large, mortgage entered into in the mid 1820s.[42] Baring Brothers, in the names of Francis, Thomas and John Baring, Humphrey St John Mildmay, and Joshua Bates, also counter-claimed under a deed of assignment to creditors of the Carnes family dating from 1807, for the compensation for sixty-four enslaved on Spring Garden estate in British Guiana, which was awarded to Charles Benjamin.[43] Sir Thomas Baring (the father of the partners Thomas and John Baring, who had himself retired from the bank in 1809) lodged a counter-claim against Eliza Edgar of Edinburgh for the compensation for 156 enslaved on the Osborne estate in St George, Jamaica and, failing in his effort with the Commission, planned to pursue Edgar for the compensation through a lawsuit.[44] Alexander Baring, the senior partner of the Barings firm

---

'may as individuals have owned slaves or had ties to slave enterprises', and of twenty partners and directors of predecessors (including Edward and Rene Payne) 'who may have had ties to slave voyages'; Citizens Financial Group and RBS Group, *Historical research report*, Appendix 4, p. 17, and Appendix 5, pp. 18–19.

[41] Citizens Financial Group Inc. and The Royal Bank of Scotland Group, *Historical research report: predecessor institutions' research regarding slavery and the slave-trade*, first published 25 May 2006, updated 29 May 2009, briefly posted at www.citizensbank.com/pdf/historical_research.pdf; *Financial Times*, 27/28 June 2009, p. 1.

[42] T71/885, British Guiana Nos. 21, 89, 270, 363, 424, 479. Baring Brothers held a mortgage dated 30 August 1824, apparently to secure Katz's Account Current with them executed by Katz for £81,717 19s 0d. Katz's replication 'denying legal execution of s[ai]d mortgage' is recorded at T71/885, British Guiana No. 21. Katz died in 1835, and all six claims totalling almost £60,000 were awarded in the names of his executors Edward Briant (Katz's son-in-law) and G. G. Lowenfeld, but T71/1252 shows the withdrawal of a claim by Katz's widow Susan Barclay Katz, and a 'consent to pay the compensation to Messrs. Baring or the exors. of Wolfert Katz who have granted a power to the said Messrs. Baring Brothers to receive the same'.

[43] Thomas Baring also signed for the compensation for 233 enslaved on Anna Catherina in British Guiana, awarded to the Voute family; T71/885, British Guiana No. 699.

[44] Claim from Eliza Edgar as 'Acting executrix and Trustee under will of James Edgar, and also as an annuitant'; counter-claim from Sir Thomas Baring, Loughnan,

prior to his retirement in 1830, was one of four London bankers to whom three estates belonging to Manning & Anderdon in St Kitts were assigned, and on whose behalf the compensation was awarded to James William Freshfield Jr.[45] Nathan Mayer Rothschild, as seen previously, had raised the public loan for the slave-compensation process, but he was also a counter-claimant as mortgagee for compensation for eighty-eight enslaved on an estate in Antigua, for which Charles Chatfield, the trustee of Rothschild's executors, was awarded £1,570 18s 0d after Rothschild's death.[46] There is no evidence, however, that Jews as a whole were disproportionate owners of slaves at Emancipation.[47] Other merchant banks that still survive, if only in name, are also present in the Compensation records.[48]

Guthrie & Pratt on mortgage to Jno [sic] Willis, a large creditor of James Edgar, T71/869, St George No. 278. Letter from Stokes & Co. informing the Commission of Sir Thomas Baring's intended lawsuit against Eliza Edgar for her compensation money, T71/1607, 19 March 1838. Sir Thomas Baring, *Dictionary of national biography*.

45 T71/879, St Kitts Nos. 206, 336, 724. The awards were made in the name of James William Freshfield Jr and Charles Bosanquet as trustees. T71/1031 shows the claims; a note with a cover letter from Freshfield & Sons of 16 January 1835 in T71/1224 sets out the background of the assignment and the associated debt of £5,000 to each of Alexander Baring, Jeremiah Harman, Sir Edward Hyde East and John Pearce. Alexander Baring, 1st Baron Ashburton, *Dictionary of national biography*.

46 T71/877, Antigua No. 390. The award is missing from the Parliamentary Return but details are shown in the underlying records. The claim was by Robert Hyndman, a bankrupt merchant from Dublin, for 158 slaves on the Matthews and Constitution Hill estates, and the original counter-claim was by Nathan Mayer Rothschild 'of the city of London merchant under a conveyance of said [Matthews] estate and 88 slaves for securing £3,000, interest to be computed at 5% on £2,650 part thereof from 2 April 1825 and on £350 from 1 November 1829 – £600 of interest has been paid'. Additional counter-claims were filed by other creditors and by the assignees of Hyndman. Nathan Rothschild and Baron James de Rothschild filed a further counter-claim for £3,878 8s 7d principal and interest, described as an amended counter-claim. After litigation in Antigua between James de Rothschild and rival claimants, Chatfield was awarded the larger part of the compensation under this claim number on 22 July 1839. Letter from Chatfield, Wingate & Hart to Commissioners re. Matthews Estate, enclosing copies of an order from the Antigua Court of Chancery on 8 April 1839 'by which the division of the slave compensation money in respect of this Estate is arranged', T71/1609, 13 June 1839. The receivers' balances in the colonial court had been invested in government stocks, 'and as soon as these are sold out we shall be enabled to acquaint you with the exact balance to be awarded to Mr Rothschild's executors'.

47 Only a handful of Jewish merchants in London were active in the compensation process as agents and principals, notably Judah and Hymen Cohen, whose links with Jamaica's Jewish communities are evident in the Compensation records. For the controversy over the extent of Jewish slave-ownership and participation in the slave-trade, see E. Faber, *Jews, slaves and the slave trade: setting the record straight* (New York and London: New York University Press, 1998).

48 Alfred Latham, the co-founder of Arbuthnot Latham, was awarded £2,921 16s 0d for 148 enslaved on Sunning Hill estate in St Thomas-in-the-East, Jamaica, together

If the City of London was important to the slave-economy, espe-cially to Jamaica and the older colonies, how important was the slave-economy to the City? Several pieces of evidence combine to provide a framework for assessing slavery's direct and indirect importance to the City, and suggest first that slave-ownership or lending against slaves was a minority interest and, second, that this minority was nevertheless disproportionately influential. It is clear that the recipients of slave-compensation constituted only a small proportion of the participants in the commercial life of the City. In December 1834, for example, over 5,000 merchants, bankers, ship-owners, traders and others con-nected with the City of London signed a 'dutiful and loyal address' to the king.[49] Of these signatories, about 250 individuals, or less than 5 per cent of the total, are identifiable in the slave-compensation pro-cess. This list of signatories is not a complete account of London mer-chants, nor is it an unbiased sample: it generally excludes merchants with Whig sympathies, for example. But, as argued above, the bulk of those involved in the slave-economy were indeed Tory, Anglican and anti-Reform. Therefore, even in a cross-section likely to have a disproportionate number of those engaged in the slave-economy, the overwhelming preponderance of London merchants did not have suf-ficiently close ties to the West Indian colonial slave-economy to have any direct involvement in the financial settlement on the extinction of the system. (They may, of course, have been tied to other slave-systems in the Americas or in other British colonies, such as Mauritius and the Cape of Good Hope).[50]

Nevertheless, several different strands of evidence indicate that the West India merchants were disproportionately represented amongst institutions generally accepted as representing the City elites. Though relatively small in numbers, the merchants closely tied to the slave-econ-omy had larger capital than the average City trader, and greater influence

---

with William Pulsford and Joshua Hobson (it is unclear in what capacity this award was made to Latham; William Pulsford and his brother Robert were assignees of a mortgage on the estate, and Latham may have been acting as a trustee or executor for Robert Pulsford); T71/867, St Thomas-in-the-East No. 192. Alfred Latham also signed for the compensation for 106 enslaved on the Lathams' estate in Trinidad awarded to Ann and Charles Latham, the executors of Thomas Latham of Thomas Latham & Co. of London (T71/894, Trinidad No. 2024). Ann Latham, the widow of Thomas Latham, also received compensation under T71/877, Antigua No. 486 and T71/882, Nevis No. 157.

[49] *The Times*, 29 December 1834, p. 5.
[50] For evidence that the slave-economy was one of many strands of activity in the equally diverse City economy of the eighteenth century, see P. Gauci, *Emporium of the world: the merchants of London 1660–1800* (London and New York: Hambledon Continuum, 2007).

appears to have been the corollary of this greater wealth. For example, of the fourteen Governors of the Bank of England elected between 1807 and 1834, nine were recipients of slave-compensation: it is noteworthy, however, that all of the first eight of these Governors between 1807 and the revival of anti-slavery agitation in 1823 later received slave-compensation, but of the six between 1823 and the Abolition Act of 1833 only one subsequently received slave-compensation. Between 1833 and 1875 (by which time the generation of City men active at the time of slave-compensation was dying out), a further eight out of twenty-one Governors were men who had received slave-compensation in the 1830s. Of the twenty-four directors of the Bank of England elected in 1821, nine later received slave-compensation; of the twenty-four elected in 1832, just prior to the Abolition Act, six were recipients of slave-compensation.[51]

Again, at the dinner to celebrate the laying of the foundation stone for the new Royal Exchange building in 1842 by Prince Albert, 100 'merchants, bankers etc.' were invited alongside the City of London Aldermen and national government ministers and officials: of these, twenty-seven had received slave-compensation in the 1830s.[52] This disproportionate importance of slavery is also indicated by the success of the West India merchants in mobilising wider support. The City was capable on occasion of engaging thousands of merchants in some limited forms of political activity, as the 1834 loyal address showed. As previously noted, there were a reported 6,000 people at the April 1832 rally of the West India interest and its City friends. When a meeting of the 'planters, merchants, ship-owners, manufacturers, tradesmen and all others interested in the preservation of the British West Indies' was called the next year in the crisis of May 1833, 189 signatories convened the meeting and 1,500 attended.[53] Of the signatories, around 100 can be identified as slave-owners or as merchants receiving slave-compensation: the other half comprises merchants with lines of business outside the West India colonial trade narrowly defined, signing either because of indirect exposure to the slave economy or potentially out of simple solidarity with neighbouring merchants. The non-compensation signatories included, for example, the stationer Letts & Son and the seedman Jacob Wrench.[54]

---

[51] For an analysis of the changing composition of the directors from 1833 onwards, see A. Howe, 'From "Old Corruption" to "New Probity": the Bank of England and its directors in the Age of Reform', *Financial History Review*, 1 (1994), 23–41.
[52] The attendees are listed in 'Ceremony of the laying of the first stone of the new Royal exchange', *The Times*, 18 January 1842, p. 5.
[53] 'Meeting of the merchants, ship-owners etc.', *The Times*, 28 May 1833, p. 5.
[54] Classified advertising, *The Times*, 25 May 1833, p. 1; 27 May 1833, p. 1.

West Indians were also prominent in the cultural and social life of the City. George Hibbert himself had entered the City in the 1770s, and his family firm were amongst the most significant of the old-line Jamaica consignees. He was a co-founder of the London Institution, conceived as a City counterpart of the Royal Institution, and served as its President. His biography betrays some social anxiety in Hibbert around these activities, characterising the London Institution as 'an ornament to the metropolis', but also 'one calculated to benefit the present and succeeding generations, especially at a period when, from the general diffusion of literature and science, the higher and middle classes of society are imperatively called upon to maintain their stations, by acquirements which, in former ages, were either neglected or very partially pursued': 'he loved to dwell upon the elevation of mind which such pursuits had produced in his own time on the mercantile character'.[55] When through inheritance Hibbert was able to leave commercial life, he also sold off his library and his art collection, both very important accumulations, on the basis that he did not have space at his new country house at Munden for them.[56]

It is important to note that London's 'West India mercantile body' was not homogeneous. It was riven by conflicts of its own. The West India merchants had divided in the late 1790s over the building of the West India Dock, a minority defecting to the rival London Dock scheme.[57] When the period of monopoly over 'tropical produce' for the West India Docks expired in 1823 and Parliament debated the renewal of its privileges, spokesmen against monopoly included the West India merchants (and slave-owners) Joseph Marryat and Alexander Glennie. The West India Committee itself suffered an upheaval in 1830 when Lord Seaford was replaced as chairman in the midst of internal controversy over how to respond to abolitionist pressure.

The identities of London merchants were not exclusively bound up with the nature of their business (such as the West Indian versus Baltic trades), but were also cut across by competing ethnic, religious, political and cultural affinities. The Highland Society of London, for example, combined Scottish grandees and a mercantile elite that included slave-owners alongside non-slave-owners.[58] There were pro-Reform recipients of slave-compensation within the City. Samuel Boddington,

---

[55] [J. H. Markland], *A sketch of the life and character of George Hibbert Esq., FRS, SA & LS* (printed for private distribution, 1837), pp. 10, 16.

[56] *Ibid.*

[57] Draper, 'City and slavery', pp. 4–5.

[58] See 'We the undersigned members', *The Times*, 5 July 1830, p. 2 for a list of Highland Society members convening a Special General Court of the Society.

for example, and (rather oddly) George Hibbert were two of ten slave-compensation recipients amongst the sixty merchants, bankers and traders petitioning the Lord Mayor to convene a meeting in support of the Reform Bill of March 1831; in an overlapping group of forty-six City signatories (amongst them Zachary Macaulay) who solicited the Lord Mayor again in September 1831 to organise a petition to pressurise the (anti-Reform) House of Lords, nine were compensation recipients, including the slave-mortgagees A. W. Robarts, Rees Goring Thomas and John Towgood.[59]

Free Trade also divided the recipients of slave-compensation, although again not evenly. The traditional consignees were protectionist and even mercantilist in their rhetoric and political activity, but a minority of merchants and bankers involved in slave-compensation were supporters of the repeal of the Corn Laws, including Henry Barkly; the bankers Price, Marryat & Co.; John Horlsey Palmer; and John Rae Reid. When this group tabled a City petition expressing satisfaction at the final passage through the Commons of the repeal of the Corn Laws, 'believing this measure to be essential to the progressive prosperity of every class of the community', their claim to speak for the City as a whole was challenged by a protectionist group heavily populated with former slave-owners and mortgagees, including T. & W. King, the Neaves, Stewart & Westmoreland and John Irving.[60] The latter was in partnership with the pro-Repeal signatory John Rae Reid.

Liverpool merchants and bankers

Liverpool had been the centre of the British slave-trade in the second half of the eighteenth century, and the networks established between the port's mercantile community and the West Indian slave-economy continued beyond 1807, so that descendants of slave-traders such as the Tarletons and the Backhouses appear as recipients of slave-compensation as owners and mortgagees in the Commission records.[61] But even in Liverpool, where the slave-economy weighed more heavily within a much smaller city than was the case with London, the port's development was not simply the product of the slave-trade and of West Indian

[59] *The Times*, 22 March 1831 p. 3; 19 September 1831, p. 4.
[60] 'News', *The Times*, 30 May 1846, p. 5; 17 June 1846, p. 6.
[61] See for example D. Richardson, S. Schwarz and A. Tibbles (eds.), *Liverpool and transatlantic slavery* (Liverpool: Liverpool University Press, 2007), especially D. Pope, 'The wealth and social aspirations of Liverpool's slave merchants of the second half of the eighteenth century', pp. 164–226; T71/880, Grenada No. 998; T71/884, St Lucia No. 624 for Tarleton and Backhouse claims.

slavery, but also of its role as the commercial and shipping centre for its hinterland.[62]

Nevertheless, Liverpool mercantile capital figures prominently in the compensation process, and the compensation in turn had a perceptible impact on the regional financial system centred on the city. Liverpool merchants collected compensation across the whole of the West Indies and the Caribbean, with the material exceptions of Grenada and Trinidad. William Shand, the surviving partner of the firm of C., W. & F. Shand of Liverpool, was a recipient of over £21,000 compensation as mortgagee in Antigua, on mortgages that largely dated from the early 1820s. Shand also appears to have owned estates in British Guiana, on which he collected a further £37,000.[63] The merchant firm of Barton, Irlam & Higginson rivalled T. Daniel & Co. as the largest mercantile recipient of compensation in Barbados.[64] William Parke and his former partner Richard Hall were major recipients of compensation in the south-eastern parishes of Jamaica around Kingston. But the heaviest concentration was in British Guiana, where fifteen Liverpudlian merchants were awarded a total of some £450,000. John Bolton received £15,391 17s 11d for 289 slaves on his Waterloo estate, and a further £8,723 12s 8d by virtue of two first mortgages dated April 1816 and May 1828 on the estate of John and Mary Ann Noble.[65] Bolton had, years earlier, been the subject of a savage personal attack by George Baillie, a bankrupt London slave-trader, who set out to humiliate Bolton by revealing his origins as a clerk in the West Indies.[66] The firm of Sandbach Tinne was the second-largest single recipient

---

[62] J. Longmore, '"Cemented by the blood of a Negro?" The impact of the slave-trade on eighteenth-century Liverpool', in Richardson, Schwartz and Tibbles, *Liverpool and transatlantic slavery*, pp. 227–51. An important part of this regional role, of course, was in serving the Manchester cotton industry, which was itself dependent by the early nineteenth century on American slave-grown raw material.

[63] T71/877, Antigua No. 3 identifies the claim by Wm Shand and Francis Shand, 'remaining partners of C., W. & F. Shand of Liverpool'. T71/885, British Guiana No. 542 shows 'Charles and William Shand, owners': the William Shand of Jamaica who gave evidence to the Extinction of Slavery Committee in 1832 and was a recipient of compensation in Jamaica was a returned Scottish planter with no apparent connection to the Shands in Liverpool.

[64] Barton, Irlam & Higginson appears primarily in the Compensation records under the name of Richard Deane, the attorney and executor of John Higginson, the surviving partner of Sir William Barton and George Irlam. George Barton Irlam and Jonathan Higginson were awarded £5,623 16s 10d for 274 enslaved on Three Houses in Barbados as trustees in which there was a tenant-for-life of the estate; T71/897 No. 2771, and additional amounts on Palmers, T71/897 No. 2751B.

[65] T71/887, British Guiana Nos. 2273 (Waterloo), 2478.

[66] G. Baillie, *Interesting letters addressed to John Bolton Esq. of Liverpool, merchant and colonel of a regiment of volunteers* (London: J. Gold, 1809).

of slave-compensation, receiving £150,000 from its claims in British Guiana.[67]

The slave-compensation money had a noticeable financial impact on Liverpool's commercial community. The 'Circular to Bankers' in March 1836 noted that compensation had resulted in 'a great accession to the floating capital of Liverpool'.[68] M. C. Reed argues that the disproportionate early ownership of railway shares in the north-west was a function not only of the re-investment of new capital from the cotton industry but also from the re-deployment of slave-compensation money, and cites *The Times*'s assertion that 'a large proportion of money paid on West India claims ... found its way into [the railway shares] market'.[69] The Grand Junction Railway borrowed £50,000 from the Gladstone family in August 1836.[70] The 1846 Parliamentary Return of those individuals investing more than £20,000 in railway shares since 1840 shows Hardman Earle (with a cumulative railway investment of £109,000), John Crosthwaite (£115,000), Robertson Gladstone (£26,300) and John Moss (£36,000), all Liverpool merchants in receipt of slave-compensation.[71]

As with London, recipients of slave-compensation were prominent in Liverpool's public life, both in political and philanthropic institutions. The two Mayors immediately preceding Emancipation (Samuel Sandbach and Charles Horsfall) were mercantile slave-owners, as were the Mayors in six of the previous thirty years. Eleven of the forty-one members of the Common Council of Liverpool in 1833 were recipients of slave-compensation. There were close family ties, as contemporaries observed, amongst this oligarchic group: Sir John Tobin, for example, and his nephew Peter Whitfied Brancker, both Common Councillors, were jointly awarded compensation for forty-seven slaves on Cold Spring in St Mary.[72] Yet, again, there were divisions of politics

---

[67] The Booker brothers, founders of the firm that later became Booker McConnell and that dominated the Guyanan sugar trade until the nationalisation of the industry in 1976, were at the time of compensation acting as attorneys and agents for slave-owners, and were only small-scale slave-owners on their own account: their large-scale purchases of estates began in 1838. Their awards include British Guiana Nos. 609, 610, 797, 929.

[68] 'Circular to Bankers', 11 March 1836, cited in M. C. Reed, *Investment in railways in Britain 1820–1844: a study in the development of the capital market* (Oxford: Oxford University Press, 1975), p. 268.

[69] *Ibid.*, pp. 262–4.   [70] *Ibid.*, p. 237.

[71] 'Railway speculation: a list of the names and descriptions of all persons subscribing to the amount of £20,000 and upwards to any railway subscription contract deposited in the private bill-office during the present session in Parliament (extracted from a Parliamentary return)', *The Times*, 13 August 1846, p. 3; 15 August 1846, p. 6.

[72] T71/856, St Mary No. 78.

amongst those who had slave-ownership in common. Thirty-six of the Council were Tory (and eight of these were slave-owners); but of the five Whigs, three (Charles Lawrence, John Ewart and Henry Ashton) were recipients of slave-compensation.[73] As noted above in Chapter 3, the question of Emancipation was divisive in the November 1830 parliamentary by-election, with the Whig candidate William Ewart (whose family firm Ewart, Myers was a lender to slave-property in Antigua) advocating immediate action towards abolishing slavery (although with compensation) and later espousing the equalisation of East and West India sugar-duties. Yet other issues brought together those who were divided over slavery. As with London itself, slave-owning (or conversely abolitionism) was only one identity amongst several available to, and at different times defining, merchants in Liverpool in competition for power and place. One dimension of organisation and identity was certainly that of the geography of overseas commerce: the West Indies traders association versus the associations for the East Indies, US, Baltic, Mediterranean and other trades. Liverpool's commercial politics at the time of the abolition of the slave-trade was marked primarily by a division between the American and West Indian traders, in which the American traders had progressively gained the upper hand.[74] But anti-monopoly cut across slave-owners and their opponents. Of forty-five Liverpool mercantile signatories of resolutions at a public meeting in 1829 seeking Free Trade to China, at which John Gladstone and James Cropper collaborated, eleven later received slave-compensation. Local allegiances – 'place-based loyalties' – against the London metropolitan interest were also strong.[75]

In philanthropy, Cropper and Gladstone – and slave-owners and abolitionists more generally – continued to co-operate. The Liverpool abolitionist Adam Hodgson served as trustee to one slave-owner in Jamaica. Joseph Brooks Yates, 'one of the leading reformers of Liverpool', the co-founder and President for twelve years of the Liverpool Literary and Philosophical Society, President of the Liverpool Royal Institution, and one of the founders of the Southern and Toxteth Hospital, was awarded almost £20,000 as mortgagee over a variety of estates throughout Jamaica, and was trustee or executor on awards of a further £20,000 of compensation, including as executor of Kean Osborn, the former

---

[73] *Liverpool Mercury*, 22 November 1833.

[74] S. G. Checkland, 'American versus West Indian traders in Liverpool, 1793–1815', *Journal of Economic History*, 18.2 (June 1958), pp. 141–60.

[75] J. Civin, 'Liverpool petitions and imperial identity', in J. Hoppit (ed.), *Parliaments, nations and identities in Britain and Ireland 1660–1850* (Manchester: Manchester University Press, 2003), pp. 187–205.

speaker of the Jamaican Assembly who had died in Switzerland in 1820.[76] John Moss, the banker and British Guiana slave-owner, was vice-president of the Liverpool Mechanics' Institute and president of the Marine Humane Society in the mid 1820s, and 'Mrs Moss' was the Lady Patroness of the Female Penitentiary or Magdalen Asylum.[77]

Bristol merchants

Bristol had lost its leadership in the slave-trade as early as the 1740s, but continued as the third port behind Liverpool and London, and its commerce as a whole remained oriented, although by no means exclusively, towards the West Indies.[78] The city was deeply inscribed by its involvement in the slave-trade and with the wider slave-economy, and its residents continued to represent a concentration of slave-ownership, both mercantile and rentier, into the 1830s.[79]

The Bristol West India merchants were generally confined to the first- and second-phase sugar-colonies, based on networks established relatively early in the seventeenth century and then reinforced in the first half of the eighteenth century in Bristol's heyday as a slave-trading port.[80] Most Bristol merchants were only marginally if at all involved in the later expansionary phase of slavery in Trinidad and British Guiana. The Pinneys, as is well known, were focused on Nevis, and Cunningham & Robley on Tobago. Amongst the Jamaican merchants, the MP and millionaire Philip John Miles was a major slave-owner in Hanover and Trelawny.

[76] Joseph Brooks Yates, *Dictionary of national biography*. The *Dictionary of national biography* refers a little coyly to John Ashton Yates, Joseph's brother and MP for Carlow and himself a recipient of slave-compensation in Trinidad, as 'author of pamphlets on trade and slavery': J. A. Yates in fact had written a proposal for Emancipation by paid manumission. For J. B. Yates's awards as beneficiary, see T71/859, Clarendon No. 404; T71/860, Manchester No. 418; T71/868, Portland Nos. 254, 259; T71/869, St George Nos. 199, 333, 334; and T71/858, Vere Nos. 37, 122B, 161. For J. A. Yates, see T71/894, Trinidad Nos. 1831B, 1893, 1895.

[77] *Gore's Directory of Liverpool and Its Environs* (Liverpool, 1827, 1841).

[78] Richardson estimated 40 per cent of the income of Bristolians derived from slavery-related activities in the late eighteenth century; D. Richardson, 'Slavery and Bristol's "Golden Age"', *Slavery & Abolition*, 26.1 (April 2005), 35–54 (p. 35). Charles Pinney claimed in 1830 that five-eighths of the port's trade was with the West Indies; P. Marshall, *Bristol and the abolition of slavery: the politics of emancipation* (Bristol: Bristol Branch of the Historical Association, 1975), p. 1.

[79] For the 'social history' of the slave-trade, see M. Dresser, *Slavery obscured: the social history of the slave trade in an English provincial port* (London and New York: Continuum, 2001). Kenneth Morgan concluded that 'the height of Bristol's connection with the West Indies came in the half century after the American Revolution'; K. Morgan, 'Bristol West India merchants in the eighteenth century', *Transactions of the Royal Historical Society*, 6th series 3 (1993), 185–208 (p. 200).

[80] Dresser, *Slavery obscured*, pp. 12–23.

However, within the Bristol merchant community, the two firms amongst the largest single recipients of slave-compensation, the Baillie family interests and Thomas & John Daniel, were not at all involved with Jamaica but spanned multiple other colonies. The Baillies, resettled from Scotland, were amongst the leading metropolitan merchants in St Vincent, and were active in British Guiana and Trinidad, as well as Grenada and St Kitts.[81] The Daniels were prominent in Barbados but collected compensation also in Antigua, Tobago, British Guiana, Nevis and Montserrat. The firm, as noted above, progressively re-located to London.

Morgan noted the propensity of Bristol West India merchants in the eighteenth century to invest in ownership of, or mortgages over, estates and slaves in the Caribbean, rather than confine themselves to intermediary functions.[82] The stability over time of the major mercantile slave-owning interests in Bristol rivals that evident in London. Of twenty-one 'West India merchants, planters etc.' at an anti-abolitionist meeting convened by the Society of Merchant Venturers of Bristol on 15 April 1789, fourteen were recognisably represented in the slave-compensation process either in person or by immediate descendants almost fifty years later.[83]

Linkages to the slave-economy could survive the end of a merchant's active career. Thus George Wear Braikenridge, Richard Honny[w]ill and John Braikenridge were awarded £2,911 8s 6d for 157 slaves as mortgagees of the Bagdale estate in St Elizabeth, owned by the heirs of James Rowe and on which William Rowe was an infant annuitant for £300 per annum. G. W. Braikenridge, the son of an American planter, had returned to Bristol as a West Indian merchant trading as Braikenridge & Honnywill, but had retired in 1820. Braikenridge & Honnywill's accounts as consignees of the Bagdale estate were challenged by G. Barnett of 6 Adelphi Chambers, who wrote on behalf of the Rowe family to the Commission that the accounts showed interest at 6 per cent per annum from 1805 to 1835 inclusive, amounting to £10,800, 'a sum more than ample to have satisfied the prior claims in their hands, in as much as their present claim is for only £12,000 and

---

[81] D. Hamilton, *Scotland, the Caribbean and the Atlantic world 1750–1820* (Manchester: Manchester University Press, 2005), pp. 178–81, 199–202.

[82] Morgan found that twenty-nine of the fifty leading sugar-merchants between 1728 and 1800 owned West Indian sugar-plantations; Morgan, 'Bristol West India merchants', p. 193.

[83] Dresser, *Slavery obscured*, p. 148, Table 8 lists the Bristolian West Indians. Of these, only Sir James Laroche, J. Maxse, [Arthur] Palmer, Ald. Brice, Ald. Daubeny, and John and G. Reid have not been found in the Slave Compensation records as owners or former owners of slaves.

upwards ... commissions are also charged on the crops [to] which as mortgagees-in-possession they are not by law entitled'.[84]

Bristol merchants also competed amongst each other for compensation. Stephen Cave counter-claimed as mortgagee against Philip and George Protheroe for the compensation on the York estate in St Thomas-in-the-East. Although Cave subsequently withdrew the counter-claim, the fact that it was his London attorney Alexander Reid Scott who signed for the compensation suggests Cave was successful.[85] Cave was described in his death-notice in *The Times* in 1838 as 'a man of unsurpassed worth and piety': his grandson, Sir Stephen Cave, was an MP and Paymaster-General in the Conservative government of 1866–8.[86] The elder Stephen Cave's son, Charles, joined the Daniels firm in London, and through marriage into the Cumberbatch family inherited estates and slaves in Barbados.

Marshall identified a total of £422,950 in slave-compensation for 15,533 slaves received by Bristolians: this study puts the equivalent figure slightly higher, at just over £500,000 for merchants and rentiers combined.[87] Marshall also suggested some recycling of Bristol's compensation into the railway boom: Charles Pinney reinvested in canal and dock shares, railway stocks and the Great Western Cotton Works. In the latter, Pinney was joined by Thomas Daniel and Robert Bright.[88] Great Western Railway subscribers included Robert Bright, John Cave, Henry Bush and George Gibbs.[89] Of these, however, only Cave appears in the 1846 Parliamentary Return of those subscribing more than £20,000 to new railway stocks since 1840.[90] The large-scale purchasing by the Baillie family of Highland estates coincided with their receipt of compensation payments.[91]

Bristol's electoral and local politics, as noted earlier, were shaped in the early 1830s by the overlapping campaigns for Reform and for the abolition of slavery. Charles Pinney was famously Mayor of Bristol at the time of the 1831 Reform riots. In 1838, three councillors for Clifton

---

[84] T71/870, St Elizabeth Nos. 371, 731, which are combined. G. Barnett to Commission, T71/1608, 12 May 1837. Braikenridge Collection, www.bristol-city.gov.uk.
[85] T71/867, St Thomas-in-the-East No. 517. NDO4/5.
[86] *The Times*, 22 February 1838, p. 7, 8 June 1880, p. 5.
[87] Marshall, *Bristol and the abolition*, Appendix I. Marshall included the Daniels as Bristolian, for £102,000; this study shows £140,000 for them, and classifies them in the tables above as London merchants. See Appendix 15 for comparison of compensation figures for other Bristol merchants.
[88] Dresser, *Slavery obscured*, p. 234.
[89] Marshall, *Bristol and the abolition*, Appendix I, p. 27.
[90] *The Times*, 13 August 1846, p. 3; 'Railway speculation', *The Times*, 15 August 1846, p. 6 .
[91] Hamilton, *Scotland and the Caribbean*, p. 201.

(Michael Hinton Castle, Robert Edward Case and Charles Payne) and one for Bristol (Peter Maze) were recipients of slave-compensation.[92]

Glasgow merchants

Glasgow was unique amongst the concentrations of compensation in major British ports in that it had no history of large-scale slave-trading to underpin its engagement in the slave-economy. Nevertheless, Glasgow merchants took just over £400,000 of the identified compensation. Their activity was concentrated in Trinidad and British Guiana, the territories attracting new capital in the 1810s and 1820s.

With the collapse of the hegemony of the Virginia tobacco lords in the 1780s, Glasgow's commercial politics came to be dominated by the West India merchants (a quarter of whom in the late eighteenth century were themselves sons of Glasgow tobacco merchants). The City's West India merchants were numerically few: only 11 out of 576 individuals enrolling as merchant burgesses and guild brethren between 1786 and 1790 and between 1801 and 1805 became partners in West India firms.[93] But they were disproportionately powerful, with a virtual monopoly over the office of Provost between 1800 and 1815.[94] Devine saw the founding of the West India Association of Glasgow, organised only in October 1807 after abolition of the slave-trade, as a defensive move, reflecting pressure building on the Caribbean trade. But the West Indians remained over-represented in the city elites: three out of seven Provosts between 1820 and 1833 received slave-compensation, and another was the scion of a West India merchant family.[95] Commentators later in the century said of the West India trade in Glasgow: 'it probably was never entitled to the consideration it got. Being in few hands, it yielded fortunes that bulked in the public eye, and less showy trades may have been of more real importance.'[96]

Despite highly visible failures amongst the West India merchants (Alexander Houston & Co., which had imported one-third to one-half of Clyde sugar in the 1770s and 1780s, failed in 1801; Robert Dunmore went bankrupt in 1793; McNeil Stewart in 1802; and John McCall &

[92] *Robson's Directory of Bristol 1838*. Extracted from *Robson's Commercial Directory of London and the Western Counties* (London, 1839).
[93] T. M. Devine, 'An eighteenth-century business elite: Glasgow–West India merchants, c. 1750–1815', *Scottish Historical Review*, 57.1 (April 1978), 40–67.
[94] *Ibid.*, p. 53.
[95] The three were William Smith (1822–4), Mungo Nutter Campbell (1824–6) and James Ewing (1832–3); Alexander Garden (1828–30) was the son of the West India merchant Francis Garden.
[96] Smith and Mitchell, *The old country houses*, Vol. LXXXIII: Possil.

Sons became insolvent in 1819 and had their assets sequestrated in 1821), the discontinuities should not be exaggerated.[97] The firms of four of the five original directors of the West India Association in 1807 were recipients of slave-compensation in the 1830s.[98] Some new firms and new capital had come forward by the 1830s. The Eccles firms (Robert Eccles & Co., William & James Eccles & Co. and Eccles, Burnley & Co.), founded in Glasgow by the sons of an Irish merchant, were major recipients of compensation in Trinidad.[99] But overall, it was the established Glasgow merchants who were prominent in collecting compensation even in the new slave-territories.

Devine has traced some of the linkages between the West India merchants and the cotton-spinning industry in Scotland. West India consignees were significant but not, in Devine's view, decisive sources of capital for the growth of the regional cotton industry; at the same time, some domestic manufacturers invested in the capital of the consignees, one of the few examples of the slave-economy providing opportunities for passive outside capital.[100]

In Glasgow, some slave-owners were associated with the cause of Reform, especially parliamentary Reform. The first MP for Glasgow in the Reformed Parliament was James Ewing, who received a total of £9,328 in compensation for slaves in St Ann, St Catherine and St Thomas-in-the-East in Jamaica.

The Scottish commercial community gave birth to a wave of new financial institutions in the first decades of the nineteenth century, especially in banking and the newly commercialised world of life insurance. Many were outgrowths of Edinburgh's financial community, including Scottish Widows (1815), the Life Insurance Company of Scotland (1825), Scottish Equitable (1831) and Scottish Provident (1837). But others were rooted in the Glasgow business community, and some in the fruits of the West India trades. Thus Scottish Amicable was founded as the West of Scotland Life Insurance Co. in 1826 by a group of Glaswegian businessmen led by William Leckie Ewing, a partner in Stirling Gordon.[101] As noted above, insurance companies as

[97] Devine, 'Glasgow–West India merchants', p. 50.
[98] Robert Dennistoun of G. & R. Dennistoun; Alex. Campbell of John Campbell Sr & Co.; Robert Bogle of Robert Bogle Jr & Co.; John Gordon of Stirling Gordon. The exception was Francis Garden of Francis Garden & Co. The secretary of the Association was James Ewing.
[99] T71/894, Trinidad Nos. 1662, 1754, 1802, 1886, 1924.
[100] Devine, 'Glasgow–West India merchants', pp. 45–6, 50–1.
[101] J. MacLehose, *Memoirs and portraits of 100 Glasgow men* (Glasgow: James MacLehose & Sons, 1886), No. 34: 'W. L. Ewing', p. 130. Scottish Amicable, which mutualised in 1833, was eventually bought by Prudential plc in 1997 for £2.78 billion.

direct participants are notably absent from the Compensation records; but these newer institutions may reflect the capital generated in the compensation process. Leckie Ewing was also a prime mover in the foundation of the Glasgow Union Banking Co. in 1830, which became through merger the Union Bank of Scotland in 1843, in turn merging with the Bank of Scotland in 1955. In contrast to the position in London, it does not appear that local Glasgow banks lent directly on mortgage to slave-owners: the banks financed the merchants, who financed the slave-owners.

Merchants elsewhere in Britain

London, Liverpool, Glasgow and Bristol dominated the mercantile recipients of compensation, but there were a handful of merchants in Dublin or scattered in other British outports with involvement in slave-owning.

In Dublin, the firm of Joseph Wilson & Sons acted as a co-ordination point for the Commission in disseminating information amongst the local West India community. Joseph Wilson & Sons was an important merchant and mortgagee to Trinidad slave-owners: under the name of Thomas Wilson (who lodged the claims with, presumably, another surviving partner, Henry Daniels Brooke), the firm was awarded compensation on nine claims in Trinidad, totalling £25,548 4s 7d. In addition, Wilson clearly intercepted another £15,896 3s 9d, awarded under seven claims to resident slave-owners in Trinidad, including the free coloured Desir Fabien, and may have intercepted a further £1,940 on one other award.[102] Nicholas Kirwan, also a Dublin merchant, was awarded £1,051 12s 2d as one of several rival claimants on the heavily litigated Bendals estate in Antigua: Kirwan's claim was as surviving executor of Patrick Kirwan for £5,454 11s 8d in unpaid purchase money.[103] John Jameson of Dublin as mortgagee and as the assignee of the bankrupt Robert and John Elliot Hyndman counter-claimed, successfully in only one case, on several Antiguan awards.[104]

Elsewhere in Ireland Samuel Nelson of Belfast was awarded £2,866 11s 9d as owner of Burke's estate and a further £252 0s 10d as mortgagee on Sawcott's estate, both in Antigua. Nelson in 1837 was also awarded £29 0s 4d on a litigated claim on Samuel Harman's estate, again in

---

[102] See Appendix 15 for detail.
[103] T71/877, Antigua No. 95.
[104] T71/877, Antigua Nos. 260, 261 (assigned by him to Warwick Pearson Hyndman) for Jameson's success; Nos. 75, 95, 390 for his failures.

Antigua. He wrote to the Commission two years later to say that he had left London without collecting it – 'as the amount was trifling, I did not trouble myself about it since' – but now asking them to pay it to his 'young friend'.[105] James Thompson, merchant of Londonderry, was awarded £713 7s 5d as an execution creditor on the Monteros estate in Antigua, together with dividends and interest on £496 5s 3d for the lifetime of Thomas Clark, Thompson's debtor, who owned the estate and the bulk of the slaves but had only a life interest in twenty-five of them.[106]

In Whitehaven, Robert and Henry Jefferson were awarded almost £7,000 as the mortgagees of two plantations in Antigua belonging to the estate of Sir William Ogilvie, Bart, York's and New Division.[107] The Jeffersons' local political rivals, the ship-owners and merchants Thomas and Milham Hartley, were awarded £14,625 8s 9d for four estates in Trelawny and St James belonging to the Minto family on which the Hartleys were mortgagees under a charge for payment of debts in the will and codicil of Robert Minto. Jarvis Minto, the heir, had not formally admitted the counter-claims of the Hartleys, they told the Commission, but 'you have his acct current with us shewing the balance due Thos and M. Hartley in 1834, and his letter acknowledging it, dated 26th May 1835 ... Mrs Minto his mother now in London will also assert that it is his wish that our claim should be paid'.[108] John Dodson of Lancaster was mortgagee on a number of estates in British Guiana, apparently as successor to the mercantile partnership of Jacob Ridley and Robert Dodson of Lancaster and William Dodgson of Starbroek, which was dissolved thirty years earlier. Dodson was awarded £14,950 for 288 slaves on Plantation Hampshire, owned by William Carr.[109]

Metropolitan agents and intermediaries

Because London was physically and administratively the centre of the compensation process, London law-firms and other agents were prominent in the compensation process as attorneys and representatives of

[105] T71/877, Antigua Nos. 391, 285. Samuel White to Commission, T71/1609, 11 April 1839.
[106] T71/877, Antigua No. 11a,b.
[107] *Ibid.*, Nos. 20, 61.
[108] T71/873, St James No. 655; T71/874, Trelawny Nos. 118, 168, 169. Letter from T. & M. Hartley to Commission, T71/1608, 3 October 1835. In 1837 Milham Hartley was awarded a further £8,741 7s 8d together with the Liverpool merchant Adam Cliff as mortgagees for 456 slaves on the Tillstone estate; T71/874, Trelawny No. 543.
[109] T71/885, British Guiana Nos. 196, 219. Dodson was also an executor of Thomas Gudgeon under British Guiana No. 289.

the owners, earning fees in this capacity. All nine signatories of a letter to Lord Glenelg in 1836 requesting that the books of the Slave Registry Office in James Street be moved to the Slave Compensation Office in Great George Street were London lawyers, including John Hopton Forbes, Freshfield & Sons and Leblanc Oliver Hook, probably the three most active legal intermediaries.[110]

John Hopton Forbes was highly involved in the compensation process as agent, but also may have been a slave-owner himself: together with another London solicitor, Charles Kaye, a partner in Freshfield & Kaye, he is shown as having bought the Hampden plantation in Tobago in 1823 and sold it in 1829 to John Gordon of Newton, who was awarded compensation for the enslaved on the estate in 1836.[111]

The role of the Freshfields' firm is particularly prominent, beyond Charles Kaye's dealings. Freshfields' was solicitor to the Bank of England, and also to Smith, Payne and Smith. It was therefore very active in the latter capacity in the wake of the Manning & Anderdon bankruptcy, to which Smith, Payne and Smith was heavily exposed.[112] James William Freshfield and John Beadnell (the manager of Smith, Payne & Smith) were awarded £7,260 for three estates in St Kitts, Bourkes, Cunnynghams and Estridge, as trustees for Smith, Payne and Smith, and a further £4,333 16s 10d for ninety-six slaves in Trinidad.[113] James William Freshfield Jr was also awarded £6,670 for himself and his co-trustee Charles Bosanquet, as trustees for a group of mortgagees for £20,000 over three estates in St Kitts.[114] The two Freshfields, together with a London merchant, were also awarded £11,106 3s 7d as trustees of the marriage settlement of John Turing Ferrier and Adriana Jonas, respectively the son of the British consul to Rotterdam and a Demerara heiress.[115] But Freshfields' involvement went beyond these extensive trustee roles. The two James Freshfields and Charles Kaye

---

[110] Letter to Lord Glenelg received 29 July 1836, T71/1603.

[111] T71/891, Tobago No. 13. It is not clear whether Forbes and Kaye were truly acting as principals. The indentures of the purchase and sale are at University of California Irvine Special Collections ms s23, California Digital Library, http://content.cdlib. org/view?docId=kt2j49q25q&doc.view=entire_text&brand=oac.

[112] R. B. Sheridan, 'The West India sugar crisis', pp. 544–5.

[113] T71/879, St Kitts Nos. 333, 525, 746; T71/894, Trinidad No. 1661. In this latter claim, Freshfield and Beadnell are described as 'owners-in-fee', but the slave-registers (T71/519, p. 2410) indicate that the estate – Brechin Castle – was owned by Smith, Payne & Smith, 'late the property of Manning & Anderdon', so again Freshfield was acting as trustee for the bank rather than as principal and beneficial owner.

[114] T71/879, St Kitts Nos. 206, 336, 724. See above, p. 247, for details of these awards. Charles Bosanquet, the son of the London merchant and governor of the Bank of England Samuel Bosanquet Sr, although named as a trustee and awardee, was not in fact active, according to a letter of 16 January 1835 from Freshfield to the Commission, T71/1224.

[115] T71/885, British Guiana No. 703.

Freshfield counter-claimed as principals under a lien for law charges for £402 15s 4d on three claims by Hugh Ryley Semper of St Kitts. Freshfields' withdrew the claim: it is not clear whether they were paid any part of the compensation either by Semper or by Reid & Dixon, the assignees of Manning & Anderdon, who were awarded the compensation money in the largest of the claims.[116] James William Freshfield, at the time MP for Penryn, had attended the anti-abolition April 1832 City rally of the West India interest.[117]

As well as the centre of activity for representatives and agents between slave-owners and the Commission, London was also the end-point for the 'farming' of compensation claims. A consistent theme both at the time and subsequently has been the allegation that small-scale slave-owners (largely assumed to be in the colonies) were being deprived of the benefit of compensation by the activity of middle-men acquiring their claims at low values. A handful of London merchant firms were prominent in what appears to be a systematic purchase of small claims from slave-owners in the colonies. William Pitcairn and John Amos, merchants of 1 Copthall Buildings, were awarded £2,774 18s 2d as mortgagees of Andrew Gregory Johnston in Portland. In addition, however, Pitcairn and Amos were awarded a further £4,000 on twenty-seven small claims in the parish of Westmoreland, at the opposite end of Jamaica. It is clear that these claims had been assigned to Pitcairn and Amos by resident small-scale owners of slaves in Jamaica, presumably in exchange for cash at a discount on the expected value of the claims.[118] In the case of St Kitts, Thomas Reynolds Bartrum and Daniel Green Pretyman, 'London hardwaremen', worked as London agents with John Bradley, who was awarded £1,550 under forty-one separate claims on St Kitts, each described as 'contested' because the Commission had advised that in such cases of assignment by the original claimant, it was necessary to file a counter-claim.[119] Thomas Reynolds Bartrum himself was a West India merchant under his own name operating from the same address as Bartrum & Pretyman, and was executor and

---

[116] T71/879, St Kitts Nos. 592, 593, 594. The three claims totalled £399 1s 8d for twenty-five slaves.
[117] Smith, *Slavery, family, and gentry capitalism*, p. 312. Freshfields Bruckhaus Deringer issued a 'Statement regarding FT article, 27 June 2009', dated 27 June 2009, in which the firm said 'Freshfields was not aware of the content of these documents [concerning slave-compensation] until the FT brought them to our attention ... we greatly regret that the firm is linked in any way to the inhumane institution of slavery', www.freshfields.com/news/mediareleases/mediarelease.asp?id=1845.
[118] T71/871, Westmoreland, various numbers. Westmoreland No. 519, for example, was originally claimed by David Kinlock, but awarded to Pitcairn & Amos on their counter-claim 'by virtue of an assignment dated 10 April 1835 for the whole compensation money'.
[119] T71/879, St Kitts, various for Bradley. St Kitts No. 30 identifies Bartrum & Pretyman as Bradley's London 'Attorneys'.

heir of Charles Bartrum, a London ironmonger and investor in the West India Docks who lent against estates and slave-property in Jamaica.[120] Bartrum & Pretyman themselves were awarded £280 under five small claims on St Kitts, as well as collecting Bradley's awards.

Such 'farming' of claims was not without risk. In August 1835, Moses Jacobs of Demerara had written to the Commission to say, 'I am the legal holder of the following [forty-two] claims on the compensation fund, by transfers and powers of in rem suam duly executed.' Seven years later, however, he wrote again from Demerara to the Commission seeking to be granted any unpaid compensation money remaining for British Guiana, 'his case being one of very great hardship'. The British government, he said, had insisted on paying the compensation in London, so Moses Jacobs had appointed the London merchant J. B. Suwerkrop, who 'within a very short time after his receiving said compensation (as can be proved on reference to John Kingston Esq. of your city, merchant) failed, by which I am loser of upwards of £5,600 sterling'.[121]

In addition to these clear cases of farming of claims, there may well have been other cases where no formal transfer of the claim took place, but where a power of attorney executed in favour of a London agent to allow him or her to collect the compensation money disguised a principal rather than agency transaction, i.e. the London intermediary had bought the claim with no disclosure. There are several London merchants who signed to collect very large numbers of small awards: some may well be cases where the merchant was acting not as a commission agent but as principal. In contrast to the larger awards, where it has been argued that evidence of mercantile interception was left in the Commission records, these cases have left no trace. Yet this would not materially distort the resident–absentee or rentier–mercantile analysis presented in this study. First, such claims, while numerous, are small; and second, the compensation was shared in some measure between slave-owner and merchant. Benefit still accrued to the slave-owner, only the precise proportion remaining unknown.

Mercantile failure in the slave-economy

The evidence for the economic decline of slavery ahead of abolition is coloured by the periodic crises of West India credit. One of these was in

[120] T71/873, St James No. 17; T71/870, St Elizabeth No. 375B for awards on Charles Bartrum's mortgages. *Robson's Directory of Bristol 1838* for Bartrum and Bartrum & Pretyman at 1 Little Bush Lane.
[121] T71/885, T71/886, T71/887, British Guiana, various. There are forty-two identifiable Jacobs claims totalling £6,067 10s 7d; letters from Moses Jacobs, T71/1610, 19 August 1835, 14 June 1842.

1831, and brought down Manning & Anderdon and at least nine other West India houses.[122] Commercial pressures and failures were inherent in the West India trade, as they were in every line of mercantile business.[123] But the imminence of Emancipation brought its own pressures. In the late spring of 1833, Duncan Brown, a West India merchant 'recently arrived in this country' from Dominica killed himself 'in a very extraordinary manner' (he was discovered by his young son, having almost severed his own arm with a razor). His surgeon, who had seen him the previous day, said that Brown 'spoke almost incessantly upon the West India question'. Brown's Glasgow agent, Thompson, had stopped the sailing of one of Brown's ships and refused to make some remittances expected by the dead man. At the inquest, Patrick Cruikshank, the London merchant who had been Brown's London agent, did not waste the opportunity both to attribute Brown's 'low and desponding state when he touched upon West India matters' to 'the impending measures which the Government has brought forward', and the actions of Thompson to the Glasgow firm's desire 'to save themselves from the general ruin which the measure alluded to would bring down'.[124]

Further failures occurred during Apprenticeship and after Emancipation. A financial crisis in 1837 in America undermined a number of firms more marginally involved in West India slavery. George Wildes of London went under in June 1837, and its affiliated firm of Wildes Pickersgill of Liverpool, in which the Fielden cotton family were partners, came under severe pressure, but survived.[125] George Wildes & Co.'s total liabilities of £2,200,000 and capital of £250,000 dwarf the slave-compensation of £3,600 that George Wilde received. The London banking house of Esdaile & Co. (previously Sir James Esdaile & Co.) entered an orderly winding-up under an inspectorship in January 1837: its main creditor was the Bank of England.[126] The Mitchells' firm in London failed, with Rowland Mitchell declared bankrupt in 1842.

---

[122] Sheridan, 'The West India sugar crisis', p. 542.

[123] See J. Hoppit, 'Risk and failure in English industry c. 1700–1800', Ph.D. thesis, University of Cambridge, 1984.

[124] 'Suicide of a West India merchant', *The Times*, 30 May 1833, p. 4.

[125] R. W. Hidy, 'Cushioning a crisis in the London money market', *Bulletin of the Business Historical Society*, 20.5 (November 1946), 131–45 (p. 138). George Wildes and John Pickersgill had been awarded £3,600 as mortgagees for fifty-one enslaved on the Wellington and Perseverance estates in Trinidad and as assignees for a further thirteen enslaved from a local slave-owner. T71/894, Trinidad Nos. 1618, 1647, 1688. Wildes and Pickersgill also acted as agent for Lewis Pantin, and filed a counter-claim against him for sixty slaves on the Concord estate, Trinidad No. 1699.

[126] *Richardson* v. *Bank of England and others*, *The Times*, 7 August 1838, p. 7.

But it was the equalisation of sugar-duties in 1846 that triggered major failures amongst the larger recipients of slave-compensation. Reid Irving collapsed in 1847, and its senior partner Sir John Rae Reid was disqualified as a director of the Bank of England, of which he had been Governor from 1839 to 1841. Of total assets of £1.12 million, Reid Irving had £466,000 tied up in advances to sundry debtors in Mauritius, and a further £91,000 in estates there and shares in the Mauritius Bank: in the West Indies, it had £195,000 in estates and £68,000 of partially secured advances to debtors there.[127] A 'Letter from Liverpool' claimed that the failure 'had occasioned no very great surprise here. The banks of this town have for the last two years taken their paper with great reserve, and never without other names believed good.'[128]

This appears to have been borne out by the low level of exposure: none amongst the Bank of Liverpool, Borough Bank and the Liverpool Banking Co. held more than £3,000 of Reid Irving's acceptances. However, when the Liverpool firm of Barton, Irlam & Higginson also collapsed in 1847, its suspension dragged down the Royal Bank of Liverpool and jeopardised the West India Bank.[129] Philip Protheroe of Bristol was bankrupt by 1849.[130]

This litany of failure appears to fit with notions of the inexorable decline of slavery and the destruction of value by the slave-system. But the mercantile failures, marked though they were, disguise a potentially different story. Amongst the top twenty-five mercantile recipients of slave-compensation in the 1830s, four had failed by 1850 (W., R. & S. Mitchell; Reid, Irving & Co.; Barton, Irlam & Higginson; and H. & J. Cohen). Another, John Campbell Sr, had faded away. But most survived, and in some cases flourished, for a half-century or more as the Caribbean sugar-economy became more corporatised in the second half of the nineteenth century.[131] Sandbach Tinne remained in business until the 1960s, and only disappeared in the fringe banking crisis that brought down its owner Jessel Securities. T. Daniel & Co. remained an active owner of sugar-plantations until its voluntary liquidation in the sugar crisis of 1896. Newer firms that emerged in the compensation period, notably Booker Brothers, became significant competitors in the sugar-industry for more than a century.

---

[127] 'General statement of the affairs of Reid Irving & Co., 17th September 1847', *The Times*, 11 October 1847, p. 6.

[128] 'Money-market and city intelligence', *The Times*, 21 September 1847, p. 3.

[129] 'The money pressure', *The Times*, 25, 28, 30 October 1847.

[130] *The Times*, 24 July 1849, p. 10.

[131] R. W. Beachey, *The British West Indies sugar industry in the late 19th century* (Oxford: Basil Blackwell, 1957), pp. 118ff.

The casualties were those who doubled up on West India property post-Emancipation with an inadequate capital base to survive the impact of the end of protection of Caribbean colonial sugar. The London West India merchant George Henry Hooper, and his partner and erstwhile clerk Alexander Denoon lost £10,000 (which broke the partnership) on a single mortgage on the Enfield plantation in Berbice, made between 1835 and 1837.[132] Those who diversified away from the slave-economy preserved the wealth that had built up from slavery. Smith for the Harewoods and Pares for the Pinneys have established how profitable over extended periods was the role of financing the slave-economy. Checkland's work confirms the wealth accumulation for the Gladstones. The compensation payments were critical to all three and to many other British slave-owners in allowing them to accelerate the realisation of the remaining value of their property and invest elsewhere. All incurred paper losses at the time of Emancipation: but by taking the compensation and redeploying it, the families survived the crash of the late 1840s.

Checkland put the losses of the Gladstones as a result of Emancipation at between £125,000 and £150,000. William Gladstone himself put the losses at £150,000. He apparently looked at the 1833 family net worth of £636,000, and extrapolated that by 1850 it 'should have' grown to £960,000 (implicitly, he assumed a 2.5 per cent annual return): in fact, the net worth must have totalled a little less than £810,000, and he attributed the shortfall to Emancipation.[133] The peak pre-Emancipation value of the family's estates in Demerara and Jamaica was £336,000 in 1833: they collected £110,000 in compensation, sold most of the estates at a loss and had only £52,850 in West India property by 1843. But the book losses do not capture the true impact of the West India property. Gladstone was earning double-digit returns from his British Guiana properties for twenty years, having recouped his initial investment in seven to eight years. Very few investments in Britain could have offered comparable sustained returns for such large volumes of capital. The capital thus accumulated was recycled into landed property in Britain and into shares, especially railway shares.[134] The Gladstone family fortune had its origins in domestic mercantile activity, but was greatly accelerated by the re-deployment into the slave-economy. The compensation process allowed the family to extract further money from

---

[132] Law: *Hooper* v. *Denoon*, *The Times*, 20 February 1849, p. 7; 28 February 1849, p. 6.
[133] S. G. Checkland, *The Gladstones: a family biography 1764–1851* (Cambridge: Cambridge University Press, 1971), p. 368.
[134] *Ibid.*, Appendix ii, pp. 414–15.

their involvement in the slave-colonies, and accelerated in turn their diversification.

Conclusion

West India merchants were not numerous, but tended to be disproportionately influential in the communities in which they operated because they were often more highly capitalised and wealthier than those active in many other trades. This remained as true of the 1820s and early 1830s as it had been in the 1790s. Their influence does not appear to have been *systematically* contested in any moral or social reaction against their involvement in slavery. Outside this core of dedicated West India merchants was a broader circle of commercial interests connected with but not reliant on the slave-economy, and capable of expressing solidarity with the West Indians in moments of crisis.

The involvement of metropolitan mercantile capital in colonial slavery on the eve of Emancipation was complex, and combined both archaic and modern elements. Separate parts within it looked back to eighteenth-century models of consigneeship and forward to vertical integration by corporate competitors in the international sugar-industry. Both facets shared a dependence on *political* intervention to secure the profitability of the system, in protecting markets, in protecting territory, in protecting the supply of labour and in suppressing slave insurgency. As these areas of protection progressively dropped away, the archaic element went into decline. Consigneeship was capital-intensive, high-risk and high-return under conditions of tariff protection. With the end of differential tariff protection, in its traditional form consigneeship dropped away. But the 'modern' forms of capitalist engagement adapted, for example in the 'Hill Coolie' deployment, which transformed Trinidad and British Guiana through another wave of labour migration – of indentured labour – primarily from the Indian sub-continent.

Compensation freed up capital, not only directly by re-paying slave-owners for some 40 per cent of the value of their slaves, but also indirectly, by injecting liquidity into the slave-economy and reviving the market in West India estates.[135] Metropolitan mercantile fortunes continued to be made from slavery after the abolition of the slave-trade,

---

[135] See K. M. Butler, *The economics of Emancipation: Jamaica and Barbados, 1823–1843* (Chapel Hill: University of North Carolina Press, 1995), Chapter 5: 'Expansion and speculation', pp. 74–91 for the impact of compensation on land values in Jamaica and especially Barbados.

although generally not in the older colonies. John Gladstone was by no means alone in his investment in slavery in the 1810s and 1820s, nor in his re-deployment of capital freed both directly and indirectly by compensation. That capital contributed to funding new industrial and infrastructure development, above all the railway boom. Yet slavery, and slave-compensation, made only one amongst many streams of wealth-creation that funded that boom. Slave-owners and slave-mortgagees were disproportionately prominent in the earliest railway projects of the 1820s and 1830s; but by the 1840s capital for railway investment was being tapped throughout Britain's economy and society.

8   Conclusion

Britain's compensated Emancipation was the first subsidised emancipation scheme in which tax-payers paid off slave-owners, in cash or in bonds.[1] It established a precedent, which was consciously followed in two other metropole/colony slave-systems, the French and Dutch West Indies.[2] The slave-owners of the Danish West Indies petitioned the Rigsdag of Denmark in June 1851 for compensation for losses on St Thomas and St John as a result of the abolition of slavery in the Danish colonies in 1848, invoking the examples of Britain and France.[3] Only in one society in which slavery was embedded rather than physically distant – Venezuela – was compensated Emancipation implemented.[4] Elsewhere, the end of slavery was accompanied by violent upheaval or civil war. In the case of British colonial slavery, however, violence both during the existence of slavery and in bringing it to an end was contained in the colonies. As a solution to a problem of domestic political economy, therefore, the compensation process was a success. As an administrative process, equally, it was an unparalleled achievement. The compensation loan was the largest single financial operation undertaken by the British state to date. The arbitration of claims and the distribution of awards to tens of thousands of slave-owners with minimal evidence of even attempted fraud were very largely achieved

---

[1] Emancipation in the northern states of the United States took place primarily by emancipation of the unborn children of slaves; R. W. Fogel and S. L. Engerman, 'Philanthropy at bargain prices: notes on the economics of gradual emancipation', *Journal of Legal Studies*, 3.2 (June 1974), 377–401 (p. 380).

[2] H. I. Priestley, *France overseas: a study of modern imperialism* (New York and London: Appleton–Century, 1938) pp. 63–9; S. McCloy, *The Negro in the French West Indies* (Lexington: University of Kentucky Press, 1966), pp. 148–52; P. Hanson Hiss, *Netherlands America: the Dutch territories in the West* (New York: Duell, Sloan & Pearce, 1943), pp. 106–9, 207.

[3] Inhabitants of the West India Islands St Thomas and St John, 'Petition for compensation for the loss of slaves by Emancipation in the Danish West Indies', June 1851, reproduced in *Journal of Negro History*, 2.4 (October 1917), 423–8.

[4] J. V. Lombardi, *The decline and abolition of Negro slavery in Venezuela 1820–54* (Westport, CT: Greenwood Press, 1971), pp. 46–53, 135–44.

within five years, at a time when Chancery cases routinely spanned decades.

What the compensation process did not set out to do, of course, was to compensate the enslaved, or make any financial provision for the transition of the enslaved to freedom. The economic and social consequences for the enslaved of the structure adopted for the abolition of slavery were therefore disappointing relative to expectations prevalent ahead of Emancipation, and are arguably still evident in the former colonies of the West Indies and the Caribbean today.[5]

The records of the administrative machinery that accompanied and implemented the end of slavery reveal the complexity of both the notion and the reality of the enslaved as 'property'. Despite challenges to the principles of 'property in men', West India property remained legally sanctioned, and subject to all the traditional devices that families used to control and manage wealth and to transmit it from generation to generation. Family, marriage and inheritance were absolutely critical to the ways in which slave-ownership was transmitted and in which slavery 'came home' to Britain. Yet West India property was also particular: it was at a distance, its returns were variable, and above all it rested on ownership of human beings. Its nature could be sanitised by monetising it, converting it into passive financial instruments of mortgage and annuity, but it remained potentially charged. At the same time, for some mercantile interests in some ports, slave-property formed a new asset class that attracted recognisably modern, mobile capital, flowing largely but not exclusively into the new colonies of British Guiana and Trinidad. Slave-property was thus both baroque *and* modern.[6] And finally, once compensation was offered, the character of ownership was transformed, because in framing the Abolition Act, Parliament legitimated slave-property and put in place direct monetary incentives to establish ownership: as a result, owners (especially male owners) moved from defensiveness, distance and reticence to assertiveness and willed identification as owners of slaves.

Slave-owning had been made an uncomfortable attribute for many British owners by the efforts of abolitionists expressing an increasingly

---

[5] See, for example, in the abundant literature of Emancipation, W. A. Green, *British slave Emancipation: the sugar colonies and the Great Experiment 1830–1865* (Oxford: Clarendon Press, 1976); T. C. Holt, *The problem of freedom: race, labour and politics in Jamaica and Britain, 1832–1938* (Baltimore: Johns Hopkins University Press, 1992); C. Hall, *Civilising subjects: metropole and colony in the English imagination 1830–1867* (Cambridge: Polity Press, 2002).

[6] R. Blackburn, *The making of New World slavery, from the Baroque to the Modern 1491–1800* (London: Verso, 1997).

accepted common sense of the abhorrent nature of ownership of other men and women. But there is little evidence that slave-owners were *systematically* subject to social sanction. Elizabeth Heyrick in 1824 had called for differentiation: 'the whole nation must now divide itself into the active supporters, and the active opposers of slavery'.[7] Yet this division never fully materialised. In many social and cultural institutions, there was clearly co-habitation between abolitionists and slave-owners, and even those who publicly quarrelled over slavery found common ground in other causes to rebuild collaboration. Ultimately, slave-owning did not constitute an *exclusive* identity for the absentee slave-owner: he or she had, and took, opportunities to assume alternative identities, local, regional, religious and philanthropic. And on compensation many, although not all, abolitionists acquiesced in the arguments that uncompensated Emancipation was tantamount to theft. It appears that it was primarily members of 'out' groups within the coalition of anti-slavery forces who both conceived slave-ownership as a single unacceptable and all-encompassing identity and resisted the principle and practice of compensation.

Analysis of the Slave Compensation records and related material suggests four main conclusions about the structure of British slave-ownership against this background. First, slave-owning was more widespread than previously understood in metropolitan Britain. Both at the time of Emancipation and subsequently, it has been assumed that the majority of the compensation passed to Britain. The detailed analysis underpinning this study confirms that at least 51 per cent and perhaps as much as 55 percent of the compensation for the West Indian and Caribbean colonies was paid to beneficiaries in Britain.[8] However, instead of this reflecting the overwhelming dominance of the metropolitan merchants, as conventionally believed, rentier-owners received and appear to have retained at least half the compensation paid to British owners. The compensation in communities in which it was concentrated represented a very material injection of liquidity.

Second, slave-owning was nevertheless not ubiquitous. The large-scale rentiers were concentrated geographically and socially, and

---

[7] Heyrick, *Immediate, not gradual abolition*, quoted in C. Midgley, 'Slave sugar boycotts, female activism and the domestic base of British anti-slavery culture', *Slavery & Abolition*, 17.3 (December 1996), 137–62 (p. 153).

[8] The figure of 51 per cent represents the identified British absentee awards of £7.75 million plus £0.4 million of Chancery awards and £0.2 million of List E awards. The upper bound would include all the £0.5 million of Chancery awards, £0.3 million of List E awards, a small increment for unidentified claims below £500 and an uplift for unidentified mercantile interception, totalling perhaps £9 million.

were powerful. But they remained a minority: consistently across the institutions analysed, slave-owning rentiers account for between 5 and 10 per cent of the relevant population. Slave-owning was not universal even within the tiers of landed gentry where it was most concentrated. Nor was slave-owning ever successfully converted into investment vehicles such as joint-stock companies capable of appealing to the urban rentier classes. But slave-ownership did permeate certain sectors of British society, where it was generally routine, unexceptional and unexceptionable. The analysis has demonstrated that the extent to which slave-ownership permeated the House of Commons, for example, has been underestimated; at the same time, slave-ownership did not automatically translate into a single political viewpoint. The identity of absentee slave-owners was not fixed or single, and they participated in many other identities: but at times of crisis or if they espoused a public defence of slavery, their identity became starker and increasingly uncomfortable.

Third, the slave-system was not homogenous. Both in economic terms and in terms of the structure of metropolitan slave-ownership, there was little in common between the old and new colonies. British Guiana and Trinidad attracted modern capitalists; the old territories remained the domain of long-standing owner and merchant dynasties. The new arenas of slavery were still creating fortunes in Britain after 1807, while many of the fortunes created earlier in the older colonies were more durable than generally assumed.

Finally, compensation appears to have been key to the dismantling of slavery. Led by slave-owners and West India merchants, an anti-abolitionist coalition was built that embraced military men, financiers and 'men of property' who were not necessarily venal but who argued that the financial system as a whole depended on the preservation of credit of the slave-economy. A combination of social pressure by anti-slavery advocates on slave-owners and insurrection or insurrectionary threat by the enslaved ultimately undermined this coalition, but the offer of compensation was crucial to satisfying the broader anti-abolition coalition, and the level of compensation awarded was attractive to many slave-owners relative to their expected economic and social returns from continuing slave-ownership.

The Compensation records represent, by definition, a comprehensive portrait of slave-ownership at a point in time. They also capture the cumulative impact of the transmission of slave-ownership over time *for those who still held slaves*. But the Compensation records, and this research, can tell us only very limited things about those families, firms or individuals who had held slaves but who had sold out by the 1830s, after extracting wealth from the slave-economy over many years.

Therefore, no claims are made here to provide a basis for a comprehensive, cumulative picture of British slave-ownership.

However, the findings from the Commission's records do force a reassessment of earlier (and indeed recent) prosopographies of British elites. As noted in the Introduction, Rubinstein, while effectively ignoring the eighteenth-century generation of wealth from slavery, has sought to wipe the slate clean of linkages between slavery and the nineteenth-century British rich: 'Very few wealth-holders earned their fortune in "immoral" trades, such as slave-trading or plantation-owning based on slaves ... No English millionaire ever made his money from the slave trade or the ownership of slaves.' These two claims are repeated in the second edition of *Men of property*.[9] The first claim is qualified by Rubinstein himself, who cites as exceptions to his own rule three half-millionaires who had in fact made their money from the slave-economy: all three were also slave-owners.[10] It is further qualified by the fact that the universe of forty-six identified half-millionaires also includes: Neill Malcolm and Richard Lee, who both certainly owed their fortunes to slavery as absentee slave-owner and West India merchant respectively; the slave-trader Thomas Leyland, described as 'Liverpool banker'; and a slave-owner who did not owe his fortune primarily to slavery (William Thwaytes, acknowledged by Rubinstein as a 'Jamaica planter' as well as grocer).[11] Rubinstein's second claim is not tenable even in its own terms, given that he acknowledges his omission of Philip John Miles, the millionaire MP, West India merchant

[9] W. D. Rubinstein, *Men of property: the very wealthy in Britain since the Industiral Revolution*, 2nd edn (London: The Social Affairs Unit, 2006), pp. 12, 141. For the fourteen millionaires (excluding Philip John Miles), see Rubinstein, 'British Millionaires 1809–1949', *Bulletin of the Institute of Historical Research* (1974), 202–23 (pp. 206–7).

[10] Henry Davidson (1771–1827), David Lyon (1754–1827) and James Ewing (1775–1853); Rubinstein, *Men of property*, p. 141. The sons of the first two were both awarded substantial slave-compensation, as was James Ewing himself.

[11] The universe of forty-six half-millioniares is identifiable by name in F. M. L. Thompson, 'Life after death: how successful nineteenth-century businessmen disposed of their fortunes', *Economic History Review*, NS 43.1 (February 1990), 40–61. Thompson started with an unpublished list of seventy-seven from Rubinstein, discarding the established landed families, women and a handful of others including a Scot (presumably James Ewing). He also discarded James Cavan, a London merchant heavily involved in the compensation process as agent, and himself a beneficiary of compensation; and Hugh Hammersley, the banker who acted as banking agent for Harry Hackshaw in St Vincent; both of whom Thompson believed to be insolvent or virtually so at their deaths in 1859 and 1840 respectively; Thompson, *Life after death*, p. 52. The forty-six half-millionaires also include John Julius Angerstein, whose slave-owning has become axiomatic in discussion of the 'tainted past' of the National Gallery, which was founded on Angerstein's own collection. However, Anthony Twist ('Widening circles in finance, philanthropy and the arts: a study of the life of John Julius Angerstein 1735–1823', Ph.D. thesis, University of Amsterdam,

and large-scale slave-owner who died in 1845, in the first edition of *Men of property*.[12] But more broadly it elides the connections between slavery and nineteenth-century British wealth: of the fourteen other British millionaires Rubinstein identified as dying between 1809 and 1859, two (Nathan Mayer Rothschild and the first Duke of Cleveland) were awarded slave-compensation by the Commission (as mortgagee and owner respectively), the firm of another (William J. Denison) acted as agent for owners in the compensation process, and two others (Sir Robert Peel and Richard Arkwright) made their money from slave-grown cotton. Nathan Mayer Rothschild himself had also of course arranged the public loan to fund the slave-compensation payments. Thus of a total of sixty-two identified 'non-landed' millionaires and half-millionaires dying in the half-century between 1809 and 1859, at least six owed their wealth to slavery, one was a former slave-trader, a further three were slave-owners, one was a mortgagee of slaves, another as banker was the agent of slave-owners and two were dependent on slave-grown cotton.[13]

At the same time, an important qualification is that Rubinstein's published work has focused on the non-landed; he estimated additional large numbers of millionaires whose wealth was solely landed. Amongst these, of course, would be an unknown number whose wealth was truly derived from the slave-economy: presumably it would include the Harewoods, the Codringtons and the Tudways. The work has yet to be

2002), argues that Angerstein was a trustee rather than owner of the one-third estate in Grenada conventionally associated with him, and that he rapidly sold other slaves his wife brought into their marriage. Angerstein, who died in 1823, appears in the Slave Compensation records in connection with the 1792 marriage settlement of Godschall Johnson, a business partner; T71/1622, Antigua No. 387. More materially, Angerstein's wealth raises the question of the linkage between the slave-trade and the growth of the maritime insurance industry, and of Lloyds of London, in both of which Angerstein was an important figure.

[12] Rubinstein, *Men of property*, p. 12.

[13] The sixty-two comprise Thompson's forty-six half-millionaires, plus James Ewing and Rubinstein's fourteen millionaires, plus P. J. Miles. The six owing their wealth to slavery are Ewing, Miles, Malcolm, Davidson, Lee and Lyon; the slave-trader was Leyland; the three slave-owners are the Duke of Cleveland, Thwaytes and possibly Angerstein; the mortgagee, N. M. Rothschild; the banker, Denison; and the two dependent on slave-grown cotton, Peel and Arkwright. For Leyland as a slave-trader, see *Dictionary of national biography*. Another half-millionaire, the tea-broker Henry Kemble, appears in the compensation process with his cousin Edward Bedwell Kemble as co-executors of Thomas Kemble (T71/865, St Andrew No. 246), although the family's West India merchant business appears separate from the source of Henry Kemble's wealth. Finally, the London merchant and half-millionaire John Tunno appears in the *Trans-Atlantic slave trade database* as the owner of a slave voyage in 1787 (the voyage of the Maria, ID No. 82460, www.slavevoyages.org). Tunno's son, Edward Rose Tunno, was awarded compensation as one of the executors of Job Matthew Raikes (T71/856, St Mary No. 262, 264–6).

done (or perhaps published) to analyse the extent to which such landed wealth had its origins in slavery. However, 23 out of 178 land-owners (13 per cent) bequeathing more than £100,000 in personalty between 1809 and 1839 were identified by Rubinstein as West India planters.[14]

This is not in any way to argue that early Victorian Britain's wealth derived entirely from slavery. As has been observed elsewhere, it is not necessarily the case that men were rich because they owned slaves (although neither does it appear true that they owned slaves simply because they were rich: in general, it was likely that in the case of rentiers such rich men came to own slaves through some prior connection to the West Indies, not as a portfolio investment).[15] But 'slave-property' permeated certain sections of British society, and it appears important to be as precise as possible about the interweaving of that property with other forms of wealth in Britain.

British colonial slavery was an economic system that generated private wealth for a narrow section of the metropolitan population at the expense both of the enslaved and of the working and middle classes of Britain. It is not at all intended to equate the exploitation of the enslaved with the costs imposed on British people through protective duties on sugar, but both were required to make the slave-economy profitable for those who participated in it as owners and agents. The slave system was maintained by political means. It was an economic system that continuously recruited new participants in the metropole through inheritance and legacies; almost invariably, those recruits retained rather than renounced their inheritance. Slave-owning was not a mass activity in the context of British society as a whole but was surprisingly common within sections of the elites. It was opposed both by other groups within the elites, but also overwhelmingly by groups outside those elites altogether.

Current debates over reparations or restitution for British colonial slavery are inevitably connected with the history of slave-compensation.[16] Men and women die: firms, families and institutions may well survive over long periods. Assets, including the compensation money

---

[14] W. D. Rubinstein, 'The structure of wealth-holding in Britain, 1809–39: a preliminary anatomy', *Historical Research* 65 (1992), 74–89. The proportion of slave-owners amongst the 1,200 land-owners who left *land* with a capital value of at least £100,000 remains unknown.

[15] J. Walvin, 'The colonial origins of English wealth: the Harewoods of Yorkshire', *Journal of Caribbean History*, 39.1 (2005), 38–53.

[16] There are also some immediate parallels in some of the processes involved. British slave-owners argued successfully for slavery as a 'national sin', a collective responsibility to which non-slave-owners had to contribute, just as it is argued once more

paid to slave-holders, have passed legitimately from generation to generation of families, partners or shareholders without exciting comment, although potentially attracting taxes on inheritance and transmission. The liabilities – the adverse moral or (potentially) financial consequences of slave-ownership – are forgotten or suppressed. But can one be separated from the other? There are firms, families and institutions in Britain today that benefited not only from the profits generated by slavery but from the compensation process that marked its passing. Some such connections are being acknowledged and worked through.[17] In many other cases, connections have remained unacknowledged. However, even in some cases in which institutions have undertaken and published research on predecessor linkages with slavery, the comprehensiveness of the findings can be open to question in the light of the Compensation records. Moreover, examination of, or self-examination by, institutions such as the Church of England (in the case of the Bishop of Exeter) and the National Gallery (in the case of Angerstein) may be flawed in their empirical base.

In the United States, as has been noted, the connections between history – especially corporate history – and the present are being made visible and have material consequences, with firms and institutions establishing and funding specific programmes in acknowledgement of their past linkages with slavery. The first step in similar discussions in Britain is surely the identification of those entities in Britain to which the debate is most relevant: those who benefited most directly from slavery. The Slave Compensation records give a unique base for such a process of identification. It cannot be more than a base, first because the records mark the end of British colonial slavery and clearly cannot capture comprehensively the eighteenth-century experience, and second because the empirical approach deployed complements rather than displaces the more conceptual and systemic approaches to 'the Atlantic economy' and Britain's economic and commercial transformation. Yet

that the legacy of slavery is a collective responsibility. Settlement of slave-compensation in the 1820s and 1830s was probably delayed by a mismatch of the demands for compensation and the nation's propensity to pay, just as now populist 'quantification' of the debt to slavery arrives at meaningless figures. See for example D. Conley, 'Calculating slavery reparations: theory, numbers and implications', in J. Torpey (ed.), *Politics and the past: on repairing historical injustices* (Lanham, MD: Rowman & Littlefield, 2003) pp. 117–125; and D. T. Osabu-Kle, 'The African reparation cry: rationale, estimate, prospects, and strategies', *Journal of Black Studies*, 30.3 (January 2000), 331–50 (pp. 344–5).

[17] For the example of the approach of the Harewood Trust, see S. D. Smith, *Slavery, family, and gentry capitalism in the British Atlantic: the world of the Lascelles, 1648–1834* (Cambridge: Cambridge University Press, 2006); Walvin, 'The colonial origins'.

they do reflect many of the processes of accumulation and transmission of wealth over long periods, and they may therefore offer the opportunity to avoid some of the pitfalls in the historical research and disclosure process evidenced to date in the USA. This study and the research underpinning it thus mark an initial contribution to a continuing process of identification and quantification of Britain's 'debt to slavery'.

Appendix 1 MPs appearing in the Slave Compensation records

Claim	MP	Own[1]	Other	Constituency	1820	1826	1830	1831	1833	1835
Antigua										
35	W. A. Mackinnon[2]	X		Lymington				X		X
"	S. Boddington[3]	X		Tralee 1807						
79	Bethell Walrond[4]	X		Sudbury		X	X			
"				Saltash				X		
101	C. B. Codrington[5]	X		Tewkesbury 1797–1812						
54	Sir Edward Codrington[6]	X		Devonport					X	X
259	James A. Gordon[7]	X		Tregoney			X	X		
"	James Gordon	X		Clitheroe 1808–12						
327	John P. Tudway[8]	X		Wells	X					
"	Robert C. Tudway	X		Wells 1855		X				
39	John Tollemache[9]	X		Cheshire South 1841						
358	Inigo Thomas[10]	X		Weobley 1796–1800						
270	Anthony Browne[11]	Xcc		Hedon 1806–18						
Barbados										
631c	J. Ivatt Briscoe[12]	X		Surrey Cty			X	X		
4925	Geo. H. Dashwood[13]		Trus.	Truro 1814–18					X	
"				Bucks. 1837					X	
270	George Anson[14]		Trus.	Lichfield	X	X	X	X		X
"	Thomas W. Coke[15]		Trus.	Norfolk	X	X	X			
3210	Abel R. Dottin[16]	X		Southampton		X	X	X		
3784	J. S. W. S. E. Drax[17]	X		Wareham 1841 & 1847						
3230	Renn Hampden[18]	X		Great Marlow 1841						
3184	Duke of Cleveland[19]	X		Totnes/Winchelsea 1788–92						
"	Lord Wm Powlett[20]	X		Durham		X	X	X		
British Guiana										
663	Rr Ad. Chas Adam[21]		Exor	Kinross-shire				X	X	X

Claim	MP	Own[1]	Other	Constituency	1820	1826	1830	1831	1833	1835
604	Geo. Hen. Laur. Dundas[42]	X		Orkney 1818–20, 1826–30		X				
865	Sir F. G. Johnstone[43]	XC		Weymouth					X	
466	Vere Fane[44]	Xm		Lyme Regis	X					
456	Duncan Davidson[45]	X		Cromartyshire		X		X		
Jamaica										
Clarendon										
358	Geo. Hibbert[46]	Xm		Seaford 1807–12		X				
3	G. H. D. Pennant[47]	X		New Romney	X	X				
189	J. B. Wildman[48]	X		Colchester	X					
284	John Wm Ward[49]	X		Bossiney	X					
156	G. G. W. Pigott[50]		Trus.	St Mawes		X	X	X		
Hanover										
19	William Feilden[51]	Xcc		Blackburn					X	
21	Geo. W. Taylor[52]	X		Devizes		X	X	X		
"				East Looe	X					
37	P. J. Miles[53]	X		Corfe Castle		X	X	X		
"				Westbury	X					
"				Bristol						X
88	James Bradshaw[54]	X		Brackley Borough	X	X	X	X		
"				Berwick-on-Tweed						X
17	Neill Malcolm Jr[55]	X		Boston		X	X			
440	R. Wallace[56]	X		Greenock					X	X
21	Ed. Antrobus[57]		Trus.	Surrey 1841						
66	Geo. Phillips[58]	X		Wootton Bassett		X				
Manchester										
65	Wm Gladstone[59]		Exor	Newark					X	X
"	Thom. S. Gladstone		Exor	Portarlington					X	
"				Queenboro'			X			

No.	Member		Constituency					
"		X	Leics. Borough	X				X
398	James Scarlett[60]		Peterborough		X	X		
"			Cockermouth				X	
"			Malton					X
			Norwich					X
Port Royal								
105	Sir John Mark F. Smith[61]	Exor	Chatham 1852–3, 1857–65	X				
St Andrew								
171	Sir E. H. East[62]	X	Winchester	X	X	X	X	X
114	Marquis of Chandos[63]	X	Bucks. Cty	X	X	X	X	X
265	Hardress Lloyd[64]	Trus. cc	Kings' Cty 1807–18					
St Ann								
84	Ralph Bernal[65]	X	Rochester	X	X	X	X	X
622	James Ewing[66]	Xm	Glasgow			X		X
"			Wareham	X				
"	Samuel B. M. Barrett[67]	X	Richmond, Yorks.	X	X			
St Catherine								
539	Lord Seaford[68]	X	Seaford	X				
309	William Burge[69]	X	Eye		X	X		
575	A. E. Fuller[70]	X	Sussex East 1841	X				
499	James Dawkins[71]	X	Hastings			X		
"			Wilton					
St Dorothy								
12	C. N. Pallmer[72]	X	Surrey	X	X			
St Elizabeth								
5	Wm Dickinson[73]	X	Somerset	X	X	X		
366	John Barham[74]	X	Kendal Borough	X			X	
"			Stockbridge			X	X	
"	Joseph F. Barham[75]	X	Stockbridge	X				X

Claim	MP	Own[1]	Other	Constituency	1820	1826	1830	1831	1833	1835
"	John F. Barham	X		Stockbridge	X					
296	Sir F. M. Ommaney[76]		Trus.	Barnstaple	X					
535	Samuel Smith[77]	X		Wendover	X	X	X	X		
"	George Smith	X		Wendover	X	X	X			
	"			Midhurst			X[78]			
1018	Alex Cray Grant[79]	X		Aldborough	X	X				
	"			Lostwithiel	X					
	"			Westbury			X			
535	John Smith[80]	X		Midhurst	X	X				
	"			Bucks. Cty				X	X	
345 & 346	J. W. Grimston[81]		Trus.	St Albans			X	X	X	
401	Henry Bright[82]		Agent	Bristol	X	X				
	"			Hertford Cty					X	
St George										
56	J. R. Grosett[83]	Xc		Chippenham	X					
278	Sir Thomas Baring[84]	Xm		Chipping Wycombe	X	X	X			
	"			Southampton				X		
St James										
549A	Sir Jos. Birch[85]	Xm		Nottingham	X	X				
185	Sir Thomas B. Birch[86]	X		Liverpool 1847–52	X					
169	R. Gordon[87]	X		Cricklade	X	X	X	X	X	X
St Mary										
336	Jas H. M. Dawson[88]	X		Clonmel	X	X				
	"			Limerick			X			
262	E. Rose Tunno[89]		Exor	Tintagel			X	X	X	X
267	Rich. Alex. Oswald[90]	X		Ayrshire		X	X	X	X	X
St Thomas-in-the-East										
549	Rowland Alston[91]	X		Hertfordshire						X

No.	Name	Role		Constituency						
118	And. Arcdeckne[92]		X	Dunwich		X	X	X		
1	John Gladstone[93]		X	Berwick-on-Tweed		X	X	X		
Trelawny				N. Woodstock	X					X
119	John Atkins[94]		X	Arundel		X	X	X		
411	Henry Dawkins[95]		X	Aldborough 1812–14	X	X				
545	Henry Dawkins		X	Boroughbridge	X					
	John Mitchell[96]		X	Kingston-on-Hull 1818–26	X			X		
278	William James[97]		X	Carlisle	X	X	X	X	X	
	"			East Cumberland 1836–1847					X	X
Vere										
122	Abel Smith[98]	Trus.		Midhurst	X	X	X			
	"			Wendover	X	X	X	X		
	"		X	Hertford Cty	X	X	X			
49	Henry Goulburn[99]		X	Armagh City	X	X	X	X		
	"			W. Looe	X					X
	"			Cambridge University						
42	Richard Godson[100]		X	St Albans		X	X	X	X	
	"			Kidderminster			X	X	X	
37	Geo. S. Byng[101]		Xcc	Chatham Borough			X	X	X	
	"			Milborne Port						
37	W. J. Denison[102]	Agent		Surrey	X	X	X	X	X	
70	Edward Littleton[103]	Trus.		Staffs/S. Staffs	X	X	X	X	X	X
Westmore-land										
265	David Lyon[104]		X	Beeralston		X	X	X		
334	Sir David Wedderburn[105]		X	St Andrews Burghs 1807–18						
66	Matthew Lewis[106]		X	Hindon 1796–1802						

Claim	MP	Own[1]	Other	Constituency	1820	1826	1830	1831	1833	1835
Nevis										
22	Chas Duncombe[107]	Xmcc		Newport, IoW	X					
102	Lord Combermere[108]	X		Newark 1806–14						X
St Kitts										
761	Henry Compton[109]		Trus?	S. Hants.						X
746	W. Manning[110]	X	Trus.	Penryn		X				
	"			Lymington	X					
461	Sir Peter Payne[111]	X		Beds.				X		
269	C. B. Percy[112]		Trus.	Newport	X	X				
635	C. Ashe A'Court[113]	X		Heytesbury	X					X
749	Geo. Rob. Smith[114]	X		Midhurst				X		
592	Jas W. Freshfield[115]	Xcc		Penryn				X		
9	W. Payne Gallwey[116]	X		Thirsk 1852						
734	Sir Gerald N. Noel[117]	X		Rutland	X	X	X	X	X	
360	John Plummer[118]	Xm		Hindon	X					X
St Lucia										
317	Martin Tucker Smith[119]		Trus.	Midhurst				X		
St Vincent										
568	James Wilson[120]	X		York City						
505	Edw. Protheroe[121]	Xm		Bristol City 1812–20		X				
572	J. I. Fortescue[122]	X		Callington 1801–3						
549	Sir W. Abdy[123]	X		Malmes 1817						
559	Sir Wm Lau. Young[124]	Xcc		Bucks.						X
644	Josias Jackson[125]	X		Southampton 1807–12						
Tobago										
6	W. R. K. Douglas[126]	X		Dumfries		X	X	X		
	"			Annan	X					
55	And. Hen. Lynch[127]	Xm		Galway					X	
	" Lachlan Maclachlan	Xm							X	

No.	Name			Constituency						
71A	P. M. Stewart[128]	X		Lancaster Borough			X	X	X	X
9	Michael Bruce[129]	X		Ilchester			X	X		
34	Alex. Murray[130]	Xm		Kircudbright 1838					X	
67	Geo. Ferguson[131]	X		Banffshire					X	X
64	Charles Brooke[132]	X		Chippenham 1812–18						
"	John Gordon[133]			Weymouth		X	X	X		
Trinidad										
643	Joseph Marryat[134]	X	d. 1824	Sandwich	X					
	Joseph Marryat Jr	X				X	X	X	X	
181B	John Ashton Yates[135]	X		Carlow 1837–41			X		X	
1684	Wm H. C. Bentinck[136]		Trus?	Notts.	X					
"				King's Lynn		X				
"				Glasgow City						X
1701	Edw. Protheroe Jr[137]	X?		Bristol City				X		
"				Evesham	X					
581	Sir Geo. F. Hill[138]	X		Londonderry	X	X				
1632	Sir Thos Cochrane[139]	Xcc		Ipswich 1837–41						
Virgin Islands										
266	Sir J. Rae Reid[140]	X		Dover		X	X	X	X	X
Total		**65**			**60**	**53**	**50**	**42**	**36**	
Higman[141]		39			40	36	31	19	–	

Dates (1820, 1826 etc.) are for the Parliaments elected in each of such election-years. Members of Parliament with no entry shown for 1820–1835 sat in Parliaments for the dates given in the 'Constituency' column.

[1] Includes any beneficial interest, such as mortgage or other debt, or holdings in right of wife: Xm = mortgagee; Xcc = counter-claim; XC = owner in Chancery award; Xmcc = counter-claim as mortgagee.

[2] W. A. Mackinnon: also came in for Dunwich, 20 February 1819.

[3] Samuel Boddington: partner in Boddington, Phillips & Sharp, and Boddington & Davis. See also Antigua No 75; Hanover Nos. 66, 508; St James Nos. 56, 564; Vere Nos. 29, 30; Nevis No. 297; St Kitts No. 219; St Vincent Nos. 485, 486.

[4] Bethell Walrond: of Dulford House, Devonshire, son of Joseph Lyons Walrond of Antigua and Caroline, daughter of Edward Codrington. Walrond claimed for 233 slaves on Lower and Upper Walrond estates, then acquiesced in a counter-claim from the trustees

Notes to Appendix 1 (*cont.*)

of his marriage settlement with Lady Janet St Clair. Walrond shared compensation for Antigua No. 54 with Mrs A. M. Bethell and Sir E. Codrington.

5 Sir Christopher Bethell Codrington (1764–1843): see also Antigua Nos. 329, 332, 334, 338, 358; Tobago Nos. 1, 32; Grenada Nos. 865–6 (Chancery).

6 Sir Edward Codrington: Admiral, Commander-in-Chief at Portsmouth.

7 James Adams Gordon came in for Tregoney, 25 February 1832: see also St Vincent No. 549. James Gordon (d. 1822) was only son of James Brebner Gordon of Antigua.

8 John P. Tudway: see also Antigua Nos. 328, 330. Claim by J. P. Tudway (d. 1835) as tenant-for-life, awarded to R. C. Tudway.

9 John Tollemache, see also Antigua Nos. 40, 58, 82, 83, 123: son and heir of J. R. D. Tollemache.

10 Inigo Thomas: claim by Inigo Thomas as tenant-in-tail, awarded to his son Freeman Thomas. See also Antigua No. 1042.

11 Anthony Browne: agent for Antigua, counter-claimed as annuitant and execution creditor, £5,126 2s 3d on Samuel Harman's estate.

12 John Ivatt Briscoe: one-third awarded to trustees of J. I. Briscoe's marriage settlement.

13 George Henry Dashwood: see also Barbados No. 2034. Trustee of sister's marriage settlement.

14 Lt-Gen. Sir George Anson: NB co-trustees = Earl of Lichfield, T. W. Coke and Viscountess Anson. Trustees together unsuccessfully counter-claimed as trustees of the marriage settlement of Sir Francis Ford with Mary Anson (sister of Sir George Anson and the Earl of Lichfield).

15 Thomas William Coke of Holkham (1754–1841): trustee of marriage settlement of Sir Francis Ford: see George Anson, above. T. W. Coke was father of Anne Margaret, Viscountess Anson, who married Thomas Anson, 1st Viscount Anson.

16 A. R. Dottin: also trustee on Barbados Nos. 4612, 4948.

17 John Samuel Wanley Sawbridge Erle Drax: awarded compensation in right of wife.

18 Renn Hampden: stood versus William Pinney, 1837, Lyme Regis; faced anti-slavery campaign. Came in for Great Marlow, 11 April 1842 in place of Sir W. R. Clayton.

19 Duke of Cleveland: awarded compensation with Lord William Powlett for Lowther estate, inherited through the Duke's mother Margaret Lowther.

20 William John Frederick Powlett of Langton Grange Durham. In 1830 he is shown as 'commonly called Lord W. J. F. Powlett'. In 1847 he is shown as WJFP, 'commonly called Lord WP of Curzon Street'. Opposed reform in 1831, did not pursue nomination at Durham in the 1831 election. Elected for St Ives, 1847.

21 Rear Admiral Charles Adam: award as executor of Francis James Adams late of Copthall Buildings, assignee of a judgement.

22 Sir Edward Cust: m. Mary Anne, daughter of L. W. Boode of Peover Hall, Cheshire and Margaret Dannett of Leasow Castle.

23 Wilbraham Egerton: trustee of Sir E. Cust's marriage settlement.

24 George Charles Grantley Fitzhardinge Berkeley came into Gloucs. County Western Division, 24 December 1832. See also British Guiana No. 493.

25 R. W. H. Dare of Cranbrook House Essex (d. 1836). Award to son (also R. W. H. Dare).

26 Thorne is only tentative on John Stewart Sr as MP for Beverley, 1826. JS of the Albany City of Westminster for Lymington, 1833, 1835. See also, for JS of the Albany, Grenada No. 449 (as trustee).

27 James Blair was also MP for Saltash (1818) and Wigtonshire (1837–41). Left his estates to his wife's family, the Stopfords [Thorne].

28 Humphrey St John Mildmay: partner in Baring Brothers; came in for Southampton Town, 9 August 1842

29 Francis Baring: partner with Thomas and John Baring, and Humphrey St John Mildmay and Joshua Bates in Baring Brothers; counter-claimed v. Wolfert Katz. See also British Guiana Nos. 21, 89, 270, 479. Alexander Baring had been senior partner, ultimately retiring in 1830 from Baring Brothers.

30 Nicholas Conyngham Tindal of 9 Brunswick Square: came in for Wigtown, March 1824; elected 1826–7 for Harwich; came in to Cambridge, May 1827; became Chief Justice of the Pleas, 1829. Appears to have been trustee for James Grant, although there is some ambiguity and a reference to slaves 'belonging to the Chief Justice'.

31 John Bent: 'commissioner of Demerara' [Thorne]; elected for Sligo, 1818–20 (d. 1848). Addresses given as Weaton House, Devon and Oathall Lindfield, Sussex; 'Surinam' in counter-claim on British Guiana No. 2398.

32 Abraham Wildey Robarts: see also Dominca Nos. 275, 288.

33 Sir George H. Rose: m. daughter of Thomas Duncombe of Duncombe Park

34 John Irving, partner in Reid Irving: see also Virgin Islands, and Vere No. 77.

35 Archibald Campbell of Blythswood (d. 1838). Grenada No. 688 shows Archibald Campbell as trustee of William M'Dowall, who was a fellow MP for Glasgow Burghs.

36 Edward Ellice: see also Tobago Nos. 14, 15, 29, 122–3; Grenada Nos. 439–40.

37 James Evan Baillie: see also St Kitts No. 48; St Vincent Nos. 491, 506, 507A; Grenada No. 591; also Chancery suits Grenada Nos. 564, 783, 864.

38 Thomas Wilson: partner with Lewis Agazziz as Grenada merchant; traded also as Wilson & Blanshard and Wilson & Co.: which moved from Jeffreys Square to Warnford Court in 1834. (Thorne): shown as trustee to Jos. Marryat. Links to Melville, Fletcher and Ambrose Wilson in Wilson & Co.

39 Sir Robert Heron, Sir Wm Edward Rouse Boughton and Sir William Alexander appear in Grenada Nos. 435, 445, 760, 771, 857 and 860 as co-proprietors alongside John Alexander Hankey and the Trevelyan family, but are most likely to have been trustees. Sir William Alexander was Lord Chief Baron of the Exchequer.

40 Samuel T. Kekewick came in for Exeter City, 9 February 1826. Trustee for marriage settlement of William James d'Urban and Mary Elizabeth Stewart Mitchell.

41 James Douglas Stoddart Douglas: of Chilston Park in Kent.

42 Awarded to Laurence Lord Dundas (later first Earl of Zetland), 'heir of the late Geo. Heneage L. Dundas' (T71/880).

43 Sir Frederick George Johnstone: *Chancery case v. Sir Christopher [Bethell] Codrington*. See also Grenada No. 862.

44 Vere Fane: of Fleet Street, counter-claimed as mortgagee with two others, possibly as trustees.

45 Duncan Davidson: see also Grenada No. 457.

46 George Hibbert: agent for Jamaica, partner in G., W. & S. Hibbert of London, mortgagee and owner in multiple claims in Jamaica.

47 George Hay Dawkins Pennant: see also Clarendon Nos. 4, 331, 362.

48 James Beckford Wildman: see also St Andrew No. 115 and Vere No. 38

Notes to Appendix 1 (cont.)

49 John William Ward, Lord Dudley and Ward, and later Earl of Dudley, MP 1802–18 for various constituencies; sat for Bossiney, 1819–23. Claim by his trustees. See also Clarendon No. 320, Vere No. 70.

50 G. G. Wandisford Pigott: trustee for the marriage settlement of Charles Devon and his wife Mary (Pigott's sister). In 1822 Pigott married Charlotte Long, daughter of Edward Beeston Long. The slave-owner Henry Lawes Long was another of Pigott's brothers-in-law.

51 William Feilden: counter-claimed with wife, the daughter of Catherine Haughton Jackson. See also Trelawny No.386

52 George Watson Taylor: see also St Kitts No. 26, St Thomas-in-the-East No. 100. MP for Newport 1816–8, Seaford 1818–20.

53 Philip John Miles: see also St Thomas-in-the-East No. 449; Trelawny Nos. 158, 183, 187–8. Came in to Corfe Castle, 6 March 1829.

54 James Bradshaw: see also Antigua No. 118 and St Ann No. 542. Came into Brackley, 1825.

55 Neill Malcolm: See also Hanover Nos. 18, 23, 86, 87, 438, 441, 451, 567.

56 Robert Wallace: see also St Elizabeth No. 741 and Westmoreland No. 266.

57 Sir Edmund Antrobus: Coutts banker, trustee of George Watson Taylor (see also Hanover No. 273, St Thomas-in-the-East No. 100, St Kitts No. 26); executor of Tully Higgins (British Guiana No. 2397).

58 George Phillips: partner in the West India merchant Boddington, Phillips & Davis (assignees of equity of redemption) but also a Manchester cotton industrialist; became a Baronet, 1828. Sat also for Ilchester, 1812–18; Steyning, 1818–20.

59 William and Thomas Gladstone: executors for Robert Gladstone, their uncle.

60 James Scarlett: made Lord Abinger in 1835.

61 Sir John Mark Frederick Smith: award as executor of his father Sir John Frederick Sigismund Smith.

62 Sir Edward Hyde East came into Winchester, February 1823: see also St Kitts No. 11; St Mary Nos. 11, 14; St Thomas-in-the-East No. 154.

63 Marquis of Chandos: Duke of Buckingham claim, awarded to trustees of marriage settlement of Marquis of Chandos (the second Duke, who succeeded his father in 1839). The first Duke was also an MP: for Buckinghamshire, 1797–1813. See also St Andrew No. 150.

64 Hardress Lloyd: trustee for Robert Hardress Saunderson and Rt Hon. Lady Maria Ann as annuitants by virtue of a marriage settlement, 18 May 1765.

65 Ralph Bernal: see also St Ann No. 435 and St Dorothy No. 19.

66 James Ewing: see also St Ann No. 550.

67 Samuel Barrett Moulton Barrett: brother of Edward Barrett Moulton Barrett, uncle of Elizabeth Barrett Browning; died Jamaica, 1837. Claimed as owner but compensation was finally awarded to the family and trustees in 1843. See also St James No. 666 for a similar award on Cinnamon Hill.

68 Lord Seaford: Charles Rose Ellis.

69 William Burge: agent for Jamaica, came in for Eye, 14 March 1831.

70 Augustus Elliot Fuller: see also St Thomas-in-the-Vale No. 289. Heir to John 'Jack' Fuller, MP for Sussex, 1801–12.

71 James Dawkins: awards went to his trustees (and possibly mortgagees) John Biddulph and Samuel Pepys Cockerell.

72 Charles Nicholas Pallmer: see also Trelawny No. 119.

73 William Dickinson: William Dickinson II (1771–1837); Ilchester, 1796–1802; Lostwithiel, 1802–6; Somerset, 1806–31. Son of WD I (MP, 1745–1806) and a daughter of Stephen Fuller of Jamaica. Awarded compensation with Ezekiel and Jeremiah Harman for St Elizabeth Nos. 5, 268, 205.

74 Hon. John Barham: see also Westmoreland No. 77. Judd shows one John Foster Barham (1800–38) for Stockbridge, 1820–6 and 1831–2; and Kendal, 1834–7. There were however two John Foster Barhams, brother and son of Joseph Foster Barham.

75 Joseph Foster Barham (died 1832). See also Westmoreland No. 77

76 Sir Francis Mollineux Ommaney: Navy agent.

77 For other Smith, Payne & Smith claims, see for example St Kitts No. 525. For Samuel Smith and Lord Carrington, see St Catherine No. 538.

78 With John Abel Smith

79 Sir Alexander Cray Grant: see also St Mary No. 260, St Thomas in V Nos. 23, 133, 289. Cambridge M.P, 1841

80 John Smith of Blendon Hill.

81 James Walter Grimston = Lord Viscount Grimston.

82 Henry Bright: collected compensation of Edward Smith on Haughton Pen.

83 John Rock Grosett of Lacock Abbey, Wilts.: see also St George No. 66 and St Thomas-in-the-East No. 503, all Chancery.

84 Sir Thomas Baring: accepted Chiltern Hundreds, 26 March 1832 from Chipping Wycombe. Came into Southampton County, 22 June 1832.

85 Sir Joseph Birch: counter-claimed by William Ward as mortgagee jointly with Sir Joseph Birch. Birch had died in 1833; the bulk of the compensation was paid to Ward alone.

86 Sir Thomas Bernard Birch: High Sheriff of Lancashire, 1841.

87 Robert Gordon: son of William Gordon, planter. Claimed for Windsor Lodge and Paisley estates on St James Nos. 169, 184, losing out to the Hibberts as mortgagees.

88 James Hewitt Massy Dawson (d. 1835): came in for Limerick County 2 February 1830, having taken the Chiltern Hundreds for Clonmel (where he was elected 1826): see also St Mary No. 387, Clarendon Nos. 66, 232 for the marriage of Massy Dawson's son.

89 Edward Rose Tunno: see also St Mary Nos. 262, 264–6 (executor of mortgagee).

90 Richard Alexander Oswald: through his wife, Lady Lilias Montgomerie, whose mother was Eleanor Hamilton, daughter of Robert Hamilton.

91 Rowland Alston: through his wife, Rose Milles, daughter of Jeremiah Milles.

92 Andrew Arcedeckne: son of Chaloner Arcedeckne; Sheriff of Suffolk, 1819.

93 John Gladstone: see also St Kitts No. 254 and British Guiana claims.

94 John Atkins: Alderman, Lord Mayor of London, 1818.

95 Henry Dawkins (1765–1852): also MP for Boroughbridge, 1806–8; Henry Dawkins (1788–1864): MP for Boroughbridge, 1824–30.

96 John Mitchell, 1781–1859 = son of David Mitchell, planter and merchant, inherited from his uncle 'King' William Mitchell (d. 1823). John Mitchell's brothers (Rowland, Samuel, William) went into the mercantile business. See also St Ann No. 128 for John Mitchell; St Thomas in V No. 60, award to John Mitchell Jr as trustee for Elizabeth Gale Vidal.

97 William James: grandson and heir of the Liverpool West India merchant William James. St Thomas-in-the-East No. 278 shows Joseph Brooks Yates as trustee of Wm James for Clifton Hill estate.

98 Abel Smith, elected for Wendover, 1831. Trustee for the marriage settlement of John F. Crewe.

Notes to Appendix 1 (*cont.*)

99 Rt Hon. Henry Goulburn: see also counter-claim under Manchester No. 432. Goulburn was elected for Cambridge University, 1831.

100 Richard Godson: awarded compensation jointly with Henry Hargreaves.

101 George Stevens Byng came in for Milborne Port Borough, Somerset, 14 March 1831; Capt. G. S. Byng of Eaton Square (re-)elected for Milborne Port, 1831. Came in for Chatham 26 June 1834. The Duke of Richmond and Earl of Wiltshire as trustees for Rt Hon. G. S. Byng counter-claimed, apparently without success, for him as mortgagee on [one-third] of Vere No. 37. John Byng was MP for Poole, 1831.

102 W. J. Denison inherited his partnership in the banking firm of Denison, Heywood & Kennard, and became senior partner.

103 Edward Littleton: as Lord Hatherton (1835) was one of trustees for the heirs of the Earl of Dudley.

104 David Lyon came into Beeralston 11 January 1831: see also Trelawny Nos. 42, 191, 374; and multiple Chancery claims in Westmoreland.

105 Sir David Wedderburn: owner of Blue Castle estate, part of the compensation for which was awarded in the name of Wedderburn's cousin and former partner Andrew Colvile, and most of which went into a Chancery suit (*Lyon v. Colvile*) in which Wedderburn and Colvile were defendants.

106 Matthew G. Lewis: 'Monk' Lewis (d. 1818); compensation awarded to his trustees who ceded one-quarter to Lewis's brother-in-law John Sheddon. See also St Thomas-in-the-East for Lewis's Hordley estate, where the compensation was paid into Chancery in *Lushington v. Sewell*. Lewis had left both estates to his two sisters, Dame Fanny M. Lushington and Mrs Sheddon.

107 Rt Hon. Charles Baron Feversham of Duncombe Park, Yorks.

108 Lord Combermere: son of Sir Robert Stapleton Cotton, MP for Chester, and former governor-general of Barbados.

109 Henry Combe Compton: awarded compensation for Mills and Golden Rock (St Kitts No. 424) estates with Sir William Pole, Bart. Pole's grandmother was Elizabeth Mills, daughter of John Mills of Woodford.

110 William Manning (d. 1835): of Manning & Anderdon; came into Lymington, June 1821. Manning claimed for St Kitts No. 746 as trustee for John Estridge, award made to Freshfields/SPS.

111 Sir Peter Payne: see also St Kitts No. 575.

112 Charles Percy, of Guy's Cliffe, Warks., came into Newport, 8 February 1826; C. Bertie Percy elected, 1826.

113 Charles Ashe A'Court: MP for Heytesbury, March–August 1820. Shown as owner with the Earl of Romney and Thomas Neave; possibly in fact trustees?

114 George Robert Smith, partner in Smith, Payne & Smith. See also St Kitts No. 752, British Guiana No. 167.

115 James William Freshfield: counter-claim by two Freshfields and Charles Kaye Freshfield, 'lien for law charges'. See also St Kitts Nos. 525, 206, 333, 336, 525, 724, 746; and Trinidad No. 1661 for other Freshfield awards as trustees etc.

116 Sir William Payne-Gallwey: second Baronet, son of Ralph Payne (the Chief Justice of St Kitts).

117 Sir Gerald Noel Noel (d. 1838): father of Rev. Gerald Noel, the abolitionist. See also St Kitts No. 705.

118 John Plummer: of Plummer & Wilson, son of Thomas Plummer (1749–1818), MP for Ilchester, 1802–3) of Plummer & Barham, and brother of Thomas William Plummer (d. 1817, MP for Yarmouth, 1806–7) of Plummer, Barham & Plummer. (Thorne: Judd shows only TWP as MP for both). See also St Elizabeth No. 137, where John Plummer is shown as assigning a mortgage to George Joad on Mt Zion estate, with counter-claims from assignees of Plummer & Wilson itself. See also St Kitts No. 73 for John Plummer as trustee.

119 Martin Tucker Smith: counter-claimed with others as trustee of Messrs. Findlay, Ballantyne & Co., mortgagees; and similarly on St Lucia Nos. 842, 872.

120 James Wilson (d. 1830): of Sneaton Castle and Cane Grove (St Vincent); deputy-lieutenant for Yorkshire, award made to his trustees.

121 Edward Protheroe: St Vincent 505 shows EP, presumably Sr, of Hill House, Newnham, Gloucs. See also Trinidad No. 1701 for EP Jr collecting, on an award for seventy-two slaves on Endeavour to EP of Hants.

122 John Ingett Fortescue: claimed with his son John I. D. Fortescue for the Hope estate on St.Vincent; lost out to mortgagees.

123 Sir William Abdy came into Malmesbury, 8 February 1817: see also Antigua Nos. 259, 342

124 Sir William Laurence Young: fourth Baronet of North Dean. See also Antigua No. 282, Grenada No. 691 ('Sir Wm Young of Upper Wimpole Street'), St Vincent No. 577 and Tobago No. 64 for Sir William Laurence Young's unsuccessful pursuit of compensation for estates owned by his grandfather, Sir William Young the second Baronet (and MP for St Mawes).

125 Josias Jackson (d. 1819): of Bellevue House, Southampton. His sons inherited (Thorne), heirs of Josias Jackson in T71/892 in Chancery suit *Baillie* vs. *Jackson*.

126 William Robert Keith Douglas: executor and trustee of his father-in-law.

127 Andrew Henry Lynch and Lachlan Maclachlan: awarded compensation jointly with one other as assignees of a mortgage. Lachlan Maclachlan's election for Galway in 1833 was subsequently voided.

128 Patrick Maxwell Stewart: see also Tobago No. 77.

129 Sir Michael Bruce: see also Tobago No. 73.

130 Alexander Murray of Broughton, came in for Kircudbright, 31 December 1838.

131 George Ferguson of Pitfour, Aberdeenshire

132 Charles Brooke: partner of John Robley, killed himself 1833. Also MP for Chippenham, 1802–3 and 1836–7; and for Ilchester, 1803–6.

133 John Gordon of Cluny: MP; counter-claimed as mortgagee. See Grenada Nos. 865, 866 and *The Times*, 5 April 1831, p. 3 for his ties to the Pulteney–Johnstone interest at Weymouth.

134 Joseph Marryat (d. 1824): see also awards to J. & C. Marryat, Trinidad Nos. 1245A, 1781, 1783, 1235 etc.; Grenada No. 762.

135 John Ashton Yates: of Liverpool firm of Yates Brothers. See also Trinidad Nos. 1893, 1895.

136 William Henry Cavendish Bentinck: commonly called Lord Bentinck. Came in for Glasgow City, 17 February 1836.

137 Edward Protheroe Jr: collected the award for seventy-two slaves on Endeavour made to 'Edward Protheroe of Hampshire' as owner-in-fee. It is unclear whether this was Edward Protheroe Jr's own award: in 1831 he was described as 'of Great Gaddesden, county Herts', and in 1837 and 1841 as 'of Forest of Dean County Gloucs.'. Edward Protheroe – presumably his father, Edward Protheroe Sr – is described in St Vincent No. 505 as of Hill House, Newnham, Gloucs.

138 Sir George Fitzgerald Hill: MP for Coleraine, 1791–5; Londonderry City, 1795–1801, 1802–30.

139 Sir Thomas John Cochrane: former governor of Newfoundland, counter-claimed as heir-at-law of Sir Alex. Inglis Cochrane.

140 For Reid Irving, see VI Nos. 95, 257, 263 266, 254, 261.

141 This row represents the totals for 'West Indian' MPs for each Parliament as calculated by B. W. Higman, 'The West India interest in Parliament 1807–33', *Historical Studies*, 13.49 (October 1967), 1–19 (pp. 3–4).

Appendix 2 MPs whose immediate families appear in the Compensation records

Claim	MP	Own	Other	Constituency	1820	1826	1830	1831	1833	1835
Antigua										
101	Chris. W. Codrington[1]			Gloucs. Cty					X	X
86	William Ewart[2]			Bletchingley		X				
"				Liverpool			X	X	X	X
26	Geo. White Thomas[3]			Chichester 1784–1812						
Barbados										
211	W. S. S. Lascelles[4]			East Looe	X	X				
3817	"			Northallerton				X		
2769	Henry Lascelles[5]			Northallerton		X	X			
3184	Henry Vane, Earl of Darlington[6]			Salop Cty			X		X	X
"	"			Tregoney	X					
270	Sir Francis Ford[7]			Newcastle 1793–6						
Grenada										
608	Wm Lushington[8]			London 1795–1802	X		X			
692	Geo. Dallas[9]			Newport 1802						
466	Henry Chaplin[10]			Lincs. 1868		X				
"	Charles Chaplin			Lincs.		X	X			
688	Wm M'Dowall[11]			Glasgow 1790–1810	X					
706	T. F. Lewis[12]			Beaumaris	X					
"	"			Radnor		X	X			
866	Sir J. Lowther Johnston[13]			Weymouth 1810			X			
Jamaica										
Hanover										
37 etc.	William Miles[14]			New Romney			X			
"	"			Somerset East				X	X	
455	Sir Jas Duff[15]			Banffshire	X	X		X	X	X

Claim	MP	Own	Other	Constituency	1820	1826	1830	1831	1833	1835
St Andrew										
514	Henry Lawes Luttrell[16]			Ludgershall	X					
St Catherine										
664	Peter Blackburne[17]			Stirling 1855					X	
539	A. F. Ellis[18]			Seaford		X	X			
St James										
5	Pascoe Grenfell[19]			Penryn	X	X				
St Thomas-in-the-East										
154	J. Buller East[20]			Winchester				X		X
Westmoreland										
27, 30, 31	Henry Fox[21]			Horsham		X				
Nevis										
41	William Pinney[22]			Lyme Regis					X	X
102	Robert S. Cotton[23]			Chester 1780–96						
St Kitts										
210	F. S. Corrance[24]			1856						
316	John G. Crosbie[25]			Co. Kerry 1795–7						
525	John Abel Smith[26]			Midhurst			X			
"	"			Chichester				X		
"	Robert J. Smith			Chipping Wycombe				X	X	X
"	"			Bucks. Cty	X					
St Lucia										
757	Gilbert E. Joliffe			Petersfield			X			
"	Hylton Joliffe			Petersfield	X	X				
"	Wm G. H. Joliffe[27]			Petersfield			X	X	X	
St Vincent										
492A	George Sinclair[28]			Caithness				X	X	X

Claim	MP	Own	Other	Constituency	1820	1826	1830	1831	1833	1835
Tobago										
27	Rob. Pulsford[29]			Hereford 1841						
Total					9	10	9	9	9	8

Dates (1820, 1826 etc.) are for the Parliaments elected in each of such election-years. MPs with no entry shown for 1820–1835 sat in Parliaments for the dates given in the 'Constituency' column.

[1] Christopher William Codrington, son of Sir C. B. Codrington, came into Gloucestershire County, 7 August 1834.

[2] William Ewart came in for Bletchingley, 1828, and to Liverpool, November 1830; the claim was by partners in Ewart Myers of 3 Exchange Alley; *Gore's Directory of Liverpool and Its Environs* (1823, 1825). S. F. Woolley, 'The personnel of the Parliament of 1833', *English Historical Review*, 53.210 (April 1938), 240–62 describes William Ewart as son of the principal partner of Ewart Rutson & Co., merchants of Liverpool (pp. 240–1). Ewart Rutson, the predecessor firm, was at 3 Exchange Alley; Gore's (1805).

[3] George White Thomas (1750–1821): father-in-law of Gen. Sir John Gustavus Crosbie. George White Thomas's kinsman Sir W. L. G. Thomas claimed for Antigua No. 355.

[4] W. S. S. Lascelles, Earl of Harewood claims: see also Barbados No. 2770. Also MP for Wakefield, 1837–41, 1842–7; Knaresborough, 1847–51.

[5] Henry Lascelles: became third Earl of Harewood in 1841 succeeding Henry Lascelles, second Earl, who was MP for Northallerton, 1818–20 (until his own succession).

[6] Henry Vane: son of second Duke of Cleveland; sat as Lord Viscount Barnard.

[7] Sir Francis Ford: first Baronet, 1758–1801. His son, also Sir Francis Ford, the second Baronet, was awarded compensation for Barbados Nos. 270 and 3258.

[8] William Lushington (d. 1823): see also Trinidad No. 1700 for Charlotte Lushington, his daughter.

[9] The award was to Sir Robert C. Dallas and Rob. W. Dallas. Sir R. C. Dallas = son of Sir George Dallas, MP for Newport, 1800–1802 (d. 1833) and his wife, the daughter of Sir John Blackwood. Geo. Dallas's brother Robert Dallas (also MP, d. 1824) married the daughter of Henry Davidson of Tulloch.

[10] Henry Chaplin, MP: son of Rev. Henry Chaplin of Blankney, Lincoln and nephew of Charles Chaplin, MP for Lincoln County, 1820, 1826, 1830. Thomas Chaplin of Welbeck St. = MP for Stamford, 1833. Award to Rev. Henry Chaplin and others as mortgagees.

[11] Thorne indicates Wm M'Dowall (III) had dissipated his fortune by his death in 1810. William M'Dowall, owner-in-fee with consent of Archibald Campbell and Ludovic Houston, trustees and exors of William M'Dowall deceased, was awarded the compensation for Mount Alexander.

[12] Thomas Frankland Lewis, elected for Ennis, 1826, came in for Radnor, 9 April 1828: brother-in-law of Sir George Cornewall, Bart., member of 1832 Select Committee, Vice-President of the Board of Trade.

[13] Sir John Lowther Johnstone, father of Sir Frederick George Johnstone. See also Grenada No. 865.

Notes to Appendix 2 (*cont.*)

14 William Miles: son of Philip John Miles. Also MP for Chippenham, 1818–20.

15 Sir James Duff, fourth Earl of Fife, of Duff House (d. 1857), MP for Banffshire, 1818–27. The Sir James Duff in this award appears to be the second Earl of Fife's (uncle of the fourth Earl) illegitimate son. The second Earl of Fife was himself MP for Banffshire, 1784–8.

16 Henry Lawes Luttrell: commonly called Earl of Carhampton, of Ireland (d. 1821), son of first Earl and of Maria, daughter of Sir Nicholas Lawes of Jamaica. HLL's sister-in-law, Maria Dowager of Carhampton, was awarded the compensation for Swallowfield, after the deaths of HLL and of his brother and heir.

17 Peter Blackburn: son of John Blackburn of Killearn: see also St Thomas-in-V No. 24.

18 Augustus Frederick Ellis (1800–41): son of Charles Rose Ellis, Lord Seaford, whom he pre-deceased.

19 Pascoe Grenfell (d. 1838): father of Pascoe St Leger Grenfell, partner in Sir James Esdaile & Co. and mortgagee of Hazelymph estate in St James. See St Elizabeth No. 296 for P. S. L. Grenfell as trustee.

20 J. Buller East: son of Sir Edward Hyde East.

21 Henry Fox of Holland House: came in for Horsham, March 1826. Claim by Lord and Lady Holland.

22 Son of J. F. Pinney: ran anti-slavery attack on Renn Hampden in the 1837 Lyme Regis election.

23 Robert Salisbury Cotton: his son was Lord Combermere, claimant on Stapleton's Estates.

24 F. S. Corrance: son of Frederick Corrance, awarded £2,770 17s 3d for 174 slaves on Needsmust as trustee for Eliza Woodley, William Woodley's widow.

25 John Gustavus Crosbie: General Sir John Gustavus Crosbie, presumed to be the son of John, married the daughter of George White Thomas, MP and was beneficiary of this award and of Antigua No. 26.

26 John Abel Smith and Robert J. Smith: members of the Smith, Payne & Smith banking family.

27 William G. H. Joliffe's father, Rev. Wm Joliffe of Merstham, conveyed the Union estate in 1822, and all claims due to Inglis Ellice, to John Bellingham Inglis. Hylton Joliffe was the Rev. Wm Joliffe's brother.

28 George Sinclair (1790–1868): of Ulbster and Thurso Castle, MP for Caithness, 1811–12, 1818–20, 1831–41. Sinclair's father, John, the first Baronet, claimed compensation for 264 slaves on Argyle and 268 on Calder (St Vincent Nos. 492A and 497A) as trustee of the marriage settlement of the Hon. A. Macdonald, John Sinclair's brother-in-law, and Jane Campbell. George Sinclair attended the 5 April 1832 City meeting of the West India interest.

29 Robert Pulsford: son or nephew of Robert Pulsford of R. & W. Pulsford, the London merchant. Robert Pulsford Sr died *c.*1835, having claimed on Tobago No. 27. See also other R. & W. Pulsford claims: Montserrat No. 42; Antigua Nos. 24, 36; and Chancery cases Antigua Nos. 97, 98; St Mary No. 25; and St Thomas-in-the-East No. 192.

Appendix 3 'West India interest' MPs, 1820–35, not appearing in the Compensation records

MP	Constituency	1820	1826	1830	1831	1833	1835
Ralph Benson[1]	Stafford		X				
Sir Francis Blake[2]	Berwick	X	X	X	X	X	
T. H. Broadhead	Yarmouth	X					
R. Hart Davis	Bristol	X	X	X			
Thomas Bilcliffe Fyler	Coventry		X	X			
W. D. Gillon[3]	Falkirk Burghs				X	X	X
Wm Holmes[4]	Bishops Castle	X	X				
"	Haslemere			X	X		
John Jackson[5]	Dover	X					
Manasseh Lopes[6]	Westbury	X	X				
G. Nugent-Grenville[7]	Aylesbury	X	X	X	X		
C. Fyshe Palmer[8]	Reading	X	X	X	X	X	
Charles Ross[9]	Orford	X					
"	St Germans		X	X	X		
"	Northampton					X	X
M. Shaw-Stewart[10]	N. Lanarkshire		X				
"	Renfrewsh.			X	X	X	X
Masterton Ure[11]	Weymouth	X	X	X	X		
TOTAL		10	11	9	8	5	3

MPs sitting in the House of Commons between 1820 and 1835 who appear in Judd's 'West India interest' but not in the Slave Compensation records; Jerrit P. Judd IV, *Members of Parliament 1734–1832* (New Haven: Yale University Press, 1955). Dates (1820, 1826 etc.) are for the Parliaments elected in each of such election-years.

[1] Ralph Benson: son of Moses Benson, Liverpool West India merchant, brother-in-law of John Bolton (Thorne).

[2] Sir Francis Blake: Baronet of Twizell Castle.

[3] William Downe Gillon of Wallhouse: seat is shown variously as Lanark or Falkirk Burghs for 1831.

[4] William Holmes (1778–1851): agent for Demerara, 1820–33. Also MP for Grampound, 1808–12; Tregoncy, 1812–18; Totnes, 1818–20; Berwick-on-Tweed, 1837–41.

[5] John Jackson (1763–1820).

[6] Manasseh Masseh Lopes: first Baronet, 1755–1831. Also MP for New Romney, 1802–6; Evesham, 1807–8; Barnstaple, 1812–20. Prosecuted and sentenced to prison for electoral bribery.

Notes to Appendix 3 (*cont.*)

[7] George Nugent-Grenville: second Baron Nugent (1789–1850). Member of Parliament for Buckingham, 1810–12; Aylesbury, 1812–32 and 1847–50.
[8] Charles Fyshe Palmer (1769–1843): MP for Reading, 1818–26, 1827–34, 1837–41.
[9] Charles Ross: shown in secondary sources as a 'proprietor'; no firm identification in Compensation records.
[10] Sir Michael Shaw-Stewart (1788–1836).
[11] Masterton Ure (1776–1863): trustee for West India property (Thorne), trustee under Sir John Lowther Johnstone's will.

Appendix 4 Other MPs aligned to the West India interest over Emancipation

MP	Constituency	1820	1826	1830	1831	1833	1835
Sir R. Vyvyan	Cornwall		X	X			
G. F. Young	Tynemouth					X	X
Hon. W. Best[1]	St Michael				X		
Vct. Stormont[2]	Aldborough			X			
"	Woodstock				X		
"	Norwich					X	
Ald. Thompson[3]	Callington	X	X				
"	London			X	X		
"	Sunderland					X	X
Ald. Copeland[4]	Coleraine				X	X	X
Col. Beresford[5]	Northallerton	X	X	X	X		
John Capel[6]	Queenborough		X	X	X		
R. A. Dundas[7]	Ipswich		X	X			X
"	Edinburgh				X		
H. Houldsworth[8]	Pontefract	X	X				
"	Newton			X	X		
"	North Notts.					X	X
J. A. Stewart Mackenzie[9]	Ross-shire				X	X	X
G. R. Robinson[10]	Worcester		X	X	X	X	X
John Young[11]	Cavan				X	X	X
B. L. Lester[12]	Poole	X	X	X	X	X	
Jas Mackillop[13]	Tregoney			X	X		
Total		**4**	**8**	**10**	**13**	**9**	**8**
GRAND TOTAL		**88**	**89**	**81**	**80**	**65**	**55**
Higman[14]		39	40	36	31	19	–

MPs sitting in the House of Commons between 1820 and 1835 identified as expressing anti-abolitionist views in the House, or speaking at or attending anti-abolition
meetings, but not appearing directly or indirectly in the Slave Compensation records
nor included in Judd's 'West India interest'. Attendees at the 5 April 1832 City meeting
of West India interest are identified from the list reproduced in S. D. Smith, *Slavery,
family, and gentry capitalism in the British Atlantic: the world of the Lascelles, 1648–1834*
(Cambridge: Cambridge University Press, 2006), pp. 311–12. Dates (1820, 1826 etc.)
are for the Parliaments elected in each of such election-years.

Notes to Appendix 4 (*cont.*)

1. Hon. W. Best: William Samuel Best (1789–1869), second Baron Wynford. Attended 5 April 1832 City meeting.
2. Viscount Stormont: William David Murray (1806–98), fourth Earl of Mansfield. Attended 5 April 1832 City meeting.
3. Alderman Thompson: William Thompson (1792–1854.) Attended 5 April 1832 City meeting.
4. Alderman Copeland: William Taylor Copeland, 'manufacturer' (Judd). Attended 5 April 1832 City meeting.
5. Col. Marcus Beresford: attended 5 April 1832 City meeting.
6. John Capel: attended 5 April 1832 City meeting.
7. R. A. Dundas: attended (and spoke at) 5 April 1832 City meeting.
8. H. [*sic*] Houldsworth: Judd and Thorne show Thomas Houldsworth, a self-made entrepreneur and cotton spinner. Attended 5 April 1832 City meeting.
9. J. A. Stewart Mackenzie: attended 5 April 1832 City meeting.
10. George Richard Robinson: also MP for Poole, 1847–50. Attended 5 April 1832 City meeting.
11. John Young: first Baron Lisgar, MP for Cavan, 1831–55. Attended 5 April 1832 City meeting.
12. Benjamin Lester Lester: grandson of Benjamin Lester of Poole, Newfoundland merchant. Attended 5 April 1832 City meeting.
13. James Mackillop: attended 5 April 1832 City meeting.
14. Totals for each Parliament as calculated by Higman, 'The West India interest'.

Appendix 5   Church of England clergymen in Britain appearing in the Compensation records

Claim No.	Clergyman	CCED[1] No.	Address/living	Beneficiary	Other
Anguilla					
205	Rev. T. Harrison[2]		6 Bloomsbury Sq.		Trus.
Antigua					
35	Rev. H. Barnes[3]	3629	Monmouth		Exor
38	Rev. Henry Jonas Barton[4]		Crichlade, Wilts.	X	
271	Rev. J. Braid[5]		Denine, Fifeshire		X
259	Rev. G. Caldwell[6]		Cheltenham	X	
387	Rev. Horace G. Cholmondley[7]		Kingston House, Dorset	X	
343	Rev. Rowland Duer[8]	56998		X	
51	Rev. Robert Hesketh[9]	11723	Epsom, Surrey	X	
324	Rev J. Kirby[10]	64145	Mayfield	X	
	Rev. H. Kirby	68660	Oakley, nr Eye	X	
131	Rev. Thomas Scott[11]	21450	Wappenham, Northants.		Rep.
363	Rev. Hon. Miles J. Stapleton[12]	543	Mereworth	X	
324	Rev. Wm Vernon[13]		Clitheroe, Lancs.	X	
339	Rev. John T. Wilgress[14]	2562	Chalke, Kent	X	
24	Rev. F. de V. Williams[15]		Wishford Magna	X	
	Rev. Dr Wrench[16]	72020	Robertsbridge		Agent
Barbados					
3619	Rev. H. Allen[17]			X	
2954	Rev. Robert Allen[18]		Barcombe, Lewes	X?	
4146	Rev. W. H. R. Bayley[19]	8132	Little-on-Severn	X	
4800	Rev. John Brome[20]		Trinity College, Cambridge	X	
2521	Rev. Renn Hampden[21]	30201	St Mary Hall, Oxford	X	
4799	Rev. Hinds Howell[22]		Hellersdon & Drayton	X	
2432	Rev. S. Isaacson[23]		Dorking	X	

Claim No.	Clergyman	CCED[1] No.	Address/living	Beneficiary	Other
391	Rev. Geo. Kemp[24]		Penryn	X	
3245	[Rev.] Richard Lane[25]		Brixton, Devon	X	
2934	Rev. Edm. Melville[26]		Great Missenden, Bucks.		Trus.
3295	Rev. John Nurse[27]	41684		X	
3296	Rev. James Nurse	41683		X	
1013	Rev. J. D. Ostrehan?[28]		Painswick, Gloucs.	X	
5310	Rev. F. F. Pinder?[29]	19038	Gosforth, Cumberland	X	
4601	Rev. Kenrick F. Saunders[30]	37549	Brighton	X	
2772	Rev. Alex Scott[31]		38 Pulteney St., Bath	X	
4196	Rev. Wm D. Sealy[32]			X	
2954A	Rev. Richard Smith[33]	72285	Sutton Rectory, Pitworth	X	
British Guiana					
277	Rev. R. Allwood[34]	8075	York Place, Clifton		
Dominica					
318	Rev. Thos Maude[35]		St Paul's, Covent Garden	X	
Grenada					
435	[Rev.] J. T. Trevelyan[36]	40744	Huish Champflower	X	
"	[Rev.] G. Treveylan	40743	Treborough	X	
466	Rev. Henry Chaplin[37]	71719	Blankney, Lincs.	X	
"	Rev. James Ellice	1814	Clothall, Herts.	X	
998	Rev. S. Crowther[38]	10405	Leamington Privis		
"	Rev. J. E. Tarleton[39]	7043	Chelsfield	X?	
955	Rev. Peter W. Pegus[40]	72398		X	
777	Rev. Edmund Waller[41]	10006	Fordingbridge	X	
Jamaica Clarendon					
410a	Rev. Geo. Chandler[42]			X	
158	Rev. C. J. Glascott[43]				Trus.
284	Rt Rev. H. Phillpotts[44]	28960	Bishop of Exeter		Trus.
291	Rev. John J. Scott[45]			X	
Hanover					
4	Rev. W. D. Longlands[46]	32583		X	
"	Rev. George Ingram Fisher	52475	Winifrith Newburgh, Dorset	X	
56	Rev. George Sandby[47]		Denton Lodge, Norfolk	X	

Claim No.	Clergyman	CCED[1] No.	Address/living	Beneficiary	Other
Manchester					
113	Rev. Edward Owen[48]	404	Lullingstone	X	
424	Rev. J. J. Rowe[49]	40485		X	
Port Royal					
30	Rev. Benjamin Guest[50]	52691			Trus.
"	Rev. Thomas Furnivall	60719			"
Portland					
231	Rev. W. Woollams Holland[51]	7157	Chichester		Trus.
"	Rev. J. Peter Rhodes		Clonmell		"
131	Rev. A. Bunting[52]			X	
229	Rev. E. C. Wright[53]	21030		X	
St Andrew					
114	Hon. and Rev. G. Neville Grenville[54]				Trus.
359	Rev. C. G. Townley[55]		Ilchester Place, Brixton		Trus.
St Ann					
524	Rev. Robt Hawthorne[56]			X	
302	Rev. Evan James[57]		Stepney		
St David					
70	Hon. Rev. W. Herbert[58]			X	
8	Rev. Robert Morgan[59]				
St Dorothy					
73	Rev. Samuel White[60]				Agent
St Elizabeth					
362	Rev. John Campbell Fisher[61]	42222	Merton Parsonage, Okehampton		Exor
360	Rev. Wm Harriott[62]				Admor
375a	Rev. John Pyke Jones[63]	13133	Alton, Staffs.		Exor
"	Rev. John D. Burdon				Exor
983	Rev. H. Nembhard[64]				
St James					
25	Rev. R. Appleton[65]		Liverpool	Xmort	
759	Rev. S. E. Bernard[66]	6534		X?	Trus.
276	Rev. John Briggs[67]	6569	Southmere, Norfolk		Trus.
"	Rev. Thomas Hodgson				Trus.
439	Rev. L. Clutterbuck[68]	71817	Newark Park, Gloucs.		
611	Rev. T. Gardner[69]	60875			
394	Rev. W. S. Halliday[70]			X	

Claim No.	Clergyman	CCED[1] No.	Address/living	Beneficiary	Other
3	Rev. Henry Mair[71]		Rawford House, Somerset	Xmort	
546	Rev. Adam Sedgwick[72]	1111			Trus.
172	Rev. R. Wetherell[73]	71489?		X	
St Mary					
1	Rev. John Mansfield[74]	18378?			Exor
252	Rev. W. Marshall[75]	53378?			
300	Rev. J. C. Shaw[76]	6303		X	
135	Rev. John Twells[77]		Gamston Rectory, Notts.		Trus.
"	Rev. J. G. Headlam				
336	Rev. J. M. Dawson[78]			X	
51	Rev. John Rate[79]				
St Thomas-in-the-East					
473	Rev. John West[80]				Trus.
"	Rev. David Laing				Trus.
129	Rev. Wheeler Milner[81]			X	
117	Rev. George Turner[82]				Trus.
287a	Rev. Thos Robertson[83]				Trus.
St Thomas-in-the-Vale					
14	Rev. Sir W. H. Cooper[84]	1767			Trus.
Trelawny					
417	Rev. H. D. Berners[85]	1035			Trus.?
"	Rev. George Capper			X	
110–15	Rev. Charles Davy[86]	55241?			Trus.
"	Rev. George Porcher				"
Vere					
63	Rev. William Biscoe[87]			X	
122	Rev. W. Crewe[88]			X	
Westmore-land					
259	Rev. Theo. Williams[89]			X	
Montserrat					
116	Rev. W. W. Parson[90]		Brandon, Suffolk	X	
Nevis					
100	Rev. Wm Butler[91]	23605	Frampton, Dorset	X	
225	Rev. John Maynard[92]	4315			Agent?
16	Hon. and Rev. Sir F. Jarvis Stapleton[93]	7167	Merewith, Kent	X	
St Kitts					
210	Rev. G. C. Hale[94]	62786	Hillingdon	X	Trus.

Claim No.	Clergyman	CCED[1] No.	Address/living	Beneficiary	Other
740	Rev. Sir H. Lees[95]		Black Rock		Rep.
705	Hon. and Rev. G. Noel[96]	71598	Farnham		Trus.
440	Rev. Geo W. Philips[97]		Wendy, Cambs.	X	
753	Rev. Benjamin Pullan[98]	8180	Hockham, Norfolk		Rep.
200	Rev. John Wilson[99]		The Queen's College, Oxford	X	
St Lucia					
757	Rev. Wm Joliffe[100]		Merstham		
St Vincent					
459	Rev. R. Coningham[101]				Trus.
554	Rev. T. S. Gumshaw[102]		Biddenham, Beds.		Trus.
688	Rev. Wm. Hutcheson[103]	41401?	Compton Martin, Dorset	Xmort	
552	Rev. Charles Paul[104]	40209	Writhlington Rectory	X	
463	Rev. Richard Warde[105]	582	Yalding		Exor
458	Rev. Arch. Alison[106]				Trus.
Tobago					
34	Rev. James Hamilton[107]		St Stephens, nr Canterbury	X	
25a	Rev. Wm. S. Wilson[108]	40926	King's Brompton.	Xmort	
Trinidad					
1234A	Rev. Edward Picton[109]	4426	Iscoed, Carmathen	X	
Virgin Islands					
151–4	Rev. Edward Cooke[110]		Bye Well Vicarage, Newcastle-on-Tyne	X	

[1] Person identification number, Clergy of the Church of England Database (CCED) http://www.theclergydatabase.org.uk/cce/apps/personQuery, last accessed 20 November 2007.

[2] Rev. Thomas Harrison: trustee for Mary Procter with Henrietta Rosco (also a London absentee) and Mary Rey. See also Antigua No. 390, where Harrison acted as attorney to Henrietta Rosco of City of London, annuitant and mortgagee on Matthews and Constitution Hill. Also involved in correspondence with Commission on Anguilla No. 174 and in St Kitts.

[3] Rev. Henry Barnes: of Monmouth, 'at present in St Sewan, France', counter-claimed as executor of Louisa Barnes, a legatee of William Mackinnon, £2,500 with interest.

Note to Appendix 5 (*cont.*)

⁴ Rev. Henry Jonas Barton: counter-claimed as 'interested under the will of Sarah Willett Hooker, formerly S. W. Ottley, & otherwise, £2,689 3s 0d with interest at 6% from March last'. Barton shared the award of £2,482 16s 2d for 199 slaves on Marble Hill with other unconnected counter-claimants.

⁵ Rev. J. Braid: identified in counter-claim as father of Helen Braid, an 'only surviving child' and annuitant of £40 per annum under the will of Thomas Gillan (the late owner of Thomas's estate). List E claim.

⁶ Rev. George Caldwell: Rector of King's Stanley, Gloucester; Fellow of Jesus College Cambridge; shared award with his brother-in-law Sir William Abdy and others. See also Antigua No. 342, St Vincent No. 549.

⁷ Rev. Horace George Cholmondley: counter-claimed for an annuity of £100 per annum bequeathed to his wife by Godschall Johnson, the London financier.

⁸ Rev. Rowland Duer: father of Elizabeth and Theodora Duer, who were awarded £306 6d 9d for 244 slaves on Big Duers. Rev. Rowland Duer's will dated 1 January 1794; V. L. Oliver, *Caribbeana*, 6 vols. (London: Mitchell, Hughes and Clarke, 1909), Vol. II, p. 240.

⁹ Rev. Robert Hesketh: awarded compensation jointly with G. W. Ledeatt as owner-in-fee for twenty-four slaves on Parson Hall. Hesketh was Rector of St Dunstans in the East in the City of London and of Acton Burnell in Shropshire (Obituary, *The Times*, 15 February 1837).

¹⁰ Rev. John Kirby and Rev. H. Kirby: awarded a £2,226 5s 0d share of compensation for 329 slaves on Vernon's with two others, all four as 'assignees for an annuity of £230 p.a. for life of John Vernon secured by a demise of slaves etc. for 100 years. Arrears due £3,517 10s 0d'.

¹¹ Rev. Thomas Scott: 'Rectory clerk', counter-claim as 'sole representative of Elizabeth Gilbert, legacy of £180 under the will of Nathaniel Gilbert'.

¹² Rev. Hon. Miles J. Stapleton: son of Sir Thomas Stapleton, sixteenth Baron le Despencer. Rector of Mereworth; Vicar of Tudeley, Kent, 1827–30. Award to Hon. Anne Byam Stapleton, Rev. Stapleton's widow (daughter of Thomas Norbury Kerby of Antigua), and the trustees of her marriage settlement.

¹³ Rev. Wm Vernon: annuitant of Vernon's estate and brother of John Vernon, the life tenant.

¹⁴ Rev. John Thos. Wilgress: counter-claim by the Potts as trustees of Rev. John Thos Wilgress and others, on Weir's. Wilgress was Vicar of Chalke, Kent, 1813–50 and of Gwinear, Cornwall, 1813–33.

¹⁵ Rev. F. de Veil Williams: counter-claimed on complex awards made on estates of Alex. Willock awarded to George Savage Martin, apparently for the benefit of all counter-claimants. See also Montserrat No. 42.

¹⁶ Rev. Dr [Jacob George] Wrench of Salehurst Vicarage, Robertsbridge: wrote to the Commission on behalf of an unnamed parishioner concerning mechanics of compensation process, T71/1594 p. 284.

¹⁷ Rev. Henry Allen: Rev. H. Allen, deceased, 'by settlement previous to his marriage conveyed, assigned and settled all his interest in sd estate' (Valley) to trustees, who received one-third compensation for 153 slaves; T71/898, Barbados No. 3619.

¹⁸ Rev. Robert Allen: counter-claimed in the name of Henry George Acklom Allen, an infant, as claimant in reversion as heir-at-law to an undivided moiety in right of his mother, the late Mary Gibbes Allen.

¹⁹ Rev. William Henry Ricketts Bayl[e]y: awarded £5,241 5s 11d for 230 slaves on Malvern estate. See also St Dorothy No. 9, where the Rev W. H. R. Bayley of

Hasleton near Bristol claimed as part of a family group as tenants-in-remainder as testamentary guardians of a minor, and as one of the residuary devisees and also as an executor of the will of Alexander Bayley Esq. The compensation of £3,272 14s 7d for 162 slaves on Wood Hall was awarded to trustees for the Bayleys and for a rival claimant, the Rev. Lewis Bowerbank of Jamaica, as annuitant of £300 per annum.

20 Rev. John Brome: his daughter married resident slave-owner Christopher Barrow, 1811; Oliver, *Caribbeana*, Vol. II, p. 132. John Brome of Hardwick House, Ham (presumably his son) received £3,833 7s 10d for 163 slaves on Bromefield, after withdrawal of the counter-claim of trustee for Rev. John Brome's widow Elizabeth Ann, his daughter Emily Arabella and her husband Charles Aldis, and £2,709 0s 0d for 122 slaves on Hannays (Barbados No. 4801).

21 Rev. Renn [Dickson] Hampden: letter from Thomas Moody, T71/1611: 'I have had a request from the Rev. Dr Hampden of St Mary Hall Oxford to enquire after some domestics left to him in Barbados, who were slaves', awarded £1 18s 10d for one slave: was King William's Reader of Theology, put forward as new Bishop of Hereford in the 'Hampden controversy' of the 1840s.

22 [Rev.] Hinds Howell: awarded £3,155 12s 10d for 160 slaves on Trent's; and a further £38 16s 9d for one slave (Barbados No. 2660), where John. G. Goding acted as attorney.

23 Rev. Stephen Isaacson: awarded £60 4s 0d for three slaves in right of wife Anna Maria Miller Killikelly. Isaacson was asked by the Commission to repay the compensation he received of £63 0s 1d for one female domestic under British Guiana No. 2651.

24 Rev. George Kemp: awarded £42 14s 5d for two slaves, originally awarded to Elizabeth Johanna Spencer, 'now to you as her husband'; Commission to Rev. George Kemp, Penryn, T71/1539, p. 164.

25 [Rev.] Richard Lane: awarded £5,538 8s 1d for 3,245 slaves on Newtons.

26 Rev. Edmund Melville: awarded £5,202 8s 9d for 266 slaves on Chapel estate and £5,458 15s 7d for 261 slaves on Carringtons as trustee (with two others) of the marriage settlement of George Carrington with Anna Maria Parris.

27 Rev. John Nurse and Rev. James Nurse: awarded £137 16s 8d for eight slaves on Kirton and £130 2s 2d for six slaves respectively. Although shown in the CCED as having taken positions in England, as curate of Northover in 1831 and curate of Lymington in 1826 respectively, they may have been in Barbados by the time of the compensation payments, when Rev. John Nurse is shown as of Christ Church.

28 Rev. Joseph Duncan Ostrehan: award to Bezsin K. Reece of £85 8s 11d for three slaves as attorney and also trustee under the marriage settlement of Rev. J. D. Ostrehan, Sheepscombe Parsonage, Painswick, Gloucester, heir-at-law to Lucretia Ostrehan.

29 Rev. Francis Ford Pinder: Francis Ford Pinder was awarded £4,307 4s 4d for 204 slaves on Hothersol estate, and £277 13s 11d for fifteen slaves on Airy Hall, which shows F. F. Pinder of Watford as one of two trustees under the marriage settlement of Eliz. B. Senhouse. These are possibly both Francis Ford Pinder – who married Elizabeth, daughter of William Senhouse – surveyor-general of the Leewards, who died in Bath in 1843 (*The Times*, 31 January 1843, p. 7) rather than their son, the Rev. Francis Ford Pinder.

30 Rev. Kenrick Francis Saunders: of Brighton, counter-claimed on the Morgan Lewis estate for a legacy left to his wife amounting to £2,740; also creditor by judgement, 11 August 1819, for £982 10s.

31 Rev. Alex Scott: awarded £2,538 2s 3d for 122 slaves on Wiltshires and £3,837 5s 4d on Bayleys (Barbados No. 2811). Scott had married Anna Maria Ellcock, and

Notes to Appendix 5 (*cont.*)

was described as 'of the Island of Barbados and Parkside Edinburgh' in a memorial in Bathwick, Bath after his death in 1858 (Oliver, *Caribbeana*, Vol. I, p. 127). See also Antigua No. 30 for Scott as trustee for Christiana Richardson, late Christiana Jarvis, of Southampton, under the will of her late father.

[32] Rev. William Drake Sealy: as remainder-man awarded £2,151 13s 3d for 105 slaves on Sealy Hall jointly with his father Thomas Sealy, the tenant-for-life, and in his own right awarded £29 2s 7d for one slave (Barbados No. 5320).

[33] Rev. Richard Smith: awarded £1,259 6s 11d for half the 123 slaves on Mapps estate.

[34] Rev. R. Allwood: wrote to the Commission to ask whether a mortgage for £20,000 by the heirs of the late James Black had been laid against Mary's Hope; 'if not can you let me have the papers to do it?'; T71/1610, 7 October 1835. See also British Guiana No. 313: together, the two awards on Mary's Hope for 229 slaves totalled £11,935 12s 10d.

[35] Rev. Thomas Maude: counter-claim by Elizabeth Stewart Maude, wife of Rev. Thomas Maude, Curate of St Paul's, Covent Garden, annuitant under the will of James Laing: £150 during the life of the counter-claimant aged thirty-one. CCED No. 18423 shows a Thomas Maude, but as ordained deacon and assistant curate of St Thomas-in-the-Town, Birmingham, 1834.

[36] Rev. John Thomas Trevelyan and Rev. George Trevelyan: sons of George Trevelyan, Archdeacon of Taunton; also shared compensation with mother Harriet and others, on Grenada Nos. 445, 760, 771, 857, 860.

[37] Rev. Henry Chaplin and Rev. James Ellice: awarded £6,388 9s 10d for 255 slaves on Clarks Court as mortgagees for £24,400 with Vere Fane.

[38] Rev. Samuel Crowther: counter-claimed under the will of Thomas Tarleton, parish curate of Knowle, Warks., 1839–54.

[39] [Rev.] John Edward Tarleton: awarded £6,526 2s 0d as trustee (and presumably beneficiary) for the late Thomas Tarleton [of Bolesworth Castle], his father. Fellow of All Souls College, Oxford, 1809–35; Rector of Chelsfield.

[40] Rev. Peter W. Pegus: awarded £1,597 2s 8d from total compensation for 153 slaves on Union estate, 'formerly of Uffington nr Stamford' (*The Times*, 18 May 1860, p. 4).

[41] Rev. Edward Waller: awarded £4993 9s 5d for 210 slaves on the Dunfermline estate, with his wife Margaret, formerly Margaret Seton, widow, in right of said Margaret as owner-in-fee.

[42] Rev. George Chandler: £5,849 6s 10d for 322 slaves on Seven Plantations awarded to a group of trustees and executors of Mary Chandler, heir and devisee of Rev. George Chandler.

[43] Rev. Craddock John Glascott: trustee with three others for Oakes's estate, owned by Edmund F. Bourke, deceased. Awarded compensation for a total of 191 slaves across Clarendon Nos. 157, 158, 160, 161.

[44] Rev. Henry Phillpotts: awarded £5,480 13s 1d for 304 slaves on Whitney; £2,412 6s 8d for 125 slaves on Rymesbury (Clarendon No. 320) with three others. Claim by 'heirs of Earl of Dudley': Phillpotts and others were trustees. See also Vere No. 70.

[45] Rev. J. J. Scott: claimed compensation for 122 slaves on Clarendon Park, which was awarded instead to trustees for the annuity of Elizabeth Scott, widow of Hon. John Scott. See also St Thomas-in-the-East No. 295, where a similar claim on 201 slaves on Retreat for £3,986 5s 11d was claimed by James J. Scott.

[46] Rev. George Ingram Fisher and Rev. Wm David Longlands: shared in £6,359 0s 6d for thirty-four slaves on New Milns, awarded to a family group of daughters (and

sons-in-law) of John Pendrill of Bath, himself son-in-law of William Campbell, the original owner of the estate.

[47] Rev. George Sandby: awarded £166 16s 11d with Mary Sandby (presumably his wife) as a share of the compensation awarded for 314 slaves on the Tryall estate.

[48] Rev. Edward Owen: awarded £1,960 2s 6d for 94 slaves on Hopetoun and £1,419 10s 7d for 69 slaves on The Wilderness (Manchester No. 222) and a further £2,326 4s 6d for 117 slaves as part of a group of beneficiaries under the will of Edward Owen, Rev. Edward Owen's father. Owen's address is given as East Hall in the parish of Orpington: he was curate of Lullingstone and of Gawsworth, Cheshire.

[49] Rev. James J. Rowe: together with his wife Elizabeth awarded £158 13s 4d for seven slaves; and under Man No. 421d, together with his wife, he was awarded £148 17s 3d as a share of the compensation for thirty-seven slaves on Old England. The Rev. J. J. Rowe of Magdalen Hall was presented to the rectory of St Mary Arches, Exeter by the Bishop of Exeter (*The Times*, 25 January 1841), and was later military chaplain of King William's town, Cape of Good Hope (*The Times*, 22 May 1876, p. 12).

[50] Rev. Benjamin Guest and Rev. James Furnivall: absentees, trustees and executors of James Willasy, awarded £5,368 1s 10d as half the compensation for 290 slaves on Orchard Plantation. The other half went to George Guest.

[51] Rev. W. Woollams Holland and Rev. James Peter Rhodes: counter-claimed as assignees of a term of 1,000 years created by the marriage settlement of Charles Forbes and his wife. List E claim. Rev. W. Woollams Holland was Vicar of Burpham in Sussex and Bapchild in Kent.

[52] Rev. Anthony Bunting: award of £126 17s 8d for six slaves to Jane E. Bunting, guardian to Sarah A. Bunting. Jane Elizabeth Bunting was the widow of the Rev. Anthony Bunting, Chaplain to the Garrison at Port Antonio, Jamaica (*The Times*, 12 January 1857, p. 1).

[53] Rev. Edward Collins Wright: claimed in right of wife with two others as absentees and owners. Wright's wife Mary was a legatee of David White of Bristol under the latter's will of 18 October 1797, and Wright assigned their claim under the will to the London merchant William Linwood.

[54] Hon. and Rev. George Neville Grenville: trustee with Marquis of Breadalbane for marriage settlement of the son of Grenville's cousin the first Duke of Buckingham to a member of Campbell Breadalbane family. .

[55] Rev. Charles Gostling Townley: awarded £339 9s 2d as committee of Elizabeth Phipps, lunatic.

[56] Rev. Robert Hawthorne: counter-claimed as judgement creditor from June 1803 for £1,727 9s 9d against St Ann Nos. 523 and 524, both estates owned by Gilbert William Sr. St Ann No. 523 was a List E claim. Hawthorne was awarded the interest and accruals only on No. 524.

[57] Rev. Evan James: counter-claimed in right of wife as owner-in-fee of one-third of the 193 slaves on Great Pond, but the compensation went to a London merchant's family.

[58] Hon. Rev. William Herbert: counter-claimed for compensation for 235 slaves on Creighton Hall in right of wife as annuitant for £5,828 10s. Awarded to two London bankers, possibly as trustees.

[59] Rev. Robert Morgan: awarded £4,321 13s 11d for 215 slaves as owner-in-fee of Radnor estate.

[60] Rev. Samuel White: apparently acting as attorney for William Beckford. George Carew of 'Rev Saml White and George Carew' signed for Beckford's compensation for 145 slaves on Bodle's Pen.

Notes to Appendix 5 (*cont.*)

[61] Rev. John Campbell Fisher: awarded £4,037 17s 5d for 214 slaves on Union and £2,543 12s 5d for 145 slaves on Luana Pen (St Elizabeth No. 730) as executor of his grandfather, the late Robert Campbell of Blackheath, whose judgement bond for £9,187 13s 7d represented a prior claim to the estates of John Fisher, the Rev. John Campbell Fisher's father.

[62] Rev. Wm Harriott: claimed as administrator for 320 slaves on Mexico Estate. List E claim.

[63] Rev. John Pyke Jones and Rev. John Dennis Burdon: awarded a £1,055 0s 0d share of the compensation for 109 slaves on Vauxhall as executors of Elizabeth Smyth, arrears of annuity £1,315 6s 0d. Rev. J. Pike Jones was Vicar of Alton, Staffs., 1829–57, and Rector of Butterleigh, Devon, 1832–57.

[64] Rev. Henry Nembhard: awarded £270 10s 5d as a share of the compensation for thirty-six slaves on Hounslow estate. Nembhard, brother of deceased owner Edward Nembhard, was at St Bees, 1842; Rector of Inslow, 1866–70.

[65] Rev. Richard Appleton: awarded £849 15s 8d for forty slaves with two others as mortgagees.

[66] Rev. Sam. Edward Bernard: awarded £316 2s 5d for fourteen slaves on Salt Spring as surviving trustee of J. A. Parnther, deceased, but as son of David and Judith Bernard of Jamaica may have had beneficial interests in other family claims.

[67] Rev. John Briggs and Rev. Thomas Hodgson: awarded £422 5s 7d, probably as trustees.

[68] Rev. Lewis Clutterbuck: Sarah Clutterbuck, late Sarah Balfour, awarded £203 2s 5d for nine slaves: she was the widow of the Rev. Lewis Clutterbuck, who died in 1820.

[69] Rev. Thomas Gardner: awarded £118 0s 0d for six slaves with his wife Margaret and two Liverpool merchants.

[70] Rev. W. S. Halliday: awarded £3,168 12s 8d for 165 slaves on Castle Wemyss.

[71] Rev. Henry Mair: awarded £4,511 17s 9d for 215 slaves on Seven Rivers and £3,604 8s 9d for 203 slaves on Old Hope (Westmoreland No. 219), both estates owned by Martin Williams, after counter-claiming as mortgagee for £16,000. The 1805 deed under which Mair claimed (possibly only as trustee but apparently as beneficiary) was between the owners of the estates and John Graham Clarke, a Newcastle merchant, and John Mair.

[72] Rev. Adam Sedgwick: awarded £3,783 1s 8d for 174 slaves on Providence after counter-claiming as devisees-in-trust under the will of Ann Hill, 10 December 1808. Sedgwick was Canon of Norwich, and Woodwardian Professor of Geology.

[73] Rev. R. Wetherell: with his wife Maria, awarded £178 14s 9d as a one-eleventh share in residual compensation for 144 slaves on Virgin Valley Estate of Charles Gordon Gray, deceased. The CCED identification is not definitive.

[74] Rev. John Mansfield: counter-claimed with others as surviving devisees-in-trust, and executor of the will of Thomas Hibbert. £3,817 6s 11d for 194 slaves on Aqualta Vale Pen were paid into Chancery in *Hibbert* v. *Hibbert*. The CCED identification is not definitive.

[75] Rev. William Marshall: £2,628 16 8d for 144 slaves on Langley estate paid into Chancery in *Rev. William Marshall* v. *James Wedderburne*. The CCED identification is not definitive.

[76] Rev. John Campbell Shaw: awarded with other devisees of Harriet Campbell four-fifths of the compensation of £895 16s 11d for forty-seven slaves on Bishops Mount.

CCED No. possibly 6056.

[77] Rev. John Twells and Rev. J. G. Headlam: awarded £413 15s 1d as part of group of what appear to be trustees for Mrs Spooner, for part of the compensation for 222 slaves on Islington Estate, and £53 15s 4d for a similar claim for 30 slaves (St Mary No. 136).

[78] Rev. John Massy Dawson: awarded £180 1s 4d and £246 2s 6d as his share of compensation to his family for 201 slaves on Prospect Pen and 260 on Pembroke Hall estate (St Mary No. 387), owned until his death by James H. Massy Dawson.

[79] [Rev.] John Rate: tentative identification only. John Rate was awarded £4,438 0s 8d for 269 slaves on Berry Hill and Rose Hill plantations with Browne Roberts, as survivors of the original four claimants and owners-in-fee.

[80] Rev. John West and Rev. David Laing: awarded £2,881 5s 0d for 152 slaves as trustees of the Mount Lebanus estate. Rev. David Laing also collected as attorney for his father-in-law John West for 202 slaves on Betty's Hope (St Thomas-in-the-East No. 29).

[81] Rev. Wheeler Milner: claim for ninety-one slaves on Wheelerfield by Charles Scott, attorney to heirs of Thomas Wheeler Milner. Rev. Wheeler Milner was the oldest son of T. W. Milner, but himself died in 1836; *The Times*, 10 May 1836, p. 7. Compensation was paid to London merchant creditors.

[82] Rev. George Turner: awarded £7,483 10s 6d for 416 slaves on Golden Grove as Trustee of Chaloner Arcedeckne with two others.

[83] Rev. Thomas Robertson: counter-claimed as trustee with others of William Bond for half the compensation for sixty-six slaves on Cardiff. Compensation paid into Chancery in *Rutherford* v. *Wilkinson*.

[84] Rev. Sir William Henry Cooper: acted as the trustee of James Dawkins until 183[5]. The trustees of Sir William Henry Cooper's widow Lady Cooper were awarded £6,379 12s 5d for 336 slaves on Duckenfield Hall (St Thomas-in-the-East No. 114). CCED No. possibly 63139.

[85] Rev. Henry Denny Berners and Rev. George Capper: with Capper's wife awarded £2,296 3s 6d for 122 slaves on Friendship, and also counter-claimed for 68 slaves on Friendship with Capper's wife, in both cases 'as entitled to the interest for their lives as stated of £10,000 sterling at 5 per cent – for arrears £2,700 to Mrs Capper'. Berners, the Archdeacon of Suffolk 1819–46, had married Sarah Jarrett, the daughter of John Jarrett of Jamaica.

[86] Rev. Charles Davy and Rev. George Porcher: awarded £4,557 7s 3d for 235 slaves on Etingdon, a further 633 5s 1d for 29 slaves on Etingdon (Trelawny No. 111), £4,387 8s 2d for 233 slaves on Hyde Hall (Trelawny No. 113), a further £1,286 19s 9d for 64 slaves on Hyde Hall (Trelawny No. 112), £1,534 7s 7d for 90 slaves on Glamorgan and Cedar Spring, and a further £244 19s 11d for 10 slaves (Trelawny No. 115), all as trustees of Henry Shirley, the tenant-in-tail. The CCED identification for Davy is not definitive.

[87] Rev. William Biscoe: awarded £5,546 9s 5d with two others after counter-claiming as mortgagees under indenture dated 20 July 1819, £7,000 sterling.

[88] Rev. Willoughby Crewe: claim as one of 'The heirs of Richard Crewe decd. as owner'. Lost to Liverpool merchant mortgagee and to trustees of the marriage settlement of Lt Col. John F. Crewe.

[89] Rev. Theodore Williams: 'interested in the estate of Joseph Stone Williams', the attorney, who was awarded £688 2s 2d for forty-two slaves on Anglesea Pen (Westmoreland No. 1); letter from Oliversons to Commission, T71/1608.

[90] Rev. Wm Woodley Parson: awarded one-seventh of the compensation for 165 slaves on Parson's estate with Geo. W. Parson, in a claim based on the will of

Notes to Appendix 5 (*cont.*)

Edward Parson of Little Pardieu in Essex, bequeathing £1,500 to his son Jasper, secured on estates real and personal. Shown in Return as Rev. Wm Woodley, but St Kitts No. 751 identifies him as Rev. Wm Woodley Parson of Brandon, Suffolk: the compensation was lost to J. F. Pinney. Death of William Parson, for 42 years Rector of Brandon; *Gentleman's Magazine*, 1838, p. 665.

91   Rev. William Butler: awarded £711 7s 11d from total compensation for 147 slaves on Grove estate. Butler was the son of Duke Butler, and claimed as mortgagee for £2,250 with two others, including the representative of Duke Butler.

92   Rev. John Maynard: collected the £633 16s 10d awarded to his father, the Hon. Walter Maynard, for forty slaves in St Paul's, Charlestown, and the £616 5s 10d awarded to Eliza F. Maynard (Nevis No. 91).

93   Rev. Sir Francis Jarvis Stapleton: counter-claimed as executor and devisee of his late father the Rt Hon. Thomas Lord le Despencer. List E claim.

94   Rev. George Carpenter Hale: awarded £2,770 17s 3d for 174 slaves on Needsmust; Hale and another were trustees for the £300 per annum annuity of Eliza Woodley, the widow of William Woodley, but also counter-claimed with his wife Arabella Louisa Woodburne Woodley, beneficially interested in the will of William Woodley for £933 19s 6d and a further sum of £817 4s 6d expectant on the decease of Eliza Woodley.

95   Rev. Sir Harcourt Lees: wrote to the Commission on behalf of the family of his absent younger brother, William Eden Lees, who 'has a claim'.

96   Hon. and Rev. Gerard [Thomas] Noel: awarded £2,925 4s 2d with another as trustees of the marriage settlement of Noel's brother Frederick and sister-in-law Mary Woodley.

97   Rev. George Washington Philips: awarded £2,678 18s 10d for 161 slaves.

98   Rev. Benjamin Pullan: representative of Edmund Fleming Akers, Chancery suit of *Pullan* v. *Manning*, £4,337 19s 4d for 278 slaves on Mt Pleasant and White Gate estates. Vicar of Sheringham, 1825–61; Weybourne, 1845–61, headmaster of Free Grammar School, Holt, 1805–57.

99   Rev. John Wilson: awarded £2,165 17s 10d for 126 slaves on Olivers.

100   Rev. Wm John Joliffe: transferred to John Bellingham Inglis all claims due to the firm of Inglis Ellice and Inglis & Co.

101   Rev. Robert Coningham: awarded £8,151 19s 7d for 305 slaves on Colonaric Vale as trustee with another of Walter Coningham, who died 9 November 1830 at the estate; *The Times*, 12 March 1831).

102   Rev. Thomas Shuttleworth Gumshaw: counter-claimed as trustee with three others for the marriage settlement of George Henry Sharpe and Caroline, his wife. Compensation awarded to G. H. Sharpe

103   Rev. Wm Hutcheson: counter-claimed unsuccessfully as mortgagee on Union Island estate. The CCED identification is not definitive.

104   Rev. Charles Paul: of Writhlington Rectory near Radstock, Bath, claimed as owner-in-fee of 126 slaves on Kingstown Park; awarded £3,480 16s 2d compensation after settling with counter-claimants.

105   Rev. Richard Warde: counter-claimed with Jane Akers as executors of Aeneas Akers, mortgagees for compensation for 136 slaves on Jambon Vale. Compensation of £3,814 0s 9d paid into Chancery.

106   Rev. Archibald Alison: with one other, Rev. Archibald Alison's sons (William Pulteney Alison and [Sir] Archibald Alison) were awarded £4,081 18s 10 for

152 slaves on the Belle Vue estate as trustees of Colonel Gerard, Rev. Archibald Alison's son-in-law.

[107] Rev. James Hamilton: claimed unsuccessfully as tenant-in-common of a moiety for £1,199 2s 7d for half the 121 slaves on the Whim estate, lost to a group of mortgagees including John Hamilton. He was awarded £4,083 1s 7d for 216 slaves on Riseland (Tobago No. 16) and £3,629 18s 10d for 186 slaves on Indian Walk (Tobago No. 36) as trustee with one other of John Hamilton, claimant and tenant-in-tail.

[108] Rev. William Wilson Sloane: counter-claimed with one other as mortgagee for two-thirds of the compensation for 122 slaves; awarded £1,639 0s 4d.

[109] Rev. Edward Picton: award of £4,268 3s 5d for ninety-eight slaves on Aranjuez to the executors of Rev. Edward Picton, devisee and universal legatee of the will of Sir T[homas] Picton (Governor of Trinidad, 1797–1803) as privileged creditor under a conveyance dated 2 January 1802 and a deed dated 1 October 1810 £4,224 11s 6d. Rev. Edward Picton had died on 28 August 1835.

[110] Rev. Edward Cooke: counter-claimed for 83 slaves on Apple Bay, 101 slaves on Cooten Bay, 70 slaves on Johnson's Gut, 116 slaves on Little Carrot Bay (Virgin Islands Nos. 151–4), and 25 on Spring Gut (Virgin Islands No. 225). Shown in Virgin Islands No. 151 as Bye Well Vicarage, St Peter, Northumberland. List E claims.

Appendix 6   Clergymen in Scotland appearing in the Compensation records

Claim No.	Clergyman	Address/living	Beneficiary	Other
Jamaica				
Clarendon 143	Rev. Alexander Whyte[1]		X creditor	
St Catherine 546	Rev. Stair M'Quhae[2]	St Enox [*sic*]		Trus.
St Elizabeth 145	Rev. Peter Robertson[3]			Exor
St Thomas-in-the-East 198	Rt Rev. Wm Skinner[4]	Bishop of Aberdeen		Exor
Trelawny 395	Minister and Elders of Kilmarnock[5]		X	
St Lucia				
3	Rev. Morris Forsyth[6]	Mortlach, Banffshire	X	

[1] Rev. Alexander Whyte: of Scotland, counter-claimed as judgement creditor for £5,552 9s 7d for 128 slaves on The Burn. A sum of £2,574 17s 11d was paid into Chancery in *Oswan* v. *Shand*. Denomination unknown.

[2] Rev. Stair M'Quhae: minister of St Enox, awarded £2,114 15s 9d for 104 slaves on Two Mile Wood as trustee and executor, with others, of Alexander M'Dowal, whose widow 'Mrs Charles [*sic*] M'Quhae, otherwise M'Dowal' was presumably M'Quhae's sister. Denomination unknown.

[3] Rev. Peter Robertson: with Duncan Robertson, awarded £3,517 2s 7d for 184 slaves on Friendship as executor and trustee of Duncan Robertson Sr. Denomination unknown.

[4] Rt Rev. William Skinner (Episcopalian, CCED No. 2249): awarded £522 13s 4d as share of compensation for 160 slaves on Friendship as one of 4 'ex[ecut]ors of [William] Lambie'.

[5] Minister and Elders of Kilmarnock: counter-claimed for a legacy of £332 under the will of Thomas Pa[t]terson on the compensation for fifty-two slaves on Down Castle.

[6] Rev. Morris Forsyth: awarded, with George Forsyth of Leadenhall St., £3,755 3s 6d for 153 slaves on Union as 'owners and proprietors'; both also awarded £343 13s 3d for 14 slaves under St Lucia No. 49 as executors of James Forsyth [late of Lansdowne Place, St Pancras: St Lucia No. 320) and £3,906 1s 0d for 149 slaves under St Lucia No. 769.

Appendix 7   Absentee clergymen elsewhere appearing in the Compensation records

Claim No.	Clergyman	Residence	Beneficiary	Other
Barbados				
2717	Rev. J. Holloway Duke[1]	Essequibo	X	
5189	Rev. Wm Prescod Hinds[2]	Philadelphia	X	
Nevis				
7	Rev. Hamble Leacock[3]	Barbados	X	

[1] Rev. John Holloway Duke: 'of Essequibo', awarded £31 1s 5d for two slaves and a further £38 16s 9d for four slaves under Barbados No. 5349.

[2] [Rev.] Wm Prescod Hinds: awarded £271 17s 6d for eleven slaves. Identified as 'Reverend' in T71/1593, Barbados No. 3663, p. 94. Moved to Philadelphia, 1834; H. Simpson, *The lives of eminent Philadelphians now deceased* (Philadelphia: William Brotherhead, 1859), pp. 532–7.

[3] Rev. Hamble J. Leacock: awarded £305 11s 1d for seventeen slaves on Long Point estate. See also Nevis No. 246 (£159 11s 1d for ten slaves), Nevis No. 295 (£19 18s 10d for one slave) and Barbados No. 5189, where Leacock was awarded £279 17s 6d for eleven slaves. Minister of Christ Church Cathedral, Louisville, Kentucky, 1840–4; left Barbados for West Africa, 1855; H. Caswall, *The Martyr of the Pongas* (London: Rivingtons, 1857).

Appendix 8   Nobility and peers appearing in the Compensation records

Rank	Claim No.	Claimant	Owner	Other
Dukes				
	Barbados 3184	Duke of Cleveland[1]	X	
	St Andrew 114	Duke of Buckingham[2]	X	
	Vere 37	Duke of Richmond[3]		Trus.
Marquesses				
	St Dorothy 6	Marquis of Sligo[4]	X	
Earls				
	Antigua 79	Earl of Rosslyn[5]		Trus.
	Barbados 270	Earl of Lichfield[6]		Trus.
	Barbados 211	Earl of Harewood[7]	X	
	Barbados 3612	Earl of Caithness[8]		
	Clarendon 284	Earl of Dudley[9]	X	
	Grenada 604	Earl of Zetland[10]	X	
	Manchester 204	Earl of Balcarres[11]	X	
	St Andrew 543	Earl and Countess of Airlie	X	
	St Andrew 514	Earl of Carhampton[12]	X	
	St Elizabeth 345	Earl of Thanet[13]		Trus.
	St Kitts 635	Earl of Romney[14]	X	
	St Mary 267	Earl of Eglinton[15]		
	Vere 122A	Earl Stanhope[16]		Trus.
	Westmoreland 82	Earl of Hopetoun[17]		Trus.
	Westmoreland 232	Earl of Northesk[18]	X?	
	British Guiana 716	Earl Brownlow[19]		Trus.
	Grenada 562	Rt Hon. Countess of Buchan[20]	X	
	St Dorothy 127	Rt Hon. Earl Talbot[21]		Exor
Viscounts				
	Montserrat 15	Viscount Henry Charles Dillon[22]		Trus.?
	St Thomas in-the-East 291	Lord Viscount St Vincent[23]		Trus.
	St David 345	Viscount Grimston		Trus.
Barons				
	Antigua 363	Hon. Anne Byam Stapleton[24]	X	
	Hanover 13	Lord Seaford[25]	X	
	Manchester 398	Lord Abinger[26]	X	

318

Rank	Claim No.	Claimant	Owner	Other
	Nevis 22	Rt Hon. Charles Baron Feversham[27]	X	
	Nevis 16	Rt Hon. Thomas, Lord le Despencer[28]		
	St Dorothy 127	Lord Sherborne[29]		Exor
	St Vincent 492A,B	Rt Hon. Lord Glenlyon[30]		Trus.
	Westmoreland 27	Rt Hon. Henry Lord Holland[31]	X	
	Antigua 266	Admiral Lord Edmund Lyons[32]	X?	
	Antigua 393	Lord James O'Bryen[33]		
	Clarendon 66	Rt Hon. Chas, Lord Sinclair[34]	X	
	Dominica 576A	Rt Hon. Lady Marjorie Saltoun[35]	X	
	Hanover 219	The Lord Rivers[36]	X	
	Nevis 102	Rt Hon. Lord Combermere[37]	X	
	St Andrew 265	Rt Hon. Lady Maria Ann Saunderson[38]	Xcc	
	St Catherine 538	Lord Carrington[39]	X	
	Trinidad 1684	W. H. C. Bentinck[40]		Trus.
	British Guiana 195	Rt Hon. Eric Lord Reay[41]	X	
	Vere 70	Lord Hatherton[42]		Trus.
	Bahamas 960	Lord Rolle	X	

Beyond the UK titled slave-owners, there were a handful of beneficiaries and trustees with European titles, such as the Prince de Polignac (the Bourbon ambassador to Britain), whose slaves came through his first wife, the daughter of a slave-owning Scottish family; the Baron George Gavin Browne Mill of Bath, MD, trustee of a marriage settlement and the former physician to the Russian Emperor (St Ann No. 565); and a counter-claim from Lydia, Countess D'Viney [sic] (St Vincent No. 473A), the daughter of Hugh Mills Bunbury and wife of the Comte Alfred Victor de Vigny, playwright and novelist.

[1] William Harry Vane, Duke of Cleveland, claimed as owner-in-fee with Lord William Powlett. Estate came in through Lowther family, to whom the Duke of Cleveland was related through both his mother and his wife.

[2] Claim by the Duke of Buckingham, awarded to Marquis of Breadalbane and the Hon. G. Neville Grenville as trustees under the marriage settlement of the Marquis of Chandos. Buckingham also claimed for St Andrew No. 150, but withdrew in favour of the mortgagee Ambrose Humphrys; and counter-claimed unsuccessfully in St Andrew No. 390, for £63 8s 4d.

[3] The Duke of Richmond and Earl of Wiltshire counter-claimed as trustees of George Stevens Byng (later the second Earl of Strafford).

[4] See also St Dorothy No. 100 for another estate owned by the Marquis of Sligo, and St Ann No. 202: counter-claim by Thomas J. Bernard, trustee of the Marquis of Sligo as judgement creditor.

[5] The Earl of Rosslyn: father-in-law of claimant Bethell Walrond, counter-claimed with Charles John Manning as trustees under the marriage settlement of Walrond and Lady Janet St Claire.

Notes to Appendix 8 (*cont.*)

6   The Earl of Lichfield, Viscountess Anson; T. W. Coke; and Sir George Anson
     counter-claimed as trustees under the marriage settlement of Sir Francis Ford and
     Mary Anson. The Earl of Lichfield was Thomas William Anson, 1795–1854, who
     married a daughter of Nathaniel Phillips of Slebech. T. W. Coke was first Earl of
     Leicester. Thomas Anson, 1st Viscount Anson, married Anne Margaret Coke, T.
     W. Coke's daughter.

7   See also Barbados Nos. 2769, 2770, 3817; St Dorothy No. 23; St Thomas-in-the-
     Vale No. 147.

8   Award was to Wilhelmina B. Traill, niece of the eleventh Earl of Caithness. Traill
     was adopted by Mary Salter Dehany, who had been engaged to be married to
     the eleventh Earl before his premature death, and inherited Dehany's estates in
     Barbados and Jamaica.

9   Awarded to trustees of the Earl of Dudley, including Henry Philpotts and the Lord
     Hatherton. See also Clarendon No. 320, Vere No. 70.

10   Laurence Lord Dundas, heir of the late George Heneage Lawrence Dundas and
     later Earl of Zetland.

11   James Lindsay, twenty-fourth Earl of Crawford and seventh Earl of Balcarres
     (1783–1869). See also Balcarres as owner for St George No. 185. In addition
     Balcarres had numerous claims for one-third of the compensation for slaves
     contracted to the government by Atkinson and Hozier of Kingston: see St Andrew
     No. 555A,B; St Catherine No. 696A,B; Hanover No. 586A,B; Trelawny No. 492A,B;
     and Kingston No. 2590A,B (Kingston No. 1978 also shows a counter-claim filed in
     error on Balcarres's behalf).

12   Claim as tenant-for-life by Maria, Countess Dowager of Carhampton, widow
     of John Luttrell-Olmius, the third Earl of Carhampton; the award was made to
     trustees in London.

13   The Earl of Thanet and Viscount Grimston were apparently trustees of the Foster
     family. See also St Elizabeth No. 346.

14   Award to Charles, Earl of Romney; Sir Thomas Neave; and Charles Ashe A'Court
     as owners. See also St Kitts No. 636 for an award to the Earl of Romney alone.

15   Eglinton's daughters Lady Jane Montgomerie and Lady Lilias Oswald were awarded
     the compensation for Pemberton Valley alongside their husbands or husbands'
     families,

16   Philip Henry, Earl Stanhope, as trustee with Abel Smith of the marriage settlement
     of Lt Col. John F. Crewe.

17   John, fifth Earl of Hopetoun, executor and trustee of Francis Grant.

18   The Earl of Northesk: shared award with John J. Carnegie, and their uncle the
     second Viscount St Vincent.

19   John, Earl Brownlow, the brother of Sir Edward Cust, was trustee and executor with
     Wilbraham Egerton of the late Mrs L. W. Boode, Cust's mother-in-law.

20   The Countess of Buchan: presumably, widow of the Earl of Buchan. See also
     Grenada No. 563.

21   The Parliamentary Return shows an award to Sir Rose Price, who died 29
     September 1834: his executors were the Rt Hon. Lord Talbot, the Lord Sherborne,
     the Hon. John Chetwynd Talbot and Viscount Jugeski. See also St John No. 64
     for an award to Talbot *et al.* as devisees and executors. Talbot and Price had both
     married into the Lambert family of County Meath. St Thomas-in-the-Vale No.

321A shows Earl Talbot, Sherborne and the Hon. J. C. Talbot as devisees-in-trust for Price.

[22] Claim by Dominick Frant of London; counter-claim by Viscount Dillon, Philip Laycock Story (Dillon's father-in-law), Henry Frant (given as Trent in the Parliamentary Return) and James Flemming, for a debt of £6,000 secured on mortgage.

[23] St Vincent and Vere Fane were trustees for Charles Blair. On St Thomas-in-the-Vale No. 292, St Vincent and Fane were trustees under the will of Charles W. Mitchell.

[24] Counter-claim by the Hon. Anne Byam Stapleton (daughter of Thomas Norbury Kerby of Antigua), the Rt Hon. Lord James O'Bryen and the Hon. Hercules Pakenham, trustees of Anne Byam Stapleton's marriage settlement with the Rev. Hon. Miles J. Stapleton, son of Sir Thomas, sixteenth Baron le Despencer.

[25] Charles Rose Ellis, Baron Seaford (whose son and heir was Lord Howard de Walden). See also St Catherine No. 539 and St James Nos. 1 and 2, and St Mary Nos. 128, 129 and 134 for awards in which it appears that Seaford as judgement creditor settled with Timperon & Dobinson, the mercantile mortgagees.

[26] James Scarlett, made Lord Abinger, 1835.

[27] Counter-claim by the Rt Hon. Charles Baron Feversham of Duncombe Park as equitable mortgagee.

[28] Counter-claim by the Hon. and Rev. Sir Francis Jarvis Stapleton, executor and devisee of his late father, the Rt Hon. Thomas Lord le Despencer: see also Antigua No. 363

[29] See above, entry for the Rt Hon. Earl Talbot, n. 20.

[30] Claim by Vans Hathorn and the Rt Hon. John Sinclair as trustees of the marriage settlement of the Hon. A. Macdonald; and the Rt Hon. James Lord Glenlyon and R. G. Macdonald, trustees of the marriage settlement of Prince de Polignac and Barbara, his wife. See also St Vincent Nos. 497A,B and 498A,B.

[31] Claim by Lord and Lady Holland as owners. Counter-claim on behalf of Sir Godfrey Webster, Bart.

[32] Son of John Lyons of Antigua and St Austen's House, Lymington, Hants. Award to Norborne Thompson and Henry Shepherd Pearson, trustees for John Lyons.

[33] Lord James O'Bryen had co-owned Matthews estate with a Mr Horsford, and sold it for £18,000; consideration paid except for £3,000, which Lord O'Bryen assigned to N. M. Rothschild.

[34] Awarded to Charles, Lord Sinclair and Francis D. Massy Dawson, Sinclair's son-in-law. See also Clarendon Nos. 232, 417.

[35] Awarded two-thirds to Lady Saltoun, the Rt Hon. Sir John Bayley and the Rt Hon. Lawrence Lord Dundas, as owners and devisees-in-trust, and executors of Simon Fraser; and one-third to Oliver Vile. See also British Guiana No. 560 for additional awards to Dowager Lady Saltoun and Sir John Bayley.

[36] George Pitt, Lord Rivers (1810–66), son of William Horace Beckford, m. Susan Georgiana Granville, daughter of Earl Granville and niece of the Duke of Devonshire. Also awarded Westmoreland No. 29.

[37] Stapleton Stapleton Cotton, son of Sir Robert Salisbury Cotton, MP, and Governor-General of Barbados. See also St Kitts No. 329 for additional award to Combermere and Barbara Yonge.

[38] Counter-claim by Robert Hardress Saunderson and the Rt Hon. Lady Maria Ann, his wife, as annuitants under marriage settlement.

Notes to Appendix 8 *(cont.)*

[39] Awarded to Lord Carrington and Samuel Smith of Smith, Payne & Smith as owners-in-fee.

[40] The Rt Hon. William Henry Cavendish Bentinck, commonly called Lord Bentinck, counter-claimed as incumbrancer under the marriage settlement of the late Marc René, Comte de Montalembert. Award to de Montalmbert's children, including Charles Forbes, Comte de Montalembert. Bentinck was the son of the third Duke of Portland, and brother of the fourth Duke.

[41] Reay was also devisee-in-trust for Robert Home Gordon on Home Castle estate (St Ann No. 498), in which capacity he was later sued by the consignee (*The Times*, 14 June 1842, p. 7).

[42] Lord Hatherton: Edward Littleton, MP, became Lord Hatherton in 1835; trustee of the heirs of the Earl of Dudley.

Appendix 9   Rentier Baronets appearing in the Compensation records

Claim No.	Claimant	Beneficiary	Other
Antigua			
259	Sir William Abdy[1]	X	
20	Sir William Ogilvie[2]	X	
19	Sir Henry William Martin[3]	X	
355	Sir William George Thomas[4]	X	
93	Sir J. E. Colebrooke[5]	X	
334	Sir Christopher Bethell Codrington[6]	X	
261	Rev. Sir Augustus Brydges Henniker[7]		Exor
350	Sir Brodrick Hartwell[8]		
728	Sir Peter Parker[9]	X	
Barbados			
631c	Sir John Gibbons[10]		Trus.
2034	Sir George Henry Dashwood[11]		Trus.
3258	Sir Francis Ford[12]	X	
4594	Sir Henry Fitzherbert[13]	X	
4917	Sir Fitzroy Maclean[14]	X	
3653	Sir George Harnage[15]	X	
3653	Sir Edward Nagle	Xm	
3777	Sir Stephen Anderson[16]		X
4310	Sir Samuel O. Gibbes[17]	X	
4584	Sir Reynold A. Alleyne[18]	X	
Bermuda			
597	Sir William C. H. Burnaby[19]	X	
British Guiana			
560	Sir John Bayley[20]		Trus.
2282	Sir Thomas Baring[21]	Xcc	
Dominica			
243	Sir George Henry Rose[22]	X	
Grenada			
441	Sir Claudius Stephen Hunter[23]	Xm	
865	Sir Frederick George Johnstone[24]	X	
706	Sir George Cornewall[25]	X	
692	Sir Robert C. Dallas[26]	X	
780	Sir James Montgomery[27]		Trus.

Claim No.	Claimant	Beneficiary	Other
445	Sir William Edward Rouse Boughton[28]		Trus.
	Sir Robert Heron		Trus.
864	Sir George Young[29]		Trus.
Jamaica			
Hanover			
21	Sir Edmund Antrobus[30]		Trus.
66	Sir George Phillips[31]	X	
St Andrew			
171	Sir Edward Hyde East[32]	X	
St Catherine			
499	Sir William Henry Cooper[33]		Trus.
St Dorothy			
127	Sir Rose Price[34]	X	
St James			
429	Sir John Gordon[35]	X	
549A[36]	Sir Joseph Birch	Xm	
185[37]	Sir Thomas B. Birch	X	
St Mary			
407	Sir William Windham Dalling[38]	X	
St Thomas-in-the-East			
417	Sir T[homas] Champneys[39]	X	
507	Sir Charles Price[40]	Xcc creditor	
520	Sir James Ferguson[41]	X	
	Sir David H. Blair	X	
114	Sir Henry Allen Johnson[42]		Trus.
94	Sir Henry Lushington[43]		
St Thomas-in-the-Vale			
296	Sir Alexander Cray Grant[44]	X	
Trelawny			
409	Sir Charles Oakeley[45]	Mortgagee-in-possession	
Westmoreland			
223	Sir John Peniston Milbanke[46]	X	
27	Sir Godfrey Webster[47]	X	
268	Sir Simon Haughton Clarke[48]	X	
334	Sir David Wedderburn[49]	X Chancery	
Nevis			
16	Sir Francis Jarvis Stapleton[50]		Exor/dev.
St Kitts			
9	[Sir] William Payne-Gallwey[51]	X	
159	Sir Henry Charles Blake[52]	X	
424	Sir William Pole[53]	X?	
734	Sir Gerald Noel Noel[54]	X	
303	Sir Wastel Brisco[55]	X	
211	Sir William Milliken Napier[56]	X	

Claim No.	Claimant	Beneficiary	Other
461	Sir Charles Payne[57]	X	
575	Sir Peter Payne[58]	X	
740	[Rev.] Sir Harcourt Lees[59]		Rep. cc
351	Sir John Lloyd Dukinfield [sic][60]	X	
St Vincent			
448	Sir Alexander Mackenzie[61]	X	
492A,B	Rt Hon. John Sinclair[62]		Trus.
559	Sir William Young[63]	Xcc	
Tobago			
9	Sir Michael Bruce[64]	X	
11	Alex. Young Spearman[65]		Trus.
74	Sir Sam. Stirling[66]		Trus./Exor
Trinidad			
901	Sir Ralph James Woodford[67]	X	
581	Sir George F. Hill[68]	X	
Virgin Islands			
256	Sir Anthony Lechmere[69]	X	

[1] Sir William Abdy: awarded compensation for 152 slaves on Lavington and for 314 slaves on Sandersons. Abdy's maternal grandfather was the slave-owner James Brebner Gordon. Abdy shared the award with his brothers-in-law (his sisters' husbands) the Rev. G. Caldwell and Sir Thomas Fellowes, and with James Adam Gordon. The same group was also awarded compensation for 248 slaves on Fair Hall (St Vincent No. 549).

[2] Sir William Ogilvie: claim for 146 slaves on York's Estate by Robert and Henry Jefferson, mortgagees of Sir William Ogilvie, Bart.; valuers' return in the name of the heirs of Sir William Ogilvie, deceased.

[3] Sir Henry William Martin: awarded compensation for 319 slaves on Green Castle. Sir H. W. Martin of 51 Upper Harley Street also counter-claimed as creditor for £214 1s 7d on Antigua No. 95.

[4] Sir William George Thomas: claim for 303 slaves at North Sound, St George by Sir W. L. G. Thomas, Bart., Co. Dorset, owner-in-fee; compensation awarded to counter-claimant Marmaduke Robinson, a London mortgagee. Sir W. L. G. ['George'] Thomas also shared in half the compensation for 147 slaves on the Hyde Estate (St Thomas-in-the-Vale No. 294) by virtue of his wife's share in legacies from her father Richard Welch to her and her sisters.

[5] Sir James Edward Colebrooke: claim by John Adams Wood for sixty-three slaves on Brecknock 'by purchase from Sir J. C. [sic] Colebrook [sic] bart.'.

[6] Sir Christopher Bethell Codrington: awarded compensation for 299 slaves on Betty's Hope.

[7] Rev. Sir Augustus Brydges Henniker: counter-claimed with Jane Roberts of Oakham as executor of James Watson Roberts for a legacy of £2,700 to James Watson Roberts under the will of James Watson. Some form of settlement was apparently reached with awardee Francis Watson.

[8] Sir Brodrick Hartwell: claim by Alicia Gunthorpe of Boulogne and James Gunthorpe of New Bond Street as executors of the Rev. W. Gunthorpe, deceased. The Gunthorpes were awarded £922 3s 0d; the remainder (£3,000) went to Hardman Earle and J. H. Turner, Liverpool merchants. Alicia Gunthorpe married Sir Brodrick Hartwell of Dale Hall in 1834.

Notes to Appendix 9 *(cont.)*

⁹ Sir Peter Parker: claim for ten slaves by Lady Parker, guardian of her late son Sir Peter Parker, Bart. A sum of £193 19s 2d was awarded to Henrietta Dallas (sister of Lady Parker) as legatee under the will of Sir Peter Parker.

¹⁰ Sir John Gibbons: counter-claim for one-ninth (£300 11s 4d) of the compensation on Lower Berney's by Sir John Gibbons of Stanwell Place near Staines, as trustee of the marriage settlement of John Ivatt Briscoe and Anna Maria Mawley.

¹¹ Sir George Henry Dashwood: one of three devisees-in-trust to the estate of Harrison W. Sober for 161 slaves on Spring estate. Dashwood's sister had married W. H. Sober [*sic*] of White Staunton in 1821.

¹² Sir Francis Ford: awarded compensation for 215 slaves on Ridge estate.

¹³ Sir Henry Fitzherbert: awarded compensation for 146 slaves on Turners Hall. See also his awards for 88 slaves on St Helens Pen (St Dorothy No. 22), for 182 slaves on Grange Hill and 307 on Blue Mountain (St Thomas-in-the East Nos. 65, 537) and 258 slaves on Perrins estate (Vere No. 56).

¹⁴ Sir Fitzroy Maclean: awarded compensation for 185 slaves on Symonds.

¹⁵ Sir George Harnage: claim for 177 slaves on Boarded Hall by attorney to the executors of Sir Edward Nagle, mortgagee of Sir George Harnage. Counter-claims from Dame Mary Nagle of Hampton Court, annuitant under the will of John Lucie Blackman, £700 per annum, and from trustees of an annuity to Lady Harnage. Settled amongst claimant and counter-claimants. Harnage was a London merchant.

¹⁶ Sir Stephen Anderson: seventy-three slaves on Byde Mill were registered in 1834 by M. W. Cromartie as 'the property in remainder of the heirs of Sir Stephen Anderson bart. on Byde Mill'. Sir Stephen had died in 1773 and the baronet title had become extinct; *A genealogical and heraldic dictionary of the peerage and baronetage of the British Empire, by John Burke* (London, 1838). The compensation was awarded to trustees of the life-tenant, Ellis Anderson Stephens, and the 'remaindermen', his four daughters.

¹⁷ Sir Samuel O. Gibbes: awarded compensation for 132 slaves on Spring Head and 156 on Taitts (Barbados No. 4311), but compensation appears to have been intercepted by the London merchants J. Nelson Wood and Benjamin Adam. Gibbes served as an assistant commissioner in Barbados in the compensation process. Edmund Lodge's *Peerage of the British Empire* shows him as of Tackley, Oxfordshire in 1843.

¹⁸ Sir Reynold Abel Alleyne: awarded compensation for 188 slaves on Bawdens, 64 on River plantation (Barbados No. 4585) and 121 on Cabbage Tree Hall (Barbados No. 4847). Resident of Barbados.

¹⁹ Sir William Crisp Hood Burnaby: awarded compensation for thirteen slaves and a further four slaves (Bermuda No. 598). Resident of Bermuda.

²⁰ Sir John Bayley: awarded one-third of the compensation for 420 slaves on Good Hope with Dowager Lady Saltoun, apparently as devisees-in-trust of the late Simon Fraser (Lady Saltoun's father).

²¹ Sir Thomas Baring: counter-claim by Baring Brothers under a deed of assignment of 1807 for compensation for sixty-four slaves on Spring Garden. Sir Thomas Baring also pursued a counter-claim as mortgages of John Willis on Osborne Estate in Jamaica (St George No. 278), and informed the Commission of his intent to pursue legal proceedings against the awardee.

²² Sir George Henry Rose: awarded, with Benjamin Aislabie, compensation for 111 slaves on Cane Field.

²³ Sir Claudius Stephen Hunter: awarded compensation for half of 112 slaves on Granton after counter-claiming as surviving mortgagee-in-fee.

²⁴ Sir Frederick George Johnstone: claimed compensation for 176 slaves on Westerhall estate as tenant-in-tail, counter-claim from Sir Chistopher Codrington as administrator of Sir William Pulteney, compensation paid into Chancery in *Codrington* v. *Johnstone*. See also the similar claim for 86 slaves (Grenada No. 866, although this appears in the Parliamentary Return as No. 862).

[25] Sir George Cornewall: awarded compensation for 139 slaves on La Taste.

[26] Sir Robert C. Dallas: awarded, with Robert W. Dallas, half the compensation for 158 slaves on Mountraven plantation.

[27] Sir James Montgomery: awarded compensation with two others as trustees of Robert Nutter Campbell of Glasgow for 223 slaves on Carriere.

[28] Sir William Edward Rouse Boughton and Sir Robert Heron: included with John Alexander Hankey and the Trevelyan family as co-proprietors in claims for 240 slaves on Beausejour, 168 slaves on Tempe estate (Grenada No. 445), 143 slaves on Simon estate (Grenada No. 771), 208 slaves on Requin (sp?) (Grenada No. 857), 231 slaves on Sagesse (Grenada No. 860) and a further 14 slaves (Grenada No. 760). It appears more likely that in fact Boughton and Heron were trustees for the Trevelyan family.

[29] Sir George Young: of Formosa Place, Bucks., counter-claimed as trustee for parties interested in the marriage settlement of Miss Colin Campbell Baillie, paid into Chancery in *Baillie* v. *Innes*.

[30] Sir Edmund Antrobus: awarded compensation for 138 slaves on Haughton Grove Pen with two others as trustees of the marriage settlement of George Watson Taylor and his wife. Similar awards were made for 272 slaves on Haughton Court (?) estate (Hanover No. 577) and for 623 slaves on Holland estate (St Thomas-in-the-East No. 100)

[31] Sir George Phillips: Manchester cotton-industrialist, and partner in London West India merchants Boddington, Phillips & Sharp; and Boddington, Phillips & Davis. Counter-claimed with Boddington and Davis as assignee of the equity of redemption. Member of Parliament, made a Baronet in 1828.

[32] Sir Edward Hyde East: awarded compensation for 220 slaves on Maryland; he was also awarded compensation for 136 slaves on Bellfield (St Mary No. 11); 146 slaves on Clermont (St Mary No. 153); 37 slaves on Koningsberg (St Mary No. 17); with the Digges Latouche family of Dublin, 212 slaves on Cape Clear (St Mary No. 14) and 184 on Koningsberg (St Mary No. 184); and 259 slaves on Rhine (St Thomas-in-the-East No. 154), with a further 17 in the same parish (St Thomas-in-the-East No. 155).

[33] Sir William Henry Cooper: claimed as trustee of James Dawkins for 199 slaves on Dawkins Caymanas; compensation was awarded to John Biddulph and Samuel Pepys Cockerell after they were added as trustees and Cooper died: see also similar claims for 160 slaves on Dawkins Salt Pond Pen (St Catherine No. 515); 107 slaves on Suttons Pasture and 162 slaves on Sandy Gully (Vere Nos. 46, 71).

[34] Sir Rose Price: awarded compensation for 79 slaves on Spring Garden. Price died in September 1834 and his executors (his wife's sister's husband – hence his brother-in-law – Earl Talbot and others) were also awarded compensation for 464 slaves on Worthy Park (St John No. 64A) and for 79 slaves on Mickleton Pen (St Thomas-in-the-Vale No. 321A).

[35] Sir John Gordon: awarded compensation for 164 slaves on Carl[e]ton. Sir John Gordon of Earlston, later also of Carleton, was the fifth Baronet, son of James Gordon of Jamaica.

[36] Sir Joseph Birch: William Ward of Liverpool counter-claimed as mortgagee jointly with Birch.

[37] Sir Thomas Bernard Birch: awarded compensation as owner-in-fee of 147 slaves on Leogan.

[38] Sir William Windham Dalling: awarded compensation for 176 slaves on the Donnington estate.

[39] Sir Thomas Champneys: claim by attorney of Sir Thomas Champneys. Champneys was shown as the owner in the 1833 Jamaica Almanac, but the compensation was awarded to Champneys' cousin, Richard Henry Cox, apparently uncontested.

[40] Sir Charles Price: counter-claim from Sir William Kay, Sir Charles Price etc., bankers, for £3,481 15s 6d against Philip Brown's one-sixth share of the compensation for 240 slaves on Morant.

Notes to Appendix 9 (*cont.*)

[41] Sir James Ferguson and Sir David H. Blair: awarded compensation without comment for 198 slaves on Rozelle estate. The Jamaica Almanacs show Rozelle (or Roselle) as owned by Sir A. Fergusson and Sir D. H. Blair in 1811, and then by 'Fergusson and Blair' through to 1833.

[42] Sir Henry Allen Johnson: awarded compensation with Robert Pitches for 336 slaves on Duckenfield Hall. Claim by attorney to trustees of Lady Cooper. Duckenfield had belonged to the Franks family: Lady Cooper's husband Sir Wm Henry Cooper (d. 1836) was grandson of Moses Franks, and Sir Henry Allen Johnson had married another member of the Franks family.

[43] Sir Henry Lushington: his wife, Dame Fanny, was co-heiress of Matthew 'Monk' Lewis for 241 slaves on Hordley, and 245 on Cornwall (Westmoreland No. 66). The compensation for Hordley was paid into chancery in *Lushington* v. *Sewell*, and for Cornwall was awarded to the trustees of Monk Lewis.

[44] Sir Alexander Cray Grant: awarded compensation for 92 slaves on Berwick and 157 slaves on Rio Magno Pen (St Thomas-in-the-Vale No. 133). See also awards for 348 slaves on Albion (St Mary No. 260), and for £211 17s 8d on Spring Vale Pen (St Elizabeth No. 1018).

[45] Sir Charles Oakeley: Governor of Madras, 1792–4, who died in 1826. Mortgagee-in-possession, award to trustees. Father-in-law and creditor of West India merchants George Reid and Roger Kynaston.

[46] Sir John Peniston Milbanke: awarded £325 6s 6d after counter-claiming with his son John Ralph Milbanke for 'a legacy of £2,000 on this Estate by the will of the claimant's father' (i.e. Julines Herring). Milbanke had married Julines' daughter.

[47] Sir Godfrey Webster: counter-claim by George Capron on behalf of Sir Godfrey Webster 'vested estate tail one third part expectant on decease of Lady Holland' against Lord and Lady Holland for compensation for 401 slaves on Sweet River (combines also Westmoreland Nos. 30, 31).

[48] Sir Simon Haughton Clarke: compensation for 324 slaves on the King's Valley estate awarded to Dame Catherine Haughton Clarke and John Haughton James after a counter-claim by Dame Catherine Haughton Clarke and T. H. Milnes as devisees-in-trust of Sir Simon Haughton Clarke (who died in 1833). Similar awards were made for 275 slaves on Fat Hog Quarter Estate (Hanover No. 403), for 150 slaves on Cacoon Castle Pen (Hanover No. 36) and for a further 147 slaves (Hanover No. 450)

[49] Sir David Wedderburn: owner of Blue Castle, defendant in Chancery suit of *Lyon* v. *Colvile* as former partner in Wedderburn Colvile and its predecessors for this and other awards in Westmoreland.

[50] Sir Francis Jarvis Stapleton: counter-claimed as executor and devisee of his late father, the Rt Hon. Thomas Lord le Despencer for compensation for thirty-two slaves on Montpellier; List E claim.

[51] Sir William Payne-Gallwey: son of Ralph Payne, awarded compensation for 137 slaves on Pond and Fancy estates. Appears simply as William Payne Gallway [*sic*] in the Parliamentary Return.

[52] Sir Henry Charles Blake: awarded compensation for fifty-nine slaves on Diamond estate.

[53] Sir William Pole: with Henry Combe Compton, awarded compensation for 170 slaves on Golden Rock. Estates may have come into Pole's family by the marriage of his grandfather.

[54] Sir Gerald Noel Noel: awarded compensation 'as owner' for nineteen slaves on Belmont.

[55] Sir Wastel Brisco: 'Sir Wastel Briscoe [*sic*] awarded, with George Stanley Carey, compensation for 205 slaves on Shadwell Park and Westhope estate, and 233 slaves on Grange (St Kitts No. 355); compensation for a further 165 slaves on Flemings Salt Pond (St Kitts No. 340) and 48 slaves on Priddies Salt pond (St Kitts No. 341) was awarded to Brisco alone. Sir John Brisco, Sir Wastel's father, had married

Caroline Alicia Fleming, who brought Shadwell into the family through her marriage settlement.

56 Sir William Milliken Napier: awarded compensation for 161 slaves on Millikens. Appears in the Parliamentary Return as Sir William Napier.

57 Sir Charles Payne: awarded compensation for 255 slaves on French Ground; the fourth Baronet of Tempsford Hall, nephew of Sir Peter Payne.

58 Sir Peter Payne: his son Charles Gillies Payne was awarded compensation for ninety-two slaves on Little Sir Gillies: Sir Peter wrote to the Commissioners to say 'I am the first claimant on the estate ... I have given it to my son ... upon certain conditions. By the time the money is payable we shall inform you to whom we wish it to be paid'; letter to Commission, T71/1609, 14 September 1834.

59 Sir Harcourt Lees: counter-claimed on behalf of the family of a younger brother, William Eden Lees, 'not at present in Ireland' for the compensation on 125 slaves on Heldens.

60 Sir John Lloyd Duckinfield [sic]: counter-claimed with Thomas Garth for the balance of purchase money for compensation for 120 slaves on Parry estate.

61 Sir Alexander Mackenzie: awarded compensation for 385 slaves on Tourama (sp?). His maternal grandfather was Colonel Sutherland of Uppat, and Mackenzie's cousin was Duncan Forbes Sutherland.

62 The Rt Hon. John Sinclair of Ulbster, Baronet: claimed half the compensation for 262 slaves on Argyle estate as trustee with Vans Hathorn of the marriage settlement of the Hon. Archibald Macdonald and his wife. Sinclair was related by marriage to Archibald Macdonald.

63 Sir William Young: of North Dean. See also his unsuccessful pursuit of compensation for St Vincent No. 577, Grenada No. 691 (counter-claim by Sir William Young, MP of Upper Wimpole Street, 'claims the legal estate in the premises under ind[entu]res of 30th and 31st July 1822'), Antigua No. 282 and Tobago No. 64.

64 Sir Michael Bruce: claim for 232 slaves on Shirvan estate, contested by John Gordon of Newton as lessee. Similar claim for 69 slaves on Telescope (Tobago No. 73). Both appealed to Privy Council.

65 Alexander Young Spearman: with David Baillie, awarded as 'Trustees and owners' the compensation for 216 slaves on Auchenskeoch. Spearman was made a Baronet only in 1840.

66 Sir Samuel Stirling: awarded two-thirds of the compensation for 123 slaves on Merchiston as trustee and executor of Archibald Napier. Sir Samuel Stirling also claimed for 113 slaves on Kings Bay in the same capacity and for 45 slaves on Lucy Vale, both lost to counter-claims.

67 Sir Ralph James Woodford: former Governor of Trinidad. Compensation for eleven slaves awarded to Antonio Gomez, Woodford's executor. Woodford had died in 1828.

68 Sir George F. Hill: awarded compensation for one slave.

69 Sir Anthony Lechmere: awarded compensation for 256 slaves. Lechmere's wife Mary Berwick was the daughter of the mortgagee of the estate.

Appendix 10   Mercantile Baronets
appearing in the Compensation records

Claim No.	Baronet	Owner	Other
Jamaica			
Westmoreland			
537	Sir John W. Lubbock[1]		Agent
Montserrat			
124	Sir Thomas Neave[2]	X	
Virgin Islands			
257	Sir John Rae Reid[3]	X	

[1] Sir John William Lubbock: Lubbock's banking firm acted as agent in collecting compensation for John A. G. Clarke.

[2] Sir Thomas Neave: awarded compensation for 92 slaves on Dagnam, 203 slaves on Rendezvous (Montserrat No. 229) and a further 66 slaves (Montserrat No. 228). Neave was also awarded compensation for 77 slaves as mortgagee (St Kitts No. 236) and for a further 15 in Basseterre (St Kitts No. 90), while the compensation for 174 slaves on the Douglas estate and 183 on another estate were paid into Chancery in the cause of *Neave* v. *Douglas* (St Kitts Nos. 207, 208). Neave counter-claimed on 119 slaves on Belmont in St Vincent (St Vincent No. 496) and for £1,600 of the total compensation for 268 slaves on Ratho Mill (St Vincent No. 509), the latter apparently settled in his favour.

[3] Sir John Rae Reid: the partners of Reid, Irving were awarded compensation for 606 slaves under this claim and for a further 112 slaves (Virgin Islands No. 263), 226 (Virgin Islands No. 266), 79 (Virgin Islands No. 95), 126 (Virgin Islands No. 254) and 80 (Virgin Islands No. 261); for 249 slaves on Mile Gully (Manchester No. 338); for 54 slaves on Milton estate (Trinidad No. 1664) and 27 on Enterprise (Trinidad No. 1650); and for 244 slaves on Paradise (Vere No. 77) and 34 on Smith's Pen (Vere No. 78).

Appendix 11   Subscribers to King's College who later appear in the Compensation records

Subscriber	Donation	Shares of £100	Capacity	Claim No.
28 June 1828				
B. Dobree	£100		Trus.	British Guiana 181, 2440
John Atkins	£100	Two	Owner	Port Royal 7, 20; St Andrew 136
Earl Brownlow	£100		Trus.	British Guiana 716
Barclay, Tritton	£100		Agent	
Sir R. Carr Glynn	£100		Agent	
John Irving	£100		Mort.	Virgin Islands 95, 253–4, 261, 263, 266
C. N. Pallmer	£100	Five	Owner	St Dorothy 12, Trelawny 119
Jeremiah Harman	£100		Owner	St Andrew 168, St Elizabeth 5, 368, 395
G. W[atson]Taylor	£100		Owner	St Thomas-in-the-East 100, 297, 457
David Lyon	£100		Owner	Trelawny 42, 143, 191
J. P. Atkins	£50	One	Mort.	St David 3, 134; St Andrew 58
Sir Claudius S. Hunter	£50		Mort.-in-fee	Grenada 441
J. H. Markland	50 guineas		Trus.	Barbados 4215
Sir Charles Price	£50		Judg. cred.	St Thomas-in-the-East 507
Thomas Wilson	£50		Trus.	Grenada 604
Hon. Col. Cust	£20		Owner	British Guiana 716
William Manning	—	One	Owner	Nevis 22 (Manning & Anderdon)
1 July 1828				
G. H. D. Pennant	£100		Owner	Clarendon 3–4, 351, 362

Subscriber	Donation	Shares of £100	Capacity	Claim No.
William King	£50	Two	Owner	British Guiana 2428–30
Lord Carrington	£100		Owner	St Catherine 538
R. W. Dare	£50		Owner	British Guiana 2358
Bishop of Exeter	£200		Trus.	Clarendon 284, 320; Vere 70
J. T. Batt	£100		Owner	Montserrat 238 (to his widow)
Sir John Rae Reid	£100		Mort.	Vere 77–8
Lord Rolle	£200		Owner	Bahamas 960
7 July 1828				
Sir H. W. Martin	£50	One	Owner	Antigua 19
Wilbraham Egerton	£100		Trus.	British Guiana 716
Spencer Mackay	—	Two	Owner	British Guiana 562, 592
10 July 1828				
Samuel Baker[1]	—	One	Cred.	St James 50
Rev. W. D. Longlands	5 guineas		Owner	Hanover 4
Rev. John Wilson[2]	—	One	Owner	St Kitts 200
14 July 1828				
John Gladstone	—	One	Owner	British Guiana 556, 650, 687
Mrs Gladstone	£20			
William Grasett	—	One	Owner	Barbados 2001
Thomas Hankey	£25	Two	Owner	Trelawny 25–7
Sir J. L. Duckenfield	£10	One	Cred.	St Kitts 351 (unpaid purchase money)
John Mitchell	£50		Owner	Clarendon 71
Rev. J. H. Mitchell	10 guineas		Owner	Vere 111
Rev. R. B. Hampden	10 guineas		Owner	Barbados 2521
Charles Devon	£20		Beneficiary	Clarendon 156 under marriage settlement
Josiah Martin	£30		Owner	Antigua 57
Robert Holford	£100	One	Mort.	Nevis 100 counter-claim
Samuel Smith	£100		Owner	St Catherine 538
21 July 1828				
[Chas] Nathl Bayley[3]	5 guineas		Owner	St Mary 262
Charles Bosanquet	£50		Trus.	St Kitts 206, 336, 704 for his brother
John Vere[4]	£50		Mort.	British Guiana 2349
George Ward	£100		"	"

Subscriber	Donation	Shares of £100	Capacity	Claim No.
John Barham[5]	—	Five	Owner	St Elizabeth 366
George Grote	£100		Agent	
28 July 1828				
William Earle	—	One	Owner	British Guiana 477
William Manning	—	One	Owner	Nevis 22 (Manning & Anderdon)
William Harrison	—	One	Owner	Trelawny 539
Joseph Marryat	£50		Owner	Trinidad 1783 etc.
John Bolton	£100		Owner	British Guiana 2478
Barnard, Dimsdale	—	Four	Agent	
Duncan Campbell		One	Cred.	St Lucia 329, 760
Rob. Wesley Hall	£50		Owner	British Guiana 2358
5 August 1828				
Rev. Dr J. G. Wrench	—	One		
Colin Campbell	—	One	Owners	Multiple British
Mungo Campbell	—	One		Guiana claims
John J. Campbell	—	One		Partners in John Campbell Sr of Glasgow
Edward Ellice	£100		Mort.	Grenada 439–40, 758
Charles Pott[6]	30 guineas			
Arthur Pott	30 guins		Trus.	Antigua 339
William Pott	30 guins			
Rev. G. Porcher	£25		Trus.	Trelawny 110–15
Rees Goring Thomas	—	One	Mort.	St James 5
19 August 1828				
Sir Geo. H. Rose	£100		Owner	Dominica 243
Eleonora Atherton	£50		Owner	St James 393
Rev. John Driggs	£10		Trus.?	St James 276
Joseph Liggins	—	One	Admor	Antigua 87, 397 (for James Adams Wood, Mary Prince's 'owner')
2 September 1828				
R. B. Pollard	—	One	Cred.	St Elizabeth 605
15 September 1828				
Trustees of Lord Crewe[7]	£500		Owner	Barbados 4943, 4944; Vere 122
Rev. James Hamilton[8]	£5		Owner	Tobago 34
1 October 1828				
Donald Mackay	—	One	Owner	British Guiana 2453

Subscriber	Donation	Shares of £100	Capacity	Claim No.
14 October 1828 Archibald Paull	—	One	Mort.	St Kitts 717–19, Grenada 700, 772–3, 775

[1] Tentative only: presumed to be Samuel Baker of Baker & Philpotts, London West India merchant.

[2] Tentative only: Rev. John Wilson of The Queen's College, Oxford was awarded £2,165 17s 10d for 126 slaves on Olivers estate; T71/879, St Kitts No. 200.

[3] Tentative only: the entry appears to read simply 'Nathaniel Bayley'.

[4] John Vere and George Ward: partners in the bankers Vere & Ward, counter-claimants as mortgagees.

[5] Tentative only: the entry is almost illegible, and appears to read 'John Brahim'.

[6] Charles, Arthur and William Pott: counter-claimed for 'Legacy of £3,000 under the will of Hamilton Kerby'; identified as trustees for the Rev. John Thomas Wilgress and others in Antigua No. 349.

[7] Trustees of Lord Crewe: The Hon. John O. Crewe was awarded compensation for the slaves on Tour Hill and The Rock in Barbados. He appears to have been the grandson of the first Baron Crewe (who died in April 1829) and son of the second (who died in 1835). In another family claim, the heirs of Richard Crewe claimed the compensation for Raymond's estate in Vere, which Richard Crewe owned. The first Lord Crewe was Richard's brother.

[8] Tentative only: more than one possible identification for Rev. James Hamilton.

Appendix 12   Donors to the National Society for Promoting the Education of the Poor in the Principles of the Established Church throughout England and Wales, appearing in the Compensation records

Donor	Address	Capacity	Claim No.
1st round, 15 August 1843			
£100			
Lord Chief Just. Tindal		Trustee	British Guiana 2382A
Rev. Gerard Noel		Trustee	St Kitts 705
Rt Hon. Earl Balcarres		Owner	St George 185 etc.
Rt Hon. H. Goulburn		Owner	Vere 49
Rt Hon. W. E. Gladstone		Executor	Manchester 65
J. Tollemache		Owner	Antigua 39–40, 58, 82–3, 123
Charles Manning[1]	New Bank Buildings	Indemnity	Antigua 257
J. H. Markland	Bath	Trus.	Barbados 4215
Rt Hon. Earl Talbot		Trus.	St Dorothy 127
Charles Bosanquet	Rock, Northumberland	Trus.	St Kitts 206, 336, 724
£50			
Mrs Maltby[2]	Bath	Mort.	Grenada 565, 684
Miss Atherton	Kirsall, Manchester	Owner	St James 393, Trelawny 539
J. P. Anderdon	Reading	Owner	Antigua 17
£25			
Alfred Latham	Norfolk St.	Trus.?	St Thomas-in-the-East 192
Sheffield Neave[3]		Agent	St Kitts 635
2nd round, 4 September 1843			
£100			
Sir Thos Baring, Bart.		Creditor cc	St George 278
Neill Malcolm	Great Stanhope St.	Owner	Hanover 17 etc.
Sir George H. Rose		Owner	Dominica 243
David Baillie	Belgrave Sq.	Trus. & Owner	Tobago 11
J. G. Boucher[4]	Shedfield, Fareham	Owner	Manchester 126–8, 156

Donor	Address	Capacity	Claim No.
William Hervey	Bradwell Grove, Oxon.	Owner	St Thomas-in-the-Vale 54, St Thomas-in-the-East 150
Archdeacon Berners		Trus.?	Trelawny 417
E. R. Tunno	Upper Brook St.	Executor	St Mary 262, 264–6
Sir R. P. Glynn		Agent	
£50			
S. T. Kekewick	Peamore, Exeter	Trus.	Grenada 449
Thos Gladstone	Cuffnalls, Lyndhurst	Exor	Manchester 65
Rev. G. Porcher	Maiden Erlegh	Trus.	Trelawny 110–5
W. C. Casamajor	Potterells, Hatfield	Trus.[5]	Antigua 275
Langford Lovel[l]	Horsley, Winchester	Owner	Antigua 108, 119
William King	Wandsworth	Owner	British Guiana 2428–30
Henry Dawes		Owner	Grenada 568
£25			
C. Heaton Ellis	Buntingford	Trus.	St Vincent 505
R. C. Tudway	Wells	Owner	Antigua 327, 328, 330

'Classified', *The Times*, 15 August 1843, p. 2; 4 September 1843, p. 3 carries lists of the donors, including 201 who donated £100 in the first round and 103 who donated £100 in the second.

[1] Charles John Manning of 3 New Bank Buildings 'claims the whole compensation money as an indemnity against the liabilities of Messrs Manning & Anderdon, they having used his name as their Trustee without his knowledge or consent'.

[2] Tentative only: identification as Louisa Maltby, widow of Rowland Maltby.

[3] Sheffield Neave collected the compensation for his father and two others for Lamberts in St Kitts.

[4] John George Boucher appears in the Compensation records as John George Crabbe: he changed his name as a condition of succeeding to the estates of Richard Boucher.

[5] W. C. Casamajor was the son of Justinian Casamajor, the London merchant who had bought the English estate of Potterells. The compensation for the Elmes estate in Antigua was awarded to Justinian Casamajor's executor James Newman, who counter-claimed on the basis that the older Casamajor had been trustee of a term for securing several annuities. The annuitants do not appear to be Casamajor's immediate family.

Appendix 13   Members of the Eyre Defence Fund connected with slave-compensation

Member	Connection
S[imon] Watson Taylor	Son of George Watson Taylor, awardee through trustees
J. H. Washington Hibbert	Son of Thomas Hibbert of Aqualta Vale
John Morant	Slave-owner, awardee
Sir Thomas Gladstone	Awardee as executor for family
Sir James Buller East	Son of Edward Hyde East, owner and awardee
John William Kaye	Son of Freshfields partner and possible slave-owner Charles Kaye
David Lyon	Slave-owner, awardee
Rev. Main Walrond	From Antiguan slave-owner family, kinsman of awardee Bethell Walrond
Charles Raikes	Son of Job Matthew Raikes, owner and awardee through trustees
Sir Samuel Baker	Son of Samuel Baker, London West India merchant and awardee

Classified, *The Times*, 1 January 1867, p. 6. carries a list of sixty-six members of the Committee of 'The Eyre Defence and Aid Fund'.

Appendix 14   Nominees as Sheriffs appearing in the Compensation records

Year/nominee	County	Residence	Role in Compensation records
1819[1]			
T. H. A. Earle[2]	Berks.	Swallowfield Place	Owner, St Kitts 93 & 95
James France France	Cheshire	Bostock	Trus. of Thos France, Clarendon 145
John Ingl. Fortescue[3]	Devon	Buckland	Owner, claim for St Vincent 572
William James[4]	Cumberland	Barrock Lodge	Heir, St Thomas-in-the-East 78
Sir Thomas Neave	Essex	Dagnam Park	Owner, Montserrat 124
Robert Westley Hall[5]	Essex	Great Ilford	Owner, British Guiana 2358
Joseph Timperon[6]	Herts.	New Barns	Owner, St Mary 310
John Biddulph	Herefordshire	Ledbury	Trus./mortgagee, Clarendon 1
John Whitmore[7]	Surrey	Epsom	Mort. Trinidad 981 etc.
Total: 9 of 102			
1822[8]			
Herbert Newton Jarrett[9]	Essex	Bromley Lodge	Owner, award to son on Trelawny 546
John Frederick Pinney	Somerset	Somerton Erle	Mort., St Kitts 751
Edward Jeffries Esdaile	Somerset	Cothelstone	Mort. cc, Tre. 538
John Barnard Hankey[10]	Surrey	Feltham Priory	Mort. cc, Westmoreland 213, 465
Total: 4 of 102			
1825			
Total: 0 of 105			
1828[11]			
John Hoskins Harper	Cheshire	Davenham Hall	Owner, Montserrat 61

Year/nominee	County	Residence	Role in Compensation records
Brice Pearse	Essex	Monkham	Trus., St Mary 262
Capel Cure	Essex	Blake-Hall	Trus. S. F. Allen, St Thomas-in-the-East 508
George Douglas	Kent	Chilston Park	Owner, award to heir, Tobago 26
James Adams Gordon	Somerset	Portbury	Owner, St Vincent 549
Sir W. G. H. Joliffe[12]	Surrey	Merstham	Father owned, St Lucia 763
Edward Collins	Cornwall	Trutham	Mort., award for Tobago 34
Philip J. Miles	Cardiganshire	Bristol	Owner, multiple awards

Total: 7 of 105 (England) or 8 of 141 (England & Wales)

1836[13]

John Nembhard Hibbert	Bucks.	Chalfont St Peter	Trus., exor and heir, St David 45
Thomas Hartley[14]	Cumberland	Gillfort	Owner, St James 655
Thomas Hibbert	Cheshire	Birtles	Trus., exor and heir, St David 45
Anthony Wilkinson	Durham	Coxhoe Hall	Owner, Manchester 306
Colthurst Bateman	Monmouth	Portholey	Owner, St Thomas-in-the-East 150
John Christian Boode[15]	Wilts.	Lucknam	Heir to awardee, British Guiana 704

Total: 6 of 108

1839[16]

Charles Snell Chauncy	Herts.	Little Munden	Owner, Grenada 693
R. C. Tudway	Somerset	Wells	Owner, Antigua 327–8, 330
John Tollemache	Cheshire	Tilstone Lodge	Owner, Antigua 39–40, 52, 82–3, 123
J. S. W. ErleDrax	Dorset	Charborough Park	Owner, Barbados 3784
John Jarrett	Somerset	Cummerten [*sic* = Camerton]	Owner, award for Trelawny 420, 544, 547

Total: 5 of 108

---

[1] 'From the London Gazette: Sheriffs for English Counties', *The Times*, 15 November 1819, p. 4.
[2] Timothy Hare Altabon Earl.

3 John Inglett Fortescue.

4 William James of Barrock Lodge: grandson and heir of the Liverpool West Indian merchant William James; the compensation for 237 slaves on Clifton Hill was awarded to Joseph Brooks Yates, another Liverpool merchant, as the trustee of William James.

5 Robert Westley Hall the younger: Robert Westley Hall took the additional name Dare, an award of £14,452 14s 1d for 273 slaves on Maria's Pleasure was made to the son (also RWHD) after death of older RWHD in 1836.

6 Joseph Timperon: awards for 156 slaves on Union Estate, 342 on New Ramble (St Mary No. 311) and 85 on Union Hill Pen (St Mary No. 312) as owner. Also awarded compensation as mortgagee with Joseph Dobinson for St Mary Nos. 128, 129, 134; and St Thomas-in-the-East Nos. 129, 134.

7 John Whitmore: London banker of Whitmore, Wells.

8 'From the London Gazette', *The Times*, 18 November 1822, p. 2.

9 Herbert Newton Jarrett: given erroneously as Robert Newton Jarrett in *The Times*.

10 John Barnard Hankey: counter-claimed as heir-at-law, residuary devisee and legatee of Thomas Hankey, mortgagee of certain of the slaves on New Hope estate and Ackindown Pen.

11 'News: Nomination of Sheriffs for the Ensuing Year', *The Times*, 14 November 1828, p. 3.

12 Sir William G. H. Joliffe: his father had conveyed Union estate to London merchants in 1822.

13 'News: Nomination of Sheriffs', *The Times*, 14 November 1836, p. 3.

14 Thomas Hartley: of Whitehaven, owner of Crawle estate and mortgagee of Minto family on several estates in Trelawny.

15 John Christian Boode: award of £14,236 for 271 slaves on De Groote to John Christian's father, Andreas Christian Boode, who bought Lucknam Park.

16 'News: Nomination of Sheriffs', *The Times*, 13 November 1839, p. 4.

Appendix 15   Notes on largest mercantile recipients of slave-compensation

Rank	Firm	Notes
1.	Davidsons & Barkly	**Includes awards under Henry Davidson, Aeneas Barkly, Henry Barkly, William Davidson singly or together:** Antigua 333; Grenada 446, 605, 609, 610, 692c, 755, 756, 1001; St Ann 201, 203; St Mary 29, 380, 381; St Thomas-in-the-Vale 117, 274, 285, 313; St Vincent 454; Tobago 50; Trinidad 1599, 1614, 1615A, 2016A; Westmoreland 233; British Guiana 16, 216, 286, 391, 491. **Adds:** Mercantile interception, Trinidad 1808, Vere 60, British Guiana 390. **Potential further awards:** British Guiana 90 (List E), St Thomas-in-the-Vale 200 (possible mercantile interception), St Mary 28 (share by mercantile interception). **Excludes:** None.
2.	Sandbach, Tinne	**Includes awards under Charles Stewart Parker, Philip F. Tinne, George Rainy, Henry Robertson Sandbach, George Parker, J. A. Tinne and J. P. M'Inroy:** British Guiana 546, 640, 641, 654, 665, 668, 680, 693, 694, 701, 702, 709, 712, 804, 1296, 2268. **Excludes:** British Guiana 2512 (Samuel Sandbach [*sic*], apparently unrelated to Sandbach Tinne); British Guiana 552, 705 (List E cases with George Rainy, apparently outside the context of the partnership); and a long list of small claims by George Rainy alone (British Guiana 804, 882, 1037, 1106, 1155, 1272, 1393, 1718, 1783, 1855, 1974, 2032, 2138, 2257).
3.	T. Daniel & Co.	**Includes awards under Thomas Daniel, John Daniel:** Antigua 268, 310; Barbados 105, 119, 139, 270, 1731, 1733, 2969, 2977, 3332, 3950, 4355, 5171B; Tobago 10; Montserrat 4, 5, 219, 221; Nevis 40; British Guiana 166, 379, 557, 578, 614, 2351, 2355; St Dorothy 75. **Adds:** Mercantile interception of Trinidad 1912, Barbados 1665, 3213, 3929; Montserrat 3, 185. **Excludes:** None. Peter Marshall's estimate (*Bristol and the abolition of slavery: the politics of emancipation* (Bristol: Bristol Branch of the Historical Association, 1975), Appendix 1) of £102,000 does not include the cases of mercantile interception, which would bring his figure up to £118,000 against the £140,000 calculated from the Compensation records in this analysis. Kathleen Butler (*The economics of Emancipation: Jamaica and Barbados, 1823–1843* (Chapel Hill: University of North Carolina Press, 1995), p. 67) gives £117,383, again excluding the £16,000 or so in mercantile interception.
4.	Chauncy & Lang	**Includes awards under Nathaniel Snell Chauncy, Nathaniel Snell, Charles Snell Chauncy, Charles Porcher Lang and Maria Lang:** Antigua 397; Grenada 433, 682, 693, 759, 761 786; St Vincent 455, 569; Tobago 2, 68; British Guiana, 2316, 2334, 2340. Mercantile interception, British Guiana 618. **Potential further awards:** St Vincent 641 (List E). **Excludes:** St Vincent 421 (Trus.).

5.	John Gladstone	**Includes:** British Guiana 556, 650, 656, 687; British Guiana 707 (with Robertson Gladstone *et al.*); St Elizabeth 534, 535A,B (with Divie Robertson); Manchester 65 (Thomas S. Gladstone and William Gladstone as executors of Robert Gladstone); St Mary 254. **Potential further awards:** Hanover 498; Westmoreland 458; St Mary 276; St Elizabeth 177, 732 (all List E), totalling a further £14,595. **Excludes:** None. S. G. Checkland, *The Gladstones: a family biography 1764–1851* (Cambridge: Cambridge University Press, 1971), pp. 320–1 gives £93,526 for John Gladstone alone, after pro-rating John Gladstone's five-sevenths share on British Guiana 707 and before including Robert Gladstone's estate. Checkland also appears to have omitted £3,059 for John Gladstone's Oxford Estate (St Mary 254) but included a half share of £4,295 awarded jointly with Divie Robertson that the database does not show.
6.	Hall, M'Garel	**Includes awards under David Hall and Charles M'Garel:** British Guiana 555, 714, 750, 2405. **Adds:** Mercantile interception, British Guiana 2278, 2370, 2371, 2372, 2453. **Excludes:** British Guiana 314, 690, 1258, 2444, 2468 under M'Garel or Hall alone. **Potential further awards:** British Guiana 545 (possible mercantile interception).
7.	H. & J. E. Baillie	**Includes awards to Hugh Duncan Baillie, James Evan Baillie, G. H. Ames:** St Kitts 48, 576, 644; Grenada 312, 591 (part), 690, 701; St Vincent 491, 506, 507A, 538, 548, 553, 661; Trinidad 1641; British Guiana 125A, 158A, 629, 2289. **Potential further awards:** Grenada 564, 783; St Vincent 644; St Kitts 657 (all awards in Chancery totalling £21,502); Nevis 5, 15, 16, 17, 18, 35 (all List E under Evan Baillie, who claimed for £4,829 against awards totalling £12,348); St Vincent 133, 222, 495, 570 (all List E) and St Vincent 463 (counter-claim on compensation in a Chancery suit) together amounting to a further £9,921. **Excludes:** None. Douglas Hamilton, *Scotland, the Caribbean and the Atlantic World 1750–1820* (Manchester: Manchester University Press, 2006), p. 201 shows James Evan Baillie receiving £53,964 in compensation, sharing in partnerships with Hugh Duncan Baillie and (George) Henry Ames, which received another £57,042, and notes further Chancery awards of £25,990. I cannot reconcile the figure for J. E. Baillie, whom the records show as receiving two awards totalling £12,967 (British Guiana 125A, 158A). Hamilton may have included the other parts of these two awards, which went to Chancery in *Elizabeth Winter v. Innes*. Marshall, *Bristol and the abolition*, Appendix 1 shows £110,000 in total, which again may include the whole of awards identified in this analysis as only partially paid to the Baillie family.
8.	J. Campbell Sr	**Includes awards to Colin Campbell; Mungo Nutter Campbell; Sir James Campbell, trustee of Robert Nutter Campbell:** Grenada 780; St Vincent 642; British Guiana 540 (awarded to A. G. Milne on behalf of J. Campbell Sr & Co.); British Guiana 2281, 2317A, 2318, 2341, 2348, 2398A, 2441, 2454. Mercantile interception, British Guiana 2292. **Potential further award:** Tobago 39 (possible mercantile interception). **Excludes:** British Guiana 2324 (Colin Campbell as executor).

Rank	Firm	Notes
9.	W., R. & S. Mitchell	**Includes awards under Rowland and Samuel Mitchell:** Clarendon 5, 25, 39, 40, 49, 93, 208, 209, 274, 275; Hanover 100; Manchester 452; St Ann 225, 561, 562B; St George 277; St Mary 149, 400, 405, 524; Trelawny 163. **Excludes:** St Ann 111B, 128; St Dorothy 17, 299; Vere 58; Trelawny 545 (all as executors of John Mitchell); St Mary 27; St Thomas-in-the-Vale 60 (executors of others, the total as executors being £33,170). Also excludes Clarendon 6 (share in small award by Samuel Mitchell), and awards to John Mitchell (Clarendon 72) and James Henry Mitchell (Clarendon 295). Butler gives £93,965 (*The economics of Emancipation*, p. 53), which clearly combines the awards of Rowland and Samuel Mitchell as principal with their awards as executors.
10.	R. Bogle, Bogle King	**Includes awards to William Hamilton, Archibald Bogle, George Bogle and Wm Bogle (partners of Robert Bogle & Co. and/or survivors of James Bogle & Co.) and to William Hamilton, David King, George Bogle and Alexander Bogle Jr (partners in Bogle, King):** British Guiana 198A, 2271, 2275, 2281, 2300, 2302; Trinidad 1475, 1632, 1884, 1901; Vere 69. **Excludes:** None.
11.	C., W. & F. Shand	**Includes awards to William Shand, and William Shand with Francis, Charles or Alexander Shand:** Antigua 3, 7, 9, 22, 36, 52, 303, 321, 351, 354, 357; British Guiana 542, 547, 553. **Excludes:** awards to William Shand in Jamaica.
12.	J. T. & A. Douglas	**Includes awards to John, Thomas & Archibald Douglas:** British Guiana 550, 568A, 692, 2020. **Adds:** Mercantile interception, British Guiana 476, 584. **Excludes:** None.
13.	Reid, Irving	**Includes awards under Sir John Rae Reid, John Irving:** St Kitts 190, 191, 644; St Thomas-in-the-East 464; Trinidad 1650, 1664; British Guiana 540; Vere 77, 78; Virgin Islands, 95, 254, 257, 261, 263, 266. **Possible further award:** St Kitts 762 (possible mercantile interception). **Excludes:** None.
14.	Wm Fraser, Alexander	**Includes awards to Wm Fraser, William Maxwell Alexander, Claude Neilson, Boyd Alexander:** Antigua 1045; Grenada 955; St Vincent 449B, 450, 451, 557, 574, 599, 690B,D, 745E; Trinidad 1838A. **Possible further awards:** Dominica 294 (possible mercantile interception by Fraser, Alexander). **Excludes:** None.
15.	T. & W. King	**Includes awards to William King or William and Thomas King:** Dominica 336A, 778; British Guiana 670, 1146, 2428, 2429, 2430, 2431; Trinidad 1636. **Excludes:** British Guiana 2527 (Wm King as executor).

16.	Pinney & Case J. F. Pinney	**Includes awards under Charles Pinney, Charles Pinney with Robert Edward Case, and John Frederick Pinney:** Nevis 36, 38, 39, 87, 97 (Pinney & Case); Nevis 92, St Kitts 398 (Charles Pinney); Nevis 155, 156 (J. F. Pinney, C. Pinney, R. E. Case); Nevis 41, Montserrat 116, St Vincent 480, St Kitts 751 (J. F. Pinney); Nevis 129, British Guiana 635 (C. & J. F. Pinney). **Possible further award:** Nevis 98 (possible mercantile interception). **Adds:** Mercantile interception Nevis 133, 134, 135, 136, 291 (C. Pinney). **Excludes:** Nevis 1 (Trustee). Marshall, *Bristol and abolition*, Appendix I adopted a total attributed to Richard Pares of £36,396, acknowledging that he himself arrived at a lower figure. Pares, *A West India fortune* (London: Longman, 1960), p. 315 shows a total of £29,069 excluding J. F. Pinney's Old Manor estate (Nevis 41), including an award on Hendricksons that is not apparent in the database, excluding Nevis 36 and 97, and before mercantile interception of Nevis 133–6. Elsewhere, however, Pares estimated £32,500 including mercantile interception for Nevis (p. 318) and identified a further £10,762 in other colonies, for a total of £43,262 against the £44,458 calculated in this study from the Compensation records.
17.	Jos. Wilson	**Includes awards under Thomas Wilson:** Trinidad 1481, 1665, 1670, 1671A, 1682, 1757, 1859, 1863, 1920A,B. **Adds:** mercantile interception, Trinidad 1338, 1747, 1755, 1760, 1762, 1843, 2020. **Possible further award:** Trinidad 1892 (possible mercantile interception).
18.	P. J. Miles	**Includes awards to Philip John Miles or Miles with Thomas Kingston:** Hanover 28, 37, 218, 402, 404, 560, 578; St Thomas-in-the-East 449; Trelawny 122, 123, 551; Trinidad 1601, 1604, 1619A. **Possible further awards:** Trelawny 35, 36 (both Chancery); Trelawny 158, 183, 187, 188 (all List E); Hanover 35 (List E); Hanover 50 (possible mercantile interception) totalling a further £18,139. **Excludes:** None.
19.	J. & H. Moss	Butler, *The economics of Emancipation*, p. 53 shows £28,188 for Jamaica alone; Marshall, *Bristol and abolition*, £36,000 in total. **Includes:** British Guiana 2455 (single award for Anna Regina).
20.	Jos. Marryat & Sons	**Includes:** St Lucia 329, 547, 760, 764, 775; St Mary 307; Trinidad 697A, 1235, 1245A, 1781, 1783, 1784. Mercantile interception, Trinidad 1088, 1637, 2063.
21.	G., W. & S. Hibbert	**Includes awards under George Hibbert, George Hibbert with William and Samuel Hibbert:** Clarendon 8 (executors of George Hibbert); Clarendon 333, 358; Hanover 432; Portland 268; St James 169, 184; St Mary 30, 132; Trelawny 126, 133, 667. **Possible further awards:** Hanover 14 (Chancery), Hanover 431 (List E) and potentially St James 173 (List E), totalling an additional £7,784. **Excludes:** Hanover 80, 81 (executors of Robert Hibbert); Portland 267; St Mary 130, 133, 149 (all Robert Hibbert Jr as executor); Hanover 138, 139; St Mary 290 (all Robert Hibbert Jr as owner); St James 168

Rank	Firm	Notes
		and Westmoreland 230 (George and William Hibbert as executors of Thomas Hibbert, totalling £9,241 combined); and St Mary 1, 3, 10 (all *Hibbert v. Hibbert* in Chancery). Butler's estimate (*The economics of Emancipation*, p. 53) of £59,545 probably includes St James 168 and Westmoreland 230, and a number of other family claims less directly related to the mercantile firm. The total family receipts of compensation were £103,000.
22.	Barton, Irlam, Higginson	**Includes awards under George Barton Irlam, Jonathan Higginson, and Richard Deane as executor of John Higginson, surviving partner of Sir William Barton and George Irlam:** Barbados 120, 264, 488, 2751B, 2758, 2771, 3048, 3999, 3601A, 4072, 4412, 4546, 4961. **Adds:** Mercantile interception, Barbados 4603. **Possible further awards:** Barbados 3101 (List E). **Excludes:** None. Butler, *The economics of Emancipation*, p. 57 gives £26,822 for Barton, Irlam, Higginson in total.
23.	T. & H. Murray	**Includes awards to Thomas Murray or Thomas Murray with Henry Murray:** British Guiana 566, 710, 844, 846, 2440, 2460, 2526. **Excludes:** None.
24.	Timperon & Dobinson	**Includes awards under Joseph Timperon and Joseph Dobinson separately or together:** St Dorothy 21; St Mary 128, 129, 134, 310, 311, 312; St Thomas-in-the-East 129, 134, 214, 215, 216 (the latter three personal to Dobinson in right of his wife). Mercantile interception of British Guiana 271. **Excludes:** None. Butler, *The economics of Emancipation* p. 53 gives £35,441 for Jamaica alone, consistent with this study's £35,468 for Jamaica alone.
25.	H. & J. Cohen	**Includes awards to Judah and Hymen Cohen together or separately:** Manchester 84, 85, 106, 229, 230, 231, 373, 377, 400; St Elizabeth 83, 108, 109, 129, 131, 195; St George 279. Butler's total of £38,247 may include some element of awards made to Henry Hymen Cohen, who operated what appears to be an independent mercantile business at 15 London Street, Fenchurch St.

This table highlights the major additions or deletions from the Parliamentary Return lists in order to provide the basis of calculation for Table 6.2 above in the main text. It also shows where there was possibly additional compensation to the merchant firm, as List E or Chancery awards or as suspected but unproven cases of mercantile interception. Finally, it seeks to reconcile where possible the data with existing estimates available in secondary sources.

Appendix 16 London bankers appearing in the Compensation records

Firm	Predecessor Firm of	Capacity	Banker	Award	Claim	Source
J. Ashley & Co.			R. Barclay for John and Henry Moss of Liverpool	£40,353	British Guiana 2455	T71/887, NDO4/8
			R. Bevan for Alexander H. Hamilton	£3,785	Grenada 685, 709	T71/880, NDO4/10
					Clarendon 291	T71/859, NDO4/1
Barclay, Bevan & Tritton	Barclays		R. Barclay for the Scott family	£6,501	St Thomas-in-the-East 295	T71/867, NDO4/5
			R. Barclay for David Langlands	£987	St Elizabeth 748	T71/870, NDO4/4
			D. Bevan for William Drummond Delap	£826	St James 189	T71/873, NDO4/5
			R. Barclay for J. B. Yates	£3,986	St Thomas-in-the-East 278	T71/867, NDO4/5
Barnard, Dimsdale	RBSG	Agent	John Barnard for Edward Huggins and Pinney & Case	£6,790	Nevis 36, 97	T71/882, NDO4/9
			W. Dimsdale for Pinney & Case	£5,108	Nevis 1, 87	T71/882, NDO4/9
Barnetts Hoares & Co.	Lloyds	Agent	J. H. Bradshaw and G. Hoare for P. J. Miles	£26,426	Hanover 28, 37, 218, 402, 404, 578	T71/872, NDO4/1
					St Thomas-in-the-East 449	T71/867, NDO4/5
					Trinidad 1601, 1604	T71/894, NDO4/12
		Agent	J. G. Hoare for Simon Barrow and E. Lousada	£2,536	St Ann 447	T71/857, NDO4/3

Name	Bank	Role	Description	Amount	Estate	Reference
Bosanquet Anderdon	Lloyds	Beneficiary	Assignees of mortgagee and judgement creditor on Clifton's, Paynes and Moreton Bay	£3,655	Nevis 132	T71/882
			Successful cc against Protheroe and Savage on Meales estate as 'the parties interested in the compensation money'	£217	Nevis 76	T71/882
			Apparently partially successful counter-claim as assignees beneficially interested under a judgement for £12,384 16s 1d in a claim made by Walter Maynard	£2,018	Nevis 42	T71/882
			Party to an undisclosed arrangement for compensation on Walter Maynard's New River estate	£1,954	Nevis 98	T71/882
Hon. Pleydell Bouverie Sir W. Call, G. R. Martin. Child & Co. Cockburn & Co.						
Cocks, Biddulph & Biddulph	Barclays	Beneficiary?	John Biddulph and Samuel Pepys Cockerell were awarded compensation as trustees of James Dawkins. Butler gives background suggesting Biddulph and Cockerell were in fact mortgagees as well as trustees[1]	£35,908	Clarendon 1, 2, 7, 11, 277	T71/859, T71/1186, T71/1187
					St Catherine 499, 515	T71/852,
					Vere 46, 71 St Thomas-in-the-Vale 14	T71/858, T71/855

Firm	Predecessor Firm of RBSG	Capacity	Banker	Award	Claim	Source
Coutts & Co.	RBSG	Trustees	For George Watson Taylor (Antrobus & Coulthurst)	£40,734	Hanover 21, 577 St Mary 26, 247 St Thomas-in-the-East 100, 297, 457	T71/872 T71/856 T71/867
		Executor	For Tully Higgins (Antrobus)	£16,800	British Guiana 2397	T71/887
		Agent	For Belfon family	£3,593	Grenada 933, 935 & 1000	T71/880, NDO4/10
			For Robert Houstoun	£5,024	Grenada 702	T71/880, NDO4/10
			For James Blair	£83,530	British Guiana 15	T71/885, NDO4/8
					British Guiana 2271, 2275, 2300, 2302	T71/887, NDO4/8
			For Bogle King & Co.	£39,284	Trinidad 1901	T71/894, NDO4/12
					Vere 69	T71/858, NDO4/2
			For John Grant	£1,548	British Guiana 1065, 1111	T71/886, NDO4/8
					British Guiana 2518	T71/887, NDO4/8
			For Charles Selkrig	£11,605	St Mary 244	T71/856, NDO4/5
			For W. Hunter Baillie	£2,451	Clarendon 323	T71/859, NDO4/1

Firm		Role	Description	Amount	Location	Reference
Cunliffe Brooks Curries & Co.	RBSG	Executor	For Robert Wallace	£4,061	Hanover 440	T71/872, NDO4/1
			For John W. Melville	£2,781	Westmoreland 266	T71/871, NDO4/1
			For Allan M'Dowall	£6,119	Dominica 151	T71/881, NDO4/9
			For Philip Gomez	£2,551	St Vincent 471	T71/892, NDO4/10
			For Wm Smith & R. Brown of Glasgow	£7,649	Trinidad 1296, 1522	T71/894, NDO4/12
			For Dennistoun family	£9,985	Trinidad 1836	T71/894, NDO4/12
					Trinidad 1627, 1652	T71/894, NDO4/12
		Trustee	Isaac Currie for his father-in-law Job Matthew Raikes	£15,379	St Mary 262, 264–6	T71/856
			Isaac Currie for J. G. Campbell	£20,027	Westmoreland 213–15, 465, 467, 468	T71/871
			John Kennard for Thos & Wm Earle of Liverpool	£10,197	British Guinea 477	T71/885, NDO4/8
					Clarendon 278	T71/859, NDO4/1
					Portland 254	T71/868, NDO4/3
Denison, Joseph & Co.	RBSG	Agent	John Kennard for J. B. Yates	£13,980	St George 334	T71/869, NDO4/4
					St Thomas-in-the-East 299, 300	T71/867, NDO4/5
					Vere 37	T71/858, NDO4/2

Firm	Predecessor Firm of	Capacity	Banker	Award	Claim	Source
Dixon, Son & Brooks						
Dorrien, Magens, Mello	RBSG	Beneficiary	Thomas Dorrien, Magens Dorrien Magens and John Mello et al., bankers of Finch Lane, mortgagees under indenture of 1818; amount claimed £3,500 and upwards on Invera and Argyle estates	£2,064	Tobago 60, 61	T71/891
			G. Drummond for Robert Farquhar	£17,934	Grenada 695–7	T71/880, NDO4/10
					Antigua 284	T71/877, NDO4/9
			G. Drummond for Mrs A. M. Bethell	£2,588	Antigua 54	T71/877, NDO4/9
					Antigua 259, 342	T71/877, NDO4/9
Drummonds	RBSG	Agent	For Sir W. Abdy et al.	£13,405	St Vincent 549	T71/892, NDO4/10
			For John S. W. Drax	£4,293	Barbados 3784	T71/898, NDO4/7
			Andrew Drummond for Elizabeth Bagnold	£1,532	St.Andrew 335	T71/865, NDO4/3
			H[?] Drummond for executors of Caleb Dickinson	£3,372	St Elizabeth 394, 545	T71/870, NDO4/4
			For E. Protheroe et al.	£8,513	St Vincent 505	T71/892, NDO4/10

Bank	Status	Beneficiary / Agent	Description	Amount	Estate / Parish	References
Sir Jas Esdaile	RBSG	Beneficiary	Mortgagees in possession on Hazelymph Estate	£4,121	St James 5	T71/873
		Agent	For J. Griffith and his wife	£685	St Elizabeth 107	T71/870, NDO4/9
Sir T. H. Farquhar, W. S. Davidson	Lloyds	Agent	Walter R. Farquhar for Rowland E. Williams	£3,569	Antigua 115, 1047	T71/877, NDO4/9
			Walter R. Farquhar for R. A. Oswald *et al.*	£5,445	St Mary 267, 269	T71/856, NDO4/5
Fullers & Co.[2] Thomas Gill & Feltham			Richard Carr Glynn for Rev. Adam Sedgwick	£3,783	St James 546	T71/873, NDO4/5
			Thos Hallifax for W. Heath	£1,371	St James 341, 342	T71/873, NDO4/5
Sir Rich. Carr Glynn, Hallifax & Mills	RBSG	Agent	George Carr Glynn for Bernard family	£14,492	Hanover 34 / St James 31, 32, 39, 163	T71/872, NDO4/1, T71/873, NDO4/5
			George Carr Glynn for Susanna James Mountague	£1,903	Trelawny 190	T71/874, NDO4/3,
Goslings & Sharpe	Barclays	Agent	Robert Gosling for Thomas B. Ricketts	£3,342	Manchester 321	T71/860, NDO4/1
Hammersley & Co.	Bank ceased on Hugh Hammersley's death in 1840	Agent	H. Hammersley of H. H. and M. J. Popplewell for Harry Hackshaw	£5,657	St Vincent 484	T71/892, NDO4/10

Firm	Predecessor Firm of	Capacity	Banker	Award	Claim	Source
Hanburys, Taylor & Lloyd			cc as mortgagee of annuity of £150 payable to James Gray of Dundee on Friendship	N/M	Hanover 7	T71/872
			cc as judgement creditors v. Edward Hyde East for £3,270 11s 10d, apparently settled	£3,270	St Andrew 171	T71/865
					St Mary 11, 14, 15, 17, 153	T71/856
Hankeys & Co.	RBSG	Beneficiary	WAH and TH bankers' owners Counter-claim by W. A. Hankey (exor of Thomas Hankey) and J. B. Hankey (heir-at-law of Thomas Hankey), both as mortgagees of certain slaves on Ackindown Pen and New Hope estate of J. G. Campbell	£5,777	Trelawny 25–27 Westmoreland 213, 465	T71/874 T71/871
Hoares						
Hopkinson, Chas Barton & Co.						
Loyd Jones						
Jones & Son						
Chas King						
G. F. Kinloch						
Ladbrokes, Kingscote						

Firm	Bank/Status	Role	Name	Amount	Estate	Reference
Lawson, Newham London & Westminster Lee, Brassey, Farr & Lee						
Sir J. W. Lubbock, Bart.	RBSG Merged with Agra Bank 1866, ceased 1900	Agent	Edward Forster of Sir J. W. Lubbock for John A. G. Clarke	£1,187	Westmoreland 537	T71/871, NDO4/1
Masterman, Peters, Mildred & Co.		Agent	W. Masterman for Anthony Wilkinson	£2,855	Manchester 306	T71/860, NDO4/1
Pocklington & Lacy						
Praed & Co.	Lloyds	Agent	B. J. M. Praed of Praeds, Sir J. Mackworth, Vere for Lt-Gen. John Mitchell	£2,652	St John 215	T71/854, NDO4/4
			Geo. Grote for William Forster Stewart	£1,287	Dominica 474	T71/881, NDO4/9
Prescott, Grote	RBSG	Agent	Geo. Grote for William Rose	£2,443	St Andrew 317	T71/865, NDO4/3
Sir Chas Price, Marryat & Coleman	Stopped payment 1866	Beneficiary	cc as judgement creditors for £3,481 15s 6d, July 1835 against Philip Brown's 1/6th of Morant estate	£3,481	St Thomas-in-the-East 507	T71/867
		Agent	Chas Price for Richard Watt	£4,485	Westmoreland 84	T71/871, NDO4/1

Firm	Predecessor Firm of	Capacity	Banker	Award	Claim	Source
Puget, Bainbridge Ransom & Co.			A. W. Robarts as mortgagee Counter-claim by Robarts	£1,517	Dominica 320A	T71/881,
Robarts, Curtis & Robarts	RBSG	Beneficiary agent	Curtis on St Toolie's estate (List E)	£3,499	Clarendon 294	T71/859, T71/915
			A. W. Robarts for Metcalfe family	£1,159	Dominica 5	T71/881, NDO4/9
Rogers, Towgood, Olding & Co.	Merged with English Joint Stock Bank, failed 1866	Beneficiary	John Towgood counter-claimed successfully for unpaid purchase money on Somersalls from free coloured, J. K. Edmeade	£1,129	St Kitts 464	T71/879
Sir C. Scott						
Smith, Payne & Smith	RBSG	Beneficiary	Lord Carrington & Samuel Smith, 'absentees, owners-in-fee' of Farm Pen	£4,908	St Catherine 538	T71/852
			George Robert Smith from claim by Samuel, George, John Abel, Samuel George and G. R. Smith for 3/8 of Holland estate	£778	St Elizabeth 535c	T71/870
			J. W. Freshfield/John Beadnell as attorneys for Samuel Smith and others on Bourkes	£2,683	St Kitts 525	T71/879

Role	Name / Description	Amount	Location	Reference
	George Robert Smith on Estridges & Estridges Bramble J. W. Freshfield/John Beadnell as trustees for SPS	£2,466	St Kitts 749, 752	T71/879
	Cunnynghams and Estridge J. W. Freshfield/John Beadnell shown in T71/894 as owners,	£4,116	St Kitts 333, 746	T71/879
	but T71/519, p. 2410 identifies SPS as owners, late the property of Mannng & Anderdon	£4,333	Trinidad 1661	T71/894, T71/519
	George Robert Smith, counter-claim by SPS as mortgagees of Plantation Friends	£14,689	British Guiana 167	T71/885
Trustee	Martin Tucker Smith counter-claimed as one amongst several trustees for Messrs Findlay Ballantyne & Co., of mortgage 1819 for £15,898	N/M	St Lucia 317	T71/884
	Abel Smith and G. R. Smith for Thomas Kirkpatrick Hall	£11,835	St James 55, 188, 652	T71/873, NDO4/5
	Geo. Beadnell for Simon Taylor	£516	St Ann 68	T71/857, NDO4/3
	Geo. Beadnell for Maurice Jones	£8,000	Portland 1	T71/868, NDO4/3
Agent	Geo. Beadnell for Philip Hearn	£1,018	St Thomas-in-the-East 4 / Portland 4	T71/867, NDO4/5 / T71/868, NDO4/3
	Geo. Beadnell for Arthur R. Jones	£594	Portland 200	T71/868, NDO4/3

Firm	Predecessor Firm of	Capacity	Banker	Award	Claim	Source
Robert Snow, Wm Strahan, J. D. Paul	Failed 1856–7	Agent	Sir J. D. Paul for Francis Acres Hyde	£667	Hanover 56	T71/872, NDO4/1
			Sir John Dean Paul for the Coulthurst family	£3,072	Barbados 4950	T71/899, NDO4/7
		Trustee?	Robert Snow [?] and William Curtis awarded compensation on Creighton Hall estate, apparently as trustees	£4,532	St David 70	T71/866
Spooner, Attwoods						
Stevenson, Salt	Lloyds	Agent	J. Salt for Geo. Johnson	£686	Hanover 477	T71/872, NDO4/1
			J. S. Salt for Viscount St Vincent's family	£3,529	Westmoreland 232	T71/871, NDO4/1
Stone, Martin & Stones	Barclays	Agent	J. Martin of G. Stone etc. for T. H. A. Earle	£3,605	St Kitts 93, 95	T71/879, NDO4/11
			J. Martin of SMS for James Kelly	£4,086	St Thomas-in-the-East 217	T71/867, NDO4/5
R. G. Twining, John Aldred						
Vere Sapte	RBSG	Beneficiary	Counter-claim from John Vere of late firm of Vere & Ward, mortgagee by assignment dated 29 January 1830 (List E)	£9,235	British Guiana 2349	T71/887
F. Wakefield						

		Role	Details	Amount	Place	Reference
Whitmore, Wells & Whitmore	Failed 1841	Beneficiary	cc as assignee of mortgage for £7,500 currency on the Harrow estate	B£7500	Barbados 2959	T71/897
			cc by Whitmores as mortgagees under agreement of 12 January 1836 v. A. Mackintosh	£1,662	Trinidad 981, 1327, 1548	T71/893, T71/894
			Other Trinidad awards	£940	Trinidad 936, 1042, 1551	T71/893, T71/894
		Trustee	Ed. Whitmore for Chas Kensington	£1,250	Tobago 57	T71/891
		Agent?	J. B. Wells for:			
			Hannah Harriott	£2,138	St Elizabeth 335	T71/870, NDO4/4
			Frances Greenwood	£546	St Elizabeth 578	T71/870, NDO4/4
			Joan L Spence	£919	St Elizabeth 729	T71/870, NDO4/4
			For J. M. H. Minvielle in appeal to Privy Council	£3,310	St Lucia 495	T71/884, T71/1609
Williams, Deacon, Labouchere	RBSG	Trustee	John Deacon of Birch Lane as trustee of J. Inglis	£9,478	Manchester 441	T71/860
					St John 206	T71/854
					St Lucia 754	T71/884
					St Thomas-in-the-Vale 41	T71/855
		Agent	J. T. H. Melville of Williams, Deacon for John Graham	£1,022	British Guiana 1114	T71/886, NDO4/8
			J. Labouchere for George Pearse, W. G. Burn, Mary K. Hewitt	£3,731	St Elizabeth 1022, 1024	T71/870, NDO4/4

Firm	Predecessor Firm of	Capacity	Banker	Award	Claim	Source
Willis Percival Wright & Co.			J. T. Melville and H. S. Thornton for Luke Thomas Crossley	£11,784	St George 44, 71, 248	T71/869, NDO4/4
					St Mary 52	T71/856, NDO4/5
			J. Labouchere for Sir Jas Ferguson and Sir D. H. Blair	£3,591	St Thomas-in-the-East 510	T71/867, NDO4/5

The complete list of sixty banks is drawn from 'Bankers', *Boyle's Fashionable Court Guide and Town Visiting Directory for April 1835* (London, 1835), pp. 690–2. The list in *Boyle's* combines City and West End bankers, traditionally defined as those east and west of Temple Bar, but excludes what became the 'merchant banks', such as Barings or Rothschild.

[1] K. M. Butler, *The economics of Emancipation: Jamaica and Barbados, 1823–1843* (Chapel Hill: University of North Carolina Press, 1995), pp. 54–5.

[2] W. H. Smith of 'Fuller & Addison' collected £2,839 for Thomas Crookenden (St Vincent No. 604). No evidence has been found to tie Fuller & Addison to Fullers & Co.

Appendix 17 Slave-owners and other connections to slavery in Marylebone

UPPER HARLEY STREET/HARLEY STREET, 1790–1850

		New Road	
Frederick Huth[1]	33	32	
	34	31	Pascoe St Leger Grenfell[2]
Gilbert N. Neyle[3]	35	30	
William T. Hibbert[4]	36	29	
	37	28	
J. H. Deffell[5]	38	27	
	39	26	
	40	25	John Lavicount Anderdon[6]
	41	24	George Cunningham[7] Samuel Cunningham[8]
	42	23	
	43(18)	22	
	44(19)	21	
Sir William Struth[9]	45	20	
		19	
		18	
		17	Joseph Timperon[10] Jos. Dobinson[11] R. W. Dallas[12]
		16	
		15	
		14	John Lavicount Anderdon[13]
		13(13)	

361

New Road

	Devonshire Street			
Chaloner Arcedeckne[14] Samuel Bosanquet[15]	46(21)		12(12)	Sir John Dalling[16] William Mitchell[17]
	47(22)		11	
	48(23)		10(10)	Mrs Baillie[18]
K. Osborne[19]	49		9	
	50		8(8)	William Dickinson[20]
Sir Henry William Martin[21]	51(26)		7	
	52(27)		6(6)	William Beckford[22]
Hans Sloane/Stephen Fuller[23] Rowland Mitchell[24]	53		5(5)	
	54		4(4)	
Spencer Mackay[25]	55(30)		3	
	56(31)		2(2)	
	57		1(1)	George Smith[26]
	Weymouth Street			
	44(38)		43	
Edward Protheroe[27]	45(39)		42	
	46		41	
	47		40(34)	Sir George Harnage[28]
Jer. Milles/Mrs Milles/Rowland Alston[29]	48(42)		39(33)	Misses Chauncy[30]
Sir Henry Martin[31] Charles Heaton Ellis[32]	49(43)		38	
	50		37	
C. Codrington[33]	51(45)		36(30)	John Oliver[34] Lady Dalling[35]
	52(46)		35	
	53(47)		34(28)	Henry John Blagrove[36]
Evan Baillie[37]	54		33(27)	
	55(49)		32	
William Mitchell Jr[38] Mrs Mitchell	56(50)		31(25)	James Dawkins[39]
			30(24)	
	Great Marylebone Street – New Cavendish Street			
[Lloyds Reading Room]			29	

New Road

	58*(51)*		28*(23)*	Henry Shirley[40]
	59		27	
Miss Deffell[41]	60*(53)*		26*(21)*	
	61*(54)*		25	
	62*(55)*		24*(19)*	
	63		23*(18)*	Alexander Baillie[42]
	64		22	
Francis Willock[43]	65		21	
Sir Wm Young, Bart.[44]	66*(59)*		20	
	67*(60)*		19*(14)*	Mrs Nasmyth[45]
Robert Taylor[46]	68*(61)*		18*(13)*	
Mrs Taylor[47]	69*(62)*		17*(12)*	Mrs Baillie[48]
Sir Abraham Elton[49]	70*(63)*		16*(11)*	Col. Delap[50]
	71		15	
			14*(9)*	

Queen Anne Street

	72		13*(8)*	James Gordon Duff[51]
	73		12*(7)*	Miss Chauncy[52]
	74		11	*Mrs Hibbert*[53] Mrs Taylor[54]
	75		10	James Lewis[55]
Simon Halliday[56] *Thomas Cussans*[57]	76*(68)*		9*(4)*	
	77*(69)*		8	
Samuel Hibbert jun.[58]	78(70)		7*(2)*	
	79*(71)*		6*(1)*	George Watson Taylor[59] C. Davison Kerr[60]
	80*(72)*		5	
	81		4	
	82*(74)*		3	
Mrs Blagrove[61]	83		2	
	84		1	
James Dawkins[62]	85*(77)*			
	86			
	87*(79)*			

Notes to Appendix 17 (*cont.*)

Harley Street and Upper Harley Street were re-numbered between 1824 and 1829. The old numbers where clearly identifiable are shown in italics.

[1] Frederick Huth. Assignee of slave-compensation. London merchant who counter-claimed, apparently successfully, for five-eighths of the compensation for 285 slaves on the Vrouw Anna estate in British Guiana (British Guiana No. 2398) in 1836–7. *Boyle's Fashionable Court Guide and Town Visiting Directory* (London, 1838, 1846).

[2] Pascoe St Leger Grenfell. Mortgagee. Partner in London banking firm of Sir James Esdaile, and awarded £4,121 19s 0d compensation with his fellow-partners as mortgagees-in-possession of 216 slaves on the Hazelymph estate in Jamaica (St James No. 5). *Boyle's* 1829.

[3] Gilbert N. Neyle. Married daughter of a slave-owner. Neyle died on 17 February 1834. His widow, Charlotte Parke Neyle (who died in Italy in 1839), the daughter of William Parke of Jamaica, was awarded £555 9s 4d for twenty-nine slaves on Beverley and £25 0s 9d for two slaves, presumably personal servants (St Ann Nos. 712, 26). William Parke himself was a major recipient of compensation. *Royal Blue Book, Fashionable Directory* (London, 1831). Gilbert N. Neyle, *Robson's British Court and Parliamentary Guide for 1832* (London, 1832). G. N. Neyle, 35 Upper Harley Street.

[4] William T[etlow] Hibbert. Slave-owner and mortgagee. Member of London merchant firm G., W. & S. Hibbert, which was paid £38,603 in compensation for several hundred enslaved over whom the Hibberts held mortgages, including Clarendon Nos. 333, 358; Portland No. 268; St James Nos. 169, 184; St Mary Nos. 30, 132; Trelawny Nos. 126, 133, 667. *Boyle's* 1829 shows William T. Hibbert at No. 36.

[5] John Henry Deffell. Slave-owner. London merchant (J. H. Deffell & Co., 3 Billiter Court; *Post Office London Directory* (London, 1836)). Received compensation as owner of 1,141 enslaved on various estates in Jamaica, including Retreat and Hampstead (Trelawny Nos. 385, 387), Salt Spring (St James No. 760) and Swansea (St John No. 69). Correspondence in *The Times* regarding mortality on Salt Spring (*The Times*, 27 March 1832 and 3 April 1832, p. 1). *Boyle's* 1824, 1829, 1835, 1838, 1846.

[6] John Lavicount Anderdon. Partner in Manning & Anderdon, the West India merchant, mortgagee and slave-owner, and son of John Proctor Anderdon. John Proctor Anderdon was awarded £2,491 16s 1d for 180 slaves on Seaforth estate in 1835 (Antigua No. 17). John Lavicount Anderdon signed for his father's slave-compensation at the National Debt Office. Manning & Anderdon was bankrupt in 1831, and the compensation for its slaves went to its creditors, notably the banking firm of Smith, Payne and Smith. *Boyle's* 1824 (old No. 14), *Boyle's* 1829 (new No. 25).

[7] George and Samuel Cunningham. Slave-owners. Together with James Cunningham of Bristol, Samuel ('of London') and George Cunningham shared the compensation for 68 slaves on Paradise Pen (as trustees) and 28 slaves on Ramble Pen as owners (St James No. 555, 562). Samuel Cunningham was also awarded the compensation for 193 slaves on Manchester, 175 on Roslin and 27 on Roslin Castle (Trelawny Nos. 45, 177, 178); George Cunningham was awarded the compensation for 228 slaves on Greenside and 155 on the Maxfield estates (Trelawny Nos. 633, 635). *Boyle's* 1829 (George) and 1835 (Samuel).

[8] Samuel Cunningham: see above, n. 8.

[9] Sir William John Struth (1762–1850). Slave-owner. Mayor of Bristol, acting Governor of St Vincent and Grenadines 1829–31. Claimed £3,527 2s 0d for 137 enslaved on Fancy estate (St Vincent No. 447) and £8,513 18s 10d for 315 enslaved on Prospect (St Vincent No. 505). *Boyle's* 1819 for Sir William Struth at old No. 20 Upper Harley Street.

[10] Joseph Timperon and Joseph Dobinson. Slave-owners and mortgagees. London merchants. Awarded a combined total of £36,575 in compensation in the 1830s (St

Mary Nos. 128, 129, 134, 310, 311, 312; St Dorothy No. 21; St Thomas-in-the-East Nos. 129, 134, 214, 215, 216). *Boyle's* 1805, 1811 for Timperon; 1819 for Dobinson.

[11] Joseph Dobinson: see above, n. 11.

[12] R. W. Dallas. Tentative identification as slave-owner. Robert W. Dallas shared with Sir Robert C. Dallas half the compensation for 158 slaves on Mountraven (sp.?) estate in Grenada (Grenada No. 692). *Royal Blue Book, Fashionable Directory* (London, 1846).

[13] John Lavicount Anderdon: see above, n. 7.

[14] Chaloner Arcedeckne (*c*.1743–1809). Slave-owner. Born in Jamaica, came to England 1765 and remained here as an absentee owner. Member of Parliament for Westbury, 1780–4. Owned Golden Grove in St Thomas-in-the-East in Jamaica; B. W. Higman, *Plantation Jamaica 1750–1850: capital and control in a colonial economy* (Mona, Jamaica: University of the West Indies Press, 2005), pp. 147–8. His son Andrew was paid compensation for 200 slaves on Golden Grove and 116 on Bachelor's Hall Pen in 1835. *Boyle's* 1792, 1796, 1805.

[15] Samuel Bosanquet. Mortgagee. With partners in the banking firm Bosanquet Anderdon, Samuel Bosanquet was awarded the compensation for 224 slaves on Clifton's, Paynes and Morton's Bay and for 19 slaves on Meales (Nevis Nos. 132, 76). The partners also shared with others in the compensation for 115 slaves under Nevis No. 42. Samuel Bosanquet of Dingeston Court, Monmouthshire, and Forest House (*Boyle's* 1829). *Boyle's* 1824 (No. 21 old), 1829, 1835, 1838 (No. 46 new); Mrs Bosanquet, *Boyle's* 1846 (No. 46 new).

[16] Sir John Dalling was governor of Jamaica, 1772–4. His son Sir William Windham Dalling, Bart. collected compensation for slaves and lived at No. 57 Wimpole Street. *Boyle's*, 1792.

[17] William Mitchell. Slave-owner. 'King' William Mitchell, Jamaica planter. *Boyle's* 1796, 1805, 1811, 1819 (William Mitchell); *Boyle's* 1824, 1829, 1835 (Mrs Mitchell).

[18] Mrs Baillie of 10 Upper Harley Street and Ealing Grove. Annuitant and widow of slave-owner James Baillie, MP, who died in 1793. James Baillie, brother of Evan Baillie Sr, was a major owner of estates in Grenada, including Hermitage and Bacolet. He bequeathed his widow an annuity of £3,000 per annum to be funded from the sale of most of his estates. *Boyle's* 1796 for Mrs Baillie at old No. 10. See also Mrs Baillie at old No. 12 Harley Street, *Boyle's* 1819 and 1824; and at new No. 17 Harley Street and Ealing Grove, *Boyle's* 1829.

[19] Kean Osborn. Slave-owner. Former speaker of House of Assembly in Jamaica. Kean Osborn of Upper Harley Street and Jamaica died near Geneva in 1820; *The Times*, 21 September 1820, p. 4. Compensation for 96 slaves on Richmond Park in Clarendon, 156 slaves on Mountpelier in St Thomas-in-the-East and for 321 slaves on Caswell Hill in Vere paid to Elizabeth Osborn and Joseph Brooks Yates as executors and trustees of Kean Osborn (Clarendon No. 278; St Thomas-in-the-East No. 299; Vere No. 65). *Boyle's* 1811.

[20] William Dickinson. Slave-owner. Awarded compensation with Ezekiel and Jeremiah Harman for three estates in St Elizabeth (Nos. 5, 368, 395). Member of Parliament for Ilchester, 1796–1802; Lostwithiel, 1802–6; Somerset, 1806–31. *Boyle's* 1792, 1796, 1805, 1811, 1819, 1824 (No. 8 old); 1829, 1835 (No. 8 new); Frank Dickinson, *Boyle's* 1838, 1846 (No. 8 new).

[21] Sir Henry William Martin (1758–1842) received £4,454 2s 6d for 319 slaves on Green Castle estate in Antigua in 1835 (Antigua No. 19). The family's slave-ownership in Antigua derived initially from his great grandfather Samuel Martin, who settled in Antigua from Dublin in the late seventeenth century. Sir Henry William Martin was an anti-abolitionist activist who published in 1823 a pamphlet, 'A

Notes to Appendix 17 (*cont.*)

counter-appeal to "An Appeal" from William Wilberforce Esq. MP', which was sold at Lloyds Reading Rooms in Harley Street. The pro-slavery pamphlet argued that the freeing of the enslaved without the consent of the slave-owners would be 'a flagrant breach of National Honour, Hostile to the Principles of Religion, Justice and Humanity and highly injurious to the planter and to the slave'. Sir Henry William Martin died at his house in Upper Harley Street in 1842; Obituaries, *Gentleman's Magazine*, May 1842, p. 552. He lived on Upper Harley Street for forty years. *Boyle's* 1805, 1811, 1819, 1824 (old No. 26); 1829, 1835, 1838 (new No. 51).

[22] William Beckford. Slave-owner. The Gothic author of *Vathek* etc. Recipient of slave-compensation in the 1830s, for enslaved on Dank's, Beckford's Rock River and Retreat (Clarendon Nos. 13, 168, 179). William Beckford of Harley Street and Fonthill, *Boyle's* 1811.

[23] Hans Sloane and Stephen Fuller. Fuller was a member of a major family of Jamaican slave-owners and the longstanding Agent for Jamaica, leading the fight against abolition of the slave-trade. Fuller was the father-in-law and uncle of Hans Sloane [Stanley], the MP. *Boyle's* 1792 and 1796 for Stephen Fuller and Hans Sloane, *Boyle's* 1805, 1811, 1819, 1824 for Hans Sloane Stanley.

[24] Rowland Mitchell. Slave-owner and mortgagee. Partner in W., R. & S. Mitchell & Co. See William Mitchell Jr at 56 Harley Street (below, n. 39). *Boyle's* 1835, 1838.

[25] Spencer Mackay. Slave-owner. Received £12,722 18s 1d for 240 slaves on Plantation Cane Grove (British Guiana No. 592) in 1835, and £10,696 7s 8d for half the 408 slaves on Plantation Lusignan (British Guiana No. 562A). Member of anti-abolitionist West India Committee; *The Times*, 11 February 1824, p. 3. *Boyle's* 1835, 1838; *Royal Blue Book* 1846.

[26] George Smith. Mortgagee. Partner in Smith, Payne & Smith, a major beneficiary of slave-compensation, MP. *Boyle's* 1811, 1819, 1824, 1829.

[27] Edward Protheroe. Mortgagee. Awarded a share of the compensation for 315 enslaved on Prospect estate (St Vincent No. 505). Member of Parliament for Bristol, 1812–20. Possibly also owner of 72 enslaved on Endeavour estate (Trinidad No. 1701) in 1836. *Boyle's* 1811, 1819.

[28] Sir George Harnage. Slave-owner. London merchant. Compensation for 177 slaves on Boarded Hall in Barbados, contested in 1830s between trustees for an annuity to Sir George's widow Lady Harnage and Sir George's mortgagee (Barbados No. 3653). *Boyle's* 1824 for old No. 34.

[29] Jeremiah Milles/Mrs Milles/Rowland Alston. Slave-owners. Rowland Alston and his son Rowland G. Alston were paid £2,505 4s 11d in 1836 for 122 enslaved on the Georgia estate in St Thomas-in-the-East in Jamaica. The estate belonged to Rose Milles, who was Jeremiah Milles's daughter and Rowland Alston's wife. Alston was elected MP for Hertfordshire in 1835. The family lived in Harley Street for over fifty years. Jeremiah Milles, *Boyle's* 1792, 1796; Mrs Milles, *Boyle's* 1805, 1811, 1819, 1824 (all old No. 42); Mrs Milles and Rowland Alston, *Boyle's* 1829, 1835 (new No. 48); Rowland Alston alone, *Boyle's* 1838, 1846 (new No. 48).

[30] Misses Chauncy. Members of slave-owning family. Misses Chauncy of Theobalds, Herts, *Boyle's* 1824, old No. 33. See also below, n. 53 for old No.7/new No. 12 Harley Street.

[31] Sir Henry Martin, who died in 1794, was the owner of slaves in Antigua and the father of Sir Henry William Martin (see above, n. 22 for Sir Henry William Martin at No. 51 Upper Harley Street). *Boyle's* 1792.

[32] Charles Heaton Ellis. Awarded part of slave-compensation for 315 enslaved as trustee for the wife of Charles Struth, who had an annuity of £300 secured on

the Prospect estate (St Vincent No. 505). Shown in Slave Compensation records as Charles Ellis Heaton, but reassumed the surname of Ellis in 1838; *Gentleman's Magazine* September 1838, p. 318. *Royal Blue Book* 1846.

33 Christopher Codrington. Slave-owner. Sir Christopher Codrington was awarded £22,422 compensation in 1835 for 1,539 enslaved on 6 estates in Antigua, including the island of Barbuda, granted by the Crown to Codrington's family (Antigua Nos. 101, 329, 332, 334, 338, 558). *Boyle's* 1796.

34 John Oliver. Slave-owner. Married Jane Catherine Sarah Long of the family that owned Longville in Jamaica. Two-thirds of the compensation for eighty-one slaves on Longville paid in 1836 to Jane Catherine S. Oliver, John Oliver's widow, and to Thomas Long Oliver, presumably their son (Clarendon No. 404). *Boyle's* 1819, 1824 (old No. 30); John Oliver, new No. 36 Harley Street and Hoole Hall, *Boyles* 1829.

35 Lady Dalling was the widow of Sir John Dalling, governor of Jamaica. See above, n. 17 for Sir John Dalling of 12 Upper Harley Street. *Boyle's* 1805 for Lady Dalling at old No. 30 Harley Street.

36 Henry John Blagrove. From a slave-owning family, inherited estates in Jamaica. Son of F. R. Coore and grandson of John Blagrove, the owner of 1,500 slaves, who died in 1824. Compensation for John Blagrove's former estate, including Cardiff Hall and Orange Bay, went into Chancery in the case of John William Blagrove, a lunatic (St Ann No. 544B, Hanover No. 503) and to John Blagrove's executors (St Ann Nos. 542, 543, 544). Compensation for 293 slaves on Frederick Richard Coore's Pembroke estate was awarded in 1837 to Foster Lechmere Coore and Thomas Fitzgerald as executors and trustees of F. R. Coore (Trelawny No. 422). 'F. L. Coore dies in Harley St.', *The Times*, 27 June 1837, p. 7. Henry John Blagrove, the Misses Coore, R. J. L. Coore, *Boyle's* 1846.

37 Evan Baillie. Member of the slave-owning Baillie family, son of Peter Baillie and grandson of Evan Baillie Sr, who died in 1835. The Evan Baillie who claimed as trustee for slave-compensation on Hermitage estate in Grenada (Grenada No. 701) was probably the grandfather rather than this Evan Baillie. *Boyle's* 1838.

38 William Mitchell Jr. Slave-owner. Partner in the firm of William, Rowland & Samuel Mitchell & Co., West India merchants who (after William Mitchell's death in 1828) were awarded £61,289 for slaves on multiple estates in Jamaica. *Boyle's* 1819, 1824 (William Mitchell Jr at old No. 50); *Boyle's* 1829, 1835 (Mrs Mitchell, new No. 56).

39 James Dawkins (1760–1843). Slave-owner. Member of Parliament for Chippenham, 1784–1806, 1807, 1808–12; Hastings, 1812–26; Wiltshire, 1831–2. Son of Henry Dawkins of Over Norton, brother of G. H. Dawkins Pennant and Henry Dawkins. Slave-compensation for several estates in Jamaica was awarded to Dawkins' trustees and possibly mortgagees, John Biddulph and Samuel Pepys Cockerell (Clarendon Nos. 1, 2, 7, 11. 277; St Catherine Nos. 499, 515). *Boyle's* 1792 for Dawkins at old No. 25 Harley Street; *Boyle's* 1796, 1805, 1811 for Dawkins at old No. 77.

40 Henry Shirley. Slave-owner. Shirley's trustees, Rev. George Porcher and Rev. Chas W. Davy, were paid compensation for slaves on Hyde Hall and Etingdon (Trelawny Nos. 110–12), on which Shirley was tenant-in-tail. *Boyle's* 1805 (old No. 23).

41 Miss Deffell. Tentative identification of 'Miss Deffell' as the woman with whom Henry, the future Cardinal Manning, had a love-affair, and as the daughter of the slave-owner and merchant John Henry Deffell (see above, n. 6 for John Henry Deffell at 38 Upper Harley Street). Edmund S. Purcell's *Life of Cardinal Manning* (1896) does not clearly identify Miss Deffell as the daughter of John Henry Deffell, but refers to her two brothers and Henry Manning as being fellow Harrovians, and to her remaining a spinster for the rest of her life. John Henry Deffell's third son was certainly at Harrow in the early 1830s (*Australian Dictionary of National Biography* for George Henry Deffell). *Royal Blue Book* 1846 and *Boyle's* 1846.

Note to Appendix 17 (*cont.*)

[42] Alexander Baillie. Alexander Baillie, 'late of Harley Street Esq., at present abroad' counter-claimed under the will of Matthew Higgins for the compensation for 294 slaves (British Guiana No. 2409) and for 165 slaves on Deutzchem (British Guiana No. 125B). *Boyle's* 1819.

[43] Francis Willock. Tentative identification only. A Francis Willock is shown in compensation claims by Sir Henry Willock as heir-at-law of Francis Willock for estates on Antigua, Mount Pleasant and Blizard's, for which Sir Henry Willock contested the compensation in 1836 (Antigua No. 24, 365). Elsewhere, however, Sir Henry is shown as the heir-at-law of his brother, Frank Gore Willock. *Boyle's* 1792 for Francis Willock at old No. 58.

[44] Sir William Young, second Baronet. Slave-owner. Governor of Tobago, 1807–15. The fourth Baronet, who pursued slave compensation unsuccessfully, lived at No. 24 Upper Wimpole Street.

[45] Mrs Nasmyth. Slave-owner. Mary Sarah Nasmyth claimed compensation as guardian of Robert Nasmyth (since deceased) for 225 slaves on Water Valley estate (St Mary No. 144); the compensation was awarded to her and trustees for Miss Nasmyth's marriage settlement. *Old Bailey Sessions* t18180506–93 shows Mary Sarah Nasmyth, widow of Lower Harley Street. Jamaica Almanacks 1826–33 show Water Valley owned by M. S. Nasmyth. *Boyle's* 1819, 1824 show Mrs Nasmyth at old No. 14 Harley Street; *Boyle's* 1829 shows her at No. 19 new.

[46] Robert Taylor (*c.*1742–1823). Slave-owner. London merchant and agent of Jamaican planter Simon Taylor; Higman, *Plantation Jamaica*, p. 145. A Robert Taylor (possibly son of this Robert Taylor) was paid £4,163 19s 7d for 209 slaves on Lucky Valley estate (Port Royal No. 53) and £2,403 0s 10d for 125 slaves on Leith Hall (St Thomas-in-the-East No. 275) in 1835. *Boyle's* 1819 shows Robert Taylor at No. 61 Harley Street and Amber [*sic*] Court, Surrey. In fact, the Surrey estate was Ember Court; Higman, *Plantation Jamaica*, p. 145.

[47] Mrs Taylor. Robert Taylor's widow. *Boyle's* 1824 for No. 61 old. *Boyle's* 1829, 1835, 1838 show her at No. 61 new; *Boyle's* 1829 shows her as 'Ambercourt Surrey'.

[48] See above, n. 19 for Mrs Baillie at 10 Upper Harley Street.

[49] Sir Abraham Elton. Fifth Baronet. Although from the Bristol family of Clevedon Court, which was founded upon the slave-trade, the fifth Baronet was a clergyman close to Hannah More and moved in Evangelical circles. *Boyle's* 1792.

[50] Col. Delap (James Bogle Delap). Slave-owner. Awarded £4,940 10s 3d for 255 slaves on Mount Eagle (Westmoreland No. 255). Col. Delap is shown in *Boyle's* 1819 (old No. 11), 1829, 1835, 1838 (Lt-Col. Delap). *Boyle's* 1829 and 1835 show also a Stoke Park address for Col. Delap. *Register of electors for Marylebone* 1840–1 identifies James Bogle Delap at 16 Harley Street. James Bogle Delap of Stoke Park Surrey = deputy-lieutenant of Surrey, b. 1779, m. 1809 Harriet Hillier, heiress of Nathaniel Hillier of Stoke Park (*Burke's* 1846).

[51] James Gordon Duff. Creditor of slave-owners, probably as trade-creditor. James Gordon Duff 'of London' was awarded £468 0s 2d for thirty-five slaves after counter-claiming with James Gordon of Madeira, Wm Henry Ingliss of London and James Bean of Madeira as judgement creditors (Barbados No. 1710). Birth of son in Harley Street to wife of James Gordon Duff of Madeira, *The Times*, 15 February 1832, p. 4. *Boyle's* 1835, 1838.

[52] Miss Chauncy. From slave-owning family. Daughter of Charles Snell Chauncy of Theobalds (1759–1809), and sister of Nathaniel Snell Chauncy and Charles Snell Chauncy the younger. The family firm of Chauncy, Lang was the fourth largest

mercantile recipient of slave-compensation in the 1830s (£121,664), lived at No. 23 Wimpole Street Nathaniel Snell Chauncy. *Boyle's* 1819 identifies Miss Chauncy as of old No. 7 Harley Street and Theobalds, Herts.

53 Mrs Hibbert. No identification, but probably widow of slave-owning Hibbert family of Jamaica and England. *Boyle's* 1811 (old No. 6).

54 Mrs Taylor: see above, n. 48 for Mrs Taylor at 68 (old No. 61) Harley Street. *Boyle's* 1829, 1835, 1838.

55 James Lewis. Slave-owner. James Lewis 'of Clifton' received compensation for 260 slaves on Lewisburgh estate in Jamaica (St Mary Nos. 75, 76). Ex-speaker of Jamaican House of Representatives. Commissioner of Compensation. 'Wedding of son of James Lewis of Harley Street to eldest daughter of James Cunningham of Rodney-place Clifton', *The Times*, 22 July 1840, p. 7. 'Death of Ann Redwood Lewis spinster, daughter of James Lewis deceased formerly of Rodney-place Clifton', *The Times*, 5 December 1848, p. 0 [*sic*]. *Boyle's* 1838.

56 Simon Halliday. Slave-owner. Owned the Castle Wemyss estate in St James, Jamaica, the compensation for which (£3,168 12s 8d for 165 slaves) went to Simon Halliday's heir, the Rev. Walter Stevenson Halliday in 1836. Simon Halliday was a banker, partner in Herries, Farquhar, Halliday, and had taken possession of Castle Wemyss in 1823. *Boyle's* 1811 for Simon Halliday at old No. 68.

57 Thomas Cussans. Tentative identification only. The Cussans family owned Amity Hall in Jamaica, and Thomas Cussans was awarded half the compensation for the 199 slaves (St Thomas-in-the-East No. 105). The heirs of Thomas Cussans claimed for 275 slaves on Winchester, but lost to Vice-Admiral R. Lambert, devisee of his mother who was the devisee of the Thomas Cussans who died in 1796 (St Thomas-in-the-East No. 119). The Thomas Cussans at 68 Harley Street in 1819 may be the Thomas Cussans who mortgaged Amity Hall to Ebenezer Maitland in 1797, but this is speculative. *Boyle's* 1819.

58 Samuel Hibbert. Slave-owner. Partner in G., W. & S. Hibbert. See notes on William Tetlow Hibbert at 36 Upper Harley Street. *Boyle's* 1819, 1824 (old No. 70, Samuel Hibbert Jr); *Boyle's* 1829 (new No. 78, Samuel Hibbert Jr); 1835, 1838 (Samuel Hibbert).

59 George Watson Taylor. Slave-owner. Married niece of Simon Taylor of Jamaica who inherited Simon Taylor's fortune from her brother. Member of Parliament for various constituencies from 1816, latterly for Devizes (1826–32). Owner of Haughton Grove Pen and Haughton Court Estate (Hanover Nos. 21, 577); Holland and Lysson's estates and Burrowfields Pen (St Thomas-in-the-East Nos. 100, 297, 457); Montrose and Flint River Pens and Llanrumney estate (St Mary's Nos. 26, 247). Compensation for 'his' enslaved was paid to his trustees after he ran into financial trouble in the 1830s. *Boyle's* 1819 (old No. 1).

60 Crawford Davison Kerr. Merchant (Baillie, Kerr, 23 Threadneedle Street). Trustee (in Slave Compensation records as Davison Kerr Crawford). Awarded compensation on behalf of Ellen Welchman for his share in 187 slaves on Philadelphia (British Guiana No. 378). *Boyle's* 1835, 1838.

61 Mrs Blagrove. Tentative identification only as widow of John Blagrove. See above, n. 37 for Henry John Blagrove at No. 34 Harley Street. *Boyle's* 1829. By the late 1830s, Mrs Blagrove is listed at 21 Welbeck Street (*Boyle's* 1838).

62 James Dawkins. See above, n. 40 for Dawkins at 31 Harley Street. *Boyle's* 1796, 1805, 1811.

Bibliography

SOURCES BEFORE c.1850

NATIONAL ARCHIVES, KEW

Records created and inherited by HM Treasury: Office of Registry of Colonial Slavery and Slave Compensation Commission Records
T71/1–671 Slave registers, 1817–32
T71/672–84 London Office miscellanea, including in-letters
T71/685–851 Valuers' returns
T71/852–914 Registers of claims
T71/915–42 Indexes to claims
T71/943–1173 Claims and certificates, original
T71/1174–1293 Counter-claims
T71/1294–1309 Adjudications in counter-claims
T71/1310–77 Lists of awards
T71/1378–99 Special awards in trust
T71/1400–22 Parliamentary Return of awards
T71/1423–1500 Commission hearing notes
T71/1501–62 Assistant commission proceedings
T71/1563–89 Accounts
T71/1590–1 Out-letters – Treasury
T71/1592–5 Domestic letter books
T71/1596–8 Out-letters
T71/1599–1601 Registers of in-letters – classified
T71/1602–20 Inward letters – original
T71/1621–31 Miscellanea

National Debt Office: Abolition of Slavery Act 1833, registers of compensation paid to slave owners
NDO4/1–37A Compensation accounts 1835–42

Records created or inherited by the Home Office, Ministry of Home Security and related bodies
HO 44/17 7a, b 'Geo. Hibbert sends to Mr Peel documents under instructions from Assembly of Jamaica, 12th July 1827'

Records created or inherited by the Treasury Solicitor and HM Procurator General's Department
TS11/978 In the Privy Council: Demerara & Berbice, Petition and Memorial of the London proprietors and mortgagees to His Majesty in Council against compulsory manumission in those colonies

Records of the Auditors of the Imprest, Commissioners of Audit, Exchequer and Audit Department, National Audit Office and related bodies: claims commissions, various claims
AO14/37–48 Slave compensation

Records of the Prerogative Court of Canterbury, and related probate jurisdictions
PROB 11 Will registers

OTHER LOCATIONS

Parliamentary papers (PP) etc.

An Act for the abolition of slavery throughout the British colonies, for promoting the industry of the manumitted slaves, and for compensating the persons hitherto entitled to the services of such slaves 28 August 1833 (3 and 4 Wm IV cap. 73)

The Debates in Parliament – Session 1833 – on the Resolution and Bill for the Abolition of Slavery in British colonies, with a copy of the Act of Parliament (London, 1834)

Report from Committee of persons interested in estates in the island of St Vincent, PP 1812–13, Vol. 3 (182)

Report from the Select Committee appointed to inquire into the working of the Apprenticeship system in the colonies, conduct of Apprentices, laws, regulations etc., PP 1836, Vol. 15 (560)

Report from the Select Committee on the commercial state of the West India colonies, PP 1831–2, Vol. 20 (381)

Report from the Select Committee on the extinction of slavery throughout the British dominions, PP 1831–2, Vol. 20 (721)

Slaves in the Colonies: return to an address of the Honourable the House of Commons dated 8th March 1826 for A Return of All the Public Functionaries ... in all the Slave Colonies belonging to His Majesty, who are Proprietors of Slaves, or of Plantations worked by Slaves; or who are in occupancy or concerned in the management of Slaves, either as Attorney, Manager, Trustee, Mortgagee, Executor or otherwise, PP 1826–7, Vol. 22.1 (111), (146)

Return to an address to the honourable House of Commons dated 12th June 1827 for extracts from the minutes of evidence taken by the committee of the council of Trinidad for enquiring into the Negro character, PP 1826–7, Vol. 23.5 (479)

Slavery Abolition Act: an account of all sums of money awarded by the Commissioners of Slavery Compensation, PP 1837–8, Vol. 48 (215)

Directories, poll books etc.

Boyle's Fashionable Court Guide and Town Visiting Directory (London, 1792, 1796, 1805, 1811, 1819, 1824, 1829, 1835, 1838, 1846)

A genealogical and heraldic dictionary of the peerage and baronetage of the British Empire, by John Burke (London: Henry Colburn, 1828)

A genealogical and heraldic dictionary of the landed gentry of Great Britain and Ireland, by John Burke and John Bernard Burke, 2 vols. and supplement (London: Henry Colburn, 1846, 1849)

A genealogical and heraldic history of the commoners of Great Britain and Ireland enjoying territorial possessions or high official rank but uninvested with heritable honours, by John Burke, 4 vols. (London: Henry Colburn, 1833)

Gore's Directory of Liverpool and Its Environs (Liverpool, 1805, 1823, 1827, 1828, 1841)

Jamaica Almanack (Kingston: A. Aikman *et al.*, 1811, 1812, 1815, 1817, 1818, 1820, 1821, 1822, 1824, 1826, 1828, 1829, 1831, 1832, 1833, 1838, 1839)

The new history, survey and description of the City and suburbs of Bristol (Bristol: W. Mathews, 1794)

The peerage of the British Empire as at present existing, by Edmund Lodge (London: Saunders & Otley, 1843)

Pigot & Co.'s National London & Provincial Directory for 1834 (London/ Manchester, 1834)

The Poll Book of the election of a representative in Parliament for the borough of Whitehaven (Whitehaven, 1832)

The poll for an election of an MP for the Borough of Liverpool, taken between Wm Ewart and J. E. Denison, to which are added history of the election etc. (Liverpool: J. Gore, 1830)

The Post Office Annual Directory for 1828–9 (Edinburgh, 1828)

The Post Office Annual Directory and Calendar 1835–6 (Edinburgh, 1835)

The Post Office Glasgow Annual Directory 1843–4 (Glasgow, 1843)

The Post Office London Directory (London, 1828, 1833, 1834, 1835, 1836, 1838)

Register of electors for Marylebone (London, 1840–1)

Robson's British Court and Parliamentary Guide for 1832 (London, 1832)

Robson's Directory of Bristol 1838. Extracted from *Robson's Commercial Directory of London and the Western Counties* (London, 1839)

Robson's London Directory, street key etc. (London, 1833, 1835, 1836, 1839)

Royal Blue Book, Fashionable Directory (London, 1831, 1846)

Periodicals etc.

Anti-slavery Monthly Reporter, 6 vols. (London, 1827–34)

The Times

Pamphlets etc.

Anon., *Abstract of the report of the Lords Committee on the condition and treatment of colonial slaves* (London, 1833)

Analysis of the Report of a Committee of the House of Commons on the extinction of slavery, with notes by the editor, printed for the Society for the Abolition of Slavery throughout the British Dominions (London, 1833)

A letter from Legion to His Grace the Duke of Richmond the Chairman of the Slavery Committee of the House of Lords containing an exposure of the character and evidence of the colonial side produced before the Committee (London, [1832])

Letters on the necessity of a prompt extinction of British colonial slavery chiefly addressed to the more influential classes, to which are added thoughts on compensation ([London], 1826)

Baillie, George, *Interesting letters addressed to John Bolton Esq. of Liverpool, merchant and colonel of a regiment of volunteers* (London: J. Gold, 1809)

Beaumont, Augustus Hardin, *Compensation to Slave Owners fairly considered in an appeal to the common sense of the people of England*, 4th edn (London, 1826)

Borthwick, P[eter], *Report of a lecture on colonial slavery and gradual emancipation, delivered at the Assembly Rooms on Friday March 1 1833* (Edinburgh, 1833)

Clarkson, Thomas, *Three letters (one of which has appeared before) to the Planters and Slave-Merchants principally on the subject of compensation* (London, 1807)

Cooper, Thomas, *Correspondence between George Hibbert, Esq. and the Rev. T. Cooper relative to the condition of the Negro slaves in Jamaica extracted from the Morning Chronicle, also a Libel on the character of Mr & Mrs Cooper published in 1823 in several of the Jamaica journals, with notes and remarks* (London, 1824)

Daniel, Thos, and Co., *A letter to His Grace the Duke of Newcastle on West India affairs called forth by the misrepresentation of the Anti-slavery society* (London, 1854)

Fitzgerald, Sir Jeremiah, *Suggestions on the Slave trade for the consideration of the Legislature of Great Britain* (London, 1797)

Grosett, J. R., MP, *Remarks on West India Affairs*, 2nd edn (London, 1825)

Hankey, William Alers, *Letter to Thomas Wilson Esq.* (London, 1833)

Inhabitants of the West India Islands St Thomas and St John, 'Petition for compensation for the loss of slaves by Emancipation in the Danish West Indies', June 1851, reproduced in *Journal of Negro History*, **2.4** (October 1917), 423–8

Page, Richard, *A critical examination of the twelve resolutions of Mr Joseph Hume, respecting the loan of fifteen millions for slave compensation* (London: Pelham Richardson, 1839)

Robley, John, *A permanent and effectual remedy suggested to the evils under which the British West Indies now labour, in a letter from a West India merchant to a West India planter* (London, 1808)

Saintsbury, George, *East India slavery*, 2nd edn (London, 1829; reprinted Shannon: Irish University Press, 1972)

[Scoble, John], *Hill Coolies: a brief exposure of the deplorable condition of the Hill Coolies in British Guiana and Mauritius, and of the nefarious means by which they were induced to resort to these colonies* (London: Harvey and Darton, 1840)

Simmons, H. P., *A letter to the Rt Hon. Earl Grey on the West India question by H. P. Simmons Esq.* (Liverpool, 1833)

Society for the Extinction of the Slave Trade, and the Civilization of Africa, *Prospectus of the Society for the extinction of the slave trade and the civilization of Africa, instituted June 1839* (London, 14 February 1840)

Sotham, Nathaniel, *Plain facts on the question of West India slavery seriously examined by the test of truth and real observation* (Cheltenham, 1825)

Stuart, Charles, *The West India question: an outline for immediate emancipation and remarks on compensation, reprinted from English Quarterly Magazine & Review, April 1832* (New Haven, 1833)

Wilmot Horton, Rt Hon. R., *1st and 2nd letters to the Freeholders of the County of York, on Negro slavery, being an enquiry into the claims of the West Indians for an Equitable Compensation by the Rt Hon. R. Wilmot Horton* (London: Edmund Lloyd, Harley Street, 1830)

    Moving for the production of evidence taken before the Privy Council upon an appeal against compulsory manumission of slaves in Demerara and Berbice (London, 1828)

    Speech of the Rt Hon. R. Wilmot Horton in the House of Commons on the 6th of March 1828 on 'Moving for the production of the evidence taken before the Privy Council, upon an Appeal against the compulsory manumission of slaves in Demerara and Berbice' (London: John Murray, 1828)

Memoirs etc.

Austen, Jane, *Jane Austen's Letters*, ed. D. Le Faye (Oxford: Oxford University Press, 1995)

Bickell, Rev. R., *The West Indies as they are: or a real picture of slavery but more particularly as it exists in the Island of Jamaica* (London: J. Hatchard, 1825)

Boddington, Samuel, Journal 1815–43, Guildhall MS 10, 823:5[c]

Carmichael, Mrs A. C., *Domestic manners and social condition of the white, coloured and Negro populations in the West Indies* (London: Whittaker & Co., 1833)

[Coleridge, Henry Nelson], *Six months in the West Indies in 1825* (London: John Murray, 1826)

Duncan, Henry, *Presbyterian letters on the West India question addressed to the Rt Hon. Sir George Murray GCB, MP, Colonial Secretary etc., etc. By Henry Duncan D. D. Rothwell* (London: T. and G. Underwood, 1830)

Gilbart, James Wilbart, 'A ten years retrospect of London banking', *Journal of the Statistical Society of London*, **18.4** (December 1855), 333–44

Greville, Charles C. F., *A Journal of the reigns of King George IV and King William IV*, 2nd edn, ed. Henry Reeves, 3 vols. (London: Longman, 1874)

Holland, Lord et al., *The Holland House Diaries 1831–40*, ed. Abraham D. Kriegel (London: Routledge, 1977).

Laurie, Sir Peter, *The Journal of Sir Peter Laurie*, ed. Elizabeth Shepherd (London: The Saddlers Company, 1985)

Lewis, Matthew Gregory, *Journal of a Residence among the Negroes in the West Indies* (originally, *Journal of a West India Proprietor, kept during a residence in the island of Jamaica*) (first published posthumously, London: John Murray, 1834; reprinted Stroud: Nonsuch Publishing, 2005).

[Markland, J. H.], *A Sketch of the life and character of George Hibbert Esq., FRS, SA & LS* (printed for private distribution, 1837)

Montefiore, Moses, *Diaries of Sir Moses and Lady Montefiore, comprising their life and work as recorded in their diaries from 1812 to 1883*, ed. Dr L. Loewe (London: The Jewish Historical Society, 1983; facsimile of the two-volume 1890 edn)

Nugent, Maria, *Lady Nugent's Journal of her residence in Jamaica from 1801 to 1805, and of subsequent events in England from 1805 to 1811* (first published 1839; reprinted Kingston: Institute of Jamaica, 1966)

Raikes, Thomas, *A Portion of the Journal kept by Thomas Raikes Esq. from 1831 to 1847* ([London], 1856)

Smith, Sydney, *Selected Letters of Sydney Smith*, ed. Nowell C. Smith (Oxford: Oxford University Press, 1956; 2nd edn 1981).

Stephen, George, *Antislavery recollections in a series of letters addressed to Mrs Beecher Stowe* (London: Thomas Hatchard, 1854)

Sturge, Joseph and Harvey, Thomas, *The West Indies in 1837* (London: Hamilton Adams and Co., 1838)

Thome, James A. and Kimball, J. Horace, *Emancipation in the West Indies* (New York, 1838)

Witts, Rev. F. E., *The diary of a Cotswold parson 1783–1854*, ed. David Verey (Stroud: Sutton Publishing, 1978; 2nd edn 2003).

Catalogues

Christie's, A catalogue of the very choice and highly valuable cabinet of Italian, French, Flemish & Dutch pictures, the genuine property of George Hibbert, Esq. Guildhall Folio Pam. 251

SOURCES AFTER *C*.1850

PRINTED WORKS

Addis, John P., *The Crawshay dynasty: a study in industrial organisation and development 1765–1867* (Cardiff: University of Wales Press, 1957)

Andreades, A., *History of the Bank of England 1640 to 1903*, 3rd edn (London: P. S. King, 1935)

Aufhauser, R. Keith, 'Profitability of slavery in the British Caribbean', *Journal of Interdisciplinary Study*, **5**.1 (Summer 1974), 45–67

Azeez, James, 'The compensation controversy', *History Gazette*, **12** (September 1989)

Ballantyne, Tony, *Orientalism and race: Aryanism in the British empire* (Basingstoke: Palgrave, 2002)

Barker, Anthony J., *Slavery and antislavery in Mauritius 1810–33: the conflict between economic expansion and humanitarian reform under British rule* (London: Macmillan, 1996)

Barrett, R. A., *The Barretts of Jamaica:, the family of Elizabeth Barrett Browning* (Winfield, KS: Armstrong Browning Library of Baylor University, The Browning Society, Wedgestone Press, 2000)

Barro, R. J., 'Government spending, interest rates, prices and budget deficits in the United Kingdom, 1701–1918', *Journal of Monetary Economics*, **20** (1987), 221–47, reprinted in R. J. Barro, *Macroeconomic policy* (Cambridge, MA: Harvard University Press, 1990), pp. 341–72

Beachey, R.W., *The British West Indies sugar industry in the late 19th century* (Oxford: Basil Blackwell, 1957)

Beckles, Hilary M., *Centering woman: gender discourses in Caribbean slave society* (Kingston, Jamaica: Ian Randle Publishers, 1999)

Beckles, Hilary M. and Shepherd, Verene (eds.), *Caribbean slavery in the Atlantic world* (Kingston, Jamaica: Ian Randle Publishers, c.1999)

Bender, Thomas (ed.), *The anti-slavery debate: capitalism and abolitionism as a problem of historical interpretation* (Berkeley: University of California Press, 1992)

Blackburn, Robin, *The making of New World slavery, from the Baroque to the Modern 1491–1800* (London: Verso, 1997)

The overthrow of colonial slavery 1776–1848 (London: Verso, 1988)

Blouet, Olwyn M., 'Earning and learning in the British West Indies: an image of freedom in the pre-Emancipation decade 1823–1833', *Historical Journal*, **34.2** (June 1991), 391–409

Bowen, H.V., 'Investment and Empire in the later eighteenth century: East India stockholding, 1756–1791', *Economic History Review*, NS **42.2** (May 1989), 186–206

Brathwaite, C.K., 'London Bourne of Barbados, 1793–1869', *Slavery & Abolition*, **28.1** (April 2007), 23–40

Brewer, John, 'Commercialisation and politics', in N. McKendrick, J. Brewer and J.H. Plumb (eds.), *The birth of a consumer society: the commercialisation of eighteenth-century England* (London: Europa Publications, 1982), pp. 197–262

Brewer, John and Staves, Susan (eds.), *Early modern conceptions of property* (London and New York: Routledge, 1995)

Brown, Christopher Leslie, *Moral capital: foundations of British abolitionism* (Chapel Hill: University of North Carolina Press, 2006)

Brown, Wallace, *The King's friends: the composition and motives of the American Loyalist claimants* (Providence: Brown University Press, 1965)

Burnard, Trevor, 'Passengers only: the extent and significance of absenteeism in eighteenth-century Jamaica', *Atlantic Studies*, **1.2** (2004), 178–195.

Burns, Arthur, *The diocesan revival in the Church of England c. 1800–1870* (Oxford: Clarendon Press, 1999)

'English "church reform" revisited 1780–1840', in Arthur Burns and Joanna Innes (eds.), *Rethinking the Age of Reform* (Cambridge: Cambridge University Press, 2003) pp. 136–162

Burns, Arthur and Innes, Joanna (eds.), *Rethinking the Age of Reform* (Cambridge: Cambridge University Press, 2003)

Burroughs, Peter, 'The Mauritian Rebellion of 1832 and the abolition of British colonial slavery', *Journal of Imperial and Commonwealth History*, **4.3** (May 1976), 244–65

Butler, Kathleen Mary, *The economics of Emancipation: Jamaica and Barbados, 1823–1843* (Chapel Hill: University of North Carolina Press, 1995)

Butler, Mary, '"Fair and equitable consideration": the distribution of slave compensation in Jamaica and Barbados', *Journal of Caribbean History*, **22.1–2** (1988), 138–52.

Cain, P.J. and Hopkins, A.G., 'Gentlemanly capitalism and British overseas expansion, I: The old colonial system 1688–1850', *Economic History Review*, NS **39**.4 (1986), 501–25

'Gentlemanly capitalism and British overseas expansion, II: New imperialism 1850–1945', *Economic History Review*, NS **40.1** (1987), 1–26

Cannadine, David, 'Aristocratic indebtedness in the nineteenth century: the case re-opened', *Economic History Review*, NS **30.4** (November 1977), 624–50

Carrington, Selwyn, 'Management of sugar estates in the British West Indies at the end of the eighteenth century', *Journal of Caribbean History*, **33.1–2** (1999), 27–53.

'The state of the debate on the role of capitalism in the ending of the slave system', in Hilary M. Beckles and Verene Shepherd (eds.), *Caribbean slavery in the Atlantic world* (Kingston, Jamaica: Ian Randle Publishers, *c*.1999)

Carroll, W.E., 'The end of slavery: imperial policy and colonial reaction in British Guiana', Ph.D. thesis, University of Michigan, Ann Arbor, 1970

Caswall, Henry, *The Martyr of the Pongas* (London: Rivingtons, 1857)

Chancellor, V.E., 'Slave-owner and anti-slaver: Henry Richard Vassall Fox, 3rd Lord Holland 1800–40', *Slavery & Abolition*, **1.3** (December 1980), 263–75

Checkland, S. G., 'American versus West Indian traders in Liverpool, 1793–1815', *Journal of Economic History*, **18.2** (June 1958), 141–60.

'Finance for the West Indies, 1780–1815', *Economic History Review*, NS **10.3** (1958), 461–9

The Gladstones: a family biography 1764–1851 (Cambridge: Cambridge University Press, 1971)

'John Gladstone as trader and planter', *The Economic History Review*, NS **7.2** (1954), 216–29

Civin, Joshua, 'Liverpool petitions and imperial identity', in Julian Hoppit (ed.), *Parliaments, nations and identities in Britain and Ireland 1660–1850* (Manchester: Manchester University Press, 2003), pp. 187–205

Colley, Linda, *Britons: forging the nation 1707–1837* (New Haven: Yale University Press, 1992)

Conley, Dalton, 'Calculating slavery reparations: theory, numbers and implications', in John Torpey (ed.), *Politics and the past: on repairing historical injustices* (Lanham, MD: Rowman & Littlefield, 2003), pp. 117–25

Cooper, Frederick and Stoler, Laura Ann (eds.), *Tensions of Empire: colonial cultures in a bourgeois world* (Berkeley: University of California Press, 1997)

Costa, Emilia Viotti da, *Crowns of glory, tears of blood: The Demerara slave rebellion of 1823* (Oxford: Oxford University Press, 1994)

Cox, Edward L., 'The free coloureds and slave emancipation in the British West Indies: the case of St Kitts and Grenada', *Journal of Caribbean History*, **22.1–2** (1988), 68–87

Craton, Michael, 'Property and propriety: land tenure and slave property in the creation of a British West Indian plantocracy, 1612–1740', in John Brewer and Susan Staves (eds.), *Early modern conceptions of property* (London and New York: Routledge, 1995), pp. 497–529

Craton, M. and Walvin, J., *A Jamaican plantation: the history of Worthy Park 1670–1970* (London and New York: W. H. Allen; Toronto: University of Toronto Press, 1970)

Dalbey, Ben, 'Slavery and the question of reparations', *International Socialist Review*, **26** (November–December 2002), 74–80

Daunton, M. and Halpern, Rick (eds.), *Empire and others: British encounters with indigenous peoples 1600–1850* (London: University College London Press, 1999)

Daunton, M.J., '"Gentlemanly capitalism" and British Industry 1820–1914', *Past and Present*, **122** (February 1989), 119–58

'"Gentlemanly capitalism" and British Industry 1820–1914: Reply', *Past and Present*, **132** (August 1991) 170–87

Davidoff, Leonore, Doolittle, Megan, Fink, Janet and Holden, Katherine, *The family story: blood, contract and intimacy 1830–1960* (London and New York: Longman, 1999)

Davidoff, Leonore and Hall, Catherine, *Family fortunes: men and women of the English middle class 1780–1850* (London: Hutchinson, 1987)

Davis, David Brion, 'The emergence of immediatism in British and American antislavery thought', *Mississippi Valley Historical Review*, **49** (September 1962), 209–30

The problem of slavery in the age of Revolution, 1770–1823 (Ithaca, NY: Cornell University Press, 1975)

Department of Research of the Association for the Study of Negro Life, and History, 'Absentee ownership in the United States in 1830', *Journal of Negro History*, **9.2** (April 1924), 196–231

Devine, T.M., 'An eighteenth-century business elite: Glasgow–West India merchants, *c.* 1750–1815', *Scottish Historical Review*, **57.1** (April 1978), 40–67

Draper, Nicholas, 'The City of London and slavery: evidence from the first dock companies 1795–1800', *Economic History Review*, **61.2** (May 2008), 432–66

'"Possessing slaves": ownership, compensation and metropolitan society in Britain at the time of Emancipation 1834–40', *History Workshop Journal*, **64** (Autumn 2007), 74–102

Drescher, Seymour, 'Cart whip and Billy Roller: antislavery and reform symbolism in industrialising Britain', *Journal of Social History*, **15** (1981–2), 3–24

Econocide: British slavery in the era of Abolition (Pittsburgh: University of Pittsburgh Press, 1977)

The mighty experiment: free labour versus slavery in British Emancipation (Oxford: Oxford University Press, 2002)

Dresser, Madge, *Slavery obscured: the social history of the slave trade in an English provincial port* (London and New York: Continuum, 2001)

Dumet, Raymond E. (ed.), *Gentlemanly capitalism and British imperialism: the new debate on Empire* (London and New York: Longman, 1999)

Dunn, Richard, '"Dreadful Idlers" in the cane fields: the slave labour pattern on a Jamaica sugar estate 1762–1831', *Journal of Interdisciplinary History*, **17.4**: *Caribbean slavery and British capitalism* (Spring 1987), 795–822

'A tale of two plantations: slave life on Mesopotamia in Jamaica and Mount Airy in Virginia, 1799–1828', *William and Mary Quarterly*, 3rd series **34.1** (January 1977), 32–65

Elbourne, Elizabeth, *Blood ground: colonialism, missions and the contest for Christianity in the Cape Colony and Britain 1799–1853* (Montreal: McGill– Queen's University Press, 2002)

Elder, Melinda, *The slave trade and the economic development of 18th century Lancaster* (Halifax, UK: Ryburn Publishing, 1992)

Eltis, David, 'The traffic in slaves between the British West Indian colonies 1807–1833', *Economic History Review*, NS **25.1** (1972), 55–64

Erickson, Edgar L., 'The introduction of East Indian coolies into the British West Indies', *The Journal of Modern History*, **6.2** (June 1934), 127–146

Evans, E. J., *The contentious tithe: the tithe problem, and English agriculture, 1750–1850* (London: Routledge, and Kegan Paul, 1976)

Faber, Eli, *Jews, slaves and the slave trade: setting the record straight* (New York and London: New York University Press, 1998)

Feinstein, Charles H. and Pollard, Sidney (eds.), *Studies in capital formation in the United Kingdom 1750–1920* (Oxford: Clarendon Press, 1988)

Fingerhut, Eugene R., 'Uses and abuses of the American Loyalists' claims: a critique of quantitative analyses', *William and Mary Quarterly*, 3rd series **25.2** (1968), 245–58

Fogel, Robert William and Engerman, Stanley L., 'Philanthropy at bargain prices: notes on the economics of gradual emancipation', *Journal of Legal Studies*, **3.2** (June 1974), 377–401

Forster, E. M., *Marianne Thornton 1797–1877: a domestic biography* (London: Edward Arnold, 1956)

Franklin, Alexandra, 'Enterprise and advantage: the West India interest in Britain 1774–1840', Ph.D. thesis, University of Pennsylvania, 1992

Furness, Alan. E., 'George Hibbert and the defence of slavery in the West Indies', *Jamaican Historical Review*, **5.1** (1965), 56–70

'The Jamaican coffee boom and John Mackeson: a Blue Mountain coffee planter 1807–1819', *Jamaican Historical Review*, **3.3** (March 1962), 10–21

Gauci, Perry, *Emporium of the world: the merchants of London 1660–1800* (London and New York: Hambledon Continuum, 2007)

Gilmore, J. T., 'The Rev. William Harte and attitudes to slavery in early nineteenth-century Barbados', *Journal of Ecclesiastical History*, **30** (1979), 461–74

Green, Abigail, 'Rethinking Sir Moses Montefiore: religion, nationhood and international philanthropy in the nineteenth century', *American Historical Review*, **110.3** (June 2005), 631–58

Green, David R. and Owens, Alastair, 'Gentlewomanly capitalism? Spinsters, widows and wealth-holding in England and Wales c. 1800–1860', *Economic History Review*, NS **56.3** (2003), 510–36

Green, W. A., *British slave Emancipation: the sugar colonies and the Great Experiment 1830–1865* (Oxford: Clarendon Press, 1976)

'The perils of comparative history: Belize and the British sugar colonies after slavery', *Comparative Studies in Society and History*, **26.1** (January 1984), 112–19

'The planter class and British West Indian sugar production, before and after Emancipation', *Economic History Review*, NS **26**.3 (1973), 448–63

Greene, Jack P., 'Liberty, slavery and the transformation of British identity in the eighteenth-century West Indies', *Slavery & Abolition*, **21**.1 (April 2000), 1–31

Gross, Izhak, 'The abolition of Negro slavery and British parliamentary politics 1832–3', *Historical Journal*, **23**.1 (March 1980), 63–85

Habakkuk, John, *Marriage, debt and the estate system* (Oxford: Clarendon Press, 1994)

Hall, Catherine, *Civilising subjects: metropole and colony in the English imagination 1830–1867* (Cambridge: Polity Press, 2002)

Hall, Catherine (ed.), *Cultures of Empire: a reader* (Manchester: Manchester University Press, 2000)

Hall, Catherine and Rose, Sonya O. (eds.), *At home with the Empire: metropolitan culture and the imperial world* (Cambridge: Cambridge University Press, 2006)

Hall, Douglas, 'Absentee proprietorship in the British West Indies, to about 1850', *Journal of Caribbean History*, **35**.1 (2001) 97–121 (originally published in *Jamaican Historical Review*, 4 (1964), 15–35)

A brief history of the West India Committee (St Lawrence, Barbados: Caribbean University Press, 1971)

Halliday, Ursula, 'The slave owner as reformer: theory and practice at Castle Wemyss estate, Jamaica 1808–1823', *Journal of Caribbean History*, **30**.1–2 (1996), 65–82

Hamilton, Douglas, *Scotland, the Caribbean and the Atlantic world 1750–1820* (Manchester: Manchester University Press, 2005)

Hancock, David, *Citizens of the world: London merchants and the integration of the British Atlantic community 1735–1785* (Cambridge: Cambridge University Press, 1995)

Hanson Hiss, Philip, *Netherlands America: the Dutch territories in the West* (New York: Duell, Sloan & Pearce, 1943)

Harling, Philip, *The waning of 'Old Corruption': the politics of economical reform in Britain 1779–1846* (Oxford: Clarendon Press, 1996)

Harris, Ron, 'Political economy, interest groups, legal institutions, and the repeal of the Bubble Act in 1825, *Economic History Review*, NS **50**.4 (November 1997), 675–96

Heuman, G., *Between black and white: race, politics and the free coloureds in Jamaica* (Westport, CT: Greenwood Press, 1981)

Hidy, Ralph W., 'Cushioning a crisis in the London money market', *Bulletin of the Business Historical Society*, **20**.5 (November 1946), 131–45

'The organization and functions of Anglo-American merchant bankers, 1815–1860', *The Journal of Economic History*, **1**, Supplement: *The tasks of economic history* (December 1941), 53–66

Higman, B. W., *Montpelier, Jamaica: a plantation community in slavery and freedom 1739–1912* (Mona, Jamaica: University of the West Indies Press, 1998)

Plantation Jamaica 1750–1850: capital and control in a colonial economy (Mona, Jamaica: University of the West Indies Press, 2005)

Slave populations in the British Caribbean 1807–34 (Baltimore: Johns Hopkins University Press, 1984)

'The West India interest in Parliament 1807–33', *Historical Studies*, **13**.49 (October 1967), 1–19

Hilton, Boyd, *A mad, bad and dangerous people? England 1783–1846* (Oxford: Oxford University Press, 2006)

Hochschild, Adam, *Bury the chains: the British struggle to abolish slavery* (London: Macmillan, 2005)

Hollis, Patricia, 'Anti-slavery and British working-class radicalism in the years of reform', in C. Bolt and S. Drescher (eds.), *Anti-slavery, religion and reform: essays in memory of Roger Anstey* (Folkestone: W. Dawson, 1980), pp. 294–315

Holt, Raymond V., *The Unitarian contribution to social progress in England* (first published 1938; reprinted London: The Lindsey Press, 1952)

Holt, Thomas C., *The problem of freedom: race, labour and politics in Jamaica and Britain, 1832–1938* (Baltimore: Johns Hopkins University Press, 1992)

Hoppit, Julian, 'Risk and failure in English industry c. 1700–1800', Ph.D. thesis, University of Cambridge, 1984

Horowitz, David, *Uncivil wars: the controversy over reparations for slavery* (San Francisco: Encounter Books, 2002)

Howard-Hassmann, Rhoda E., 'Moral integrity and reparations for Africa', in John Torpey (ed.), *Politics and the past: on repairing historical injustices* (Lanham, MD: Rowman and Littlefield, 2003), pp. 193–215

Reparations for Africa (Philadelphia: University of Pennsylvania Press, 2008)

Howard-Hassmann, Rhoda E. and Lombardo, A. P., 'Framing reparations claims: differences between the African and Jewish social movements for reparations', *African Studies Review*, **50**.1 (April 2007), 27–48

Howe, Anthony, 'From "Old Corruption" to "New Probity": the Bank of England and its directors in the Age of Reform', *Financial History Review*, **1** (1994), 23–41

Hunt, Bishop C., 'The joint-stock company in England, 1800–1825', *Journal of Political Economy*, **43**.1 (February 1935), pp. 1–33

Hyndman, Henry M., *The record of an adventurous life* (London: Macmillan, 1911)

Inikori, Joseph E., *Africans and the Industrial Revolution in England: a study in international trade and economic development* (Cambridge: Cambridge University Press, 2002)

Inikori, Joseph E., Behrendt, Stephen D., Berg, Maxine *et al.*, 'Roundtable: reviews of Joseph Inikori's *Africans and the Industrial Revolution: a study in international trade and economic development* with a response by Joseph Inikori', *International Journal of Maritime History*, **15**.2 (December 2003), 279–361

Jones, Wilbur Devereux, 'Lord Mulgrave's administration in Jamaica, 1832–1833', *Journal of Negro History*, **48**.1 (January 1963), 44–56

Judd, Gerrit P., IV, *Members of Parliament 1734–1832* (New Haven: Yale University Press, 1955)

Jupp, Peter, *British politics on the eve of reform: the Duke of Wellington's administration 1828–30* (London: Macmillan, 1998)

Kitson Clark, G. S. R., *The making of Victorian England* (London: Methuen, 1965; first published 1962)

Laidlaw, Zoe, *Colonial connections 1815–45: patronage and the information revolution in colonial government* (Manchester: Manchester University Press, 2006)

Lambert, David, 'The "Glasgow king of Billingsgate": James MacQueen and an Atlantic proslavery network', *Slavery & Abolition*, **29**.3 (June 2008), 389–413

    White creole culture: politics and identity in the age of Abolition (Cambridge: Cambridge University Press, 2005)

Langford, P., *Public life and the propertied Englishman, 1689–1798* (Oxford: Clarendon Press, 1991)

Lester, Alan, *Imperial networks: creating identities in nineteenth-century South Africa and Britain* (London and New York: Routledge, 2001)

Lester, Alan and Lambert, David (eds.), *Colonial lives across the British empire: imperial careering in the long nineteenth century* (Cambridge: Cambridge University Press, 2006)

Levy, Claude, 'Barbados: the last years of slavery 1823–33', *Journal of Negro History*, **44**.4 (October 1959), 308–45

Lipscomb, Patrick C., 'Party politics, 1801–1802: George Canning and the Trinidad question', *Historical Journal*, **12**.3 (1969), 442–66

Lobdell, Richard A., 'The price of freedom: financial aspects of British slave Emancipation 1833–38. Notes on research in progress', unpublished paper delivered at the Annual Meeting of the Social Sciences History Association, Pittsburgh (October 2000)

Lombardi, John V., *The decline and abolition of Negro slavery in Venezuela 1820–54* (Westport, CT: Greenwood Press, 1971)

Longmore, Jane, ' "Cemented by the blood of a Negro?" The impact of the slave-trade on eighteenth-century Liverpool', in D. Richardson, S. Schwarz and A. Tibbles (eds.), *Liverpool and transatlantic slavery* (Liverpool: Liverpool University Press, 2007), pp. 227–51

MacLehose, James, *Memoirs and portraits of 100 Glasgow men* (Glasgow: James MacLehose & Sons, 1886)

Maehl, William H., Jr, 'Augustus Hardin Beaumont: Anglo-American radical (1798–1838)', *International Review of Social History*, **14** (1969), 237–50

Malcomson, A. P. W., 'Absenteeism in eighteenth-century Ireland', *Irish Economic and Social History*, **1** (1974), 15–35

Marks, Shula, 'History, the nation and Empire: sniping from the periphery', *History Workshop Journal*, **29** (Spring 1990), 111–19

Marshall, P. J., 'Parliament and property rights in the late eighteenth-century British empire', in J. Brewer and S. Staves (eds.), *Early modern conceptions of property* (London and New York: Routledge, 1995), pp. 530–44

Marshall, Peter, *Bristol and the abolition of slavery: the politics of emancipation* (Bristol: Bristol Branch of the Historical Association, 1975)

McAlmont, Cecilia, 'Peter Rose: the report of 1850', *History Gazette*, **20** (May 1990), 1–15

    'Peter Rose: the years before 1835', *History Gazette*, **19** (April 1990), 2–9

McCloy, Shelby T., *The Negro in the French West Indies* (Lexington: University of Kentucky Press, 1966)

Meany, E. S., *Origin of Washington geographic names* (Seattle: University of Washington Press, 1922)

Michie, R. C. (ed.), *The development of London as a financial centre*, 4 vols. (London: I. B. Tauris, 2005)

Midgley, Clare, 'Slave sugar boycotts, female activism and the domestic base of British anti-slavery culture', *Slavery & Abolition*, **17**.3 (December 1996), 137–62

Mitchell, B. R. and Deane, Phyllis, *Abstract of British historical statistics* (Cambridge: Cambridge University Press, 1962)

Moohr, Michael, 'The economic impact of slave Emancipation in British Guiana, 1832–1852', *Economic History Review*, NS **25**.4 (November 1972), 588–607

Morgan, E. V., *The theory and practice of central banking 1797–1813* (Cambridge: Cambridge University Press, 1943)

Morgan, Kenneth, 'Bristol West India merchants in the eighteenth century', *Transactions of the Royal Historical Society*, 6th series **3** (1993), 185–208

Morris, R. J., *Men, women and property in England 1780–1870: a social and economic history of family strategies amongst the Leeds middle classes* (Cambridge: Cambridge University Press, 2005)

'Voluntary societies and British urban elites, 1780–1850: an analysis', *Historical Journal*, **26**.1 (March 1983), 95–118

Murch, Jeron, 'Memoir of Robert Hibbert', in *The book of the Hibbert Trust* (printed by direction of the trustees for private circulation, 1933)

O'Donoghue, J. and Golding, L, 'Consumer price inflation since 1750', *Economic Trends*, **604** (2004), 38–46

Oliver, Vere Langford, *Caribbeana*, 6 vols. (London: Mitchell, Hughes and Clarke, 1909)

Osabu-Kle, Daniel Tetteh, 'The African reparation cry: rationale, estimate, prospects, and strategies', *Journal of Black Studies*, **30**.3 (January 2000), 331–50

O'Shaughnessy, Andrew Jackson, *An empire divided: the American Revolution and the British Caribbean* (Philadelphia: University of Pennsylvania Press, 2000)

'The formation of a commercial lobby: the West Indies, British colonial policy and the American Revolution', *Historical Journal*, **40** (1997), 71–95

Palmer, Norman D., 'Irish absenteeism in the eighteen-seventies', *Journal of Modern History*, **12**.3 (September 1940), 357–366

Pares, Richard, 'Merchants and planters', *Economic History Review*, Supplement 4 (Cambridge: Cambridge University Press, 1960)

A West India fortune (London: Longman, 1950)

Parker, Sarah E., *Grace and favour: a handbook of who lived where in Hampton Court Palace 1750–1950* (East Molesey: Hampton Court, 2005)

Paton, Diana, 'Decency, dependency and the lash: gender and the British debate over slave Emancipation 1830–1834', *Slavery & Abolition*, **17**.3 (December 1996), 163–84

Pearsall, S. M. S., '"The late flagrant instance of depravity in my Family": the story of an Anglo-Jamaican cuckold', *William and Mary Quarterly*, **60.3** (July 2003), 549–82

Penson, Lillian M., *The colonial agents of the British West Indies* (London, 1924; reprinted London: Frank Cass and Co., 1971)

'The London West India interest in the eighteenth century', *English Historical Review*, **36.143** (1921), 373–92

'The origin of the Crown Agency Office', *English Historical Review*, **40.158** (1925), 196–206

Petley, Christer, 'Boundaries of rule, ties of dependency: Jamaican planters, local society and the metropole 1800–1834', Ph.D. thesis, University of Warwick, 2003

Phillips, Glenn O., 'Barbadian legacy: the unacknowledged earlier life of William Hinds Prescod', *Cheltenham Local History Society Journal*, **16** (2000), 14–17

Pigou, A. C., 'Problems of compensation', *Economic Journal*, **35.140** (December 1925), 568–82

Pitman, Frank Wesley, 'The treatment of the British West Indian slaves in law and custom', *Journal of Negro History*, **11.4** (October 1926), 610–28

'The West Indian absentee planter as a British colonial type', *Proceedings of the Pacific Coast Branch of the American Historical Association* (1927), 113–27

Pope, D., 'The wealth and social aspirations of Liverpool's slave merchants of the second half of the eighteenth century', in D. Richardson, S. Schwarz and A. Tibbles (eds.), *Liverpool and transatlantic slavery* (Liverpool: Liverpool University Press, 2007), pp. 164–226.

Porter, Bernard, *The absent-minded imperialists: Empire, society and culture in Britain* (Oxford: Oxford University Press, 2004)

Pressnell, L. S., *Country banking in the Industrial Revolution* (Oxford: Clarendon Press, 1956)

Priestley, Herbert Ingram, *France overseas: a study of modern imperialism* (New York and London: Appleton–Century, 1938)

Proctor, J. H., 'Scottish missionaries and Jamaican slaveholders', *Slavery & Abolition*, **25.1** (April 2004), 51–70

Ragatz, Lowell, 'Absentee landlordism in the British Caribbean 1750–1833', *Agricultural History*, **5** (1931) 7–24

The fall of the planter class in the British Caribbean, 1763–1833: a study in social and economic history (New York and London: The Century Co., 1928)

Ranston, Jackie, *The Lindo legacy* (London: Toucan Books, 2000)

Rawley, James A., *London, metropolis of the slave trade* (Columbia and London: University of Missouri Press, 2003)

Reed, M. C., *Investment in railways in Britain 1820–1844: a study in the development of the capital market* (Oxford: Oxford University Press, 1975)

Richardson, David, 'Slavery and Bristol's "Golden Age"', *Slavery & Abolition*, **26.1** (April 2005), 35–54

Richardson, D., Schwarz, S. and Tibbles, A. (eds.), *Liverpool and transatlantic slavery* (Liverpool: Liverpool University Press, 2007)

Robinson, Randall, *The debt: what America owes to Blacks* (New York: Plume, 2001)

Rooke, Patricia, 'Slavery, social death and imperialism: the formation of a Christian black elite in the West Indies 1800–1845', in J.A. Mangan (ed.), *Making imperial mentalities: socialisation and British imperialism* (Manchester: Manchester University Press, 1990), pp. 23–45

Rubinstein, W.D., 'British millionaires 1809–1949', *Bulletin of the Institute of Historical Research* (1974), 202–23

'The end of "Old Corruption" in Britain 1780–1860, *Past and Present*, **101** (November 1983), 55–86

'"Gentlemanly capitalism" and British industry 1820–1914', *Past and Present*, **132** (August 1991), 150–70

Men of property: the very wealthy in Britain since the Industrial Revolution, 2nd edn (London: The Social Affairs Unit, 2006)

'The structure of wealth-holding in Britain, 1809–39: a preliminary anatomy', *Historical Research*, **65** (1992), 74–89

Rupprecht, Anita, 'Excessive memories: slavery, insurance and resistance', *History Workshop Journal*, **64** (Autumn 2007), 6–28

Schama, Simon, *Rough crossings: Britain, the slaves and the American Revolution* (New York: HarperCollins, 2006)

Schneer, Jonathan, *London 1900: the Imperial metropolis* (New Haven: Yale University Press, 1999)

Semmel, Bernard, *The Governor Eyre controversy* (London: MacGibbon and Kee, 1962)

Seymour, Susanne, Daniels, Stephen and Watkis, Charles, 'Estate and empire: Sir George Cornewall's management of Moccas, Herefordshire and La Taste Grenada 1771–1819', *Journal of Historical Geography*, **24.3** (1998), 313–51

Sheridan, Richard B., 'The commercial and financial organisation of the British slave trade 1750–1807' *Journal of Economic History*, **53.1** (March 1987) 249–63

'The rise of a colonial gentry: a cast study of Antigua 1730–1775', *Economic History Review*, NS **13.3** (1961), 342–357

'Simon Taylor, sugar tycoon of Jamaica 1740–1813', *Agricultural History*, **45** (1971), 285–296

'Sir William Young (1749–1815): planter and politician with special reference to slavery in the British West Indies', *Journal of Caribbean History*, **33.1–2** (1999), pp. 1–26

'The wealth of Jamaica in the eighteenth century', *Economic History Review*, NS **18.2** (1965), 292–311

'The wealth of Jamaica in the eighteenth century: a rejoinder', *Economic History Review*, NS **21.1** (1968), pp. 46–61

'The West India sugar crisis and British slave Emancipation, 1830–1833', *Journal of Economic History*, **21.4** (December 1961), 539–51

Simpson, Henry, *The lives of eminent Philadelphians now deceased* (Philadelphia: William Brotherhead, 1859)

Sires, Ronald V., 'Sir Henry Barkly and the labor problem in Jamaica, 1853–1856', *Journal of Negro History*, **25.2** (April 1940), 216–35

Slinn, Judy, *A history of Freshfields* (London: Freshfields, 1984)

Smith, John Guthrie and Mitchell, John Oswald, *The old country houses of the old Glasgow gentry* (Glasgow: James MacLehose & Sons, 1878)

Smith, S. D., 'Merchants and planters revisited', *Economic History Review*, NS **55.3** (2002), 434–65

Slavery, family, and gentry capitalism in the British Atlantic: the world of the Lascelles, 1648–1834 (Cambridge: Cambridge University Press, 2006)

'Sugar's poor relation: British coffee-planting in the West Indies 1720–1833', *Slavery & Abolition*, **19** (1998), 68–89, reprinted in Gad J. Heuman and James Walvin (eds.), *The slavery reader* (London and New York: Routledge, 2003)

Solow, Barbara L. and Engerman, Stanley L. (eds.), *British capitalism and Caribbean slavery: the legacy of Eric Williams* (Cambridge: Cambridge University Press, 1987)

(eds.), *Sotheby's, Important silver, gold boxes and objets de vertu* (London: Sotheby's, 2007)

Staves, Susan, 'Resentment or resignation? Dividing the spoils among daughters and younger sons', in J. Brewer and S. Staves (eds.), *Early modern conceptions of property* (London and New York: Routledge, 1995), pp. 194–220

Steel, M. J., 'A philosophy of fear: the world view of the Jamaican plantocracy in a comparative perspective', *Journal of Caribbean History*, **27.1** (1993), 1–20

Stoler, Ann Laura, 'Rethinking colonial categories: European communities and the boundaries of rule', *Comparative Studies in Society and History*, **31.1** (January 1989), 134–61

Sturtz, Linda L., 'The "Dimduke" and the Duchess of Chandos: gender and power in Jamaican plantation management – a case study or, a different story of "a man [and his wife] from a place called Hope"', *Revista/Review interamericana*, **29.1**–4 (1999), n.p.

Sugarman, David and Warrington, Ronnie, 'Land law, citizenship and the invention of "Englishness": the strange world of the equity of redemption', in J. Brewer and S. Staves (eds.), *Early modern conceptions of property* (London and New York: Routledge, 1995), pp. 111–43

Sussman, Charlotte, *Consuming anxieties: consumer protest, gender and British slavery 1713–1833* (Stanford: Stanford University Press, 2000)

Taylor, Clare, 'The journal of an absentee proprietor: Nathaniel Phillips of Slebech', *Journal of Caribbean History*, **18.1** (1984), 67–82

Taylor, D., '"Our man in London": John Pollard Mayers, agent for Barbados, and the British Abolition Act 1832–3', *Caribbean Studies*, **16** (1977), 60–74

Temperley, Howard, 'Capitalism, slavery and ideology', *Past and Present*, **75** (May 1977), 94–118

Thomas, Robert Paul, 'The sugar colonies of the Old Empire: profit or loss for Great Britain', *Economic History Review*, NS **21.1** (April 1968), 30–45

Thomas, Sue, 'Pringle v. Cadell and Wood v. Pringle: the libel cases over "The history of Mary Prince"', *Journal of Commonwealth Literature*, **40.1** (2005), 113–35

Thompson, F. M. L., 'Life after death: how successful nineteenth-century businessmen disposed of their fortunes', *Economic History Review*, NS **43.1** (February 1990), 40–61

'Stitching it together again', *Economic History Review*, NS **45**.2 (May 1992), 362–75

Thorne, R. G., *The House of Commons 1790–1820*, 5 vols. (London: Secker and Warburg for the History of Parliament Trust, 1986)

Torpey, John, *Making whole what has been smashed: on reparation politics* (Cambridge, MA: Harvard University Press, 2006)

Torpey, John (ed.), *Politics and the past: on repairing historical injustices* (Lanham, MD: Rowman and Littlefield, 2003)

Turley, David, *The culture of English antislavery 1780–1860* (London: Routledge, 1991)

Twist, Anthony, 'Widening circles in finance, philanthropy and the arts: a study of the life of John Julius Angerstein 1735–1823', Ph.D. thesis, University of Amsterdam, 2002

Tyrrell, Alex, 'A house divided against itself: the British abolitionists revisited', *Journal of Caribbean History*, **22**.1–2 (1988), 42–67

Walvin, James, 'The colonial origins of English wealth: the Harewoods of Yorkshire', *Journal of Caribbean History*, **39**.1 (2005), 38–53

Ward, J. R., *British West Indian slavery, 1750–1834: the process of amelioration* (Oxford: Clarendon Press, 1988)

'Emancipation and the Planters', *Journal of Caribbean History*, **22**.1–2 (1988), 116–37

'The profitability of sugar planting in the British West Indies 1650–1834', *Economic History Review*, NS **31**.2 (1978), 197–213

Wastell, R. E. P., 'The history of slave compensation 1833 to 1845', M.A. thesis, London University, 1933

Watts, David, *The West Indies: patterns of development, culture and environmental change since 1492* (Cambridge: Cambridge University Press, 1987)

Wesley, Charles H., 'The neglected period of Emancipation in Great Britain 1807–1823', *Journal of Negro History*, **17**.2 (April 1932), 156–79

Williams, Eric E., *Capitalism and slavery* (London: Andre Deutsch, 1964)

Wilson, Kathleen, *Englishness, Empire and gender in the eighteenth century* (London and New York: Routledge, 2003)

Wilson, Richard G., *Greene King, a business and family history* (London: Bodley Head and Jonathan Cape, 1983)

Woolley, S. F., 'The personnel of the Parliament of 1833', *English Historical Review*, **53**.210 (April 1938), 240–62

Databases, online publications etc.

ABN AMRO Bank NV, *Predecessors of ABN AMRO Bank NV and their connection to African slavery in the United States and the Americas* (April 2006), www.abnamro.com/com/about/history/pdfhai_report.pdf

Aspey, Melanie, 'Nathan Rothschild's company: Jews, Quakers and Catholics', *Rothschild Archive: Annual Review*, April 2003–March 2004, pp. 24–9, www.rothschildarchive.org/ib?/doc=/ib/articles/annualreview

BBC, 'Church apologises for slave trade', http://news.bbc.co.uk/1/hi/uk/4694896.stm

Braikenridge Collection, www.bristol-city.gov.uk

Bristol City Council, PortCities Bristol, www.discoveringbristol.org.uk

Brown University, *Slavery and justice: report of the Brown University Steering Committee on Slavery and Justice* (n.d.), www.brown.edu/slaveryandjustice

Census of England and Wales, www.ancestry.co.uk

Clergy of the Church of England Database, www.theclergydatabase.org.uk

Citizens Financial Group, Inc. and The Royal Bank of Scotland Group, *Historical research report: predecessor institutions research regarding slavery and the slave trade*, first published 25 May 2006, updated 29 May 2009, www.citizensbank.com/pdf/historical_research.pdf

Flaherty, Peter and Carlisle, John, *The case against reparations*, National Legal and Policy Centre, www.nlpc.org/stories/2009/04/29/monograph-case-against-slave-reparations

Glasgow Digital Library, www.gdl.cdlr.strath.ac.uk/glasgowebooks.html

History Associates, www.historyassociates.com

Horowitz, David, 'Ten reasons why reparations is a bad idea for blacks – and racist too' (1 March 2001), www.frontpagemag.com/Articles/Printable.aspx?GUID={23D875BO-65A3-44

Jamaica Family Search, www.jamaicafamilysearch.com

MLN Testaments, www.scottap.com/family/Lanark/MLNTestaments/MLNTestaments1E.html

O[ffice] of N[ational] S[tatistics] time series data online, www.statistics.gov.uk/StatBase/TSDseries1.asp

R[oyal] B[ank] of S[cotland] Archive Guide, www.rbs.com/about02.asp?id=ABOUT_US

Trans-Atlantic slave trade database, www.slavevoyages.org

University of California, *California Digital Library*, http://content.cdlib.org/

Victoria County History, www.victoriacountyhistory.ac.uk

Index